Love's Subtle Magic

Love's Subtle Magic

An Indian Islamic Literary Tradition, 1379–1545

ADITYA BEHL

Edited by

WENDY DONIGER

OXFORD
UNIVERSITY PRESS

OXFORD
UNIVERSITY PRESS

Oxford University Press is a department of the University of Oxford.
It furthers the University's objective of excellence in research,
scholarship, and education by publishing worldwide.

Oxford New York
Auckland Cape Town Dar es Salaam Hong Kong Karachi
Kuala Lumpur Madrid Melbourne Mexico City Nairobi
New Delhi Shanghai Taipei Toronto

With offices in
Argentina Austria Brazil Chile Czech Republic France Greece
Guatemala Hungary Italy Japan Poland Portugal Singapore
South Korea Switzerland Thailand Turkey Ukraine Vietnam

Published in the United States of America by
Oxford University Press
198 Madison Avenue, New York, New York 10016

Library of Congress Cataloging-in-Publication Data
Behl, Aditya, 1966–2009.
Love's subtle magic : an Indian Islamic literary tradition, 1379–1545 / Aditya Behl ;
edited by Wendy Doniger.
pages cm
Includes bibliographical references and index.
ISBN 978-0-19-514670-7
1. Sufi literature, Hindi—History and criticism. 2. India—Civilization. I. Doniger,
Wendy. II. Title.
PK2035.B45 2012
891.4'309921297—dc23
2012003729

ISBN 978-0-19-514670-7

1 3 5 7 9 8 6 4 2
Printed in the United States of America
on acid-free paper

Contents

The Reconstruction of the Text

ADITYA BEHL FINISHED a draft of a text that he called *Shadows of Paradise* in 2001; this was a greatly expanded revision of a text he had completed in 1995, his doctoral dissertation, "Rasa and Romance: The *Madhumālatī* of Shaikh Mañjhan Shattari." But by 2001 he had extended it to include three more Sufi poems. He began with the *Madhumālatī*, of which he had by then published a translation (*Madhumālatī: An Indian Sufi Romance*, translated by Aditya Behl and Simon Weightman; Oxford: Oxford University Press, 2000). Then there was Quṭban's *Mirigāvatī*, of which his translation was published posthumously in 2011 (*The Magic Doe: Shaikh Quṭban Suhravardī's Mirigāvatī. A New Translation by Aditya Behl*, edited by Wendy Doniger; New York: Oxford University Press, 2011). Next came Malik Muḥammad Jāyasī's *Padmāvat*, of which he had completed a partial translation at the time of his death, and, finally, Maulānā Dā'ūd's *Cāndāyan*. That 2001 version of the book consisted of ten chapters: three general chapters as well as one chapter each on *Cāndāyan* and *Mirigāvatī* and two each on *Padmāvat* and *Madhumālatī*.

He continued to work on the text, and in 2004–05 he delivered, at the École des Hautes Études in Paris, seven lectures, now renamed *Love's Subtle Magic*, consisting of revised versions of seven of the chapters of the 2001 text. Then, in 2008, at the School of Oriental and African Studies at the University of London he delivered four lectures, of which we have only one in a complete draft, "The Landscape of Paradise and the Embodied City" (a revision of one of the Paris lectures) and two in partial draft: "On Rupa: Form, Embodiment and Technique in the Hindavi Sufi Romances" (which was published, posthumously, in 2011, as the centerpiece of the introduction to his translation of the *Mirigāvatī*), and "The Seasons of Madhumālatī's Separation" (a revision of one of the original 2001 chapters). He also made a new outline of the book he intended to finish, still devoting one chapter each to *Cāndāyan* and *Mirigāvatī* and two each to *Padmāvat* and *Madhumālatī*, now framing them with four general chapters, two introductory and two at the end. He died, in August 2009, before he could finish revising that book.

In editing this book, my basic principle has been to follow his final plan for the book and to include the latest available version of each of the ten chapters that he sketched in that plan. So I have taken six of the 2004–05 Paris lectures as my basic text (Chapters 1, 2, 3, 4, 6, and 7) and added to that core the two unpublished 2008 London lectures, "The Landscape of Paradise and the Embodied City" (Chapter 5) and "The Seasons of Madhumalati's Separation" (Chapter 8). Following Aditya's intentions as expressed his final draft of the introductory chapter and his final outline, I constructed Chapters 9 and 10 out of portions of the 2004 draft of Chapters 4 and 2, respectively.

Because Aditya kept coming back to the book over the years and never edited the final copy, there were a number of duplications, not only between different versions but between chapters in a single version, and on the level of both phrases and whole paragraphs. In order to minimize such repetitions, I cut words, sentences, sometimes paragraphs, and to clarify the structure of the arguments within each chapter I moved paragraphs, sometimes sentences, sometimes words, sometimes whole sections. I added nothing but subheadings and a few explanatory parenthetical paraphrases. How often I longed to ask Aditya what he meant by a certain puzzling phrase, and since he could not answer I usually left it in enigmatic form, hoping that other readers would be able to tease out the meaning better than I had; and rarely, when I thought I did know what he was getting at I rearranged clauses to clarify the passage.

The result is, as I am painfully aware, not the book he intended to write, but it is not a patchwork. Eight of the ten chapters are taken from one text (the 2004–05 Paris lectures), and the other two are from a draft made four years later. Moreover, the basic materials and ideas remained consistent in tone and substance between the earliest and latest versions; what he added were new interpretations and insights that enriched but did not cancel out his earlier understandings.

I think he would have gone on finding new meanings in these texts for years to come; the process was cut short only by his death. As I edited his text, I found myself falling under the spell of his perfectionist ghost, going over the chapters again and again to trim the excess, fit the pieces together more snugly, smooth the transitions. It was hard to stop, in part because it was hard for me to end our collaborative effort, first begun when Aditya was my student twenty years ago. The result is still unfinished, imperfect. But what he was writing is a book of stunning originality, scholarly depth, and intellectual excitement, of great importance for our understanding of Sufism as well as of the relationship between Hindus and Muslims during a marvelously fruitful period of Indian history. It is his legacy to us, and a very precious one.

Wendy Doniger

Acknowledgments

ADITYA DID NOT get around to writing a file of acknowledgment of the many people who helped him write his book, and I cannot construct such a file, but I am sure they know who they are, and I hope they will take pride in this book. For my part, I acknowledge, with gratitude, the generous and expert help of John Stratton Hawley, Philip Lutgendorf, Aradhna Behl, Ayesha Irani, A. Sean Pue, Francesca Orsini, Carl Ernst, Thibaut d'Hubert, and Vasudha Paramasivan in assembling and editing this text. Thanks to Katherine Ulrich for making the index. And I believe that Aditya would have wanted to dedicate this book to his parents, Colonel S. K. Behl and Mrs. Purnima Behl, to his sister, Aradhna, and his nephew, Anhad, and his niece and namesake, Aditi. And so we dedicate it to them.

Wendy Doniger

Note on the Romanization of Sanskrit, Avadhi, Persian, Arabic, and Urdu

Aditya Behl wrote the chapters of this book at different times, and often spelt the same word differently in different languages; moreover, he transliterated Avadhi, Persian, Arabic, and Urdu in several different ways. In romanizing Indic languages, we have not changed the transliteration of words within quoted material, which therefore still show a great range of systems of romanization, but we have tried to make the text as consistent as possible, while retaining Behl's own preferences. We have followed his custom of leaving out the diacritics on words that are well known to English-speakers as well as on place names and clan names. We have kept his preferred spelling of "Mañjhan," using the Avadhi rather than Persian (Manjhan) romanization, and we have honored his preference for spelling 'Alāuddīn, 'Abdul, 'Abdullāh, and Sher Shāh as such rather than as 'Alā' al-dīn, 'Abd al, 'Abd Allāh, and Shīr Shāh.

For Sanskrit, we have used the International Alphabet of Sanskrit Transliteration. In order to avoid romanizing a single term differently across linguistic contexts, Sanskrit spelling has been preferred over Hindi, with a few exceptions, including titles and proper names. For Hindi, the system followed is the one laid out in R. S. McGregor, *The Oxford Hindi-English Dictionary* (Delhi: OUP, 1993).

Transliterated terms and names in Persian follow the transliteration scheme for the Arabo-Persian letters laid out in F. I. Steingass' *A Comprehensive Persian-English Dictionary* (London: Routledge & K. Paul, 1892). In the case of consonants, we have made a few substitutions to reflect Behl's choices. For ث, where Steingass uses "s̤", we have used "s̱." For غ, Steingass' "gẖ," we have used "ġh", and for the letter و in its consonantal form, we have replaced Steingass' "w" with "v." For vowels and diphthongs, we have used *a, ā, i, ī, u, ū, a´*, o, e, *ai*, and *au*. For the sake of consistency, the transliteration of the occasional Arabic or Urdu name, book-title, term, and quotation also follows the same transliteration scheme for the Arabo-Persian letters laid out for Persian above. In the case of Urdu, *e* is used to indicate the final ی in words like *banāe*, and the letters common to Urdu and Hindi are romanized according to the conventions for Hindi. Throughout, we have retained Behl's preference for the final "h" in terms like *silsilah*. We have indicated elision of the Arabic definite article when preceded by a vowel. *Iẓāfah* is indicated, in Persian, Arabic, and Urdu, according to the Library of Congress's conventions for each of these languages.

Love's Subtle Magic

I

Studying the Sultanate Period

LOVE'S SUBTLE MAGIC can change nature, and even tame that most intractable beast, human nature. This is the simple mystery (*sahaja bheda*) that the Sufis (Islamic mystics) of sultanate India taught through their spiritual and worldly practice, the principle they illustrated through composition and recitation of their verse romances, written in Hindavī and sung in courts, salons, and Sufi shrines from the fourteenth century onward. Their challenge was to make their spiritual agenda comprehensible and appealing in an Indian cultural landscape, using local terms, symbols, concepts, techniques, and gods. The poets were members of the Persian-speaking courtly élite of the Delhi sultanate and the regional kingdoms that followed in its wake, as well as disciples of the Sufi masters who sanctified the landscape of north India through their austerities. Written and performed in Delhi, Jaunpur, and the eastern provinces of the Indo-Gangetic doab, the Hindavī Sufi romances (*prema-kahānī*, "love stories") mark the inauguration of a new literary and devotional culture in a local language. The major romances of the genre date from the fourteenth century till the middle of the sixteenth, when the Mughals took over the rulership of north India. This is a book about those fictional narratives and the cultures of performance and reception that produced them, aristocratic local courts and the hospices of Sufi shaikhs.

The Cultural Landscape

The poems, recited in the evenings in elegant storytelling sessions or ritually performed in Sufi shrines to awaken the novice to spiritual realities, were entertaining stories as well as suggestively erotic narratives about ascetic self-transformation. Although this powerful genre of Indian Islamic poetry inspired numerous retellings in later centuries, it has remained enigmatic to modern interpretation.

Three linked historical processes—cultural assimilation and transformation, creation of new literary media and canons, and articulation of spiritual practice using local terms and concepts—are central to understanding the Hindavī love stories. Although characterizations of the period emphasize the rhetoric of war, the Islamic conquest of northern India prompted a much subtler process of competitive cultural assimilation. No matter how strident the triumphalist rhetoric of conquest, the courts of the Delhi sultanate were situated in a landscape not entirely under their control, a contact zone of cultures and languages. Not only was desire frequently expressed over frontiers of war, but once the incomers were settled in India they reimagined community, polity, and religious belief and practice within an Indian landscape. Conquest also entails setting mutual terms of understanding, styles of accommodation that allow people to live together, interact, be transformed by one another. Encounters, battles, erotic desire, political rapprochements, and competitive expressions of cultural or religious supremacy are marks of such a diverse, contested, and multilingual world. The authors of this particular élite-sponsored Hindavī literary tradition were operating in a world in which many groups of people occupied the same cultural landscape, in constant dialogue with one another and with their own perceived and real pasts and presents.

Creation of new literary languages has to be understood within this complex cultural landscape, in which Persian, Arabic, and Sanskrit were the "classical" or cosmopolitan tongues that predefined generic and poetic expression in Hindustan in the fourteenth century. These languages were not the sole means of expression, however, and across the subcontinent a range of new literary languages and cultures were created in the first part of what Sheldon Pollock has memorably termed "the vernacular millennium."[1] By expressing themselves in these newly emergent media and thereby shaping them decisively, Sufis and aristocrats participated in the literary and linguistic transformation of their world. The poets of the genre created a sophisticated Indian Islamic literary tradition, a genre containing a set of *desī* or indigenous literary and religious terms, and a narrative universe to express the distinctive Sufi agenda within the local landscape in which the Chishtis and Shattaris worked hard to establish themselves. (The Chishtis were an order of Sufis who came from Afghanistan to India in the twelfth century C.E.; the Shattaris, whose name means "lightning-fast," were a Sufi order that originated in Persia in the fifteenth century but became codified in India.) Explicating the Hindavī Sufi romances entails understanding the genre's form and content, its place in the social relations and lived experience of a past time, the conditions of its reception and transmission, and its links to larger processes of linguistic choice and canon formation during the period of the Delhi sultanate.

Understanding these historical transformations, however, involves us in a host of conceptual and interpretative problems. On one side lies the philological direction of specifying how something new is created out of an older, mixed repertory of literary and religious sources, breaking it down into its component parts: Sanskrit, Persian, and Arabic, as well as regional poetic forms and spoken languages. By doing this, one is refusing it the status of the new, showing that it is old after all and not distinctive and novel. Moreover, one falls into the trap of using the fragmentary remains of one of the least-understood periods of Indian cultural history, the age of the Delhi sultanate and the regional Afghan and Turkish kingdoms that followed in its wake, to constitute philological objects floating free in time and space, the *ur*-texts of classical Indology or Oriental studies. Even a genre of fantasy as seemingly liberated from everyday experience as the Sufi romance betrays the marks of historical process, time, and place. One has to set even the most fantastic narrative against the cultural horizons of its production.

The other tendency, into which cultural historians of the period have mostly fallen, is to list events, kings, battles, and literary and religious texts in chronological order, neatly divided into separate compartments such as Hindu and Muslim, subdivided in each case into art, architecture, languages, and history.[2] This compartmentalized history, based on the tendency to list, a *Listenwissenschaft* posing as cultural history, has made it difficult to account for, or even to discern, larger cultural processes or smaller episodes of interaction and assimilation: creation of new literatures, growth of material culture and technology, the clearly joint production of what is now called Hindustani classical music, changes in cuisine and eating habits with the adoption of new foodstuffs, what constituted aesthetic pleasure, common stereotypes—in short, the everyday culture of the area Indian Muslims called Hindustan, the Indo-Gangetic doab north of the Vindhyas.[3] A stage play of essentialisms substitutes for any understanding of the feel of cultural life in the period.

There are also real difficulties in drawing linguistic boundaries between the various dialects and languages prevalent in northern India. As Colin Masica has indicated in a discussion of the development of the new Indo-Aryan languages, the historical situation in South Asia is shaped differently from Europe and involves a slippery distinction between dialect and language:

> Lacking clearcut geographical units of the European type where dialectical variants can crystallize in semi-isolation, or longstanding political boundaries, the entire Indo-Aryan realm (except for Sinhalese) constitutes one enormous dialectal continuum, where continued contact inhibits such crystallization, and differentiated dialects continue to influence one another. The speech of each village differs slightly from the next, without loss of mutual intelligibility, all the way from Assam to Afghanistan. Cumulatively the differences are very great, but where do we draw the dialect, let alone the language, boundaries?[4]

Linguists have addressed this situation through elaborate classificatory schemes and studies of morphology, syntax, and linguistic change. Literary critics, however, do not have the advantage of a living laboratory; their materials for studying the historical transition into the new Indo-Aryan languages are shaped by generic conventions and the aesthetics created by poets in the new literary languages.

Understanding the genre involves also setting it within the political and social context of its inauguration. The Delhi sultanate, established by the invading armies of the Ghaznavids and later the independent Turkish and Afghan sultans, introduced a system of political appanages (*iqṭā'*) and built massive forts to garrison the northern Indian countryside.[5] The generals and noblemen in charge of these provinces (*iqṭā'-dārs*), dependent on their superior technology of warfare and the efficacy of their mounted cavalry, assessed the land under their control for revenue and sent regular tribute to the Sultan in Delhi. Sultans and generals also pushed what recent scholars have called the "moving frontier of Islamic expansion"[6] relentlessly forward to conquer new provinces, loot them for treasure, and set up new forts and garrisons. Once these provinces were acquired, however, their rulers remained a small élite that attempted to control local chiefs and rajas as well as local communities that did not give up their religious beliefs or cultural practices. The forts and their rulers were points in a landscape that was only gradually susceptible to ideological and religious change as well as cultural exchanges. Despite the self-projections of a new set of rulers, control over provinces held as *iqṭā'* remained uncertain, porous, and constantly subject to renegotiation. The role of Turkish slaves who gradually took over administrative and military control; the rise of local, converted noblemen and pressure groups; and ethnic and tribal rivalries at the court in Delhi meant that dynastic and military control was also negotiable.[7] An overly centrist or dualistic perspective must therefore be avoided, particularly in examining the evidence of mutual assimilation and the rise of many local composite cultural forms.

The Indian Islamic literary tradition of the Hindavī Sufi romances is part of this complex process of intermingling and territorial conquest, which generated new polities, created a set of new literary and devotional traditions, and transformed the subjectivities of both conquerors and conquered. Elucidating these processes involves exploring the thematic content and narratives of the Sufi romances, as well as asking how they represent their contexts of production and reception.

The Chishti Sufis

The first poets of these romances, the Chishti Sufis, were powerful figures in the cultural and religious life of the Delhi sultanate. At the core of their mystical activity and contemplation was the transcendental monotheism of belief in Allah, the invisible center, cause, and creator of the visible world. In order to achieve closeness to Allah, the Chishtis aimed at transforming themselves through ascetic practice, which involved a hard regimen of spiritual exercises, fasting, and extra prayers performed at night. The objective of this ascetic self-mortification was to view ordinary physical reality as imbued with divine presence and subject to manipulation by figures that were close to Allah, watched over by his invisible agents.

Whether at the level of the concrete landscape or the physical body, the Chishtis were in a sense trying to resolve the intractable dilemma posed by a transcendental monotheism within a material world. Put simply, the problem had to do with the nature of the transcendence of Allah: since this strictly monotheistic, invisible God created the physical, sensible world and yet stayed apart from it and was different in essence from the world, how could a seeker have access to the presence of Allah? Muslims on that cultural scene had to grapple with similar problems and come up with their own solutions: What gave meaning to their lives? What was love? What was aesthetic pleasure? How were these notions linked with divine presence, with embodiment? In common with the other religious groups on the cultural landscape of northern India, the Sufis emphasized surrender, the true spiritual meaning of *islām* or "submission." The term is matched by *prapatti* ("surrender") among the Vaiṣṇavas and similar notions among other devotional poets in India. The Chishti Sufis tried to resolve their particular dilemmas through the cultural and spiritual means at their disposal: through sanctification of the landscape, or through a bodily regimen of piety with which a special sense of Allah's nearness could be cultivated, or through training the mind to read the world for signs of invisible spiritual processes, or, finally through listening to erotic poetry and letting it transform their being. Attendant on the ritual performance of the Chishti *samā'* or audition was opening up the self to the music and poetry that celebrated the erotics of the relationship to an impossibly distant beloved.[8] Other *silsilahs* (lineages of teachers) such as the Naqshbandis did not practice *samā'* but had their own distinctive style of spiritual training that created awareness in the trainee or novice.

The material and political sponsorship for these mystical agendas came from the sultans and aristocrats of the Delhi sultanate and the provinces ruled from Delhi in the thirteenth and fourteenth centuries. Ever since K. A. Nizami's pioneering study on Indian Sufi thought, *Some Aspects of Religion and Politics in India During the Thirteenth Century*, a separation between the realms of mysticism and politics has defined the field. Citing the Chishti compendium of praxis and belief (Muḥammad Kirmānī's

Siyar-al-'Auliyā or "Biographies of the Saints"), Nizami underscores the Chishti abhorrence for court politics:

> Shaiḵh Nizām-ud-din 'Auliyā of Delhi, who lived to see more than half a dozen rulers occupy the throne of Delhi, never visited the court of any Sultan. He even refused to grant interviews to them.... However great the Sultan may be and however insistent his requests, the Shaiḵh would never deviate from his principle. The Shaiḵh refused to see Sultan 'Alā-ud-din Khiljī and when he insisted, his reply was: "My house has two doors. If the Sultan enters by one, I shall make my exit by the other one."[9]

This attitude persisted as a prescriptive ideal in the Chishti *silsilah* until at least the seventeenth century and was prevalent among latter-day Sufis. However, the relation of precept to practice is a difficult one, and a number of scholars have suggested that over time the central organization of the Chishti *silsilah* broke down into "a conglomerate of smaller and bigger autonomous principalities."[10] Many of the Chishti Sufis accepted royal patronage and even expected sultans to provide tax-free land grants for them.[11]

With these facts in mind, the insightful studies of another scholar of Indian Sufism, Simon Digby, have pointed the way to a different sort of answer: that the sources mark a complex, contradictory relationship between kings and Sufis. On the one hand the Sufis admit their dependence on the structures of political authority; yet on the other, they assert a superior claim to authority because kings frequently gain their power from the blessings of a Sufi shaikh.[12] The Chishti strategy of holding on to a public rhetoric of *tark-i duniyā* or abandonment of the world while accepting economic support and even playing at kingmaking embodies the social tension between political and spiritual claims to authority[13] that is apparent in the literature of the period.

The Sufi shaikhs of Delhi and the provincial *vilāyahs* (territorial jurisdictions) of Hindustan created a male-centered ascetic culture. Within the lands conquered by the armies of the Delhi sultanate, the great shaikhs of the Chishti *silsilah* were able to command a following and set up hospices where they gave spiritual instruction and trained disciples. Several aspects of the Chishti social and spiritual agenda are noteworthy: their relations with rulers and the flow of material gifts, their belief in cultivating consciousness of God and of the invisible world of saints and adepts that surrounds the visible order of things, their regimen of ascesis and prayer, and their musical practice, which was aimed at transforming the novice into a man with a taste for things spiritual (*ẕauq*).

The first of these aspects, their relation with rulers and the new landed aristocracy, is intrinsically linked with the carving up of Hindustan into provinces by a class of Turkish military aristocrats. Sufi shaikhs often pressed superior claims of spiritual authority over territory, using the idea of their divine jurisdiction over land

and reminding kings that they were on their thrones because of the blessing of a holy man.[14] Such holy men were special because they lived in two realms at once, the visible and the invisible, and could interpret signs from the invisible world for the select disciples and the throngs who frequented the Sufi *k͟hānaqāh* (the Sufi lodge, cloister, or hospice): "Above the authority of mundane rulers there is ordained a hierarchy of those with supernatural powers, perpetually watchful over the welfare of all regions of the world...such claims to the *wilāyat* of a specific territory were actively and vigourously pursued by Shaikhs in Khurasan...and the concept is very common in fourteenth-century and later Indian Sufi literature."[15]

This notion of territorial jurisdiction (*vilāyah*), and the superior relationship of the shaikh to the world of material affairs (*duniyā*), coexisted with a contradictory notion. In order for the Sufi hospices to function, they were dependent on the economic largesse of rulers, in the form of tax-free land grants (*madad-i ma'āsh*), as well as on the regular flow of alms or *futūḥāt*.

The distinctive way in which the Chishtis handled this inflow of material goods was to insist on a spiritual principle of redistribution. Thus, for instance, Shaikh Niẕām al-dīn Auliyā' had the following to say about amassing and dispensing worldly goods:

> "One must not collect worldly goods except that which is necessary, such as the cloak that resembles a woman's veil. That much is legitimate, but no more than that. Everything else that one receives should be dispensed with rather than hoarded." Then on his blessed lips came the following couplet:
> Gold is there just for giving, my son.
> For keeping, what's the difference between gold and stone?[16]

Spiritual merit is connected, in this system, only with giving up the goods and cash that flow into the *k͟hānaqāh*. The discourses of Chishti shaikhs are full of stories in which wealth proved an impediment to worship and spiritual practice. Any regular expectation of money was a hindrance in the sense that the Sufi then expected to be paid for his mystical practice. Along with this explicit devaluation of material goods, the Chishtis took a distinctive view of the concrete world: it was only an overlay for the invisible world, whose spiritual principles could be seen here at work in visible ways.

The invisible world and its hierarchy of adepts and saints was, for the Chishti shaikhs and their disciples, a source of guidance as well as an explanatory factor for concrete occurrences. For instance, there are numerous references to figures from the invisible world (*mardān-i ġhaib*) intervening in the visible world:

> The conversation turned to men of the invisible world, who, when they see someone is capable and of high resolve in acts of devotion and

> striving, carry them off. The master then told the story of a young man named Nasir in Badayun. "I heard about him that he said that his father was united with God. One night they called him before the door of his house. He came out, and from inside I heard salutations and greetings, and then heard my father say, 'I will just say farewell to my son and to the people of my house.' They said, 'The moment is passing.' After that I knew nothing of them, nor where my father went!"[17]

Stories such as these allowed the Chishtis to attach a spiritual significance to material objects, acts of devotion or ascesis, or events such as the appearance and disappearance of people. The ability to appreciate the true significance of the visible and the invisible worlds was what distinguished men of insight and discernment. The capacity of corporeal things or stories to exemplify or to allegorize (*tamṣīl*) invisible or hidden spiritual principles is also of course a common theme in Sufi literature in Persian and Arabic. Poets used it effectively to compose texts such as Farīd al-dīn 'Aṭṭār's *Manṭiq al-Ṭair* ("The Conference of the Birds") and Jalāl al-dīn Rūmī's *Maṣnavī*, both poems full of stories, exempla, and allegorical clues to the decipherment of mystical experiences and doctrines.[18]

For the Chishtis, the key was to immerse oneself in Allah (*mashġhūlī-yi ḥaqq*) to the exclusion of all other work and all other kinds of knowledge:

> Conversation then turned to immersing oneself in God. That is the true work, and everything else not related to it is but an obstacle to that blessing. The master noted: "Once concerning those books that I had read and studied, a fear arose within me and I said to myself, 'What has become of me (from all that reading)?'" In this connection he told the following story: "Shaykh Abu Sa'id Abu'l-Khayr—may God have mercy on him—when he had reached a perfect spiritual state took all the books that he had read and put them in a corner. Others say that he washed them (i. e. the writing) away." The master paused. "It is not correct to say that he washed them, but he did keep them in a particular place until one day he wanted to study something from one of those books. A voice from the Unseen declared: 'O Abu Sa'id, let us annul our pact, for you are immersing yourself in something else!'" The master, when he reached this point in the story, began to cry and these two lines of poetry came upon his blessed tongue:
>
> O shadow of enmity, how can you ever be contained, in that place
> where even the thought of the Friend is a bother?

> That is to say, in a circumstance where even books on the Shaykhs, not to mention tomes on jurisprudence and legal statutes, become a veil, how can one make room for things other than them?[19]

The intervention of the voice from the Unseen was only to exhort Abū Saʿīd to throw away all his books, even the books about Sufis of the past. As the Persian verse puts it, even thought is an obstacle to the direct experience of being constantly mindful of Allah, the divine presence with which the Sufis sought to sanctify the landscape of Hindustan.

Such asceticism also involved transformation of all the physical drives such as sex and hunger. In this anecdote, which Nizami discusses as an example of the Chishti principle of living only for God, the attitude of the dervishes who are engrossed in God changes the physical experience of being in the world:[20]

> A saint lived on the bank of a river. One day this saint asked his wife to give food to a *darwesh* residing on the other side of the river. His wife protested that crossing the water would be difficult. He said: "When you go to the bank of the river tell the water to provide a way for you due to respect for your husband who never slept with his wife." His wife was perplexed at these words and said to herself: "How many children have I borne this man! Yet how can I challenge this directive from my husband?" She took the food to the bank of the river, spoke the message to the water, and the water gave way for her passage. Having crossed, she put food before the *darwesh*, and the *darwesh* took it in her presence. After he had eaten, the woman asked, "How shall I recross the river?" "How did you come?" asked the *darwesh*. The woman repeated the words of her husband. On hearing this, the *darwesh* said: "Go to the river and tell it to make way for you out of respect for the *darwesh* who never ate for thirty years." The woman, bewildered at these words, came to the river, repeated the message, and the water again gave way for her passage. On returning home, the woman fell at her husband's feet and implored him: "Tell me the secret of those directives which you and the other *darwesh* uttered." "Look," said the saint, "I never slept with you to satisfy the passions of my lower self. I slept with you only to provide you what was your due. In reality, I never slept with you, and similarly, that other man never ate for thirty years to satisfy his appetite or to fill his stomach. He ate only to have the strength to do God's will."[21]

The Problem of "Hindu" and "Muslim"

Where is one to place a single emergent literary genre in a regional language? Nineteenth-century colonial scholarship, which made available the Hindavī texts and the Persian materials on premodern Indian history and religion, represents them as examples of popular synthesis between "Hindu" and "Muslim" cultures.

Sir George Grierson, the scholar who discovered the Sufi romances (*premākhyāns*), was the first to place them within a chronological history of the formation of genres and to convert them from manuscripts written in Persian script into critical editions that represented this poetry as written in "the purest vernacular of the time."[22] Although Grierson accomplished the monumental *Linguistic Survey of India*, he displayed less than his customary acuity in constructing the category of vernacular populism under which the Hindavī romances, sophisticated exemplars of a self-conscious literary tradition, have labored since his day. Grierson's account of Sufi universalism fits the poem into a populist stereotype of folk devotionalism and ignores the élite courtly patronage of the Hindavī Sufi poets.

Grierson's efforts created the models of literary classification and analysis for the nationalist Hindi critics who were to follow; he assumed that the past contained a single language called Hindi or Hindustani and fitted the literary documents of the past into the development of this language.[23] In 1896, in collaboration with Pandit Sudhakar Dwivedi, he began to publish the text of the Sufi poet Malik Muḥammad Jāyasī's *Padmāvat* (ca. 1540). Grierson's work in converting into printed editions manuscripts taken from Sufi shrines provided an influential model for later scholars: the drive to edit more and more *premākhyāns*. His collaborator, Pandit Sudhakar Dwivedi, established another interpretive strategy for explicating the romances: he added to the printed text a line-by-line gloss of the poem, which he called the *Sudhākar-Candrikā* ("The Moon That Spreads the Nectar of Illumination"). These procedures wrenched the poetic text from its context of authorship and reception, the proper place for understanding why and how such a romance was written and received historically and socially. Instead, Grierson and Dwivedi concentrated scholarly attention on classifying and constructing complete, philologically accurate texts, a tendency that dominates Hindi scholarship on the tradition to this day.

Propagation of modern standard Hindi as the national language of India in the first decades of the twentieth century was an enterprise that involved equipping Hindi with a literary history and a canon of masterpieces. Prominent in the struggle were organizations such as the Nagari Pracarini Sabha, which promoted the use of the Devanagari script and sponsored scholarly editions of literary texts.[24] Nationalist critics such as Ramchandra Shukla drew on colonial models of literary history to classify the Hindi canon, placing the Hindavī Sufi romances within a teleological scheme of the evolution of modern standard Hindi. Shukla also edited Jāyasī's texts but attacked Dwivedī's gloss as spreading darkness (*andhakāra*) rather than the nectar of illumination. Shukla subsumed the five major literary languages[25] of premodern Hindi poetry into a new nationalist construction of the canon, and he collected and edited texts that would fit within this canon. These nationalist critics invented modern standard Hindi on the model of the European nation-states with their own national languages and literary canons, classifying earlier literary and linguistic forms in conformity with primordialist notions of national identity.

When Shukla published his landmark *Hindī Sāhitya kā Itihās* in 1929, he prefaced his account of the Hindi canon by linking language, national consciousness, and history in an evolutionary scheme: "If every nation's literature is a collective reflection of the consciousness of its people, then it is necessarily true that as there are changes in the people's consciousness, the form of their literature changes also."[26]

Although the spoken tongues that emerged as vehicles of literary expression after 1200 did develop into the various regional languages of South Asia, reading the newly constituted discourses of Hindu nationalism back to constitute a unified and linear history for modern standard Hindi creates a telos for the earlier languages that is unjustified. Moreover, given the links between the movement for propagation of Hindi and Hindu revivalism, where do Muslim Sufis fit into an account of the development of modern standard Hindi? What is the precise relation of the literary traditions of Arabic and Persian to the formulation of a Hindavī Sufi poetics? If Hindi and Urdu were historically linked with the formation of separate "Hindu" and "Muslim" literary and social identities, how does one begin to understand a major body of premodern literature that is both "Muslim" and in "Hindi"?

This difficult crux led Shukla to propose that the Hindavī Sufi poetic tradition was derived from Persian *maṡnavīs* or verse narratives and was therefore "un-Indian" in inspiration and in the kind of love depicted in the stories. As a later critic, Ganapatichandra Gupta, put it, "In Acharya Ramchandra Shukla's opinion, the Indian tradition of love takes as its ideal the marital love of Rāma and Sītā, whereas in the *premākhyāns* premarital, socially unstigmatized, spontaneous love is depicted. Therefore this [argument] cannot be accepted against the Indian tradition of love."[27]

The embarrassment with the Islamic identity of a major genre of Hindi poetry, as well as with its lush eroticism, led Shukla to ignore the specifics of the Sufi romances. Although the Sufi poets depicted the heroine's body as a sensuous shadow of divinity, Shukla chose to classify the *premākhyāns* as narratives of love for an unqualified or formless divine essence (*nirguna-prema-mārga*).

These classificatory confusions yielded an extraordinary dilemma for the Hindi critics following Shukla: Are the Hindavī Sufi romances truly "Indian" or not? Shukla's view is challenged by Ganapatichandra Gupta, who offers numerous examples of extramarital love from poetry dedicated to Kṛṣṇa in Indian languages. Gupta traces a tradition of "spontaneous love" (*svacchanda prema*) back to the *Ṛgveda* and the *Mahābhārata,* citing the love stories of Uṣā and Aniruddha, Nala and Damayantī, and so on. More ink than one would care to acknowledge has been spilled on the fruitless debate between partisans of the Indian and non-Indian factions.

Setting these richly suggestive and multivalent texts within the contexts of their production and reception is a difficult proposition because of the models of cultural history that we have inherited from colonial and nationalist accounts of the Indian past. The difficulty is compounded by the near-exclusive focus on political history and chronicles of conquest and dynastic rule, with lack of attention to the discursive assumptions framing other sorts of narratives and texts.[28] The bias is apparent even in the founding moments of the academic study of the period, as in Sir Henry Myers Elliot's 1849 preface to the eight-volume sourcebook entitled *The History of India as Told by Its Own Historians*:

> We have to lament the entire absence of literary history and biography, which in India is devoted only to saints and poets. Where fairy tales and fictions are included under the general name of history we cannot expect to learn much respecting the character, pursuits, motives, and actions of historians. Even in Europe this deficiency has been complained of; how much more, then, is it likely to be a subject of regret, where despotism is triumphant.... [These chronicles] comprise, for the most part nothing but a mere dry narration of events, conducted with reference to chronological sequence, never grouped philosophically according to their relations. Without speculation on causes or effects; without a reflection or suggestion which is not of the most puerile and contemptible kind; and without any observations calculated to interrupt the monotony of successive conspiracies, revolts, intrigues, murders, and fratricides, so common in Asiatic monarchies, and to which India unhappily forms no exception.... [they] will make our native subjects more sensible of the immense advantages accruing to them under the mildness and equity of our rule.[29]

It is totally incorrect as well as highly objectionable to characterize the cultural landscape as a zone of Oriental despotism, battling essentialisms, and irrational prejudice. The assumptions made explicit in this severely biased indictment of premodern "Oriental despotism" are a useful entry into the problems that beset any attempt to shed light on what unfortunately still remains a "dark period" in Indian history.

To begin with, the colonial notion of the despotic rule that the British sought to displace in India[30] centered all effective power in the person of the tyrannical ruler. Removing him allowed the imperium to be reconstituted around the supposed "mildness and equity" of British rule rather than the savage and pointless actions of previous rulers. In addition to the untenable focus on élite history, there is another noteworthy assumption in Sir Henry Elliot's words, representing a colonialist attitude that has generated much misunderstanding and politically motivated scholarship.[31] In the same preface, he anachronistically divides the populace into Hindu and Muslim nations, corresponding to nineteenth-century views of nationalism based on race, religion, and language:

> The few glimpses we have...of Hindus slain for disputing with Muhammadans, of general prohibitions against processions, worship, and ablutions, and of other intolerant measures, of idols mutilated, of temples razed, of forcible conversions and marriages, of proscriptions and confiscations, of murders and massacres, and of the sensuality and drunkenness of the tyrants who enjoined them show us that this picture is not overcharged...[T]hese deficiencies are more to be lamented, where, as sometimes happens, a Hindu is the author. From one of that nation we might have expected to have learnt what were the feelings, hopes, faiths, fears, and yearnings, of his subject race...[T]here is nothing to betray his religion or his nation.... He is so far wedded to the set phrases and inflated language of his conquerors, that he speaks of "the light of Islam shedding its refulgence on the world," of "the blessed Muharram," and of "the illustrious Book."[32]

Two points are central here: the change in cultural forms and conventions after the change in polity, and the idea of Hindus and Muslims as two nations divided by race and religion.

The adoption of Persianate literary forms by a "Hindu" author is part of the same process of cultural assimilation and interaction that causes a "Muslim" author to use the conventions of a local Indian language to express his message. In either case, the religious identity of the author serves as no guarantor of ideological position. It is only when groups of people share the same cultural landscape that we have mixed or boundary-crossing literary and devotional traditions of poetry. It is entirely congruent, on such a cultural scene, to have a range of competitive attitudes toward conquest, religion, and the politics of cultural change. The formation of creolized or mixed literary genres implies a world of conversion and conflict, dialogue and intermingling.

Moreover, the idea of Hindus and Muslims as two nations[33] sets up an overdrawn opposition between religious communities in a history in which class, caste, occupation, language, and sectarian affiliation have always also determined social position and attitude. As Gyanendra Pandey has noted about the colonialist construction of Hindu and Muslim communalism, it "captured for the colonialists what they had conceptualized as a basic feature of Indian society—its religious bigotry and its fundamentally irrational character. . . . 'History' happens to these people; it can hardly be a process in which they play a conscious and significant part."[34] Pandey's analysis is exemplary in that he distinguishes a range of colonialist positions, from the liberal or rationalistic to the more racist and essentialistic.[35] The colonialist construction of a communally divided past, as Pandey points out, shared many elements with subsequent nationalist critiques of colonialism.

Competing nationalist historians have taken these positions to the extreme, as for instance the distinguished Pakistani historian of the Delhi sultanate, Ishtiaq Husain Qureshi: "How could two people with such divergence in their outlook, beliefs, mores, tastes, and inclinations be moulded into one [without sacrificing] something that had entered into the innermost recesses of their souls?"[36] According to this view, Indian history has been an armed struggle between Hindus and Muslims in the interests of their separate identities. On the other hand, secular Indian historians such as Tara Chand characterize the cultural life of premodern India as exemplifying the modern Indian nation's idea of religious harmony and unity: "The effort to seek a new life led to the development of a new culture which was neither exclusively Hindu nor purely Muslim. It was indeed a Muslim-Hindu culture."[37] This joint culture is often also characterized as hybrid or syncretistic, denoting an indiscriminate mingling of elements in new cultural forms.

These visions of history have had a real impact on our understandings of the cultural monuments of the past and their links with polity and religion. Thus, Aziz Ahmad places his treatment of the premodern texts that deal with the Turkish conquest of northern India within a radically dualist view of the division between "Hindu" and "Muslim" literatures:

> Muslim impact and rule in India generated two literary growths: a Muslim epic of conquest, and a Hindu epic of resistance and of psychological rejection. The two literary growths were planted in two different cultures; in two different languages, Persian and Hindi; in two mutually exclusive religious, cultural and historical attitudes each confronting the other in aggressive hostility. Each of these two literary growths developed in mutual ignorance of the other.[38]

This separatist view of genre and history, between groups of people who overlap significantly in both cultural and physical space, simplifies complex identities into a static, unchanging opposition. The highly questionable assumption of "mutual ignorance" leaves unasked all the questions about how people interact; how genre, history, and imaginative geography shape one another; and how emergent literary canons in the new Indo-Aryan languages are implicated in this moment of transition in Indian history.

On the other hand, studies of the new literatures in the regional Indian languages commonly contrast Sufis with narratives of Islamic conquest and military brutality and portray them as populists preaching universal love and brotherhood. For example, Annemarie Schimmel characterizes the users of *bhākhā*, the spoken language of north India, as follows:

> The expansion of this newly emergent language was largely due to the activities of wandering preachers, both Muslim Sufis and representatives of Hindu *bhakti* mysticism. The first great leaders of Sufi orders, like Mu'īnuddin Ćiśtī and Bahā'uddīn Zakariyā, reached the subcontinent around 1200. They taught the love of God and man and stressed the equality of all human beings before God, and they advocated religious tolerance: hence their appeal to members of a caste-ridden society.[39]

These characterizations of the Sufis as tolerant "popular" figures are often linked with the Orientalist assumption of a division of society into élite and masses, which ignores the complex and often contradictory relations of Sufi groups with ruling groups and with audiences. Thus Asim Roy describes Bengali syncretic literature in the following manner: "This literature is characterized by an anxiety to illumine the masses of Bengali Muslims, who were found ill-grounded in their religious traditions and steeped in pre-existing non-Muslim tradition. The root of this problem lay, in the agreed opinion of these writers, in the Bengali Muslims' inability to follow the religious and other works in Arabic and Persian."[40]

The difficulty with such accounts is that they ignore the specific social relations that form the context of particular syncretistic formations and assume that those whom such texts addressed were equally ignorant of those factors. Rather than single statements of Islamic conquest or Indo-Islamic assimilation, we need to understand the range or spectrum of discourses of antagonism or syncretism along with their underlying political, literary, and religious implications.[41]

At stake here is the problem of "religious syncretism," a category used to explain overlaps between the retrospectively defined categories of "Hindu" and

"Muslim" in premodern India. As Shantanu Phukan has perceptively noted about the *Padmāvat,*

> *Padmavati* has been discussed by critics...as an example of a Hindu-Muslim syncretism, or fusion. Also commonly placed in the category of "syncretic" are texts like Kabir's *Bijak,* the songs of such Sufis as Abdul Latif of Bhit, and the scriptures of the Sikh tradition since all of these are perceived as sharing the common feature of straddling the boundary between the Hindu and the Islamic traditions....Often the mere fact of co-existence in a contiguous space is held responsible for an inevitable seepage of influence from one tradition to another....Such discussions offer inadequate analysis of literary works because they fail to contextualize the relationship between a text, its author and its readers.[42]

The Sufi poets of the *premākhyāns* do not fit simply or easily into the scholarly stereotype of populist syncretic religion. In the small and select reading communities of court and *k͟hānaqāh,* they redefined Indian notions of the sympathetic response to poetry (*rasa*) in order to translate Sufi cosmology and metaphysics into narratives in a local language. The social implications of this act can best be understood within the formation and expansion of the Delhi sultanate, which generated romances as well as stories of conquest. This twin impulse, of subjugating the local population and eroticizing the landscape, poetry, and music of India, is apparent also among the Chishti Sufis who were carving out their own territories of spiritual jurisdiction. The public rhetoric of these territorial takeovers tended to be dualistic, positing an ineradicable gap between the Turkish and Afghan Muslim élite and the local population. Such a public rhetoric of polity formation concealed a much subtler process of indigenization and cultural assimilation, exemplified in the adaptation of local literary and artistic forms to express new poetic and religious agendas within a complex multilingualism of religious and symbolic vocabularies.

Since it was a composite or mixed world, culturally and linguistically, we should expect to find connected records among the different languages of the period. We find, however, that scholars of Islamic India have focused largely on the Persian and Arabic historical and linguistic record. They have produced groundbreaking studies of the establishment and institutional history of Sufi *silsilahs,* exploring the social and political roles of Sufis in the conquest of new territories,[43] the institutional and historiographical traditions shaping transmission of Sufi teachings,[44] the individual biographies of Sufi holy men[45] and the Persian literature that they left.[46] But the writings of Sufis in the emerging new Indo-Aryan languages have been little examined. The situation is complicated by the refusal of the early Chishti Sufis to write books, and it is not until the fourteenth century that there is an explosion of Persian and new Indo-Aryan Chishti mystical literature.[47] Literary critics and historians such as Mahmud Shirani and Abdul Haqq[48] have been quick to list the genres and languages that the Sufis used, but without explaining fully how they interacted with the political establishment of Turkish and Afghan sultanates in India and with preexisting literary and religious traditions. As Carl Ernst has pointed out, "the Indian environment was the world in which these Sufis lived. From it they took attractive materials, whether *pān* leaves or poems, which in this way became ancillary to Sufi teaching and practice."[49] People living together within the same environment continually define and redefine themselves and others, and these processes in turn reshape their larger social narratives and contexts.

But present-day Hindus and Muslims see themselves as separate religious communities, divided by nationality, religion, and language. In a groundbreaking analysis of attitudes toward Hindu-Muslim differences, Cynthia Talbot points to the difficulty: "No one would deny that modernization has led to the sharper articulation of identities encompassing broad communities or that such identities have been 'imagined' and 'invented' to a large extent. Nor can we uncritically accept the primordialist view that postulates the inherent and natural roots of national and ethnic identity."[50] Today's public narratives are based on sources that have been twisted to meet a communalist constitution of India's past and present. These biases also frame our readings of the sources and chronicles from the past that necessarily recognize religious difference and attempt to shape particular collective identities. Our attempt must be to disaggregate the unified readings, the two-nation theory writ large on the Delhi sultanate, or the secular liberalism of Indian historians who wish away the oppositional others and expressions of prejudice, hostility, or disgust.

Modern scholars often employ primordialist notions of identity to explain the polities and symbolic forms of premodern India. In my view, any attempt to link particular genres to particular communities must refuse to begin with primordialist notions; it must take seriously the evidence of cultural mixing and interaction on the ground. In the case of the Hindavī Sufi romances, written by local Muslim poets, this definitional issue is complicated by the fact that all the characters in every story are ostensibly "Hindu" in name and cultural and religious practice. These distinctive literary forms have been an awkward embarrassment because they do not fit neatly into the little boxes of "Hindu" or "Muslim" tradition, or "Hindi" and "Urdu" defined as separate, standardized languages. As Phukan has pointed out, this fact has led scholars such as Aziz Ahmad, in his study of the *Padmāvat*, to ascribe to the poet Jāyasī a "rural lack of sophistication which inclined [Ahmad] to accept 'in all simplicity, at a non-sectarian level, the bardic legends of Rajput heroism...'"[51]

It is only when one reads these sophisticated romances that one finds that, far from being nonsectarian, they use local mythologies, narratives, and religious practices to express their competitive and distinctive agenda of Sufi love. But their presence in the world of Indian myth and ascetic practice leads them to use local imagery and aesthetics to express their own distinctive local tradition, in what was by then an Indian Islamic literature.

Interpreting the Hindavī Sufi romances, therefore, is complicated by historiographical perspectives that characterize the cultural world of sultanate India as divided between élite and masses or Hindus and Muslims, as well as perspectives that emphasize the syncretic or separatist tendencies of the Sufis in order to create a genealogy for present-day nationalisms. Separating a particular historical moment from the overdetermined trajectory of the unfolding of "Islam"[52] allows us to focus, as I have done in this book, on a local language and idiom of self-fashioning and cultural expression. In his discussion of what he calls Indian Islamic traditions, Richard Eaton has given us this supple formulation:

> The traditions...were discursive traditions, in the sense that they were rooted in written or oral genres that had sufficient historical depth to lend them the weight of authority. And they were Islamic traditions inasmuch as they all related themselves in some way to the Qur'ān or the Traditions of the Prophet. Thus, when a writer of a compendium of Sufi biographies sat down to do his work, there would already have existed in his mind an established model of what such a work should be like, and that model would in turn have had its roots in formulations and explications of piety traceable to the foundational texts of the religion. The same was true of visual arts, such as miniature paintings, or mosque architecture, inasmuch as their creators, too, had inherited models for their endeavors, though of course there was always room for innovation within the framework of these models.[53]

This formulation allows us to account for the wholesale introduction of Persian and Arabic symbolic and literary forms into India and their use as models and prototypes for various kinds of local cultural production.

The texts of this genre exemplify a process of double distancing, in which the Indianness of the Hindavī and the pleasures of the local tongue are celebrated over the classical literary traditions of Persian and Sanskrit. My subject is the distinctive new voice that emerges from this double distancing, reusing yet rejecting older languages in creating a new literary genre. Recent work has emphasized that classicism as an "oppositional discourse" in India contains within it many impulses—toward defining the mother tongue as "classical," as "Indian," or even racially as "Turk" or "Hindu," "Dravidian" or "Aryan."[54] Similarly, this classicizing Hindavī genre has multiple religious and literary valences and intersects with different sets of locative maps: Hindustani, Muslim, Sufi, Indian poetic, and devotional culture.

The darkness that has surrounded the historiography of the sultanate period is, in part, a result of the Mughals shattering and reconstituting Afghan rule, a process parallel to the later conquest and retelling of history, culture, and narrative under British imperialism. In addition to the multiple competitive voices that clamor to be heard from the sources of the period, we have inherited stereotypes and distortions about the Turkish and Afghan sultanates from both subsequent periods. The combination of all these unfortunate tendencies has clouded our vision. Cultural historians have wrenched earlier fictions out of their contexts of production and reception and made them into the bedrock of colonial and nationalist views of the Indian past.

Needless to say, the relations between Hindus and Muslims are a major concern in the partitioned subcontinent today. I have sought to enrich that debate not by hammering the issue on the head but by building a sense of a shared literary culture that was not monolithic, monolingual, or monoreligious. Rather than the overdrawn crusades of conquest and resistance, or the stereotypes of harmonious coexistence, this shared culture was a result of collisions, encounters, convergences, and interchanges between these seemingly incompatible traditions. Then, as now, we have a much more complex cultural and religious scene than the essentialistically conceived notions of "Hindu" and "Muslim" convey. Representations of religious difference or sameness are like the engines of war paraded ritually every few years in front of the ramparts of the Indian forts during the sultanate period. They are used as rhetorical figures to make a point about identity or collective notions of honor, and therefore they cannot be taken innocently and at face value.

A New Literary Language and Tradition

The genre of the Hindavī Sufi romance embodies an Indian Islamic literary tradition, the acculturation of a monotheistic faith and a literary model into a local landscape. Poets during the period drew on the three classical (or, in Sheldon Pollock's term, "cosmopolitan") languages of law, religion, and literature: Arabic, Persian, and Sanskrit. Each of these has complex hierarchies of generic forms that continued to predetermine literary and religious expression in the subcontinent and to circulate widely among the different polities and linguistic communities formed during the period. There were in addition the particular regional literatures in Apabhraṃśa and the various Prakrits, elements from which were adapted by various poets in the new Indo-Aryan languages.[55]

Through their use of generic conventions, the Hindavī Sufi poets linked the genre to the Persian prototype of the *maṡnavī*, the long romantic, martial, or didactic poem in rhyming couplets. However, they also felt free to take concepts, models of praxis, generic conventions, imagery, poetic techniques, and themes from local universes of discourse to create their *desī* Muslim literary tradition. The poetic universes of their romances had their own specific logics of use and understanding, distinct from their various literary sources.

But these genealogies do not begin to address other questions: How are texts linked with larger ideological formations that are not necessarily nationally or even linguistically defined? How are literary genres formed at particular moments? How do they come to embody wider social concerns and attitudes? As Pollock notes, what is required is a situated study of the formation of literary language and its links with particular social and political forms: "To study vernacularization is to study not the emergence into history of primeval and natural communities and cultures, but rather the historical inauguration of their naturalization. For it was during the course of the vernacular millennium (ca. 1000–2000) that cultures and communities were ideationally and discursively invented, or at least provided with a more self-conscious voice."[56] The discursive invention of community or literary culture is difficult to understand without clarifying the thematic and formal links of genres with particular places, languages, and social agendas.

As for the language of the Sufi romances, modern linguists often classify it as Avadhi or eastern Hindavī, but we need to set the term within a larger dialectal continuum. Avadhi was spoken in the area around Ayodhya, Allahabad, and Jaunpur, and its features have been traced to Ardhamāgadhī, itself classified as a point on a spectrum between Śaurasenī Prakrit and the Bihari dialects that developed out of Māgadhī.[57] However, in the usage of the poets of the sultanate period, Hindavī can be seen as an umbrella term that carries a broader range of associations:

> Hindī, Hinduī, and Hindavī were the terms used for the language of the country as against Persian during the rule of the Delhi Sultans and later in the Mughal period: thus the usage of the term by Amīr Khusrau (1253–1325) in the thirteenth century who is traditionally regarded as the first writer of distinction in Hindi/Hindavī.... [Hindavī] was the collective designation for the indigenous group of northern Indian languages, and it was used to demarcate it from Persian. However, when its distinction from Sanskrit was to be emphasized, the poets who composed in the language spoke of it as bhāṣā [the spoken tongue].[58]

The Sufi use of Hindavī as a literary language was thus a double inauguration: the definition of a particular colloquial or spoken literary idiom (*bhāṣā*/

bhākhā) as opposed to Sanskrit, and the indigenization of ideas and themes taken from Persian narrative poetry but reused in the Indian language known as Hindavī.

Several assumptions are common to modern criticism on the genre: that these texts constitute a single coherent genre modeled on Persian *maṣnavī*s or verse romances, that they express a syncretic mingling of elements between Indian and Islamic poetic and religious traditions, and that they are somehow "allegorical" (*saṅketātmaka*) in equating human and divine love. Scholars have concentrated on classifying the genre within larger canons of Indian literature and finding some sort of schema to explain its spiritual meaning. Beyond these basic points, all agreement ends, and critics have adopted a number of schemata to explicate the surviving Hindavī Sufi romances. These strategies include interpreting the texts as examples of vernacular populism,[59] of love for a formless divinity (*nirguṇa-prema-mārga*) and simultaneously of "un-Indian" sensuality,[60] of premarital love,[61] of the indigenization of Persian romances,[62] of adaptation of the Alexander romance into Indian literature,[63] of allegory understood as a point-for-point correspondence between two levels of meaning,[64] of numerical symmetry,[65] of "image-ism" (*pratibimba-vāda*),[66] of religious syncretism[67] or its opposite,[68] and of deployment of multiple metaphoric systems toward a moral and didactic purpose.[69] We cannot resolve these interpretative confusions without understanding literary meaning as the poets of the genre defined and used it.

The various Sufi *silsilah*s whose members composed Hindavī poetry in north India were part of a literary and devotional culture fully steeped in the conventions and symbolism of the various genres of Persian poetry, both lyric (*ġhazal*) and narrative (*maṣnavī*). That culture regarded the works of Persian poets as delicate, full, and richly suggestive poems, but lacking the graphic allure and frank eroticism of the *desī* Hindavī. The Hindavī poets celebrated the sweet, straightforward *desī* tongue, in which it was possible to express concretely the particulars of life in the provinces of Avadh and Bihar. They were poets observant of nature, frequently using intensely local flora and fauna to create multiply suggestive imagery. One can imagine rural audiences listening spellbound to the romances as an evening's entertainment in assemblies sponsored by sultans, nobles, and landed gentry, or accompanied by musicians, at the shrines of the Sufi shaikhs who had taken over the spiritual jurisdiction of the various territories of Hindustan. The *Cāndāyan* of Maulānā Dā'ūd, the first surviving Hindavī Sufi romance (ca. 1379), even mentions a *bājir*, a wandering minstrel who sings the beauty of the seductively lovely heroine Cāndā through the kingdoms of the land. Audiences would have understood and enjoyed the sly and constant allusions and hints of spiritual and erotic meanings, the scary demons and seductive women, the adventures and fights, the exotic landscapes, and the conventional set pieces like the head-to-foot description of the beloved and the song of the worldly heroine's twelve months of separation from her Lord.

The historical agents who formed this Indian Islamic literary culture were not just courtiers and kings of the Delhi sultanate and the Afghan regional polities in the fifteenth and sixteenth centuries. They were also disciples in Sufi orders, guided by shaikhs who set themselves up as commanding spiritual jurisdiction (*vilāyah*) over different parts of the territory of Hindustan. The army of prayer (*lashkar-i du'ā'*), as it is sometimes called, led by these shaikhs, formed one dominant cultural force during the period. Sufi shaikhs played at being kingmakers and established themselves in hospices (*k͟hānaqāhs*) at a calculated distance from royal courts. Here they trained disciples to attain nearness to Allah by teaching them spiritual exercises and cultivating their taste for things spiritual (*z̤auq*) through ritually controlled exposure to music and poetry. They recreated their own Persian and Arabic models of poetry and ascetic praxis in an effort to communicate within their Indian cultural context. They reimagined these models in terms of local religious and poetic practice, "going *desī*" by creating outwardly Hindu or Indian characters and narrative universes, yet maintaining a mystical interpretation in which the suggested referents of plot and character were distinctively and competitively linked to Sufi asceticism. If the Chishtis or the other *silsilahs* promoted a surface liberalism of outlook, they also "asserted the finality and supremacy of their faith"[70] vis-à-vis other ascetics and the various orders of Sufis.

The Genre of the Hindavī Romance

The Hindavī poets themselves belonged to different *silsilahs*, who were in competition with each other and sought out areas and populations to which they could minister. But since there was no single or central institution, court or shrine, to which all the poets belonged, repetition of the same generic logic compels us to think of the romances as a common narrative and literary phenomenon.

In the generic formula, the first encounter of the hero and the heroine is treated as a way of conveying allegorically the Sufi concept of the first meeting of the immortal spirit with divinity in the phenomenal world.[71] Erotic desire is aroused between the hero and the heroine in this initial encounter, but in order to transform it into love, the hero and the heroine have to pass through several trials or ordeals. They have helpers, who commonly exemplify spiritual values such as mystical absorption (*sahaja*) or the abstract quality of love (*pema/prema*). And there are demons to fight and trials of strength that the lovers must pass through in order to attain each other. The action is usually set in fantastic and exotic landscapes, described through a sensuous erotic poetics.

All the plots have certain formulaic elements that allude to earlier canons or to common stereotypes about gender and culture that the Hindavī poets reshaped into a distinctive formula. These include the moment of the awakening of love through a vision, a dream, or a description of the heroine's beauty as a divine manifestation, a convention common to both Persian and Indian romances. Description of the heroine's body follows the order of the *sarāpā*, the head-to-foot description of the heroine in Persian poetry, but uses much of the imagery of the *nakha-śikha varṇana*, the toe-to-head description of human heroines in Sanskrit, Middle Indic, and new Indo-Aryan poetry. The necessary transformation of the hero into a yogi on an ascetic quest draws on the poetry of the Gorakhnāth *panth*. The hero's abandonment of a first wife in order to consummate his love with the divine heroine is a motif that draws on the common sultanate cultural stereotype of the jealousy between co-wives (*sautana*) in a harem. The message that the deserted wife sends, describing her agony through the twelve months of the year, uses the convention of the *bārah-māsā*, taken from oral songs in the various regional languages. The hero's resolution of the strife between the co-wives, his death, and the burning of both his wives on his funeral pyre uses the stereotype of the self-immolation of the Indian *satī* to signify mystical annihilation.

Each of the poets of the Hindavī romances used the elements of this generic formula differently. From the period of the Delhi sultanate and the Afghan kingdoms, works by four poets survive. The inauguration of the genre may be seen in the *Cāndāyan* of Maulānā Dā'ūd, composed in 1379 at the provincial court of Dalmau in Avadh. It is followed by Quṭban's *Mirigāvatī* (1503), composed under the patronage of Sultan Ḥusain Shāh Sharqī of Jaunpur. Although there are scattered references to two romances from the early sixteenth century entitled the *Paiman* and the *Jot Nirañjan*, these have not survived.[72] Malik Muḥammad Jāyasī emulated the model of the *Cāndāyan* and the *Mirigāvatī* in several poems that are still extant, preeminently the *Padmāvat* (1540), which tells the story of King Ratansen of Chittaur and his quest for the princess Padmāvatī. Jāyasī also composed a version of the life of Kṛṣṇa called the *Kanhāvat*, as well as a number of shorter poems, including the *Akhrāvat* ("Alphabet Poem"), an acrostic composed out of the beliefs of a millenarian group of Sufis (the Mahdavis of Jaunpur), and the *Ākhirī Kalām* ("Discourse on the Last Day"), a foreshadowing of the events of doomsday. There is also the short poem *Citrarekhā*, a romance between Prītam Kuṉvar and Princess Citrarekhā, with a happy ending. Finally, there is the *Madhumālatī* (1545) of Mīr Sayyid Mañjhan Rājgīrī, a Shattari Sufi who was attached to the court of Islām Shāh Sūrī[73] and was a member of the Shattari *silsilah*. Although poets continued to compose romances on this model until the early twentieth century, they did not, by and large, reproduce the formula of the two heroines or the elaborate Sufi ideology of the earlier works.[74]

The main lines of the argument in this book are organized around the different facets of a common generic logic. This logic, of the love triangle of the hero and his divine and earthly wives and the final self-immolation of the three major characters, must have appealed to some cultural longing, some perceived tension of the day. An upper-class Muslim consciousness or subjectivity for which this was important must have informed the mind of the ideal reader or listener, who would have been excited by the romances of the genre, alert to its nuances. Many critics have pointed to the tendency of romance genres to resolve larger social and ideological contradictions and oppositions, whether they personify these oppositions as denizens of superhuman and subhuman worlds or as the principles of dialectical materialism.[75] Our sensibility inclines us to adopt a rigid dualistic division between the things of this world and the hereafter. But we can think of this general contrast between *dīn* and *duniyā* as one among a series of rhetorical dualisms such as Turk and Hindu, conqueror and conquered that were important to the cultural world of sultanate India. As in many situations created by acts of conquest, the poets used these dualisms as rhetorical figures to make a point about identity or collective notions of honor.

Since the Hindavī Sufi romances are only fragments of the entertainment, spiritual and literary, of a past age, the picture they give us is only a partial and slanted one. Trying to understand the sultanate world through these romances is like trying to understand contemporary India by watching Bombay films, inspiring the curious spectator in a later century to ask, "But didn't people do dance routines in the street, to the sound of playback music?" In some places the Hindavī documentation is thicker, as in the case of the Shattari materials that we will consider in Chapter 7. Here, we can discern not only the poetic form (the allegorical centerpiece of Madhumālatī's body) but also the larger cosmological, political, and mystical world of the poem. We have to read the texts through categories of interpretation that would not have sounded strange to the historical agents who produced and enjoyed the Hindavī Sufi romances.

Although the authors of the Sufi romances used the inflated rhetoric of the conquest narratives of Hindustan, they reimagined themselves as the "natives," the Rajputs who defended their forts to the last and created narratives such as the fictive sacrifice of Padminī at Chittaur (see Chapter 6). In these stories of the sacrifice of Rajput women, the ultimate preservation of their women from the enemy functions as a palliative for their loss of symbolic honor after they were forced to admit the suzerainty of the Delhi sultans. It is remarkable that within two centuries of the conquest the conquerors should take on the opposing viewpoint, that of the conquered, and use it to create their own local literary tradition. The victors were vanquished by the seductive charm of the languages and literatures of India, by the culture that contained exquisite *bārah-māsās* and folk songs as well as a cultivated Sanskrit aesthetics and narrative poetics. These poets' mixture of Persianate literary notions, Sufi ideology, and *desī* symbolic and literary forms fits well within the cosmopolitan and cultured literary world of sultanate India, a world that was predominantly rural but dotted with forts controlled by aristocrats and crisscrossed by fighting armies as well as by wandering Sufis and minstrels.

The distinctive narrative logic of the Hindavī Sufi romances linked bodily discipline to stereotypes of gender to express a male-centered mystical agenda as well as the resolution of uneasy political relationships with rulers and other religious communities. Gavin Hambly, the editor of a volume of essays on women in Islam, has remarked on "the stereotypical assumption that in traditional Islamic society women were somehow 'invisible.'"[76] The difficulty of making women visible through fictional sources such as the ones analyzed in this book are evident. As Hambly remarks, the representation of women in literature "raises questions of great complexity: the extent to which fiction reflects some kind of reality; the authenticity of different voices; and the imposition by male authors of a particular point of view."[77] We have to set the élitist Indian Muslim male-authored narratives of the Sufi romances against other narratives from the period, to see if we can begin to isolate a larger cultural logic of gender relations. One pattern that is distinctly observed is the general assumption of male superiority to women, and of women's complete subservience in some idealized domestic realm.[78] To what extent this is idealized, we cannot say, but what else can we expect from the fantasy literature of a male aristocratic élite? Tentative and slanted as such a reconstruction may be, at least it helps us understand the authors' assumptions about gender, understand deeper misogynies that run through the stories that people told during the sultanate period, and understand how eroticism is powerfully shaped socially and culturally, even in the moment of renouncing the world to become an ascetic.

These fictional narratives demonstrate that alterity, desire, opposition, mutual understanding, material and symbolic competition, and sexual fantasy were very much part of the historical interaction between ethnic and religious groups during the period of the Delhi sultanate. The genre exemplifies the gradual transformation of conquerors and conquered as they met on the landscape of the soul, defining its pleasures and possibilities. The literary past of modern standard Hindi was a shared past, to which the Sufis contributed a major literary tradition, reinventing themselves as *desī* Muslims in the process.

Enigmatic texts conceal within them multiple layers of meaning and intention, as well as an architectonics of form that governs their use, allowing the producers and performers of the text to control access and understanding but confounding attempts to systematize or map them. Thus the pluralism of readings has also a limit condition, which is set by the makers of these texts. One can identify specific contexts and conditions of reception that show quite clearly how the contact between text and audience works in each case, triggering and shaping a spiritual process behind closed shrine doors and presenting lovely romantic narratives in musical salons, bazaars, courts, and the public or outer spaces of the shrines. In other words, one cannot just derive any random meaning from the text, and it is the interplay between pluralism and its limiting that the genre allows us to explore.

The Chapters of This Book

The chapters focus on the four major sultanate romances. My main objective is to provide a reading of the major texts of this unjustly neglected literary tradition.

Chapter 2 examines the religious and political structures of address in the prologues of the Hindavī Sufi romances, using a set of frames derived from Persian models and adapted into the new literary language Hindavī, as well as the schemes of meaning they invoke through their discussions of the ideal reading or listening subject. The Hindavī poets framed their literary efforts through the prologues to their romances, which offer clues to place them socially, linguistically, and ideologically. The structures of address embodied in these prologues allow us to elucidate an indigenous Islamic theology and poetics expressed in Hindavī, as well as a social place for the Sufi romances.

The ensuing chapters present the texts, in chronological order, and their meanings. The first presentation of each romance offers a detailed reading of the narrative, intended to give the reader a basis for understanding the ensuing hermeneutical discussion, in which I place textual particulars within larger frameworks of cultural and literary understanding. Thus Chapter 3 investigates the creation of a new genre in Maulānā Dā'ūd's *Cāndāyan*, reconstructing the sources for his narrative and delineating the generic formula that he created in his romance of Lorik, Cāndā, and Mainā. Dā'ūd's use of *rasa* allows us to specify a Sufi poetics of ordinate love. He links eroticism and ascetic transformation through the multiple meanings of the "juice" or "essence" (*rasa*) that runs through Indian notions of poetry and praxis, reimagining the Chishti theology of *'ishq* (love)[79] in richly suggestive language. Setting his use of *rasa* and embodiment within a range of other Indian devotional poets allows us to see the distinctive Sufi use of common literary and religious vocabulary.

Dā'ūd's text inaugurated a narrative formula that was important to later poets as they created their own literary fantasies. Chapter 4 is about the *Mirigāvatī* of Quṭban, written at the court-in-exile of Sultan Ḥusain Shāh Sharqiī of Jaunpur. Quṭban combined the formula of the hero and his two wives with story motifs that are also found in the voyages of Sindbād the Sailor and other narrative traditions from around the Indian Ocean. These motifs have their own histories in local and global storytelling traditions. I trace the Sindbād stories back to a Sanskrit source, the Sānudāsa stories of the *Bṛhat-kathā*, and place them within the cultural encounters of the trading world of the Indian Ocean. This enables us to see how the intensely local world of Quṭban's romance is part of wider global mercantile and cultural trajectories and the circulation and exchange of stories and trade goods.

The fifth chapter uses several notions of landscape—interior, imaginative, and concrete—to read the suggestive poetics of the first half of Malik Muḥammad Jāyasī's *Padmāvat*. In narrating the ascetic quest of the hero Ratansen and his winning of the beautiful Padmāvatī, Jāyasī's distinctive use of coded language creates a suggestive map of the body as a city within the paradisal isle of Singhala-dvīpa. On one level, the imagined landscapes of the embodied city of Ratansen's quest can be interpreted as metaphors for the stages of an interior journey toward spiritual realization. On another level, they suggest the appropriation of the territory traversed by the hero into the spiritual jurisdiction of Sufi authority. Using aspects of Jāyasī's spiritual lineage, I then set the text against facets of the Chishti ascetic regimen, especially the sanctification of the north Indian landscape by Chishti Sufi masters such as Shaikh Ashraf Jahāngīr Simnānī. Here I emphasize the competitive aspects of this spiritual ideology, especially as represented in encounters with local ascetics that end with their conversion and submission to Islam. The imaginary landscapes of the romances are thus articulated within a concrete historical space of transformation, the cultural landscape on which the *Padmāvat* was composed and disseminated enthusiastically through assemblies of eager listeners.

Chapter 6 examines this transformation of selves and others through the controversial ending of the *Padmāvat*, which thematizes the conquest of Chittaur by 'Alāuddīn K͟haljī and the death of the lovely queen Padminī or Padmāvatī on a funeral pyre. Jāyasī brings his story to a conclusion by invoking the stereotypic narratives of the Turkish conquest of Hindustan, yet he valorizes the Sufis as the brave Rajput defenders of the land. In the conflict of might versus right, the women are sacrificed on a funeral pyre, a symbol for mystical annihilation. I compare Jāyasī's ending with prior narratives of the conquest of India: a story of the Scythian conquest of India popular among Jains in the sultanate period, a Persian verse romance by Amīr K͟husrau, and an Apabhraṃśa text from one of the Rajput kingdoms that fell to the superior cavalry and military might of the Turkish army of Delhi. These texts interweave conquest and romance, spelling out a wider cultural politics in which possession, rejection, or sacrifice of women marked the negotiations of opposed ideologies and notions of male honor.

The next two chapters, 7 and 8, are about the *Madhumālatī* of the Shattari Sufi Mīr Sayyid Mañjhan Rājgīrī, the final text of the four romances under discussion. The seventh chapter presents a detailed reading of the allegorical centerpiece of the *Madhumālatī*, the head-to-foot description of the heroine's body as it unfolds in front of the enraptured gaze of the seeker. My aim is to understand the poetics of embodiment and erotic union in the context of Shattari cosmology, politics, and spiritual practice, which I reconstruct in this chapter from rare manuscript materials. I link the lush eroticism of the allegorical set piece to the ascetic culture that produced it, the regimen of the author's group of Sufis, the Shattari *silsilah.*

Chapter 8 turns this knowledge of the Shattari mystical context to an exegesis of certain key passages in the romance, set within a complete reading of Mañjhan's text. The *Madhumālatī* differs from the other romances of the genre in that the hero does not have two wives; nor is there a final annihilation. Instead, Mañjhan structures his story around a double plot: two couples come together in the end, and the poetic description of marriage and the journey to the beloved's land signifies the ascent to a paradise of eternal love. There is a poetic play between the secret mysteries of divine presence and what can be publicly told. The hero and heroine swear a binding oath of silence, and Mañjhan exploits this to hint at the greatest mystery of all: the dissolution of boundaries between God and human beings at the higher levels of spiritual perfection. My reading focuses on the way in which poetic personification suggests spiritual mysteries, showing how the hero's meeting with Pemā or "Love" in a dark forest evokes spiritual macrocosms and self-transformation. Love's descent into this world from the paradisal mango grove of her father's kingdom slyly hints at larger cosmologies, and the hero's conquest of the evil demon who brought pemā there advances him on the quest for perfection. I also highlight the generic set piece of the *bārah-māsā*, which is set here in the voice of the divine heroine rather than the worldly wife.

The ninth chapter reconstructs the contexts of reception and performance for these sensuous romances. Common understanding of the multiple meanings of poetry allowed the poems to be performed in both courtly and Sufi circles, each with its own protocol of reception and interpretation. Not all readings are created equal, however, and in this chapter I attempt to isolate a hierarchy of response in which the Sufi shaikhs were the most privileged interpreters of these poems. A discussion of the Chishti practice of audition or *samā'* shows how ritual manipulation of the listening self was the most valued part of the reception of the Hindavī Sufi romances, making the Sufi novice under the guidance of a teaching shaikh the ideal reader of the romances. The final chapter considers the sources of the stories in the wider culture of the Indian Ocean, their translations into Persian, and their subsequent impact on the wider world.

All in all, the various chapters delineate a number of aspects of the genre: formation of a Hindavī poetics of multiple meanings with a distinctive slant, creation of a generic formula, use of narrative motifs, use of landscape and coded language to denote interior and imaginative journeys, cultural and literary understandings of the Turkish conquest of Hindustan, gender stereotypes used to denote spiritual transformation as well as mystical love, the cosmological and ascetic context for the lush eroticism of the texts, and finally, the audiences for whom the pleasure of listening to narrative poetry was mediated by the Sufi practice of audition and theological interpretation.

The poets of the Hindavī Sufi romances commonly use the phrase "the shadow of paradise on earth" (*janu kabilāsa utari bhui chāvā*)[80] to describe elements of their fictional landscapes. These include golden cities gleaming in the sun or lush visions of paradisal islands with the flora and fauna of north India:

And if anyone ever comes to that isle,
he seems to approach paradise: on every side
are planted thick mango-groves,
rising from the earth to meet the sky. . . .[81]

The heroine's body sometimes flashes with the light of divine revelation:

Her body was wave upon wave of tenderness,
anointed with sandal and nutmeg mixed together.
She looked as if she truly came from paradise,
and was poised to fly away there. . . .[82]

And, when the heroes of these works run to catch these heavenly nymphs:

"I ran to fall at her feet, but she saw me coming and flew away.
When she left, there was a shining of light and a tinkling of bells,
and I fainted dead away!"[83]

These references to shadows of an elusive paradise are the hallmark of a genre of Sufi romance that is assumed to put forward "the equation of human love and love for a divine being."[84] In these shadows we will seek this great and wrongly neglected genre.

2

Inaugurating Hindavī

The Prologues of the Hindavī Sufi Romances

This chapter presents a detailed reading of the prologues of the four major Hindavī Sufi romances from the fourteenth to the sixteenth centuries: Maulānā Dā'ūd's *Cāndāyan* (1379), Shaikh Quṭban Suhravardī's *Mirigāvatī* (1503), Malik Muḥammad Jāyasī's *Padmāvat* (1540), and Shaikh Mīr Sayyid Mañjhan Shaṭṭārī Rājgīrī's *Madhumālatī* (1545). Setting them against the backdrop of earlier Sanskrit and Persian models of poetic understanding emphasizes the Hindavī poets' continuity with these earlier canons, as well as their distance from them. They signal their uniqueness and novelty by using the terms *Hindavī, Hindukī*, or *Bhākhā* ("the spoken tongue") to describe their courtly and patterned verse. Since they represent *rasa* or the idea of sympathetic response as the cornerstone of their aesthetic agenda, the prologues of these works are invaluable as a statement of aesthetic intention.

The following pages use the theological, political, and aesthetic frameworks set out in the Hindavī prologues to specify the particular generic conventions drawn on and transformed by the poets and to connect these conventions to various contexts of reception. First, I set out the convention borrowed from Persian verse narratives or didactic poems (*mas̱navīs*), which serve as the generic model for the Hindavī poet, examining the opening verses of the prologues to establish the metaphysics and distinctive Islamic religious vision of the Hindavī poets. Then I show how the convention was translated into Hindavī in the prologues of the four major romances. Finally, I look at the praise poems to the rulers and noblemen who sponsored the poets, showing how the genre creates the material circumstances for its production through the ideal forms of the panegyric.

Inaugurating any new genre of poetry is a complex phenomenon, often justifying itself in terms of earlier canons or celebrating its freshness and novelty vis-à-vis scriptural or classical languages. Often, poetic inaugurations are signaled in framing statements that serve both to introduce the poetic text and to place it within a larger sociohistorical context. The Hindavī Sufi romances are a case in point, for they belong self-consciously to a single genre of poetry and open with elaborate prologues that create aesthetic and cultural frameworks for understanding them. The authors addressed the works both to their spiritual guides and to the rulers and noblemen who provided material support and an important audience. These prologues present us with a set of metaphysical, historical, and literary frameworks that allow us to gauge the sources, the aesthetics, the social place, the religious vision, and the ideological constraints of the Sufis who were composing this kind of poetry.

Rasa

Even while they were transcreating a Persian generic model in a local language, however, the poets of these prologues also inaugurated a Hindavī poetics that established its distance from Persian romances by drawing on the Indian aesthetics of *rasa*, the literary flavor or juice of a poem or play, the mood or essence of a poetic or dramatic text in Indian poetics, the aesthetic taste of a literary text. *Rasa* was defined famously in Bharata's eighth-century Sanskrit aesthetic treatise, the *Nāṭya-Śāstra*, as the juice or flavor of a poem arising from "the combination of the *vibhāvas* (sources of *rasa*), the *anubhāvas* (actions, experiential signs of *rasa*), and the transitory emotions (*vyabhicāribhāvas*)."[1] *Rasa* also meant the sap or semen that runs through the natural world and the human body and was the essence that Indian yogis sought to control through the channels of their subtle bodies.

Rasa is "the poem's capacity to elicit a deep response from a sensitive reader."[2] The cultivated reader was the *sahṛdaya*, the "person with heart" who could open himself up to the meanings and nuances of poetry, music, and dance. The aim of reading or listening was to have an experience of the dominant *rasa* that animates the poem, and the *sahṛdaya* feels the emotions of the parted lovers in the poem. The *sahṛdaya*'s response is shaped by the sources of *rasa* depicted by the poet. These include monsoon clouds indicating the season of love, the experiential signs of love such as bodies trembling and perspiring from desire, and the transitory emotions that attend the progress of the main emotional mood of a poem: apprehension, envy, contentment, shame, joy, and so on. A reader can approach the poet's vision, the literal, figurative, and suggested meanings of the poetic imagery, and the feelings of the characters only because the ideal reader is a *rasika* or connoisseur of *rasa* at heart. A reader or listener who was a *rasika* would understand the spiritual, ascetic, and erotic dimensions of the poetry and appreciate the cunning interweave of meaning and interlinguistic resonance in the Sufi love stories in Hindavī.

The poets of the Hindavī romances used this concept in their own distinctive way and without the elaborate superstructure of Sanskrit literary criticism. They used *rasa* to anchor a poetics of suggestion and secrecy, linking ascetic practice and eroticism in particular narrative patterns. These patterns, called *rūpas*, "forms," are the basis of an aesthetic practice in which form and beauty structure response to the poetry and imprint the consciousness of the listener with a sequential revelation of the emotional truths embodied in the narrative. Spectators and listeners in a poetic or dramatic performance understood the words, music, and movements through a transsubjective communication of the *rasa* of a performed or recited piece. By using a spoken language, Hindavī, rather than Sanskrit, the poets distanced themselves from the classical literary language controlled by Brahmin ritual specialists. But at the same time, by appropriating aesthetic models and conventions from Sanskrit and Persian, they laid claim to literary and social prestige, classicizing Hindavī and transforming it from an everyday spoken vernacular into a courtly language.

Maulānā Dā'ūd, writing in 1379, uses the term *rasa* as the keystone of his narrative poetics, the pleasure that he expects his audiences to savor in his love story. The full extent of Dā'ūd's indebtedness to classical Sanskrit models of *rasa* or their Middle Indic approximations can be known only through the incomplete and damaged text of the *Cāndāyan*, as we have hardly any contextual information about the poet. There are verses in the *Cāndāyan*, however, indicating that the poet was familiar not only with *rasa* as the "meaning" or *ma'ānī* of Hindavī music and poetry but also with a range of Sanskrit poetic techniques such as *dhvani* or suggestion.[3]

Earlier theorists of meaning in Sanskrit distinguished *abhidhā*, the denotative power of a word, from the secondary or figurative meanings (*lakṣaṇā*) that arose when the primary denotation was blocked.[4] The ninth-century Kashmiri critic Ānandavardhana clarified the aesthetic effects of poetic utterance by developing a third linguistic function or meaning, the *dhvani*, or suggested sense of the poem. As Edwin Gerow puts it, this third sense is bound up with "the emotional response to the work of art, the *rasa*":

> The affective response is...linked with the non-denotative utterance: not accidentally, as an attribute of a content itself poetic, but essentially, and simultaneously with the content that is apprehended through the other modes and thus is not (as such) poetic. The co-existence of poetic (*dhvani*) modes of apprehension with others (*abhidhā* etc.) thus

becomes not an obstacle to the theory, but a token of the complexity of the language and of the paradigmatic essential character of poetry itself.[5]

In other words, aside from the literal meanings of a poetic text, there are varieties of implied or suggested meanings that are simultaneously apprehended by the reader who is aware of the limits of denotative meaning in understanding a poem.

In this kind of poetry, the expressed meaning (*abhidhā*) interacts with the suggested meaning (*vyaṅgyārtha*) that resonates from the verse. An example of such a verse, attributed to king Vikramāditya and commented on by the critics Ānandavardhana and Abhinavagupta, would be:

What a unique river of allurement is this,
where waterlilies float together with the moon;
from which arise an elephant's cranial lobes,
and where new trunks of plaintain trees
and stems of lotus fiber grow.[6]

In this Sanskrit verse, the luxuriant images used to describe the river are not completely coherent at the level of expressed meaning. Only the sensitive reader who thinks beyond the direct imagery can grasp the hidden suggestions of the limbs of a woman's body: branches as arms, trunk as body, waterlilies as eyes, elephant's cranial lobes and fruit as breasts, plaintain trunks as thighs, and so on. The poet counts on the slow dawning of the implications of these images in the minds of sensitive readers or listeners to achieve his aesthetic effect.

At the heart of the Hindavī love stories is a Sufi poetics of the notion of *rasa*. For, aside from being a literary category, *rasa* in Indic religious systems also serves to underpin yogic and Tantric ideas of spiritual practice[7] and the attainment of immortality. Within the musical and poetic culture of fourteenth-century Delhi and the provinces under its rule, the Chishti Sufis adapted to their own ends the imagery and sense of this mystical attainment. They used a Hindavī poetics of *rasa* to compose verse that was sung during the spiritual training and eventual transformation of novices through the practice of *samā'* or musical audition. The poets of the genre exploited the multiple referentiality inherent in poetry to give desire and love an extra fillip by their association with Sufi love, linking the sensuous eroticism of their images with the rigorous ascetic practice of the Sufi *silsilahs*.

These poets produced self-conscious reflections on language that emphasized its links with both the transitory world and the eternity of Allah. Images can disappear in the twinkling of an eye, but the experience of mystical love lives beyond the play of forms. This complex use of language and its inherently multiple meanings enabled the authors of this genre to straddle the two major institutional contexts of reading and sponsorship, court and Sufi hospice. The poems also circulated in contexts outside these interpretive communities, for cultivated readers appreciated the Hindavī poets for their lush imagery and their ability to tell a good story. In the Sufi shrine, however, the internal principle of the proliferation of endless meanings was limited by the logocentric bias of Sufi commentators and their insistence on the training of the self toward a monotheistic godhead.

The Persian Conventions of the *Cāndāyan*

Although we have no evidence documenting Dā'ūd's sources for the *Cāndāyan*, the text demonstrates the complex reimagining of a Persian genre in terms taken from Indian poetry. The opening verses of Dā'ūd's story of the love of Lorik and Cāndā, written in 1379 at the provincial court of Dalmau in Avadh, set up a model that is followed by later poets but is itself patterned self-consciously on the Persian *maṡnavī*s or verse romances. The most famous of these form the *Khamsah* or "Quintet" of five *maṡnavī*s by Niẓāmī Ganjavī (1141–1209), widely circulated and imitated throughout the Persian-speaking world.[8] Niẓāmī's romances (*Laylī va Majnūn*, *Khusrau va Shīrīn*) are preceded by elaborate prologues that sing the praises of Allah, the Prophet Muḥammad, and the ruling king. The terms in which these panegyrics are framed draw on Islamic theology, the traditions of the Prophet, and the literature of the "mirrors for princes"[9] that taught rulers how to be ideal and just kings. Dā'ūd and the Sufi poets of the Delhi sultanate used tropes from both Indian and Islamic theology and theories of statecraft. The later poets, however, show both greater self-consciousness of an Indian Islamic identity and an elaboration of a distinctive Hindavī poetics of *rasa*.

Niẓāmī's famous romance, *Khusrau va Shīrīn* (KS, composed 1177–1181), opens with an intricate set of conventional panegyrics: a *ḥamd* or praise of Allah, a description of divine unity (*tauḥīd*), the poet's prayer to Allah; a *na't* or praise of the Prophet Muḥammad; a praise poem to the Saljuq rulers of Azerbaijan; and finally the poet's reason for composing the book. *Mutatis mutandis*, his other *maṡnavī*s follow the same pattern, except that they are dedicated to different princely patrons. In addition, the prologue to *Laylī va Majnūn* includes a description of the Prophet's night journey (*mi'rāj*), while that of the *Haft Paikar* contains a discussion of poetic speech (*sukhan*). Amīr Khusrau, who composed his own *Shīrīn va Khusrau* (SK) in his *Khamsah* in response to the works of Niẓāmī, follows a similar pattern in his prologues, with one significant difference. He always includes a section in praise of his spiritual guide, Shaikh Niẕām al-dīn Auliyā' (d. 1325), pointing to the importance of the Sufi *silsilahs* in the cultural and spiritual life of the military aristocracy of the Delhi sultanate.

Each element in the model sketched out here presupposes an elaborate theology and ideology of rulership, as well as a sophisticated poetics. To begin with Niẕāmī's prologues, we see that his praise poems to Allah (*ḥamd*) ground the world in an Islamic metaphysics replete with Qur'ānic references. The *Laylī va Majnūn* (LM) opens with a long series of exhortations to Allah:

> *O You, whose Name is the best at the beginning!*
> *Without Your Name, how can I begin my story?*
> *O You who make every task easy!*
> *Your Name is the key to everything that is closed ...*
> *O knower of the secrets of the world of might!*
> *The world is from you, both below and above.*
> *O You, who are endowed with your attributes!*
> *Your prohibition cancels out even a known command!*
> *Your command pervades (everything) absolutely.*
> *From your command, the universe is derived ...*
> *O You, on whose page the lesson of the days*
> *is received from the beginning to the end!*
> *You are the master, the others are slaves!*
> *You are the Sultan, where are the others? [LM 1–2, 10–13, 15–16]*[10]

Here the divine Name functions as the key to all difficult tasks and the anchor of the universe. Niẕāmī uses the language of the divine attributes (*ṣifāt*) to delineate the different aspects of Allah's might and majesty. Allah, in the metaphysic the poet sketches out, is the Keeper of the book of days.

In his *Shīrīn va Khusrau*, Amīr Khusrau begins each *masnavī* with a similar series of exhortations, each calling on aspects of Allah's power and praying to Allah to grant spiritual knowledge and grace. Thus, his prologue opens:

> *O Master! Open the eyes of my heart!*
> *Show me the way to my ascension of faith!*
> *Through your compassion, open your treasury!*
> *...Give me a heart full of praise for You,*
> *and a tongue that stays far away from the praise of others! [SK 1–3]*[11]

Amīr Khusrau follows his initial prayer with a paean to divine unity (*tauḥīd*) and another long prayer (*munājāt*) following Niẕāmī's model. His other *masnavīs* follow the same pattern. His *Deval Rānī Khiẓr Khān* (DRKK), a story about the love of Prince Khiẓr Khān and the Princess of Gujarat, opens with these lines:

I place at the head of my story the name of that Lord God,
who gave to hearts their attachment to beauties.
He adorned the tablet of water and clay with love,
and in that life, he granted life to the heart.
From the letters kāf *and* nūn, *which are a difficult mystery,*
he brought out the single dot, which is the heart.
From dark locks of hair and cheeks, he gave to the idols night and day,
and from the sight of these fair ones, he brought pleasure into our lives.[12]

Here the poet makes the *ḥamd* into an extended figure for the attachment of the human heart to divine beauty. The image for humanity, the "tablet of water and clay" (*lauḥ-i āb-va gil*), places the faculty of love at the center of God's shaping of Adam in the Qur'ān, and the second couplet links that faculty with the heart of life. Rather than the difficult mysteries of the letters *kāf* and *nūn*, the poet focuses on the single effulgent dot (*nuqtah*) that stands at the center of the letter *nūn* and contains divine love. Lovely women are here embodied as seductive idols (*but*), enchanting to the eyes, potentially leading one down the path to heresy, but ultimately part of Allah's creation. Vision is the source of pleasure in life, yet it enables one to approach invisible divinity through the layers of materiality.

In his *Cāndāyan* (C), Maulānā Dā'ūd translates this model into the spoken language of Hindavī or Bhākhā and begins to develop an indigenous set of theological terms for Allah's might and majesty:

First I sing of the Creator,
who has made this country and this land.
He made the heavens and the earth,
the mountains Meru, Mandara, and Kailāsa.
He made the radiant sun and moon,
and all the necklaces of stars in heaven.
He made the shade, the cold, and the sunshine,
and all the forms and bodies there are.
He made the clouds, the wind, and the darkness.
He made the lightning that flashes forth.
I sing of the One who created the entire world.
My heart is full and my mind rejoices;
no other comes to mind [C 1.1–6].[13]

Dā'ūd takes a Hindavī term for the Creator, *sirjanhārū*, the "one who emits or creates the world," and uses it to describe Allah's creative power. The repeated verb *sirjasi* ("He made/created") begins each line after the first couplet, approximating something of the repetitive power of the openings of the Persian *masnavīs*. In this and the following verses, Dā'ūd sings the praises of the Creator by making all the elements of creation dependent on their Maker to put them in place.

Dā'ūd adapts the rhymed couplets of the Persian *masnavī* into the new form of the Hindavī *caupāī-dohā*, each set of five short rhymed couplets followed by a longer summary couplet. Used before him in Jaina Apabhraṃśa works, the four-foot *caupāī-dohā* becomes after Dā'ūd the standard narrative form for Hindavī poetry.[14] He also introduces into the Persianate model of the praise poem many Indian mythological and cosmological elements: in the verse above, the Creator is responsible for creating the cosmic mountains Meru, Mandara, and Kailāsa. In the verses that follow, he realigns the indigenous cosmology around Allah:

He created the earth and the nine continents.
He created the rivers, all three hundred and sixty.
He created the [seas] of water, milk, and salt.
He created oceans whose depth I know not.
He created hills and mountains and trees.
He created the forests and the lakes.
He created gems, precious metals, and pearls ...
He created the entire world, and all the waters and lakes in it.
He is the One whose place we cannot know, yet without him
place would not exist [C 2.1–4, 6].

Dā'ūd fits the Sanskritic notion of the nine continents (*nava khaṇḍa*), as well as the seas of water, milk, and salt, into a string of elements of creation that build up to a finale in the *dohā*, the couplet at the end. Dā'ūd makes clear to his audience that although he is sketching out the elements of place using commonly understood terms, his distinctive notion of divinity exists beyond place. Allah is *lā-makān*, "placeless," although he is the anchor of every place that the poet can name.

Dā'ūd also appropriates another convention from Persian poetry: the *na't* or the praise of the Prophet Muḥammad. The second section of Niẓāmī's prologue to the *Laylī va Majnūn* praises the seal of the prophets:

O Seal of the messengers sent from on high!
O final sweetness and first salty beauty!
O first fruit of the garden of primal power!

O commander of the final covenant! ...
O chief enthroned in both the worlds!
Prayer arch of the earth and sky! [LM 2.2–3, 12]

Niẕāmī uses the language of the Qur'ān to assert the primacy of Muḥammad in Allah's creation. The imagery suggests that sending Muḥammad is Allah's latest act of mercy toward humankind (*ḥalvā-yi pasīn*), along with the first flash of divine beauty in a humanly accessible form (*malḥ-i avval*). The reference is to the famous Sufi tradition that God's light was first refracted in the form of Muḥammad, an idea continued in the image of the first fruit. Earth and sky turn toward him when they wish to worship Allah. Niẕāmī follows the *na't* with a long section in praise of the night-journey (*mi'rāj*) of the Prophet, a convention that is frequently used by Amīr Khusrau but not by the Hindavī Sufi poets.

Amīr Khusrau's response to Niẕāmī uses the same grand language to convey many of the same ideas, as in his prologue to the *Majnūn va Laylī*:

O emperor of prophethood and healer sent from on high!
(You are) the latest sun and the first light.
Companion of the lamp of vision,
equal to the lamp of creation.
Emperor of the heavenly throne,
read out from the secret tablet! (ML 2.1–3)

Amīr Khusrau also draws on the language of the first and last things created by Allah to praise the Prophet, and in the second line he echoes Niẕāmī directly. Muḥammad is both the final sun (*khurshīd-i pasīn*) and the first effulgence of divine light (*nūr-i avval*). The figure of the lamp (*chirāġh*) plays on the Verse of Light from the Qur'ān (24:35): "Allah is the light of the heavens and the earth. The parable of his light is as if there were a Niche and within it a Lamp: the Lamp enclosed in Glass; the glass as it were a brilliant star, lit from a blessed tree." The Prophet's name is the secret message on Allah's tablet, written there by the Creator and read out for humanity's benefit. In Khusrau's *Deval Rānī Khiẕr Khān*, the *na't* on the Prophet Muḥammad praises him as the one to whom the angels pay homage, astonished at his perfection, and the stars are lovers of his perfect beauty (DRKK 8–9). Muḥammad's night ascension to heaven (*mi'rāj*) is described as an extended planetary journey: the moon rends the veil of his sleep, Mercury carries him up on the dark night on which he witnesses divinity, the planet Venus is intoxicated with the divine mystery, and the sun yields its place to him out of respect (DRKK 11).

Dā'ūd adapts these conventions and ideas in a way that was to form the prototype for the Hindavī Sufi romances. He takes the language of light and divine effulgence, and reimagines it in characteristically Indian, intensely local imagery:

> *He created a radiant man of light.*
> *His name is Muḥammad, the beloved of the world.*
> *For him the entire world was created,*
> *and his name resounded throughout creation.*
> *The one whose tongue doesn't take his name*
> *should cut off his head and fling it into the fire!*
> *After him God created those people*
> *to whom he spread the word and gave the true path [C 6.1–4].*

Dā'ūd is shorter and pithier than the long praise poems of the Persian poets. For him Muḥammad embodies Allah's command. According to the famous tradition, "If you had not been, I would not have created the heavens" (*laulāka mā khalaqtu 'l-aflāka*), Allah created the world for Muḥammad. The verse follows Sufi tradition in depicting the Prophet as the radiant light of the first manifestation of God. In a phrase that recurs through the genre, the drum of Muḥammad's name resounds throughout creation. Further, the name of the Prophet Muḥammad goes along with a faith and a true path (*sharī'ah*) that Muḥammad declared and the community of believers must walk.

In the next verse, Dā'ūd introduces a new item, something not always found in the Persian *masnavīs* but certainly comprehensible within the armature that he inherits from them: the praise of the first four caliphs, the righteous rulers of the first years after the death of the Prophet. Dā'ūd praises Abū Bakr (*r.* 632–634), 'Umar ibn al-Khaṭṭāb (*r.* 634–644), 'Usmān ibn 'Affān (*r.* 643–656), and finally 'Alī, the son-in-law of the Prophet (*r.* 656–661), as the four friends or "companions" of the Prophet Muḥammad:

> *Four friends met and had one thought,*
> *so that he gave them the true scripture.*
> *Whatever they heard, they transmitted faithfully …*
> *Count all four of them as one wise man (*paṇḍita*).*
> *Do not admit any fifth into their company.*
> *Only he could read scripture whom they instructed,*
> *and gain access to the true path…*
> *Abū Bakr, 'Umar, 'Usmān, and 'Alī are the four lions…*
> *who destroyed the enemies (of the faith?) [C 7.1–4, 6].*

Although some of the readings of this verse are fragmentary, the general sense is clear. Dā'ūd uses a structure of scriptural authority comprehensible in local terms as his way of conveying the importance of the four righteous Caliphs. They are the four friends to whom Muḥammad entrusted the scripture, for which Dā'ūd uses the Sanskrit term *beda purāna* (= *Veda Purāṇa*), rather than the Arabic word *Qur'ān*. By the process of instruction, the poet suggests, the four become collectively *paṇḍitas* or learned men. Dā'ūd uses a biographical fact from the life of the third Caliph, 'Us̱mān, who commissioned the second and final version of the Qur'ān, and collapses it into the general sense of the four Caliphs imagined as a single entity, learned men controlling the only righteously authorized scripture. The community of believers, then, has access to the true path and true book only through the four "companions" of the Prophet Muḥammad.

The Prologue of the *Mirigāvatī*

The three other Hindavī poets whose romances survive follow Dā'ūd's sequence of topoi fairly closely, using greater elaborations and a much more developed set of theological tropes and language but most of the same tropes and structure of praise. Throughout, the general sense is of a divinity and a prophet praised in terms comprehensible within the terminology of Indian devotional poetics yet embodying a distinctive Islamic monotheistic faith. Although the first folios of all the available manuscripts of the second surviving Hindavī love-story, Quṭban's *Mirigāvatī* (1503) (M), seem to be damaged, the edition by D. F. Plukker reconstructs the first few lines of the prologue:

Creator of the world, invisible God,
you pervade the world in the one sound 'Oṃ'!
Unseen, beyond qualities, you cannot be seen.
Whoever sees you in the form of light
forgets himself. Absolute God,
perfect one, highest divinity,
you do not take man's form or woman's.
God does not have mother, father,
or kinsmen. One alone, God has
no match or second [M 1.1–4].[15]

The terms used here for the formless, ungendered, attributeless divinity translate Islamic theology effectively into Hindavī. The term *ekoṃkāra*, "the one sound of Oṃ," translates the Arabic word with which Allah began the creation of the universe, for in the Qur'ān's account of creation Allah said "*kun!*" ("Be!"), and the world came into existence ("*fayakun*"). Absolute divinity (*parama brahma*) on the highest plane does not take on a gendered form, and

Quṭban transforms the Qur'ānic notions of Allah's absolute divinity, unity, and peerlessness into a statement that Allah has no mother, father, or kinsmen (*mātā pitā bandhu nahi koī*).

The first manifestation of divine essence is in the form of light (*joti sarūpa/nūr*). In the fourth verse of his prologue, Quṭban mentions the philosopher Ibn 'Arabī's[16] notion of the Muḥammadan light (*nūr-i Muḥammadī*):

First He created the light of Muḥammad,
then, afterwards, He made everything for his sake.
For his sake, He manifested himself,
and created Śiva and Śakti in two bodies.
The one whose tongue does not take his Name
will burn in the flame, never be liberated!
The one who recites the Name in his heart,
and calls out the profession of faith, is saved,
and gains the throne of Indra! [M 4.1–4]

Here Quṭban expresses Ibn 'Arabī's idea of the "reality of Muḥammad" (*ḥaqīqat-i Muḥammadiyyah*), the first refraction of light from the divine. The world is created because Allah is a "hidden treasure" who longs to be known, and this desire brings into existence first the "reality" of Muḥammad and then all other things in their turn. The moving force within this metaphysic is desire, and in the phenomenal world Allah's desire is echoed in created beings who wish to return to the source of their being. Śiva and Śakti are the two genders, a statement that shears the overtly Śaivite superstructure off an elaborate local mythology of godhead and refits it into an Indian Islamic literary framework. Similarly, Quṭban makes the throne of Indra, king of the Hindu gods, the ultimate spiritual reward for reciting the words of Muslim faith, the *kalmah-yi shahādat*. This proselytism is characteristic of the Hindavī Sufi poets, who use Indian myth, religion, and literary and social convention freely, yet with a distinctive and sometimes missionary slant.

Like Dā'ūd, Quṭban goes on to praise the four "companions" of the Prophet, the first four righteous caliphs. Unlike Dā'ūd, he takes care to differentiate among their respective achievements:

Listen to my account of the four friends:
Abū Bakr was known as an adept.
'Umar took the second place after him,
and his justice is renowned even now.
'Us̱mān wrote down the word of God,
that he had learnt at the command of Muḥammad.

'Alī, the lion, used his intelligence,
and conquered even the most difficult forts [M 5.1–4].

'Abū Bakr is distinguished for his capacity of *siddhi* or spiritual perfection, 'Umar for his justice, 'Us̱mān for rectifying and fixing the text of the Qur'ān, and 'Alī for his conquests (*futūḥ*). Thus Quṭban brings into Hindavī some historical vestige of the biographies of the caliphs. In the concluding couplet, however, he brings them all together by acclaiming them as wise men (*paṇḍita*) who show the disciple the true path.

The Prologue of the *Padmāvat*

Quṭban is elegantly brief in his treatment of the generic form. The third poet to take up the genre, Malik Muḥammad Jāyasī in his *Padmāvat* (P; 1540), carries his prologue to greater heights of complexity. He uses the *caupāī-dohā* form, but with seven short rhymed couplets and a longer rhymed *dohā* at the end. In ten elaborate verses, he praises the Creator as the Maker of all things that exist in the universe. Like Dā'ūd, he uses a repeated verb, *kīnhesi*, "he made," to knit a string of created things together:

In the beginning I remember the Creator,
Who gave us life and made the universe.
He made the first light shine out.
For love of the Prophet, He made the heavens.
He made fire, air, water and earth.
He made all the colors that are.
He made earth, heaven, and the nether world.
He made all the kinds of living beings.
He made the seven continents and the cosmos.
He made the fourteen divisions of creation.
He made the day and the sun, the night and the moon.
He made the constellations and their lines of stars.
He made the sunshine, the cold, and the shade.
He made the clouds and the lightning in them.
The One who made this entire creation, and whose sole glory it is:
Such a Name do I first invoke, and then I start my tale [P 1.1–8].[17]

All the elements declare the glory of the sole Creator. The next three verses go through the visible cosmos in the same manner, pointing out signs of the power and majesty of Allah.

Then the poet turns to forging a set of terms within Hindavī to express the theology of Allah. Some of the tropes repeat Quṭban's prologue, but within a more elaborate framework:

> *The Creator is invisible, without form or color.*
> *He acts in all creatures, all act through him.*
> *Manifest or hidden, he pervades all things.*
> *The righteous recognize him, but not the sinful.*
> *He has no son, no father, no mother,*
> *no family nor any relations.*
> *He was not born from anyone,*
> *and no one was born from him.*
> *All of creation is of his making [P 7.1–5].*

Here a theology is being defined by translating the Arabic Names of Allah into Hindavī, stressing all the while God's inability to be defined or represented in words. Describing divinity as *alakha arūpa abarana*, invisible, formless, and colorless, stresses Allah's difference from the embodied and colorful local gods. We see here the invention of a set of Indian Islamic theological terms, using *desī* Hindavī words. Nature presents a visible, manifest face to the senses but also has a hidden or secret side known only to God. As we shall see, the poets and audiences of the Sufi romances exploit this notion of hiddenness to go beyond the glittering surface of poetry in order to convey invisible and hidden meanings.

Jāyasī follows the remaining conventions much more briefly, using single verses for the *na't* and the praise of the Prophet's companions. He praises the Prophet as the *puruṣa nirmarā* or radiant man of light:

> *He created a pure and spotless man,*
> *whose name is Muḥammad,*
> *a digit of the full moon.*
> *God created his radiance first,*
> *and for love of him, He made the universe.*
> *God lit a lamp to light the world.*
> *Recognizing his luster, the world knew the path [P 11.1–3].*

Here Jāyasī is drawing on the imagery of the *āyat al-nūr*, the "Light Verse" of the Qur'ān, in which God's radiance is compared to a lamp placed in a niche, to make Muḥammad the lamp of creation:

> Allah is the Light of the heavens and the earth. The parable of His Light is as if there were a Niche and within it a Lamp: the Lamp enclosed

> in Glass; the glass as it were a brilliant star: lit from a blessed Tree, an Olive, neither of the East nor of the West, whose Oil is well-nigh luminous, though fire scarce touched it: Light upon Light! God doth guide whom He will to His Light: God doth set forth parables for men: and God doth know all things.[18]

Jāyasī goes on to specify the ideal community of believers (*ummat*) and the teaching handed down from on high to the Prophet:

In the second place, God has written his name.
Whoever listens to his teaching, becomes righteous.
God made him the path for the community.
Whoever takes his name, crosses both the worlds [P 11.5–6].

In these lines Jāyasī mixes terms freely, using the *desī* term *dharmī* for "righteous," and *desī* words to suggest the Arabic *sunnat*, the way of Muḥammad, yet referring directly also to the *ummat* or community of believers. He implies that those who follow the path of Muḥammad are following the true *dharma*, the true religion. His verse on the four "companions" of the Prophet is very similar to Quṭban's verse above. He praises the four caliphs for similar achievements, Abū Bakr for his sincerity and wisdom, 'Umar for his justice, 'Uṣmān for fixing the text of the Qur'ān, and 'Alī for being the brave warrior and lion of God (P 12.2–5). In conclusion, he upholds the Qur'ān as the only true scripture for the world (P 12.8).

The Prologue of the *Madhumālatī*

The fourth and final poet of the genre, Mīr Sayyid Mañjhan Rājgīrī, uses these by now well-established conventions with a deceptive simplicity in his poem *Madhumālatī* (MM; 1545). He does not attempt to go through the diverse elements of creation as Maulānā Dā'ūd and Malik Muḥammad Jāyasī did before him. Instead, he uses the Hindavī theological terms that the previous poets of the genre forged:

God, giver of love, the treasure-house of joy
Creator of the two worlds in the one sound Oṃ,
my mind has no light worthy of you,
with which to sing your praise, O Lord!
King of the three worlds and the four ages,
the world glorifies you from beginning to end.
Sages, the learned, thinkers on the Absolute,

all have failed to laud you on earth.
How can I accomplish with a single tongue
what a thousand tongues could not in four ages?
Manifest in so many forms, in all three worlds, in every heart,
how can my senses glorify you with one tongue alone? [MM1.1–6][19]

Mañjhan's praise of Allah links the Creator first with "love, the treasure-house of joy" (*prema prītī sukhanidhi*), the central value of the love story. Then he sketches out the attributes of the ruler of the universe and the four ages (*juga*). As we have seen, the term *ekoṃkāra*, the one sound, refers to the Qur'ānic account of creation, in which God said "Be!" and "It was." The Hindavī Sufi poets translate the divine command in Arabic (*kun fayakun*) into the local Hindavī word for the *nāda* or sound that sets the universe in motion.

Mañjhan goes on to find Hindavī approximations for the widespread Sufi theory of *vaḥdat al-vujūd* or the unity of all existence, playing on the Lord's unity (*vaḥdat*) and his multiplicity (*kas̱rat*):

In every state the Supreme Lord is One,
a single form in many guises.
In heaven, earth, and hell, wherever space extends,
the Lord rejoices in multiplicity of form.
The Maker makes the universe as He wills.
He came as Death, comes still, will always come.
Placeless, He is present everywhere.
Unqualified, He is Oṃ, the singular sound.
Hidden, He is manifest everywhere.
Formless, He is the many-formed Lord.
One Light there is which shines alone, radiant in all the worlds.
Countless are the forms that Light assumes, countless are its names
[MM 2.1–6].

The verbal structure of this verse plays with the literal Arabic attributes of Allah and mimics them in Hindavī. Thus the fourth couplet invokes the Arabic *lā-makān*, the "placeless" one, and reproduces it as *bāju ṭhāṉva* (also "placeless"). The concluding couplet brings up the "Light" verse as well as the Names of Allah. Here Mañjhan is referring to the *a'yān al-s̱ābitah*, the eternal hexeities or patterns, the divine Names, which Ibn 'Arabī regarded as prototypes of all things in existence. Mañjhan's use of this term has a special referent, however, because his Sufi order, the Shattaris, formulated an elaborate system of letter mysticism and cosmology based on the Names of Allah, using them to inculcate divine qualities or attributes in the practitioner.

Finally, Mañjhan uses the convention of the *na't* and the praise of the "companions" of the Prophet to suggest Muḥammad's true nature:

Muḥammad is the root, the whole world a branch,
the Lord has crowned him with a priceless crown.
He is the foremost, no other is his equal.
He is the substance and the world his shadow.
Everyone knows the Maker, the hidden mover,
but no one recognizes the manifest Muḥammad!
The Invisible One, whom no one can see,
has assumed the form of Muḥammad.
He has named this form Muḥammad,
but it has no meaning other than the One [MM 8.1–5].

Mañjhan uses the paradoxical logic of Ibn 'Arabī's theory of the refraction of divine light into the forms of this world to declare the sole substantial reality of Muḥammad's body (*sarīra*) and the shadowiness of the concrete, sensible world: "He is the substance, and the world his shadow." Further, he uses the Hindavī word *rūpa* ("form, beauty") to skirt, dangerously, the language of incarnation. Allah is *alakh*, the invisible one, but the form that can be seen is that of Muḥammad, which suggests the divine presence. Significantly, *rūpa* is also used extensively in the erotic encounter in the romance to refer to the divine and human aspects of the love that blossoms between the hero and heroine. Mañjhan ends his *na't* with the standard, simple words of praise for the first four righteous caliphs.

Mañjhan's Hindavī poem marks the end of a long process of competitive assimilation of the courtly culture of the Delhi sultanate and the Afghan kingdoms into an Indian landscape. Beginning with Dā'ūd's *Cāndāyan*, which created the paradigm for the literary tradition out of the romances of Niẓāmī Ganjavī and Amīr Khusrau, we can trace the elaboration of the model in the works of the later Hindavī poets. Dā'ūd took the *ḥamd* and *na't* of the Persian romance poets and used it to invent a Hindavī Islamic theology and terminology. Quṭban developed and embellished the formula in his *Mirigāvatī*, to be followed with greater degrees of skill and elaboration by Malik Muḥammad Jayāsī and Mīr Sayyid Mañjhan *Rājgīrī*.

But what of the politics and historical placement of these poets? Who were their audiences, and how were their poems understood and performed? To answer these questions, we must turn to the remainder of the prologue, paying attention to literary form, multiple linguistic and theoretical sources, and performance contexts.

Protocols of Praise in the *Cāndāyan*

The rest of the prologue of the *Cāndāyan* moves from praise of the Creator of the world and his Prophet to praise of earthly kings and their accomplishments. Dā'ūd composed his poem in 1379 at the provincial court of Dalmau in Avadh, whose *iqṭā'-dār* (general or provincial governor) was tributary to Sultan Fīrūz Shāh Tuġhlaq at Delhi. The Tuġhlaq cultivation of Hindavī verse in the Delhi sultanate was one of a set of wider cultural changes taking place during the thirteenth and fourteenth centuries. The rise of a new set of literary genres in the spoken languages was attendant on the conquest of north Indian territories by Turkish military and aristocratic élites, the consolidation of a political and revenue-collecting structure in which local landholders paid tribute to the generals of the Delhi sultans (the *iqṭā'* system), and the setting up of hospices and sanctification of local landscapes and populations by Sufi shaikhs of different lineages.

Maulānā Dā'ūd was a member of this Indian-born and Hindavī-speaking Turkish aristocracy, affiliated with the ruling sultan and his ministers and with the shaikhs of the Chishti order. In a world in which such poems were promoted by royal patronage, *qāẓīs* (Muslim officials who preach and preside over ceremonies) and more orthodox sorts of jurisconsults must have been kept in check by rulers, brought out to legitimate their rule when needed but not allowed to exercise much real control over military and administrative power.[20] Cultural value and pleasure were vested in the mystical and musical assemblies that convened in the cool of the north Indian evenings to listen to polished verse in Hindavī or Persian in these courts or within the Sufi hospices. Material patronage for these assemblies came from the rich and powerful nobles of the Delhi sultanate, who are praised in the panegyric sections of the prologue to Dā'ūd's Hindavī poem. There was a saying popular in Delhi, reputed (almost certainly apocryphally) to be a tradition of the Prophet Muḥammad, which ran, "If there be no sultan, the people will devour each other."[21] It is thus not difficult to reconcile the political reading of the panegyrics presented below with the populist ideology of the sultan's benevolent paternalism and claim to just rule.

Adapting the language and conventions of the Persian *maṣnavī* tradition into Hindavī, Dā'ūd places himself vis-à-vis the established order in his panegyrics to political authorities. In his prologue, he praises the sultan Fīrūz Shāh Tuġhlaq, his minister the Khān-i Jahān Junā Shāh, the nobleman in charge of the provincial court of Dalmau, Malik Mubārak, and the Chishti shaikh Zain al-dīn 'Alī. The poetic prologues of Persian *maṣnavīs* themselves draw on the "mirrors for princes," the manuals of statecraft and governance that set the tone for ideal rulership and political order during the period.[22] These include such works as the famous *Qābūs Nāmah* of Kai Kā'ūs bin Iskandar,[23] Niẕām al-Mulk Tūsī's *Siyāsat Nāmah,*[24] and numerous anonymous works such as the *Baḥr al-Favā'id.*[25] As Julie Meisami has noted in her distinguished study of Persian court poetry, "the proliferation of mirrors for princes during the period in which Persian romances flourished (from the advent of the Saljuqs to the Mongol invasion) testifies to the widespread interest not only in establishing the practical ethics of kingly conduct, but in defining the nature of kingship and the qualifications of the ideal sovereign."[26] In Meisami's account of genres, panegyric poems are the ideal forms through which poets construct a prescriptive poetic ethic designed to praise kings as well as to instruct them in their duties and responsibilities. But since it was commonly accepted during the period that poets were much given to lies, exaggeration, and hyperbole, what was the precise discursive and political status of this poetic ethic of kingship?

The panegyric was an ideal form that set the style and laid out the content of political authority but also created the material circumstances for its own production. The praise of kings and noblemen, and particularly of the military nobility of the period, gave poets access to the resources and sponsorship they needed to compose poetry within a courtly culture that patronized skilled literary figures, calligraphers, scholars, and artists. In return, the poet composed poetry that gave the patron pleasure and allowed him to establish his political authority through the symbolic forms and the cultural style of the period.

The concern with establishing political authority and defining cultural style grew especially acute as conquests of territory in the name of Islam ranged further and further from the spheres of the near-defunct 'Abbasid caliphate and the Saljuqs. In his masterful history of the Delhi sultanate, Peter Jackson has commented incisively on the problem of political authority in the regional sultanates after the disintegration of 'Abbasid rule from Baghdad. As Jackson notes:

> In the majority of caliphal territories power passed into the hands of semi-independent, hereditary governors. Such rulers, who initially bore no title higher than *amīr* (literally "commander"), usually went through the formality of obtaining a patent of authority (*manshūr*), a robe (*khil'at*), and a sonorous title (*laqab*) from the 'Abbasid Caliph, in return for inserting his name in the public Friday sermon (*khuṭba*) and, more notionally, remitting an annual tribute.[27]

As the territories that were acquired in the name of the Caliph grew ever more far-flung, the problem of legitimacy became more acute, especially in view of the recently converted status of many provincial rulers. As Jackson comments,

> To bolster their dubious legitimacy, the provincial amirs had to act (or pose) as champions of Sunnī Islam and its caliph against both the infidel and the heretic. These functions were exercised most successfully by rulers of Turkish origin. Most of the regional dynasts imitated the 'Abbasid Caliphs, and buttressed their own power, by maintaining regiments of Turkish slave guards (Arabic sing. *ghulām, mamlūk;* Persian *banda*) from the pagan steppelands of Central Asia. Ghulam status, it must be emphasized, bore none of the degrading connotations associated with other kinds of slavery. The Turkish peoples enjoyed a particularly high reputation for martial skill and religious orthodoxy, and ghulams were highly prized by their masters, receiving both instruction in the Islamic faith and a rigorous military training. Nor was such confidence misplaced...[T]he forging and preservation of an independent Muslim power in India were to be in large measure the work of Turkish slave commanders and their own ghulams.[28]

The gradual expansion of Ghaznavid rule into the Punjab and, after the thirteenth century, the establishment and consolidation of the Delhi sultanate was largely the work of such men. Fundamental to their system of political legitimation and their sense of ideological superiority were projections of the triumph of Sunni Islam, to which they had recently converted, as well as the claim to just rule according to the numerous manuals of statecraft composed during this period.

It is against this backdrop that one has to set the inflated claims and rhetoric of the prologues to both the Persian and the Hindavī romances. The prologues of both sets of works draw on the elaborate language of polity to wax eloquent in praise of various courtly patrons. They praise the ruling sultan and his noblemen as generous sponsors, as well as guarantors of justice and stability. Their political ideology linked state, religious law, and military might in an institutional structure that draws revenue from its subjects and in return guarantees order and justice. The idea that the king's justice provides the criteria for determining right and wrong and for maintaining order in the land comes from Persian definitions of kingship such as the one found in Fa<u>kh</u>r al-dīn Rāzī's *Jāmi' al-'Ulūm*, cited and translated by Richard Eaton:

> *The world is a garden, whose gardener is the state [*dawlat*];*
> *The state is the sultan whose guardian is the Law [*shar'īa*];*
> *The Law is a policy, which is protected by the kingdom [*mulk*];*
> *The kingdom is a city, brought into being by the army [*lashkar*];*
> *The army is made secure by wealth [*māl*];*
> *Wealth is gathered from the subjects [*ra'īyat*];*

The subjects are made servants by justice ['adl];
Justice is the axis of the prosperity of the world ['ālam].[29]

The images here construct, as Eaton notes, a "unified theory of a society's moral, political, and economic basis—a worldview at once integrated, symmetrical, and closed."[30] The perfect order of kingship invoked here is therefore an ideal that is part of the conventional set of expectations for a Muslim king's authority. As Eaton demonstrates in his study of the consolidation of Turkish rule in Bengal, sultans initially used this Persian political symbolism to bolster their authority. As the lineage of Raja Gaṇeśa demonstrates, however, the Bengal sultans were very much a mixed bag—some from outside Bengal, but others, such as Raja Gaṇeśa, converts to Islam. It should come as no surprise, then, that they adopted indigenous practices of royal legitimization (such as being crowned after bathing in Ganges water) and patronized artistic and literary endeavors in several languages—Arabic, Persian, Sanskrit, old Bengali—as part of their mixed Indian and Islamic ideal polity.

In the five poems of his *Khamsah*, Niẕāmī lavishly praises the powerful Saljuq sultans and their provincial governors of his native land of Azerbaijan, the Eldigüzids.[31] The Eldigüzids were *atabegs*, tutors (literally "father-commanders") to the young Saljuq princes, and they exercised power through their status as advisors and effective rulers of the extensive Saljuq domains. Thus, the *Khusrau va Shīrīn* contains among its opening sections praises of Sultan Tuġhril III Arsalān-Shāh (*r.* 1176–1190), his *atabeg* Jahān Pahlavān Abū Ja'far Muḥammad Eldigüz (*fl.* 1175), and the tutor's son Qizil Arsalān. In praise of the sultan, Niẕāmī writes:

Illuminator of the throne of the realm of meaning,
seizer of the territory of the kingdom of life,
King Tuġhril is the Darius of existence,
the fortune of the state and the ocean of generosity.
The refuge of his country is the emperor Tuġhril.
He is the master of the world and the just sultan [KS 7.2–4].[32]

Whatever the real limits of his power, in Niẕāmī's idealized rhetoric Tuġhril Arsalān is the moral and political center of the state as well as a generous patron.

Niẕāmī then praises the power and munificence of the tutor Jahān Pahlavān Abū Ja'far Muḥammad Eldigüz and his son Qizil Arsalān:

From that grace that has made mercy for all,
two masters of the name Muḥammad were created.

One became the seal of prophecy in his essence,
the other the seal of worldly kings in his life.
One was the moon of the Arab heaven for eternity.
The other became the eternal ruler of 'Ajam (Persia).
*One freed the true religion (*dīn*) from the darkness.*
The other established the world with his justice [KS 8.9–12].

The poet draws on the dualism of *dīn* and *duniyā*, the true religion and the world, to suggest that Abū Ja'far Muḥammad is the sun that illuminates the world, comparing his status in the political realm with that of the Prophet in the religious sphere. In light of the fact that Abū Ja'far poisoned the Sultan's father in 1176 to set the Sultan up as the new king, the line about "the seal of worldly kings" has a certain grimly ironic ring to it. The section is followed by the *khiṭāb-i zamīnbūs* ("address of obeisance") to the patron, in which he asks for his generous support and calls down blessings on him, as well as by a section of praise dedicated to the *atabeg*'s son, Qizil Arsalān.

This pattern is fairly standard and varies only with the commissioning patron of the poet. Thus, in his *Haft Paikar* (HP, "The Seven Beauties"), Niẓāmī waxes eloquent in the praise of 'Alāuddīn Körp Arsalān (*fl.* 1170), the Ahmadili ruler of Maragha in southwestern Azerbaijan:

Both land and sea his rule commands,
his praise sung by their denizens.
His noble nature soars to heights
unreachable by flagging thoughts.
In greatness like an angel he,
the sphere's twin in nobility.
Shroud-stitcher for his foes, his blade,
like lightning, sets their mail ablaze.
Before him conquest bows its head;
sedition drowns in his sword's waves...
But when he opens bounty's mine,
he gives great wealth, forgives great crime.
Sea-like, not grudging, ever true,
the whip and sword his ebb and flow [HP 5.20–4; 29–30].[33]

The Ahmadilis were a minor dynasty who played a role in Saljuq politics from their power base in Maragha. Thus the generic conventions of praise extend to provincial nobility and lesser rulers, who either are placed in a political hierarchy with the sultan at its apex or mimic the imperial style as the central figures in their provincial courts.

Amīr Khusrau's prologues in his *Khamsah* in imitation of Niẓāmī similarly extol the Sultan's authority. Since the poet was a courtier in Delhi, however, his panegyrics do not extend to the provincial nobility. His *Shīrīn va Khusrau* (SK) contains fulsome praises of Sultan 'Alāuddīn Muḥammad Khaljī (*r.* 1296–1316). The section opens with the planet Mercury approaching the poet with a heavenly patent of authority (*manshūr*), which bestows on him the emperorship of the realm of meaning (*mulk-i ma'ānī*) and authorizes him to recognize 'Alāuddīn as the second Alexander and the shadow of divinity on earth:

The exaltation of the world and of religion is he, the supreme emperor,
under his royal parasol he is the shadow of the Almighty ...
With his sword he has adorned Islam,
and with his shield he has shaded the world [SK 251].

This passage brings to the fore 'Alāuddīn's military might and the image of the holy warrior, as well as the insignia of royalty and power that signal his might. Amīr Khusrau pushes this triumphalist rhetoric to unprecedented heights, particularly in his *maṡnavīs* that deal directly with conquest. Thus, in the *Deval Rānī Khizr Khān*, he extols the reign of 'Alāuddīn as coterminous with the victorious rule of Islam:

Happy is Hindustan, and the liveliness of its religion!
The sharī'ah *has here the perfection of majesty and glory.*
From knowledge put into action, Delhi is now Bukhara,
and because of its emperors Islam has become manifest!
The entire country, because of the warlike sword,
is like a land of thorns rendered free of thorns by fire.
Its land has been watered by the luster of the sword.
Now dust rests above, and infidelity to Allah below.
The powerful Hindus have been subdued and made compliant [DRKK 46].

Here the king is the military power through whose prowess the *sharī*'ah rules supreme. As we know from another source in the period, *jihād* or holy war was considered an obligation for a Muslim adult man,[34] irksome and potentially dangerous, but necessary nevertheless to ensure regular flows of booty and revenue into the capital, Delhi. The images are militaristic and strong: the warlike sword puts all the infidel Hindus to rest below the dust. The poet represents the territory of India as *dār al-Islām*, a land of Islam. From the inflated rhetoric, one would never guess that 'Alāuddīn fought campaign after campaign to subdue India, large parts of which would still remain *dār al-ḥarb*, the territory of war.

This generic model preshapes Dā'ūd's panegyrics to Fīrūz Shāh Tuġhlaq, his minister Jūnā Shāh, and Malik Mubārak, their appointed *muqṭa'* or noble in Avadh. The Hindavī verses, though brief, establish the hierarchy that sponsored his poetic efforts and therefore allow us to place the composition of the poem in the year 781/1379, at the provincial court of Dalmau:

> *It was the year seven hundred and eighty-one,*
> *when I proclaimed this poem endowed with* rasa.
> *Shah Fīrūz is the Sultan of Delhi,*
> *and Jūnā Shāh is known as his chief minister.*
> *Dalmau is built as a city of nine colors,*
> *the fort above, the Gaṅgā flows below.*
> *The people of the faith live here, fortunate,*
> *and it is a famous town, one which appreciates virtues.*
> *The son of Malik Bayān, steadfast in war,*
> *is Malik Mubārak, the ruler here [C 17].*

The verse situates the poem within an oral performance in court (*kabi sarasa ubhāsī*), a point to which we shall return. It praises Dalmau on the Ganges as a provincial utopia, home to the people of the faith, a stronghold that is held securely despite rebels and large tracts of territory that were only tenuously controlled by its *iqṭā'-dār*.

The personages mentioned in the verse require a brief historical aside. The scant information available about Dā'ūd from other sources indicates his closeness to the court and his involvement in the politics of Fīrūz Shāh's succession to royal power. At the time of Sultan Muḥammad Tuġhlaq's death in Sind, his minister Khvāja-i Jahān Aḥmad bin Ayāz placed a pretender on the throne of Delhi. After his own accession to the throne, Fīrūz Shāh advanced on Delhi with an army at his back. The Khvāja-i Jahān sent four messengers including Maulānā Dā'ūd to reason with him. Fīrūz Shāh kept three of them in captivity and sent Dā'ūd back with a message saying the Sultan had no son (i.e., he did not recognize the claims of the pretender). Although the Khvāja-i Jahān opposed Fīrūz Shāh, the future Sultan was victorious with the help of a faction at court led by the deputy (*nā'ib vazīr*) to the Khvāja-i Jahān, Malik Maqbūl,[35] who also patronized literature in Telugu and was a Brahmin convert to Islam. After Fīrūz Shāh's accession in 1351, Maqbūl was rewarded with the chief ministership and given the title of Khan-ī Jahān, while Aḥmad Ayāz was put in prison in Hansi.[36] At the time of Malik Maqbūl's death in 1370, his son Jūnā Shāh succeeded to his father's post.[37] Maulānā Dā'ūd was evidently part of the winning faction in Delhi, since he is extravagant in his praises of Jūnā Shāh in the prologue to the *Cāndāyan*.

Dā'ūd's panegyrics include the address of obeisance (*khiṭāb-i zamīnbūs*) to these people, in particular the Khān-i Jahān Jūnā Shāh and his appointee in Dalmau, Malik Mubārak, son of Malik Bayān:

> *The Khān-i Jahān is a steadfast pillar of the earth.*
> *If God had not created him, the world would move*
> *from its place. He is created as a ship*
> *upon which the world climbs, and he*
> *draws virtue over to the other side.*
> *Hindus and Turks he treats equally,*
> *and speaks the truth to both of them.*
> *In his reign, the cow and the lion walk*
> *on the same path, and drink at the same ghat [C14.1–4].*

Jūnā Shāh is thus the guarantor of the circle of justice, the fair ruler who treats Hindus and Turks alike and upholds the truth. The trope of the cow and lion walking and drinking together, an ideal metaphor for his justice, is repeated in the terms of praise of the other Hindavī prologues. Other verses focus on the ruler's bravery and the force of his sword (the military might that underwrites his just rule), as well as the courage and generosity of his *iqṭā'-dār* Malik Mubārak.

Tropes of Praise in the Other Three Prologues

This literary pattern and the tropes of praise are repeated in the later romances of the genre, even though there were significant political shifts in the Delhi sultanate after the invasion of the Mongol conqueror Timur in 1398 and the eclipse of Tuġhlaq power. The Sayyid and Lodī sultans of Delhi could not assume even a titular sovereignty over the rulers, landholders, and *iqṭa'-dār*s of the different regions of northern, central, and eastern India. Preeminent among the sultanates of the east was the Sharqi kingdom of Jaunpur, founded in the 1390s by Malik Sarvar, a eunuch or *khvājah-sarā* in the service of Fīrūz Shāh Tuġhlaq. Appointed custodian of the town of Jaunpur, he played an important part in the succession disputes following Fīrūz Shāh's death in 1388 and eventually consolidated his own position as ruler of Jaunpur. His successors through an adoptive son strengthened the realm and ruled the region as independent sultans till the accession in 1458 of Ḥusain Shāh Sharqī, who involved himself in a protracted and ill-fated struggle to conquer Delhi from the Lodī sultans Bahlol (1451–1489) and Sikandar (1489–1517).[38] Ḥusain Shāh was dethroned by Bahlol Lodī's capture of Jaunpur in 1483 and fled to a small enclave in the town of Chunar in Bihar. The Bengali Sultan 'Alāuddīn Ḥusain Shāh later gave him Kahalganv or Colgong in Bhagalpur district in Bihar, and he had coins bearing his name issued until his death in 1505.[39]

In 1503, Quṭban, a poet attached to Sultan Ḥusain Shāh's court in exile, dedicated the *Mirigāvatī* to him as an ideal patron and ruler. The dedication should be placed against the larger historical background of the establishment of regional sultanates such as Malwa, Gujarat, Jaunpur, Bengal, and the Deccani states. These new polities employed the languages and courtly styles of the fourteenth-century Delhi sultans as well as local idioms and aesthetic media. Ḥusain Shāh Sharqī himself was a poet and a noted patron of the distinctive Sharqī style of architecture. He was also an accomplished musician, credited with creation of Rāga Jaunpurī, the various Syāms, and four versions of the morning Rāga Toḍī in north Indian or Hindustani classical music.[40] The prologue to the *Mirigāvatī* places him at the center of a multilingual and cultured court:

> *Shāh Ḥusain is a great king.*
> *The throne and parasol add to his luster.*
> *He is a* paṇḍita, *intelligent and wise.*
> *He reads a book and understands all the meanings.*
> *He is adorned by Yudhiṣṭhira's sense of duty.*
> *He provides shade for our heads,*
> *may he live as the world's king!*
> *He gives generously and does not count the cost,*
> *Bali and Karṇa cannot match him...*
> *He is clever and wise, and speaks many languages. I have not seen his equal.*
> *Listen attentively, all of you in his assembly, then*
> *I will tell you about him! [M 7.1–4, 6]*

Here Ḥusain Shāh is the ideal patron and cultured listener, cognizant with languages and able to comprehend subtle points and multiple meanings. The mythological references from the *Mahābhārata* introduce an Indic ideal language of kingly authority: Ḥusain Shāh is equal to Yudhiṣṭhira, as a model of *dharma* or royal duty, and surpasses Karṇa as an exemplar of generosity. As part of the context of oral performance, the poet addresses his audience directly as the *sabhā* or court of Ḥusain Shāh.

These conventions are also part of Jāyasī's *Padmāvat* (*circa* 1540), addressed to Sher Shāh Sūrī, the Afghan king who forced Humāyūn to leave India in 1540, and Mañjhan's *Madhumālatī*, written at the court of Sher Shāh's son

Islām Shāh Sūrī in 1545. For both, the elements that go to build up an ideal polity are military might, a claim to just rule, and possession of great treasure. Jāyasī addresses Sher Shāh Sūrī in polished verse:

Sher Shāh is the Sultan of Delhi.
He illuminates the four quarters like the sun.
The throne and parasol adorn him alone.
All the kings bow to the ground before him.
He is a Sūr by name and a hero by his sword.
He is intelligent and full of all the virtues.
He has humbled the heroes of the nine continents.
The earth with her seven islands bows before him [P 13.1–4].

Jāyasī plays on the multiple lexical meanings of *sūra* or "hero" in his panegyric to the Sūrī conqueror of north India, comparing him, in the following lines, to Alexander and to the subduer of jinns (genies), King Solomon. He wishes eternal rule for Sher Shāh in the couplet to this verse, and he praises his treasure and generosity, as well as his valor, in the following verses. Although critics have taken these to be purely formulaic, a glance at the career of Sher Shāh Sūrī and his constant jockeying to gain control of forts that contained treasure shows that these were indeed the elements on which he based his power and effectiveness as a military commander and ruler.[41] Jāyasī is also a poet with an unusually large range of allusions, all part of the same overlapping set of discourses about the cultural symbolism of political authority in Hindavī, in which Allah is definitely on the side of the big battalions.

Might and right similarly coincide in Mañjhan's *Madhumālatī*, articulated within the charmed circle of an Afghan court and the poets it patronized. His romance is dedicated to Sher Shāh's son Islām Shāh Sūrī. Mañjhan combines the language of praise with Persianate notions of the power of Islām Shāh's army. He makes justice or *'adl* the moral basis of kingship:

The fame of his justice resounds high and clear,
lamb and wolf graze together at peace.
I cannot describe his just rule, where the lion
plays with a cow's tail in its paw.
Through his austerities, his kingdom is strong,
a garden come to flower without any thorns.
His policy in the world ensures
the strong cannot oppress the weak.
Right is known from wrong as milk from water.
The man who knocks on his door, finds it open.

Joy and happiness, enthusiasm and delight: everyone accepts these here.
Poverty, grief, oppression and fear have left the land and fled away [MM 12.1–6].

Mañjhan uses the conventionalized tropes of the lion and cow playing together, of lamb and wolf grazing together in peace, and describes Islām Shāh's state as a "garden without thorns," echoing Fakhr al-dīn Rāzī's closed and integrated notion of kingship. The remaining verses repeat the mythological references to Yudhiṣṭhira, Karṇa, and the great King Bhoja of Ujjain. They also praise the Afghan nobleman and military commander Khiẓr Khān, who may have patronized the poet and supported him at his own court.

These four poets' addresses to their patrons are not just a prescriptive ethic for kingship but a generic form that enables its own production through praise of discerning, cultivated, and rich patrons. Moreover, the kings and noblemen thus addressed were not just the material sponsors of the Hindavī poets but also the sympathetic patrons of a courtly culture that reveled in music, poetry, and art.

Conclusion

Our reading of the sources and structures of the prologues of the Hindavī romances has allowed us to specify the inauguration of a distinctive *desī* Muslim aesthetics on the local landscape of Hindustan in the fourteenth, fifteenth, and early sixteenth centuries, an Indian Islamic literary tradition. On the one hand, these poets referred to and used important ideas, generic conventions, and techniques from the Sanskrit poetics of *rasa* and suggestion. But then, setting themselves against Sanskrit, they proclaimed the unique sweetness of their *desī* spoken language. While applauding the delicately subtle imagery of the Persian, they were mesmerized by the colorful and erotic flora and fauna of their native Hindavī, the flowering night jasmine and lotus for which they named their graphically described "divine" heroines.

The following chapters examine a number of aspects of the genre: the use of Sanskrit and Persian erotologies and story motifs from multiple traditions to create a distinctive narrative pattern, the structure and sources of their stories, the imaginary landscapes created in the romances, the links between themes of conquest and gender, and the spiritual transformation of the male seeker through the imagery of the erotic body of a woman. Whether in the ritual context of Sufi *khānaqāhs*, in which audience response was controlled and texts were made to conform to metaphysical schemes of interpretation, or at royal courts where poets vied with one another to recite elegant and polished poetry for their patrons, or among groups of cultivated people who met for an evening's entertainment, savoring the royal *rasa* of love and the taste of things spiritual (*ẕauq*) meant understanding the multiple references of the poetry and training one's heart to be open to the Sufi message. All one had to do was to learn how to listen.

3

Creating a New Genre: The Cāndāyan

Manuscripts and Paintings

The openness of the possibilities, and the intractability of the fragmented remains of the text of the *Cāndāyan*, the first surviving Hindavī Sufi romance, make the task of interpreting it as a model for an entire genre a peculiarly tentative and caution-inducing exercise in judgment. The extended fragments of a now-lost original serve almost as an allegory of the difficulties of explicating the cultural history of the sultanate period. Reading the poem is like trying to make one's way across a swiftly flowing river, large parts of which remain shrouded in darkness and obscurity, on the stepping stones of a few secure textual fragments. The later Hindavī poets had the advantage over us in having complete texts of Maulānā Dā'ūd's original Hindavī *prema-kahānī*, written and recited in Dalmau's provincial court in 1379. Dā'ūd created an Indian narrative genre for cultivated people who already enjoyed the exquisite Persian romances of the great Niẓāmī Ganjavī, with their subtly suggestive texture and imagery, as well as Indian music, poetry, and dance. The later Sufi romances that followed Dā'ūd's formula sought to emulate and surpass the popularity and allure of their predecessor. Within the sultanate court cultures of Turkish and Afghan nobles and the Sufi hospices they frequented as disciples and novices ready to develop their spiritual taste (*ẕauq*), the generic formula of the *Cāndāyan* was to have a tremendous appeal and impact.

In addition to later poems modeled on the *Cāndāyan*, Dā'ūd's rhymed Hindavī story inspired several courtly illuminated manuscript traditions, minimally exemplified in the respective styles of the Bharat Kala Bhavan, Staatsbibliothek and Lahore-Chandigarh leaves of the *Cāndāyan*, the Prince of Wales Museum manuscript in Bombay, and the John Rylands Library manuscript in Manchester, England.[1] When confronted by this mass of fragmentary evidence, none with a very clear provenance, and no extended account describing any particular artistic culture, scholars have not been able to reconstruct anything approaching a complete cultural picture of the romance or its context. General accounts of sultanate culture operate by listing thematically elements of food, dress, custom, and so on.[2] A discussion of the various illuminated manuscript traditions, none of them complete, and their relation to the printed editions of the text is outside the scope of this chapter,[3] which reads the fragments put together in the printed editions to reconstruct the distinctive narrative pattern of the *Cāndāyan.*

However, the intermingled presence of painting and poetry in the first fragments of the genre may be an occasion that warrants reflection on the shape and form of the books that embodied the Sufi romances. Rulers not only patronized authors, musicians, and dancers but also sponsored production of illuminated and beautifully calligraphed copies of texts such as the *Cāndāyan.* Books circulated as handwritten manuscripts that were read out loud in select Sufi gatherings, recited in poetic assemblies, or enjoyed as luxurious illustrated objects at royal courts. One approach has been to examine the Persian historical chronicles in conjunction with the painted and built remains.[4] For instance, from B. N. Goswamy's incisive study of a particular illustrated manuscript, the so-called Jainesque *Shāh Nāmah,* we learn that Dā'ūd's patron's overlord, Sultan Fīrūz Shāh Tuġhlaq (whom we have already noted as a patron of music, poetry, and astrology) was hostile to painting:

> There is little in painting that is firmly associated with the important Delhi Sultanate, possibly because of the orthodox attitude in the Islamic world towards the art of painting: something that a ruler like Feroze Tughlaq (1351–1388) upheld when he had traces of all figurative paintings removed from the walls of his palace. He showed marked hostility towards all painting, for instance by having a Brahmin who was carrying around a portable painted device—obviously a 'picture showman'—burned alive for his crime. However, in the other Sultanates the rulers of which were not burdened with carrying the flag of Islamic orthodoxy with the same zeal as the Sultan of Delhi, the attitude towards painting seems to have been far more tolerant as is evidenced by surviving examples of Sultanate work.[5]

Despite these isolated instances, the larger aristocratic culture knew, enjoyed, and sponsored the arts of painting, music, poetry, and manuscript illumination. Whatever the individual attitudes of rulers who projected an image as protectors of an anti-iconic Islam, there is evidence of the cultivation of painting on walls and paper within the ruling aristocratic culture of the day.

Indeed, as Simon Digby has pointed out:

> The literary evidence indicates that a tradition of mural painting was transmitted from the court of Ghazna to the Delhi Sultanate; this probably included the representation of amorous scenes on the walls of the inner apartments of the Sultans, and of ceremonially accoutred servants and warriors on those of the public halls of audience. Persian script manuscript illustration existed...[and]...a lively Hindu tradition of wall-painting depicting scenes of the epics and of popular folktales survived and was familiar to Muslims.[6]

As with other arts, a technique from Central Asia that was already known in the subcontinent was transmitted to local artisans, who interpreted and recreated it according to their native iconography and conventions. Courtly patrons were thus responsible for the creative minglings and reformulations that flourished in the arts of poetry, wall painting, music, architecture, and manuscript illumination.

When not interrupted by the exigencies of war, invasion, and the struggle to keep one's place at the court in Delhi, local aristocrats sponsored a richly mixed set of regional artistic, spiritual, and literary cultures. There were also related artistic and narrative traditions such as the various Jain sects and their illustrated *Kalpa-sūtras* and other doctrinal texts, of which more later.[7] There are many works in Apabhraṃśa and the developing literary traditions of the regional spoken languages, exemplified in the repertory and abilities of the bards and professional poets who flocked to the courts of the dynasties that called themselves Rajputs, dynasties that commissioned retrospective genealogies for themselves hailing to the sun and the moon.[8]

Within this diverse and fragmentary set of textual and manuscript traditions, shattered fragments of a world now irretrievably lost, stands the text of the *Cāndāyan*. The illuminated courtly manuscript traditions that surround it, incomplete as they are (and the manuscripts of the *Cāndāyan* are all damaged), illustrate at least two processes of artistic composition: the courtly and sophisticated mingling of Persian models and Indian painting techniques exemplified in the Prince of Wales Museum and John Rylands Library manuscripts, and the use of indigenous painting conventions to illustrate Persian texts. The text was copied and disseminated among people who were multiliterate and multicultural.

Persian and Hindavī: Composite Texts

There were also two partial translations of the *Cāndāyan* into Persian, for the Indian-born Persian speaking aristocratic élite of the Delhi sultanate. The discourses of a later Chishti shaikh, 'Abdul Quddūs Gangohī (1456–1537), attests to the popularity of the *Cāndāyan* in the fifteenth century. According to the account given in *Laṭā'if-i Quddūsī* ("Quddūsī's Graces/Subtleties"), written by his son Rukn al-dīn Quddūsī, the shaikh began a translation of the *Cāndāyan* into Persian verse couplets in his youth and completed a substantial portion of it.[9] A partial motivation for the translation was that Dā'ūd's Hindavī *maṣnavī* included an account of the Prophet's ascension to heaven (*mi'rāj*), which the Persian *maṣnavī* prologues lacked. The verses quoted in the *Laṭā'if-i Quddūsī* come from this section of the *Cāndāyan*, as do three Persian couplets translating the following Hindavī lines:

I saw a great tree, its fruits in the sky,
no hopes of plucking them with one's hands.
Tell me, who is powerful enough
to stretch out his arms around it?
Who can encompass the branches of that tree?
Night and day, guards keep watch,
and whoever sets eyes on it, is killed [C 57].

The verse is modeled on Sanskrit verses allegorizing the power of suggestion,[10] and 'Abdul Quddūs Gangohī reproduces it with a fairly close literal translation into Persian. The handwritten manuscript of the translation was destroyed in the military campaigns and countercampaigns of Bahlol Lodī and Ḥusain Shāh Sharqī over Jaunpur. In addition, regional songs from Avadh, central India, and Bihar used the *'Iṣmat Nāmah* or "Account of Chastity,"[11] a Persian translation of the *bārah-māsā* section of the *Cāndāyan*, to illustrate the sufferings of Mainā Satvantī, the "chaste Mainā" of that romance.

Explaining the logic of the generic formula through the social and cultural logics of Dā'ūd's day is an approach not without its dangers. On the one hand, one runs the risk of taking the part for the whole, of imagining that what one can say about the distinctive Indian Islamic literary tradition of the Sufi *prema-kahānī*s will go for the period as well, a simple homology between text and context. On the other hand, one does not want merely a formalist account of the text as a floating isolated object within a larger world that one cannot explicate. The answer must lie in integrating genre and history, in understanding the social and cultural themes of Dā'ūd's Hindavī *maṣnavī* not just as literary conventions but as new canons of literary and devotional poetry in an Indian language. Dā'ūd expresses a Sufi mystical ideology through a Hindavī devotional aesthetics.

We can trace the rough outlines of the distinctive generic formula of the poem through the model that was complete for the composers of the later Hindavī romances, and in that way we can delineate its component parts and themes, its address to various contexts of reception. This formalist analysis must take into account the necessarily mixed or composite nature of the conventions and tropes Dā'ūd used.

In the words of M. M. Bakhtin, "Utterances are not indifferent to one another, and are not self-sufficient; they are aware of and mutually reflect one another."[12] In the Sufi romances, the Chishtis and other Sufi groups are competing in two ways: externally, with other religious groups who also produced powerful and appealing poetry, such as the *bhaktas* or votaries of incarnationist (*saguṇa*) deities Kṛṣṇa and Rāma and the devotees of the attributeless (*nirguṇa*) absolute; and internally, with other Indian-born or émigré Muslims in the form of materially and militarily potent rulers or other Sufi *silsilahs*. There was also significant internal competition in claims to sovereignty between Sufi shaikhs and the political rulers of northern India.

Love, in Dā'ūd's formula, reverberates with the concerns of this world and the hereafter, *duniyā* and *dīn*, or the claims of kings and Sufis to symbolic and real authority. Dā'ūd creates a complex narrative within which he places generic set pieces from diverse sources, such as the *bārah-māsā* or the description of the twelve months of separation from one's lord and lover, and the *sarāpā* or the head-to-foot description of the beloved, a set piece that goes back in Persian to the works of Niẓāmī, Amīr Khusrau, Mas'ūd Sa'd Salmān, and Abū' l-Faraj Rūnī, and is continued in Urdu in the works of Mīr Taqī Mīr, Qalandar Bakhsh Jur'at, and a host of others.[13] These pieces are both assimilative and competitive. On the one hand, Dā'ūd uses the terminology of *rasa* and love, like the other groups operating in Hindustan at the time. On the other, he uses these terms and concepts in a very particular way, creating a distinctive Sufi poetics of *prema-rasa*, a *desī* Islam, in which narrative, the pleasure of telling and listening to a good story, employs Indian aesthetics and erotology. And they are both internally and externally competitive. Externally, Dā'ūd takes elements from the local groups the Chishtis encountered in north India, an interaction in which we can put together only one side of the encounter through the generic form of the *Cāndāyan*. Internally, the formula of the two wives works out the somewhat tense relationship between Sufi teachers and aristocratic élites in the Delhi sultanate. Thus Dā'ūd gives the totalizing claims of religious rhetoric a local habitation and a name.

The Sufi Poetics of Prema-Rasa

The distinctiveness and power of Dā'ūd's poetics of *prema-rasa* emerges when we define his poetics of the *rasa* or juice of love, compare it to other visions of *prema-rasa*, and demonstrate the connections of his aesthetics with Chishti mystical ideology.

Sanskrit and new Indo-Aryan poetry to Kṛṣṇa contemporary with the *Cāndāyan* contains a fully worked out range of theologies and aesthetics. But in the incarnationist theology of the Vaiṣṇava poets, the seeker or devotee transforms his subjectivity by imagining himself in a relationship with an embodied divinity. By contrast, Kabīr and the *nirguṇa* poets imagine a formless godhead, and self-recognition through the meditative practice of the divine Name. The Hindavī Sufi poets fall somewhere in between these two poles. In their poems, the erotic body of the heroine signifies divinity in a temporary revelation that is intended to draw the seeker out of himself and on to the ascetic path. Their metaphysics assumes a transcendent principle that cannot be embodied. And since the Chishtis believed in a notion of ordinate love, in which each object of desire is loved for the sake of the one higher to it, their poetry requires narrative stages in which the seeker advances toward the highest object through a series of ordeals.

Although there are no poetic treatises in Hindavī that describe Indian Sufi aesthetics, Maulānā Dā'ūd offers his audience his own definition of *rasa* through an exchange between two characters in the *Cāndāyan*. At one point in the story, the heroine Cāndā ("the Moon") is sorely afflicted by separation from the hero, a brave warrior named Lorik whom she has seen recently. Lorik has routed the wicked King Rūpcand, who besieged the city of Govar to satisfy his lust for Cāndā, and has saved her from submitting to Rūpcand. She appeals to her nurse, Biraspati (the planet Jupiter), to assuage the physiological effects of desire (Hind. *kāma*/Ar. *shauq*) on her body by telling her a diverting tale of love:

> *Cāndā called Biraspati to her,*
> *"Come and tell me a tale of love,*
> *full of love's savor, its taste,*
> *that I may forget my mind's insipid state,*
> *and light the lamp of* rasa *in my heart's niche.*
> *Give me the food of* rasa, *do not tire,*
> *only* rasa *can put out the flames of separation.*
> *I have tried many medicines and powders,*
> *now tell me a story full of flavor and juice.*
> *In its* rasa, *the night will pass quickly,*
> *and sweet sleep will come to my eyes.*
> *O Biraspati, speak sweet words of* rasa, *sweeten my bitter mind—*
> *divert me with an hour of* rasa, *that this pain, this burning*
> *and agitation, may go!" [C 172]*

Cāndā's appeal invokes *rasa* in two senses: as a term adapted from Indian aesthetics into the poetics of a new genre in Hindavī, and, in conjunction with the word *prema* ("love"), as the remedy for the existential condition of *viraha* or separation. Just as savoring the *rasa* or juice of a story is what gives a reader pleasure in a text, so savoring the *rasa* of love removes the burning and pain of separation between lovers. In these two senses, *rasa* signifies an aesthetic relation between reader and text as well as between lovers, a relation that marks both the circulation and reception of the text among sensitive readers and the consummation of desire between characters in a love story. In Dā'ūd's text, however, *prema-rasa* signifies not just human love but also Chishti Sufi notions of love for God. For instance, in Cāndā's words to Biraspati, she uses the image of lighting the lamp of *rasa* in the heart's niche. The image suggests the verse of the Qur'an (24:35) in which God's radiance (*nūr*) is likened to a lamp placed in a niche (*mishkāt*), illuminating the heavens and the earth.[14]

This third sense of *rasa*, the relationship between the invisible Allah and the visible world, is put forward more clearly in Biraspati's response. She plays further on the word, using the rural mixture of jaggery and ghee (unrefined sugar and clarified butter) as the especially sweet *desī* combination or taste of *prema-rasa*:

> *"What do you know of taste or tastelessness?*
> *It's only* rasa *when you wet it with love,*
> *sweet like ghee in sugar-cane molasses,*
> *sweet like moon-nectar you could taste, Cāndā!*
> *You may avoid* rasa, *push it away,*
> *but the world is sunk only in love's savor!*
> *Deep and dark is the lake of* rasa *into which*
> *your yogi has fallen—he will die sinking in*
> *its waters. Cāndā, stretch out your arm and pull*
> *him out!" [C 173]*

The nurse proposes the theological sense in which *rasa* signifies in the *premākhyān* texts: it is the mark of the circulation of desire between Allah and the world. As the famous tradition (*ḥadīs̤ quds̤ī*) has it, Allah created the world as a mirror for divine beauty (*jamāl*). It is Allah's longing that is reflected in human desires, just as it is Allah's radiance that spreads from the niche in which it is placed into the heavens and the earth. The nurse's response to Cāndā also contains the following observation:

> *To the one burnt by* rasa, *food and water are distasteful.*
> *If you relish this savor, bring along its remedy.*
> *If this taste is truly established in your heart,*
> *never would you know an insipid hour! [C 173]*

The taste for *rasa*, then, allows the reader or listener to pass many instructive and delightful hours interpreting individual lines and sets of images for their suggestive resonances. The genre redefines *rasa* as the relation of desire between characters and transforms it into *'ishq* or love.

Sacred and Profane Attitudes Toward *Rasa* and Devotion

The poetics of the day linked the valence and use of *rasa* to notions of embodiment. The Sanskrit poetry to Kṛṣṇa famously sets the tone for the merging of sacred and profane modalities of love in the period. In Līlāśuka Bilvamaṅgala's *Kṛṣṇakarṇāmṛta*[15] and Jayadeva's twelfth-century *Gītagovinda*,[16] the lyrics work on two levels at once. The poet holds in suspension the question of whether the love play of Kṛṣṇa is sacred or profane, and the reader/devotee approaches the embodiment of God through a sacralized human love. As Lee Siegel has remarked in his study of the *Gītagovinda*, "within the Kṛṣṇa-cults a love-mysticism, a love-symbolism, developed. The human and the divine became inextricably intertwined in love, in *bhakti*, no longer *bhakti* simply as 'devotion,' but *bhakti* as fervent, passionate love."[17] A poetic delight in the multiple resonances of embodiment marks verses that celebrate the handsome dark god:

With a bright peacock plume hair ornament and a
face as if dipped in sweet tenderness,
The Light takes life in that budding youth found
where the nectar of full flute sounds swell
and, on all sides, the milkmaids of the full bud-like
breasts adore (him).
The Light is the one wonder and the one delight of
the world; let it shine in our heart.[18]

Here Līlāśuka simultaneously delineates a scene of the beloved Kṛṣṇa and his adoring *gopīs* or milkmaids and an incarnationist theology. Although the sacred biography of Kṛṣṇa in the tenth chapter of the *Bhāgavata Purāṇa* created a basic narrative, model, and proof text for what Friedhelm Hardy has called the "emotional *bhakti*" of the Kṛṣṇa sects,[19] much of the poetry devoted to Kṛṣṇa is not in the form of long narratives. Rather, as in the *Gītagovinda*, the poems describe and celebrate a succession of moments in the passionate love play of Kṛṣṇa and the strong and elemental village girls who fetched water and milked cows and drove herds of cattle for grazing:

When he quickens all things
to create bliss in the world,

his soft black sinuous lotus limbs
begin the festival of love
and beautiful cowherd girls wildly
wind him in their bodies.
Friend, in spring young Hari plays
like erotic mood incarnate.[20]

Jayadeva suggests that the Lord in his love play is the embodiment (*mūrti*) of the erotic mood in poetics, *śṛṅgāra*. In this he turns the classical aesthetics of *śṛṅgāra* toward *prema*, the pure transformative love of the *gopīs* for Kṛṣṇa. In Jayadeva's imagery, as Siegel puts it, *prema* is gold: "the 'night manifests [itself] as a touchstone for the gold which is love for him' (XI.12). The correlation *prema* = gold and *kāma* = lead, suggests the alchemical process—the goal of the Vaiṣṇavas was the transmutation of the baser emotion into the pure emotion."[21]

The Sanskrit poetry of Līlāśuka and Jayadeva and the *padas* or lyric poems to Kṛṣṇa in the regional languages created a new aesthetics of *bhakti*, based on a revaluation of the literary category of *rasa*.[22] They elaborated the vocabulary of *kāma* and *prema*; the mythology of Kāma-deva, god of love, with his bow and arrows; and the celebration of moments of passion and separation in love, and creatively mingled that erotic love with devotion, as in this poem to Kṛṣṇa (Dāmodara) by the fifteenth-century Maithili poet Vidyāpati:

Who would go so far away from me?
Thousands of co-wives live in Mathura, city of sweetness.
The treasure comes by itself into my hands.
The prayers I have recited for ages are fulfilled today.
A good thing has happened, the bad days are over;
the moon and the waterlily have seen each at last.
Where is the god Dāmodara, the lord of the forest,
and where am I, a rustic cow-herding girl?
Today, all at once, our glances have met.
Destiny has favored us completely.
Vidyāpati says: "Listen, O excellent woman,
the bad times stay only for a few days."[23]

Here the jealous co-wives (*sautana*) are imagined in a structure different from that of Dā'ūd's formula of warring wives. Kṛṣṇa satisfies all sixteen thousand wives in his love play in the paradise of Mathura, as the lovelorn *gopī* attests. Her time has come after eons of prayers (*japa*). The god Dāmodara and she have glanced at each other, and that first moment of vision granted her the grace of the Lord. She has attained *siddhi* or fulfillment (both spiritual and physical). The symbolism of glances, of the water lily opening to the moon's rays, and the love play that will ensue all underscore the way that classical erotics have here been transformed into the *rasa* of devotion to Kṛṣṇa.

The concept of *rasa*, as Siegel has indicated, links the "psychological and physiological aspects of love—*rasa* is both the emotional pleasure of love and the biological manifestation of that pleasure, i. e. semen."[24] The different sects that sought to use *rasa* in their lyrics and to execute a direct and concrete erotico-mystical practice invoked the sexual, aesthetic, spiritual, and psychological aspects of *rasa* simultaneously. As Edward C. Dimock has pointed out about the Sahajiyā Vaiṣṇavas of Bengal:

> To the Sahajiyās, the body is full of rasa, of the bliss of union, or, speaking purely physiologically, of semen. The place of rasa at the beginning of *sādhana* is in the lowest lotus, the seat of sexual passion. By *sādhana*, rasa is raised from lotus to lotus along the spinal column, until it unites with the thousand-petalled lotus in the head; there, in pure experience and pure consciousness of Rādhā and Kṛṣṇa in union... is full and eternal realization of their bliss. Here there is no longer even the seeming distinction of human and divine; here man knows completely the divine *ānanda* within himself.[25]

Here we begin to see the practical implications of the Vaiṣṇava *rasa* theory, as human and divine collapse into each other at the level of *ānanda* or bliss.

The sects devoted to Kṛṣṇa used these notions differently, creating interpretive schemes and theological commentaries around the various songs to Kṛṣṇa and the sacred biography contained in the *Bhāgavata Purāṇa*. Although the Sahajiyās practiced a form of Tantric mysticism, the Rādhā Vallabha sect followed nine stages of devotion to Kṛṣṇa: listening to the deeds of Kṛṣṇa (*śravaṇa*), singing his names (*kīrtana*), remembering the Lord (*smaraṇa*), worshipping the feet (*pāda-sevana*), worshipping (*arcana*) and paying homage (*vandana*) to the image (*svarūpa*) of Kṛṣṇa, servitude to Kṛṣṇa (*dāsya*), companionship with Kṛṣṇa (*sākhya*), and finally, dedicating oneself completely to Kṛṣṇa (*ātma-nivedana*).[26] Devotees sang various *padas* or songs to Kṛṣṇa as part of this nine-step program, designed to help the devotee transform his soul (*jīva*) into a loving worshipper of Kṛṣṇa. The *Subodhinī*, Vallabhācārya's elaborate sixteenth-century commentary on the *Bhāgavata Purāṇa*, supplies the theological superstructure for this regimen of worship.[27] Vallabhācārya interprets the love games of Kṛṣṇa as transcendent in their very physicality, and makes Kṛṣṇa the summation of all the aesthetic moods and concepts found in classical *rasa* theory.

Other forms of devotional poetry emphasize the inability of language or form to capture the transcendent. Preeminent among these is the fifteenth-century poet Kabīr, with whom the Sufis also share a certain amount of the technical vocabulary of devotion.[28] Like the Sufis, Kabīr uses negative terminology to name the highest level of reality: Alakhā (the invisible one), Nirañjanā (the untainted one), Nirākārā (the formless one). He also takes terms for practice from the Gorakhnāthī yogis (the followers of Gorakh, the thirteenth-century leader of the Nāth yogis) and the Tantric adepts (*siddhas*): Śabda (the Word), Anāhadā (the unstruck sound), Sahajā (the state of pure spontaneity), and Śūnya (the void). Kabīr's verses subvert the outward forms of ascetic practice to express his devotion to the worship of Rām, the absolute divinity:

Kabīr, that path is difficult,
no one can follow it:
Those who went never came back
none ever came back to tell about it!
Kabīr's house is on the top,
where the path is slippery:
An ant cannot hold its footing
and they go with loaded bullocks!
...In that Forest where no lion roars,
where no bird takes to flight,
where there is neither day nor night,
there dwells Kabīr, entranced.
...Between Gangā and Yamunā,
on the ghat *of 'Absorption' [*Sahaj-śūnya*],*
There Kabīr has built his hermitage
while the Sages search for a path![29]

The image of Kabīr building his house above worldly distinctions, in the *śūnya-maṇḍala* or "circle of emptiness," expresses the difficult path of absorption in the void. In the symbolic geography of the body, this circle lies between the eyes and on top of the *cakras* along the spinal column.

Kabīr negates exterior forms of religion and places meditation on Rām's name at the center of his esoteric practice:

Kabīr, why are you afraid?
Why let your soul be shaken?
Drink the nectar of Rām's Name,
of Him who is the Lord of all joy.[30]

The love of Rām is the simple love in Kabīr's devotional practice, and the devotee repeats Rām's Name while practicing breath control to attain the state of absorption (*sahaja*).

Like the Sufis, Kabīr frequently uses the tropes of a bridal mysticism to express his passionate love (*prema*) for the attributeless (*nirguṇa*) Rām. In a song strikingly reminiscent of the divine heroine Cāndā's longing for a lover, Kabīr uses the tropes and conventions surrounding the practice of child marriage. In this widespread Indian practice, it was usual for the bride to remain with her parents after her first wedding ceremony until she reached the age of puberty. After this there was a second ceremony, the *gavana* or "going," in which all good-byes were said and she set out for her husband's home after the ritual of consummation as a sexually mature woman.[31] Union itself, as in other mystical literatures, is described in terms of both mystical marriage and sexual union:

To my Father-in-law's house,
as a new bride I came,
But I couldn't unite with my Lord
and my youth passed in vain!
The Five erected the wedding-canopy,
the three fixed the marriage's date,
my girl-friends sang the wedding songs
and smeared my brow with the turmeric of Joy and Sorrow.
Clad in motley array, I circled the sacred Fire,
the knot was tied, true to my father's pledge:
Without a Bridegroom, I entered wedlock—
on the marriage-square I stood as a widow by my Lord's side!
My husband's face, I've never seen,
yet people urge me to be the perfect wife.
Says Kabīr, I'll raise a pyre and I'll die on it:
clinging to my Spouse, I'll cross over, playing the trumpet of Victory![32]

Here all the signs and symbols of an Indian wedding are turned toward the practice of absorption in the invisible Lord. The bride acquires a father-in-law's house (*sasurāla*) as a new bride, but cannot consecrate her marriage until she has come of age. The five senses erect the canopy, while the three strands that make up all creation (*guṇas*) bring the couple to the fated date (*muhūrata*). But the groom remains invisible, and she circles the fire without him. In the end the bride sacrifices herself on a funeral pyre to "cross over" to the other side of this world of separation, union with the Beloved in the next world.

Dā'ūd's Use of Islamic and Sanskritic Erotologies

Dā'ūd constructs an erotics of asceticism in which both verbal description and vision excite desire in the anxious suitors of the divine heroine, and both lover and beloved display conventional signs of love such as fainting and lovesickness. He uses yogic imagery to suggest the Chishti novice's ascetic quest to savor the *rasa* of love. But his poetic version of desire and fulfillment draws upon the Islamic and Sanskritic erotologies that determined the cultural and literary representation of love and sexuality in his day.

The earliest works on love in Arabic, such as al-Jāḥiẓ's ninth-century treatise the *Risālah fī 'l-'Ishq va 'l-Nisā'* ("Essay on Love and Women"), speak of the excessive nature of love:

> *'Ishq* is the name for what exceeds that which is called *ḥubb* (affection) and every *ḥubb* is not called *'ishq*, for *'ishq* is the name for what exceeds that degree, just as *saraf* (prodigality) is the name for that degree which is more than that which is called *jūd* (liberality) and *bukhl* (stinginess) is the name for what falls short of the level of *iqtiṣād* (economy) and *jubn* (cowardice) is the name for what falls short of the quality which is termed *shajā'a* (courage).[33]

This excessive and violent emotion, exceeding ordinary attachment, is often described as invisible to the eye: "It is too sublime to be seen and it is hidden from the eyes of mortals, for it is concealed in the breast like the latent fire in a flint, which when struck produces fire, this fire remaining hidden as long as it is left alone."[34]

Further, Persian and Arabic sources define *'ishq* as comprising a number of feelings, both sacred and profane, and a complex of emotions centering on madness and violent obsession:

> And in the *Kitāb al-Mutayyamin* of al-Marzubānī: Someone said to Zubair al-Madini, "What is *'ishq*?" He said, "Madness and submissiveness, and it is the malady of refined people (*ahl az-zarf*)." And he (al-Marzubānī, probably) said, "A person ardently in love looked at his beloved and violent emotion overcame him and he fainted, so someone present asked a learned man, 'What happened to him?' He said, 'He looked at the one he loved and his heart dilated greatly and then the body was agitated by the great dilatation of the heart.' So someone said to him, 'We love our children and our spouses and nothing like that happens to us.' He answered 'That is the love that comes from the mind (*muḥabbat al-'aql*), but this is the love that comes from the soul (*muḥabbat ar-rūḥ*, or spirited love).'"[35]

This "love that comes from the soul" must be distinguished from ordinary attachment and also from lust (*havā*), which is connected with the lower soul (*nafs*), an important distinction among Sufis, who tried to promote the former at the expense of the latter.

This definition of *'ishq* as excessive love or an excess of feeling, with an exclusive character, was among the common topoi used to describe love. Other themes that recur in Islamic theories of love are the characterization of love as a divine madness that is neither fair nor foul, the ennobling power of love, love as progressive apprehension of the stages of beauty, and the concept of ordinate love in which each object except the last is loved for the sake of another higher than itself. The classical Greek philosophical question of whether the happy and self-sufficient man needs friends was adapted in the Islamicate cultural context into the question of whether God as self-sufficient can be described as loving. The corollary to the self-sufficiency of God was denial of love between God and man, or the contrary assertion, that love is the means of all intercourse between God and man. Factors that were held to excite love included contemplation of beautiful faces, especially those of beardless boys and women at whom it is not lawful to look. As J. N. Bell points out, these topoi were brought into Arabic through translation of the classical Greek sources on love.[36] Moreover, as Annemarie Schimmel indicates,

> The discussions on mystical love became more complicated in Baghdad circles around 900, with the introduction of the notion of *ḥubb 'udhrī*, "platonic love." Jamīl, a noted poet from the tribe of 'Udhrā in the late seventh century, had sung of his chaste love for Buthayna in delicate verses that almost foreshadow the love lyrics of French and Spanish troubadours; and soon a *ḥadīth* was coined, according to which the Prophet had said: "Whoever loves and remains chaste, and dies, dies as a martyr." It was Muḥammad ibn Dā'ūd, the son of the founder of the Zahirite law school, who composed, in Ḥallāj's day, a book on the ideal chaste love, containing one hundred chapters of poetry about *ḥubb 'udhrī* and stressing the necessity of the "martyrdom of chastity." He and his followers denied the possibility of mutual love between man and God and excluded every human object from mystical love.[37]

Later writers on love often discussed Muḥammad ibn Dā'ūd's *Kitāb al-Zahra*, exemplifying the concept of the martyrdom that attended chaste love. They drew incessantly on systematic and unsystematic anthologies of maxims, anecdotes, and verses about love such as the *Maṣāri al-'Ushshāq* of Abū Muḥammad Ja'far ibn Aḥmad al-Sarrāj.[38] Manuals on the subject treated the physical signs and terminology of love, as well as the progress of love affairs, and often described desperate lovers dying of unconsummated love.[39]

Dā'ūd's poem draws on these texts and on this tradition of mystical love, as we shall see, and also on the Sanskrit tradition exemplified by Vātsyāyana's *Kāma-sūtra* and the enormous literature on erotics in Sanskrit and Prakrit.[40] As the *Kāma-sūtra* tells us, erotic desire (*kāma*) "consists in engaging the ear, skin, eye, tongue, and nose each in its own appropriate sensation, all under the control of the mind and heart driven by the conscious self."[41] In general, however, poets and critics frowned on explicit descriptions of lovemaking in Sanskrit poetry:

> In dealing with love, both physical and emotional, the Sanskrit poet sought always to avoid vulgarity. This conscious effort at refinement appears in the poet's choice of individual words, in the speech and gestures of the lovers he portrays, and in the selection he makes of fact from actual sexual experience. Words that refer to bodily functions are avoided unless they are to be used metaphorically. Clouds may spit lightning but when humans spit the poet must turn away.[42]

By and large, Dā'ūd follows this prohibition against describing the actual physical details of sex in his own poem. He models his imagery on the poetry of *śṛṅgāra*, both love-in-enjoyment (*saṃbhoga-śṛṅgāra*) and love-in-separation (*vipralambha-śṛṅgāra*).

Dā'ūd's use of Indian erotics to express a Sufi message was thus based on a key distinction in Sanskrit poetry. Actual sexual practice, the *ars amandi* laid out in the *Kāma-sūtra*, the *Koka-śāstra*, and related texts, is separate from its emotional and aesthetic representation in poetry:

> The Sanskrit poet was chiefly interested in the sentimental or emotional development of sex. But he recognized that the basis of all sexual emotion lies in sight and touch and regularly describes sufficient physical details to form a base for the non-physical development...[C]ertain words may not be used, e. g., *kaṭi* for hip, certain parts of the body may be mentioned only by euphemisms (e. g., *nābhimūla* "base of the navel," *ūrumūla*, "base of the thigh"), while the sexual organs themselves may not be mentioned even indirectly. More to the point, the actions and occurrences that are mentioned are chosen because they reveal an abiding sentiment. The poet is not interested in the simple copulation of humans any more than of animals, but in an event which affects the personality of those engaged in it. Hence the constant mention of the sweating and horripilation of the lovers, symptoms which seem to a

> European far from poetic. To the Indian they were significant. Sweating and bristling of the skin are involuntary actions...They cannot be simulated; they are criteria of the true state of the affections.[43]

Even though a fourteenth-century Chishti disciple, Ẓiyā' al-dīn Nakhshabī, translated the *Koka-śāstra* into Persian as the *Lazzāt al-Nisā* ("The Delights of Women"),[44] the art of love is not Dā'ūd's central purpose in the *Candāyan*. Dā'ūd uses the conventions of *śṛṅgāra-rasa* with their elaborate classificatory schemes and exquisitely detailed descriptions of an idealized love, but goes a step further in his Hindavī poem: he transforms *śṛṅgāra* into the emotion of *prema*, emphasizing the emotions and sentiments surrounding the erotic experience, rather than its physical details. He does not follow the rules of propriety (*aucitya*) so carefully laid out by the Sanskrit critics but uses the Perso-Arabic theory of *'ishq* and the Sanskrit poetics of *śṛṅgāra-rasa* to express his own Hindavī poetics of love and separation, which has its own signs and stages of love, its own erotology.

The eleventh-century *Kashf al-Maḥjūb* of 'Alī Usmān al-Hujvīrī attests to the several valences of passionate love in Indian Sufi contexts. The author restricts the relation between Allah and humans to *maḥabbhah* (love or affection) but does not allow *'ishq* (passionate love) between a subject and object who are so unlike each other:

> You must know that the term "love" (*maḥabbhah*) is used by theologians in three senses. Firstly, as meaning restless passion for the object of love, and inclination and passion, in which sense it refers only to created beings and their mutual affection towards one another, but cannot be applied to God, who is exalted far above anything of the sort. Secondly, as meaning God's beneficence and His conferment of special privileges on those whom He chooses and causes to attain the perfection of saintship and peculiarly distinguishes by diverse kinds of His miraculous grace. Thirdly, as meaning praise which God bestows on man for a good action.[45]

Much of al-Hujvīrī's chapter on love is a collection of sayings about love from the great Sufis and theorists of his day. Only occasionally does he allow the notion of *'ishq* to be applied to Allah, whose essence is generally held to be imperceptible and unattainable and therefore far above passionate love (*maḥabbhah*).[46] By the fourteenth century, however, the Chishti Sufis had collapsed the distinction between the two terms, seeing them as sequential rather than radically different. The chapter on love in the *Siyar al-Auliyā'* begins its section on *'ishq* by quoting Niẓām al-dīn Auliyā' on the relationship between the two: "*'Ishq* is the last of the stages of *muḥabbat,* and *muḥabbat* is the first of the stages of *'ishq.*"[47]

What is also clear from the *Siyar al-Auliyā'* is that love was valued for its utility in Chishti mystical practice. Muḥammad Kirmānī skillfully deploys the idea of ordinate love:

> It is necessary for the practitioner to be a lover, and passionate, and in love with the beauty of the *vilāyah* of his pir, so that little by little, with practice and with the exercise (or abundance) of his neediness (*ba-andak 'amalī va kas̱rat-i niyāz*) he may reach more quickly the original goal which the seekers of this road have reached.... He must strive in the work of Almighty God for many years. He must burn his lower soul (*nafs*) with fasting and observance, and worship and effort...[and] be sincere towards that Beloved so that the light of that [other] world may illuminate him.[48]

The seeker's path leads first to an engagement with his teacher's *vilāyah* or *valāyah,* a word that encompasses both the notion of spiritual jurisdiction and the friendship of Allah, the power to dispose and to command.[49] Little by little, by applying the Chishti regimen of worship and fasting, he approaches the real beloved, God. Finally, the invisible world is illuminated to him, and the ways of divine providence. Though there is no exact allegorical scheme of the stages of love that can be mapped on to Dā'ūd's poem, the events in his story resonate with the Chishti formulations of mystical love and ascetic practice. These events draw the reader into the hero's erotic/ascetic quest for the invisible divinity that is temporarily revealed in the beautiful form of the heroine Cāndā.

A fantastic story in Ḥamīd Qalandar's *Khair al-Majālis* demonstrates the ideological link between this ascetic regimen and Hindavī and Persian poetry. This text contains the collected discourses of Shaikh Naṣīr al-dīn Muḥmūd Chirāgh-i Dihlī ("The Lamp of Delhi"), the spiritual preceptor of Dā'ūd's guide Shaikh Zain al-dīn. Even though the shaikh was known to be generally opposed to poetry and music,[50] he recounted in one of his discourses the parable of a young man who died from unrequited love. After his death an autopsy was carried out, and a stone was extracted from his stomach. The emperor who had ordered the autopsy had two rings made from the stone, one to wear and the other to keep in his treasury. Once, while listening to singers in *samā'* (ritual audition),[51] the ring on his finger melted and turned to blood. His clothes were all stained red with blood. Puzzled, the emperor summoned wise men, who told him that the young man had been in love. If *samā'* had been performed for him, they opined, he would have become well. For demonstration, the other ring was fetched from the treasury, and it too melted in front of the singers and became blood. The moral of the story is that to the people of *samā'*, *samā'* is the medicine for all ills.[52] The medico-moral discourse of the Chishtis on *'ishq* represents love as both physical and emotional, a congealed substance in the body that can be melted by the power of music and then directed toward Allah.

How does this Chishti mystical agenda translate into Hindavī poetic conventions in Dā'ūd's poem? At this point it may be helpful to read another passage from the romance, in which a wandering singer has just seen Cāndā's dazzlingly lovely body at a window of her palace and has fainted in response to it. The singer's response to Cāndā's revelatory beauty is widely known both in Islamic and Sanskritic theories of love; this was how one scholar analyzed it:

> The *Maṣāri' al-'Ushshāq* of Abū Muḥammad Ja'far b. Aḥmad as-Sarrāj probably did more than any Arabic book to popularize the theme of tragic, passionate love. The word *maṣra'*, verbal noun of the root *ṣ-r-'*, comes from a root which has the connotation of "throwing down to the ground." From this derive the meanings "to fall down in an epileptic fit," "to go mad," or "to be killed in battle." The word is particularly appropriate in the title of this book, for it embraces almost all the afflictions described in its pages: the lovers faint, fall down in a spasm of rapture or painful longing, never to regain consciousness, or they go mad.[53]

Similarly, both the aesthetic theory of the *Nāṭya-Śāstra* and the practical prescriptions of the *Kāma-sūtra* include fainting (*jaḍatā* or *mūrchhā*) as the penultimate stage of *kāma*, to be followed, if the desire is unfulfilled, by death (*maraṇa*).[54] Fainting as a response to a vision occurs frequently in the Hindavī Sufi romances; lovers fall to the ground in rapture or agony, and they recover only after they attain the object of their desire.

The *Sarāpā* or Head-to-Foot Description

Desire is aroused, in Dā'ūd's poem as well as in older schemes of erotics, through descriptions and visions of the beloved. Dā'ūd uses the convention of *adṛṣṭa-kāma* or "love without seeing" the object of desire. The wandering singer knows that he is not of the correct social status to marry Cāndā. The only way he can communicate his desire is by singing the beauty of Cāndā far and wide. He leaves Govar and enters Candragiri, a town ruled by King Rūpcand. Here he sings all night, in hauntingly beautiful words, about the supernatural beauty he has just seen. Nobody in the town is able to sleep, and in the morning the king summons him to his court. In response to the king's questions, he replies that he has seen a vision of exquisite beauty. A restless desire (*caṭpaṭī*) is aroused in the king's heart, and he orders him to continue. The musician depicts Cāndā in the generic set piece of the head-to-foot description:

> *"Let me first tell of her blessed parting,*
> *from whose red color, the world plays Holi.*
> *Her parting is full of vermillion,*
> *creeping along on her head like a centipede.*
> *Or, like a lamp's radiance in the dark night,*
> *it shines like a jewel in the blackness...."[C 64]*

Here begins a description of Cāndā's attributes (*ṣifāt*), which, as we know from the Chishti interpretive principle of verbal transfer (*taḥmīl-i alfāẓī*), was understood as referring to the attributes or Names of God (*asmā'-yi ilāhī*). The Divine Names, which form the prototypes of all things in existence, are divided into His wrathful and destructive attributes (*ṣifāt-i jalālī*) and his gentle and comforting ones (*ṣifāt-i jamālī*). The poetic images employed here to describe the various parts of Cāndā's embodied form fluctuate between the fierce and gentle aspects of her beauty.[55] At the festival of Holi, revelers would throw red powder and red water on one another.

Next he describes her flowing black locks, which are like stinging black serpents guarding a treasure of nectar:

> *"Then I saw her hair, the color of black bees,*
> *or poisonous serpents rolling about on a treasure.*
> *Her long black locks reached from her head to her feet,*
> *like vicious cobras stained red with vermillion.*
> *Her black braid hung down so dangerously,*
> *that those who saw it rolled about in agony.*
> *The poison rushed up to their foreheads.*
> *When she opened her dark knot of hair,*
> *day shaded over into black night" [C 65].*

The indication that these are fierce, *jalālī* attributes comes from the account of their effect upon King Rūpcand:

> *The king was stung viciously, the poison mounted,*
> *and he writhed about in agony.*
> *As he heard the singer's words, the venom rose;*
> *what could the snake-bite charmer do? [C 65]*

According to Sufi metaphysics, God yearns to be known and loved, and human desire is only a mirror of divine desire (*shauq*). The agony of desire in which the king finds himself signifies the interaction of divine revelation with human vision, the seductive appearance of divinity to attract human love. A later Sufi gloss on the Hindavī images for feminine beauty, the *Ḥaqā'iq-i Hindī* of Mīr 'Abdul Vāḥid Bilgrāmī, indicates that the beloved's dark locks can also signify the dark night of sin. The lover has to escape from the night in order to follow the mystical path, which is often represented as the shining white parting in the hair of the beloved.[56]

The next part of Cāndā's body described is her forehead, which suggests the radiant divine manifestation in the form of light:

> *"Her forehead shone like the moon*
> *on the second night of the month,*
> *or purest gold, tested and refined.*
> *The drops of moisture on her forehead,*
> *were like stars shining on the moon.*
> *It could not be looked at directly,*
> *like the flame of a lamp,*
> *or the blinding sun at noontide." [C 66].*

The poison that had rushed through the king's arteries is arrested by this sight, and he recovers himself:

> *When this sun rose in the sky, the venom subsided,*
> *and the king rolled over.*
> *As he heard about her forehead, he sat up and*
> *rewarded the singer with purest gold [C 66].*

The effect of her beautiful form on the king suggests the circulation of desire between God, who wants to be seen, and the created being who sees in beauty the reflection of divinity. On another level, the singer's verses indicate what can happen to readers or listeners in the context of reception of such mystical poetry, if the listeners are able to appreciate the *rasa* of the poem.

The singer continues to describe Cāndā's beautiful body, and the king's reactions fluctuate with the verses. Her teeth flash lightning, like glittering diamonds, and are full of juice (*rasa*) and perfectly formed as pomegranate seeds. If her speech is sweet, it is because she has drunk much of the *rasa* of fruits. Indeed, her mouth is described as a pool full of nectar. In response the King cries out, "Catch her! Catch her!" But she remains elusive. Her ears shine like golden lamps, and flashes of light from her jeweled ear studs illuminate the heavens. The king revives and sits up, but then he sees the mole on her face:

> *"Between her eye and her ear lay a mole,*
> *a spot of blackest ink,*
> *as if put there by separation incarnate!*
> *Her face was fortunate, in bliss from that mole,*
> *which looked like a bee on a lotus flower.*
> *He sat there drunk on the blossom's scent...*
> *I think I'm going to die, scorched*
> *by separation's blaze, bloodless, burnt to a cinder!"*
> *When that arrow had struck the singer, he lay stunned, tossed*
> *to one side.*
> *And the king burnt with a terrible flame, a fire that none could*
> *extinguish [C 74].*

The Persian title for this verse is "*ṣifah̲-i k̲h̲āl-i bīmis̲āl,*" a "description of the incomparable mole." The mole is without a *mis̲āl,* an allegory, exemplum, or likeness, a word that was commonly used to suggest the process of abstraction in the literature of the period. The images the poet uses to describe the mole suggest the sexual encounter of the male black bee and the female lotus that the bee penetrates, intoxicated by its scent. This cruel image has a double impact: on the singer, who lies stunned, and the king, who burns in the terrible flames of separation. The singer moves on to describe Cāndā's peerless throat, which looks as if it has been perfectly shaped on a potter's wheel, and is so beautiful that all the gods have declared the impossibility of embracing it. The king immediately declares he will embrace her lovely neck, even if he has to conquer Govar to do so.

Throughout this entire passage, in which the poet has heightened the *rasa* to suggest the multiple allegorical resonances of Cāndā's beauty, the reader/listener is never sure of the status of Cāndā's embodiment. Dā'ūd's skillful use of imagery allows a logic of embodiment and a transcendent formless absolute to work together in the imagery of the female body.[57] The *sarāpā* draws to a close with a verse that sums up Cāndā's beauty by describing the heavenly grace of her body, balancing her corporeal (*saguṇa*) and transcendent (*nirguṇa*) aspects:

> *"Her body was wave upon wave of tenderness,*
> *anointed with oil of sandal and nutmeg.*
> *She looked as if she had come down from paradise,*
> *and was poised to fly away there any moment.*

She was as if cut from a grove of swaying bamboo,
graceful as a heavenly nymph standing there.
The flower-scent of her beautiful body
made spring break out in all four directions" [C 82].

She is an allegory and mirror of the transcendent divinity, which is momentarily reflected in her body: she looks as if she has come down from paradise, but is also poised to fly away at any moment. Dā'ūd's imagery skirts the Islamic prohibition against the embodiment of Allah, instead describing Cāndā's body as reflecting flashes of divine essence. The singer's description has the effect of triggering an invasion by Rūpcand, who is violently (and ultimately unsuccessfully) offered to Cāndā to transform her desire into *prema* and to savor the *rasa* of a mutually fulfilling love.

The Chishti Ideology of Love

The notion of the reciprocal relationship of desire between God and man, as well as its corollary, the interchangeability of lover and beloved, was well known in Chishti circles. The *Lavā'iḥ* ("The Lights") of Qāẓī Ḥamīd al-dīn Nāgaurī (d. 1244), one of the successors of Haẓrat Mu'īn al-dīn Ajmerī, provides valuable glimpses into the Chishti ideology of love. As Bruce B. Lawrence notes in a pathbreaking article, the work survives only as a fragment quoted in the larger *Ma'ārij al-Vilāyah* of Ġhulām Mu'īn al-dīn 'Abdullāh K͟hvīshgī Quṣūrī.[58] In Lawrence's translation of the excerpt, one of the key passages is the play of coquetry and dalliance between Creator and created being:

> The coquetry and dalliance of the Beloved reach the lover, whom He has created because the lover, before he came into existence, did not wish for the Beloved. But the Beloved, before the existence of the lover, was himself a lover. God wanted someone to want Him.
>
> *Without a lover and love, the labor of the Beloved is lost.*
> *While there is no lover, where is the coquetry of the Beloved?*[59]
>
> And again they say: when the Beloved preens himself and dallies before the eye of the lover, He produces commotion and anxiety in the lover. Yet for the Beloved, there is pleasure in that exchange. And when the lover in the presence of the Beloved appears weak and submissive and destitute, there appears world after world of delight for the Beloved, and therein lies the happiness of the lover.[60]

The passage puts forward as the very reason for man's existence his role of lover (*'āshiq*) of God as beloved (*ma'shūq*). The narratives of the Hindavī love stories are centered on awakening and transforming this basic human desire or *shauq* (translated into Hindavī as *kāma*) into divine love.

The fragment of the *Lavā'iḥ* illuminates also the hidden causes for the arising of love in man:

> Love appears in connection with man for two reasons. One reason is manifest. Man is dominated by passions and desires. The seeker of Truth, by nature, tries to hold these tendencies in check, just as he tries to curb his hunger for bread and his thirst for water, but he succeeds only by inclining to excess toward the Possessor of all beauty. The second reason for the appearance of love in man is hidden. It exists as a secret in the very nature of man. It is a divine secret, expressed in the *ḥadīs̱ qudsī*:
>
> al-insān sirrī va anā sirrahu
> *Man is my secret, and I am his secret.*
>
> Neither verbal expression nor written commentary can unravel that mystery. Related to it is the *ḥadīs̱* from the Prophet Muḥammad:
>
> k͟halaqa allāh ādam ilá ṣūratahu
> *God created man in his own image.*
>
> For this reason the soul of man hastens with a thousand steps toward that other world in order to acquire a scent of its aroma.[61]

Women, in this misogynistic formulation, are beside the point; they are good for marriage and procreation, or seductively arrayed to excite the ascetic on his mystical quest for the juice of love. Although the literal application of the traditions that Ḥamīd al-dīn Nāgaurī quotes here skirts the limits of heresy, *rasa*'s capacity to refer to invisible emotional realities allows poets of this genre to suggest the secret identity of lover and divine beloved. The seeker's need to die to all else on the mystical quest constitutes the central symbolic value of *prema-rasa*.

The necessary journey of self-transformation points strongly to the centrality and importance of storytelling and narrative elaboration in Hindavī Sufi poetry. Dā'ūd's Sufi vision requires the long narrative, the constant deferment of desire in order to draw the seeker into the process of self-realization. This lures the reader or listener into the narrative, working to arouse his desire so that a spiritual mentor may guide him appropriately to transform his subjectivity. Hence the emphasis in Dā'ūd's text on *viraha*, the constant and nagging feeling of longing for and separation from the beloved. As S. M. Pandey points out:

> Philosophical interpretations have been given to this pain of separation in Sufi literature. In Hindi what is called *virah*, is called *firāq* or *judā'ī* in Persian-Arabic literature. This *virah* or *firāq* takes place as soon as the soul separates from God. The soul strives to reunite with God and its separation is painful.... In fact *virah* (separation) and *prem* (love) in the *Cāndāyan* are one. All the Hindi Sūfī poets who succeeded Maulānā Dāūd describe *virah* more profoundly than love. Maulānā Dāūd declares that birds, beasts, earth and sky all can burn through the fire of *virah*.[62]

Dā'ūd expresses the theology of devotion by introducing the figure of the lovelorn yogi, Lorik, who became an ascetic for the sake of his beloved. Lorik must be pulled out of the deep, dark waters into which he has fallen, and union with Cāndā should be the fruit of his austerities.

The religious and poetic vision of the *Cāndāyan* is not of a fully embodied divinity with whom a personal relationship is imagined by the author and his audience, like the vision of the poets who used *rasa* poetics to compose lyrics in praise of Kṛṣṇa. Dā'ūd's poem does not try to realize the Sahajīya Vaiṣṇava union of Rādhā and Kṛṣṇa within the seeker, or, as in Kabīr, to awaken the formless divine within man through breath control and constant repetition of the name of Rām. The Sufi poetics of the *Cāndāyan* are in the narrative, the pleasure of telling and listening to a story, through which the audience realizes *prema rasa*.

Narrative is important in this composite poetics because the Chishtis do not believe in an absolute union between devotee and Allah, as do the other devotional poets who use *prema-rasa*, but in the notion of ordinate love. The desire of the novice is first for a beautiful woman or man as an object of longing, then for the shaikh, and then on through stages until Allah. The stages follow no set schema, as each poet invents ordeals for his laboring and lovelorn yogi prince; there is only the necessity of narrative elaboration, deferment, and invention. There is no absolute meeting with Allah; rather, there are stages of desire and longing that are eventually consummated in union with the divine heroine, who has then to be balanced with the worldly wife. The Chishti notion of ordinate love requires narrative elaboration.

Lorik, Cāndā, and Mainā

Sources of the Tale

The *Cāndāyan* contains motifs and conventions from Persian and Apabhraṃśa poetry, the imagery of the Gorakhnāth yogis, a plot taken from a story orally extant among the Ahīr group of cowherders in Avadh and central India, lyric genres such as the regional songs of the twelve months of separation (*bārahmāsā*), and cultural stereotypes about gender relations from the period. To read the *Cāndāyan* as the textual record of a historical interaction with various social groups on the scene, we first compare his plot to the oral poetic versions of the love of Lorik, Cāndā, and Mainā; then see how Dā'ūd creates a distinctive Sufi poem out of different sources and poetic conventions; and finally set his story within the larger cultural logics implied by the themes of his poem.

The heroine Cāndā is offered several options for fulfillment of her own longing. As R. S. McGregor notes, the symbolism of casting the lover and beloved as the sun and the moon resonates with the Nāth-yogic practice of the raising of the "sun" toward the "moon" in the symbolic geography of the yogic body. In the circulation of desire between lover and beloved, the raising of the sun/Lorik works along with the descent of the moon/Cāndā, which imitates in poetic form the descent of the divine absolute into the world of concrete forms.[63] Lorik has to bring Cāndā, the moon, down into the world in order to consummate his love for her. Playing on the double meaning of *sūra*, "sun" and "hero," Dā'ūd uses the symbolism of light and the physical structure of Cāndā's shining white palace (*dhaulāgiri*) to portray Lorik's ascent to Cāndā's bedroom as a Sufi journey linking the twin themes of love and self-annihilation through ascesis. Before this journey can happen, the poet creates a complicated narrative that functions through interplay among the three types of love offered to Cāndā: marriage to a dirty impotent dwarf, submission to the lustful Rajput King Rūpcand, or a mutually fulfilling love with the brave warrior Lorik. Lorik is also married to another woman, Mainā, whom he abandons in order to elope with Cāndā.

If the relation between Lorik and Cāndā is the relation between the Sufi and Allah, then the relation between Lorik and Mainā is the relation between the Sufi and the world. The later poets of the genre repeat this triangular relationship of the hero and his two wives, and the Sufi reading communities and even the larger culture explained this triangle as the hero's reconciliation of this world and the next.[64] This love triangle assumes a social arrangement in which women were seen as the symbolic repository of honor (*'izzat*) and are contained within the *zanāna* or women's quarters, where they must compete for their lord's attention and love. Co-wives within the harem were stereotypically inimical and hostile to one another, and reconciling them was as difficult for the Sufi as was the reconciliation of this world and the next. In the masculinist poetics of the *Cāndāyan*, women were simultaneously idealized and subordinated. The male élite reader identifies with the hero, the seeker who is lured into becoming a yogi and reaching the distant "divine" heroine, then bringing her back and reconciling her with the world. In the contemporary cultural logic of gender relations, he has become transformed through ascetic mortification into the master of his two wives and of this world and the hereafter.

Maulānā Dā'ūd adapts a number of generic conventions from Persian and Indic traditions into this masculinist narrative pattern. As we saw in Chapter 2, he opens his story with a prologue that follows the model of the Persian *masnavī*s. He also employs Indic literary conventions such as descriptions of cities and landscapes (*nagara-varṇana*) and descriptions of the twelve months of the year (*bārah-māsā*), the head-to-foot description of the heroine's beauty (*sarāpā*), the description of her palace as paradise (the locus of divine revelation), and Mainā's account of her painful separation through the twelve months of the year, which moves Lorik to come back to her along with Cāndā. In addition, he draws on preceding Apabhraṃśa poetic works that contained a rich and highly developed set of narrative conventions for describing all the stages of action in a plot as well as common motifs such as description of towns, lakes, gardens, pavilions, and markets.[65] Finally, he uses meters, figures of speech, and topoi that the local Indian traditions of *kāvya* or poetry considered suitable. The story is set in four-foot Apabhraṃśa meter, in *caupāī*s to which are added *dohā*s or longer couplets, a form that remains standard for narrative verse in Avadhi.[66]

The transfer of these forms into Hindavī before the *Cāndāyan* is attested by an early-fourteenth-century poetic manual in Maithili or eastern Hindavī, the *Varṇa-Ratnākara* ("Ocean of Descriptions").[67] The Sanskrit author Kaviśekharācarya Jyotirīśvara Ṭhakkura composed the *Varṇa-Ratnākara* at the court of the Raja of Tirhut in northern Bihar. The text, a poet's manual in which Jyotirīśvara translates into Maithili the Sanskrit conventions for writing poetry, is organized in eight chapters called *kallola*s or waves, each dealing with the figures of speech and words appropriate to particular poetic topoi: describing cities (*nagara-varṇana*), heroes and heroines (*nāyaka-nāyikā*), palaces and royal courts (*āsthāna*), the seasons (*ṛtu*), military campaigns (*prayānaka*), poets (*bhaṭṭa*), and cremation grounds (*śmaśāna*). In each chapter Jyotirīśvara gives many other topoi, such as how to describe a lake, a garden, the companions of the heroine, morning, afternoon, evening, the sleeping quarters of the princess, a rainy night, darkness, the moon, and so on. As the only critical text in eastern literary Hindavī available to us, the *Varṇa-Ratnākara* is a valuable indication of the adaptation of Sanskrit and Apabhraṃśa poetic categories into the spoken language of the fourteenth century.

The *Varṇa-Ratnākara* also includes, as part of the description of the noise of a town, the singing of ballads about the adventures of Lorik,[68] so the tale must have been widely known even at that time and considered suitable matter for versification and public performance. The text mentions the dance of Lorik, "*Lorika nāco,*" which indicates that the ballad was also performed as a play with dancing and singing. Dā'ūd's *Cāndāyan* can be seen as a response to this local performance tradition, albeit with a distinctive slant of his own. He elevates this local performance tradition of Lorik and Cāndā into a courtly poem using the established "classical" literary conventions of the day, both Sanskrit and Persian.

The *Varṇa-ratnākara* is a revealing analogue to this classicizing process, reproducing a "high" literary tradition in a local language through use of classical forms and conventions. It is a useful manual through which to understand the horizons of poetic convention for a fourteenth-century poet at a regional court in Hindustan. Jyotirīśvara devotes the sixth chapter to the ideal qualities and education of a poet: he had to know prosody, rhetoric, works on erotics, literary appreciation (*rasa* and *dhvani*), and the classics of Sanskrit and Prakrit literature. The ideal poet was also a boon companion to the king, as well as a genealogist and bard. Dā'ūd draws on many of these ideas and conventions, as we shall see, and must have been, at least temporarily, a "poet-in-residence" at Malik Mubārak's court in the fort of Dalmau on the Jamuna. Even when he does not use the exact imagery Jyotirīśvara prescribes, Dā'ūd does use many of the topoi listed in the *Varṇa-Ratnākara* to embellish his narrative.

The Plot

To begin with the plot itself, Dā'ūd based the *Cāndāyan* on the Ahir story of Lorik and Canvā, available in many versions throughout northern and central India[69] as well as Bengal.[70] Oral renditions of the story are still widely recited in public. As S. M. Pandey, the veteran collector of extant sung versions, has pointed out, "the oral epic *Loriki* or *Candaini* is sung by the Ahir singers of Northern India in the Avadhi, Bhojpuri, Maithili, Magahi, and Chattisgarhi dialects of Hindi...The singers are mostly Ahirs, who are either milkmen or farmers. They are called *Gvalas*, i. e., cowherds, as they keep cows. All these singers are male and hardly any of them can read or write. Women are generally not permitted to sing the epic."[71] The question of the continuity and shape of the narrative is a difficult one, and Pandey has demonstrated, through detailed comparison, the many points of difference between the oral poem and Dā'ūd's text.[72] McGregor has suggested that an earlier folk tale may underlie both the literary Sufi romance and the oral versions: "The folk character of this story, which served as the basis for a sūfī romance, is . . . evident. . . . [T]his story must (to judge from modern versions) have differed considerably in style and substance from the tales underlying the sixteenth-century sūfī romances. . . . A comparison of the narrative of Candāyan with that of the modern story suggests an early folk tale."[73] Without further information, it is impossible to specify the hypothetical ancestor of written and oral versions.

Although we do not have access to the folk tale on which Dā'ūd must have based his courtly poem, we can identify two major extant oral performance traditions that have many elements in common with Dā'ūd's plot, one from eastern Uttar Pradesh or Avadh and the other from the central Indian region of Chhattisgarh.[74] The modern Ahir versions are elaborate and episodic, since this is an orally transmitted tale that can be adapted to many performance conditions.

The basic story[75] in the two local dialects of modern standard Hindi, Bhojpuri and the far older Avadhi, centers around the exploits of the hero Lorik of Gaura and his step-brother Savarū, a devotee of Durgā. One day Lorik goes to play Holi in the neighboring village of Kusumapur. He sprays colored water on Canvā, the daughter of King Sahadeva. The angry Canvā taunts him, "Fool, you do not know the tradition. Go and get your brother married. He is getting old and nobody comes to him with a proposal of marriage. You can then play Holi with your sister-in-law." Lorik finds a bride for Savarū in the person of Satiyā, daughter of Bamarī. But the father of the bride is opposed and there is a great battle in which Lorik and his friend Ajai take on the forces of Bamarī. After a series of battles, they win the bride and take her home.

In another section of the story, Lorik himself marries Majarī, the daughter of an Ahir named Mahar who lives in the realm of a tyrant king Molagat. Molagat demands the sexual services of all the girls of his kingdom, but when it is Majarī's turn she appeals to Lorik to save her honor. Lorik dispatches Molagat and his army with his powerful sword. As Joyce Flueckiger notes,[76] this episode occurs in the Bhojpuri version of the story, but not the Avadhi. In the latter, Majarī's father loses her in gambling to a non-Ahir Thakur warrior, and Lorik has to save her from an out-of-caste marriage by defeating the Thakur in armed combat. What is common to both versions is the overwhelming concern for the woman's honor (*'izzat*) and the honor of the Ahir subcaste, an ideological valence of the modern story that differs from Dā'ūd's Sufi tale. The next episode of the story describes Lorik's happy life in Gaura with Majarī, until the day he meets Canvā again. She has been married to an impotent Ahir named Sivadhar, whom she rejects. She returns home, but on her way home she is harassed by Bātha, who tries to violate her; she cleverly tricks him, but Bātha will not leave her alone, and she appeals to Lorik, who beats Bātha to death.

Lorik and Canvā are overcome with desire for each other and begin meeting in secret. She becomes pregnant and they run away together to the neighboring kingdom of Haldī. On their way to Haldī, Canvā's husband Sivadhar comes to fight Lorik, but Lorik defeats him. A snake stings Canvā, but Lorik prays for help and she is saved. They arrive in Haldī and Lorik distinguishes himself by his invincible strength and bravery in freeing the soldiers of the king from their enemies. In the meantime, Lorik's mother, Khoilanī, and his wife, Majarī, are persecuted by the village and reduced to extreme poverty. They send a desperate appeal to Lorik. He returns secretly to Boha, a place near Gaura, and announces that he wants to buy milk and curds at a very high price. All the Ahir women go to him, including Majarī. On her way to Boha, Majarī crosses a river by ferry; the boatman tries to violate her. She invokes the goddess of chastity and prays to her: "O Goddess, if I am a chaste and truthful woman, make this river dry up." The river dries up. The boatman falls at her feet and begs for his livelihood back. She forgives him and proceeds to Boha. Lorik recognizes her, and they are reunited. He returns to Gaura and regains his wealth and land by fighting his enemies. In the fighting, he discovers he has lost his former strength. He gives all his wealth to his two sons and burns himself to death in Gaura.

The Deeper Meaning

The Chhattisgarhi versions of the story mute the martial aspects of Lorik's fight for honor in order to emphasize the loving relationship of Lorik and Candaini and the powers of the heroine Candaini as an initiator of action.[77] In her ethnographic study of the performance and reception of the Laur-Cāndā cycle, Flueckiger notes the shift in emphasis as well as the use of the story by other castes:

> In Chhattisgarh, *candainī* is the love/elopement story of the hero Lorik and heroine Candaini, both from the Raut cowherding caste. The hero and heroine are each married to other partners, but Candaini leaves her husband when she learns that he has been cursed by the goddess to be impotent for twelve years. On her way back to her maternal village, Candaini is accosted in the jungle by the untouchable Bathua. She cleverly escapes his evil intentions, but he chases after her and terrorizes the inhabitants and cattle of the village. In desperation, the villagers ask Lorik to rescue them; ultimately he defeats Bathua through nonmartial (and, I might add, rather dishonest) means. During this contest, Candaini first lays eyes on the hero, falls in love, and proceeds to seduce him. After some delays, primarily due to Lorik's hesitancy

> and cowardice in decision making, the hero leaves his wife Majari, and he and Candaini elope to Hardi Garh. In Chhattisgarh, *candainī* performances center on and elaborate various adventures from this elopement journey (*urḥāī*; literally, flight).[78]

Although this Chhattisgarh version retains most of the narrative elements recounted in other versions, the slant of the story shifts. It is likely, given the emphasis on love and elopement in this version, that Dā'ūd's source was closer to the Chattisgarhi narrative tradition than to the Avadhi.

The plot of the *Cāndāyan* retains some elements of these different Ahir versions, but presents the reader with a story in which the literary aesthetics of *prema-rasa* is paramount. Dā'ūd's poem, recited and sung in court and Sufi hospice, has the martial and erotic elements of the local original, as well as a new emphasis on asceticism and mystical love. The narrative tension of the poem, as we shall see, comes from the transformation of awakened desire into love through the vicissitudes of battle and lust. Lorik abandons his other wife, Mainā, in order to elope with Cāndā, but in the end he does come back to Mainā, who is famously tested for her chastity as Majarī is in the Ahir tale. The episode, versified as the *Maina Satvanti* ("The Chaste Mainā") in some regional songs, was later also translated into Persian as the *'Iṣmat Nāmah* or "Account of Chastity."[79]

The story begins with a topos taken from the conventions of *kāvya* that are set up in the *Varṇa-Ratnākara*: the description of the town (*nagara-varṇana*) of Govar, home of the Princess Cāndā. The poet describes the town's gardens with their shady trees blossoming with many fruits and flowers. There are birds crying out in many languages in the trees, and shining lakes where beautiful women come to draw water (C 21). All of the social groups who inhabit the town—Brahmins, Khatris, Agravals, traders, Cauhans, and Rajputs—are described in terms of their distinct *jātis* (subcastes), and are shown plying their business in the town's markets, gardens, and squares. Within all this urban order and activity, surrounded by doorways guarded by fierce stone lions, stands the shining white royal palace, painted with red lead dye (*īngur*).

The birth of Cāndā in this royal palace suggests the metaphysical manifestation, the *jalvah* or *maẓhar*, of the divine absolute into the world of concrete forms, and the poetic imagery depends on the lexical meaning of her name. The Pleiades attend her, and the planets and constellations all serve her and pay her homage; Rāhū and Ketu, the two demons of eclipse, hover about her. Like the heroine of the later *Padmāvat*, Cāndā is a Padminī or "lotus-woman," the best kind of woman according to Sanskrit erotic theory and the new Indo-Aryan devotional poetry. Since she is as radiant as the moon, the world experiences two nights when she assumes a body and comes into existence:

> *In the house of Sahadev, the moon became incarnate,*
> *earth and heaven were radiant with moonlight.*
> *Since she was born in the first watch,*
> *two moons adorned the world's two nights.*
> *The seven Pleiades shone in the parting of her hair.*
> *Her limbs shone with the radiance of the sun.*
> *She was the full moon of the fourteenth night,*
> *Cāndā, the princess, a Padminī among women.*
> *Rāhū and Ketu served her diligently.*
> *Venus and Saturn were at her beck and call.*
> *All the constellations were present at her doorstep to pay homage.*
> *Her beauty stunned all passers-by; the entire world was full*
> *of light [C 32].*

The verbal phrase "*cānda avatārā*" ("the moon became incarnate") in the first half-line (*ardhālī*) of the *caupāī* indicates the adaptation into Hindavī of the Islamic theological term for manifestation (*ẓuhūr*). Cāndā's supernatural beauty is distinctive because it is endowed with form (*saguṇa*), but the revelatory flashing of light that attends it suggests a divinity that cannot be contained in physical form (*nirguṇa*). Dā'ūd's use of form or beauty (*rūpa*) is expressed through a language of incarnation but leads ultimately to the folding back of this form into the formless.

This local revelation of stunning beauty quickly becomes known to all the regional sultanates. Dvārasamudra, Tirhut, Avadh, Malabar, Gujarat, and Badayun all hear of her beauty, and marriage offers begin to pour in. The key criterion for her potential husbands is status: her father, King Sahadev, does not count anyone as his equal. The astrologers who cast her horoscope predict that she will go to her death in the prime of her life, but her beauty will be so incandescent that kings and warriors will flock to her like moths to a flame. The first type of love for Cāndā is presented to her father in the form of a marriage offer from a neighboring king, Jaita. There are astrological difficulties with the offer, foreshadowing a troubled marital future. In the end, however, King Jaita's emissaries prevail and Candā is married to Bāvan, King Jaita's son.

Bāvan (Sanskrit *vāmana*, "dwarf") is one-eyed and impotent, a dwarf who never washes and never comes near her even when she comes of age.

Although desire moves through her body, her husband completely ignores her and she is frustrated and angry:

And though she had been married a year and a day,
this moon had never been looked at by the sun.
She thought, "The woman whose man is elsewhere,
is always unhappy in bed at night.
Bāvan never even talks to me—
I don't even know whether he's black or red!
...I should just go back home,
anything is better than this ridicule." [C 44].

Her sister-in-law hears her complaining and reports the matter to her mother. What ensues is the stereotypical *sās bahū kā jhagṛā* (the fight between the mother-in-law and the daughter-in-law), which Dā'ūd portrays skillfully as a family quarrel:

When she heard this, the Queen came to Cāndā,
"Daughter-in-law, why are you angry?
...You are ignorant and don't know men.
How can you make barley-water without water?
You can put on gold and silver and roam about
every day with a freshly-washed sari on—
but until my Bāvan is of age,
you'll have to satisfy yourself with fruits and flowers." [C 45].

Their dispute revolves around Cāndā's desire, with the bride saying that she needs to be satisfied sexually, and the mother-in-law that she is an evil wanton who would seduce her innocent son (*dūdha kī phoī*):

"I knew what was on your mind
when you were shameless enough to talk to me like this.
You want a godling as a husband,
but can you ever get butter without churning curds?
My Bāvan is still a pap washed in milk,
how can he sleep with you?
I've never seen such an upstart bride,
but then, a horse can't be controlled without a rein!" [C 47]

In its cultural logic, the fight reflects a world in which mothers and wives fight over the favors of men, who are the ideological guarantors and providers of security for women. The theme is elaborated later on in the poem through the misogynistic gender politics of polygamy, in which the male has the power of choice between jealous co-wives.

Finally, her mother-in-law drives Cāndā out of her husband's house, and a message is sent for her brother to come and fetch her. In the internal narrative logic of the plot, one attempt to transform Cāndā's desire into love has failed, and the ordinary structure of marriage has disintegrated. Yet the moon requires a sun to love her, a lover who can consummate her desire. This mutual fulfillment, the true *prema-rasa*, cannot be attained by those unworthy of love, and Cāndā returns home in disappointment. After this, the second type of love in the *Cāndāyan* is brought to life when one day Cāndā leans out of her balcony in all her radiant beauty. A wandering musician (*bājir*) who is passing by happens to look up and is transfixed. A glimpse of the supernatural beauty of Cāndā makes him faint with desire and fall to the ground in what seems to be an epileptic fit or an episode of snakebite. As we have seen, the wandering singer uses the set piece of the *sarāpā* to excite desire in King Rūpcand for Cāndā without his ever having seen her (*adṛṣṭa-kāma*). Dā'ūd uses the tropes of love through description rather than direct vision and the convention of head-to-foot descriptions to suggest the divine revelation that is temporarily embodied in Cāndā. The singer's description triggers the second option that is offered to Cāndā for the transformation of her desire into *prema*.

King Rūpcand starts crying, calls Bānṭh, his chief minister, and orders him to muster the army so that he can conquer Govar and obtain Cāndā's hand in marriage by force. Rūpcand's grand and imposing army sets out to besiege Govar. There are bad omens on the way: a crow cries out, a jackal howls in the direction of the rising sun, and the path of the advancing army appears red with blood. When they camp outside the city of Govar, they go on a rampage, cutting down all the mango groves that make the city a paradise and destroying all the sacred temples. There is panic in King Sahadev's realm, and he sends emissaries to ask what Rūpcand wants. He asks for Cāndā. The emissary asks him not to lust after another man's daughter (i.e., a respectable maiden); he responds by threatening to cut off the emissary's head and feed his flesh to the dogs. The emissary's response emphasizes Cāndā's inaccessibility:

"Govar is a sea, deep, unfathomable—
You could drown in it, O King,
and never reach the bottom.
Even if you climb up to the sky,
you would not find even a trace
of the dust of Cāndā! The very stars
circle the moon at night, looking on her....

Even if you go to heaven and search, O King! You would
not see her.
You'll sink in and die, but will never
plumb the depths of this sea." [C 98].

But Rūpcand persists in his intentions of forcing Cāndā to satisfy his lust, and vows that Govar is a heaven he will destroy. His army begins to fight Sahadev's army, and his best warriors carry the day for him by killing Govar's best fighters.

Once the situation is desperate, the people of Govar go to the heroic Lorik, who lives with his mother, Kholin (called Khoilanī in the Avadhi version), and his wife, Mainā. At first his wife and mother will not let him go. Kholin argues that since he does not hold his land in tenancy from the king or share his crops with any landlord, why should he put his life at risk? But the demands of the town are insistent, and Lorik girds himself for combat. His first guide in the tricks of fighting is a fellow warrior called Ajay (the "Invincible"), who shams sickness but gives Lorik instructions on shielding his body. Ajay is like a Sufi *pīr* who guides the hero along on the path of spiritual perfection (*siddhi*). Here Dā'ūd introduces a motif that becomes characteristic of the later formulaic genre: allegorically named emblematic helpers such as nurses and companions, who aid in resolving problematic situations.

Ajay teaches Lorik how to keep his guard up in battle. As the hero, Lorik has to fight and vanquish illicit desire in order to gain the love of Cāndā. When he comes into the field, he is likened to the sun that has come to save the moon. Ranged against him is the very best warrior on Rūpcand's side, the formidable chief minister Bānṭh. Lorik is accompanied by his band of armored warriors, and Bānṭh leads Rūpcand's army. Vultures gather and call their kin for a feast, kites fly overhead, and jackals invite their entire species (*jāti*) for the ritual feed that will propitiate their dead ancestors (*pitṛpakṣa*). Single combat to the death ensues between various warriors. Lorik goes after Rūpcand and brings his sword down on his head, splitting his helmet in two. The cowardly Rūpcand runs away, and eventually Bānṭh and Lorik face off against one another. The fight is close and intense. Lorik strikes blow after blow, cuts off Bānṭh's arm, and finally defeats and kills him. Rūpcand's army is routed and flees along with its king.

Brute armed force, the second option for winning *prema-rasa* within the narrative logic of the *Cāndāyan*, is here defeated. Cāndā cannot be won by anyone unworthy of her, or by violence. She needs a worthy lover who will win her through the right means. Here the final narrative option for obtaining the "love that comes from the soul" (*maḥabbah al-rūḥ*) is activated, as is Dā'ūd's own erotology, his description of the ideal love affair and its mystic resonances. The ideal love affair, whether aroused through words or a dream or a vision, sends the lover into a spasm or fainting fit, then into a prolonged and obsessive period of lovesickness in which he can think only of the beloved. These are common symptoms in both Islamic and Sanskrit erotologies, where they occur at different moments but are part of the cultural vocabulary for how love is experienced. But Dā'ūd takes the conventional signs of love and links them to ascetic practice and to the rigors of a climb up to heaven to meet the divine heroine.

After Lorik's victory, there is jubilation in Govar. Lorik, the hero of the day, is paraded around town in procession on an elephant. Cāndā appears like the moon on the balcony of the royal palace:

Cāndā appeared above, on the shining white palace,
with her nurse Biraspati at her side.
Evening was falling and the world grew dark,
but the moon illumined all with her radiance.
She asked Biraspati, "Where is that hero
who killed an army for my sake?
Where is the lion who vanquished that elephant?
Blessed is the mother who gave birth to him.
Nurse, listen to me, tell me just one thing:
where is Lorik in this throng?
What does he look like, and where is his house? Tell me,
O Biraspati!
Sister, I am dying for Lorik, please show me where he is!"

Biraspati said, "Dear Cāndā,
Lorik is the sun's radiance.
His earrings glisten with elephant-pearls.
His forehead appears with the moon shining on it,
and the flash of his smiling teeth is entrancing.
Lovely locks flow down from his head.
His waist is like a lion's, and cannot be grasped.
His eyes are limpid and clear,
like bowls of shining white milk,
his pupils are black bees on their surface.
His body is lustrous with golden color.
He shines like an image of Kāmadeva,
clear of the dust that is flying about.
Red silk is stretched across the back of his howdah, he sits
on an elephant.
He has a dashing turban on his head, and his scimitar gleams
handsomely on him."

Cāndā looked down and saw him.
She lost her senses and fainted,
her eyes burning, her face withering.
Food or water were useless,
for the moon had fainted for love of the sun.
Biraspati came and sprinkled water on her...[C 136–38]

The passage gives us a *sarāpā* of Lorik in miniature, and reverses the earlier situation in which Cāndā's body was the object of the lustful singer's gaze. The vision of Lorik's handsome form arouses a burning desire in Cāndā, who insists that her nurse arrange a meeting for them. The nurse suggests a ruse: she tells Cāndā to ask her father to give a feast celebrating the great victory, and makes sure that Lorik is invited as the guest of honor. When the day of the feast dawns, the entire town comes to the royal palace to be fed in grand fashion.

The Otherworldliness of Cāndā

Cāndā decks herself out in splendid jewels and a beautiful sari, and appears on the balcony and looks down at the rows of feasting people. Her action suggests God's appearing in splendor to seduce man. Lorik looks up at the balcony and is struck senseless with desire. He exclaims that she is an *apsaras* or nymph from heaven, and falls over. He has to be carried out on a stretcher, and when he reaches home Mainā and Kholin put him to bed. He lies in bed weeping, and no doctor or physician can cure him.

This is a common theme in Islamic and Sanskritic theories of love: "Every lover who is sincere in his affection, if he be barred from union with his beloved either through separation or as the result of a breaking off, or because for some reason or another he has to conceal his attachment, must necessarily fall in consequence into sickness, wasting away, and emaciation; not infrequently he is obliged to take to his bed."[80] As we know from Sanskrit poetry, lovesickness is a dangerous affliction. The stages of love laid out in the classical Indian sources begin with longing for the beloved, which is then heightened to anxiety (*cintā*), recollection (*anusmṛti*), and an enumeration of the beloved's virtues (*guṇakīrtana*). After this the lover feels distress (*udvega*) and laments his lot (*vilāpa*). Then insanity (*unmāda*) descends on him, then sickness (*vyādhi*), then stupor (*jaḍatā*) and finally, if love is not satisfied, death.[81] These are not far removed from Persian and Arabic lists of the stages of love, which go from attachment (*ulfah*) to excitation of the heart (*mavaddah*) and an obsessive focus on the beloved (*fikr-i maḥbūb*) to passionate desire for him or her (*havā*). Later stages include violent affection (*shaġhaf*), exclusive attachment (*khullah*), and then affection (*maḥabbhah*) leading to passionate love (*'ishq*). Finally, the lover is totally enslaved by love, falls into bewilderment and madness, and destroys himself utterly out of unrequited love.[82]

Now that desire has been awakened on both sides, the burning pain of separation is mutual. Lorik and Cāndā are still in the early stages of love, where they have seen each other and conceived a passionate attachment to each other. They will have to suffer the pangs of longing and burn in agony until they are able to meet in bed as lovers.

Biraspati the nurse visits Lorik and recognizes that he is suffering from the malady of desire. She speaks to him in secret, here acting as the spiritual guide who can unite the lover and the beloved. Much like the Chishti shaikhs instructing their disciples, she will prescribe a period of asceticism and mindfulness, a channeling of Lorik's desire through a regimen of bodily mortification. The knowledge about love she is about to impart has to remain secret, like the mysterious Chishti Sufi ideology. If Lorik speaks out in public it will cause their death, since Cāndā is the royal princess:

> *"Listen to me, Lorik, and I will teach you wisdom.*
> *Go to the temple and serve there faithfully,*
> *and I will bring her there to worship the gods.*
> *Become an ascetic and sit there, ashes rubbed on your frame.*
> *When you are granted a vision of her, you can*
> *sate your eyes" [C 161].*

Lorik becomes a yogi, puts a basil-bead necklace around his neck, and dresses in the saffron robes of the followers of Gorakhnāth. He serves at the temple for one whole year, concentrating faithfully on the image of Cāndā.

The Hindavī Sufi poets use the yogic disguise of the hero to structure the stages of a mystical journey. In using the local language of asceticism,[83] they create a narrative motif that is instantly recognizable and comprehensible to audiences in Hindustan in the fourteenth century and afterward, yet slanted toward expressing the Sufi ethic of practice. There are numerous instances in the Persian hagiographic literature about competition between Sufis and yogis.[84] In the *Cāndāyan*, the motif also suggests identification of the hero with the spiritual seeker:

> *Lorik put on the garb of a yogi.*
> *He took up the steel circle and the patched cloak,*
> *and on his feet he wore the wooden sandals*
> *of the followers of Gorakhnāth.*
> *He rubbed ashes on his face, and picked up*
> *the wooden crutch to support his yoga.*

He sat on a deerskin in ascetic pose.
Accompanied by stick and horn whistle,
he sang the song of love and burned.
He played the stringed kiṅgarī *at the same time,*
fixing in his mind the image of Cāndā's face [C 164].

Lorik's ascetic practice has a different valence from that of the wandering *sādhūs* of the Indian countryside. Although he has assumed the external signs of asceticism, his song is about the burning pain of *'ishq*. He meditates on the image of Cāndā's face instead of a god or goddess. The poet goes on to say that he eats nothing but fruits and leaves from the forest, and Cāndā's name is his "*tat sāra*" or essence of essences, the essential element or *tattva* on which ascetics meditate. Thus the poet uses the highest spiritual value in yogic language to suggest a Persian mystical concept, reimagining Islamic ideology in Indian dress.

Dā'ūd turns this symbolic vocabulary away from the Nāth-panth and uses it to express the Sufi mortification of self. Peter Gaeffke has pointed out that the Sufi adaptation of the motif of the Gorakhnāthī yogi runs counter to Indian traditions of renunciation because it shows the renunciant reentering the world after gaining his object.[85] But Dā'ūd reuses elements from local traditions in his *maṣnavī*, sometimes without great regard to accuracy. Thus he combines repetition of Cāndā's name with the technique of visualization so common among yogis. Lorik's song is a lover's song, and he must go through a year of asceticism to purify himself and burn off the impurities of his carnal or lower self (*nafs-i ammārah*), so often mentioned in Sufi thought and practice. As Lois Anita Gifften has noted:

> (al-Ghazali said:) "Everyone who gives himself wholly to God (*tadjarrada lillahi*) in the war against his own desires (*nafs*), is a martyr when he meets death going forward without turning his back. So the holy warrior is he who makes war against his desires as it has been explained by the Apostle of God. And the 'greater war' is war against one's own desires, as the Companions said: We have returned from the lesser war unto the greater one, meaning thereby war against their own desires."
>
> Long before Ghazali, however, Hasan al-Basri (d. 110/728) is supposed to have voiced a similar opinion. According to Ibn Qayyim al-Jauziya, a man asked Hasan, "O Abu Sa'id, which *jihad* is most meritorious?" He said, "Your battling against your *hawa*." Ibn al-Qayyim adds that Ibn Taimiya said, "Fighting against your lower nature (*nafs*) and against *hawa* is fundamental to (or takes precedence over) the fighting of infidels and 'the hypocrites,' for a man cannot fight them until he first fights his *nafs* and its *hawa* (lusts). Then he may go out and wage war against them."[86]

The Chishti *silsilah* vigorously championed the idea of this kind of *jihād*.

The events that ensue distinguish this ethic of asceticism from the Nāth system of mortification. On the festival of Divali, Biraspati brings Cāndā and her friends and maids to worship at the temple with offerings of rice and flowers. Cāndā's necklace of lustrous pearls breaks, and she is in a panic because she cannot go home without them. The girls and Biraspati advise sheltering in the temple while they gather the pearls. They go in to the handsome yogi:

> *"O moon," said the stars, "come and have a vision of the sun.*
> *Gazing upon such beauty burns away all your sins!" [C 167]*

Cāndā descends from heaven—the royal palace—,enters the temple where embodied forms are worshipped, and salutes the ascetic. Here Cāndā is not equivalent to the fully incarnated deity, but rather suggests a superior principle of divinity that is only temporarily and blindingly visible to the seer. The handsome Lorik faints dead away.

Cāndā herself is disturbed but cannot understand why the ascetic fainted because she does not know him. She leaves the temple and goes home but remains perplexed and upset. When Lorik comes to, he asks the image in the temple what happened: "Was it a dream I saw, or something real?" The god replies:

> *"Lorik, listen to this marvel*
> *which was real even in your dream!*
> *A throng of heavenly nymphs came down,*
> *and you could not look at them.*
> *When you saw them you fainted,*
> *and I became rapt in the vision of their beauty.*
> *There was a magic jingling of bells,*
> *and nature flashed with golden light!*
> *They stayed to play but for a moment. . . ." [C 171]*

The heavenly manifestation ended, the temple is empty again except for the meditative Lorik and the image of the god. The exchange with the animated image shows the local deity acknowledging the superiority of the new Islamic religious vision that is embodied in the flashingly beautiful form of Cāndā. At a later point in the story, when Cāndā enters the temple again, the images run away in terror from the splendor of her revelation.

Meanwhile, Cāndā sits at home burning in the flames of separation. She asks Biraspati for a story full of *rasa* to assuage her pain, and the nurse responds by telling her to pull out the ascetic who is sinking in a pool of *rasa* for her sake. Cāndā asks her nurse to bring her and Lorik together. Biraspati goes to Lorik, who has been in the temple chanting "I die! I die!" since Cāndā's departure. The nurse tells him that his ascetic practice, his battle for internal purification, has been successful. She advises him to throw off the clothes of a yogi, to come to the palace at night, and to climb up to Cāndā's bedchamber if he wishes to consummate his love.

The poet uses the imagery of the path to heaven (*sarag-panth*) to indicate the spiritual direction of Lorik's quest. In the words of Biraspati:

> *"When you climb up to the sky, O Lorik, you could put a noose around your neck,*
> *or you could enjoy the moon herself; either way, you will be in heaven!" [C 185]*

The nurse's words suggest that Lorik's quest will involve *fanā*, the Sufi practice of dying to the lower self and turning toward God:

> Man should recover the state he had on the Day of the Primordial Covenant, when he became existentialized, endowed with individual existence by God, which, however, involved a separation from God by the veil of createdness.... The Sufi experiences the return to the moment when God was, and there was nothing else.[87]

The Chishti seeker "must strive in the work of Almighty God for many years...(and)...burn his lower soul (*nafs*) with fasting and observance, and worship and effort."[88] Lorik sets out on a dark and rainy night, armed with an intricately woven rope ladder, to scale the steep height of the royal palace. The rain pours down thick and heavy, and frogs and birds call out. A flash of lightning illumines the palace, and Lorik throws the iron grappling hook of his rope ladder up. When it catches, Cāndā wakes up, and she laughingly undoes the grappling hook and throws it back at him, testing his patience and endurance. Her teasing echoes the coquetry and dalliance of the divine beloved, but she relents when he becomes discouraged, and lets him climb up.

The palace is a wondrous structure with glittering lamps and jewel-encrusted surfaces. These images are prescribed in the *Varṇa-Ratnākara* as appropriate to the bedroom of a princess, which should be a *citraśālī* or painted room similar to the house of the king of the gods (*devarājagṛha tatsamāna*).[89] When Lorik reaches the top, Cāndā is in bed feigning sleep:

> *Lorik hid behind a pillar, and peeped out:*
> *he saw that which cannot be seen.*

Sixty lamps burned on nine pillars,
and gems and gold glittered all over.
Around her neck a precious necklace gleamed,
and her beautiful maids slept around her
like stars in heaven, or lustrous pearls.
The maids on watch were sleeping
like the Pleiades around the moon [C 192].

When his vision shifts to the bed and he sees her sleeping there with her black locks in seductive disarray, he faints again. She wakes up, grabs his hair, and yells, "Thief! Thief!" When Lorik protests that he is merely enamored of her beauty, she responds, "If you set one foot on my bed, you'll lose your life!" Lorik responds by saying he has already died in order to climb up to heaven.

The Persian title for this section in manuscript sources is *"tamṣīl dādan-i Lorik,"* i.e., "Lorik's allegory" or explanation of hidden meanings. This framing word indicates the importance of the notion of *tamṣīl* or exemplification, the shorter allegorical segments that were part of a larger narrative centered around *rasa.* The poets of the genre could show off their skill through these short allegorical segments and hint at invisible spiritual realities to deepen the audience's understanding of the nuances of love. Thus, Cāndā continues to test Lorik by accusing him of betraying his valor, his caste, and his lord master the king (*svāmi-droha*), but Lorik insists that the love he seeks is higher than any structure of rulership. Finally she agrees to consummate their love, but only if it is true (*satya*). The proof of the "true" or divinely sanctioned love is that the seeker has to die to the world and to his self. Thus Cāndā's demands, and Lorik's responses, seal a pact of *fanā* or annihilation of self between them. But before Lorik can possess his heart's desire, Cāndā's pearl necklace breaks again and they have to gather all the pearls. Dawn breaks, and Lorik has to hide under the bed all day, keeping absolutely silent for fear of discovery.

On the second night after his ordeal, he and Cāndā consummate their desire:

The day that God created me, Cāndā,
I have been steeped in your color!
. . . Separation from your color has come to dwell in my heart.
Its leaves are in the sky, roots in the earth; if my life goes now,
it goes! [C 210]

Lorik and Cāndā feel a kinship that has existed between them since the beginning of time, and the figure of speech of the great tree pulls together heaven and earth, love and death. Cāndā offers herself to him, and they make love:

> *She bit half the betel leaf and gave it to Lorik,*
> *and snatched up half with her own two lips.*
> *Sometimes he would lay down his head on her,*
> *or pull her into his arms and kiss her.*
> *Sometimes she would turn her back, annoyed,*
> *and he would laugh and loosen her locks....*
> *In an excess of* rasa *the* rasika *roamed the bed, and gave Cāndā*
> *her nuptials [C 216].*

Vision and the gaze are central to the circulation of desire in Dā'ūd's scheme, but the lovers do more than look at each other. In this moment of lovemaking, the poet links the *rasika*'s taste of the essence or juice of love with the erotics of eating *pān* or betel and with the exchange of saliva between lovers. Saliva or the red *pān* juice was also sometimes passed from the mouth of a shaikh to the mouth of a disciple to incite a mystical vision. When morning dawns, however, Lorik goes away down his ladder. Cāndā is left with the traditional Indian poetic signs of love on her body: nail marks and love bites. Her serving maids notice that she has enjoyed a secret lover, although she protests that she was mauled by a neighbor's cat. When people come to visit her, they adduce two reasons for her shame: she has left her lawfully wedded husband, and now she has taken a lover in secret.

The Worldliness of Mainā

Now the poet uses the misogynistic cultural stereotype of the two wives of a man battling it out for his affections to suggest the struggle that a Sufi has to undergo in order to balance the concerns of this world and the next. Sociological information about gender relations in the period is somewhat limited,[90] but such poetry indicates a deep cultural misogyny in which women's erotic bodies draw the seeker out of himself and on to the path to God, while the women themselves are ultimately sacrificed in the annihilation of the narrative universe. One popular source of advice on bringing up children from the period, Yūsuf Gadā's *Tuḥfah-i Naṣā'iḥ*, asserts that when women are married, they are completely subject to the will of their masters and husbands, "an ideal of almost total male dominance and female subservience."[91]

In a Sufi sense, however, the two wives of the hero are made to signify, on the one hand, the connection of the *nafs-i ammārah* or lower or carnal soul with this world, the perishable world of reprehensible pleasures (*duniyā-i murdār*); and, on the other hand, the *rūḥ* or immortal soul's link with the next world and with the more permanent spiritual quest of ascetics and Sufis.[92] As Shaikh Naṣīr al-dīn Chirāġh-i Dihlī, the spiritual preceptor of Dā'ūd's guide Shaikh Zain al-dīn, put it, "one must not love this perishable world in one's heart. Whatever one receives on the path of truth/God (*ḥaqq*), one should give it away."[93] This attitude is part of a larger pattern of thought among the Chishti Sufi shaikhs of the Delhi sultanate in which claims to authority over the holders of worldly power and material goods were advanced on the basis of spiritual prowess:

> In this period there was an unavoidable conflict between professed aims and necessary practice in the pursuit of the role of a great Shaikh.... The Chishtī Shaikhs were committed to a lifestyle of personal austerities, poverty or even deliberate indebtedness, inaccessibility, avoidance of cities and of contact with worldly people—and especially of avoidance of contact with the rich and the powerful, and to the concealment of *karāmāt* (miraculous powers). Their charisma largely derived from the widespread conviction that they possessed these qualities, but for this charisma to be recognized they had often to proceed in exactly the opposite way. Prestige also depended on the ability to construct, extend, and organize a *Khānqāh*; to feed, accommodate and attend to the material and spiritual needs of disciples and often numerous dependants; and to accommodate travellers according to Muslim precept and the expectations of hospitality. The principal means to support such necessarily expensive establishments were likely to be offerings from the wealthy and powerful, sometimes by a system of monasterial labour.[94]

For the Sufi *k͟hānaqāhs* to function, therefore, they were dependent on the economic largesse of rulers, in the form of tax-free land grants or *madad-i ma'āsh*, as well as on the flow of alms or *futūḥāt*. Thus the Sufis were dependent on courts in practice even when their rhetoric was vigorously oriented toward poverty and avoidance of worldly rulers.

The Chishti strategy of holding on to a public rhetoric of *tark-i duniyā* or abandonment of the world while accepting economic support and even playing at kingmaking embodies the social tension between political and spiritual claims to authority[95] that is apparent in the literature of the period. For instance, there was a story extant about the Slave King Shams al-dīn Iltutmish (*r.* 1211–36), who lived in straitened circumstances in Baghdad in his youth. Every night, he would serve a group of ecstatic dervishes headed by Qāẓī Ḥamīd al-dīn Nāgaurī and weep during the assemblies of *samā'*:

> As the service of Malik Iltutmish pleased the dervishes, they cast a (kindly) glance (*naẓar*) on him. Due to the spiritual power (*barakat*) of

> that glance, Almighty God, the Exalted, raised him to the rank of Sultan (of Delhi). After an age, when he sat on the throne of empire in the country of Hindustān, and Qāẓī Ḥamīd al-dīn Nāgaurī was engaged in instructing seekers after truth in Delhi, the dervishes always sang and danced in his assembly.[96]

Challenged about the legality of this practice, Qāẓī Ḥamīd al-dīn Nāgaurī justified it by saying it was illegal for men who were rationalistic (*ahl-i qāl*), but legal for men of spiritual emotion (*ahl-i ḥāl*). He then reminded the Sultan of the true source of his power: "It would be in the auspicious recollection of your Majesty, that one night dervishes and men of emotional experience were engaged in spiritual exercises, and you...served the people in that meeting, and wept in the exaltation of your feelings. The dervishes cast a glance on you, and you have reached your present high rank on account of the spiritual power of that glance."[97] All mundane power, within this mystical ideology, lies in the spiritual gift of holy men. Kings and the visible world are therefore subordinate to the spiritual dictates of the invisible world of the Sufis.

Dā'ūd carries this tension over into the narrative logic of the *Cāndāyan*, using it to color the triangular relationship among the hero and his two wives. His triangle reflects a masculinist fantasy in which one cannot think about the politics and praxis of asceticism without using women as vehicles for ideology and ultimately sacrificing them. He is interested not in actual sexual practice, but in emotional manipulation of sexuality toward the élite Indian Muslim male seeker's progress on the ascetic path.

Evidence from Sufi glosses of Hindavī poetry indicates that they interpreted the jealous co-wives vying for the hero's love as representative of the claims of this world and the next.[98]

All of Govar is gossiping about Lorik's love of the princess, and Mainā burns with jealousy. Any resolution of the love between Lorik and Cāndā has to include Mainā. A festival day dawns and all the women of the town go to the grand temple of Somnath to offer prayers. Dā'ūd reimagines the temple of Somnath—sacked by the armies of 'Alāuddīn Khaljī, and a symbol of the religious strife between the Turkish invaders and the Indian defenders they encountered—as the place where Cāndā and Mainā fight. Cāndā decks herself out and goes to worship in a splendid palanquin. She is so beautiful that even the images in the temple fall in love with her. She prays that she may get her man. Mainā comes up to the temple just as Cāndā is leaving, and accuses her of being a whore (*chināl*) while she herself is a chaste woman (*satī*). Cāndā claims that she is the divine beauty who can entrance the world, while Mainā responds by asserting that at least she is legally married to the man she sleeps with. They descend to fisticuffs, and Lorik has to separate the two. Mainā goes back home and tells Lorik's mother, Kholin, about the incident at the temple. Kholin sends a message to the king complaining about his daughter's behavior. Cāndā threatens to take poison and kill herself if Lorik does not help her to run away from Govar and escape the wrath of the king and Lorik's family. She sends Biraspati with a message to Lorik, and Lorik prepares for the elopement.

He goes to a Brahmin astrologer, who calculates an auspicious time for him to run away, safe from Śukra (the planet Venus, the dwarf), and predicts that he will gain *siddhi* (spiritual power and perfection) abroad. Lorik plans and executes a midnight raid on the heavenly palace to steal the moon. The sun and the moon escape by cover of night wearing black clothes and baskets on their heads. The news that another man has eloped with his wife reaches the dwarf Bāvan, and he follows them in hot pursuit. The fleeing couple come to a river, snatch the ferryman's boat, and ferry it across. Bāvan threatens them angrily from the other side and shoots arrows at them. He has three arrows in his quiver; the first one shatters Lorik's shield, shield strap, and arm, the second blows away the mango tree under which Lorik and Cāndā are sheltering. The third arrow goes wide, and Cāndā taunts him: "Venus has set, the sun has risen, and all the world knows it!" (C 294) The dwarf responds by lamenting that he has lost them, and drowns himself in the river Gangā. Before dying, he curses them: "You will rule the kingdom of death, Lorik, and Cāndā will be stung by a deadly snake!" (C 296)

In another reference to the original Ahīr story, Dā'ūd has Lorik and Cāndā flee to a place called Haldī Pāṭan. Here, the city suggests a realm of the heart where the lovers can stay and satisfy their love for each other. They intend to pass the spring season in the city. On the way they make a night halt and camp:

> *On a moonlit night, in the light of the full moon, on a bed*
> *of flowers they slept.*
> *A snake, attracted by the scent of the flowers, came up and*
> *stung Cāndā.*
> *When it stung her, the moon darkened,*
> *she fell down senseless, and the snake fled,*
> *hissing and spreading its deadly hood.*
> *Lorik heard, and ran to avenge her [C 308–9].*

Lorik kills the snake just as it is about to go into its hole, and then begins to grieve over Cāndā as she lies there senseless. Desperate, he loosens all her clothes and ornaments and begins to lament her death. He starts to build a pyre of sandalwood for her, but then a *guṇī* or skilled healer appears and restores her to life.

They continue on their journey and camp in a forest underneath a fig tree. At the crack of dawn, another snake stings her, and she succumbs to the deadly venom.[99] All she can say before she falls senseless is, "I sinned when I attached myself to you" (C 313). By the Sufi logic of transformation, she must purify herself of this sin (*kukarma*) by passing through her own near-death ordeal before she can enjoy the love of Lorik freely. He is desolate, and again builds a pyre of sandalwood and prepares to cremate her. Since his life and soul have left his body with the death of Cāndā, he prepares to burn himself alive to expiate the sin of sleeping with another man's wife. The transformation of desire into love is not possible without holding to the notion of truth (*ḥaqīqat*, or in its Hindavī translation, *sat*):

> *"I am not her husband, and I've left aside truth, harmed*
> *my family's good name.*
> *To be brave, I have to bring this love of another's wife*
> *to its ultimate end [C 317].*

He prepares the pyre, and is just about to climb on it, when another *gāruḍī* or snake venom specialist appears and restores Cāndā to life again. And so perhaps the only male who attempts to become a *satī* in the history of Indian literature is prevented from doing so.

The incident marks both the purification of Cāndā through her passage into death and the willingness of Lorik to sacrifice his all on the path of true love, about which Lorik says:

> *Love is a blaze which, with a single spark from a single ember,*
> *can burn heaven, earth and hell to ashes in an instant [C 323].*

Clearly, Dā'ūd's text is centered around both *fanā* or destruction (of the self, of sins, of the ego) and the ability to valorize *prema-rasa* above all ordinary conventions of society and the world.

Transforming desire into this kind of love can also involve absolute chastity, as Mainā's experiences make clear. She suffers terribly from Lorik's absence and his elopement with Cāndā. She sits at home, not going anywhere, not eating properly, and not adorning herself. She spends the nights crying in bed and her days staring at the road that will bring her beloved Lorik back home. Kholin, her mother-in-law, is desperately worried about her and at a loss for what to do. She knows that Lorik and Cāndā are in Haldī Pāṭan, but she does not know how to reach them. A caravan of traders comes through town, on their way to Haldī Pāṭan. Kholin invites Surjan, the caravan leader, home and begs him to take a message to Lorik from Mainā.

The Sufferings of the Twelve Months (Bārah-māsā)

Here Dā'ūd embellishes his poem with another generic set piece popular with the regional literatures of north India, depiction of the sufferings of the deserted wife through the twelve months of the year (*bārah-māsā*). Mainā describes how she passed the long days and nights of separation in each season that passed on the earth. The *bārah-māsā* brings up the other side of *prema* or *'ishq*: *viraha* or, in Persian, *hijr*, the radical, ineradicable difference between the Creator and created beings, between lover and beloved. In Chishtī metaphysics, Allah and creatures share in the same essence, but are not the same being. The divine essence (*z̤āt-i ilāhī*) is refracted through the layers of manifestation, but the essence itself is unknowable and radically other from human beings.

Dā'ūd's *bārah-māsā* is not based on the description of the six seasons (*ṣaḍṛtu-varṇana*) so common in Sanskrit poetry and described in detail in the *Varṇa-Ratnākara* as one of the conventions a poet was expected to master.[100] Instead, in an innovation, he draws on the sung poetry that became part of so many Apabhraṃśa and regional literary genres. The *bārah-māsā* reconfigures the yearly cycle of time in order to represent the deserted wife's separation. The imagery of the female body meshes with the cycle of nature.

Thus, in the month of Sāvan, the rains come and invade Mainā's eyes, so that she weeps incessantly like the clouds in the sky. In Bhādoṉ, her heart breaks as the lightning flashes in the pitch darkness of the night, and her empty house eats away at her. In the month of Kuṉvār, the rains stop and cranes and wagtails appear, but no lover comes to assuage her loneliness. Kārtik comes with its silvery moonlight, and passionate women spread beds outside to sleep with their lovers. For Mainā, however, the moonlight only burns her already suffering body. Winter begins with the month of Aghan, and her body wastes away pining in the cold. In Pūs, quilts are taken out and beds arranged for warm comfort with lovers, but nothing suits Mainā. In the month of Māgh, she shrivels up like a lotus without the sun to warm her, since the moon has stolen away her sun. In the happy month of Phālgun, all the young women adorn themselves and dance, but she is desolate. She cries tears of blood till her blouse is all wet and stained. When spring comes, and the month of Caita, she has no lover—and what is spring without a lover? In Baisākh, her body blooms like a mango orchard, but her husband is not there to sample the juice. The hot summer sun of Jeṭh burns her, and neither sandal paste nor cool water can calm the fire in her body. In Āṣāḍh, dark clouds gather but no relief is at hand, for her Lorik is not nearby.

Mainā asks Surjan to take this message to Lorik in Haldī Pāṭan, and to tell him to leave the wicked Cāndā and return to her. The caravan leader accepts the commission, which the poet describes as "a cargo of burning desire," and sets off for Pāṭan. On his way, from the sheer intensity of Mainā's sorrow, the deer he passes become smoke-colored, and the birds are burnt as black as coal. The sea he crosses burns up, along with all its fish, and his boat and oars along with it. The sky incinerates spontaneously, and the clouds that form above are represented as the smoke from the fire. Nevertheless, he perseveres. He enters Pāṭan and seeks Lorik.

The End of the Story

Surjan presents himself to Lorik in the guise of a Brahmin astrologer. Appropriately enough, in a tale where much of the imagery hinges on astrological symbolism, the resolution of the impasse among Lorik, Cāndā, and Mainā is triggered by a horoscope. Surjan casts Lorik's horoscope and gives the following reading:

> *"The Moon is in Aries, your birth sign,*
> *And the Sun is in your third house.*
> *Mars dwells in the seventh house,*
> *and Jupiter shines in the ninth mansion.*
> *The astrologer counts four constellations in the southern direction.*
> *Mars and Mercury, Jupiter and the Moon especially mark your birth.*
> *Mercury in your fourth house signifies happiness,*
> *and you will rule in glory like Jupiter.*
> *In the second, Mars will make you gain your object,*
> *make you leave the path of sin and return to the truth.*
> *Saturn's presence in the sixth house*
> *will bring lost wealth back into your hands.*
> *Rāhu and Ketu will make you wander about,*
> *but then you will return home and meet your family.*
> *I would stake my life if this not be so,*
> *if my calculations are false, I'll tear up my almanacs!*
> *You have been sucking on a sour lemon, but now you should eat sweet* drākṣa *fruit.*
> *Lorik, leave this pool of sin, and bathe in the pure, good Gangā! [C 367–68]*

Surjan's conclusions from the planetary positions reflect, of course, the message he has been sent to give to Lorik, but they seem astrologically accurate.[101] The seventh house is the house of marriage, and the evil aspect of Mars[102] has caused a disruption in Lorik's marriage. Now the astrologer begs him to return to his wife, and by implication, to the path of truth. He ends by exhorting him to leave the pool of sin in which he has been bathing and to return to the pure Gangā. Lorik is stricken with remorse. He takes his leave of the

King of Haldī Pāṭan. Lorik and Cāndā set out, accompanied by a huge escort and laden with gifts given to them by the king.

When this unknown army reaches Govar, there is some alarm, but Mainā has a dream in which she sees her husband returning to her. The women of Govar go out to the camp to sell milk to them. Mainā goes along with the other women, and Lorik, disguised, devises a test for her. He asks Cāndā, who is buying the milk, to reward the women of Govar by putting vermillion (*sindūra*) and sandal on them. The entire row of women receives this honor happily, but Mainā refuses, saying:

> *"Only the woman whose man is by her,*
> *can adorn her hair with* sindūr.
> *My master has gone to Haldī Pāṭan.*
> *While he is away from home,*
> *how can I make myself beautiful without him?*
> *Day and night, I cry tears of sorrow...." [C 388]*

Through her chastity, Mainā proves herself worthy of the love of Lorik and completes the transformation of her desire into a transcendentalized Sufi *'ishq*. Lorik is happy with her fidelity and reveals himself, and the two women also recognize each other. They begin to fight, but Lorik calms them down by assuring them that he loves both of them. They all go home to Govar happily, and he proves his love and his masculinity by sleeping with both of them and recognizing them as his two wives.

Unfortunately, all the manuscripts of the text are incomplete, and none tells us what happens next in Dā'ūd's version. As the editor M. P. Gupta notes, in some folk versions Lorik engages in a fight with another warrior and is killed. He is then cremated and his wives become *satīs* by burning themselves to death on his pyre. In other versions, Lorik wins the battle but goes to Benares as an ascetic and immolates himself.[103] Both of these possible endings underscore the connection of *prema-rasa* with the ultimate annihilation (*fanā*) of the seeker and this world and their absorption back into God.

Whatever the ending Maulānā Dā'ūd may have chosen for his poem, the *Cāndāyan* sets a model for one of the major literary traditions of the subcontinent. Incomplete and gap-ridden as it is, Dā'ūd's text does create a generic formula that the later poets follow in greater or lesser degrees of elaboration. The fragments of narrative and the lines of the larger story sketched out here proved formative for the genre. Dā'ūd used the rules of propriety creatively to invent a new *rasa*, one that demonstrates the Muslim internalization of an Indian theory of poetic response, expressing the new Sufi message in terms of the *desī prema-rasa*.

There is no single allegorical scheme for Sufi practice that directly maps on to the *Cāndāyan* or on to the later texts of the genre. The multiple resonances of each *sa-rasa* line of poetry are also tied to the Sufis' internal competition with the military and aristocratic élites who sponsored their efforts and created the material circumstances for them to write their poems of love in Hindavī. In Dā'ūd's distinctive formula of the two wives, the Sufis express a claim to superior symbolic authority and hegemony over cultural and literary production in north India. Dā'ūd himself was able to maintain his dual roles as a poet at a provincial court and a Sufi and follower of the Chishti Shaikh Zain al-dīn, as a Persian-speaking Turkish Muslim with a Central Asian ancestry and a *desī* speaker of Hindavī and eager enthusiast of local poetry. The fantasy of Lorik's reconciliation of his two wives, like the Chishti *silsilah*'s claims of independence, is part of a negotiation of social tensions between Sufis and rulers, between Indian and Islamic identities.

Composed at a time when the centralized Turkish sultanate controlled various provinces from Delhi, the poem constructs a social order containing many local kingdoms with ruling aristocracies. Dā'ūd is part of a new ruling group that establishes a power base among the kingdoms and people of this Hindustani landscape. The poem he wrote not only redefines the local language and traditions by translating the Perso-Arabic theory of *'ishq* into the eastern Hindavī or Avadhi *prema-rasa,* but also contains a temporary embodiment of Sufi divinity in the form of Cāndā, who is depicted as more powerful than all the idols in the temples. The *Cāndāyan* marks the historical transformation of the canons of Indian poetry through sponsorship of an aristocratic class that is itself being transformed by Indian culture, a far cry from the narratives of military conquest associated with the earlier phases of the Muslim presence in India.

The chapters that follow trace four aspects of Dā'ūd's formula through the later romances of the genre and their contexts of articulation: the use of narrative motifs, notions of landscape and technical language, the system of gender relations implied by the genre and by comparable narratives from the period, and the role of vision and embodiment in the self-transformation of the hero/reader of the romance.

4

Oceans and Stories: The Mirigāvatī

The Structure of Fantasy

Succeeding generations of poets put the narrative formula of Maulānā Dā'ūd's *Cāndāyan* to complex uses. The next surviving Avadhi Sufi romance, Shaikh Quṭban Suhravardī's *Mirigāvatī* (ca. 1503), recreates the formulaic pattern of the *Cāndāyan.* The text, embodied as a fifteenth-century illuminated manuscript now held in the Bharat Kala Bhavan in Benares, is probably from some eastern provincial town with a musical and poetic culture like that of Kahalganv, the Bihari court in exile of the talented musician and patron of the arts, Sultan Ḥusain Shāh Sharqī. In reading the *Mirigāvatī,* we have to come to terms with the conventionality, the multiple origins, and the range of responses to the fantastic universes created by the poets of eastern Hindavī. The Avadhi *premākhyāns* circulated among a variety of audiences and used narrative formulae and terminology that were commonly recognizable and had a wide appeal. This chapter investigates Quṭban's formulaic construction of the fantasy world in his tale of the love between the handsome Prince of Candragiri and the beautiful Mirigāvatī, the magic Doe-woman.

Although very little is certain about Quṭban, we know that he dedicated his romance to his cultivated patron Ḥusain Shāh Sharqī (1458–1505), the ousted ruler of the regional sultanate of Jaunpur, north of Benares on the Gomatī river, and the center of a refined court-in-exile in Bihar. The local world in which he lived was dominated by the political and military struggle between Ḥusain Shāh Sharqī and the Lodi sultans of Delhi for control over Avadh and Jaunpur.[1] Nothing of this struggle appears in Quṭban's literary fantasy. Yet Quṭban goes a long way from the cowherding origins of the Ahīr story of Lorik and his two wives in mythological and literary sophistication. He creates an aristocratic social world, in which all the ritual, social, and emotional discussions between characters display a nice understanding of social distinction and the commonly understood valences of élite society.

As we shall see in the first section of this chapter, the quest for the elusive object of desire is structured through contrasted and contradictory narrative options. The repetition of the pattern of the *Cāndāyan* in the later Sufi Hindavī romances suggests the existence of a generic formula, a set of narrative expectations that such romances had to fulfill in order to please their audiences. An entire court and hospice-sponsored regional literary culture must have surrounded the dissemination and performance of these poems. For the audiences who gathered in the scented cool of the summer nights of Avadh to listen to poetry in Hindavī and Persian, this was one of the options for entertainment with or without using intoxicants of various kinds or engaging in a fashionable and potentially spiritually transformative practice of opening up the self to erotic mysticism and poetry. But these Sufistically charged stories about seductive heroines, evil demons, good nymphs, and handsome princes-turned-yogis were not the only literary fantasies or devotional verse available. There were many kinds of erotic and mystical poetry, many shrines and hospices competing for audiences and followers, many groups of pilgrims and devotees within many lineages, many languages encoding their crisscrossing and separating religious and poetic visions.

Within these fictional universes, characters are frequently emblematic types, exemplifying abstract qualities such as love, wisdom, mystical absorption, and spiritual guidance. Ordinate love requires stringing together narrative motifs into an organized story. There is no set schema the stages have to follow, as each poet invents ordeals for his lovelorn yogi prince; there is only the necessity of narrative elaboration, deferment, and invention. And even though the primary purpose of the poet who creates an imaginary universe may not be to represent historical events, poetic uses of individual motifs and larger narrative sequences are linked with wider historical processes and have a history of their own. Stories are part of larger historical worlds with their own struggles and interactions. The balancing act might reflect the necessary psychological conflict between the received genealogy of conquest and migration and the feeling of rootedness in the soil of Hindustān. The formulaic narrative positing of dualism, repeated again and again in the later romances, lines itself up against the other perceived dualisms of the age: the world and religion, *duniyā* and *dīn*, women and men, Turk and Hindu, foreign and native, fair and dark, exotic and familiar. Rather than taking these oppositions at face value, we must see them as rhetorical dualisms, wheeled out like ritual siege engines whenever enmity is to be portrayed on stage. The tendency toward oppositional thought dominates also the narrative universes of the Hindavī Sufi romances: good and bad love, love by consent or violence, ups and downs, demons and helpers, always a good choice and an evil one.[2]

These narrative options or choices between progress and regress on the ascetic path are propelled along in the consistent narrative drive toward the consummation of desire aroused in an initial dream, vision, or encounter. First, inspired by Persian *masnavīs*, they relate the story of a spiritual quest that proceeds through the deferment of desire and the enticement of the hero/reader further and further on the journey of self-transformation. There are many narrative motifs that are not precisely allegorical or symbolic, but are nevertheless integrally part of the narrative design. Characters and places can also personify abstract states of being, or sometimes stock types,[3] but without being locked into a rigid allegorical scheme. The notion of *tamsīl*, allegory or exemplification, and the emblematic characters that exemplify general Sufi values reveal the Sufi meanings of the shorter allegorical or suggestive segments.

The Plot of the Mirigāvatī

Let us turn now to the story of the *Mirigāvatī* to illustrate these narrative processes through the plot and the principles of its advancement.

Perhaps as a result of the war between his patron Ḥusain Shāh and the Lodī sultans, Quṭban's narrative does not open with the traditional topos of the *nagaravarṇana*, a description of the idyllic town where the poet is nurtured in a political utopia by his princely patron. Instead, the Prince of Candragiri, Rāj Kuṉvar, sees a seven-colored magic doe while out hunting in the forest, and he wants her. When he follows her he sees her sink deep into a lake and disappear. The poet describes this lake as the site of the flash of divine manifestation (*tajallī*), where Mirigāvatī and her band of heavenly nymphs come to play. Episode after episode describes the near-death experiences of the prince in his effort to convert into love the desire (*kāma/shauq*) that has been aroused in him by his vision of Mirigāvatī.

For the prince, Mirigāvatī represents the seductive temporary revelation of divine presence:

He said, "That cannot possibly be a doe,
born with a skin so marvellous!
All the ornaments she wears are of gold
and she walks like a beautiful woman."
Seeing the astonishing marvel in the distance, the prince spurred on his horse.
He thought, "Should I kill it with an arrow?
Or dismount and capture it by force?"

When he saw her heavenly form,
love seized his heart. He dismounted

and followed her on foot, thinking,
"If only I could approach and capture her!
I'll die if I cannot get that beautiful doe.
I'll come at her from the front and catch her."
But the doe skipped away and evaded him.
He rubbed his hands in disappointment,
began to rue in his heart the spell she had cast.
He mounted up again and followed her close,
but the saffron-colored doe ran away again.
He followed her for seven yojanās, *all alone and apart from the company.*
The nobles and followers thought he was hunting, but the prince went on alone.

The prince and the doe were alone in the forest.
No third person was around there with them.
The prince was enraptured, in love with the doe,
his intelligence forgotten, all sense fled his body.
He saw a great green tree in the forest,
with a clear pure lake flowing beneath it.
As the prince approached, the doe grew skittish.
She sank into the waters of the Mānasarodaka.
She hid herself completely in the pure water.
She wouldn't come out again, but was absorbed.
The prince tied his horse to the tree, disrobed and put his clothes on the shore.
He jumped into the pure lake quickly, hoping to find the vision he had seen [M 19–21].

Desire for the magic doe with the heavenly form (*rūpa*) is an external force that seizes him in its cruel grip. Characteristically, it is entwined with the Sufi notion of annihilating the carnal soul, then the self itself, *fanā*: the prince exclaims that he will die if he does not gain the doe. When he searches for the beautiful shimmering form he has seen, however, he cannot find it:

He searched the lake and did not find his desire.
He forgot everything but his mind's longing,
"Since the doe has escaped me utterly,
I shall not die, nor live, just stay at this spot!"
His senses left him and his intelligence was forgotten.
The story of love had seized his mind.

He could not forget the picture in his thoughts,
it was etched there in lines in stone.
Minute by minute, love engulfed his mind,
for that spotless moon of the second of the month.
He longed for her deeply, but could not find her, came out and stood on the shore.
He cried tears upon tears of sorrow and grief, his body bereft of sense [M 22].

Although the prince jumps into the lake to find her, she disappears completely and he is left lamenting. The poet uses a visual technique reminiscent of miniature painting to depict the prince's sense-numbing grief:

He longed and looked only for his love.
The prince leant against the green tree and wept.
He cried like a spring cloud in Bhādoṉ
and the world was filled with his liquid tears.
Clouds came massing out in the sky,
great and small, and filled the heavens.
The world clouded over with the rain of his tears.
His eyes rained more and more, never lessening.
He prayed, "God, give me wings,
that I may fly wherever I hear she lives."
Burning with longing, he stood up and sat down, unable to think of anything at all.
He renounced his home, his family and other people, began to forget the world [M 23].

Playing with poetic opposites, the poet describes the prince as burning with longing, yet bringing on a monsoon flood in the world through his tears. His companions find him under a tree that glitters like a royal canopy. The shimmering lake by which he sits is the purifier of sins and of those who drink from it, and many lush images are used to describe it: black bees hover over its white lotuses, drunk with love, and lovely fragrances pervade the atmosphere from its camphor- and *khus*-scented water. The prince will not return to court with them, and sits by the lake meditating on the vision he has seen.

When the company returns to court and informs the prince's father, the entire town comes out to the forest to reason with the prince. The prince will not return and instead wants a boon. He asks his father the king to build him a seven-story red and gold palace around the shining lake. The king assents, and craftsmen, painters, architects, and goldsmiths arrive to construct the fantastic gold-encrusted palace that will encompass within its painted and sculpted form the formless absolute that has flashed in the prince's eyes. The palace has seven levels, with four-colored steps on all four sides. Over them stretches a gold and red *caukhaṇḍī* or four-cornered pavilion that is painted with scenes from the *Rāmāyaṇa* and the *Mahābhārata*. The decoration of the pavilion, with its depictions of scenes from the epics such as Bhīma's slaying of Kīcaka, is indicative of the familiarity of the Hindavī poets with the range of local mythology and custom.[4] Interlaced through these mythological scenes are depictions of the golden doe, which the prince keeps looking at and weeping. His nurse (*dhāī*), performing the function of a Sufi *pīr* or guide as usual in these narratives, comes to him to ask what is wrong.

Although at first he cannot respond to his nurse because his mind and heart are concentrated on the golden doe, he describes his sorrow through the seasons of the year in an abbreviated form of the *bārah-māsā*. In the dark nights of the season of the rains, he cannot sleep because of the lightning flashing in his eyes, an elusive flickering of divine essence that he cannot catch. In the winter, the fire of separation (*viraha agni*) keeps him wailing with its intensity all night. The prince's fire sears winter itself, the personification of cold, and covers the season with ashes. The cold retreats to a distance of twenty *kosas* from the prince, and the earth becomes green again. Summer comes, and the month of Jeṭh, but the fire burning in the prince's body does not subside. He burns constantly, like a smoldering ember, and sandal paste does not cool his agony. He stays on by the lakeside, ignoring all human company, oblivious to all but the desire that has him in its grip.

After a year, seven heavenly nymphs come to play in the magic lake, all of them perfect in their beauty, each like the full moon on the fourteenth night. Fairest among them is Mirigāvatī, and they play about in the lake like the moon and all the constellations come down to earth. Mirigāvatī notices that there is a new palace there, and they are all amazed because not even the shadow of a human has ever fallen on the place. The prince is struck dumb with their beauty, losing his fair color and turning to a blackened cinder. When he rushes forward to catch Mirigāvatī, the entire group of lotus-faced nymphs flies away to heaven. He lies stricken by the lakeside, with no one intelligent enough to give him what he needs to alleviate his condition, "words full of *rasa*, a love story that would awaken him" (M 48). His nurse comes again to him, revives him with nectar (*amṛta*), and makes him sit up in her arms. She is like a mother to him, since she eases his transformation and rebirth into a life with love. To her he confides the vision that has flashed in his eyes like lightning.

The prince uses both the generic set piece of the *sarāpā* or head-to-foot description and the language of analogy to describe, through poetic imagery, the unrepresentable divine essence in bodily form:

"I saw that which cannot be spoken,
and desire burnt my mind from within....
The sun rose blinding in the east,
and I could not distinguish her features.
Lightning flashed in my eyes, and I broke all controls and restraints!
Let me describe that beauty: the parting in her hair, her breasts,
and her hands and feet [M 49].

From the parting in Mirigāvatī's hair, described as a line of cranes against a dark monsoon cloud, to her cruel black-tipped breasts and her golden limbs dusted with vermillion, love's inventory describes the fierce (*jalālī*) and gentle (*jamālī*) attributes of her body and its physiological effects on the prince. The nurse is sympathetic to the severe effects of this revelation on the prince, and advises him how to go about obtaining the golden doe.

She is confident that the nymphs will return to the lake for the religious observance of breaking their fast on *nirjalā ekādaśī*, the eleventh day of the hot Indian summer month of Jeṭh. On that occasion, she tells him, he must steal Mirigāvatī's sari, and she will be in his power. Here Quṯban employs a motif that occurs frequently in folk and fairy tales, the story of the Swan Maiden who can be overpowered by robbing her of her swan coat.[5] This narrative motif, which occurs in Indian folk tales as the seduction or wooing of a bathing girl by stealing her clothes, is found in stories from Kashmir to the south and in the Assam hills,[6] as well as in the mythology of Kṛṣṇa and the bathing cowgirls. Quṯban's use of it serves to show what Vladimir Propp called the capacity for transformation inherent in such formulaic tales: "If our observations about the exceptionally close morphological kinship of tales are correct, it follows that no single theme of a given genus of tales may be studied either morphologically or genetically without reference to others. One theme changes into another by means of the substitution of elements according to its forms."[7] For the use of formulaic sequences of action makes us insist on their completion, just as the prince whose mind and heart have been captivated by the magic doe waits faithfully for her return by the lakeside.

When the eleventh day of Jeṭh dawns, Mirigāvatī is drawn irresistibly to the lake in the forest. She persuades her fellow nymphs to fly there with her. They do so, and the prince is again dazzled by the play of lights. Like Purūravas with Urvaśī, the prince runs away with Mirigāvatī's sari while she is in the water. She cannot now return with her friends. He brings her to the palace and lives with her, feasting his eyes on her beauty but unable to consummate his desire.

Even though he has captured her and they live in the painted palace by the magic lake, they do not make love, for Mirigāvatī defines the *rasa* of love in an interesting new way:

Rejoicing, the prince entered his palace,
and sat down on his golden throne.
He said to his nurse, "Look!
This is that very one whose love
has overshadowed my heart and mind."
The couple sat on the golden throne, revelling in each other's company.
Till the prince reached out his hand through her necklaces to touch Mirigāvatī's breasts.

Mirigāvatī said, "O prince, control yourself,
and follow what I tell you.
You are a king's son, and desire me,
but I am of noble birth myself.
Stop, I tell you, listen to me,
just let my girlfriends arrive.
Force does not count; only through rasa
can you enjoy the savor of love
within this world and the hereafter.
Rasa *cannot be enjoyed through violence,*
it is a savor which only comes through rasa.
If you talk of enjoying rasa, *I have told you what* rasa *means.*
Only those who are colored with rasa *can savor it now or hereafter" [M 85–86].*

Mirigāvatī's description of *rasa* not only stays the prince's hand but also defines the transformation of desire into love, through *yoga* (asceticism) or *bhoga* (sensual enjoyment through divine grace).

One day the prince's father, who dotes on the prince and has given many gifts to Mirigāvatī as her father-in-law, sends a message to the prince asking him to visit the royal court. Despite adverse omens, the prince rides out, and in his absence the nurse is left to look after Mirigāvatī. Mirigāvatī confuses the nurse by telling her far-fetched stories and sagas, and then sends her on an errand. Mirigāvatī then finds her magic sari and puts it on. When the nurse returns, she cannot see the nymph anywhere. Finally she happens to look up and sees Mirigāvatī perched on a roofbeam outside the palace. Before flying off, Mirigāvatī tells the nurse that the prince will have to work hard to earn what he has so far enjoyed through tricking and constraining the doe. The town over which her father rules is Kancanpur, and she instructs the nurse to tell the prince that he can find her there. Love does not work through force or violence, but through cultivation of a sympathetic understanding among lovers, Sufis, and listeners.

The larger narrative design for the structure of the story entailed by the generic model of Dā'ūd's *Cāndāyan* involves the hero's accomplishment of his quest by leaving the world as a yogi and the conflict between the two wives who represent this world and the hereafter. Here Quṭban does not disappoint his audiences. When the prince returns to the magic lake, he is devastated, and he and his nurse consider the future together. At this time, the poet tells us,

> *In his worried state, the method of* yoga
> *came to the prince and attached itself to him.*
> Bhoga *ran away, hearing of the onset*
> *of ascetic rigor....[M 105]*

The prince's period of closeness to the object of his desire is over, and now he must work his way toward the golden city, Kancanpur. He puts on a yogi's guise, with all the accouterments of the Gorakhnāth *panth*: the matted locks, the basil-bead rosary, the stick, the begging bowl, and the deerskin on which to meditate. He sets off singing of his pain in separation from his love, accompanying himself with his stringed *kingarī*.

On his quest he comes to a grove with mangoes sweet as nectar hanging from its trees and a matchless palace built within their shade. When the prince goes up to the palace, he discovers in it a lovely young woman, as beautiful as a half-opened lotus, crying like a spring cloud. The young woman's name is Rūpminī, and she tells him she is held there in captivity by an evil demon who has terrorized the town over which her father rules. The demon demanded the sacrifice of the young princess, and her parents agreed in order to save the town. Rūpminī is terrified that the demon will eat her up, but the prince tells her not to worry. He promises to save her with "a pure mind." Suddenly the ferocious demon appears, with fourteen arms and seven heads, ready to fight. He attacks the prince, who shoots his *cakra* or steel ring at him seven times, decapitating a head at each throw, and the demon falls dead. Rūpminī guesses that he is no yogi but a king or prince in disguise, and she extracts the story of his love for Mirigāvatī from him.

The prince tells her all and escorts her home, but refuses to marry her or to touch her in a carnal way. Rūpminī's father, however, is delighted at the eligible bridegroom who seems to have appeared from heaven and offers him his daughter's hand in marriage and half his kingdom. The prince refuses, for he is a yogi and has no desire for earthly things. He informs the king that he has given up the path of *bhoga* or sensual pleasure. The king is enraged and puts him in prison, promising him freedom on the condition that he marry Rūpminī. Against his will, he agrees, but does not consummate the marriage because he wishes to keep his love chaste and spiritual. Although Rūpminī is burning with desire for him, he whiles away the nights with her in making sweet excuses, keeping himself pure. He has a guesthouse built for wandering ascetics and *sādhūs*, and asks all who pass if they know the way to Kancanpur. A great company of ascetics comes in, bound for the banks of the Godāvarī river, and they inform him that Kancanpur is not far from there.

The prince's quest and his journey to Kancanpur are the subject of detailed analysis in the next section of this chapter. Once there, he gains the love of Mirigāvatī and lives there happily with her. In part, this represents consummation of the characters' passion, but it is only a partial solution to the problem of the relation of story and history. A more productive line of inquiry is suggested by the next move that Quṭban makes in his narrative, weaving smaller formulaic motifs into the larger narrative design of the plot.

One day Mirigāvatī is called to the wedding of a friend of hers, and she leaves the prince in her palace with the warning that he can go everywhere in the palace except for one room. In an episode that is strikingly reminiscent of Bluebeard's castle[8] with gender roles reversed, the prince is unable to resist the temptation. Inside the room is a large wooden chest, within which there is a *dānava*, a fierce evil ogre. He pleads with the prince to set him free, promising that he will serve him faithfully. The prince does so, but the ogre once released carries the prince off and dashes him into a great gulf of the sea in order to kill him. When Mirigāvatī returns she is distraught, and does not know where the ogre can have cast him down. Now the roles of seeker and sought on this quest are reversed, suggesting the Sufi interchangeability of lover and beloved, God and man. Mirigāvatī sets out in search of the prince. By a fortuitous chance, the wind acts as a messenger between the two. It finds the prince clinging precariously to life and informs Mirigāvatī, who rushes to him and rescues him. The two are compared to a bee and a lotus finally coming together.

Formulaic fictions set up narrative patterns that form the generic expectations of their audiences and limit the innovations possible within the form. The formula that Quṭban has chosen to use is Dā'ūd's pattern of the hero with his two wives. Accordingly, he has to bring the plot to a close with a resolution of the prince's unconsummated marriage with Rūpminī. In his absence, she burns with the pain of separation, and spends her time on the ramparts of her palace looking for her lost love in the distance. She sees instead a caravan of traders, and sends a tearful message in the form of a *bārah-māsā* through the leader of the caravan.

The prince is full of remorse, and with Mirigāvatī and one of his two sons by her he retraces his path to his father's kingdom. They leave the other son in charge of the kingdom. Finally they are reunited with Rūpminī, and the three of them return to Candragiri where the prince's father is king. The two wives fight, as in the *Cāndāyan*, but the prince separates them and calms them down, sleeping with both of them in turn to satisfy their jealous desire. This happy romantic resolution, however, contains an unusual twist at the end. One day, the prince goes out hunting in the forest, and gets into a fight with a tiger. Although he wounds the tiger, the fierce beast is enraged and kills him in its own death agony. The prince dies, and the whole universe is saddened by his death. The entire kingdom mourns, and both Mirigāvatī and Rūpminī fling themselves in anguish on his funeral pyre. The three of them burn to ashes, with love consummated, desire satisfied, and the narrative options of *yoga* and *bhoga* transformed into the *rasa* of love.

The traditional plot of the *premākhyāns* is static in its repetition of the formula of the *Cāndāyan*. Without becoming an ascetic, no prince or king can attain the divine heroine of the story; the hero has to have two warring wives between whom he has to make peace. Within this larger narrative design, however, Quṭban's plot in the *Mirigāvatī* shows a great deal of inventiveness in reinterpreting the formula. Fantasy worlds are also linked to particular historical circumstances. Quṭban's restaging of the dynamics of the conflict between Sufis and kings raises the question of the relevance of the social order to the order of events in the narrative. There is no single key that would allow us to posit a homology between narrative and social form. In the Sufi logic of the story, the Sufi's relation with God and with the world has been resolved in this utopian ending in which two hostile co-wives have been brought into an amicable truce and the Sufi seeker has united with his God.

Homer in the Indian Ocean

Quṭban also reinscribed the Arabic genre of the marvels of India in the adventures of the *desī* hero of the *Mirigāvatī*. Along with exchanges of gems, cloth, spices, and other merchandise through the sea lanes of the Indian Ocean, there was an ongoing and global exchange of narrative motifs between Indian and Islamic traditions of storytelling. Multiple uses of the same set of motifs demonstrate the links of fiction with the global historical processes of trade and cultural encounter.

R. S. McGregor has remarked on how "Quṭban's work appears as the product of a composite culture in which Muslim and Islamic elements have been

Indianised."[9] The Arabic genre of the marvels that travelers encountered in India was reinscribed in the adventures of the hero of the *Mirigāvatī*. Like the beast fables and mirrors for princes that traveled from India to Europe, so too these sailors' yarns about the marvels of the Indies circulated in the Islamicate and pre-Islamicate world of the Indian Ocean.

But the prince's quest and his successive ordeals are also modeled on the seven valleys of spiritual quest in 'Aṭṭār's famous Persian poem *The Conference of the Birds*.[10] Each of the prince's ordeals is designed to test him in some particular Sufi virtue such as chastity, trust in God, or the power of rigorous meditation. On his travels, the first place he comes to is a kingdom whose king is so deeply moved by the yogi's song and the power of the prince's words that he loses consciousness, and the audience is entranced. When the king recovers, he wants to reward the singing yogi with great wealth and a beautiful wife, but the prince wants only news of Kancanpur. Even though the king protests that it is a difficult path, full of dark forests haunted by ghouls and man-eating demons, impassable oceans, and inaccessible roads, the prince is not daunted. If he dies on the difficult path of asceticism, he says, he will attain spiritual perfection (*siddhi*). He has no life to lose, because *prema* has taken his life away. So they lead him to a dark seashore with a boat moored at it, which is the only way to Kancanpur. Here he has to remember the Names of Allah (the Sufi *ẕikr*) and rid himself of fear. Only if he proves himself absolutely fearless will he reach the farther shore. As he climbs in and begins to row, the sea's waves begin to rock the boat more and more furiously. All at once he is in the grip of a fierce whirlpool. The boat is about to sink, but the prince concentrates his attention and prays to Allah to release him from the whirlpool. A huge wave rears up and washes him ashore, saving his life.

On the shore he notices a great mountain, and two men come to greet him. They are bound on the same path as the prince, but the mountain in the distance has no ghat or landing place at which to dock a boat. They inform him that the shore they are on is the lair of a vicious serpent who comes daily in search of a man to eat. The prince is afraid and begins to weep, but then remembers Mirigāvatī and her sorrow should he be killed. He recovers himself and begins to pray to Allah, and while he is doing this the serpent appears. The prince feels happy to die for love, but by the grace of the supreme One another serpent appears and begins to fight with the first one. While they are locked in combat, another great wave sweeps the two out to sea, and carries the prince on his boat to the mountain. Saved from death for the second time, the prince leaves his boat on the mountainside and heads on to Kancanpur.

On his way, he meets the fair Rūpminī, rescues her from the demon, and marries her while remaining chaste. He has now conquered fear and lust, but does not know the way to Kancanpur. He has a guesthouse built, and asks all who pass if they have ever heard of Mirigāvatī's kingdom. One of a band of wandering adepts advises him:

> *"Kancanpur is not far from where we're bound.*
> *Between us and that city, there lies*
> *a deep ocean and a dark forest,*
> *like a blind well with no way out.*
> *If you walk steadily you'll gain the path, but only if you walk in truth.*
> *If you are true, truth will be your friend, and the lions and tigers will not eat you" [M 158].*

He takes from the adept his yogic garb, and seizes his chance to escape from his marriage while on a hunt outside the bounds of the town. He abandons his horse and princely attire, and puts on the adept's clothes. He walks away from his virgin wife and into that dark forest of death. He wanders round and round, seeking a path out of the forest. But first he must acquire another spiritual value, the ability to keep to the path of truth (*ḥaqīqat/sat*). His steps falter in the dense shades of the trees, and he walks a long way, constantly meditating on his love. When he finally gives up all and trusts to God (the Sufi quality of *tavakkul*), he reaches the end of the forest and sees before him the slopes of a sunlit country.

He sees flocks of goats and sheep grazing on the grassy slopes before him, and thanks God because he has come to an inhabited land. A herdsman grazing his flock comes up and offers hospitality to the yogi. The herdsman leads him to the cave that is his home, and the prince follows unsuspectingly. Once the prince is inside, the herdsman rolls a huge rock across the entrance and traps him inside, just as Polyphemos does to the wandering Odysseus in Homer's *Odyssey*.[11] The prince looks around him and sees a number of other prisoners in the cave. They are all extremely fat, so fat that they cannot walk, or even crawl. On questioning them he finds that they have all been fed a druglike herb by the herdsman, which has made them so fat as to incapacitate them. They warn him that the herdsman is a cannibal, and that the prince should not accept the drug from him if he wishes to stay alive. The prince is distressed, but realizes that losing his life on the path of truth will gain him spiritual perfection. He prays and mentions the name of truth in his Sufi *vird* or *ẕikr*, trusting to God to release him from the herdsman's cave.

Just then the herdsman comes in, catches one of the imprisoned men, and bangs his body against the cave floor to kill him. He roasts the man and eats him up, chewing up even the hard parts of his body. The prince is terrified. The herdsman belches contentedly after his meal and goes to sleep. The prince puts a pointed pair of metal tongs in the fire to heat them. When the tongs are red hot, he takes them out and puts them into the herdsman's eyes, blinding him instantly. The herdsman screams in agony, but since he is blind he cannot catch the prince. He vows revenge, however, and sits by the mouth of the cave to prevent the prince's escape, like the Cyclops in the Greek epic. The deadlock continues for three days, but finally the prince thinks of a stratagem. He kills one of the largest he-goats in the herd, skins it, and dries the skin. Then he puts it on, and, when the cannibal herdsman releases his herd for grazing, the prince slips out among the goats and sheep. The herdsman feels the back of each animal to make sure it is not a man, but does not feel underneath. When he comes to the prince he is suspicious, but the prince runs out before he can stop him. He continues on his way, vowing not to trust anyone but God, and praying to God to unite him with his beloved.

How is one to read the appearance of this Homeric narrative motif in a sixteenth-century Indian romance? Does the explanation lie in the deep structure of the unconscious, or the archetypal patterns of folklore?

In the Arabic literature of the marvelous, the sense of astonishment over events and things with unknown reasons or causes (*sabab*) is encoded within an ideological framework in which visible marvels fit into the ultimate reality of the invisible divine creator. This totalizing frame, however, allows a very wide latitude for the construction of fictive and geographical accounts that depend on astonishment for their effect on the reader. Shahrāzād's nightly revelations of ever-more astonishing marvels to create suspense are a good example of the variety and complexity of the uses of astonishment, as well as the containment of such marvels within a compendious framework.[12] To return to our Homeric motifs in Hindavī, we can begin to explain their presence in two ways: first, by tracing the motifs to see if we can establish a historical genealogy; and second, by examining their uses and the ideological frames within which they occur in each place. I apologize to the reader in advance; the remainder of this chapter involves a considerable amount of storytelling, all extremely pertinent and vitally important to the larger discussion.

Sindbād in Arabic

Quṭban's narrative of the ascetic quest of the Prince of Candragiri draws on motifs found also in the voyages of Sindbād the Sailor.[13] The adventure of the giant serpents, the boat that drifts about, and finally the cannibalistic herdsman who traps people in his cave and is blinded by the hero before he can make his escape—these ordeals appear also in that rambling and copious collection of stories, the Arabic *Kitāb Alf Lailah va Lailah* ("The Book of the Thousand Nights and a Night," widely known as the *Arabian Nights*) in the travels of the intrepid Sindbād. In his third voyage, Sindbād is washed up on an unknown island shore with his shipmates:

> [W]e saw a stately mansion situated in the middle of the island. We found it to be a strong castle, with high walls and a gate of ebony, with two leaves, both of which were open. We entered and found inside a large courtyard, around which there were many high doors, and at the upper end of which there was a large, high bench on which rested stoves and copper cooking pots hanging above. Around the bench lay many scattered bones. But we saw no one and were very much surprised. Then we sat down and soon fell asleep and slept from mid-morning till sundown when suddenly we felt the earth trembling under us, heard a rumbling noise in the air, and saw descending on us from the top of the castle a huge figure in the likeness of a man, black in color and tall in stature, as if he were a huge palm-tree, with eyes like torches.... When we saw him, we fainted, like men stricken dead with anxiety and terror.
>
> When he descended, he sat on the bench for a while, then he got up and coming to us, grabbed my hand... and lifting me up in the air, turned me over, as I dangled from his hand like a little morsel, and felt my body as a butcher feels a sheep for the slaughter. But finding me feeble from grief, lean from the toil of the journey, and without much meat, he let me go and picked up one of my companions... he kept turning us over and feeling us, one by one, until he came to the captain of our ship, who was a fat, stout, and broad-shouldered man. He was pleased by the captain and he seized him... and throwing him on the ground, set his foot on his neck and broke it. Then he fetched a long spit and thrust it through the captain's mouth until it came out through his posterior. Then he lit a big fire and set over it the spit on which the captain was spitted, turning it over the coal, until the flesh was roasted. Then he took the spit off the fire and, placing the body in front of him, separated the joints, as one separates the joints of a chicken... and devoured all the flesh and gnawed the bones, and nothing was left of the captain except some bones, which he threw on one side. Then he sat on the bench for a while and fell asleep, snoring like a slaughtered sheep or cow, and slept till morning, when he got up and went on his way.[14]

Sindbād and his companions are terrified, especially since the giant cannibal repeats his gruesome actions on the next day. They try to escape, but there is no place to hide from the giant anywhere on the island.

Mia Gerhardt has noted that the voyages of Sindbād are structured around an initial calamity, followed by an adventure or adventures, the description of a wonder, and a final return.[15] Ferial Ghazoul has faulted her analysis for doing violence to the text and setting up a rigid pattern that is not borne out by all seven voyages. She prefers instead to draw parallels between structure and psychological process in the Sindbād cycle and the frame-tale of Shahrāzād's nocturnal storytelling sessions.[16] In the story at hand, however, what is at issue is the very survival of the mercantile culture that Peter Molan has perceptively identified as the context of the production and reception of these narratives.[17] Significantly, the shipwrecked sailors' motivation in their crisis is to make the place safe for other Muslim merchants and travelers who might pass by the island on their own voyages. One of them says, "Listen to me! Let us find a way to kill him and rid ourselves of this affliction and relieve all Muslims of his aggression and tyranny."[18] Guided by Sindbād, they come up with a plan to save themselves and Muslim shipping. They will try to kill the giant, but first they need to build a raft so that they can escape from the island and secure passage with any ship that goes by.

In their response to a hostile situation, Sindbād and his companions temper their astonishment (*ta'ajjub*) with skillful action and trust in God (*tavakkul*).[19] They begin to carry wood out of the castle, build a raft, and tie it to the island shore. After putting some food on it, they return to the castle:

> When it was evening, the earth trembled under us, and in came the black creature, like a raging dog. He proceeded to turn us over and to feel us, one after one, until he picked one of us and did to him what he had done to his predecessors. Then he ate him and lay to sleep on the bench, snoring like thunder. We got up, took two of the iron spits of those set up there, and put them in the blazing fire until they became red-hot, like burning coals. Then, gripping the spits tightly, we went to the black creature, who was fast asleep, snoring, and, pushing the spits with all our united strength and determination, thrust them deep into his eyes. He uttered a great, terrifying cry. Then he got up resolutely from the bench and began to search for us, while we fled from him to the right and left, in unspeakable terror, sure of destruction and despairing of escape. But being blind, he was unable to see us, and he groped his way to the door and went out. When he went out, we followed him, as he went searching for us. Then he returned with a female, even bigger than he and more hideous in appearance...[W]e were in utmost terror. When the female saw us, we hurried to the raft, untied it, and, embarking on it, pushed it into the sea. The two stood, throwing big rocks on us until most of us died, except for three, I and two companions.[20]

Dodging the rocks that the giants throw at them, they float to another island. Here, when it is night, they fall asleep. They are barely asleep, however, before they are aroused by an enormous serpent with a wide belly. It surrounds them, and, approaching one of them, swallows him to his shoulders, then engulfs the rest of him until they can hear his ribs crack in the serpent's belly. The next night, the same thing happens to Sindbād's only remaining companion. Sindbād is able to escape only by tying long pieces of wood to his limbs so that the giant snake is unable to swallow him, and by hailing a passing ship to carry him to safety.

Scholars of Arabic literature have long known that the Sindbād cycle in the *Alf Lailah va Lailah* is derived from Arab mariners' tales of the wonders of India. The earliest available manuscript of the *Nights*, which Muhsin Mahdi reconstructed from a fourteenth-century Syrian version, is one of many no longer extant written and oral texts from which later storytellers, writers, and redactors drew.[21] As Hussain Haddawy, the translator of this version, notes, the story of Sindbād's voyages is not found here and constitutes a later addition to the *Nights*.[22] The cycle of the voyages can be traced back, instead, to a specific genre of Arabic literature: books of the wonders and marvels of the world (*'ajā'ib*), which drew on classical Greek and Roman geographers such as Pliny and Diodorus Siculus, as well as the sailors' yarns told around the coffeehouses and taverns of Basra and Baghdad in the ninth and tenth centuries. Increasing Arab involvement in the profitable Indian Ocean trade meant that sailors visited India and the islands beyond with greater frequency, and brought back tales of the wonders they found there. In this account of travelers' tales, and tales that travel through the Indian Ocean, it is entirely fitting that one should find a common source for the Sindbād cycle and the ordeals of the ascetic prince of the *Mirigāvatī* in the stories of a frequent traveler.

Buzurg bin Shahryār, a sea captain and merchant, was based in the port of Ramhormuz in the Persian Gulf in the tenth century. We know almost nothing about the good captain, except that his father came from the Persian province of Khuzistan. He did, however, leave a work entitled the *Kitāb 'Ajā'ib al-Hind*, "The Book of the Wonders of India." Reconstructed from a unique manuscript in the Aya Sophia mosque in Istanbul, the book contains stories and anecdotes of varying lengths, many of which are to be found as adventures in the voyages of Sindbād. The mercantile interests of both texts are repeatedly signaled by constant references to the products of each island or country visited: tin, diamonds, spices, coconuts, slaves, and so on. We have the following story in the *Kitāb 'Ajā'ib al-Hind*, about a giant shepherd encountered by a sailor:

> I heard a Basra man, who lived in the middle of the Street of the Quraysh, say he left Basra for Zabaj or some nearby place, [and was shipwrecked]. He escaped, and was thrown up on to an island.

> I landed, he said, and climbed a large tree, and spent the night there. In the morning I saw a flock of about 200 sheep arrive. They were large as horned cattle. They were driven by an extraordinary looking man. He was fat, tall, and had a horrible face. He had a stick in his hand, with which he drove the sheep.... He wore nothing but a leaf, like a banana leaf, but larger. He had it round his waist like a loincloth. Then he went up to a sheep, held it by its hind legs, took its udder in his mouth, and sucked it dry. He did the same with several others. Then he lay down in the shade of a tree. While he was looking at the tree, a bird settled on the one where I was. The man took a heavy stone, and threw it at the bird. He did not miss, and the bird fell from branch to branch, and stopped just beside me. He [saw me and] made me a sign to come down. I was so afraid that I hurried. I trembled all over, half dead with fear and hunger. He took the bird and threw it on the ground. I reckon it weighed about 100 *ratl*. He plucked it while it was still living. Then he took a stone that weighed a good twenty *ratl*, hit it on the head, and killed it. He went on hitting until it was in bits, and then began to bite it with his teeth, like a wild beast devouring its prey. He ate everything, and left only the bones.
>
> When the sun began to go down, he got up, took his stick, drove his sheep in front of him and shouted [at them]. He took me with him. The sheep gathered in one place. He led them to a sweet-water stream that there is on this island, watered them, and drank himself. I drank too, although my death seemed certain to me. Then he drove again, to a sort of wooden enclosure, with a kind of door. I went in with the sheep. In the middle was a kind of log hut, of the type weavers use, about twenty cubits high. His first act was to take one of the smallest and thinnest sheep, and hit it on the head with a stone. Then he lit a fire, and dismembered it with his hands and teeth, like a wild beast. He threw the pieces into the fire, still covered with skin and the wool. He ate the entrails raw. Then he went from sheep to sheep, drinking their milk. Then he took one of the largest ewes in the flock, seized her around the waist, and took his pleasure with her. The ewe cried out. He did the same with another. Then he took something to drink, and finally fell asleep, and snored like a bull.[23]

In the sailor's account, Zabaj is a reference to the island of Java. The sailor's most immediate reaction in this tale of cultural encounter is of shock at the dietary and sexual habits of the man he meets. Both tend toward bestiality, and are very far from the norms of Islamic law and diet that are familiar to him. Moreover, the islander has other habits that seemed far from civilization as the sailor knew it: "I noticed that he gathered the fruit of certain trees that grew on the island, steeped them in water, strained them, and drank the liquor. After that he was drunk all night, and lost consciousness."[24]

How were the sailor and the islander to communicate across this ideological divide, this scene of cultural encounter that could not progress beyond a few gestures and a marveling at the other's strange ways? They tried to speak to each other in Arabic and the islander's language, but with little success. After two months, the sailor climbed up on some overhanging branches and escaped from the enclosure. He walked as far and as fast as he could, and came to a grassy plain that was frequented by large birds. Like Sindbād with the giant roc, he caught one of them and flew over the sea to a mountain by attaching himself to the bird's claw. Then, he tells us:

> I went down from the mountain, and climbed a tree and hid.
>
> Next morning I saw smoke. I knew there is no smoke without people, and went down towards it. I had not gone far when a group of men came to meet me. They took hold of me, saying words I did not understand. They led me to a village. There they shut me up in a house, where they were already eight prisoners. These asked me about myself. I told them, and asked them about themselves. They told me they had been on board a certain ship, going from Sanf or Zabaj. They had suffered a gale, and twenty of them escaped in a boat, and arrived at this island. The natives had seized them, had drawn lots for them, and had already eaten several of them. Considering that, I realised I was in greater danger than I had been with the giant shepherd. It was some consolation to have companions in misery. If I had to be eaten, death seemed nothing to me. We consoled ourselves that we had hard luck in common.
>
> Next day they brought us some sesame, or some grain that looked like it, as well as bananas, *samn* (clarified butter, *ghī*) and honey. They put it all in front of us.
>
> There, the prisoners said to me, this has been our food since we fell into their hands.
>
> Each one ate some of it to support himself. Then the cannibals came, and looked at us one by one, and chose the one that seemed to them to be plumpest. We said good-bye; we had already made our final farewells to each other. They dragged him into the middle of the house, anointed him with *samn* from head to foot, and made him sit in the sun for two hours. Then they gathered round him, cut his throat, cut him to pieces in front of us, roasted him, and ate him. Part of him was made into a stew, another part was eaten raw, with salt. After the meal they drank a drink which made them drunk, and went to sleep.

> Come on now, I said to my companions in misfortune; come, let us kill them while they are drunk. Then we can walk away. If we escape, glory to God! If we die, better to die than to remain in our present misery. If the local people recapture us, we cannot die more than once.
>
> My words could not decide them, and night fell without anyone leaving. Our masters brought us food as usual. One day, two days, three days, four days dragged on by without there being any change in our state. On the fifth day they took one of us, and treated him as before. This time, when they were drunk and asleep, we went and cut their throats. Each of us provided himself with a knife, some honey, some *samn* and some sesame, and, when night shrouded the earth in darkness, we escaped from the house.[25]

Some time later, they came across a shipwreck. They caulked the boat, made a mast from a tree, laid in a stock of coconuts and sweet water, and escaped to an inhabited island and thence to Basra.

Motifs in these two stories have been combined to create the composite figure of the cannibalistic shepherd and the enclosed house, cave, or compound that is the scene of the cannibalistic countdown. Buzurg bin Shahryār lived in a world in which Arab traders repeatedly crossed the Indian Ocean and sailed the China seas in search of exotic merchandise, jewels, spices, and articles of trade that would fetch high prices in the lands of the west. Cultural contact called up wonder in the presence of radical difference. It is not surprising that these sailors' yarns of the strange encounters they had with the peoples and marvels of the Indies should circulate through encyclopedias of marvels and travelers' tales. They were also used by the authors of sophisticated literary works such as the *Mirigāvatī* to create a sense of wonder and mystery, a fantastic landscape against which a heroic Sufi quest could be played out.

The particular tale at issue here, Sindbād's encounter with the cannibalistic herdsman, has been a subject of scholarly debate for some time. Antoine Galland, the first eighteenth-century translator of the *Nights* into French, noticed the similarities between the story and the episode in the *Odyssey*, and since then scholars have tried to show that the Arabs knew Homer and the Greek epics well. Indeed, the popularity of the *Nights* in the eighteenth century was also a measure of the wholesale adaptation of this markedly "foreign" material into the concerns of the age. The English essayist Joseph Addison, for instance, was an advocate of anything that was popular:

> In his capacity as prolific essayist and popularizer, Addison considered popularity a sign of worthiness and, accordingly, he found himself committed to digest the new genre and to pamper his audience's susceptibility by reproducing as many of Scheherazade's pieces as possible.

> It is true that Addison retold "The Story of the Graecian King and the Physician Douban" and the story of al-Naschar's daydreams to lecture his readers upon the usefulness of bodily exercise and the vanity of extravagant hopes; yet, the real significance of these and numerous other contributions lies in the fact that he lent the tremendous prestige of the *Spectator* to fiction in this mode.[26]

It is the ubiquity and inventiveness of this kind of fictive production that I wish to emphasize. Thus the first fictional universe of the Hindavī Sufi romances, the story of Lorik and Cāndā, was partially Ahīr in composition, partly drawn from the poetry and practice of the Gorakhnāth *panth*, and partly from song genres in regional dialects and local translations of Sanskrit literary theory. This rich mix enhanced its popularity in Hindavī and the popularity of the Persian *'Iṣmat Nāmah* or "Account of Chastity" that described Maināʼs sufferings throughout the Persian-speaking world, in elegantly rhymed couplets.

To return to the voyages of Sindbād: G. E. von Grunebaum declared magisterially in his *Medieval Islam* that

> instances... culled from the first four *Voyages* of the adventurous mariner can with certainty be assigned a Western, that is, a Greek source, at the very least in the sense that the motives, whatever the region of their invention, made their literary debut in Greek and were taken up and developed by the oriental narrator from the form they had been given by the classical author.[27]

Robert Irwin has contradicted this by invoking the survey made by the tenth-century bookseller and cataloguer Muḥammad Ibn Isḥāq al-Nadīm in his comprehensive list of literature in Arabic, the *Fihrist*:

> The ninth-century translator, Hunayn ibn Ishaq, was able to recite sections of Homer by heart, presumably in Greek, yet he never translated him into Arabic. Although there are indications in the *Nights* and in the writings of al-Biruni, al-Shahrastani and others that the contents of Homer's epics were known to some, Homer was only a name to the cataloguer Ibn al-Nadim, and neither the *Iliad* nor the *Odyssey* was translated into Arabic until the present century.[28]

The question is not as simple as these contrasted views make out, however, and entails a brief excursus into the exceedingly complicated history of the *Arabian Nights*, the *Alf Lailah va Lailah*.[29]

The work is first noticed in *Murūj al-Ẕahab* ("Meadows of Gold"), by the geographer al-Mas'ūdī (896–956), who mentions that there

> are collections of stories that have been passed on to us translated from the Persian, Hindu, and Greek languages. We have discussed how these were composed, for example the *Hazār Afsāneh*. The Arabic translation is *Alf Khurafa* ("A Thousand Entertaining Tales").... This book is generally referred to as *Alf Layla* ("A Thousand Nights'). It is the story of a king, a vizier, the daughter of the vizier and the slave of the latter. These last two are called Shirazad and Dinazad. There are also similar works such as *The Book of Ferzeh and Simas* which contains anecdotes about the kings of India and their viziers. There is also *The Book of Sindibad* and other collections of the same type.[30]

Al-Nadīm's *Fihrist* also mentions The *Nights*, and gives a slightly longer synopsis of the frame-story of the Persian *Hazār Afsānah*.[31] His account is an early version of the familiar frame-story, in which a king named Shahryār, much disenchanted by the faithlessness of women, marries a fresh virgin every night and has her beheaded in the morning. Once his marriage is arranged to an intelligent woman named Shahrāzād, who has a helper or sister in the palace called Dīnārzād or Dunyāzād, she begins the cycle of telling him a tale every night and breaking it off before morning. The basic narrative anticipation on which the frame-story is built propels the reader along with the king, in expectation of the more astonishing entertainment the next night will bring.

The last of the books that al-Mas'ūdī mentions, *The Book of Sindbād*, is not the cycle of tales that concerns our familiar sailor. It is, rather, a cycle of stories about the wicked wiles of women, and is available to us in multiple versions. In the words of W. A. Clouston:

> The leading story of the 'Book of Sindibád,' or the 'Seven Wise Masters,' is briefly as follows: A young prince having resisted the importunities of one of his father's favourite women—his stepmother in the European versions—like the wife of Potiphar with Joseph, she accuses him to the king of having attempted her chastity. The king condemns his son to death; but the seven vazírs (or wise men) of the king, believing the prince to be innocent, and knowing that he is compelled by the threatening aspect of his horoscope to remain silent for seven days, resolve to save him till the expiry of that period, by each in turn relating to the king stories showing the depravity of women, and the danger of acting upon their unsupported assertions. This they do accordingly, but the woman each night counteracts the effect of their tales, by relating stories of the deceitful disposition of men; and so each day the king alternately condemns and reprieves his son, until the end of the

seventh day, when the prince is free to speak again, and the woman's guilt being discovered, she is duly punished.[32]

Exhaustive analyses of the migrations and transformations of this story, as well as its origins in Indian stories, have been based on the accounts of al-Mas'ūdī and al-Nadīm and on its extant versions.[33] The frame-story of the entire *Hazār Afsānah* has also been demonstrated to have been put together from two or three Indian frame-stories.[34] However, not much attention has been paid to the other Sindbād cycle, which concerns the adventures of the sailor and merchant of Baghdad.

Sindbād in Sanskrit

Could both versions of the Sindbād cycle have been translated from Sanskrit?[35] Al-Nadīm's *Fihrist* contains a tantalizing textual ambiguity about translating Sindbād's story into Arabic from Indian sources: "There was the book *Sindbādh al-Ḥakīm* ('Sindbād the Wise') which is in two transcriptions, one long and one short. They disagreed about it, too, just as they disagreed about the *Kalīlah wa-Dimnah*. What is most probable and the closest to the truth is that the Indians composed it."[36] The word used in Arabic for the two forms of the book, the larger (*al-kabīrah*) and the smaller (*al-ṣaghīrah*), is *nuskhah*. This word can have a range of lexical meanings: an edition, a copy, a manuscript, an example or exemplar, a transcription, and so on. Therefore one cannot say whether two books, each named after the main character Sindbād, were extant in ninth-century Baghdad, or merely two forms of the story of the seven wise masters and Sindbād. Perry states in exasperation: "It is impossible to say with any certainty what was meant by these terms, or whether either of the two editions to which they refer can be identified with any extant version of the book."

If we turn to an earlier set of stories, we get some important, hitherto unnoticed clues to the story of Sindbād and his marvelous adventures. To follow the trail of Sindbād before he appears in the Islamicate world of the Indian Ocean, we must look to the history of transmission of another great compendium of stories, the eleventh-century Somadeva Bhaṭṭa's *Kathā-sarit-sāgara* ("Ocean of the Streams of Story"), a recasting of an earlier lost original called the *Bṛhat-kathā* or "Great Story."[37] Composed by Guṇāḍhya between the first and the fourth century, it was redone twice in Kashmir, once by Somadeva Bhaṭṭa and once by Kṣemendra in his *Bṛhat-kathā-mañjarī* ("A Bouquet from the *Bṛhat-kathā*," *circa* 1037). No one resembling Sindbād appears in these collections, but there is also a little-known Nepali Sanskrit recension of an abridgement of the *Bṛhat-kathā* called the *Bṛhat-kathā-śloka-saṃgraha* ("Collection of Verses from the *Bṛhat-kathā*"), which contains extensive accounts of the seafaring world of India and the islands of the eastern seas (*dvīpāntara*). The date of the text, the identity of its author, Budhasvāmin, and his religion (Buddhist or non-Buddhist) are matters of some controversy. His summary of the lost *Bṛhat-kathā* of Guṇāḍhya could have been composed any time between the fifth and eighth centuries.[38]

The *Bṛhat-kathā-śloka-saṃgraha* tells the story of the many voyages of a figure called Sānudāsa the Merchant, who travels around the Indian Ocean to many lands, sees many marvels, loves many women, and brings back cargoes of costly goods from dangerous and exotic places. As in the frame-story in Sindbād's narrative of his seven voyages, the setting for Sānudāsa's story is an evening's entertainment at his own home where he tells his guests about a beautiful and mysterious woman named Gandharvadattā. One of his guests has won her in a musical competition, and Sānudāsa narrates his travels to explain how he found her. He is the son of the rich merchant Mitravarman and lives in the ancient Indian city of Campā. He seems initially to lead a charmed existence, until his dissolute friends play a trick on him. First they make him drunk on lotus mead. Then they hire a prostitute named Gaṅgā to seduce him and to convince him that she is a nymph from heaven. Slowly, he becomes more and more enmeshed in her love, and squanders his entire family fortune on her. The procuress who manages the bawdy house where Gaṅgā lives eventually throws him out on his ear. He is forced to abandon his widowed, destitute mother and go on multiple sea voyages to restore his fortune. The general ethos of mercantile exploration and adventure, as well as many motifs and the frame-story, appear as they do in the Sindbād cycle: giant birds that carry sailors around and across the ocean, islands where ships anchor that turn out to be giant fish, and the many frightening and strange ordeals and experiences that are encountered in the islands of the Indian Ocean.

Sānudāsa's travels, set within the three oceans (*trisamudra*) of the Bay of Bengal, the Arabian Sea, and the sea between the islands, contain many details of the maritime trade of India. Voyages of groups of merchants in a profit-sharing venture are common, often bound for Suvarnabhumi, the Land of Gold (mainland Southeast Asia), or the islands beyond. The commodities they trade in include pearls, gems, gold, textiles, and spices. The historical processes that form the backdrop for these exchanges are the Indian Ocean trade along maritime networks that stretched from Rome to China,[39] the Indianization of the mainland and islands of Southeast Asia, and the establishment of Buddhist and Hindu kingdoms there, with the help of ritual specialists from India.[40] The trade and settlement of these lands are the context for Sānudāsa's difficult journeys, in which our hero has to use all available modes of transport. These include what the Sanskrit grammarian Pāṇini classified as *aja-patha*, a path so steep and inaccessible that it can be negotiated only with the aid of a goat. (Other kinds of paths are those that can be negotiated with the aid of birds, the gods, and so on.)[41] Coming to such a crux on one journey led by the caravan leader Acera, Sānudāsa faces, on a narrow mountain pass, a traveler coming from the other side on his goat. Unfortunately there is only room for one of them to pass.

Here the larger cultural frames of the encounter are brought into play. In a sermon as long as the *Bhagavadgītā*, the caravan leader Acera urges Sānudāsa to an act of cruelty, just as Kṛṣṇa did with Arjuna. Sānudāsa is reluctant to kill another man, but in the end he strikes the other man's goat lightly across the legs and both man and goat sink into the dark mountain precipice. When the caravan reaches the other side, they come to a river and rest. The story, narrated by Sānudāsa, continues:

> When the leader woke us up, our eyes were still heavy from too little sleep. "These goats," he said, "have to be killed. We shall eat the meat; the skins we turn inside out and sew up to form sacks. Then we wrap ourselves in these sacks—no room for squeamishness here, it will only delay us!—in such a way that the bloody inside is turned outside. There are birds here as large as the winged mountains of legend, with beaks wide as caverns. They come here from the Gold Country. They will mistake us for lumps of meat and carry us in their beaks through the sky all the way to the Gold Country. That is what we must do."
>
> I said, "It is true what people say, 'Throw this gold away that cuts your ears!' How could I be so cruel as to kill my goat, this good spirit that has saved me from peril as virtue saves a man from hell? I am done with money and done with living if I have to kill my best friend to save the life he gave me."
>
> Acera said to the travelers, "Everyone kill his own goat. And take Sānudāsa's goat out of the way." One of the traders took my goat somewhere and came back with a goatskin hanging from his stick.[42]

The adventure that follows is played out in the Arabic Sindbād cycle with giant birds, lumps of meat, and diamonds. Sānudāsa's objective, however, is the Land of Gold:

> ... Soon all the heavens were filled with huge gray birds thundering ominously like autumn clouds. Under the wind of their wings the heavy tree trunks on the mountain were crushed to the ground as though they were the mountain's wings being cut by the blades of Indra's arrows. Seven birds swooped down and carried the seven

> of us, each with his heart in his throat, to the sky. One bird was left without its share, and, cheated out of its expectations, it started to tear me violently away from the bird that had got me. This started a gruesome fight between the two vultures, each greedy for its own share.... I was torn between the two birds, passing from beak to beak and sometimes rolling over the ground. I prayed to Śiva. Their pointed beaks and claws, hard as diamonds, ripped the skin until it was worn like a sieve. I was dragged from the torn skin bag and tumbled into a pond of astonishing beauty.
>
> I rubbed my bloodsmeared body with lotuses and bathed. Next I made a thanksgiving offering to the gods and the fathers, and only then tasted the nectar of the pond. I sank down on the shore and lay until I was rested. My eyes wandered over the woods that had been the scene of prodigious adventures and forgot the anxieties of the battle between the giant birds, forgot them like a man who has escaped from the Hell of the Swordblades to stroll in Paradise. There was not a tree with a withered or faded leaf; not one was burned by lightning and brushfire or empty of bloom and fruit.[43]

After traveling through this and many other marvelous adventures, Sānudāsa eventually comes back home a rich man, like Sindbād. He finds that his ordeals have been planned by his family in order to teach him about the ups and downs of life in the world, or, one might say, the Indianized world system of the maritime trade among India, Rome, and the islands of Southeast Asia. Within his immediate cultural context, there are numerous other tales of cosmopolitan travelers that share some of the motifs and structure of Sānudāsa's journeys, such as the voyages of the merchant Cārudatta in the Jain Prakrit *Vāsudeva-hiṇḍī*.[44] As a narrative about coming of age, the travels of the dashing and well-traveled Sānudāsa the Merchant have affinities with stories about the education of the main character, analogues of which are found as far away from fifth-century India as the modern *Bildungsroman* and the European chivalric romance.

The Goddess of Maritime Trade

But what of the wonder, the astonishment at the marvelous others that sailors and merchants encounter? Is it all domesticated into the narrative of Sānudāsa's coming to maturity? If the trading world of the Indian Ocean produces stories like those of Sindbād and Sānudāsa out of maritime adventures, surely encounters with radical otherness must occur in other places in the literature of the region. Indeed, given the subcontinent's propensity toward deification, is there not a goddess of maritime trade?

In the adventures of a courtesan's daughter of a philosophical bent, the Tamil *Maṇimekhalai,* written by the merchant-prince Shāttan in the fifth century, we find another set of analogues to the ordeals suffered by the hero of Quṭban's *Mirigāvatī.* The heroine, Maṇimekhalai ("Girdle of Gems"), is named after a goddess who also appears in a few of the Buddhist Jātakas or stories of the Buddha's former births. In the words of Sylvain Lévi,

> Maṇimekhalā is the name of the heroine, but it is also the name of a deity who is her guardian angel. The young girl is the issue of a tragic love affair between a merchant and a dancing girl. She is the ideal of chastity, charity, and faith. She lives at Puhār, also called Kāverīpaṭṭanam, the port of Kāverī, situated at the mouth of the this river, which was one of the great markets between India and the Far East since the time of Ptolemy at the end of the second century A.D.... The beauty of the young girl kindles love in the heart of prince Udaya who pursues her and intends to take her away during the joyful tumult of the festival of Indra. Her tutelary deity Maṇimekhalā descends from the heavens to protect her. She carries her away over the seas to a sacred island called Maṇipallavam.[45]

The adventures of Maṇimekhalai, who discovers an inexhaustible magic bowl on the island and escapes from Prince Udaya's clutches to travel to Java, offer fascinating glimpses of the maritime networks that criss-cross the Indian Ocean and reaffirm the importance of the sea trade in the prosperity of the region. Presiding over the sea as guardian divinity was the goddess Maṇimekhalai, whose worship was celebrated in the Tamil port cities of South India.

One episode from the text, which portrays Maṇimekhalai's gradual progress toward spiritual realization and the truths encoded in the eightfold path of the Buddha, is particularly striking. It occurs not in Maṇimekhalai's story, but in one of the subsidiary or "branch" stories that form the components of the larger narrative.[46] A merchant, Sāduvan, sells his wife's jewels to finance his affair with a dancing girl, is ruined, and goes to sea to seek his fortune. He is shipwrecked on a desert isle, where he encounters a people whom he labels Nāgas, subterranean serpents, or half-serpents (from the waist down; anthropomorphic above), a different species of humans in Indic schemes of classification:

> On reaching the island, Sāduvan was exhausted after struggling so long in the sea where the clouds come to draw their water. He painfully climbed along the sheer side of a mountain which plunged into the

> sea, and, reaching a tree hanging to a rock, he fell deep asleep. The cruel inhabitants of the country, who live naked without clothes and are known for their ferociousness, discovered him and woke him with their shouts of joy. They said, "This man has come here alone, with no companion. His well-covered body will make us an excellent meal."
>
> During his journeys, Sāduvan had had the chance to learn their dialect. Forthwith he spoke a few words. Surprised at hearing their tongue spoken, the savages kept at a distance without harming him and spoke warily."Noble lord of rare strength, hear us! Our chief lives nearby. It is better that you go and present yourself to him." Accepting their invitation, Sāduvan followed them to the Nāgas' guru, whose dwelling was a cave. He found him seated naked on a bed of boards, with his wife at his side, as naked as he. They could have been a bear and his companion. They were surrounded by small vessels in which palm-wine was fermenting. Other pots contained morsels of tainted meat. Whitened bones were scattered on the ground, spreading a fetid smell. Speaking to the chief in his own tongue, Sāduvan managed to impress him favorably. The chief invited him to sit next to him in the shade of a tree with dense foliage and questioned him as to why he had come.
>
> Sāduvan explained that he had come from the sea with its mighty tides.
>
> The chief then said, "This worthy man has undergone great tribulation without food, in the midst of the sea. He is weary and deserves our pity. Tribesmen! Give him a girl for his pleasure, some of our strongest palm-wine, and as much meat as he desires." Overwhelmed by the barbarous customs of his host, Sāduvan refused his benevolent offer. "Your words," he said, "hurt my ears. I can accept nothing of what you offer."[47]

What is significant in this episode is that Sāduvan is able to communicate with the others, since he speaks their language. He recognizes in their customs a social order and an uncivilized way of being. To him, their life is clearly based on eating human flesh, drinking palm toddy, and practicing free love. Yet there are hierarchies there, both the masculinist one in which girls are used for male pleasure, as well as the one based on the authority of the chief, who is their leader as well as their guru.

Despite the ease of communication, however, Sāduvan is horrified by the whitened bones and the fetid smell of rotting food and drink. Like the Arab sailors stranded on these distant isles, he is revolted by the dietary and sexual habits of the people he encounters. The common set of narrative motifs is here put to a different use as the interaction with the chief continues. The chief is furious at his refusal of the generous hospitality offered him, and asks what he desires aside from sex, flesh, and intoxicating liquor. Sāduvan explains:

> The sages who have attained a higher vision of things do not use inebriating drink and avoid destroying life. In this world, we can see that everything that is born has to die and whatever dies is born again. Life and death are phenomena similar to the states of sleeping and waking. Those who have accomplished meritorious acts are reborn in a better world and sometimes know the delights of earthly paradises, while those that committed evil deeds descend into the infernal world where they undergo unspeakable tortures. Such is reality, and this is why wise men give up intoxicating liquor and refuse to feed on the flesh of living beings. These are the facts you should consider.[48]

The Nāga chief is not convinced, but Sāduvan goes on to explain the Buddhist doctrine of reincarnation to him, showing him how it is necessary to practice nonviolence (*ahiṃsā*) in order not to incur harmful *karma*. In a technique common to most preachers who seek to popularize their religious doctrines (*dharma*), he explains how they can modify the *dharma* to suit their ways. They are not to kill travelers who are washed up on their shores, or to eat them. Even Sāduvan recognizes the futility of preaching vegetarianism to cannibals, however, so he allows them to eat animals that have died of old age.

In a final dialogue, the now-converted cannibal chief acknowledges the appropriateness of the virtuous path that Sāduvan has taught them, and offers him in exchange cargoes of aloes and sandalwood, bales of cloth, and precious gold and gems looted from wrecked ships. The language of value and exchange permeates this last moment of encounter. In the words of the chief,

> "We will follow this virtuous path that is appropriate for us here, and you take these precious things that are appropriate for you there. Often in the past we have eaten shipwrecked people. We got all these valuable things from them. Take these fragrant woods, soft clothes, piles of treasure, and other things."[49]

This moment of barter, the true *dharma* for cargoes of gold and precious goods, encapsulates both the supposed naïveté of the peoples that Indian merchants and Buddhist monks encountered throughout the islands of the eastern seas, and the Indian hegemonic drive to civilize the "savages." Sāduvan's encounter with the Nāgas is part of the larger narrative of Maṇimekhalai's realization of the ultimate value of spiritual renunciation.[50] Any sense of wonder is tamed by the grand scheme of Buddhist philosophy, and by the practical prescriptions left behind by Sāduvan. The tale fits well into the larger historical process by which Indianized rulers and states tamed the jungles and peoples of the Southeast Asian mainland and islands in order to build kingdoms based on rice cultivation and grand schemes of irrigation, as well as splendid temple complexes and palaces such as Angkor Wat and Borobudur.

Fantastic Exchanges

Before we return to the marvels of the *Mirigāvatī*, one final question: Did these cross-cultural encounters and exchanges always end in the victory of the civilizers? Were the indigenous people and the marvels encountered by travelers always subordinated to various schemes of literary representation or religious doctrine? Were the Indian travelers and merchants ever overwhelmed by radical cultural difference? A last example, one final story, from the Buddhist Jātakas in Pali, a set of texts that precede both the *Bṛhatkathā-śloka-saṃgraha* and the *Maṇimekhalai*, should demonstrate that the exchange was not always favorable for the traveling merchants. In the "Valāhassa-Jātaka," the Buddha relates a story that is ostensibly about the magical powers of women to tempt practitioners away from the path laid down by Buddhist doctrine. The story is about the she-devils (*yakkhinīs*) that inhabit a certain town on the island of Lanka. They command powers of illusion through which they can make shipwrecked merchants imagine they are seeing a prosperous city of human beings, with peasants tending fields and herds of cattle grazing peacefully. Whenever a ship is wrecked on their shore, they go up to the merchants carrying food, with their children on their hips. They make them believe that their husbands have all gone away to sea and they have long since despaired of their return home.

Once the merchants are under their spell, they make them believe that they would make good wives, and they take them home. The Buddha relates the experiences of a group of five hundred merchants:

> The she-devils came up to them, and enticed them, till they brought them to their city; those whom they had caught before, they bound with magic chains and cast into the house of torment (*kāraṇaghare*). Then the chief she-devil took the chief man, and the others took the rest, till five hundred had the five hundred traders; and they made the men their husbands. Then in the night time, when her man was asleep, the chief she-devil rose up, and made her way to the house of death, slew some of the men, and ate them. The others did the same. When the eldest she-devil returned from eating men's flesh, her body was cold. The eldest merchant embraced her, and perceived that she

> was a she-devil. "All the five hundred must be she-devils!" he thought to himself: "we must make our escape!"[51]

He is able to convince only half of the merchants of the necessity of flight, and 250 traders elect to stay back on the island. Since their ship is in pieces, however, the others cannot make their escape until a magic flying white horse appears, who is the Bodhisattva or Buddha-to-be in a previous birth. As the horse flies through the air, he calls out repeatedly, "Who wants to go home?" Two hundred fifty merchants climb up on his back and lay hold of his tail and mane, and by his power he carries them to their home. The merchants who are left on the island are devoured by the she-devils.

This text gives the story motif of the encounter with the cannibal islanders a gendered slant, and the only possible salvation is through the supernatural intercession of the Bodhisattva. This tale of gendered terror refracts a set of experiences common in the trading world of the Indian Ocean: meeting with strange groups of people on distant isles. The Buddha uses this incident only to point out the nature of *māyā* or illusion, and the salvific power of his own intervention. What is remarkable is that the merchants here have no power to transform or civilize the cannibals, or even kill them; they have only the capacity to escape if they can recognize the true nature of the women they have encountered. In our own long trajectory of tales of cross-cultural encounters and marvels, it is fitting to stop at a place where the would-be civilizers have to flee in order to keep from being eaten, to preserve their lives.

In all these cross-cultural encounters, similar sets of narrative motifs are put to complex uses in the service of a religious, mercantile, or literary agenda. Fantasy and the fantastic are still inscribed in the metaphysics of the real and the imaginary, what Todorov called the "bad conscience of the positivist era." What is it that causes astonishment (*'ajab*) within different historical limits? For many cultures, fantasy does not mean hesitation between the real world and the imaginary one. The fantastic voyages of Sindbād, for whose marvels scholars have even tried to find "real" scientific and geographical analogues,[52] are a useful indicator of how mercantile and ideological purposes can be mixed with the experience of wonder.

Sindbād's voyages were probably put together with a frame-story inspired by the travels of Sānudāsa the Merchant and embellished by many narrative motifs and marvels taken from diverse sources and collected in encyclopaedic books of the wonders of the cosmos. The final adventure of the hero of the *Mirigāvatī*, which involves ingenious mechanical devices, or automata, is evidence of the reinscription of these marvels or *'ajā'ib* in the regional literary traditions of India. The prince comes to a place of enchantment and great danger, a moonlit palace built by magic, where he sees a wondrous sight. Four doves appear in the palace, twisting about and then turning into four beautiful women. They speak a mantra, and beds appear and walk up to them. The beds are made ready for sleep without any human hands. Another mantra is spoken, and four dancing peacocks appear. They turn into men and sit on the beds with the women, laughing and flirting and spending the night in pleasure. After four watches of the night have gone by, a runner appears to them and reports that the herdsman has been blinded. The prince realizes that they are connected with the evil cannibal, and flees in terror. He runs as far and as fast as he can. Finally he reaches a shady tree, and sits under it considering what to do next. He has passed through five near-death experiences, and proved himself as a seeker by purifying himself of fear and lust and holding to the path of truth and trust in God (*tavakkul*).

Sindbād's voyages and the travels of the Prince as a yogi appear in many unlikely and unexpected places, from Homer's *Odyssey* to the nineteenth-century versions of the *Arabian Nights*, from sailors' yarns told in the coffeehouses of Basra and Baghdad to the ancient Indian tales of Sānudāsa the Merchant. This suggests not (or not just), as Roland Barthes puts it, that "narrative is everywhere, like life itself," but that the travels of narrative motifs mark the many ongoing interactions between the peoples and languages along the rim of the Indian Ocean, the global economy of the Islamicate world system. People exchange stories as easily as trade goods, technology, food and spices, music, craft techniques. In a global economy where there is constant movement between sultanates and kingdoms, it is no surprise that we can locate the ordeals of the Prince of Candragiri, told in a *desī* Hindavī romance, within these narrative exchanges of wonder, hostility, negotiation, alterity, desire.

In examining how the formulaic fantasies of the Sufi romances are structured, and where the narrative motifs come from, my concern has not been a merely antiquarian dissection of sources. These stories have both a motor and an aesthetic purpose. Rather than a large schematic allegory, shorter sections of the text like the Prince's quest are allegorically suggestive of particular Sufi values. Narrative in the Hindavī Sufi romances comes out of and adds to deep and long-standing storytelling traditions. The intensely local world of the Jaunpur and Delhi sultanates and the literary genre of the eastern Hindavī romances are thus part of the larger global pattern of exchange and cultural encounter that characterizes the world of the Indian Ocean. The fictive, even when constructed within an anti-mimetic poetics, indicates the historical experience of the encounters with radical otherness that characterize a world with plural cultures, languages, and religions. The poets of the Hindavī romances reinscribe the Arab sense of the marvelous into a concrete historical agenda as well as a genre grounded in a transcendentalized aesthetics. The fantastic in the Hindavī romances makes the reader hesitate between the illusory domain of visible events and the palpable reality of Allah as the mysterious and invisible essence of the world of phenomena.

5

The Landscape of Paradise and the Embodied City: The Padmāvat, *Part 1*

Landscapes of Conquest and Piety

Narrative requires a spatial expansion, a spreading out of consecution over place. The Hindavī Sufi poets constructed distinctive fantasy landscapes on which the quest of the hero is played out. The poets of the Delhi sultanate and the regional Afghan kingdoms represented Hindustan as a stage for triumphal narratives of conquest, a landscape to be conquered as well as eroticized. Moreover, the *premākhyān* poets lived in the mental maps of their imaginary homelands in Central Asia, Arabia, and Persia—homelands that grew more imaginary with every succeeding generation in India. How was their sense of the world as landscape, their space of fantasy and their fantasy of space, produced, and what did they try to achieve through it?

How is the Sufi poets' vision of the *'ālam-i ġhaib* or "unseen world" linked to the visible, historical world? What was the goal of their "production of space" (to use Henri Lefebvre's phrase[1])? In his daring and insightful attempt to found a unified theory of space, Lefebvre approaches the problem of the relationship between language and space through a threefold conceptualization. Distinguishing among spatial practices, representations of space, and representational spaces, Lefebvre analyzes the role of space in the formation of subjectivity as a triad: space perceived, conceived, and lived.[2] Living involves interacting with representational systems, systems of symbolism and signification that are built into social and architectural space. The "naturalness" of space is represented through linguistic systems: "Perhaps what have to be uncovered are the as-yet concealed relations between space and language: perhaps the 'logicalness' intrinsic to articulated language operated from the start as a spatiality capable of bringing order to the qualitative chaos presented by the perception of things."[3]

Lefebvre grounds this call for disarticulation, for opening up the "natural" landscapes presented to us in texts and other forms of social representation, and provides a thorough analysis of the material and ideological process of producing spatiality. His analysis, however, stops short at premodern and non-Western societies because of the difficulty of working out the relationship between representations of space and systems of ideology in these societies.

The problem involves historical agency, the formation of subjects within spatial or representational worlds. Studies of the religious and social orders represented in premodern landscapes have tended to focus on centered locative maps of the world. As Jonathan Z. Smith points out in his groundbreaking essay, "Map Is Not Territory":

> I would term [such a] cosmology a locative map of the world and the organizer of such a world, an imperial figure. It is a map of the world which guarantees meaning and value through structures of congruity and conformity. Students of religion have been most successful in describing and interpreting this locative, imperial map of the world.... In most cases, one cannot escape the suspicion that, in the locative map of the world, we are encountering a self-serving ideology which ought not to be generalized into the universal pattern of religious experience and expression.[4]

Although I share Smith's suspicion of the cosmological systems that are so frequently held to be homologous with the entire structure of a society, it is not a simple matter to open up political or religious cosmologies to include the incongruous or the out-of-place. Where there are significant overlaps between the symbolic vocabularies and discursive worlds of different religious groups, how is one to intuit the conflictual process of subject formation and social dialogue? Approaching this problem often requires reading the available map through a different optic, at an angle to the expressed purpose of the author.

Defying simple notions of religious purity and syncretism, overlaps between the symbolic systems of different communities and religious groups present the complexity of particular historical situations. In his study of a South Asian urban landscape and its contested representations through time, James Duncan remarks: "The translation of cultural beliefs into the visible motifs of landscape exteriorizes that which was hitherto internal vision and thus helps to shape, control, and reinforce the internalization of vision. It is through tropes such as these...that landscapes do much of their ideological work."[5]

The most thoughtful and excellent studies of sultanate India, such as those of Richard Eaton and André Wink, use the trope of "the moving frontier of Islamic expansion" to characterize the cultural history of the period. But the sultans who led armies in the name of Islam into India and acquired province after province viewed the world not as a frontier but as territory, to be conquered and assessed for revenue. Their efforts were authorized by the public rhetoric of Islamic conquest and the activities of Sufi shaikhs who set up hospices and sanctified the terrain of northern India. Yet this was not, as in other situations of colonization, *terra nulla* or empty land. It was an inhabited landscape with cultural, religious, and linguistic parameters that the incoming adventurers, soldiers, and missionaries had to negotiate. The dualistic rhetoric of conquest concealed a much subtler process of cultural and linguistic assimilation and internalization, as well as intermarriage and conversion to Islam on the part of local populations. It should come as no surprise, then, that the literary universes of the Hindavī romances should betray a concern with negotiating a local landscape, not as a frontier of conquest but rather as a contact zone, a place where many maps overlap.

The Sufi Landscape

The Chishtis and the other *silsilahs* of sultanate India sanctified the landscape by taking over particular areas as their *vilāyahs* or spiritual territories, the spiritual jurisdiction of particular shaikhs over particular areas. Patronized by local landholders and aristocrats as well as sultans, these *vilāyahs* made the physical landscape an object and vehicle of Sufi ideology and testify to the independent yet interlinked claims to authority of kings and Sufis. The notion of *vilāyah* was famously defined in the eleventh-century manual of Sufism, the *Kashf al-Maḥjūb* of Shaikh 'Alī al-Hujvīrī:

> You must know that the principle and foundation of Súfism and knowledge of God rests on saintship, the reality of which is unanimously affirmed by all the Shaykhs.... *Waláyat* means, etymologically, "power to dispose" (*taṣarruf*) and *wiláyat* means "possession of command" (*imárat*)... God has saints (*awliyá*) whom He has specially distinguished by His friendship.... He has made the Saints the governors of the universe; they have become entirely devoted to His business, and have ceased to follow their sensual affections. Through the blessing of their advent the rain falls from heaven, and through the purity of their lives the plants spring up from the earth, and through their spiritual influence the Moslems gain victories over the unbelievers.[6]

As Simon Digby has perceptively remarked about this notion of divine "friendship":

> Above the authority of mundane rulers there is ordained a hierarchy of those with supernatural powers, perpetually watchful over the welfare of all the regions of the world....[S]uch claims to the *wilāyat* of a specific territory were actively and vigorously pursued by Shaikhs in Khurasan in the eleventh and twelfth centuries, and the concept is very common in fourteenth century and later Indian Sufi literature....[W]ith this concept of territorial jurisdiction, it was difficult for a locally established Shaikh to tolerate the presence of another Shaikh of powerful charisma in his vicinity.[7]

Moreover, going to the provinces or territories conquered in *iqṭā'* entailed carving out a *vilāyah* for oneself in parallel with the armed conquest of Hindustan.

One of the ways in which Sufi holy men interacted with their Indian environment emerges from an episode in the life of Shaikh Aḥmad Khattū Maġhribī, the charismatic Chishti Sufi who was one of the four Ahmads famous for transforming the Gujarati city of Asawal into Ahmadabad. The slave general whom Sultan Fīrūz Shāh Tuġhlaq deputed there invited Shaikh Aḥmad to Gujarat. The shaikh meditated with some companions for some time in the mosque of Khān-i Jahān in Delhi. Ordinarily, Shaikh Aḥmad fasted all day, but his companions pressed him to make arrangements for food. He replied, according to his own account:

> "I am a guest of the holy Prophet (peace be upon him!) here, therefore I do not need to make any arrangements for food. Be responsible for yourselves." Therefore those people went to the bazaar, ate some food, and came back. We all read the night prayer together, and those people went to sleep. I washed my hands and began counting off my rosary beads. Suddenly, somebody called out, "Who is the guest of the holy Prophet?" I thought perhaps some other person was being called, so I remained silent. The voice came a second and third time, so I thought I was myself the guest of the holy Prophet, so I stood up in my place and went to the man who had called out. He was standing there with a platter in his hand. He said to me, "The holy Prophet has sent me to you." I spread out the skirt of my gown, and he dropped some dates from the platter into my lap, emptying the platter, and went back. When I ate those dates, they were so sweet that their sweetness and taste cannot be expressed in words. After that I also went to sleep. The dream I saw near dawn was the same dream which came to my three companions. The dream was this: The holy Prophet was present in a

> well-lit and well-ventilated place, and his magnificent companions were standing around him. A beautiful woman, well-dressed, perfumed, and loaded with jewelry, was in front of the holy Prophet. The Prophet said, "Accept this woman." I said, "Even my father did not accept her." The holy prophet gestured and said, "But your father is here, behind you." I turned around and saw 'Alī, may the kindness of God be on him, was standing there astonished with his finger in his mouth and he said, "Bābā Aḥmad gives you to her, accept her." I accepted the woman, and immediately the thought came to mind, "This woman is in actuality the world, and that all-powerful Allah, through the kindness of his holy Prophet, has opened the doors of the world to me."[8]

This premonitory dream, after which Shaikh Aḥmad did go on to Gujarat and become the leading Sufi of the province, points to a deep connection between land, sex, and territorial authority. Shaikh Aḥmad, a Sufi who consciously rejects the world, is offered control over the world in the form of an alluring woman. His control over the world is likened implicitly to his erotic ownership of the woman offered, and the whole episode occurs on the eve of his departure for a new territory. He has an invitation from Ẓafar K͟hān, who owes his rule to the conquest of the kingdom of Anhilwāṛā Paṭṭan in 1296 by the armies of Sultan 'Alāuddīn K͟haljī. Territorial jurisdiction and spiritual authority over the land are brought together as two linked facets of the Islamic presence; the spiritual and political conquest eroticizes the land or the world, and Allah gives it to the Sufi in the material form of a bejeweled bride. As Chapter 6 will make clear, in the narratives of contestation and hostility that laid claim to the land of Hindustan in the sultanate period, political and religious discontinuities were negotiated through exchanging women, tokens of symbolic honor, between opposing sides.

The Landscape of the *Padmāvat*

Several contextual and interpretative maps impinge on the landscape of paradise in the *Padmāvat* of Malik Muḥammad Jāyasī (c. 1540). The *Padmāvat* offers us at first glance a grand mystical progress through a fantasy landscape and an interior landscape of the self. The technical poetic language of the first half of the *Padmāvat* does much more than create a fantasy landscape; in the opening verses, Jāyasī praises Allah in terms that are fully engaged with and rooted in his local environment:

> *He made the agallochum, musk, and vetiver.*
> *He made both camphors, Bhīmasenī and Chinese.*

He made the snake, in whose mouth lives venom,
and also the charm that relieves a serpent's sting.
He made the nectar of immortality, which gives eternal life,
and also the poison that kills the eater.
He made the sugarcane, sweet and juicy,
and the bitter gourd, a creeper with many fruit.
He made honey, which the bee brings and stores,
as well as blackbees, moths, and winged creatures.
He made the fox, the mouse, and the ant,
and all those who dig and burrow in the earth.
He made demons, haunters, and ghosts.
He made ghouls, Devas and Daityas.
He made eighteen thousand kinds and species, all different in their genus.
After he had adorned all of creation, he bestowed food and provender to all [P 4.1–8].

This is a local, Hindustani landscape, and its use of words in dialect intrinsically reproduces the view from a small provincial center in Avadh or Bihar, in this case the town of Jais. It is a crowded landscape, full of the denizens of the Indian countryside, both natural and supernatural. The oppositional imagery can be appreciated only by an inhabitant of Hindustan who has tasted both raw juicy sugarcane and the *karelā* or bitter gourd that children hate to this day. The supernatural and natural beings are all local ones; if Islamic referents are intended they are reimagined and presented in Hindavī, hence transformed into locally comprehensible beings. There is a larger transformation of subjectivity indicated here, in which a "foreign" religion is reimagined in purely local terms.

As a practicing Sufi of both the Chishti and Mahdavi orders, Jāyasī tries, as Thomas de Bruijn notes, to convey his "vision of the unseen world."[9] His major strategy is to use words and imagery with multiple resonances to express the *rasa* of his story:

The poet, the bard, and the lotus full of rasa—
those who are near them are really far away,
and the distant are very close to them.
Too close, they are thorns with the flower.
From afar, they are drawn to them
like greedy ants to brown sugar.
The bee comes from the forest to smell the fragrance of the lotus.
The frogs will never get it, though they live next to the flower [P 24.6–8].

The poet uses the image of the lotus full of *rasa* to represent the poetic persona as a purveyor of the subtle fragrance of meaning. Aesthetic pleasure is connected with the scent of the unseen world, the *'ālam-i ġhaib*, which can only be hinted at through suggestion. Those who are too close to the flower see only its literal surface, while the fragrance of the invisible world spreads far and wide to connoisseurs who can appreciate it.

Jāyasī's own aesthetic purpose, his use of the Sufi poetics of *rasa* and *dhvani* (suggestion), fits well within the literary tradition of the Hindavī Sufi romances. How a work as a whole can suggest a *rasa*—the formation of an appropriate plot, the creative freedom to change a narrative pattern in accordance with the *rasa*, the creation of plot segments to enhance the *rasa*, intensifying and relaxing the *rasa* at appropriate moments, and using suitable figures of speech to enhance the *rasa*[10]—are all part of Jāyasī's poetic repertory. His use of many local symbolic vocabularies has often been read as a mark of his vernacular populism, or, even worse, his religious tolerance, a sign that he was, in A. G. Shirreff's phrase, the "prophet of unity."[11] Reading the text within the Sufi arrogation of the actual physical landscape demonstrates that Jāyasī was a competitor within a diverse religious and literary scene, not an apostle of religious unity. If his combination of elements constitutes a "syncretism," it is a competitive syncretism rather than a peaceful one.

Jāyasī's poem can also be understood within both Persian and Arabic systems of literary understanding. But there are other, more fantastic mappings in the *Padmāvat*, for Jāyasī creates a paradisal landscape on the faraway island of Singhala-dīpa as the locus of the action. This imaginary landscape conceals many levels of signification, since Jāyasī uses coded tantric, yogic, and *bhakti* devotional terms to suggest that the imaginary landscape on which Ratansen advances to attain Padmāvatī is also an interior landscape,[12] within which Ratansen crosses stages in the symbolic geography of the body (imagined as a city) to reach the Sufi goal.

Jāyasī has also an acute sense of social position, of power and the politics of social interaction in Hindustan. Of the status-ridden, male-centered, and martial world of the Indian Muslim élite, he has this to say in his prologue, in the section in praise of Allah:

He made man, and gave him dominion.
He made grain for food and provender for him.
He made the king who enjoys his realm.
He made elephants and horses and their trappings.
He made for him many pleasures.
He made some lords, and the others slaves.
He made wealth, from which comes pride.

He made longings, which none can satisfy.
He made life, which all desire always.
He made death, from which none escape.
He made happiness, and delight and pleasure.
He made sorrow and anxiety and doubt.
He made some wealthy and others beggars.
He made property, and adversity, and wealth.
He made some powerless, and others lords of strength and might.
From ashes did He create them all, and to ashes did He return them all [P 3.1–8].

This self-confident and dominant mapping of the cosmos and world intricately interweaves the metaphysics of Allah, the supreme lord of the universe, with the feel of inequality and social mastery. The verse weaves together motions and power structures to comment on social inequality while subordinating all to the monotheistic Creator; in other words, there is an established social order, in which kings and men are on top, and that is the will of Allah. No prophet of unity, our poet, but a man deeply conscious of social distinction and struggling to make the *Padmāvat* the most ornately poetic and elaborate Sufi romance in Hindavī, even through his protestations of modesty in the prologue.

Jāyasī's Lineage

A heated controversy rages around Jāyasī's precise Sufi affiliation. In the elaborate set of spiritual lineages in his prologue, he praises the Chishti Shaikh Ashraf Jahāngīr Simnānī (d. 840 A.H./1436–37 A.D.) as a radiant man of light who illuminated his heart with the light of love and divine knowledge. But the lifetime of this famous and peripatetic Sufi shaikh is separated from Jāyasī's own by several decades.[13] Sayyid Ashraf eventually settled down in Jaunpur after wandering through most of north India and Bengal. His legendary biography has a bearing on the *Padmāvat*, for there are episodes in this hagiography concerning the Chishti takeover of the physical landscape of Jaunpur as well as describing life inside the hospices that the poet Jāyasī frequented as a disciple.

Ashraf Jahāngīr's guide was Shaikh 'Alā' al-Ḥaqq, among whose disciples was Shaikh Nūr Quṯb-i 'Ālam of Pandua.[14] Three disciples of Ashraf Jahāngīr are mentioned in the prologue to the *Padmāvat*, a certain Hājī Shaikh, called a "flawless jewel," and Shaikh Mubārak and Shaikh Kamāl, referred to as "shining lamps" (P 17). The hagiographical literature provides details of a Kamāl Jogī, who becomes Shaikh Kamāl al-dīn; his tomb is outside Jais, and Jāyasī names him as one of his spiritual ancestors. Shirreff notes that "the tomb of Shaikh Kamāl, one of Jaisī's spiritual ancestors, on the outskirts of Jais, is locally known as Pandit Kamal's tomb."[15]

We know quite a bit about the identity and activities of this Pandit Kamāl or Shaikh Kamāl of the lineage descending from Ashraf Jahāngīr. Digby has traced, from Niẓām Yamanī's *Laṭā'if-i Ashrafī* (the "Subtleties of Ashraf," an early-fifteenth-century hagiographic collection about Ashraf Jahāngīr), a Kamāl Jogī who was tamed by the shaikh and converted to Islam. The episode underscores the competition between religious beliefs as well as the importance of establishing authority over particularly charged symbolic sites:

> Before Ashraf Jahāngīr took final leave of his *pīr*, Shaikh 'Alāuddīn 'Ganj-i Nabāt' Chishtī ("Treasury of Sugar") of Pandwa in Bengal, the latter showed him in a vision where his tomb would lie... [W]hen Ashraf Jahāngīr arrived in Jaunpur, the local landholder Malik Maḥmūd welcomed him and accompanied] him on his search for the place which he had seen in his vision. There then came into view a circular tank, upon seeing which the Shaikh said that this was the place that his *pīr* had revealed to him. [Malik Maḥmūd] suggested that there was a difficulty, in that a Jogi resided there, and the Shaikh could only settle there if he had the power to confront him. The Shaikh said, "The Truth came and falsehood perished: lo, falsehood perishes! What is difficult about driving out a body of unbelievers?"
>
> [When the Shaikh sent for his servitor Jamāl al-dīn Rāvat, he was reluctant to face the Jogi.] The Shaikh called him close to him and took some *pān* (betel) from his own mouth and put it in Jamāl al-dīn's mouth with his own hand. As Jamāl al-dīn ate the *pān* he was overcome by a strange exaltation, and he bravely set out for the battle. He went to the Jogi and said, "We do not think it becoming to display miracles (*karāmāt*), but we will give an answer to each of the powers (*istidrāj*) which you display."
>
> The first trick that the Jogi displayed was that from every direction swarms of black ants advanced towards Jamāluddīn; but they vanished when Jamāl-aldīn looked resolutely at them. After which an army of tigers appeared, but Jamāluddīn only said: "What harm can a tiger do to me?"
>
> At this all the tigers fled. After various other tricks the Jogi threw his staff into the air. Jamāluddīn then asked for the staff of the Shaikh and sent it up after it. The Shaikh's staff beat down that of the Jogi until it was brought to the ground. When the Jogi had exhausted all his tricks, he said, "Take me to the Shaikh! I will become a believer!"[16]

The text further refers to the newly converted 'Shaikh' Kamāl as a *jāmi'-i riyāẓat-i shadīdah va ṣāḥib-i mu'āmalah-i jadīdah*, which can be translated as "a combiner of severe disciplines and possessor of a new enterprise." As Digby indicates, these unusual epithets probably refer to the novel combination of "a previous mastery of Yogic techniques to which had been added progress on the Sufi path."[17] Shaikh Kamāl was given the spiritual charge of the town of Jais, and may have been the source of Jāyasī's use of yogic concepts and cosmology.

In addition to the spiritual descendants of Shaikh Ashraf Jahāngīr, a second Sufi genealogy is given in the prologue in the person of a Shaikh named Burhān, mentioned as the actual *pīr* of Malik Muḥammad Jāyasī. Shirreff traced Shaikh Burhān's spiritual lineage back to Shaikh 'Alā' al-Ḥaqq, Shaikh Ashraf Jahāngīr's *pīr*, via the alternative Bengali Chishti line descending through Shaikh Nūr Quṭb-i 'Ālam, Shaikh Husām al-dīn Mānikpurī, Rāja Ḥāmid Shāh, Shaikh Dāniyāl, Sayyad Muḥammad, and Shaikh Allahdād. In a brilliant rereading of the lines of the prologue which refer to Shaikh Burhān, John Millis has established that Shaikh Burhān was a Mahdavi. He belonged to the millenarian movement started by Sayyid Muḥammad Jaunpurī, who declared himself the Mahdī or "divinely guided one" in 1495.[18] The Mahdavi affiliation explains also the mystical content and ideas expressed in Jāyāsī's shorter poems such as the *Akhrāvat* ("Alphabet Poem"), an acrostic composed out of the elements of Mahdavi ideology, and the *Ākhirī Kalām* ("Discourse on the Last Day"), a foreshadowing of the events of doomsday and an expression of Jāyasī's millenarian faith.

Millis has persuasively suggested that Jāyasī's double affiliation was part of the common phenomenon of multiple initiation into *silsilahs*, and he links Shaikh Burhān to the historical Shaikh Burhān al-dīn Anṣārī of Kalpi:

> Jāyasī's Shaikh "Burhānū" was the historical Sufi saint Burhān ud-dīn Ansārī (usually called Shaikh Burhān) of Kalpi. He was quite famous; al-Badaoni has mentioned him in *Muntakhabu-t-tawārīkh*, as has Abu-l Fazl in the *Ā'īn-i Akbarī*. A fact which has been neglected by scholars studying Jāyasī is that Shaikh Burhān was quite likely Jāyasī's instructor or at least his inspiration for writing *premākhyāns* and for using Awadhi.... Jāyasī wrote that it was through Shaikh Burhān's help that he "found his talent," that his tongue was freed, and he began to compose "love poetry" (*prema kabi*). The possibility of Shaikh Burhān instructing Jāyasī on such literary matters is confirmed by what is known about the Shaikh. According to al-Badaoni Shaikh Burhān was not schooled in Arabic, but he did write beautiful poetry in Hindi on mystical topics...[S]uch verses in Awadhi by him have been found in old manuscripts.[19]

Shaikh Burhān al-dīn lived, in al-Badāyūnī's words, in a small, dark cell (*ḥujrah-yi tang va tārīk*), and was famous for his interest in Hindavī poetry and his skill in versifying and reciting it. He was also the author of the *Firāq Nāmah* ("Account of Separation"), a Hindavī work that has not survived. The qualities for which his verse was prized were, according to al-Badāyūnī, "exhortation, admonition, mysticism (*taṣavvuf*), the longing of the human soul for God (*ẕauq*), the Unity of God (*tauḥīd*), and withdrawal from the world."[20]

Jāyasī composed the *Padmāvat* under instruction from and among these teachers and shaikhs who were sanctifying the lush physical landscape of northern India and using Hindavī and other local languages to express their Sufi message. For the slow cultural transformation entailed in this process, both of the conquerors and of the conquered, we would do well to remember what Peter Brown has remarked on in another context, the Christianization of the late antique pagan world:

> [M]any...fourth-century persons lived in a universe bustling with the presence of many divine beings. In that universe, Christians, even the power of Christ and his servants, the martyrs, had come to stay. But they appear in a perspective to which our modern eyes take some time to adjust—they are set in an ancient, pre-Christian spiritual landscape.[21]

Within such a crowded landscape of beliefs as Hindustan as their stage, it is no wonder that the Sufis who traced their lineages and sources of authority back to Central Asia should also fight to establish themselves in an Indian landscape, squabbling over local holy places that were normally inhabited by yogis or ritual specialists of various descriptions, and who had to be conquered in order to sanctify Hindustan.

Cats, Yogis, and Conversions

Episodes of contest and conversion are common in the hagiographic literature of the Delhi sultanate,[22] and they point to two important features of Sufi ideology: the need to sanctify the physical landscape by establishing the *vilāyah* or spiritual authority of the *pīr*, and the competition with yogis and other itinerant holy men who laid claim to the same sites. This literature also offers an account of the transmission of spiritual authority through the takeover of the physical landscape with the collaboration of the local landholder. This site is the very one inhabited by a yogi, who has to be tamed and converted by the Sufi who intends to establish his hospice. Taking over a site meant that the previous inhabitants of the site had to accept the authority of the shaikh, a process that is often characterized as accepting or converting to Islam (*Islām qubūl kardan*). As we shall see, the term conceals a wide variety of positions and beliefs, putting into question any rigid notions of mutually exclusive religious worlds.

These patterns of interaction with the Indian landscape—the competitive production and marking of space in order to legitimate Chishti spiritual claims—continued beyond the period of the six great Chishti shaikhs who established the order in India. After this period, which ended with the death of Shaikh Naṣīr al-dīn Maḥmūd Chirāg̲h̲-i Dihlī in 1356, Chishti networks of authority and allegiance were dispersed throughout the subcontinent via the successors and disciples of the order. In the words of I. A. Zilli, the Chishtis were not

> an integrated and centralized empire but a conglomeration of smaller and bigger autonomous principalities. When a disciple was raised to the status of a *khalifa* (successor), he was entitled to enroll disciples in his own right and organize his affairs according to his own judgement; he was not at all answerable to anyone except his own *pir*, bonds of love and affection notwithstanding.[23]

Chishti networks of spiritual authority were changed further during the establishment of local regional sultanates such as Jaunpur in the fifteenth century and challenged by the consolidation of other Sufi *silsilah*s such as the Mahdavis, the Naqshbandis, the Shattaris, and the Suhravardis.[24] In 1540, when Jāyasī was composing his romance, the Chishtis were still well established in Delhi and much of northern India, though they were only one of the many groups competing for disciples.

The Chishti pattern of interaction with the physical landscape and its human and animal denizens continues to invest these living objects with supernatural causality. As Chishti holy men and their followers in competition with other groups construct hospices and tombs, even animals get drawn into this sanctification of the physical landscape, as the *Laṯā'if-i Ashrafī* makes clear in its account of the activities of Kamāl Jogī's pet cat in Shaikh Ashraf Jahāngīr's hospice:

> It had occurred to a disciple of Shaikh Ashraf Jahāngīr... that in former times there were Shaikhs whose glance had power over animals and birds; but he did not know whether such people existed at the present day. The Shaikh when he heard of this smiled and said: "Perhaps!" Now Kamāl the Jogī had a cat that sometimes used to pass in front of the Shaikh. The Shaikh ordered the cat to be brought into his presence and began a discourse on a holy topic. The Shaikh's face gradually assumed such an expression that all present were struck with fear. The cat also listened to the discourse and was so affected that it fell down unconscious. When it came to its senses again, it began to rub the

feet of the Shaikh and then those of its other companions. After this it became a habit that when the Shaikh was talking upon divine mysteries, the cat never left the holy gathering.[25]

From this account, which places the cat's spiritual perspicacity within the pedagogical practice of the shaikh, we learn that an animal may be a more devout believer than hypocritical human beings, and that the shaikh's power extends beyond the hearts and minds of human beings to the animal and heavenly worlds. This story echoes the famous couplets by the poet Ḥāfiẓ about the abilities of the cat of his rival 'Imād-i Faqīh, an animal that the jurisconsult had trained to follow him in all his actions when he said his prayers: "The Sufi lays his snare and opens his box of tricks; he inaugurates his deceits with the juggling heavens. O graceful partridge, who walks so proudly and prettily, don't be deceived because the ascetic's cat has said its prayers!"[26] The triumphant "conversion" of this yogi, and the sanctity and perspicacity of his pet cat, are emblematic of a larger process of spiritual conquest that includes the sanctification of the animals as well as the people in the local landscape.

Further anecdotes about the power of Kamāl Jogī, and of his cat, illustrate the ongoing work of training disciples and converting unbelievers:

> When travellers were about to arrive at the *khānaqāh*, the cat used to indicate their numbers by mewing. From this the servitors of the *khānaqāh* would know for how many guests to lay the cloth for a meal. At the time when the food was served, the cat also was given a portion equal those of the others who were present, and sometimes it was sent to bring members of the company who had been summoned. It would go to the cell of the person who had been called, and by mewing insistently or banging against the door would make him understand that the Shaikh had summoned him.
>
> One day a party of dervishes had arrived at the *khānaqāh*. The cat mewed as usual, but when the food was brought it appeared to be short by one portion. The Shaikh turned to the cat and said, "Why have you made a mistake today?"
>
> The cat immediately went around and began to sniff at each of the dervishes of the party. When it came to the head of the band, it jumped on his knee and pissed. When the Shaikh saw what had happened, he said, "The poor cat has done nothing wrong: this man is a stranger [an unbeliever]!"
>
> The head of the band immediately cast himself at the feet of the Shaikh and said: "I am a *Dahriyya* [materialist]. For twelve years I have travelled through the world wearing the garments of Islam. It was my

> intention that if it should so befall that some Sufi recognized me, I would accept Islam. Till now none has known my secret, but that cat has revealed it. Today I accept Islam!" The Shaikh taught him the words of faith, made him his disciple, and gave him austerities and spiritual exercises to perform. Some time afterwards, when it appeared that his interior self had been cleansed, the Shaikh honoured him with his *ijāzat* [license] and *ḳhilāfat* [succession], and entrusted to him the spiritual guidance of Istanbul [*sic!*].[27]

This fascinating and somewhat fanciful episode has several important implications. First, historical agents are capable of multiple religious affiliations. Changes from one system to another do not necessarily involve renunciation of all the beliefs previously held. Rather, the convert recasts the old beliefs and practices into a new framework, overtly Sufi and Islamic but containing important elements of other religious systems. As Richard Eaton has demonstrated, old-fashioned theories of force, political patronage, or the social liberation offered by Islam are simply inadequate to describe the mass conversions that took place.[28] Instead, we have to look at the evidence of slow growth and mutual assimilation, of generational patterns of change that span anachronistically imagined religious divides.

Second, once converted, disciples were routinely entrusted with the task of establishing the beliefs and spiritual practices of their *silsilah* in ever-more-far-flung territories. Aside from establishing the living presence of the *silsilah* in new lands and marking them as the spiritual territory of the *pīr* (*vilāyah*), Sufis were buried in tombs that became the focus of devotional cults for local populations. These concrete remains of holiness were perceived as reservoirs of spiritual power or *barakah* to be tapped by petitioners in any exigency. All who were associated with the cultus of the shaikh were drawn into these tomb cults, as the account of the martyrdom of Shaikh Kamāl's holy cat indicates:

> The cat remained alive until after the death of the Shaikh. One day the *sajjādah-nashīn* [successor] of the Shaikh had put a pot of milk upon the fire in order to cook *shīr-birinj* [rice-pudding], and it chanced that a snake fell into the pot. The cat saw this and prowled around the pot. It would not budge from the place and it mewed several times, but the cook did not understand and drove it out of the kitchen. When the cat saw that there was no way of making the cook understand, it leapt into the pot and surrendered its life. The rice then had to be thrown away, and in it the black snake was discovered. The *sajjādah-nashīn* remarked that the cat had sacrificed its own life for the sake of dervishes, and a tomb should be built for it. So the cat was buried near the tomb of Sayyid Ashraf Jahāngīr, and a structure was erected over its grave.[29]

Along with the tombs of Shaikh Ashraf Jahāngīr and Shaikh Kamāl, the cat's tomb too was presumably the object of veneration for devotees. It is not known whether the tiny structure still survives, but the account is a perfect cap for the dynamic of contest, conversion, and the marking of spiritual territory. A similar impulse may be seen in the drive to build aristocratic tombs near the dargahs of Sufi shaikhs in Delhi, the medieval necropolis *par excellence.* Jāyasī as a historical figure can be set within these larger impulses toward the competitive arrogation of Avadh and Bihar, the eastern extremities of the local landscape of Hindustan, and the production of a distinctive regional literary and devotional culture. This competitive cultural landscape and its politics are an essential part of the mystical progress of the hero in the narrative of the *Padmāvat.*

Language and Landscape: The Island of Singhala-dīpa

In the first half of the *Padmāvat,* the poet uses charged language—tantric, yogic, and *bhakti* devotional terminology—and symbolic vocabularies for spiritual progress and romantic fantasy, in order to map the paradisal landscape of Singhala-dīpa. Jāyasī begins by invoking the Sufi theology of manifestation in an elaborate formulaic prologue. God is the Creator, *Kartā* or *al-Khāliq,* who has two aspects, Manifest (*Prakaṭa* = *al-Ẕāhir*) and Hidden (*Guputa* = *al-Bāṭin*), which pervade all reality. Nature thus presents a visible, manifest face to the senses, but also has a hidden or secret side known only to God. Using an impassioned Hindavī phrase, Jāyasī calls Allah the *nirmala nāṉva,* the "spotless name" (P 8.7). The term is common to many north Indian devotional poets, but in the literary tradition of the *premākhyāns* this divine absolute is represented as the heroine of the love story, who is born in a paradisal landscape.

The story opens with a landscape of paradise, the fabulous Singhala-dīpa, where the heroine Padmāvatī will be born, a shadow of the Qur'ānic *jannah* on earth. The seeker has to cross many shifting stages within this symbolic geography, which makes use of whatever materials come to hand. In this case, since their closest contacts, competitors, and collaborators were the yogis, it is yogic symbolism that is deployed to express the distinctive Sufi agenda. Jāyasī's opening verse maps onto a woman's body the classical Indic cosmology of the seven islands or continents of the world. The reference to "description" (*barana*) as a reflecting mirror signals the momentary glimmering of the "true form" (*rūpa*) in its shining surface:

> *Now I shall sing a tale of Singhala-dīpa,*
> *and describe for you the beauty of Padminī.*

Description is a mirror, that is its specialty.
It shows whatever exists in its true form.
Blessed is that land, where the women are lamps,
and where God made Padminī incarnate.
Everyone describes the seven islands,
but not one comes close to rivaling that one.
The isle of lamps is not as radiant.
Serendib, the isle of gold, doesn't compare.
The isle of Jambu, the rose-apple tree,
does not come close to it, I tell you.
The isle of Laṅkā cannot match this reflection.
Kumbha, the island of pitchers, fled to the forest.
And the honeyed isle of Madhu destroyed man [P 25.1–7].

Jāyasī here uses the technique of resonance or suggestion as it is found in Sanskrit poetry. The parts of a woman's body sparkle like lamps in the mirror of suggestion: the lamps on the isle of lamps, *diyā-dīpa* (itself a pun on lamp and island, *dīpa*), could be eyes, while Serendib can also mean the island of ears, and the black rọse-apple in its epithet signifies a woman's raven hair. Laṅkā or *laṅka* is also waist, while Kumbha-dvīpa or "pitcher-isle" suggests breasts. The final image of the destruction of man lays the blame on the island of Mahu-sthala or Madhu-sthala, the secret parts of a woman. The figures used to reflect both form and landscape in the mirror (*darpana*) of Jāyasī's poem give the reader clues to multiple meanings. The best island of all is the home of the heroine Padmāvatī.

The ensuing description of the island approximates in poetic terms the Qur'ānic notion of paradise as a garden.[30] Here Jayasī creates an imaginary landscape, a lush garden with lakes, mango orchards, sandalwood trees, and beautiful pavilions set among colorful flowerbeds:

And if anyone ever comes to that isle,
he seems to approach paradise: on every side
are planted thick mango-groves,
rising from the earth to meet the sky.
Everywhere there are fragrant sandalwood trees,
world-shadowing, they make day into night.
Scented breezes blow in their pleasant shade
and even the hot month of Jeṭh feels wintry.
Their dark shade is so much like night
that the blue sky seems green under them.
When a traveler comes there, faint from sun,

he forgets his troubles, rests at ease.
Whoever finds this perfect shade,
never goes out to face the sun's rays.
Those dense mango groves, impossible to describe, are endless.
They blossom and bear fruit all year long, in an eternal springtime [P 27.1–8].

The language here reimagines into an Indian landscape the garden described in the Qur'ān. As Sūrah 77, verses 41–42, makes clear, the true believers shall enjoy the afterlife: "As to the righteous, they shall be amidst (cool) shades and fountains, and (they shall have) fruits, all they desire." The first couplet in this passage of Jāyasī's text, however, indirectly suggests *jannah* or paradise: "And if anyone ever comes to that isle, he seems to approach paradise" (P 27.1).[31] He uses the Avadhi term *kabilāsa* (Sanskrit Kailāsa, Śiva's heaven) to suggest the Qur'ānic *jannat*, and reimagines the heavenly shade and fountains and fruits as shady mango orchards (*amarāī*) blossoming and bearing fruit "in an eternal springtime."

Jāyasī goes on to recast into Hindavī the widespread Sufi convention that the birds of the world praise their Creator in their different tongues. The theme is already well known in Persian poetry, as for instance in Ḥakīm Sanā'ī's "Litany of the Birds,"[32] in which every bird has its own way of praising Allah. Similarly, Jāyasī uses Indian birds and their special calls to suggest that the new garden that praises Allah is in Avadh:

Birds live there, singing in many tongues,
joyous whenever they see the branches.
At dawn, the honey-suckers pipe up,
and doves cry out, "One alone, only You."
Mynahs and parrots play about chirping,
and pigeons coo in their own voice.
"My love, my love!" cries the papīhā,
and the warbler sings, "Just You, just You!"
The cuckoo coos "Ku-hu, ku-hu!"
while blackbirds speak in many tongues.
"I burn, I burn!" says the maharī,
the green pigeon, plaintive, cries his woe.
The peacock shrills pleasantly,
and the crows caw noisily.
In the whole garden, all the birds of the world sit praising the Creator, each in his own tongue [P 29.1–8].

The doves' cry of "One alone, only You!" and the songs of the warblers and *papīhās* fit the Qur'ānic attestation that "everything was created in order to worship God. Everything praises God with its own voice."[33] Even when the tongue is silent or lacking, the *lisān al-ḥāl* or "tongue of one's state" comes into play, a nonverbal language through which everything involuntarily and constantly praises God, by means of the "state" in which He created it. Peacocks and cuckoos, whose calls ordinarily signify the monsoons and the summer, here join a chorus of birds proclaiming the message of Islamic monotheism.

Jāyasī goes on to place his imaginary Sufi landscape within a full range of Indian religious renunciants, the competitors of the Chishti Sufis. The passage that follows harnesses the cartographic impulse in Indian religions, which reimagines place in terms of pilgrimage sites (*tīrthas*), to demonstrate the superiority of the holy landscape of Singhala-dīpa:

> *At every step, there are wells and step-wells,*
> *built fine with seats and broad steps.*
> *Everywhere there are beautiful lakes,*
> *named for all the fords of pilgrimage.*
> *Around them are well-adorned temples and pavilions,*
> *with yogis and ascetics all sitting in meditation.*
> *Some are sages, some are renunciants,*
> *some are focussed on Rāma, others stay for a month.*[34]
> *Some are on the path of celibacy,*
> *and some are Digambaras, who remain naked.*
> *Śaivas and wanderers and mendicants are there,*
> *and those who are disappointed in the path of love.*
> *Some cover themselves with ashes like Śiva,*
> *others go everywhere as mendicants.*
> *Some try left and right paths to the Goddess, Śakti.*
> *White-clad* sādhūs, *Jains, and forest-dwellers, adepts, seekers*
> *and* avadhūtas,
> *all sit there solemnly in meditation, burning their mortal bodies*
> *to ash [P 30.1–8].*

The variety and all-inclusiveness of Jāyasī's list spans the religious spectrum from naked Jains to devotees of the god Rāma, Nāth panthī yogis, wandering mendicants, tantric worshippers of the goddess Śakti, and all manner of holy men. All of them come to Singhala-dīpa in order to pray and mortify themselves at its holy sites, hoping to gain salvation at its fords and step wells.

Jāyasī next represents the spiritual center of Singhala as a holy lake, the Mānasarodaka or Mānasarovara. In Sanskrit poetic convention, the Mānasa lake near Śiva's mountain home Kailāsa is the true home of the soul, to which it flies from the toils and travails of this mortal world. The human soul is imagined as a migratory *haṃsa* bird or goose who longs to return home. But the Mānasarovara is also an internal station in the yogic body, just below the tenth door or *dasam dvāra* (the secret opening):

How can one look at Mānasarodaka, the holy lake?
It is fuller than the ocean, and fathomless.
Its water is pure and lustrous as pearls—
nectar does not equal that camphor-scented water.
They took rare lapis lazuli from Lanka
to make the broad ghats around the lake,
and set winding stairs on all its sides
for people to climb up and down.
Crimson lotuses flower there,
and each bloom has a thousand petals.
When a shell opens up to yield a pearl,
beautiful geese peck it up and play,
golden birds swimming on the water,
like pictures etched in gold.
Trees with ambrosial fruit grow on all its four banks.
Whoever sees that beautiful lake feels no hunger or thirst [P 31.1–8].

The geese playing on the lake, suggesting human souls in paradise, are "pictures etched in gold" among the crimson lotuses. The flowering lotuses with a thousand petals refer to the thousand-petaled lotus (*sahasra-dala kamala*) of the yogic body where the ascetic can taste the rain of nectar through controlling and redirecting spiritual energies. The easing of hunger and thirst is a reference to the frequently expressed Qur'ānic idea that believers in heaven will get ample food and drink and all their needs will be satisfied in the garden of delights (38:49–52, 79:41).

Jāyasī uses words that are loaded with resonances of the religious systems with which his audiences were familiar. He uses technical terms freely at various junctures to suggest invisible spiritual meanings. The birds warble the Names of Allah, and complain of their burning desire and their separation from their loves. All the flowers of India—the fragrant screwpine (*kevṛā*), the golden magnolia (*campaka*), jasmines of various kinds, *kadamba*, marigold, dog-roses, *maulasiris*, and citrons—add their color and fragrance to the enchanting island paradise and excite both the audience and the characters in the story to anticipate the erotic *rasa* (*śṛṅgāra*), here recast into Jāyasī's central aesthetic of *prema-rasa*.

Within this imaginary landscape of paradise, Jāyasī now invokes another symbolic plane: the interior landscape of the ascetic's body, imagined in terms borrowed from tantric, alchemical, and yogic practice. The most important of these symbolic vocabularies derives from the songs of the Buddhist and tantric

Siddhas, as exemplified in the *Cāryā-gīti-kośa* and the poems of Kāhṇipā and other adepts of the ninth and tenth centuries.[35] David White has noted the coincidence of these systems in the later literature of the Nāths, stating that "the language of... *haṭha yoga* is often nothing other than a projection of alchemical discourse upon the human body. The human body is an alchemical body."[36] Jāyasī evokes the sense of alchemical and spiritual transformation as he describes the island of Singhala-dīpa as an imaginary and an interior landscape. The *Padmāvat* is part of the historical formation of different sets of new Indo-Aryan poetic traditions out of the ascetic terminology and praxis of the Gorakhnāthī yogis, using Nāth *panthī* as well as Islamic terms.

Jāyasī's spatialization of the subtle body through the technical language of yoga and tantra creates the effect of internalizing vision through the tropes of a built and embodied landscape. His idea of the body as a city can be traced back to the songs of Kāhṇipā:

> *Kāhṇa, the kāpālī ascetic, entered into ascetic practice.*
> *He wanders in the city of the body in non-dual form.*[37]

The *Gorakhbānī* greatly elaborates on the "city of the body" (*deha-nagarī, kāyā nagara*), the symbolic body of the practitioner, who must master breath control to enter within:

> *Adept, such is our city, look there at its door!*
> *Gorakh declares this after much thought:*
> *the traffic in its market is inhalation and exhalation!*
> *Nine doors appear plainly to the sight,*
> *but the tenth door cannot be seen.*
> *Eighteen kinds of wood crown the fort,*
> *built up in countless chambers.*
> *Over the nine doors, chains are set and engines spin*
> *so that the fortress cannot be conquered.* [38]

The nine gates are the nine openings of the body, the mouth, eyes, ears, nostrils, and the organs of excretion and reproduction. The tenth door is the secret opening (*brahma-randhra*) between and above the eyes in the subtle body, through which the practitioner can enter the microcosmic universe within.

Similarly, Jāyasī's description of the city of Singhala represents both the yogic body and a lofty fortress:

> *The sun and the moon cannot fly over it.*
> *They hold themselves back and circle that high fort,*

else their chariots would crash into dust.
Nine gates it has, made of adamant,
with a thousand soldiers at each.
Five captains of the guard make their circuit,
and the gates shake at the tread of their feet.
...Golden slabs inlaid with blue lapis
are set as the stairways of the sparkling fort.
The nine stories have nine gates, each with its doors of adamant.
Four days it takes to climb to the top, if one climbs on the path of truth [P 41.1–3, 7–8].

The five captains suggest the five senses that guard the body. The four days suggest obliquely the four stages of the Sufi path, *sharī'ah* (following the law), *ṭarīqah* (the Sufi way), *ma'rifah* (gnosis), and *ḥaqīqah* (realizing the truth). Alternatively, they could be a reference to the four states of existence, *nāsūt* (the human world), *malakūt* (the angelic world), *jabarūt* (the heavenly realm), and *lāhūt* (absolute divinity).[39]

The next verse continues to map onto the paradisal city all of these esoteric Sufi terms for practices. The seeker has to climb up above the nine gates of the city/body to the secret or hidden tenth door, the *brahma-randhra,* through which he can escape into the *brahmāṇḍa* (the mundane egg = the cosmos) within:

Above the nine stories is the tenth door,
where the royal clock strikes.
When each hour is over, the clock is struck,
and so it continues through the watches [P 42.1–2].

The royal clock or clepsydra marks time for the fort/body. In the *Gorakhbānī*, too, the clock marks the unstruck or mystic sound within:

The clock of the unstruck sound reverberates,
and the two lamps of the primal light stay burning.[40]

Jāyasī uses these elements in new ways. In his text, as Millis notes, the clock's regular chimes suggest the regulation of the *bindu,* semen or nectar in the yogi's symbolic body, which the yogi must control in order to arrest time and mortal decay.[41]

In consonance with the absence of a consistent "allegorical" scheme, the next verse refers ambiguously to two rivers that flow in the fort. These could refer to the Qur'ānic rivers of milk, water, wine, and honey (47: 15) at the center of the garden of paradise, which believers enjoy in the afterlife: "In it are rivers of water incorruptible; rivers of milk of which the taste never changes; rivers of wine, a joy to those who drink; and rivers of honey pure and clear." Jāyasī's verse reads:

At the fort there are two rivers,
that flow perpetually with milk and water,
never-ending, like Draupadī's platter.
And there is a lake of crushed pearls,
its water like nectar, camphor its clay.
Only the King drinks its water,
and never grows old as long as he lives [P 43.1–3].

The lake of crushed pearls suggests the yogic *amṛta-kuṇḍa* or pool of nectar that is located between the eyes in the symbolic geography of the yogic body.[42] As Charlotte Vaudeville has noted,

> Potions of Immortality play a great part in Tantric theories. *Amṛt* (ambrosia) is conceived as a Liquor flowing from the Moon, i. e. the *sahasradal* formed by a thousand petals. The Nāth-yogīs believe that, from the *sahasradal*, flows a wonderful Liquor: by the blockade of the breath, the Yogī forces the liquor along the *suṣumnā-nādī* into the *sahasradal*, where it is drunk by the *jīvātmā*, the living Soul which then obtains Immortality.[43]

Jāyasī's rivers and the pool of nectar also resonate with this symbolism of the left, right, and central mystical channels (*nāḍīs*) in the subtle body, the *Iḍā*, *Piṅgalā*, and *Suṣumnā*. The goal of yogic and tantric practice is to channel vital fluid (*rasa* or semen), breath, and heat and to move it up the central channel until it reaches the thousand-petaled lotus between the eyes. In the words of David White, "It is this nectar that gradually fills out the moon in the cranial vault such that, at the conclusion of this process, the lunar orb, now brimming with nectar, is possessed of its full complement of sixteen digits...[T]his transformation of semen into nectar wholly transforms the body, rendering it immortal."[44]

If the body is a fort, its ruler the king is the soul (*rūḥ*), who can be transformed through the appropriate spiritual practices. The symbolism is again traceable to the *Gorakhbānī*, in which the allegorical references are made explicit:

Hari, emperor of the vital breath, is its lord,
thought is the qadi, *and the five senses are ministers.*
The mind and the breath are horse and elephant,

and knowledge is its inexhaustible treasure.
Call our body a city, and the mind is its minister.
Awareness is the captain on guard there—
no thief can even peep through the door!
...Gorakh, grandson of Ādināth and son of Matsyendra,
has established this city of the body.[45]

In Jāyasī's text, the King is well established in his city, with vassals who are lords of horses, elephants, forts, and men. The interlinear Persian gloss of the Rampur manuscript interprets these as the equivalents of the four chief Islamic angels: Jibrīl, Mikā'īl, Isrāfīl, and 'Azrā'īl.[46]

Jāyasī uses this vision of orderly rule in his own symbolic geography of the body, adding elements to the basic image. At the holy lake, the Mānasarodaka, flowers a golden tree:

Near the lake is a golden tree,
like the wishing-tree from Indra's heaven.
Its roots go down to the nether world,
and its branches up to heaven.
The vine of immortality grows on the tree,
who can attain that immortal creeper?
The moon is its fruit and the stars its leaves
and its radiance spreads till the limits of the city.
Only the one who does many austerities,
can taste its fruit, become a youth from an old man [P 43.4–7].

The celestial tree suggests the *sidrat al-muntahá* or lote tree of the furthest extremity, the magical tree that is radiant with God's light and is the point of demarcation between the manifest world and the unseen. The tree is here translated into Hindavī as the *kalpataru* or wishing tree of Indra's heaven, where the creeper of immortality (*amarabeli*) grows. The slender creeper suggests also the personification of *ṯūbá*, the tree of blessedness in the Qur'ān (13:29): "parallel to the *sidra* tree...the wonderful tree in Paradise, more slender and elegant than a cypress, and conveying shade to those who draw near to it."[47] Only the Sufi who can mortify himself can realize truth, harvest the creeper on the golden tree. Different audiences would understand this polysemous poetic symbol either as Indra's wishing tree or as the Qur'ānic lote tree.

Jāyasī adapts elements from Nāth *panthī* notions of the body, from the Qur'ānic idea of Paradise, and from Indian mythologies of heaven into a Sufi ascetic body that has its own logic of transformation into immortality. As

Annemarie Schimmel notes, "notwithstanding its enormous spatial extension, Paradise seems rather an enclosed garden, as were the gardens in the East: surrounded by God's greatness, the garden becomes...in mystical interpretation the *Weltinnenraum*, the inner aspect of creation."[48] Thus the landscape of paradise can refer simultaneously to Singhala, a fabled island, to the Qur'ānic idea of heaven, to the interior geography of the symbolic body, and to Jāyasī's distinctive embodied city.

The Parrot as Sufi Spiritual Guide

Within the landscape of paradise with its many resonances, the beautiful Padmāvatī is born, stunningly lovely and a reflection of the divine light:

> *Singhala is called a* dīpa, *an island,*
> *because such a lamp,* dīpa, *shone in that place.*
> *First that light was created in the heavens,*
> *then shone as a jewel on her father's forehead.*
> *That light descended into her mother's body,*
> *and in her womb it received great honor.*
> *As the months of pregnancy were fulfilled,*
> *she became more radiant day by day.*
> *Like a clay lamp shaded by a thin veil,*
> *just so her heart was shining with light [P 50.3–7].*

Here the poet suggests God's light, which is incarnated in Padmāvatī, yet separate from her as a lamp is separate from the cloth that screens it (*jasa añcala jhīne manh diyā/ tasa ujiyāra dekhāvai hiyā*). The verse also hints at the *mishkāt al-anvār*, the niche for lamps in the famous Light verse of the Qur'ān (24:35).[49] Rather than a brilliant star, however, the poet goes on to compare Padmāvatī to the moon in its splendor on the second day of the month (when there are no marks on it), for the moon functions as a mystical symbol.[50]

The princess is a *padminī* or lotus woman in terms of Sanskrit erotic theory, the best of the four classes of women. She personifies the ideal of beauty described, for instance, in the *Rati-mañjarī* or "Bouquet of Passion": "she is lotus-eyed, with small nostrils, with a pair of breasts close together, with nice hair and a slender frame; she speaks soft words and is cultured, steeped in songs and [knowledge of] musical instruments, dressed well on her entire body, the lotus-woman, the lotus-scented one."[51] The poet constantly plays on the similarity between Padminī and Padmāvatī, using both names for his heroine and frequently inventing ingenious imagery connected with lotuses. Her father, King Gandharvasen, keeps her in a seven-storied tower, where the golden parrot Hīrāman tutors her in all the traditional arts and sciences. He is the Brahmin among all the birds, wise beyond compare. Gandharvasen does not consider anyone equal to his daughter in status, and so will not accept any marriage proposals for her. As she grows older she begins to be tormented by longing, by desire for a lover worthy of her. Hīrāman offers to fly over all the lands of the earth for her, to find her an acceptable husband. The king hears of the dangerous knowledge that the parrot is imparting and threatens to have him killed. But the princess protects him by protesting to her father that he is but a bird who repeats what he hears others say, having no reasoning intelligence of his own. For the moment, Hīrāman is safe, but his days in Singhala-dīpa are numbered.

One day the princess and her friends go to play at the fabulous lake, the Mānasarodaka. The virgin girls are like innocent souls in paradise, and their play suggests the divine flashes of manifestation upon the beautiful surface of the lake. One of the games that they play is to dive for pebbles in the lake. Unfortunately, one of the women loses her jeweled necklace, but the lake generously gives it back. Jāyasī's description animates the landscape and makes the lake speak out to the players as a character who has been purified by a touch of divine beauty:

Said the lake, "I have gained what I desired.
Beauty, the philosopher's stone, has touched me.
I have become pure at the touch of their feet.
Seeing their beauty, I have become beautiful.
A sandal-scented breeze came from her body.
I have become cool, my burning anguish is gone.
I don't know who brought this fragrant breeze here,
but my state is now pure, all my sins are lost."
Instantly, he gave up the necklace.
Her friends picked it up, and the moon smiled.... [P 65.1–5]

Beauty (*rūpa* or the Sufi quality of *jamāl*) functions as a philosopher's stone, turning lead into gold, mud into pure water, human beings into spiritually realized beings. Padmāvatī's participation, in consonance with the imagery describing her birth and incarnation, suggests the unfolding of divine essence into the world of phenomena. The sight of her beauty is enough to cause anxious lovers to swoon and lakes to bloom with lotuses.

But all is not well at the palace, for Hīrāman the parrot sees a large, ferocious cat on the prowl. He flees from his cage in terror and flies away to the forest, where he lives happily in the trees with the other parrots. Padmāvatī is informed, and mourns the empty cage Hīrāman has left behind. She and her friends think he is dead. Meanwhile Hīrāman is trapped by a fowler who walks around in the forest to catch birds with a decoy tree whose foliage artfully conceals forks smeared with birdlime. The parrot is sold to a Brahmin merchant who has arrived from Chittaur, where King Ratansen rules. The Brahmin sells Hīrāman to King Ratansen for a hundred thousand rupees, and the King makes the parrot his favored counselor in all matters. One day, when the King is out hunting, Queen Nāgmatī comes to the parrot and asks him who is the fairer, she or the fabled Padmāvatī who lives in Singhala-dīpa. The parrot laughs at her and tells her that she is like the night compared to Padmāvatī's day. Nāgmatī is enraged, and fearful that the parrot may excite desire for Padmāvatī in the king's mind. She sends her maid to kill him, but the maid puts Hīrāman in a place of safety.

When Ratansen returns from the hunt, Nāgmatī tells him a cat has carried off the parrot, and he is distraught. He threatens Nāgmatī with death and commands her to produce the bird. Nāgmatī goes to her maid in desperation. Playing on the similarity between the words *rasa* and *risa* (anger), the maid tells her that anger produces discord and is the enemy of love. She has, however, saved the bird's life, and brings Hīrāman back. The king questions the parrot, and Hīrāman tells him about the path of truth (*sat*) and love. As Thomas de Bruijn notes, Jāyasī's use of *sat* or truth (*ḥaqq*) in connection with love (*prema*) draws on the Sanskrit words *sattva* (essence) and *satya* (truth, goodness), to suggest "the divine essence" within all human beings.[52] Moreover, the use of this Hindavī equivalent for *ḥaqq* (truth) suggests that the true meaning of the journey to Singhala-dīpa is the voyage of self-discovery.

Hīrāman begins the process of instructing Ratansen:
"O King, how can I tell you about it?
The isle of Singhala-dīpa is like Paradise.
Whoever goes there is entranced
and cannot return, though aeons pass.
In every house there are Padminīs
of all the thirty-six castes.
Every day is springtime, day and night.
All the flowers of the world
blossom there as fragrant maidens.
Gandharvasen is the mighty King,
like Indra among his apsarās.
Padmāvatī is his daughter.
and she is the most radiant of all lamps...." [P 95.1–6]

King Ratansen is immediately excited to hear of her, and asks the parrot to describe the beauty of Padmāvatī, and what he means by love, since his heart is now aflame with desire.

Hīrāman goes on to indicate that the path of true love is a path on which one has to annihilate oneself, a reference to the Sufi value of *fanā* or dying to one's lower self. He defines the connection between love and death:

> *"Listen, O King, and don't forget:*
> *love is difficult, and one has to die,*
> *to give one's head for it.*
> *If one falls into love's noose,*
> *the noose will not break,*
> *though many have given up their lives" [P 97.1–2].*

The king protests, and says that he is willing to brave all sorrows to gain the honey of love. He heaves a deep sigh and responds to the parrot's instruction:

> *"Do not speak these hopeless words!*
> *Even though love is so hard and difficult,*
> *whoever plays this game safely traverses*
> *both this world and the hereafter. . . ." [P 98.1–2]*

He demands that the wise parrot describe Padmāvatī's matchless beauty to him from head to foot. Hīrāman launches into an elaborate description of her charms, proceeding, in the manner of the *sarāpā*, from the dark fragrant locks on the top of her head to the jingling anklets on her feet.

The king faints away, overcome with passion, and when he comes back to consciousness, he wants Padmāvatī. The parrot advises him that the path of love is a difficult one, and in order to gain his desire he will have to renounce the world. Singhala-dīpa, says Hīrāman, functioning as his spiritual guide, cannot be gained by force or conquest; Ratansen will have to become a yogi and conquer it by austerities. Despite the protestations of his wife and mother, Ratansen sets out on the long and difficult voyage to Singhala-dīpa, along with a company of men of his kingdom who also become yogis. To gain the lovely Padmāvatī, they will have to pass through wild tracts and sail across the ocean. Jāyasī describes a path from the desert fastness of Chittaur through the jungles of central India to the kingdom of the Gajapatis of Orissa, keeping the kingdom of Vijayanagara to the south. There the company of ascetics meets King Gajapati, the lord of elephants, who offers to outfit them with ships for their sea voyage to Singhala-dīpa.

The Oceans of the Spiritual Voyage

To describe the voyage out from Jambudvīpa or India, Jāyasī uses the ancient Indian geographical convention of the seven continents (*dvīpa*), which are traditionally depicted as islands, each surrounded by a sea of a particular fluid. Thus, Jambūdvīpa has the sea of Lavana (salt), Plakṣadvīpa the sea of Ikṣu (sugarcane juice), Śālmalidvīpa the sea of Surā or Madya (liquor), Kuśadvīpa the sea of Ghṛta (clarified butter), Krauñcadvīpa the sea of Dadhi (curds), Śakadvīpa the sea of Dugdha (milk), and Puṣkaradvīpa the sea of Jala (fresh water).[53] Jambūdvīpa, the island of the rose-apple tree,[54] lies in the center of all the continents and the golden mountain Meru stands in the middle of it. These are all internal stations in the yogic subtle body. David Cashin has also noted that the Bengali Sufi poetry imagined these oceans as lying within the human body:

> There are salt, milk, and marshy (*jala*) rivers, these three oceans ever abide in the body. At the base of the tongue is a sweet river, the ocean/jewel (*ratnākāra*) [sic] in the eye, much is written in the Sind (concerning) the milk ocean. The milk ocean of semen flows forth through the penis, the salt river as urine flows with great force.... Consider now...the matter of the moons (*maṇi*), the moon (*candra*) is called *maṇi* in Arabic. These moons, menstrual blood and semen, are water. The same moons are spoken of in many languages. The body, color, passion, strength and mantra are derived from the moons, as is the length of life, as everyone knows. The lord has said, you will find it in the Quran, "I drink the fluid lest this blessing be poured out." The one who expends the moons by making love, his body becomes weak and powerless. The moons, as you know, are an ocean, a sea of nectar, when one drinks the nectar he becomes immortal, indestructible.[55]

Stressing the continuity of Indian Tantric practice with the Qur'ān (!) through an apocryphal quote, this author emphasizes the physicality of *rasa* and its links with the four elements that make up the human body. Certain Bengali Sufi *silsilahs* ingested these bodily substances ritually, very much in continuity with ordinary Bengali Tantric practice.

Other eastern Sufis chose to adopt and reimagine local terms such as *rasa* for their practice. One approach was to consider *prema-rasa* as a psychological process, a "means for transforming the attitude of the worshipper from separate to being in union with the divine":

> Of the many different *rasas* in the three worlds the actor of love (*premer nāgara*) is the essence of them all. By enjoying various *rasas* one dies, (having had) an unfulfilled life, dying having enjoyed the *prema rasa* is

the goal of a *sādhu*. The one who has a beginning in this rule, such a *sādhu* is highest, enjoying the lord's love (he) merges (with him).[56]

In these forms of Sufi practice, the adept eschews the physical consumption of bodily fluids: "Yogis do not consume the physical *rasas*. One does not gain perfection by the physical essences of the *cakras*. The precious flower of wisdom is entrapped by the consumption of *rasa*, this is why yogis do not eat them."[57] This is similar to the sublimation suggested by the Hindavī Sufi poets, who represented *prema-rasa* as a process for abstracting an emotional state and directing the soul toward God.

Jāyasī uses the ancient Indian spatial scheme of seven oceans to suggest seven stages through which the seeker must pass in order to reach the Mānasa lake, the true home of the soul. Jāyasī changes one of these oceans to what he calls the Kilkila, a sea thirty thousand *kosas* wide, spanned by a narrow bridge fine as a sword blade. To negotiate this dangerous bridge (a suggestive reference to the Pūl-i Sirāṯ across which the souls of the dead are said to cross the abyss to paradise), one needs a guide with whom one can travel in the path of truth. The company of saffron-clad ascetics finally lands at Singhala-dīpa after crossing the seventh ocean, their journey fulfilled by the glimpse of their true home, the Mānasa lake blossoming with lotuses. Hīrāman describes this lake, alluding to the fragrance of the lotus that has reached the bee, Ratansen:

> *In the lake of the sky, the lotus is the moon, and stars blossom like night-lotuses.*
> *You, O sun, have risen up as a bee—the breeze has brought you its fragrance [P 160.8].*

The scent of the invisible world, the fragrance of Padmāvatī, has reached Ratansen, who has come from afar like a bee to the lotus. The imagery recalls Jāyasī's characterizations of his own suggestive poetics, grasping the invisible scent of the lotus.

Hīrāman advises the king to meditate at the temple of Śiva while he goes to tell Padmāvatī about the sun he has brought to illumine her life:

> *O my queen, you are the moon, the golden bud,*
> *and he is the spotless sun, the gem [P180.1].*

The sun, moon, and lotus suggest the yogic practice of drawing down the moon, semen, and nectar or lunar energy through the ascetic heat of the sun.

In order to make the thousand-petaled lotus blossom, Padmāvatī must open herself to the newly arrived sun.

The king consults the deity in the temple, Mahādeva or Śiva, who tells him of the Sufi path of love (*prema*) and devoted service (*sevā*). The god proclaims the superiority of Jāyasī's aesthetics of the *rasa* of love:

> *Humans dwell in paradise through love.*
> *Otherwise, what are they? A handful of ashes.*
> *Love is permeated by the* rasa *of separation,*
> *just as the ambrosial honey dwells*
> *within the waxen honeycomb [P 166.2–3].*

The deity then redefines *prema, rasa,* and *viraha* for Ratansen; only through service can the seeker become a true inhabitant of the landscape of paradise (*baikuṇṭhī*) and taste the joys of love and separation. This involves constant breath control and difficult self-mortification; Ratansen practices austerities, and Padmāvatī's passion increases under the force of his yoga.

Padmāvatī comes to worship at Śiva's temple on the day of the spring festival, and wishes for a suitable bridegroom. Ratansen, meditating in one corner of the temple, swoons away at the approach of the heavenly maidens. She puts sandal paste on him and writes in magic letters over his heart that he fell asleep at the wrong moment; now he will have to satisfy his desire by climbing up, like the sun, across seven heavens to gain the moon. When he wakes up, he is distraught to find that the object of his desire has left, and in his desperation he builds a flaming pyre and is about to fling himself on it. The monkey god Hanumān takes the news of his impending death to Śiva and Pārvatī in heaven, and even the gods are astonished at his persistence. Jāyasī's characteristic strategy of using the symbolic vocabularies and even the gods of different religious systems in his own fantasy landscape is much in evidence.

Ratansen realizes the importance of a guide at the critical juncture he is in, referring to the *pīr* as Gorakhnāth:

> *Without a guru, one cannot find the way, whoever disregards*
> *this is lost.*
> *The* jogī *becomes a perfected* siddha *only when he meets*
> *Gorakhnāth [P 212.8].*

When Ratansen is in need of a guide to explain the intricacies of spiritual perfection, the god Śiva appears to him and imparts the true esoteric knowledge of the high citadel of Singhala that he will have to capture in order to gain his love. Śiva uses the coded word "crooked" (*baṅka*) to refer to a "curved duct" (*baṅka nāla*)[58] within the yogic body along which energy (*kuṇḍalinī*) flows:

The fortress is as crooked as your body.
Examine it and see: you are its very reflection.
One cannot gain it through fighting and obstinacy.
Only he wins it that knows himself.
There are nine gates within that fortress.
Five guards roam all around it.
There is a tenth door, a secret vantage point.
Its ascent is difficult, its way is crooked.
Only he who can penetrate the secret
can breach the fort and climb through like an ant.
Beneath the fort there is a passage
and a fathomless pool, within which is the path
of which I speak now to you [P 215.1–6].

Śiva thus explains the symbolism of the nine doors of the embodied city through coded words that refer to the yogic subtle body and the practices for transforming it. The poet characterizes Śiva's instruction as the *siddhi-guṭikā*, the magic pill of the Nāth *panthī*s that transforms the seeker and gives him the eight powers or *siddhi*s.

Śiva tells the king the method of restraining his breath and his mind in order to get through the tenth door and reach the secret pool of nectar, the *amṛta-kuṇḍa* that is within him. Śiva's instruction also reveals that the Chishti Sufis are not actually becoming yogis. They adapt some of the concepts and practices of yoga, but the verse goes on to fit the yogic practices within the framework of the Sufi destruction of the ego and purification of the lower soul (*nafs*):

The tenth door is like a palm tree.
Only he who reverses his vision can see it.
... Suppress your breath and control your mind.
If you are to die, destroy yourself first!
Speak outwardly of worldly things,
but secretly, fix your mind on love.
Everyone is drunk saying, "I, I!"
But when there is no "you," there is only God.
For the man who has once died,
what is death? Who can kill him?
He is himself the guru and the disciple,
he is everyone, yet all alone [P 216.1, 2–7].

To progress on this mystical path, the king-turned-ascetic must destroy egotism and fix his mind on the beloved even while conducting the affairs of the world. As Śiva puts it, "When there is no 'you,' there is only God." The king is enlightened by Śiva's instruction, and although his body has wasted away, Padmāvatī and Hīrāman feed him a magic herb ("Sanjīvanī") to bring him back to life from his ascetic mortification.

Ratansen Reaches Padmāvatī

Once enlightened and revived, the king breaks into the fortress with his yogis. Padmāvatī's father is outraged and has them bound and brought into the city to be burnt at the stake. But Ratansen is not disturbed by the death sentence and does not swerve from his meditation on Padmāvatī. The princess, like Ratansen, is afflicted with *viraha*, and through the force of meditation her desire for him increases to an unbearable heat. Her handmaidens bring her news of her hero, and she is ecstatic at the prospect of meeting her lover at last:

The lotus blossomed when he named the "sun,"
and the bee returned to enjoy its nectar and scent.
Her face shone forth like the autumn moon.
Her eyes, like wagtails on the wing,
began to play about seductively.
Her separation did not let her speak.
She died, but then her soul cried out.
Her heart trembled at separation's forest-fire,
but she could not reveal her hidden sorrow [P 251.1–4].

She is afraid that Ratansen might die, and sends her old nurse to summon the wise parrot Hīrāman to counsel her. Hīrāman tells her about the funeral pyre that is being built. He reminds her that she and Ratansen are bound in a reciprocal relationship of true love: now the yogi is the body and she is his soul. Death cannot touch him now, since he has annihilated himself in the being of his guide (*fanā fi 'l-shaikh*).

Throughout, Jāyasī refers to multiple religious systems; although Hīrāman has been Ratansen's guide, here the parrot calls Padmāvatī the guru:

"Why, Princess, you are his guide,
and he is your disciple.
...
You are in his body, he is in you.
Where can death find even his shadow?

That yogi has now become immortal, through entering into another's body.
If death comes it will see the guru in his body, salute him, and return" [P 258.1, 7–8].

Guru and disciple, lover and beloved, share the same refracted light. The identity of Padmāvatī with Ratansen thus conceals references to many layers of mystical ideology.

Ratansen is about to be impaled when Śiva appears in the form of a singer and intercedes for him to King Gandharvasen, Padmāvatī's father. He reveals the truth to the angry king, and tells him that Ratansen is a prince from Jambudvīpa or India, not a yogi at all. The king relents. Ratansen throws off his ascetic garb and puts on the clothes of a Rajput king. The wedding is carried out with great pomp and fanfare. When they come together on their wedding night, Jāyasī uses the language of alchemy or *rasāyaṇa* to describe their union:

My body of mica was made vermillion,
but you have put it in the fire again.
When one meets the beloved and parts, one burns with separation.
Either I will meet her and put out the fire, or die and thus find peace [P 294.7–8].

Fortunately, no such exigencies are needed. She responds by saying:

When I saw your beautiful form,
O yogi, you cast a spell on me.
You took control of my vision
with your magic pill of immortality.
You mixed the mercury and silver,
and enthroned your beauty in my eyes [P 314.4–5].

The *siddhi guṭikā* or pill of immortality is, in alchemical systems, treated mercury mixed with silver. Eating it reverses the flow of time, makes the body hard and immortal. They consummate their marriage in ecstatic union:

When they had revealed their true feelings
they embraced, just as gold mixes with borax.
The jogī *was an expert in the eighty-four positions,*
a taster of the six tastes, clever and accomplished [P 316.1–2].

They play the game of love, the poet says, like two besotted Sarus cranes, or the sun and moon becoming one in the heavens. In this manner they enjoy themselves through a whole year, an entire cycle of six seasons.

Jāyasī recounts their love play in verse full of puns, double entendres, and cunning allusions, employing vocabularies from different areas of social life. When Padmāvatī is flirting with Ratansen on their wedding night, she coyly refuses to believe that he is a prince at all. She uses the imagery of *causar* or *caupar*, a game of dice played on a cross-shaped board like *paccīsī*:

> *"Not so will I believe you are a prince.*
> *Take up the long dice and the round pieces—*
> *play with me and I will acknowledge you.*
> *When you throw a* kaccā *twelve points,*
> *you will wander round and round.*
> *Throw a* pucca *twelve and you won't stop.*
> *. . . The one who plays seven/the truth*
> *is a true player. Whoever throws eleven*
> *cannot be killed by anyone. In your mind*
> *you have fixed on the deuce, and so*
> *you wish to touch my two round pieces!"* [P 312.1–2, 4–5]

Here Padmāvatī uses the several throws of the dice game to suggest the game that is unfolding between the lovers. A *kaccā* or "raw" twelve is a simple throw adding up to twelve, but a "*pucca*" twelve is a throw of six, six, and one. This enables the player to move two pieces forward six spaces and one piece forward by an additional two spaces, a significant move in the game of love, while a *kaccā* twelve can improve the position of only a single playing piece, only one step further in the erotic advance. She puns further on the word *sat*, which generally refers to the true path but here refers to the throw of seven. Finally, paired pieces cannot be killed, so it is advantageous to keep pieces together by throwing the same number on more than one die. Padmāvatī, of course, is also suggesting that he wishes to touch her breasts, and the prince responds using the same vocabulary and protesting that he has already lost the game to her. In the lovers' final union, Jāyasī evokes the symbolic vocabularies of yoga, alchemy, tantric sexual practice, and Ratansen's quest through the geography of Singhala-dīpa as well as through the terrain of his own body.

The Return to Chittaur

Meanwhile, back in Chittaur, Nāgmatī is suffering from separation (*viraha*) and cannot bear her husband's absence. Burning flames of separation consume her body and let her know no peace. She cries out her agony through the twelve months of the year, recounting the torments that the changing cycle of seasons occasions her—a set piece of the genre, the *bārah-māsā*.[59] Her *bārah-māsā* is so intense in its affective power that she can find no messenger to take it to Singhala-dīpa. Finally, one night bird accepts the commission and blazes a great trail of fire as she flies to the distant isle in the south. Ratansen is in despair when he hears her, as he remembers his wife and the land of Chittaur. He has to return to earth, as fantasy has to contend with the reality of worldly life. He respectfully begs leave of King Gandharvasen. When Padmāvatī hears of it she is unhappy, because she does not wish to leave paradise to come down to earth, yet if her lover compels her she is helpless.

The couple set off for Chittaur with a cavalcade of horses and elephants laden with much wealth. On the way, during the sea journey, an evil demon attacks their ships and breaks them into pieces. Their lives are in danger, but a magical roc (*rājapankhī*) rises up and kills the demon so that they can continue. Padmāvatī floats away on a plank and is washed up half-conscious on an unknown shore. Ratansen draws his sword to take his own life, but the Ocean appears to him in the form of a Brahmin adorned with all the twelve auspicious marks and begs him not to commit this grave sin. Instead, he offers to take him to the shore where Padmāvatī is languishing and gives him five miraculous gifts: a gem impregnated with ambrosia for curing snakebite, a swan that can pick up pearls from water, a bird that surpasses all hunting falcons in its voice and vision, a philosopher's stone to transmute base metals into gold, and a valiant tiger cub for hunting.

They reach the shore, but before Ratansen can meet his wife the proverbially fickle goddess of fortune, Lakṣmī, appears to him as Padmāvatī and tests him by asking him to come to her. He recognizes that she is not his wife, and Lakṣmī is pleased with his faithfulness and reunites them. Padmāvatī is overjoyed and revives; the verse describing this suggests her descent from paradise and her embodiment in human form:

When Padmāvatī obtained her beloved,
it was as if the spirit returned to her body,
and a dead body was given back life.
She saluted him and offered herself up,
body and mind at her love's feet.
She said, "God has given me a new birth today,
from ashes I am restored to human form."[60]

Padmāvatī has come down to the human realm, compelled by her lover. Now that they are in the earthly world, her stunning beauty will have its effect on humans. When they reach Chittaur, Nāgmatī is overjoyed to see her husband again. But Padmāvatī is insanely jealous of Nāgmatī, and the two women fight bitterly over Ratansen's affections. He calms them down by sleeping with both of them in turn, and they are persuaded to live together in peace; figuratively speaking, the demands of this world and the next are fulfilled.

Ratansen does not become a yogi; he only adopts the guise of a yogi. The poet uses an "as-if" logic. When Ratansen takes off the yogic disguise, the poet tells us that his earrings were only attached with wax, not hung from pierced lobes as was the custom of the "pierced-ears" (Kānphaṭa) Nāth yogis. And although his austerities can be understood as if they were the yogic practices familiar to audiences within a northern Indian context, they suggest Sufi ascetic exercises intended, like the night prayers and fasts undertaken by Chishtis, to awaken the consciousness of the seeker to spiritual reality. The characters in the story, and by implication the Sufis, are not exactly yogis; they are like yogis, only better, as they can use yogic practices and language framed within a Sufi romantic poetics. Through this seeming logic Jāyasī spells out the Chishti Sufi claim to superiority within a local religious landscape.

The use of various symbolic vocabularies, physical and imaginative, tempered by their place within the Sufis' arrogation of the physical landscape of Hindustan, allows us a glimpse into the transformation of literary and religious categories in sixteenth-century India. The fanciful stories of cats, tombs, and rice pudding and the revelation of unbelievers are entertaining, but they also point to a larger process of religious competition. This *desī* Islamic tradition represents Islam in local dress, "as-if" imagined through local gods and goddesses, a thorough integration of a monotheistic faith into a polytheistic cultural landscape.

Tropes of landscape within the text narrativize place. The imaginary paradise of Singhala-dīpa and the subjective terrain along which Ratansen progresses to self-realization constitute an ideologically charged space. Those in the know could interpret Jāyasī's spatialization of internal vision through the loaded vocabularies that expressed hidden referents, the scent of the invisible world. Religious worlds can overlap, and agents themselves can assert notions of selfhood and self-realization through the shared language of competing systems and through literary suggestion, the subjects' own theory of meaning. This phenomenon becomes even clearer in the second part of the romance, when Jāyasī uses the motifs and themes of the Rajput martial literature and the narratives of the Islamic conquest of Hindustan to bring his own tale to a powerfully tragic conclusion. But that, as all storytellers say, is a story for another day....

6

The Conquest of Chittaur: The Padmāvat, *Part 2*

Padminī/Padmāvatī: Myth and History

The fall of the fortress of Chittaur, ruled over by King Ratansen and his lovely Queen Padminī or Padmāvatī, has inspired many contesting accounts since the Sultan of Delhi, 'Alāuddīn Khaljī, sacked it in 1303. Chittaur's doomed siege, its heroic defenders, and the queen's final act of self-sacrifice (*jauhar*, more precisely a Hindu woman's action of throwing herself alive on a funeral pyre so as not to be taken alive and desecrated by the Muslims) have become commonplaces in our thinking about the sultanate period. Amīr Khusrau, who accompanied the sultan on the historical campaign, describes it in his *Khazā'in al-Futūḥ* ("The Treasures of Victories"), a panegryical account of the Khaljī campaigns that subjugated northern India.[1] Khusrau does not mention any actual Padmāvatī or Padminī in Chittaur, although he refers to 'Alāuddīn Khaljī as Solomon and himself as the *hudhud* (hoopoe) who brought news of the beautiful Queen of Sheba to the fabled king.

Khusrau does insist, however, that King Ratansen's person and family were spared once the fort was taken and 'Alāuddīn's son Khiẓr Khān was made the governor of the newly renamed Khizrabad. Contemporary chroniclers such as Baranī and 'Iṣāmī are silent about Padminī[2] and instead recount that Chittaur continued under the military governors and garrison set there by 'Alāuddīn Khaljī, who went back to Delhi after forgiving Ratansen and his family for their resistance against him. The historical Padminī/Padmāvatī, if she ever existed, never sacrificed herself at the fall of Chittaur but continued to rule as the queen of a vassal lord. The question then becomes: Why do so many people need to invent stories about her fictive sacrifice? What are these stories enacting in their own contexts of articulation? Do they have a common ancestor?

These are complex and difficult questions, since they have a bearing on one's stance vis-à-vis the current-day nationalisms that inflect the politics of the subcontinent. The major source of the retrospective creation of Rajput chivalry and the ideological construction of the Rajputs as the last "Hindu" bastion of resistance against the invading Turkish armies, James Tod's *Annals and Antiquities of Rajasthan*, waxes eloquent about the lovely, if fictive, Queen Padminī and the tragic resistance of the defenders of Chittaur.[3] As Ramya Sreenivasan has made clear, Tod's work was

> ...governed by a fundamental desire to justify British intervention in the princely states of Rajputana, in its representation of late eighteenth-century Rajasthan as bordering on chaos, and of British intervention as bringing in immediate and sharp improvement. It was still enormously influential, however, not only in providing the intellectual basis for British intervention in Rajasthan, but also in the other task it achieved—systematically compiling all the accounts available to its author about the past and present socio-cultural life of the region, and fitting these into a structured understanding of Rajput society, even if it was fundamentally wrong in omitting all mention of Mughal suzerainty and therefore seeing all Rajput history as Hindu defence against Muslim invasion.[4]

Sreenivasan, in tracing the afterlife of Tod's work, as well as the reception and afterlife of the poem in its various translations and recreations, notes that although the story was not centrally taken up in Rajasthan, it became a stock narrative in late-nineteenth-century Bengali nationalist accounts. It fit well into the wider Hindu nationalist attempt to find past narratives of heroic resistance to imperial domination:

> It has been suggested that writers in nineteenth century Bengal were unable to directly criticize the imperial domination of the British, and that they therefore substituted another set of invaders....This substitution also fitted in neatly with the emergence of communalism with its consistent interpretation of all Indian history as perennial Hindu-Muslim conflict...[T]he story of the heroic queen committing jauhar also assumed significance in the context of the prolonged and intense debates about widow-immolation, in which gender was reconstituted as a key component of the intersecting debates on colonialism, nationalism, and social reform.[5]

The implications of this skewed and prominent later recasting of Queen Padminī's ritual sacrifice or *jauhar* are not hard to grasp. Tod's views imply that historians would do well to divide up the past into a dualistic battlefield between Hindus and Muslims, crusaders of brutal Islam against the brave chivalric indigenous defenders of the land.

Similarly, Aziz Ahmad, in his account of the "epics and counter-epics" of conquest, posits a fundamental disjuncture between the consciousness of Hindus and Muslims:

> Muslim impact and rule in India generated two literary growths: a Muslim epic of conquest, and a Hindu epic of resistance and of psychological rejection. The two literary growths were planted in two different cultures; in two different languages, Persian and Hindi; in two mutually exclusive religious, cultural and historical attitudes each confronting the other in aggressive hostility. Each of these two literary growths developed in mutual ignorance of the other; and with the exception of eclectic intellectuals like Abu'l Fazl in the 16th century, or the 17th century Urdu poets of the Southern courts of Bijāpūr and Golconda, the relationship hardly ever converged. The Muslim and the Hindu-epics of Medieval India can therefore hardly be described as "epic" and "counter-epic" in the context of a direct relationship of challenge and response. Yet one of them was rooted in the challenge asserting the glory of Muslim presence, and the other in the response repudiating it.[6]

This radically dualist view of genre and history, between groups of people who overlap significantly in both cultural and physical space, simplifies complex identities into a static, unchanging opposition. It leaves unasked all the questions about how people interact; how genre, history, and imaginative geography shape each other; and how emergent literary canons in the new Indo-Aryan languages are implicated in wider transitions in Indian history.

A further irony is that Jāyasī's poem is the earliest extant narrative of the last stand of Padmāvatī and Ratansen. He based the first part of the story on the Rajput bardic narratives of the *Pṛthivīrāja Rāsāu* ascribed to Cand Bardai, a complex text that comes down to us in four variant manuscript traditions that differ radically in length. Although the *Rāsau* relates events ostensibly from the twelfth and thirteenth centuries, none of the manuscripts predates the reign of Akbar (1556–1605), so that analyzing and dating the *Rāsau*'s language and component parts is a daunting task. The episode of Padmāvatī, called the "Padmāvatī Samaya," does not occur in the shortest versions. In outline, the brief episode relates how Padmāvatī falls in love with Pṛthivirāja Cauhān, King of Delhi, because her talking parrot describes him to her. When Padmāvatī's father arranges her marriage, she sends a letter through her pet parrot to Pṛthivirāja, who arrives with an army at his back to win his bride. After propitiating Śiva and Pārvatī, he elopes with her on his horse. On his way back to Delhi he has to face a Turkish army from Ghazni, which he defeats. He enters Delhi triumphantly, marries Padmāvatī, and lives happily with her. In form, the episode seems to repeat the narrative logic of Pṛthivīrāja's much more famous elopement with Saṃyogitā, the daughter of King Jaicand of Kannauj.[7]

Jāyasī may have had a bardic Rajput source (possibly a Jain one) for the second part of the story, the conquest of Chittaur, but that is now lost. Later versions such as the Bengali Sufi poet Ālāol's romance *Padmāvatī* and the reference to the fall of Padminī and Chittaur in the seventeenth-century verse chronicle, the *Muhta Naiṇsī rī Khyāt*, are based on Jāyasī's popular and widely circulated version of the Padmāvatī story.[8] If we accept the evidence that the story was first constituted in textual form by Jāyasī, we may ask: What is a Chishti Sufi poet doing inventing, or at least retelling, one of the key historical fictions of later Hindu nationalism? To answer this complex question, we need to consider how Jāyasī brings his tale to a conclusion through his elaborate reuse of the themes and motifs of the Rajput martial literature, and take into account the wider contextual resonances of his narrative resolution. In effect, Jāyasī takes up what was formulated as a literature of Rajput defeat and consolation for the loss of power and adapts it into a generic form created within the context of the consolidation of the power of the Turkish sultanate of Delhi.

Rajput martial literature is constructed around the notion of symbolic honor (*māna*), in part as a palliative for the loss of power and for the necessity of accepting Turkish overlordship and living within the new social and political arrangements. This symbolic honor is invested in the women of the lineage, and possession or exchange of these women becomes a key trope in the narratives of the fall of various Rajput forts to the invading armies. For Jāyasī to express this notion through the generic form of the Hindavī romance implies that he is taking the symbolics of defeat and reimagining them through a formula of success, performing a balancing act between Sufi concerns and the self-image and cultural sponsorship of the new aristocracy in the forts and garrisons of the Delhi sultanate.

The indigenization of this aristocracy, the Sufi sanctification of their new landscape, and their successful reframing and adaptation of local elements into new literary frameworks have been the subjects of previous chapters. But if the genre of the Hindavī Sufi romance implies a spiritually justified Turkish victory, what does the invention of a story of defeat by a poet writing for the Afghan inheritors of the Turkish imperium imply? At the level of the narrative that Jāyasī puts together, he uses the death of Padmāvati and Nāgmatī and the *jauhar* of all the women of the fort to suggest the supremacy of the Sufi values of self-annihilation (*fanā*), love, and asceticism. Jāyasī appends to the formulaic narrative of the hero and his two wives an account of Sultan 'Alāuddīn Khaljī's conquest of Chittaur, the city to which King Ratansen takes his Padminī after winning her in Singhala-dīpa. To the "matter" of a Rajput king's quest for Padmāvatī, princess of the fabled island of Singhala-dīpa, drawn from the bardic narratives of the *Pṛthivīrāja Rāsau*, Jāyasī adds the themes of the Rajput martial literature surrounding the *Hammīra Mahākāvya*, the *Kānhaḍade Prabandha*, and other poems that treat the resistance of various Rajput Ranas to the Muslim invaders.[9]

By using Sultan 'Alāuddīn K͟haljī and his lust for Padmāvatī as the cause for the siege of Chittaur, the second part of the *Padmāvat* takes up the sultanate narrative of the conquest and eroticization of northern India. Scholarly readings of this part of the text have been marked by an innocent acceptance of the dualisms of the public rhetoric of the Turkish conquest and its reversal by Jāyasī. To get around this we must isolate a broader cultural logic within which these representations of war make sense. Accordingly, in the first part of this chapter I lay out three other narratives from the period that treat various conquests of India and link war with the "traffic in women." The first is the Jain *Kālakācārya-kathā*, the story of Kālakācārya, the monk whose sister Sarasvatī was carried off by the King of Ujjain and who in response invited the Scythians or Śakas to invade India. Two other narratives from the period concern the erotic liaisons of the children of 'Alāuddīn K͟haljī: Amīr K͟husrau's *Deval Rānī K͟hiẓr K͟hān* and Padmanābha's retrospective account of the fall of the Rajput kingdom of Jalor. A reading of these narratives concludes the first section of the chapter, setting the stage for Jāyasī's elaborate reworking of these themes. The final part of this chapter presents a reading of the war over Chittaur and the ending of the *Padmāvat*, highlighting the multiple meanings of Sufi self-identification with the brave Rajput warriors against the wicked Turks. At issue is the Chishti Sufi claim to symbolic dominance over political rulers, as well as the ability of the Sufi poet and his readers to adopt the personae of Rajputs, yogis, and all the figures and concepts of the Indian cultural landscape. Conquering a landscape may be represented as an expression of dominance over a subject population, but eventually the conquerors find themselves transformed beyond recognition by the landscape they have taken over.

Three Contemporary Narratives of "Traffic in Women"

The theme of the lustful seizure of another's woman as *casus belli*, understanding the cause of conquest as the abduction of a woman, points to one dominant trope in all three narratives of conquest that were told and retold in Hindustan during the period, in Apabhraṃśa, Persian, and Sanskrit. The stories, composed and recited within communities of interpretation as diverse as monastic orders, Sufi shrines, and aristocratic courts, focus on the cultural logic of exchanging women. The texts objectify women as counters of exchange between opposing sides and embodiments of symbolic honor, to be fought over to the death. Political and religious discontinuities, within the cultural landscape of Hindustan, are negotiated through the taking and retaking of women, of images, of sites charged with religious meaning. How did this "traffic in women" inflect the poetics and politics of the Sufi romances? Did control over women and control over territory intersect on the ideal plane of the romance world? Women become poetic embodiments or symbols of divinity in the Sufi romances; seeing them arouses the desire for ascetic self-mortification in the hero's heart.[10] Viewed against the larger culture of Hindustan, this embodied image is the symbol through which the poet can evoke and address other social tensions, between conquerors and conquered, Sufis and kings. Such a negotiation of larger social meanings is possible only in a world in which women were understood as vehicles of ideology, a cultural logic whose misogynistic outlines these three narratives help us to delineate.

Kālakācārya, the King of Ujjain, and the Magic She-Ass

In our consideration of narratives leading up to the "absent origin" of the fictive *jauhar* of the Queen of Chittaur, it is fitting to begin with the *Kālakācārya-kathā*, itself endowed with the complex history of oral and literary renditions that W. Norman Brown has treated in his critical edition and translation. As Brown says, "It seems impossible to ascribe all the known versions of the Kālaka cycle to a single written source, whether that source should be one of these versions or some other lost original."[11] The story of Kālaka, who is supposed to have lived in 78 A.D.,[12] was put together before the tenth century and circulated widely in the sultanate period, in at least seventeen versions and redactions in Sanskrit and Jain Mahārāṣṭrī Prakrit.[13] The story, which formed the ninth chapter of the larger *Kalpa-sūtra*,[14] was recited at the Paryuṣaṇā festival in the month of Bhādrapada as part of a Jain ascetic regimen of moral instruction. Frequently illustrated and recopied in Sanskrit and Prakrit in the pre-Mughal period and later in Gujarati, the text allows us to see how an ancient set of concerns and narrative motifs is told and retold.

The *Kālakācārya-kathā* is divided into four episodic segments:

> In the first, we have Kālaka's conversion and initiation under [his preceptor] Guṇākara and the dealings with Gardabhilla, the wicked king of Ujjayinī, whose overthrow Kālaka effects with the help of the Sāhis (Sanskritized as Śākhis [Scythians/Śakas]). In the second we have the events at the city of Kings Balamitra and Bhānumitra, and the alteration of the date of the Paryuṣaṇā festival; in the third we read of Kālaka's reproof to his vainglorious spiritual grandson Sāgaradatta; in the fourth Kālaka expounds the Nigoda doctrine to Śakra.[15]

Brown has convincingly demonstrated that the later anecdotes are about two latter-day Kālakas, whom he dubs Kālaka II and Kālaka III, and that they were melded together with the episode of the Scythian conquest sometime before the tenth century C.E. The episode of conquest has always been an embarrassment for Jains because of its overt condoning of violence, so much against the Jain ethic of *ahiṃsā* or nonviolence.

Our Kālaka, as he appears in the "Long Anonymous Version" (earliest mss. copied ca. 1278 and 1279) that Brown deemed authoritative, is a young prince of the city of Dharāvāsa (Dhar).[16] Riding in the forest, he encounters a saintly Jain Ācārya named Guṇākara with his following of monks. Guṇākara teaches the young prince all the Jain moral teachings on right knowledge and right action. As if anticipating the necessary violence that will be the result of Kālaka's actions, Guṇākara's moral framework prohibits causes of sin such as the taking of life and emphasizes control over mind, speech, and body. The prince renounces the world. Guṇākara trains him and initiates him as a Jain Suri. Kālaka the Suri goes to Ujjain to preach Jain moral principles, and his group of monks is soon joined by a group of nuns that includes his younger sister Sarasvatī. One day King Gardabhilla spots her going to the latrine and forcibly abducts her into his harem (*anteura*, from Sanskrit *antaḥ-pura*, inner quarters).

Kālaka tries to teach the king the right path and urges him strongly not to besmirch his family and good name. Violating the wife of another is "forbidden like flesh of the body." But the lustful and infatuated king will not listen, and Kālaka swears a mighty oath to uproot him violently from his kingdom. He goes to the "Scythian shore" (*Śaka-kūla*) of the River Indus and mobilizes a group of ninety-six disaffected Śaka nobles to follow him south to the land of Hinduka. He then advises them to take Ujjain, the "key to the splendid land of Mālava." They invade the city, but on the eighth day the ramparts fall silent. Kālaka knows the secret: he reveals that the king is conjuring up a Magic She-Ass. Asses or donkeys are notorious for their lewd nature, and the king is also significantly named Gardabhilla or "Donkey," from the word *gardabha* (donkey). The Magic She-Ass he conjures up has "a mighty bray, and every biped or quadruped belonging to a hostile army that shall hear it will without fail fall down upon the ground vomiting blood from its mouth."[17]

Kālaka has a military solution to neutralize the Magic She-Ass, however. He instructs everyone in the army to retreat beyond the reach of the braying, a distance of two leagues, except for 108 sharpshooting archers. These he instructs to shoot as soon as they see the She-Ass open her mouth to bray, thereby preventing her from making a sound. They do so, and by her magic art the She-Ass now turns upon the man who raised her by sorcery, King Gardabhilla. She rained "urine and ordure upon the conjuror himself, kicked him, and straightway left." Kālaka attempts to follow the rout of Gardabhilla with a sermon on the evils of lust and violence, not to mention destroying a nun's virtue, but the king is so hedged about with painful *karma* that he will not listen and leaves the kingdom to wander in exile.

Among the Jain communities of interpretation that recited and recopied this story, it is easy to see that this tale would be immediately susceptible to allegorical interpretation. King Donkey can signify lust, his Magic She-Ass the world of sensory illusion, and the 108 archers can refer to the 108 precepts or rules with which delusion can be defeated. In the final exchange between Kālaka and the recalcitrant king, the monk curses him in punning language: "You are free on the spot. Go now, you, exiled from your land." The other meaning of this utterance is, "You are saved on the spot. Go now, you, no longer attached to the objects of the senses."[18] The story can thus be made to fit into a Jain moral framework of nonviolence and the overcoming of delusion through right perception and right action, despite the narrative of the brother who invites violent conquest because his younger sister, herself a chaste Jain nun, has been abducted and violated by a conqueror. Similar tales of the seizure or capture of women form the etiology of many other narratives from the sultanate period. The Jain tale therefore fits into a larger cultural universe in this period in which women are objects of exchange, trophies of war, or tokens of symbolic honor, a stereotypic logic of gender relations in which the erotics of sexual conquest coincide with martial conquest.

The Children of Sultan 'Alāuddīn Khaljī

The first accounts of Islamic conquests in northern India have two remarkable features: detailed descriptions of military warfare and the articulation of romantic desire between opposing sides. In the years following 'Alāuddīn Khaljī's accession to the throne of Delhi in 1296, the sultan repulsed a number of Mongol invasions into Sind and Punjab[19] and undertook a series of campaigns designed to expand his rule into the Indian provinces south of Delhi. In 1297, after defeating an incursion of Mongols into Sind, the sultan dispatched the generals Ulugh Khān and Nuṣrat Khān to Gujarat. They captured and looted the great capital at Anhilvāṛā Paṭṭan, also called Pāṭan, as well as the trading port of Khambāyat or Cambay. The temple at Somnath, famously sacked by Maḥmūd Ghaznavī, was again taken by the generals and its images smashed. Among the spoils of Gujarat were a handsome slave, Malik Mānik, later called Malik Kāfūr Hazārdīnārī; and Kaṉvalā Devī, the wife of Raja Karṇa of Anhilvāṛā Paṭṭan. Sultan 'Alāuddīn was infatuated with Malik Kāfūr, who became one of his leading generals and favorites, and he took Queen Kaṉvalā Devī into his harem. Both were assimilated into the booty of conquest, taken as prizes to the victor's capital to be his property, mementos of the acquisition of a province.

These military victories sent shock waves through the Indian kingdoms that were easy targets for the superior cavalry and arms of the Turkish armies.[20] The chroniclers and poets of the Rajput kings took up the task of making sense of the conquerors and the conquests, casting their poetic efforts in the form of Sanskritic *prabandha-kāvyas* (court poems) and other Indic genres. Their dominant concern in these texts was to preserve a sense of Rajput symbolic honor, especially in the face of recurrent defeat. They did this through narratives in which control over Rajput women was the key factor in the preservation of honor. In text after text, the Rajput men go into battle to fight to the death when the situation is beyond retrieval, and the women commit *jauhar* or ritual suicide rather than fall into the hands of the Turkish armies. In both Rajput and Persian representations, then, women were crucial as markers of victory or signs of preserved honor in defeat. Amīr Khusrau recounted these conquests and other victories in Bengal, Malwa, Telengana, and Dvara-samudra in his *Khazā'in al-Futūḥ*, a prose history of 'Alāuddīn's campaigns framed by elaborate panegyrics (*madḥ*) to the sultan and written in an ornately figurative style.[21] His *Deval Rānī Khiẓr Khān* explicitly linked the motif of conquest with romance, creating a fantasy where conqueror and conquered approach each other on the territory of the imagination as lover and beloved rather than as the spoils of war.

Two narratives from the period treat of the erotic liaisons of the children of the sultan 'Alāuddīn Khaljī, who came to the throne of Delhi after brutally murdering his uncle Jalāluddīn in 1296 and was one of the major figures in the military struggle over northern India that ensued after Maḥmūd Ġhaznavī's invasions into India. The prolific Amīr Khusrau, who was 'Alāuddīn Khaljī's court poet, composed a series of prose and verse narratives commemorating his patron's advances.[22] Among 'Alāuddīn Khaljī's opponents were the Rajput kings of Jalor, Ranthambhor, Chittaur, and the rulers of Gujarāt and Warangal. The bards (*bhāṭs*) of these rulers and their descendants also composed their versions of the Muslim conquests, including poems such as the *Kānhaḍade Prabandha* of Padmanābha, Nayacandra Suri's *Hammīra-mahākāvya*,[23] Naiṇsī's *Chitāi Vārtā*, and the cycle of the *Prithvirāj Rāsau* and related tales.

'Alāuddīn Khaljī appears as a character in some of the Rajput poems in which the topos of romance is directly linked with the wars he fought against the Rajputs and other Indian kings. His children's romantic entanglements, intertwined with military conflicts over territory, are the subjects of two other texts from the period that we are about to consider: Amīr Khusrau's *Deval Rānī Khiẓr Khān* (1316) and Padmanābha's *Kānhaḍade Prabandha* (1455).

Prince K͟hiẓr K͟hān and Deval Rānī

To begin with the view from the conqueror's court, Amīr K͟husrau's *Deval Rānī* is a Persian historical *maṣnavī* or verse narrative, which K͟husrau introduces with the usual panegyrics. The story begins when Prince K͟hiẓr K͟hān, the son of 'Alāuddīn, asks the poet to compose a verse narrative of his passionate love for Devaldī or Deval Rānī. The poet sets the plot in motion by mentioning the triumphs of 'Alāuddīn at Devgir and Sind, and then tells how 'Alāuddīn sent Uluġh K͟hān to Gujarāt. Rivers of blood flow as the region is brought to heel and Uluġh K͟hān destroys Somnath and the other cities of Gujarat (DRKK 64ff). The victorious army heads home through Jhain and Ranthambhor, bringing Kaṇvalā Devī home as a prize to the harem of 'Alāuddīn. As booty, she is a symbolic marker of the military triumph of Islam over Gujarat. But the queen is lonely in the new harem. She longs for her daughter Deval Rānī, who is just eight years old and her only surviving child.

Deval Rānī is sent for from her father, Raja Karṇa, in Gujarat, and love begins to grow between the young Prince K͟hiẓr K͟hān and the princess. The poet describes the progress of their love through a set of generic interruptions to the narrative flow of the *maṣnavī*. The prince and princess send lyric poems to each other, *ghazals* in Persian in the same meter and rhyme as the rest of the *maṣnavī* (*hazaj maḥẕūf*). The prince spends sleepless nights pining for the princess, and the courtship proceeds through *ghazals* that implore her to come to him:

> What radiant face is this that illumines my eyes?
> What fragrance makes this gathering a rose-garden?
> The moon in the sky does not have such a face,
> nor the highest heaven any fragrance such as this.
> I look at your face, which gives life to my life,
> but sends to my heart the news of its imprisonment! [DRKK 88]

He receives a curt reply from the princess: "Look at the age we live in, how can I do this? How can I open the doors of happiness to you?" (DRKK 89)

But passion is excited in Deval Rānī when her own youth begins to blossom. The poet describes this as a form of madness, in which love is expressed sometimes through the curve of an eyebrow, sometimes through the reproachful eyelashes of the beloved. Everyone in the palace notices the progress of the love affair as the two exchange *ghazals* through confidants, some of whom inform the prince's mother, the Malikah-i Jahān. Once she suspects the truth, she disapproves, and moves swiftly to separate the two passionate lovers by persuading the sultan to send Deval Rānī to the Kūshk-i La'l, the Red Palace. Deval Rānī herself, playing on the similarity of the Persian words for a tongue (*zabān*) and fire-ball (*zabānah*), wonders:

> *It is necessary for the grass to burn in the fire...*
> *but whose tongue has rained fire on me?*
> *Should one call it a tongue or a ball of fire? [DRKK 142]*

The prince's mother arranges his marriage with the daughter of her brother Alp Khān. The marriage is celebrated with great pomp and ceremony, with splendid fireworks, music, and dancing. But the two lovers are not happy apart from each other, and Khiẓr Khān cannot forget his childhood sweetheart.

Finally, some well-wishers persuade the queen not to sacrifice her son's happiness, and she allows the lovers to be married quietly. They are happy at last. The story, set in the context of conquest and war between 'Alāuddīn and various Hindu kings and based on historical personages, works through a simple narrative pattern of love followed by separation, resolved by love triumphant.[24] Even though Khusrau could have exploited the common oppositional trope of Turk and Hindu[25] effectively to refer to the historical context of the *masnavī*, he focuses instead on the simplicity and tenderness of longing and love within a political context of war and conquest.

But the happy couple's idyll is not destined to last. Amīr Khusrau originally ended his *masnavī* with the triumph of love and presented it to the prince in that form, but subsequent events compelled the poet to compose a historical epilogue bringing the story to a close. For Sultan 'Alāuddīn fell sick in 1315, and as he neared the end of his life he looked for a successor in his son. In Khusrau's narrative, the prince, rather than expressing any interest in generalship or statecraft after his marriage, spends his days happily with his beloved Deval Rānī. In these circumstances, the inevitable battle for succession begins between 'Alāuddīn's generals. One of them, the powerful Malik Nā'ib (the title of Malik Kāfūr, the handsome slave captured from Gujarat with Kanvalā Devī), falsely implicates Khiẓr Khān in a conspiracy against the sultan and has him imprisoned in Gwalior fort. He passes his time there tenderly with Deval Rānī, exchanging with her verses of *ġhazal* poetry such as these:

> *O friend who is in my heart, come and sit by me for an instant....*
> *If my days make me a prisoner, I would be happy*
> *to be imprisoned in the chains of your black locks [DRKK 254].*

In 1316, soon after the happy couple are imprisoned, Sultan 'Alāuddīn Khaljī dies. Mohammad Habib has summarized the ensuing events in Amīr Khusrau's narrative:

> Alauddin died soon after and the Malik Naib placed Shihabuddin 'Umar, the Sultan's youngest son, on the throne. At the same time he sent one, Sumbul, to blind Khizr Khan at Gwalior. The ex-heir-apparent...accepted his fate with a pious resignation. "He sat smiling calmly at the decree of fate instead of attempting to run away from it like a fool. 'Maybe, the Emperor is dead,' he remarked when Sumbul and his men, covered with the dust of the road, appeared before him...'But why this hurry with which you have come to do me honor in my prison?' His eyes, which were soon to be blinded, were moist with tears. 'I have no hope of regaining my freedom, for who will place his enemy on the throne? But if you have an order for depriving me of my life or my eyesight, I am ready.' Sumbul pleaded that he was a mere instrument in the hands of others...The prince willingly offered his eyes to Sumbul. They laid him on the ground; and when his eyes were pierced by the needle, the sockets were filled with blood like a wine-glass." Sumbul rushed to Delhi in haste to win the rewards promised for his deed,...[but]...within forty days of Sultan Alauddin's death, the Malik Naib was assassinated by the guards of the Palace, who elevated Mubarak Shah, a son of the late Sultan, to the Regency and, later on, to the throne.[26]

After his gruesome blinding, the prince lives on with Deval Rānī in the fort at Gwalior. Malik Kāfūr Hazārdīnārī, though powerful and a favorite of 'Alāuddīn, does not outlive him by more than forty days.

Mubārak Shāh consolidates his power against his rivals and rules from Delhi, until another palace conspiracy makes him determined to wipe out all potential opposition. He sends a message to Khiẓr Khān asking him to send Deval Rānī to his court, offering the prince his freedom in return. In the interchange between Mubārak Shāh and Khiẓr Khān, Deval Rānī becomes a pawn between the two men: she embodies Khiẓr Khān's life, love, and honor. Mubārak Shāh knows that Khiẓr Khān cannot let her go, and the prince's angry refusal gives Mubārak Shāh the excuse to order the prince's final execution. In the last scenes, the officers dispatched to kill the doomed prince chase him around his room, and then a low-born Indian attendant finally stabs him. The story comes to an end with the prince's burial in a tower in Gwalior fort, while Kanvalā Devi and Deval Rānī spend the rest of their days there together quietly.

In this symbolic resolution, the woman who comes as the spoils of war becomes the embodiment of tender love and the honor of a powerless and defeated prince. The love between the two, though it does not use the common imagery setting the fair Turk against the dark Hindu, is nevertheless articulated within the disputes over territory between Islamic and Indian rulers in the thirteenth and fourteenth centuries. Thus conquest does not simply mean brute appropriation of the spoils of war; K͟husrau uses the generic logic of the *masnavī* to play out the desire between social and religious others, setting up a cultural model for thinking about men exchanging women as they exchange kingdoms or provinces. Since the Persian text is spoken from the perspective of the victors, the subordinated woman is linked with the assimilation of new territory by conquest. As Kanwar Muhammad Ashraf notes, the "victor had a perfectly valid right of marrying the wives of the deposed Sultān, and there are records of such marriages against the express wishes of the wife or mistress in question."[27] Deval Rānī is taken as a prize that signals the public triumph of the K͟haljī rule, a rule that Amīr K͟husrau's ideal representation of kingship connects with the victory of Islam over unbelief. The woman is objectified as property, changing hands with the political transfer of power, but she is also the underpinning of the militaristic system of conflict over territory and booty. Discontinuities between political territories are thus transacted over the body of a woman, here represented as a focus of romantic desire.

Princess Furūzān and Prince Vīramade of Jalor

Such a fantasy about the intersection of geography, desire, and the body is also evident from a fictive romantic liaison between another of 'Alāuddīn's children, the Princess Furūzān, and an Indian ruler, Prince Vīramade of Jalor, set within the history of the siege and conquest of Jalor and expressed in verse by a Rajput poet. The *Kānhaḍade Prabandha* (KP) of Padmanābha, composed in 1455 in a western dialect of Apabhraṃśa, recounts events that occurred almost a century and a half before the poet's time. Padmanābha was a Nāgar Brahmin attached to the court of Akhairāja, the Chauhan Rajput king of Visalnagar. Although information about both the poet and his patron is limited, it seems from the text that they were living in the small town of Visalnagar after the treacherous capture of Jalor by the Lohani Afghans in 1394. Akhairāja was descended, through the Princes Vīramade, Megalde, Ambarāja, and Khetsi, from Rāval Kānhaḍade, the king of Jalor whom 'Alāuddīn K͟haljī defeated in 1311. In form, the poem is a *prabandha-kāvya*, the name for a courtly ornate poem in Sanskrit, Prakrit, or Apabhraṃśa recounting the life and deeds of a king or hero.[28] Genealogy, political memory, and loss are invoked in this ideal biography as Padmanābha remembers the events that led to the passing of Jalor into Turkish hands and the death of Rāval Kānhaḍade, the heroic ancestor of his patron, Akhairāja.[29]

The text begins with an invocation to Gaṇeśa, the elephant-headed god who removes obstacles, and Sarasvatī, the goddess of learning. The poet,

Padmanābha Paṇḍita, asks them to grant him a clear intellect so that he may recount the heroic story of Rāval Kānhaḍade (KP 1). He praises the Sonagiri Chauhan lineage and their capital as the city of gold (*kaṇayācala*), named after the local yellow rock that forms the hill and from which the fortress of Jalor is hewn. Then he moves into a narrative of the events of 1296, when 'Alāuddīn Khaljī ascended the throne of Delhi after his conquest of Gujarat, and the poet begins his story with the cause of that war. According to him, the Baghela king of Gujarat one day insults Mādhava, his favorite minister, and Mādhava swears vengeance upon his former master. He goes to Delhi, where 'Alāuddīn interrogates him about conditions in Gujarat, to which he responds:

> "The *kshatriya dharma* has vanished from there. Rāo Karṇade has become insane and has developed an infatuation for the pleasures of the body. Every day he takes the aphrodisiac Vachhanāga, and struts about with an unsheathed sword in his hand!...The Rāi first humiliated me. Then he killed my brother Keśava, and even took away his wife and kept her in his palace. Such a provocation is beyond toleration! I will wage war against Gujarat and pray you to send an army with me for the purpose. I will attack the Hindūs, drive them into jungles, killing them and enslaving them!...Either I will conquer Gujarat by force or perish" [KP 3].

In this Indian view of polity, what Mādhava is advocating is the sultan's use of a feud in a neighboring king's realm as an occasion to invade his kingdom. Further, the ideology that is invoked to condemn Karṇadeva is his deviation from the *dharma* of a warrior or *kṣatriya*, which would involve his protecting the wives of other men rather than preying on them. In the poetics of this non-Persian text, the *casus belli* is a woman, specifically the woman of his brother Keśava. By killing Keśava, Karṇadeva has insulted his family's honor, which Mādhava will avenge. Moreover, in the classical Indian system of polity to which Padmanābha refers, the king's relationship to the land is that of a *pati* or husband to the country, which is represented as the submissive female awaiting domination.

'Alāuddīn enthusiastically agrees to Mādhava's plan and sends envoys to ask safe conduct from all of the Rajput kings through whose territory his army would pass on its way to Gujarat. Kānhaḍade of Jalor alone refuses, on the grounds that allowing the Muslim army to pass would contravene the *dharma* of a warrior:

> "This is contrary to our *dharma*! Kings do not give passage when by doing so villages are devastated, people are enslaved, ears of women torn (for their ornaments), and cows and Brāhmaṇas are tortured" [KP 4].

Kānhaḍade is thus made into the good king, the one who is a protector of right religion, cows and Brahmins, as well as the honor and safety of the women of his realm. The conflict between him and the forces of Islam is thus set up at the very beginning in terms of narrative causality; the cause of the historical quarrel will be the conflict between religious truth and evil conduct rather than the political exigencies of control over territory. This single narrative cause simultaneously legitimates rulership and introduces the events from which the story flows.

The grand army of cavalry, elephants, and foot soldiers, equipped with the latest technology of war—siege towers and catapults for flinging naphtha over fortress walls—marches through Rajput territory. On his way to Gujarat, Uluġh K̲h̲ān destroys in a brutal battle the only Rajput who offers him any resistance, the brave chief Bataḍa of Moḍāsā. When he reaches the city of Anhilvārā Paṭṭan, the Baghela capital, King Karṇa flees the fort in the dead of night. The fort is destroyed, its temples torn down and made into mosques, and the rule of Sultan 'Alāuddīn proclaimed everywhere. Uluġh K̲h̲ān goes on to Somnath and sacks the town, emptying the prosperous and fertile land in the wake of his marauding army. When the Muslims come to the temple of Śiva in the center of the town, all the priests give up their lives to defend the image of God. The stone *lingam* is dispatched to Delhi to be smashed as an object lesson in the ideological superiority of Islam. Meanwhile, in Jalor, Śiva and Pārvatī appear to Kānhaḍade in a dream and tell him that God is being taken from Somnath through his territory (*deśa*). He must rescue the image.

On his way back to Delhi, Uluġh K̲h̲ān has the first of several military encounters with the Chauhan Rajputs of Jalor. Rāval Kānhaḍade sends his nobles as envoys to spy out the camp at Gujarat, which is described as one of the grandest military assemblages. With the army of Gujarat are hundreds of thousands of lamenting Hindu prisoners, being taken to Delhi as slaves. The Rajputs muster all the Rais and Ranas from the neighboring principalities and prepare to attack Uluġh K̲h̲ān's army, who are described as *asura*s or demons. The goddess of the Gujarat fort, Āsāpurī Devī, gives her blessing, and Kānhaḍade and his brother Māladeo rout the Muslims. They take alive two prominent nobles, Sa'dullāh K̲h̲ān and Sih Malik, and recover the Śiva-*lingam* from Uluġh K̲h̲ān's clutches. The poet adds a commentary on the effects of *puṇya*, meritorious action:

Indeed, the Chauhan clan has unmeasured *puṇya* to its credit. It is on account of *puṇya* that Rāval Kānhaḍade destroyed the Mlecchas (a derogatory name for Muslims). It is indeed due to *puṇya*, the merit earned for good and virtuous acts, that people enjoy rich food and drinks, wealth grows in the house, and one marries a lady of good lineage....Those

> without *puṇya* roam about confused and confounded...It is by virtue of *puṇya* that grain and provisions in one's house are never exhausted. It is due to *puṇya* that one is blessed with a son. Again, it is on account of *puṇya* that the king gives honor and the Pradhāns (noblemen) become favorable....At the house of a *puṇyavanta*, all the three times of the day—morning, noon, and evening—one hundred and eight auspicious rituals and ceremonies are performed [KP 25–26ff].

The meritorious action of the king underpins an entire ritual economy of virtue and right behavior. It is only through good actions that merit can be gathered, but once one has it, then all sorts of natural and human bounty flow from it: the kingdom works perfectly, one's house is never empty of food, a son is born who can perform the funeral rites that let his parents cross over to the further shore, and the proper order or *dharma* of the universe is maintained through the 108 rituals performed daily at the house of a person who possesses merit.

At the center of this ritual economy is God, who is embodied in the stone image seized by the Muslims from Somnath. Rāval Kānhaḍade, the god of flesh who keeps the ritual order working, goes to the camp and brings the *lingam* into Jalor with all due reverence. He bathes it with his own hands and adorns it with sandal paste, flowers, and vermillion. Pieces carved out of the *lingam* then bless the entire territory (*deśa*) with embodiments of God:

> Five images were carved out of the Ekalingam, which saves one from falling into hell and from dire troubles and afflictions; there is no sixth one like them. One of these was ceremoniously installed at Soraṭha and another at Lohasing in Vāgaḍa. One was sent to a pleasant spot on Ābū hill for consecration, while one was installed at Jalor where the Rāi built a temple and one was sent to Saivāḍī. At all these five places, worship of Lord Śiva is performed [KP 28–29].

These multiple ritual centers consecrate the kingdom, making the God Śiva present throughout Kānhaḍade's realm. In Padmanābha's imaginative geography, Jalor is the land where the concrete embodiments of Śiva anchor the ritual economy that it is Kānhaḍade's responsibility to run. The move not only legitimates the Rajput ruler but also establishes proper order throughout the king's territory and marks the land as his. Ritual and political sovereignty reinforce each other through this politics of embodied religious devotion.

The Turkish armies return to Delhi in disarray, where 'Alāuddīn, incensed at the actions of the Rāval, sends the renowned Nāhar Malik and Bhoja to lay siege to the fort of Sivānā or Sāmiyāṇā in Kānhaḍade's kingdom. The fort is held by Sātala, the Sutal Dev of Amīr Khusrau's *maṣnavī.* Unfortunately for 'Alāuddīn's generals, however, Sātala's forces defeat them utterly and kill Nāhar Malik and Bhoja. When the sultan hears the terrible news, he decides to besiege Sivānā himself. The poet again describes in great detail the grand army of 'Alāuddīn and the fearsome siege they undertook. The end of the protracted campaign comes one night when the Goddess Āsāpurī appears to Sātala in a dream and shows him around the enemy camp. There the Rajput prince sees the Turkish emperor as a form of Rudra-Śiva:

> The Bhūpa (ruler) at that time was fast asleep. Sātala saw Śiva's three eyes, and five faces, and large brown matted locks. The Lord wore a necklace of skulls and had in his hands an alms-bowl. Sātala also saw the Lord's ample forehead. He saw the Ganges in the crown of the locks of Lord Śiva, ashes smeared on his body, a tiger skin as a mattress, and also his trident. Sātala was wonder-struck. He thought for a moment, happy to obtain a vision of Lord Śiva, and bowed reverently.... "The Sultān has appeared in the form of Rudra! How can I strike a blow against him?" he thought, and decided to retrace his steps [KP 42].

Supernatural agency is made into the narrative cause for a historical event, enabling Padmanābha to explain why Sātala lost the fort of Sivānā to 'Alāuddīn. Indeed, events did progress badly for the Rajputs, and finally the women were forced to commit *jauhar.* Meanwhile the men rode out on a suicidal raid from which they did not return, in the customary Rajput last stand. Here again, investing the women with the Rajputs' symbolic honor (*māna*) meant that they could not be captured alive but had to sacrifice themselves.

To return to the narrative, which has so far been an exclusively martial and religious poem staking the Rajputs' claim to their land, we now come to the story of love intertwined with these political and religious battles. A skirmish leads to further bloodshed, and the sultan is angry enough to wish to march directly on to the fort of Jalor. But his daughter Furūzān, variously called Piroja and Sītāi, comes to him and pleads with him against another expedition:

> "By virtue of remembering past lives, I know the science of divination. Now I shall take the omens for your campaign....The God Viṣṇu took bodily form in nine different incarnations, one after the other, each time destroying the *asuras.* The tenth time, the Ādi Puruṣa has been incarnated in the Chauhan clan. You know, honored Sir, when a moth jumps into a flame, it burns its wings and body. In the same way, if you march to Jalor, Kānhaḍade will certainly take your life" [KP 56].

Here, the narrative circle of God, territory, and rulership is closed with Kānhaḍade identified as the tenth incarnation of Viṣṇu, the primal person or Ādi Puruṣa for the current age. He literally becomes, in the religious causality behind events in the story, a god of flesh who cannot be attacked. Further, the poet uses a mythic referent to represent social and religious alterity: the reference to *asuras* or demons implies that the Muslims are the demons of the historical age of Kānhaḍade.

Furūzān expresses her desire to be married to the handsome Vīramade, the crown prince of Jalor. Sultan 'Alāuddīn answers: "Good daughter, do not be mad and talk like that. You are mistaken in your affection for him. You know well that marriage between a Hindū and a Turk cannot take place. In Yogininagar (Delhi) there are Muslim princes and distinguished Khāns. Whomsoever you like amongst them, I will call him and you may marry him" (KP 56). But the princess swears that she cannot marry anyone but Vīramade: "There is a great difference between the Hindūs and Turks: Hindūs alone know how to enjoy the good things of life, like Indra . . . I have no desire to wed a Turk. . . . Either, my dear father, I will marry Vīramade, or else I shall end my life!" (KP 56–57). The sultan sends an envoy to Kānhaḍade with an offer of marriage and a grand dowry: the wealthy province of Gujarat and fifty-six crores of gold and silver. Land, woman, and money come wrapped up in the same package—the matrimonial proposal, in which these are the articles of exchange.

Vīramade, however, laughs to himself and spurns the Sultan's offer indignantly:

> The Emperor has now thought of a new strategy to bring Jalor under his sway. He has such a large army! But is this the way to conquer countries, without any fighting? I cannot agree to this offer of marriage and thereby incur dishonor! I will never unite with a Turkish woman in wedlock. Even if the pinnacles of Mount Meru were to crash down, Chauhan Vīramade will not sit at the sacred fire to marry the Sultan's daughter, nor clasp her hand in the *hathlevā* ceremony, or dine in the marriage pavilion! . . . By such an act, all the thirty-six Rājpūt clans will be shamed and the luster of all twenty-one Rājpūt kings will be dimmed. . . . Our great ancestor, Chāchigadeva Chauhan, will be disgraced. . . . Such a thing has never happened in the past, nor shall it ever happen in the future! [KP 57–58]

In rejecting the Sultan's offer, the prince invokes his mythicized ancestor, the honor of the thirty-six Rajput clans, and the twenty-one dynasties of the kingdoms of Rajputana. The contours of power in Vīramade's understanding are significantly different from the model of the Islamic state that Amīr Khusrau described. Here, the bonds of kinship, marriage, and relations between lords and vassals link together a loosely knit confederacy of feuding rulers, who sometimes come together against a common enemy.[30] Further, the prince constructs a great religious divide that can never be bridged by marriage or alliance; it seems war is the only course open to Jalor.

But the princess will not have it so. When the envoy returns with news of Vīramade's refusal, 'Alāuddīn at first orders another raid into Jalor. In the course of the raid, 'Alāuddīn for the first time sees the golden city of Jalor. By Kānhaḍade's orders, the city has been adorned especially to show the sultan the grandeur and might of the Chauhan kingdom:

> Broad woven silk sheets of the color of the clouds were hung up, two on each bastion, and so also were *chandovās* (canopies) studded with jewels, with pendants of pearls dangling from them. The golden triple spires on the towers shone brightly. The earthen lamps on the battlements looked like so many stars, shimmering tremulously, their light mingling with that of the stars. A variety of minstrelsy (*gītagāna*), sung in melodious tunes, could be heard. On the bastions, dances and plays were enacted. No one knew with what to compare these spectacles! Indeed, the fort looked like Indra's *vimāna* (flying chariot), or like Lankā perched on the Trikuṭā mountain, so it seemed to the Ġhorī Sultan ('Alāuddīn). Delicate gold images studded with jewels were dangling here and there.... The royal palaces and temples were whitewashed and had here and there beautiful wall paintings... Kānhaḍade's fort had many bastions on which rows of lighted earthen lamps shed golden light around, while *chāmaras* (yak-tail fly whisks) were being waved over the Chauhan ruler's head, the protector of the clan [KP 59–60].

The Sultan marvels at this heavenly city, which is lavishly described in the fashion of the *nagara-varṇana* (description of a city) of Sanskritic *kāvyas*. The poet uses the convention effectively to show the Rajput resistance to 'Alāuddīn, constructing a golden utopia of song, dance, architecture, painting, and, at the center of it all, the figure of the ideal king.

The Rajputs then attack a Turkish encampment and carry off Shams K̲h̲ān and his *begam* (queen). To prevent a military raid, the princess again approaches her father:

> "My beloved father! I pray you listen to my request. Vīramade was my husband in my previous birth. They have captured my sister and her husband and taken them to Jalor. By telling them all the signs and proofs of our past births, I will surely obtain their release."

> The Emperor asked: "How could Vīrama be your husband?"
>
> ..."Long ago, he was Bāpal's son, known as Singharāja, while I was born as Surjande, the daughter of Jai Chand. We entered into wedlock, full of ardent love for each other, in Yogininagar (Delhi). On his death, I entered fire in Antaraveda (Doāb), a beautiful country, and thus upheld the true traditions of *satī dharma*....The second time, Vīramade was born as Kelhaṇa in the house of the Kāśī ruler while I was Ajaipāla's daughter...I again entered fire following my consort's death....[Details of three more births, formulaically recounted] Again, the sixth time,...he was born as Pṛthivīrāja while I appeared as Padmāvatī. In that life I committed a grave sin. I had a cow killed and conjured magical incantations on the fetus to charm my lord and make him subservient to my wishes. This deranged his mind, and we indulged in amorous dalliance night and day, throwing all propriety to the winds. I had the Pradhāns murdered and usurped power. Later, Sultan Shihāb al-dīn killed the Rāi on the banks of the Ghaggar, so I heard....I ascended the pyre in Ayodhyā, which brings immeasurable *puṇya*, and it was for this reason that I was born in a royal family. But because I had committed the two great sins, I was born in the house of a Turk" [KP 64].

The seventh time is the princess's present birth, in which she feels she has to join her husband again. This extraordinary account of reincarnation provides the beginnings of the narrative resolution of the story, as well as a fascinating reshaping of historical causality. The love that Prince Vīramade and the princess have felt for one another during their last six births must be continued in this one, but her sins—killing a pregnant cow and usurping power—have led her to be born as a Turk. Here the princess is being assimilated into the structure of death and reincarnation, which explains her current political situation through *karma*.

Although the princess goes on an embassy in Kānhaḍade's realm and is received with great respect, courtesy, and royal hospitality, Prince Vīramade refuses even to look at her. He spurns her again, and she accepts her fate for the sake of the sins she has committed. She does, however, secure the release of all the prisoners and returns to her father, having done the job of an envoy. After this, preparations begin for the final assault on Jalor, which is taken by treachery in 1311. The illustrious Kānhaḍade falls to the forces of the sultan, and all the women of the fort commit *jauhar*. The princess had, however, sent her nurse Dādā Sanāvar with the army, with instructions to save Vīramade if she could. If she could not, she was to bring back his head to the princess. The nurse searches through the rubble of the fallen city and comes upon the body of Vīramade. She puts his head tenderly into a basket of flowers and bears it to Delhi. When the head is presented to the princess on a platter, she addresses it:

> "Earlier, the Chauhan had vowed that he would never look at my face. Now, at least today, he will have to break his word!"
>
> Those who are brave and of good lineage do not give up their plighted word even after death. The moment the princess came in front of Vīramade's face, it turned away! [KP 101–2]

The princess weeps sadly over the loss of her brave and resolute love, then goes to enter a funeral pyre on the banks of the Yamuna, holding the head of Vīramade in her lap. The story comes to an end with the genealogy of the rulers who follow in the line of Vīramade.

Padmanābha and Amīr Khusrau thus set within opposing narrative frames the historical transition of the period, the carving out of political territories from which a new Islamic polity with its capital at Delhi could collect revenue. Unlike the earlier Jain tale with its moral philosophy, these later romances are framed in terms of Islamicate and classical Indian notions of the ideal polity.[31] In Amīr Khusrau's poems about Sultan 'Alāuddīn Khaljī, the achievement of the sultan is precisely that he has managed to make India into an Islamic land (*dār al-Islām*). Padmanābha's *Kānhaḍade Prabandha* sets the Rajput ruler within a ritual economy of kingship in which political rule and legitimacy is intrinsically bound up with saving the images of Śiva that are being smashed by the iconoclastic Turks.[32] In this tragic romance, where political and military enmity is never bridged, the Turkish princess becomes the active go-between who negotiates between the two sides, mediating between two systems that, although rooted in differing religious ideologies, share a symbolic investment in land and women.

Although the generic forms and the provenances of the Jain Mahārāṣṭrī Prakrit tale, the Apabhraṃśa *prabandha-kāvya*, and the Persian *masnavī* are quite different, together they imply a common understanding. Exchanging women can redress political and social imbalances; it can make important social statements about alliance or hostility, about ascetic values and symbolic honor. Prince Khiẓr Khān makes a sacrifice for male honor, while Vīramade refuses to give up the machismo of Rajput honor even after death. Both poets use the figure of crossing over to the other side in a fantasy in which true but tragic love transcends conflicts over political borders. The images that Persian poetry praised as infidel seductresses (*but-i kāfir*) had to be smashed in the iconoclastic logic of the conquest narratives, but this did not lessen their allure and fascination. The stories of the children of 'Alāuddīn Khaljī fetishize the woman belonging to the enemy, who becomes the repository of symbolic honor for her own side and the object of romantic desire and fascination for the other side.

It is here that we begin to glimpse the wider political and cultural context of Sufi attitudes toward territory and sexuality. Bruce Lawrence has emphasized in an important article the dual role of women for Sufis of the Delhi sultanate, as obstacles to spiritual progress through their embodiment of the baser instincts of the lower soul (*nafs-i ammārah*) and as helpers to mystical perfection through their own saintliness.[33] The Persian sources give us only partial answers to questions about Sufi self-mortification and its links with eroticism and sexuality. But the elaborate Sufi romances in Hindavī and the other Indo-Aryan languages reveal the degree to which the Indian Sufis subscribed to common cultural understandings of society and sexuality. For the Sufi poets of the Hindavī, *premākhyāns* created the fictional image of an Indian landscape with the eroticized body of an Indian woman as its centerpiece. And as we shall see presently, this figure becomes a symbol of mystical annihilation in her final (and fictive) sacrifice on a flaming pyre in Chittaur.

The Erotics of War

In telling the story of Ratansen's journey to Singhala-dīpa and his triumphant return to Chittaur with Padmāvatī in the first part of his poem, Jāyasī follows the generic pattern of the other Hindavī Sufi romances such as the *Cāndāyan* and the *Mirigāvatī*, at the same time reshaping the Padmāvatī episode from the tale cycle of the *Pṛthvirāja Rāsau*. In the second part, he again draws on the Rajput narratives of the Turkish conquest of northern India such as the *Kānhaḍade Prabandha* and the Hammīr cycle.[34] But rather than adopting the Turko-Afghan stance of the victory of Islam over unbelief, he instead portrays Sultan 'Alāuddīn Khaljī, the emblem of military power, leading the wicked and treacherous Turks to the destruction of Chittaur. Read in the context of Sufi sanctification of the physical landscape of Avadh and projections of the imagined and interior landscapes that we considered in Chapter 5, the negative treatment of 'Alāuddīn Khaljī makes sense as a political statement and an assertion of symbolic independence from the ruling élites of early-sixteenth-century India. The dualistic rhetoric of conquest, so important to the narratives of polity formation articulated during the thirteenth and fourteenth centuries, is here reimagined from the Rajput side and subverted by Jāyasī's valorization of the defenders of Chittaur. Within the internal logic of the transformation of subjectivity, self and other merge into each other on some imagined and real landscape of interaction.

In an article about the numerous "epics" and "counter-epics" of conquest between Hindus and Muslims, Aziz Ahmad notes that:

> This allegorical epic of Rājpūt chivalry, written by a Muslim, ends with an anti-Islamic finale: "and Chitore became Islam." As the author is a Muslim, the array and might of the Turks is not belittled, though his sympathy lies with the Rājpūts. He makes an open reference to Hammīr, sees in the Rājpūt struggle something of the epic grandeur of the Mahābhārata and quotes without contradiction Gorā and Bādal's version of the inherent treachery of the Turks. Much more remarkable is his complete self-identification with the sense of tragic intent in a Rājpūt epic-theme, and its view of his own culture and religion; for the outwardly simple phrase "Chitore became Islam" signifies, in its allegorical equation, the unsubstantial victory of illusion.[35]

I would like to consider more carefully what this "self-identification" with the Rajputs implies in the narrative and context of the *Padmāvat*, as well as the final "unsubstantial victory of illusion" over the citadel of Chittaur. Since Jāyasī's poem does not present an essentialized "Hindu" view of "Islam," a presentist and communalist reading of the poem fails to do justice to the complex aesthetics and politics of the text. Instead, Jāyasī's poem is a mystically suggestive romance that uses themes of conquest to make a claim to Chishti superiority in a local context and to undermine subtly the political power of its sponsoring patrons[36] and all competing religious groups.

Ahmad's discussion of the poem has two basic thrusts. First, he takes at face value the allegorical verse from the envoi to the poem, the key or *kuñjī* to the narrative formula, which Mataprasad Gupta and the tradition of modern Hindi scholarship have proved to be a later interpolation. Second, Ahmad draws on the Urdu scholarship of Kalb-i Mustafa to consider events contemporary with Jāyasī that resonate with motifs in the story:

> Ratan Sen (1527–1532), the Rana of Chitore, was a contemporary not of 'Alā al-dīn Khaljī, but of Jāisī himself and of Sher Shāh Sūrī. The ruse of warriors entering an enemy fort in women's palanquins, though a motif paralleled in epic and romance, had also some historical basis as it was used by Sher Shāh to capture the fort of Rohtās. In 1531, nine years before the composition of *Padmāvat*, a case of mass *satī* had occurred in a Rājpūt fort sacked by Sultan Bahādur of Gujarat to avenge the dishonor of two hundred and fifty Muslim women held captive in that fort. There might have been a conscious or unconscious confounding in Jāisī's mind of 'Alā al-dīn Khaljī with Ghiyāth al-dīn Khaljī of Mālwa

> (1469–1500) who had a roving eye, and is reported to have undertaken the quest of Padminī, not a particular Rājpūt princess, but the ideal type of woman according to Hindu erotology. Ghiyāth al-dīn Khaljī, according to a Hindu inscription in the Udaipur area, was defeated in battle in 1488 by a Rājpūt chieftain Bādal-Gorā, multiplied by Jāisī into twins.[37]

Ahmad's effort to historicize the *Padmāvat* rightly refers to events that are matched by narrative motifs in the text. But the approach is problematic because Ahmad explains in a directly referential way a narrative pattern that has its roots in the generic tradition of the Hindavī romances, confusing literal and literary truths. As we shall see, the ending of the poem has more to do with the pattern set up in Quṭban's *Mirigāvatī* than with any "actual" *jauhar* or *satī*, and the motifs that Jāyasī uses are drawn from the Rajput martial literature. Finally, the idea of any putative "confounding in Jāisī's mind" of the two very different Khaljī sultans must surely be discounted.

The sacking of the fort of Raisen in 1532 by Sultan Bahādur Shāh (1526–1537) and the *jauhar* of the Rajput women are, however, highly relevant to the second half of the *Padmāvat* in one respect. In a discussion of Bahādur Shāh's sack of Raisen, Dirk Kolff has emphasized the role of women as embodiments of symbolic honor and the role of Rajput warlords as power brokers in the world of the Afghan sultanates. The presence of Muslim women as an accepted part of Purbiya Rajput households causes theologians and ulema in Bahādur Shāh's realm to pester him for vengeance. Even though Silhadi, the lord of Raisen, has converted to Islam and, after protracted negotiations, is offered a fief as the *muqṭa'* of Baroda, his mother Queen Durgāvatī and the women of Raisen commit *jauhar* rather than give up the very real political independence the family enjoyed in northern Malwa. Kolff points out that

> the events leading up to the holocaust of Raisen are related by Persian historians of the age of Akbar as a contest between muslim orthodoxy and Rajput honor. Yet it would be anachronistic to suggest that the episodes...attest to the fundamental irreconcilability of two ideologies. Rather, they tell a story of Rajputs groping about for terms that would allow them to preserve their identity as exuberant and conspicuously living warriors while at the same time enabling them to be associated with the unchallenged power of the day, an assertive Muslim sultanate.[38]

Well worked-out strategies of accommodation and patronage enabled Afghans and Rajputs in sultanate India to live and to fight side by side, appealing to the dualistic rhetoric derived from conquest narratives only in extreme cases such as Raisen.

The End of the Padmāvat

The Offended Brahmin Counselor and the Padminī Woman

Jāyasī puts these notions to effective use by combining them with another motif that is also found in Padmanābha's *Kānhaḍade Prabandha* and the Hammīr story, the treachery of the offended Brahmin counselor of a good Rajput king. One of King Ratansen's counselors, a Brahmin called Rāghav Chetan, is wise and learned beyond compare. On a certain new-moon day, the king happens to ask his assembled counselors, "When will the second day of the month fall?" (P 447) From Rāghav's mouth unthinkingly comes, "Today," but the other pandits say, "Tomorrow." But such is Rāghav Chetan's arrogance that he refuses to take back his words. Instead of admitting he is wrong, he propitiates a *yakṣinī* by black magic and makes the moon of the second night of the month appear in the sky by illusion. The other Brahmins are not convinced, and when on the next night the moon of the second night appears again, they inform the king that Rāghav is a black magician who uses spells to cheat and to trick people. The king condemns Rāghav Chetan as a sorcerer and sentences him to banishment from his kingdom of Chittaur.

But Padmāvatī is worried that Rāghav will cause some mischief by his black magic, and summons him to a tower in the palace, ostensibly to have him accept an offering on the occasion of a solar eclipse. When Padmāvatī comes to the window lattice, her radiant beauty stuns Rāghav out of his senses:

> *At that moment Rāghav blessed her.*
> *He was like a* cakora *bird*
> *who had seen the face of the moon.*
> *The moon wore a necklace of stars.*
> *Earth and heaven were radiant with her light.*
> *She wore on her hands a pair of bracelets,*
> *on which each gem was worth nine crores.*
> *She took off a bracelet and threw it down,*
> *and her necklace broke and fell with it.*
> *Along with the stars, the moon was falling.*
> *A stream of death was loosed from heaven [P 451.2–6].*

Rāghav falls down on the ground, and passers-by wonder whether he is an epileptic, or possessed, or poisoned by some drug. He remains senseless, and it is only with much difficulty that he awakens. When he comes to, he curses the cruel beauty who has robbed him of his senses and resolves to destroy the kingdom. He goes to Delhi with the intention of getting Sultan 'Alāuddīn

Khalji, famous as a conqueror and subjugator of resistant provinces, to attack Ratansen with all his might. He leaves, taking with him the jewel-encrusted bracelet, and he arrives in Delhi as a mendicant wearing the glittering band on his arm.

When Rāghav arrives at the sultan's court in Delhi, he comes to a grand imperial center. The emperor is the lord of all he surveys, with an awesome machinery of information and rule at his command. Thirty thousand elephants and hundreds of thousands of Turkish horsemen, the cavalry that was a sign of military superiority in sultanate India, attend him. He greets Rāghav as a beggar, but laughs at his account of getting the bracelet from the lotus princess of Singhala-dīpa:

> *"When a beggar finds a piece of glass,*
> *he raises it to Mount Sumeru as gold.*
> *You are a beggar so your tongue has been spared.*
> *Now control yourself and speak the truth.*
> *Where is there a woman above the world,*
> *whom the sun and moon cannot match?*
> *If there is a Padminī, she is in my palace,*
> *where all the seven continents dance attendance.*
> *I have picked them out of all seven continents.*
> *I have sixteen hundred queens in my harem" [P 461.2–6].*

The emperor is referring here to the best type of woman in the Indian systems of erotic classification, the Padminī or lotus woman. Rāghav responds by asserting that all the other types of women in the world pale in comparison with Padmāvatī of Chittaur: "Where is the Padminī, so like a lotus, around whom the bees hover?" (P 462.8)

After recounting for the sultan all the erotic types of women, Rāghav describes Padmāvatī as a woman beyond all others. He describes her beauty in a second *sarāpā* or head-to-foot description, in which Jāyasī projects a lush sensuality:

> *She opens her braid and shakes out her tresses.*
> *Night falls, lamps are lit throughout the world.*
> *Her locks fall to the ground from her head.*
> *Darkness descends on the whole country.*
> *Her locks roll about like poisonous snakes,*
> *imbued with the fragrance of her sandal limbs.*
> *They ripple and wave like snakes full of venom,*
> *flowing about, very fragrant and jet black [P 470.1–4].*

Jāyasī uses the imagery of snakes on the sandalwood trees of the Malabar coast to portray her black tresses on her soft golden limbs. He goes on:

> *Her lips, brightly colored, are delicate*
> *as betel leaves. They are red*
> *and moist with the* rasa *of nectar.*
> *Dyed and wet with betel juice,*
> *her lips sparkle like* gulāl *when she smiles [P 476.1–2].*

Padmāvatī's shining lips suggest the sparkling *gulāl* powder that is mixed with mica and thrown in red clouds at the festival of Holi. Rāghav takes his inventory only down to her waist, for, as he coyly suggests to the sultan, he has seen her only at her window lattice (*jharokhā*). His description works well to arouse the sultan's lust, in contrast with Hīrāman's exhortations to the seeker Ratansen in the first part of the romance. In the mystical quest, Ratansen is excited to gain Padmāvatī through ascetic mortification; in the evil version of mystical *sarāpā* and arousal, the wicked sultan hopes to capture her by force of arms. The militaristic language of lust and conquest, Jāyasī will begin to suggest, is another way of trying to gain the joys of *prema-rasa*; its inadequacies will become clearer in the ensuing narrative.

The aroused sultan sends a letter to Ratansen demanding his wife and the treasures of Chittaur on threat of siege. "No one demands the wife of another man!" Ratansen thunders, and continues:

> *"If the lady of the house leaves,*
> *what remains of the house?*
> *What is Chittaur and the realm of Chanderi?*
> *Why should anyone despoil a man's house*
> *while he is still alive? Only a yogi leaves his house.*
> *Am I Hammīr, the lord of Ranthambhor,*
> *who cut off his head and gave up his body?*
> *I am Ratansen, a man of power!*
> *I pierced the fish and gained Sairandhri.*
> *I have borne a mountain, just like Hanumān.*
> *I have bridged the ocean like King Rāma....*
> *He can seize my treasure and I would accept it, serve him as his slave.*
> *but if he wants a lotus woman, let him go to Singhala-dīpa himself!"*
> *[P 491.1–5, 7]*

Padmāvatī is the one inalienable object for whom Ratansen would fight to the death. Unlike Hammīra, he will not cut off his head in defeat. He compares himself to Arjuna, who pierced the eye of a fish with a single arrow even though he was blindfolded, and to other legendary heroes. Even though his counselors remind him of the capture of Princess Chhitāī from Devagiri[39] and Hammīr's death at Ranthambhor, he will not agree to give up Padmāvatī. Boiling with anger, Ratansen sends back a peremptory refusal.

But the sultan, the powerful lord of the world, is resolved to gain by brute force what Ratansen earned through asceticism. The Turkish army that is mustered in response is fierce and mighty. There are horses of every breed, mighty elephants, and siege engines, and all the sultan's vassals join in the muster. The forts of the Rajput Rais and Ranas that surround Delhi tremble at the sultan's approach: Junagarh and Champaner, Mandu, Chanderi, Kalinjar and Gwalior all quake with fear like leaves in the wind. But 'Alāuddīn Khaljī's intention is to subjugate Chittaur and gain the beautiful Padmāvatī.

The Battle for Padmāvatī

These themes resonate within the dualistic rhetoric and narrative motifs of the earlier conquest narratives. As the sultan's army comes to camp below the walls of Chittaur, all the military might of the Delhi sultanate is on display. In response, Jāyasī tells us, all the Rajput lineages and clans gather:

Ratansen was equipped in Chittaur.
Accompanied by music, all the kings
came to join him in the fort.
Tomars, Bais, and Panvārs came,
and Gahlots, their heads bowed in reverence.
Here were Khatris and Panchbāns,
Agarvāls, Chauhans, and Chandelas....
Ḍhāṛhīs stood in front, making music.
At the back, the death-flags were on display [P 503.1–3, 5].

The noisy and grand spectacle of the Rajput lineages mustering matches the Turkish army's show of strength. Many of the lineages that Jāyasī mentions, such as the Gahlots and the Panvars, were significant power brokers in the fifteenth and sixteenth centuries rather than at the time of the siege of Chittaur. Jāyasī retrospectively fits them into the topos of the muster of the armies before the grand battle outside a Rajput fort.

Moreover, he lavishes attention on description of the martial combat and the sultan's cannons as they advance and are trained against the fortress walls.

Jāyasī begins to suggest that the cannons are devastatingly beautiful women, ready to cause destruction wherever they go:

> *I will tell of their adornments as if they were women.*
> *Easily intoxicated, they drink powder like wine.*
> *When they breathe out, they breathe fire.*
> *No one stays with them out of fear.*
> *Fire stains the tops of their heads, like vermillion.*
> *Their wheels are their earrings, flashing as they go.*
> *Their breasts are the cannon balls,*
> *that stay in pairs close to their hearts.*
> *Their flags wave out like veils in the breeze.*
> *Although they have no tongues,*
> *they keep their mouths open.*
> *And when they speak, Laṅkā burns.*
> *Their tresses are the chains that wind*
> *all about their necks, and the elephants*
> *that drag them forward, break their shoulders.*
> *The erotic* rasa *and the martial are both one here.*
> *The cannons' names are "Foe-bane" and "Fort-breaker."*
> *The beauty-spot on their forehead is the fuse, and their teeth*
> *are adamantine darts.*
> *Wherever they look, they cause a tumult; if they laugh out loud,*
> *who can withstand them? [P 507.1–8]*

Punning on *dārū*, the word for wine and gunpowder, Jāyasī carries his extended metaphor through the parts of the cannon. The double imagery eroticizes battle and the machinery of battle in terms of the Sanskrit system of aesthetics, when Jāyasī says that cannons embody the erotic and the martial *rasas* in their elaborately decorated forms.

Jāyasī does something quite different in the rest of the conclusion to the *Padmāvat*, where the grand battle between the Turks and Rajputs signifies the contest between the narrative options of love by force and love earned through Sufi practice. The sultan's attempt to taste the joys of *prema-rasa* is in stark contrast to the approved mystical quest narrative of the genre. These warring sides signify much more than ethnic or religious groups; they embody might versus right on the battlefield:

> *Here the king gathered his army.*
> *From the other side, the Shāh approached.*
> *The vanguard advanced rapidly forward,*

while the rearguard stayed ten leagues behind.
The Shāh came and attacked the fortress,
twenty thousand elephants in his train.
Both armies came down thundering.
Hindus and Turks faced each other in battle.
Both were oceans, like the seas of milk and curd,
or mountains, like Meru and Kiṣkindhā.
Enraged, the warriors fought each other.
Elephants faced their enemy elephants.
Their goads glittered like lightning.
The elephants roared like dark clouds thundering.
Heaven and earth fought each other, army upon army,
regiment on regiment.
Neither force could move the other, as if they were masses
of adamant [P 516.1–8].

The armies of Chittaur, defending the rightful and honorable Ratansen, are not able to withstand the onslaught of the sultan's vast army and his machinery of war. Jāyasī compares the sultan to the sun, in front of whom the moon (Ratansen) is eclipsed and withdraws into his high fortress. The sultan's forces advance inexorably through the passes surrounding Chittaur, leaving countless dead behind. His archers let loose crores of arrows against the fort, thick as constellations of stars in the sky.

Finally, the sultan's forces are camped all around Chittaur with catapults and siege engines at the ready, and they have dug underground mines and tunnels to take the fort. Although it seems that Ratansen will be defeated, he does not give up in his heart. In defiance, he orders a dance performance to be held on the ramparts of the fort. The sequence of events that follows is taken directly from the Rajput poetic accounts of the siege of Ranthambhor as exemplified in texts such as Nayacandra suri's *Hammīra Mahākāvya*. The *Hammīra Mahākāvya*'s retelling of 'Alāuddīn Khaljī's siege of Ranthambhor contains the episode of the dancing girl Rādhā Devī,[40] who performs for Hammīr on the ramparts of Ranthambhor and turns her back on the sultan as a planned insult. Enraged, the sultan has one of his archers shoot her down. Jāyasī introduces the motif with five dancing girls performing at Chittaur and an elaborate typology of melodies and instruments. Then:

When the Shāh was watching the performance,
a dancer whirled and turned her back to him.
When he saw this, he thundered from his throne,
"How long shall the moon enjoy the doe?

My men will shoot their arrows and climb up.
The head of pride should always stay low."
As he spoke, a hundred thousand arrows shot up.
Some reached the ramparts, some only to its gates.
Malik Jahāngīr was the lord of Kannauj,
and his was the arrow that shot down the dancer.
The arrow hit home and her leg moved as if dancing.
Her spirit went to heaven, and the mould fell to earth.
When the dancer died, the dance also ceased.
The Turks were delighted, and clapped their hands [P 529.1–7].

In both these narratives, shooting down the dancing girl functions as part of the etiology of the conflict and siege, one of the causes for the emperor's ire against the Rajputs. It is not found in the Persian accounts of the conquests of Ranthambhor or Chittaur, but within the cultural logic of the Rajput texts it is one way to explain the conquest. Jāyasī accepts this causation and reuses the motif in his depiction of the conflict between right and might.

The Negotiations

Now it truly appears as if Chittaur's cause is lost, and Ratansen and his men prepare for a suicidal last stand. They build pyres of sandalwood and aloes, and the women make ready for *jauhar* in the king's harem. The men anoint themselves for the final battle. But before this can happen, Jāyasī introduces another classic motif from the Rajput narratives: cessation of hostilities for negotiations. The lustful and treacherous sultan thinks to win over Ratansen by friendship and somehow gain his aim by trickery. So he sends an envoy to Ratansen giving up his demand for Padmāvatī and presenting conditions for a truce. In exchange for lifting the siege, he asks for the five objects that the Ocean gave to Ratansen, the treasures of Chittaur: the hunting tiger and bird, the swan, the philosopher's stone, and the ambrosial gem that cures snake bite. Ratansen's response is still defiant and ready for an extended siege or the ultimate sacrifice:

"We have foodgrains that will last for sixty years.
The hill gushes with water without our asking.
Moreover, even if the fort were to be breached,
the truth of a man of might will not falter" [P 535.3–4].

But his counselors prevail on him and he agrees to treat with the sultan. He has the swan brought from its golden cage, as well as the ambrosial jewel, the philosopher's stone, the golden bird on a golden perch, and the hunting tiger in a silver cage. Envoys bring all these to the sultan's camp, and 'Alāuddīn accepts them as marks of a vassal's homage. He sends a message to Ratansen to tell him that he will come on the morrow to meet him in friendship and to inspect the fort.

Here Jāyasī introduces another motif familiar to us from another Rajput conquest narrative, Padmanābha's *Kānhaḍade Prabandha*: entertaining enemy royalty within the fort. Just as Padmanābha recounted the lavish entertainment and feast that was prepared for Princess Furūzān in Jalor, Jāyasī devotes a long section to the grand preparations for the emperor's banquet in Chittaur. Fish are caught, every sort of viand and vegetable is gathered, and fruits and sweets of all kinds are made ready. The emperor inspects the paradisal fort before the banquet, looking at all the lush orchards, lakes, and jewel-encrusted palaces carefully. He remarks on the beauty of Padmāvatī's heavenly mansion: "How lovely must be the queen who lives in such a beautiful palace!" (P 555.8) They sit down to eat, but all the while the sultan thinks only of Padmāvatī and how he can make her his own. Two warriors of King Ratansen, Gorā and Bādal, warn the king: "Do not make friends with the Turk, for in the end he will turn out to be treacherous!" (P 558.4) But the king does not listen, for he believes that friendship drives out baseness and that he can bring the Turk around from evil to good by doing good himself.

At the banquet, dancing girls as beautiful as heavenly *apsaras*es perform for them. But the sultan is deaf and blind to all other women, and asks Rāghav: "Where is the lotus lady among all these?" (P 560.8). When he is told that she is not among them, he knows no peace. He cannot enjoy the feast, for his mind is lost in thoughts of Padmāvatī. After the feast is over, he thinks of a stratagem. He speaks sweetly to the king and offers him betel as a mark of friendship. He then suggests a game of chess (*shatranj*, Sanskrit *caturaṅga*). The sultan has a mirror affixed to the wall so that he may look at Padmāvatī whenever she comes to her lattice to look down at the court. They sit down to play chess together. The poet puns on the moves that are unfolding in the game to gain Padmāvatī:

The intoxicated lover moves like a pawn:
he takes a step forward, but kills sideways.
The shāh moved his knight and threatened the queen.
He had the pieces exactly as he wanted them.
The king advanced his elephant and called check,
so the shāh moved his knight back again.
Castle threatened castle, both locked tusks like enraged elephants.
The king wished for a stalemate, but the shāh was hoping for checkmate [P 567.4–8].

The stalemate between the two is, however, figuratively broken by Padmāvatī. Her serving maids tell her that the Sultan of Delhi has appeared in court, and that he is handsome and resplendent beyond all the assembled kings and warriors. When Padmāvatī goes to her lattice to look at him, she appears in the mirror in the shah's line of vision. This is Jāyasī's textual mirror of description, which reflects the true form or symbol of divinity. The shah falls down unconscious, blinded by the divine beauty that has granted him a fleeting vision.

Even though the sultan represents lust and brute force, his sighting of Padmāvatī suggests a divine revelation, a temporary drawing aside of the veils of human vision for readers and listeners who can catch the implicit suggestions in his words. This is consistent throughout the genre and is as common as, say, the wet sari scene in contemporary Bombay films. The love-struck 'Alāuddīn calls for Rāghav Chetan and describes to him what he has seen, using poetic suggestion to communicate the ineffable mystery of revelation that is embodied in Padmāvatī:

"I have seen an amazing sight.
It was behind a veil, yet there was no veil.
I saw a lake that contained water,
yet there was nothing to drink in it.
Heaven came down to earth as a shadow.
It was earth, yet not a part of the earth.
It seemed there was a lofty pavilion within,
within one's reach, yet inaccessible.
I saw an image within that temple,
without body and without life,
yet made unlike any others in spirit.
It glowed radiantly like the full moon,
revealing itself like the philosopher's stone,
and then it was hidden from sight.
Now my life is with that full moon.
How can the sun gain her during the new moon?
The lotus blossomed in the heavens, and flashed like lightning
in the night.
Here too the sun went into eclipse. Believe this, Rāghav,
in your mind!

I saw her standing there, marvelously strange.
She etched her picture in my mind
and robbed me of my life.
A lion's waist, two elephants' temples,

a snake as goad and a peacock as mahout.
Over these a lotus was blossoming.
The flying bee took in the fragrance
of the rasa *of the flower.*
A parrot sat between the two wagtails.
The moon of the second night of the month
rose along with its bows.
A doe revealed herself, then departed.
The moon became a serpent, the sun a lamp.
As I gazed, she rose higher and higher.
I could not grasp her; I saw her, and she left" [P 571, 572.1–7].

The constant assertion and denial of physical form—earth, yet not a part of earth—is a characteristic strategy of the poets of the genre. Padmāvatī is like an image in a temple, but without the sense of immediate presence that is so much a part of image worship. Her essence is elusive, the poet suggests, a marvelously strange body composed of hyperbolic elements, not just a token of material exchange. In his response, Rāghav explains each of the parts: her breasts are elephants' temples, her tress is a serpent, and her neck has the grace of a peacock. The lotus is her face, and its scent is the scent of her body. The wagtails are her lively eyes, and the parrot (whose beak often suggests a sharply etched nose) is her nose. The crescent moon is her forehead, its bows her eyebrows. As she revealed herself like a doe, the serpent was her braid and the lamp was the sultan's thought. Since he saw her image in the mirror, this was the image in which there was no life. Now the sultan must think of a ruse so that he may taste the *rasa* of Padmāvatī's lips.

The sultan leaves, and keeps up a warm friendship with Ratansen. He invites him to his own palace and lavishes gifts and kindnesses on him. Giving him gems and fiefs of land, ʻAlāuddīn Khaljī lures him deeper and deeper in. Then he treacherously has him chained and fettered and thrown into a dark dungeon. An Abyssinian slave is Ratansen's jailor, and he uses all the machinery of torture to break Ratansen. Ratansen is asked to render loyal service to the sultan as his vassal, but he refuses. Finally, the surrender of Padmāvatī is made the condition of his freedom. Meanwhile, back home in Chittaur, Padmāvatī and Nāgmatī lament and suffer greatly due to their separation from Ratansen. Ratansen's neighbor, King Devapāl of Kumbhalner, nurses a vendetta (*baira*) against Ratansen. He decides to take advantage of Ratansen's absence to capture Padmāvatī. Jāyasī comments, using the cultural logic of the time, that:

The long-nursed hatred in an enemy's heart,
is satisfied if the foe's wife comes to his house [P 584.3].

Devapāl asks Kumudini, an old messenger woman (*dūtī*) in his house, if she can bring the fabled Padmāvatī to his house. The old woman compares herself to a famous witch, Lonā Chamārin, and prepares her tricks and incantations. She takes all manner of foods, sweets, and wheat cakes and savories, and crosses over the border to Chittaur. She enters the women's quarters of the palace by using her charms and spells. Once inside, she insinuates herself into Padmāvatī's confidence by alleging that she was present at her birth in Gandharvasen's palace. Kumudini claims to be the daughter of Gandharvasen's family priest, Benī Dube. Padmāvatī welcomes her as a person from her own natal home (*naihar*), embraces her, and tearfully tells her about Ratansen's imprisonment in Delhi. She cannot even touch any of the sweets and savories that Kumudini has brought as gifts to cozen her, since she is so affected by separation from her lord.

Kumudini craftily begins to suggest to her that youth is fleeting and that she should enjoy herself while she can. Artfully she compares her to a drooping lotus that has enjoyed the attentions of only one bee. If Padmāvatī will consent, she could bring another bee to her, namely Prince Devapāl of Kumbhalner. Padmāvatī angrily repudiates her as a whore and tells her to go back to her husband's enemy. In her eyes, no one can compare with her beloved husband Ratansen. Following her angry eviction of Kumudini, Padmāvatī establishes a charitable house for wandering ascetics (*dharmaśālā*). She hopes to hear news of her captive husband from travelers, as well as to earn merit to release him from captivity. Back in Delhi, 'Alāuddīn hears of this and engages a harlot to disguise herself as a wandering ascetic and to bring Padmāvatī to him. This whore comes to Chittaur in the guise of a *yoginī*, a female ascetic, completely equipped with the external marks of Gorakhnāth's path: the horn whistle, the begging bowl, the yogi's crutch (*ādhārī*), and the ascetic's viol (*kiṅgarī*). She tells the queen of Ratansen's grievous imprisonment and torture, hoping to entice her to come back to Delhi with her. Padmāvatī is ready to become the *yoginī*'s disciple and set out on a quest for her lord, but her companions dissuade her. They dismiss the *yoginī* and advise the queen to seek the help of her husband's preeminent warriors, Gorā and Bādal.

In desperation, Padmāvatī goes to the house of Gorā and Bādal. The warriors are amazed that the queen has deigned to come from her palace to their house. Jāyasī makes much of the beautiful Padmāvatī's descent to earth, and Gorā and Bādal set her on a golden throne and attend her with the yak-tail chowries due to royalty. They repeat their warning about the perfidy and treachery of the Turks, and advise her not to become a *yoginī* herself. Instead, they offer to obtain Ratansen's release by going to Delhi and fighting with the Turks themselves. Together, they think of a way to get Ratansen released from the sultan's dungeons.

They use a trick that we find also in sources contemporary with Jāyasī or later, such as the historian Firishtah's account of the fall of Chittaur. Firishtah makes Padmāvatī the clever daughter of King Ratansen, and relates that she used the stratagem of visiting the king accompanied by armed warriors concealed in the women's palanquins. Once inside the fort, the warriors jumped out and overpowered the guards, allowing the king to make his escape.[41] As Aziz Ahmad has also noted, Sher Shāh Sūr used the same trick during his military struggle against Humāyūn. When Humāyūn seized the strong fort of Chunar in 1538, Sher Shāh got his men into the fortress of Rohtas in Bihar by asking the Raja for shelter for the women of his harem and smuggling warriors into the fort in palanquins.[42] It is very probably this contemporary event that Jāyasī recasts into a moving episode in which Gorā and Bādal reassure the distressed Queen Padmāvatī and use the trick against 'Alāuddīn Khalji.

Even though Bādal's beautiful new bride has just arrived with her wedding train, he goes to war rather than consummate his new marriage. The two warriors make their way to Delhi with sixteen hundred women's litters. Young armed warriors are seated in all of them, ready to do battle once they are inside the sultan's palace. When they arrive in Delhi, Gorā and Bādal bribe the jailor to inform the shah that Padmāvatī will make herself and the keys of Chittaur over to him if she is allowed half an hour alone with her husband. Jāyasī's presentation of these events, in common with several of the Rajput and Persian narratives, shows that Rajputs, Turks, and Afghans understood in common the mechanisms for negotiation, hostage taking, entertainment of enemy envoys, safe conducts, and in general mutual accommodation, the whole code of warfare, siege, negotiation, and parley. Despite frequent campaigns and jockeying for advantage, these parties had worked out the arrangements for power sharing, communication, tribute, and the everyday business of life in shared space. Thus the message of Gorā and Bādal is immediately understood and acted on; they are allowed to meet Ratansen in his dungeon. Once inside, they overpower his jailors and escape from the palace before anyone realizes what is going on.

The Final Battle

As they flee Delhi, the sultan's army swoops down on them and a melee like the *Mahābhārata* war ensues. Gorā and a thousand brave youths make a last stand, fighting a rearguard action so that the others may get away. The sultan's forces kill them, but Bādal and the king escape and make their way back to Chittaur. Bādal is reunited with his newly wedded wife. Padmāvatī is delighted to see her true love again, and tells him of Devapāl's attempt against her virtue:

> *"My lord, your boat fell into a whirlpool.*
> *But now listen to the sorrows of your lotus love.*
> *You went and left me in the lake,*
> *and the lake dried up around me without you.*
> *The goose that used to play there flew away,*
> *and the friendly sun became my enemy....*
> *Above all this, how can I tell you*
> *of the blows that struck me—a heavy grief*
> *fell on me like a rugged mountain.*
> *Devapāl sent a woman messenger to me.*
> *She put on the guise of a Brahmin woman*
> *and tried her utmost to deceive me.*
> *She told me she was my friend from long ago.*
> *She offered to take me, the clinging vine,*
> *to where the black bee awaited.*
> *Then I realized, truly, that her words*
> *were steeped in poison" [P 643.1–3, 644.1–4].*

Ratansen is enraged, and his response brings up again the imagery of the bee, the frog, and the lotus that Jāyasī has already used to indicate the mystical significance of his poetics of *rasa*:

> *"When has the frog ever looked at the lotus?*
> *The bat never sees the face of the sun.*
> *The peacock dances in his own color,*
> *but can the rooster copy him successfully?*
> *Before the Turks come to attack the fort,*
> *I will seize him, else I am not a king!" [P645.2–4]*

Ratansen evokes the symbolism of the fragrance of the lotus that only the true lover or connoisseur (the bee) can grasp. Like the bee, he traversed a long distance to Singhala-dīpa to win Padmāvatī, the lotus lady. Devapāl is merely a frog, who lives next to the lotus but cannot appreciate the subtle scent that wafts through the earth because of Padmāvatī's revelatory beauty. He is just a common rooster trying to imitate the peacock's dance. The angry Ratansen attacks Devapāl's fortress of Kumbhalner, and the two kings engage in single combat. During the fight, Devapāl treacherously uses a poisoned spear and wounds Ratansen. And although Ratansen captures Devapāl and beheads him for the insult he has offered his wife, he is fatally wounded. On his way back to Chittaur, he breathes his last and is carried home on a litter.

Padmāvatī and Nāgmatī, lamenting and wailing, put on fine silken clothes and ascend his pyre, sacrificing themselves as *satīs*. Love consummated, in the generic logic of the *premākhyāns*, leads to a final annihilation and a return to the divine realm. Here the stereotype of what is due from an obedient Hindu wife, becoming a *satī* for the sake of the dominant male, is yoked to the mystical value of *fanā* or the destruction of self. Padmāvatī and Nāgmatī are *mahāsatīs*, faithful wives of great loyalty. As they mount the pyre they say:

"Today the sun has set in the day, and the moon is sinking at night.
Today let us give up our lives dancing for joy; today the fire for us is cool."

They prepared the funeral pyre
and gave generously in alms and charity.
Seven times they circled the pyre.
"There was one kind of circle at our wedding;
now there is another as we go with you.
In life, beloved, you embraced us.
We will not leave your embrace in death.
And the knot that you, our lover, tied,
let it never be untied from beginning to end.
What is this world but non-being in being?
We and you, lord, will be together in both worlds."
They embraced him and lit the Holi fire.
They were burnt to ashes, but did not flinch.
They left this world, steeped in their love, and heaven glowed ruby red.
Whoever had arisen, had now set; no one remained in the world
of the living [P 649.8–650].

The real violence of the act is obliterated like the bodies of the women, and a symbolic edifice is created on the ashes. In a sense, the Sufi poets of the romances use the misogynistic poetic symbol of the *satī* to assert their spiritual superiority over the material and political dominance of their élite patrons. The speech Jāyasī puts in the mouths of the burning wives, characteristically, makes them happy to burn themselves alive for love. In dying on the pyre, they reaffirm the ultimate value and eternity of mystical love (*prema*) over the transience of this world. The knot of faith and love endures from the beginning to the end of existence. Indeed, the speech asserts that though the world is eventually folded back into nonbeing, love lasts forever. In a generically consistent ending, all the major characters disappear from this world, demonstrating the interconnection of love and death, the path of Sufi mysticism and final annihilation.

The emperor, who has laid siege to the fortress again, enters the city walls to find nothing but useless cinders. He demolishes the fort, and Chittaur is converted to Islam. Violence is of no avail, and all that remains for the wicked sultan in the end is ashes:

> *When they had departed, going with their lord,*
> *the sultan came and attacked the fortress.*
> *By then, the occasion had passed already.*
> *Rāma and Sītā had vanished away.*
> *The shah came into the assembly hall....*
> *He picked up a handful of ashes*
> *and threw it in the air, declaring*
> *"Earth is vanity! Until ashes fall on it,*
> *Desire for the world cannot be extinguished!"*
> *His whole army raised earth,*
> *and built causeways over the fort's passes.*
> *They attacked, and there was a confused battle.*
> *Bādal came to the gate and died fighting.*
> *All the women committed* jauhar, *and all the men died in the battle.*
> *The Emperor demolished the fortress, Chittaur became Islam [P 651].*

The final *fanā*, in which all of Chittaur is consumed and "becomes" Islam, signifies the Sufi martyrdom of a figure such as al-Ḥallāj, as well as the nostalgic identification with the Rajputs who fought bravely and sacrificed everything. By implication, only seekers on the path who give up even their lives can achieve the symbolic goal of spiritual love. But the famous last words also contain a pun on the word Chittaur, which can be broken down into its component parts of *citta* and *ura*, mind and breast, or by implication, heart.[43]

As Shantanu Phukan has pointed out, these last words imply "the theological concept of the complete surrender of the human heart and mind to the will of God (*islam*)."[44] Moreover, placing this assertion of the "true" meaning of Islam as submission within the imaginative and interior landscapes of self-transformation implies that lovers and mystics who have tasted *prema-rasa* survive beyond the destruction of the world, that is, they go beyond *fanā* (annihilation of self) to *baqā'*, subsistence in God. As Padmāvatī and Nāgmatī cry out on the funeral pyre, the knot that they have tied with Ratansen will last beyond the beginning and end of all things. As for the sultan, he embodies a "false" Islam. Although he has triumphed over Ratansen and the Rajput army, all he gets for his trouble is ashes. The spiritually justified victory belongs to the Rajputs, who gave their all for love. The subjectivity of the conquerors is here transformed so that they assume the roles of the defenders of the land, an interesting contrast to the fourteenth-century narratives of the victory of an idealized and militaristic Islam. Thus Jāyasī valorizes defeat as a spiritual value. Externally, Chittaur has "become Islam," but the internal victory belongs to the martyrs of love.

Jāyasī's depiction of the tragic fall of Chittaur implies a complex sort of indigenization of the Chishti and Mahdavi Sufi circles among whom he composed his poem. The hero Ratansen puts on a yogi's guise before he goes on his quest, only to shed the saffron robe and the earrings attached with wax when he wins Padmāvatī. Ratansen is a Sufi seeker, and though he has become just like a yogi in his appearance (*bhesa*), he is actually better than a yogi because he can use yogic and alchemical language and techniques to gain a superior goal: union with the divine Padmāvatī. The "as if" logic of this operation implies that Jāyasī is using the generic formula established by Maulānā Dā'ūd and Quṭban to bring local tales of the fabled Serendib and stories of Rajput resistance to the Turks into the formulaic narrative of the hero and his two wives and the different sorts of love. But this is only a fictional image. The Sufi reinscription of themselves as indigenous figures implies an elaborate masquerade of going *desī*.

Jāyasī takes up all the classic tropes and motifs of Rajput martial literature (the offended Brahmin minister, the impudent Turkish demand for a woman who embodies symbolic honor [*māna*], its furious rejection, woman as *casus belli*, the overwhelming military superiority of the Turks, and the evil sultan in Delhi who subordinates small regional kingdoms to satisfy his greed and his lust) but reads them within the Chishti arrogation of the physical landscape of Avadh. His poem can therefore also be read as a critique of political power: although political élites proclaimed their dominance through the sponsorship of art and literature, the Hindavī Sufi romances concealed within them a covert Sufi claim to spiritual superiority over the kings who supported them. The contest between love rightfully gained and love wrested through violence sends a clear message to political élites about the symbolic independence of Sufi *silsilahs* despite their reliance on those same élites for patronage. The relationship was one of mutual dependence, for Sufis played important roles as guarantors of the spiritual legitimacy of rule during the period of the Delhi sultanate and the regional Afghan kingdoms.

Padmāvatī represents a Sufi courtly poet's erotic fetishization of India, while the hero in his yogic disguise signifies the courtly élite "going native." Malik Muḥammad Jāyasī used all the tropes and figures native to India to create a "false" or seemingly native image of an Indian romance, which is only a front for the "true" Sufi message of the poem. And although the historical

Padmāvatī did not ascend the flaming pyre, and her *jauhar* is a historical fiction, and the final martyrdom uses the theme of Rajput resistance to Turkish invaders to convey the message of the spiritual struggle to taste *prema-rasa*, the larger conflation of erotic fetishization and military subjugation makes the text a powerful statement of the actual cultural logic of its period.

The story caught the imagination of audiences, poets, patrons, and imitators, and became an emblem of the successful and tragic conquest of Hindustan. Padmāvatī meant many things to many people in the centuries that followed. For the Rajput chroniclers following Jāyasī, she was the lovely queen who died rather than submit to the wicked Sultan 'Alāuddīn Khaljī, thus preserving the symbolic honor of a defeated people. For the Afghan and, later, the Mughal courts, she was an erotic object and the centerpiece of an Indian landscape, the crystallization of the beauty and allure of a subjugated people. Ironically, for the nationalists she was the emblem of a heroic resistance to foreign imperialism, a key figure in the narrative of the recuperation of "Hindu" honor despite the tragic fall of the Rajput states to the sultans of Delhi.

7

Bodies That Signify: The Madhumālatī, *Part 1*

Erotic/Ascetic Sufi Narratives

Erotic union, failed or fulfilled, is at the heart of any romantic text. But the reception of sophisticated mystical poems to the accompaniment of music in courtly settings as well as in the *kh̲ānaqāhs* of Sufi shaikhs raises questions. How did these various audiences—and how should we ourselves—understand the complex linking of asceticism and eroticism implied by the passages of love play in these romances? We have already noted the coincidence between the imaginary landscape and the eroticized female body that is its centerpiece, as well as the yogic dress adopted by the seeker to progress on his ascetic quest. In the only published treatment of the sexuality of South Asian Sufis in the period of the Delhi sultanate, Bruce Lawrence has remarked on the contradictions inherent in attitudes toward women in Sufi thought and practice:

> Women are the topical focus for expressing attitudes on sexuality, not only in Shaykh Nizam ad-din Awliya's case but also in the case of other South Asian Sufi masters. There is at once delight in women's beauty and fear of their power, yet there is no sense of enjoyment in the physical dalliance or consummation of the love relationship. For the South Asian Sufi masters, and for South Asian society as a whole, we find scant evidence of the pleasure principle applying to or deriving from sexual experience. Sexuality therefore means something other than coitus in our evidence. It would be more apt to say that sexuality becomes the achievement of social expression through gender interaction, while asceticism is at once the recognition of the role of sexuality in society...and its partial curtailment, or...its outright rejection, on the part of holy minded individuals.[1]

Lawrence sets this judgment within a nuanced reading of the discourses of Shaikh Niẕām al-dīn Auliyā' and his expressed attitudes toward women as facilitators of chastity and true repentance for wayward men. He cites the shaikh's atypical renunciation of sex and marriage and his respectful attitude toward a certain holy woman in Delhi, Bībī Fātimah Sām, making him "a celibate male feminist of pre-Mughal Indian Islam."[2] But Shaikh Niẕām al-dīn was unique; most Sufis were married and had families, exemplifying the tradition of the Prophet: "there is no monkery in Islam."

As Lawrence maintains, "sexuality... means something other than coitus in our evidence." How did sexuality figure in the ideas of married Indian Sufis, the largest part of our sample population? The Persian Sufi sources from the sultanate period list several saintly women whom the various Chishti shaikhs venerated; some of these are the pious mothers of the shaikhs themselves,[3] others female exemplars of piety such as Rābi'ah of Basra.[4] The Hindavī Sufi romances of the period must be included alongside the Persian and Arabic discourses and manuals of practice. For these elaborate vernacular fictive narratives express cultural stereotypes about gender and asceticism as they were thematized in the imagination of poets and their audiences at courts and *k͟hānaqāhs*. The erotic encounters and poetic description of love play between heroes and heroines in the Hindavī Sufi romances contain many suggestive clues and coy references to theology and Sufi mysticism. And certain cultural stereotypes were commonly understood and cut across religious lines.

For instance, in the Hindavī form of *prema*, ordinary marriage and procreation were simply social structures that were beside the point. In a representative anecdote, Shaikh Rizqullāh Mushtāqī, a contemporary Shattari disciple, relates the story of a dervish and a newlywed bride who were obsessed with each other:

> In Jaunpur, a certain person got married and took his bride to his house in Zafarabad. He stopped the palanquin under a tree outside the city for rest and for eating a meal. He took his seat near the palanquin and the bride put aside the curtain to look around.... A recluse who was resting under the same tree cast his eye on the beautiful face of the girl and was completely captivated. He fixed his eyes on her face. Every time the girl looked at him she found him as if in a trance and constantly staring at her face. She guessed his condition and was surprised. She inquired from the nurse: "When shall we return to this place?" She said: "We shall come back after four days...." After four days, the recluse continued to wait for her the whole day. At... sunset, he got disappointed and began to sigh: '"Ah, ah, she has not come back," and passed away in this state. When the Muslims found him

> dead, they buried him after performing religious rites. The palanquin of the girl arrived in the evening just after his burial.... They told her that he suddenly died, and pointed to his grave at a little distance.... They said: "He only repeated, 'Ah, ah, she has not come,' and at last passed away"...[D]eeply moved, she said to the nurse: "[S]how me the grave of the recluse, so that I may visit and offer the *Fātihā* prayer for the departed soul." People created a curtain of sheets on all sides, so that she might visit the grave without exposing her face to people. When she visited the grave, she placed her head upon it. After some time, the nurse thought to call her back. When she looked for her inside the sheets, she did not find her there. She told people about it and every one of them was surprised; they considered it a miracle of *'ishq*. They unearthed the grave and found to their surprise the dead body of the recluse, wrapped with the embroidered garments of the bride, and his hands and feet dyed with henna. But there was no sign of the bride.[5]

The disappearance of the bride into the spiritual remains of the dervish points both to the evanescence of *'ishq* (love[6]) and the fact that the erotic body of the woman is part of the whole complex of male asceticism and sexuality. Bodily disappearance signifies sublimation of the erotic to theology, unification with the divine. Obsessive passion or ideal love (*'ishq*), leading even to death, is the most valued part of sexual and ascetic experience. It is the incitement of this obsessive emotion within the seeker that allows him to progress on the spiritual path and the narrative quest, putting *'ishq* (or, in the poetics of the Hindavī romances, *prema-rasa*) at the pinnacle of theology, the goal of the narrative, and the core of Sufi experience.

The Madhumālatī, *Part 1*

Nowhere is this better illustrated than in Shaikh Mīr Sayyid Mañjhan Shaṯṯārī Rājgīrī's *Madhumālatī*, a romance completed at the Afghan court of Islām Shāh Sūrī within five years of Malik Muḥammad Jāyasī's *Padmāvat*. Both Iqtidar Husain Siddiqui and S. C. R. Weightman have demonstrated that the poet Mañjhan has been confused with the Shaikh Mañjhan, whom the *Gulzār-i Abrār* mentions as the *qāẓī* of the town of Chunar.[7] As Weightman has noted, the poet Mañjhan (the "middle" son) was the maternal grandson of Shāh 'Abdullāh Shaṯṯār's *khalīfah*, Shaikh Muḥammad Qāẓin 'Alā':

> Manjhan's mother was Bibi Khunja Daulat, the daughter of the renowned Shaikh Muhammad Qāzin 'Alā who, although reared in both the Madārī and Chishtī traditions, later proved to be one of the

principal exponents and propagators of the Shattāriyya order in Bihar. Manjhan's father was Sayyid Muhammad 'Alī Manjhan Danishmand, the son of Sayyid Muhammad Chakkan of Jaunpur.[8]

Regrettably, very little else is known about the poet Mañjhan, except what he himself tells us in the prologue to the *Madhumālatī*. We do know that he was attached to the Shattari Sufi master Shaikh Muḥammad Ġhauṣ Gvāliyārī (d. 1562), and received instruction from the charismatic shaikh in Gwalior. The mystical culture of the Shattaris is an intrinsic part of the *Madhumālatī*.

The heroine of the first part of the poem is a princess of the mystical city of Mahāras, the "great *rasa*." Heavenly *apsara*ses ("nymphs" or peris) transport Manohar, Prince of Kanaigiri, to the bedroom of the sleeping Madhumālatī. The vision of beauty before him stuns him. The poet uses the generic set piece of the head-to foot description (*sarāpā*) to detail what Manohar sees, portraying the body of Madhumālatī as the unfolding of divine revelation before Manohar's eyes. The Princess awakes and they fall instantly, completely, in love. Promising eternal love, they exchange their rings as signs of their oath to be true to one another. Manohar falls asleep, only to wake up in his own city of Kanaigiri. His nurse Sahajā ("absorption in the inborn reality") counsels him to become an ascetic to win the beautiful Madhumālatī, and he sets out in the garb of a yogi to attain the love that his vision of Madhumālatī promised him. The logic of embodiment that runs through Mañjhan's poetic images matches male ascetic body to female erotic object and echoes in the various contexts of cosmology, ascetic practice, politics, and poetic literature.

Shattari cosmology hierarchically orders the stages of emergence from and return to Allah (*mabda' va ma'ād*) in concentric circles, fitted within the larger circular structure of emergence and return. These circles within circles are elaborated as the stages of mystical ascent and descent for the Shattari novice. Citing the *Gulzār-i Abrār*, an important Shattari hagiographical collection completed in 1612, S. A. A. Rizvi indicates that the shape of religious practice for the Shattaris was circular:

> According to the Shattāriyya technique, the neophyte at the very beginning of his training is required to consider himself at the very *'ain* [essence] of the Being and then descend step by step from the realm of the self-manifestation of the Absolute to the phenomenal world. Then step by step he re-ascends and reaches the Divine sphere, effacing all traces of the stages of descent. In contrast to this method, the other Sufis direct their disciples to ascend step by step from the realm of humanity to the realm of *Wahdat al-Wajūd*.[9]

In a pioneering article, Weightman has pointed out the similarity between this religious practice and the plot of the *Madhumālatī*. The disciple's initial state of absorption or *jaẕbah* is represented as the first meeting of the hero and heroine, Manohar and Madhumālatī. The neophyte must work his way back to the realm of the Absolute Divine, just as Manohar's progress describes a circular movement from the initial moment back to the point when the lovers can be united again.

At the first meeting of the lovers, the hero is required to fix "within his deepest awareness the image of God and of Divine Beauty (Madhumālatī)":

> The neophyte has then to descend step by step from the realm of self-manifestation of the Absolute to the phenomenal world. This process is paralleled in Manohar setting out, being shipwrecked and cast up on an unknown shore alone "save for the pain of his suffering in separation and the mercy of God." Then he discovers love, Pemā, portrayed as young, innocent and unawakened, but imprisoned by a demon. Manohar kills the demon by destroying the source of its powers of renewal, suggesting that a very radical transformation of the disciple's nature is here signified...[he] is able to have a second meeting with [Madhumālatī]. This point can be taken as the beginning of the ascent back to the Divine sphere.[10]

Mañjhan's text is loosely suggestive of such a circular movement, although elements of the narrative fall outside a strictly "allegorical" explanation. Thus, for instance, at one point Madhumālatī's angry mother bewitches Manohar and sends him back home, an event that violates the easy progression of mystical stages set out in the Shattari practical manuals. Simultaneously, Madhumālatī is separated from Manohar and becomes the seeker, wandering the world in the shape of a bird in search of her mate. In this form she sends him a message using the generic set piece of the *bārah-māsā* (the description of the twelve months of separation), which impels him to come back to her.[11]

The ascetic body that is the site for self-transformation in this formulaic text is anchored in a system of belief and religious invocation. Shattari uses of the body are relevant both to their way of remaking themselves and to the larger cultural dynamics of Sufi practice. In accordance with the generic pattern of the Hindavī romances, the hero's path to spiritual attainment is through the awakening of love through a dream, vision, or poetic description. In a sense, the male subject can be transformed only by using the woman's body as the erotic and aesthetic impetus to draw him out of himself. Similarly, the description of Madhumālatī's body, in which the poet itemizes the limbs of her body and describes their effects on the seeker, is a formal requirement of the genre of the Hindavī Sufi romance. Both bodies signify, and are part of the process of, concretizing an invisible Sufi spiritual cosmos. The Shattari manuscripts take up cosmological and bodily structures, elaborate them, and fit them to particular needs: interior practice or the Hindavī poetics of love. As Pierre Bourdieu and other anthropologists remind us, practice involves a dynamic intermeshing of structure and agency.[12] Cosmology is not an essentialist form that endures through the ages, but a changing structure that different people use differently, that they internalize and live through varying structures of habitus, whether it is court ritual or the poetics of obsessive love or Sufi ascetic discipline.

In the Hindavī romances, the woman as erotic object is part of the politics of conquest of an Indian landscape, but she is also the carrier of theological and spiritual meanings. What makes the Hindavī Sufi romances different from, say, European colonialism and its fetishizations of native objects are the complex interminglings of theology and politics, indigenous and foreign, implicit in the yogic garb of the Sufi seeker and his sensuous meeting with the divinely beautiful heroine. This chapter considers the logic of embodiment in Shattari poetics, politics, and practice through a reading of the allegorical centerpiece of the romance, the head-to-foot description of the heroine Madhumālatī. It will then analyze the elaborate Shattari macrocosm and the order's ideology in the context of their involvement with court politics and ascetic practices.

Madhumālatī Described

The allegorically suggestive description of Madhumālatī's body, a formal requirement of the genre of the Hindavī Sufi *premākhyān*, works simultaneously as a Hindavī head-to-foot description (*śikha-nakha varṇana*) and a site for divine self-disclosure, making visible an invisible Sufi spiritual cosmos. In the logic of the Shattari worldview, hidden nature is more real (*ḥaqīqī*) than the forms (*ṣūrat*) that are apparent to the senses. This distinction between *ḥaqīqat* and *ṣūrat* or reality and appearance, neo-Platonic in origin, enables the Sufis to interpret sensible forms literally as well as spiritually. The theory of representation that makes possible this move is contained in the term *tamṡīl*, which may mean allegory, exemplification, or embodiment, depending on its context. The plain text (*'ibārah*) may contain a reference (*ishārah*) or an exemplification of an abstract concept (*tamṡīl*).

These principles of reading for multiple signification are signaled right at the beginning of the story with the birth of Manohar, prince of Kanaigiri, the Mountain of Gold. Prince Manohar is born to the childless Sūrajbhānu, king of Kanaigiri, as the result of an ascetic's boon. The prince is the apple of his father's eye. The king summons a pandit to educate him in all the classical texts. Included in his education are the principles of interpreting texts for multiple meanings:

The pandit taught the prince well
that each word had several meanings.
He taught him yoga and the science of sex,
drew pictures and explained their meanings.
Soon the prince became so clever
he could explain many levels of mystery in scripture [MM 57].

In this passage, Mañjhan introduces a view of language basic to the polysemy of the text. Each word (*bacana*) has multiple meanings (*artha*), which the prince learns to read. The prince learns the explication of many levels of mystery in scriptural texts as a basic interpretive strategy. This vernacular *'ilm-i bāṭin*, or knowledge of the inner secrets of divinity, is fundamental to the polysemic Sufi poetics of the *Madhumālatī*.

The pandit teaches Manohar all the classical sources, introducing another useful notion:

He taught him the true meanings
of the Yogasūtra *and the* Amarakoṣa,
poetics and prosody and the Koka-śāstra.[13]
Who could match the prince
in grammar, astrology or the Gītā,
in the arts of meaning, poetry or song? [MM 57]

Here Mañjhan uses the term *sat-bhāva* ("true meaning/essence"), which anchors the poetic practice of referring to double or multiple meanings in the text. The literal events of the narrative of the *Madhumālatī* have true or *ḥaqīqī* meanings that the poet obliquely suggests. The Shattari idea that the cosmos is only a veil for the secrets of the divine is thus the sanction for the text's poetics of oblique reference. Reading becomes a process of unveiling the secrets locked in concrete forms. These passages on the young prince's education refer self-reflexively to how reading is understood within the poetic culture of the Afghan courts and Sufi *k͟hānaqāh*s of the sixteenth century.

Once the prince's education is complete, he takes over the kingdom from his father, Sūrajbhānu. One night, Manohar is fast asleep in his bedroom after watching an entrancing dance performance in court. Some celestial *apsaras*es (nymphs) who are flying about catch sight of him and are struck by his beauty. They decide that he is a suitable match for the beautiful Madhumālatī, the princess of the city of Mahāras. So they pick up his bed and carry it to Madhumālatī's bedroom. Their purpose is to compare the beauty of both to determine which is better. They are confounded when they discover that the prince and princess are a perfectly matched pair. At this point they refer to the allegorical significance of the meeting through a series of analogies:

> *"If God should let them come together,*
> *the three worlds would echo with celebration.*
> *To look on them is to taste the joy*
> *of yogis in the state of mystical union.*
> ...
> *He is the sun and she the moon. She is the sun and he the moon.*
> *If love were born between them, kettledrums would sound through creation" [MM 72].*

Their inability to decide whether the prince or the princess is preeminent in beauty is conveyed through the poetic image of sun and moon: Whose light or spiritual effulgence is reflected in whom? The sun and moon here could refer to the internal geography of the yogic body, to the channels of Iḍā and Piṅgalā that run inside the body and that the practitioner harnesses in his austerities. As the Shattari stages of manifestation show, concrete forms (*ṣūrat*) exemplify and are shadows of spiritual processes on higher planes.

As Manohar opens his eyes, he has a vision of the divine unfolding before him. Alternately, he faints and recovers consciousness, as the beauty that is shown him awakens in him a deep response:

> *The moment that he saw Madhumālatī*
> *she possessed his heart completely.*
> *His soul bowed down to her beauty.*
> *Seeing her lying in sweet sleep,*
> *the fire of love engulfed his body,*
> *consuming him utterly, from top to toe.*
> *Like a lotus opening towards the sun, he blossomed as he saw her face.*
> *Love from a past birth, like a green shoot, sprouted in the prince's heart [MM 75].*

The image of a lover blossoming like a lotus when he sees the beloved's face signifies, according to a 16th century Sufi gloss on Hindavī poetry, the *Ḥaqā'iq-i Hindī*, the opening up of a religious community (*ummah*) to the spiritual truth taught by the Prophet Muḥammad.[14] Here, the prince becomes aware of love from a previous birth, the mystic love that is responsible for the creation of the world and that dwells within the hearts of all beings. The words the poet uses for Manohar's response mirror, in reverse, the description of Madhumālatī. He is consumed with the fire of love from top-to-toe, *nakha-śikha*, just as the *tajallī* of Madhumālatī describes her from head-to-foot. If the body of Madhumālatī represents the *jalvah* or brilliant revelation of the divine, Manohar represents the believer who witnesses this effulgent manifestation. During the *mushāhadah* or witnessing, he faints and recovers. Like Lorik in the *Cāndāyan*, he is blinded by a woman's brilliance.

The text views her body through a characteristic play between denial and affirmation:

> *If someone describes this as God's self-disclosure, then understand the nature of God:*
> *The Lord is hidden in this world, and no one has ever seen Him [MM 88].*[15]

The poet's denial works as a way of affirming a truth that cannot be conveyed in ordinary language. In other words, the text implies that if the beautiful description of Madhumālatī were to inspire someone to exclaim, "Why, she is the manifestation of God!" the poet would kindly explain to the reader that no one has seen God in this world. But the reader would not be wrong in supposing that her disclosure mirrors the *prasāra* or *tajallī* (self-disclosure) of God, that it is the description of a form (*ṣūrat*) in a world in which true reality is elusive and invisible. She is simultaneously a concrete form and a shadowy mirror of a spiritual reality that no one has ever seen except through analogy, allegory, or likeness. Her body signifies both an accepted set of poetic topoi in Avadhi and a spiritual cosmos, bridging the gap between *ṣūrat* (appearance) and *ḥaqīqat* (reality).

When the veil of the invisible is rent, the whole world reels before the flash. Madhumālatī smiles slightly in her sleep and her *jalvah* or manifestation is blinding:

> *When she smiled slightly in her sleep,*
> *lightning flashed from the heavens.*
> *When her lips parted, her teeth shone:*
> *the sages of the triple world were blinded*
> *and lost all recollection of themselves [MM 88].*

How can one decipher the signs inscribed upon the "signifying body" of the heroine? Some indications are given by a near-contemporary Sufi gloss on Hindi poetry, the *Ḥaqā'iq-i Hindī* of Mīr 'Abdul Vāḥid Bilgrāmī, written in 1566 and concerned precisely with interpreting the sensuous portions of *dhrupad* and *viṣṇu-pada* poetry for Sufi readers, useful in reading the *sarāpā* of Madhumālatī.

According to this text, in this parting of Madhumalati's lips Allah's divine attributes or Names are manifested. These are divided into two sorts: those related to his divine beauty and grace (*asmā'-i jamālī*) and those related to his astounding might and majesty (*asmā'-i jalālī*). God is al-Raḥmān ("the Beneficent"), al-Raḥīm ("the Merciful"), al-Ġhaffār ("the Forgiver"), al-Muḥyī ("the Giver of Life"), al-Nūr ("the Light"), al-Karīm ("the Generous"). All these qualities nourish and protect the believer. At the same time, Allah is al-Qahhār ("the Subduer") al-Jabbār ("the Compeller"), al-Mumīt ("the Bringer of Death"), al-Muqtadir ("the Powerful"). These are the destructive attributes of Allah, which excite fear in the believer and wreak vengeance for wrongdoing.

The *Sarāpā* or Head-to-Foot Description (Reprise)

The poetic imagery used to describe the parts of Madhumālatī's body, using the same conventions of the *sarāpā* that Dā'ūd used to describe Cāndā in the *Cāndāyan*,[16] similarly alternates between fierce and gentle (*jalālī* and *jamālī*), paralleling the manifestation of the Names of Allah. Starting at the top of her head, the poet begins his description of her with her *māṉga* or parting:

> *Let me first tell of the parting in her hair*
> *difficult of ascent as the path to heaven.*
> *As he looked at her parting and flowing locks*
> *he kept straying from the path and returning to it.*
> *Strikingly lovely was the parting on her head,*
> *like the keen edge of a sword stained with blood.*
> *Who could traverse the path of that parting?*
> *At every step, ringlets and curls set snares for the traveller [MM 77].*

The poetic reference or *ishārah* here is to the famous narrow bridge (the Pūl-i Sirāṭ) of the Qur'ān, the bridge between heaven and hell that all must pass over after death. Only the righteous can cross the infernal abyss on this narrow path, so difficult of access; and it is as difficult to attain the parting in the black locks of the beautiful Madhumālatī as it is to walk over the Pūl-i Sirāṭ. Further, her shining white parting, adorned with red *sindūra* or vermillion, is likened to the keen edge of a fierce sword stained with blood, which has been used to dispatch lovers eager to walk along it. The ringlets and curls are described as *phaṉsihārā*, fierce thugs who set snares for travelers and strangle them. The killing that goes on here can also refer to the necessary annihilation of the ego or self (*khvudī*) of the seeker (*fanā*).

To this display of *jalāl* or ferocious cruelty, the poet adds another image in the next verse, one specifically related to the circular structure of the Shattari spiritual quest:

> *A ray of sunlight was her beautiful parting.*
> *When it had won all the world, it moved heavenwards [MM 78].*

Her parting as a ray of sunlight mimics the descent of divine essence into the world and the eventual return of all things to God.

Lest one think that the beautiful Madhumālatī was all fierce cruelty and no *jamāl* or grace, the poet compares her parting to a stream of nectar:

> *Where did this stream of nectar flow from,*
> *the source for her moon-face's inexhaustible radiance? [MM 78]*

The text goes on to describe her beautiful black tresses as poisonous serpents that cruelly sting away the lives of lovers:

> *Her scattered locks were poisonous serpents*
> *gliding over the pillows in excitement*
> *gem-bearing snakes, moving so quickly,*
> *viciously, full of deadly venom.*
> ...
> *Whoever in this world saw her locks,*
> *lost all awareness of his own condition [MM 79].*

Her locks embody the vicious, sinful darkness of this world, and gather the sorrows of lovers into themselves. They are like poisonous snakes, but snakes who sting seekers out of all awareness of their own condition, making them receptive to the revelation in the next verse:

> *Her forehead was as spotless as the moon*
> *on the second night of a month,*
> *shining through nine regions and three worlds.*
> *Beads of perspiration shone brilliantly on her face,*
> *as if the Pleiades had engulfed the moon [MM 81].*

For the prince, and all others who look on with the right eyes, this revelation of light (*nūr*) is the first specification of divine essence. Her shining forehead, spotless as the moon, with pearllike beads of moisture on it, signifies the site of the first revelation (*ta'yīn*). According to the *Ḥaqā'iq-i Hindī*, her forehead (and by extension her body) is the writing of the mysterious invisible (*ġhaib*) on the surface of this world.[17] This textualized embodiment works as both the *'ibārah*, the plain text, and the *ishārah*, or reference, to the spiritual cosmos of the Shattaris.

There is allegory (*tamsīl*) in the description of Madhumālatī's eyebrows:

Love happily took his bow in his hands
and broke it into two with his strength.
Without any alchemy, he put them point to point,
arranging them as Madhumālatī's eyebrows.
How beautifully her eyebrows graced her face,
as if Love's bow had been embodied on earth [MM 82].

The line of her eyebrow suggests the line that is drawn between the two aspects of the revelation of the Divine, oneness and unification (*aḥadiyah/vāḥidiyah*). The eyebrows are the site of the *barzakh-i kubrá* or intermediary state between these two. According to the *Ḥaqā'iq-i Hindī*, the space of the eyebrows is the length of "two bow-lengths or less" (*qāb qausain au adná*), the space between God and the Prophet on the *mi'rāj*, or night journey of the Prophet Muḥammad.[18] Their embodiment suggests both the all-conquering bow of Kāmadeva, the God of Love, and the space of revelation between God and the believer; love is the bond that ties them together across this space.

The poet moves on to talk of her crookedly seductive eyes, large, lively, keen, and intoxicating (*capala bisāla tīkha ati bāṇke*), which captivate the souls of lovers with their play. According to Bilgrāmī's gloss, her eyes suggest the *karishmah-yi chashm-i maḥbūb*,[19] the deceptive glitter in the eyes of the divine beloved containing within it a shadow of the invisible. They embody both the vision to see spiritual reality and the play between ferocity and loveliness (*jalāl* and *jamāl*):

They were a wondrous paradox that could not be resolved:
her eyes were does that lay fearlessly, each one beneath a hunter's bow [MM 83].

Space forbids exploration of the bloodthirsty description of Madhumālatī's eyelashes, each like an arrow that pierces the heart of the poor lover and reduces him to a sieve; or a description of her nose, which the text links with the mystic channels of Iḍā and Pingalā in the symbolic geography of the yogic body. Madhumālatī's cheeks suggest the site of the witnessing (*mushāhadah*) of the revelation of the divine. Their unveiling overwhelms the seer's capacity to find similes or words. Below these two lovely cheeks is a pair of red lips, dripping with nectar, the source of the primordial grace of God (*luṭf-i sābiqah*), sustainer of life and love:

> *[Her lips] were tender, juicy, red in color,*
> bimba *fruits placed against the moon.*
> *No, no, this simile does not suffice:*
> *God squeezed the moon's nectar to form them.*
> *Her lips, full of nectar, were yet untasted.*
> *When the prince saw them, he felt*
> *his life drain away, and cried aloud:*
> *"When will the Lord grant my life be restored?" [MM 87]*

Allah's mercy (*raḥmaḥ*), which restores life to wounded lovers and hope to believers, is in the nectar dripping from Madhumālatī's lips.

Madhumālatī's body embodies Allah but is only a weak shadow of divinity, embodying the interplay between *nirguṇa* and *saguṇa* aspects of vernacular theology. It is not merely a female body taken up as an object of the poet's gaze.[20] The Sufi text recognizes the power of the female gaze as overwhelming the male looking at her. This interlocked set of gazes signals a mystical ideology in which God/woman also has the power to look at man and transform his being. The unfolding religiosity in which subject and object, lover and beloved, divinity and created beings, can change places is played out in the description of the mole on Madhumālatī's face:

> *The prince's eyes were enamored of its beauty;*
> *they became transfixed, and would not leave it.*
> *"It is not a mole, but the reflection of my eye,*
> *with which her face appears ever more lovely.*
> *Her face is a clear, unblemished mirror;*
> *in it my eye's shadow appears as a beauty-spot.*
> *The pupil of my eye is soft and dark.*
> *It has fallen as a mole on her pure, spotless face" [MM 89].*

Here the very materiality, the dense blackness of the mole on her shining white face, is imagined as the transposition of the pupil of Manohar's eye onto the face. If Manohar's gaze is embodied on the mirror of her face, the face also has the power to see him. If the world was created, in the famous Sufi tradition, as a mirror for Allah's beauty, here beauty becomes a mirror for the seeing gaze. The interlocked visions suggest that divine revelation needs a witness as much as human beings need a mirror for their desire.

Divinity, like the beautiful Madhumālatī, is not merely an open book to be read for the allegory of every letter. There are mysteries, places difficult to reach or to unravel with poetic image or reasoning intelligence. One of these sites is the black tips of Madhumālatī's breasts:

Pointed, sharp, and unscrupulously seductive,
her breasts entered lovers' hearts on sight.
Lovely they looked, with darkened arrows on their tips.
Famous as brave fighters through the three worlds,
they wanted to dispute their boundary in war,
but then a necklace came between them [MM 95].

According to Bilgrāmī's gloss, the dark tips of her breasts signify divine mysteries (*sirr-i bārīk*) whose unveiling the Sharī'ah forbids. They are mysteries beyond the senses, contained in the words describing Allah's power and might, *jabr* (al-Jabbār, the Compeller) and *qadr* (al-Muqtadir, the Powerful). The cruel black tips are ready to fight on their boundary line to prevent an invasion into their sphere. The necklace that is trapped between them manages to mediate, to separate them so that they do not fight each other. As the embodiments of the unattainable mysteries of Allah's being, their beauty does not pain "her on whom they grew, but those who look on their loveliness."

Between her titillating breasts and her lovely hips lies Madhumālatī's waist, thin and delicate to the point that the weight of her hips might cause it to snap. The text refers to the inability of mortal hands to grasp her fine waist. The *Ḥaqā'iq-i Hindī* describes her thin waist also as a *barzakh* or intermediary state between Allah and the world.[21] On her waist is the fine line of her *romāvalī* or line of hair, which also suggests an intermediary chord (*barzakh*) in the circle of manifestation:

The line of hair on her navel
was a venomous serpent released
from its lair, roaming dangerously.
When it fell into her navel's pool,
it curled around, unable to climb out [MM 96].

The pool of nectar below the navel (*nābhi kuṇḍa*), out of which the fine line of hair rises, suggests the *amṛta kuṇḍa*, the pool of nectar that, in the Shattari mystical body, is imagined to be between the eyes (at the *brahma-randhra*). This is the place where nectar rains on the seeker, where he can enjoy the fruits of his austerities. The *romāvalī* combines the *jalālī* qualities of divinity with this pure and sacred site of union, since it is represented as a poisonous black snake, roaming about dangerously on her beautiful white stomach and ready to sting the man who lays his hand on her.

The final verse in the *sarāpā* of Madhumālatī is the description of her thighs and legs, as well as of her intoxicating "treasury of love" (*madana bhaṇḍāra*). The poet adroitly sidesteps an exact description:

For fear of immodesty before my elders,
I shall not describe her treasury of love.
The sight of her hips aroused the mind,
excited passion in the body in an instant.
Seeing her thighs plunged one's being
into utter confusion, struck one dumb [MM 97].

The never-perfect catching of the elusive divine that the seer attempts reduces him to utter confusion and silence. But the passionate desire excited in the believer's mind was an important component of the Sufi training of the self, which inculcated love in a novice toward any worldly object of desire and then sought to train it toward the divine beloved, moving from love of the *ṣūrat* or apparent form to the *ḥaqīqat* or reality behind appearances.

The embodiment of Madhumālatī is a mapping of precisely this double step, of concentrating desire in a concrete form and then showing how the concrete form is only a shadow of a spiritual reality. What enables the poet to accomplish this is a theory of meaning based on likeness (*upamā/tashbīh*) and reference. The head-to-foot description of Madhumālatī is a set of poetic images that play with analogy, exemplification, and likeness to construct her body as a field of meaning, or rather, double meaning.

The plain text (*'ibārah*), reference (*ishārah*), and allegory/exemplification (*tamsīl*) cannot be separated. As the nineteenth-century Urdu poet Ġhālib once famously remarked in a couplet,

Everything she says, Ġhālib, is a calamity she wreaks on my life—
What plain speech, what reference, what a manner![22]

The *sarāpā* fits into the narrative logic of the text as the moment when desire is awakened, between Manohar and Madhumālatī, Allah and the world, and reader and text.

Macrocosmic Geometries

The Key to Hidden Treasuries

Mañjhan dedicates several verses in the prologue of his *Madhumālatī* to the praise of his teacher, the renowned Shattari Shaikh Muḥammad Ġhauṣ

Gvāliyārī (d.1562), the fourth in a line of Shattari Sufi masters,[23] the dynamic spiritual guide to the first Mughal emperors Bābur and Humāyūn and to many nobles in the 1530s and 1540s. Shaikh Ġhauṣ̱ and his brother, Shaikh Phūl, were disciples of Shaikh Zuhūr Hājī Ḥamīd. Under him they learnt the Shattari methods of *ẕikr* and meditated in the jungles around the town of Chunar in central India. In the cosmological treatise *Kalīd-i Makẖāzin* ("The Key to Hidden Treasuries"), written in 1533, Shaikh Muḥammad Ġhauṣ̱ Gvāliyārī indicates this view of the body: "Man's body is like a book, and every letter is the form of an allegory. You will find in it everything you seek, and will not return empty-handed."[24] Each part of the body is a sign to be interpreted for a spiritual referent.

The *Kalīd-i Makẖāzin* also works out the most fully elaborated Shattari cosmology. In it, Shaikh Ġhauṣ̱ describes a pair of midnight visions that led him to write his key to the spiritual cosmos:

> One night in the year 932 (1523), I was thinking of the stages of descent and ascent, and meditating on the arrangement of the manifestation and progression of the hidden and the manifest, when suddenly I found myself in a state which was not annihilation (*fanā*) nor the annihilation which is subsistence (*fanā al-baqā*), neither sleep nor dream, when the Eternal Friend, the Everlasting Messenger of God, came to this *faqīr* and showed him all the hidden and the manifest stages, the emergence from and the return to God from the beginning without beginning to the end without end, and ordered, "After you emerge from this vision, proclaim it forth...."[25]

The shaikh was able to complete the book as ordered only after a few years, but then fell into a quandary about the right choice of name for it:

> No name occurred to me at all for naming this treatise, when suddenly the veil of the invisible was rent and, on the night of the eleventh of Ramaẕān, 942 (1533), the heavenly court was revealed to me. Muḥammad, the Lord of the worlds, whose breast is...the storehouse of the most ancient secrets, was enthroned in majesty and his noble companions and the great shaikhs were all present. The Messenger of God asked Abū Bakr, the Commander of the Faithful, to ask Shaikh Muḥammad Ġhauṣ̱ for the key to hidden treasuries. The Commander came to this *faqīr* and said, "Give me the key to hidden treasuries." I said, "I don't have it." And he extended his noble hand to my side and brought out this manuscript and said, "This is the key to hidden treasuries. Whoever opens it will find it a guide to the realities of the world and his way will be made clear to him."[26]

The shaikh's key to hidden spiritual treasuries, written and named in these nocturnal flashes of vision, reflects a well-worked-out Shattari cosmological scheme. It forms the basis of the Shattari system of interior discipline and letter mysticism, of the historical and social placement of the Shattari Sufis during the reigns of the first Mughal emperors.

Shattari Sufis thematize the descent of the divine Absolute into the world of phenomena as a succession of concentric circles (*dā'irah*, pl. *davā'ir*). To construct their image of a spiritual cosmos, they drew heavily on Ibn 'Arabī's formulation of *vaḥdat al-vujūd*, or unity of being,[27] which can be traced back to the neo-Platonic theory of the self-manifestation of the Absolute. Ibn 'Arabī's theology set up a correspondence between microcosm and macrocosm, using the geometry of circles to order the stages of divine manifestation hierarchically. The stages map a continuum between the plane of Absolute Essence (*z̤āt*) and the plane of material forms and sensible experience. In the highest degree or circle, the divine Absolute is nondetermined (*lā ta'yīn*), beyond all attributes, specified forms, and revelations, absolutely one (*al-Aḥad*).[28]

The first determination (*tajallī* or *ta'yīnn*) is the Absolute's manifestation in the form of light (*nūr*), unity (*vāḥidiyah*), or the archetypal reality of Muḥammad. On this plane, all the Divine Names and Attributes exist in the divine presence and are identical with it; the divine unity and the principle of multiplicity (*kaṣrat*) share in the same Essence. The Divine Names contain in summary the multiplicity of forms, which exist as receptacles for them in more concrete planes of existence. The second determination is the plane of the divine unity in the eternal Names, the *a'yān al-ṣābitah*, which form the prototypes for the multiple forms of creatures in existence. This is the plane where the forms are determined and distinguished one from the other, though they never come into concrete existence except through their shadows on the more material planes of the divine descent.

Following these two manifestations, the divine essence is refracted through three planes of existence, which gradually assume greater concreteness. The third determination of the divine essence is in the world of spirits (*'ālam al-arvāḥ*), in which the spirits know each other and recognize their prototypes (*al-a'yān*) as their masters. The next determination is that of the subtle forms (*ṣūrat* or *ams̤āl*) and imagination (*k͟hyāl*), which exemplify within their imaginal forms their prototypes on higher planes. They are not identical in being to their prototypes, but rather combine a shadow or analogy of the spiritual with their subtle material forms. Finally, the world of bodies (*'ālam al-ajsām*) is the plane of corporeal existence, in which the senses and sensible experience come into play (*mushāhadah*). Each of these planes is bound to the higher planes by a relationship of *tams̤īl* (exemplification). The processes of creating spirits, or subtle forms, or bodies, mirror analogically the process of creation by which the Divine Names come into existence.

Each plane of manifestation has both a hidden (*bāṭin*) and a manifest (*ẓāhir*) aspect, and Shaikh Muḥammad Ġhaus̱ Gvāliyārī works out the relation between them as the relation between a point and a circle:

> A point is the secret essence, and a circle is its manifest form. The point is the center of the circle which the pen of power draws and makes itself into a circle... [T]he circle is, in summary, the point. When you look at the point, it is the greatest mystery. When you come into the circle, and open the door of the point, you see that the circle is precisely the point, equal from every side.[29]

The hidden aspect of divine Being, unknowable, beyond representation or language, is unfolded in the manifest form of a circle or *dā'irah*, transforming Essence (*ẕāt*) into Attributes (*ṣifāt*). (This is the circular structure that the quest of the novice, and of Manohar, mirrors.) The contradictory relation between point and circle, the one containing and mirroring the other without being identical, extends through every plane of divine emanation. The Sufi can determine the inner meaning of the manifest forms by a process of *ta'vīl* or symbolic interpretation, a meditation on the exterior and manifest forms, the concentric circles, to know the hidden interior.

Another concept expressed in geometric shape in the Shattari cosmological diagrams is the idea of the intermediary state or *barzakh*, which the Shattaris sketch out as a chord dividing the circle of manifestation in half. This idea is, as William Chittick points out, fundamental to Ibn 'Arabī's thought:

> A *barzakh* is something that stands between and separates two other things, yet combines the attributes of both. Strictly speaking, every existent thing is a *barzakh*, since everything has its own niche between two other niches within the ontological hierarchy known as the cosmos... [E]xistence itself is a *barzakh* between Being and nothingness. In the hierarchy of worlds which makes up the cosmos, the term *barzakh* refers to an intermediate world standing between the luminous or spiritual world and the dark or corporeal world.[30]

Reality is represented, first, as the reality of Muḥammad (*ḥaqīqat-i Muḥammadīyyah*), and second, as the human reality (*ḥaqīqat-i insānī*), the Perfect Man (*insān-i kāmil*).[31] The human reality contains within the bodily frame all of the stages of divine manifestation; it is a microcosm that functions as the *barzakh* or intermediary between the notion of divine unity and the multiplicity of created sensory forms. The appropriate spiritual practices enable the Sufi to transform and perfect the human body as a receptacle for the divine Names.

The World-Showing Cup

In addition to the general theories of Ibn 'Arabī, the Shattaris based much of their cosmological structure directly on a short prose treatise, the *Jām-i Jahān Numā* or "The World-Showing Cup," written in 1385 by the Persian poet Muḥammad Shīrīn Maġhribī.[32] This magic cup, which belonged to the mythical Persian King Jamshīd, showed faraway places and events distant in time. Maġhribī's treatise constructs a macrocosm by integrating the circles of manifestation with the letters of the Arabic alphabet. Soon after he wrote the treatise, a certain Shaikh Rashīd read it and wrote a long work on it entitled the *Davā'ir-i Rashīdī* ("The Circles of Rashīd"). In it Shaikh Rashīd, about whom nothing else is known, extended Maġhribī's ideas and elaborated a scheme for invoking the divine Names.[33] The Shattaris in India took up Maġhribī's treatise and seem to have taught it extensively in Shaṯṯārī *kh̲ānaqāhs*. The *Jām-i Jahān Numā* was the subject of at least three Shaṯṯārī commentaries, one by the famous Shaikh Vajīh al-dīn 'Alavī Gujarātī, a second by a Shaikh Ibrāhīm Shaṯṯārī, and a third by a Shaikh Bahlūl.[34] Maġhribī's cosmological structure was also adapted into Shattari practice by a later Shattari shaikh named Ḥaẓrat Ibrāhīm Shaṯṯārī 'Gāẕur-i Ilāhī,' "the washerman of God."[35]

Maġhribī's text sketches out the Shattari macrocosmic framework in terms of two circles, or *dā'irahs*, which are successive stages of the self-manifestation of divine Essence (*ẕāt*). Before these circles come into existence, divine Essence exists in a mysterious, unmanifested state beyond human comprehension. Building on Ibn 'Arabī's idea of the chord (*barzakh*), the text gives visible form to the first manifestation (*tajallī*) of the invisible mystery as a circle divided by a chord; the divine mystery is first manifested into the twin arcs of oneness (*aḥadiyah*) and unification (*vāḥidiyah*). The chord between them represents the distance between these two aspects of divinity, which Maġhribī characterizes as "two bow-lengths or less." The allusion is to the Qur'ānic account of the ascension (*mi'rāj*) of the Prophet Muḥammad, when the ultimate distance between Allah and the Prophet was described as "*qāb qausain au adná*," or "two bow-lengths or less." The text makes this intermediate state (*barzakh*) the locus of the reality of Muḥammad (*ḥaqīqat-i Muḥammadīyyah*).

This intermediate state is termed the *barzakh-i kubrá*, or the greater *barzakh*. The chord also divides the divine quality of oneness from the most important qualities of divine Being (*ẕāt-i Ilāhī*). These are the faculties of existence (*vujūd*), knowledge (*'ilm*), light (*nūr*), and witnessing or sight (*shuhūd*). Although each refers to a different aspect of divinity—existence and knowledge to Essence and Attributes, and light and witnessing to the divine Names and actions—they are all indissolubly part of the same invisible perfection of Essence.

The circle of the first *tajallī* or manifestation is succeeded by a second circle of manifestation, which the *Jām-i Jahān Numā* represents as the second *dā'ira*. This second circle is to the first circle as the manifest exterior is to the secret interior. It too is divided into two arcs, manifest being (*ẓāhir-i vujūd*) and manifest knowledge (*ẓāhir-i 'ilm*). Each arc has twenty-eight sections. In the arc of manifest being, the twenty-eight sections are filled by twenty-eight Names of Allah, ranging from the Unique to the Hidden, the Manifest, the Knower, the Seer, the Powerful, the Subtle, and on to the Sublime in Rank. On the side of manifest knowledge, the twenty-eight sections are all the divisions of created things, from universal reason (*'aql-i kull*), universal soul (*nafs-i kull*), universal nature (*ṭabī'at-i kull*), primal matter (*jauhar-i habā*), universal form (*shakl-i kull*), the universal body (*jism-i kull*), down through the throne of God, heaven, the seven planets, the four elements, the three kingdoms (animal, vegetable, and mineral), angels, jinns, men, and the station of combinations of the aforesaid elements. In the higher ranks of the arc of manifest knowledge, the world is conceived as a universal body or a "macro-man" (*insān-i kabīr*), with a universal soul, reason, and all the faculties of a human body. Maġhribī's account relates the two arcs of manifest being and manifest knowledge, one to another, as hidden interior to manifest exterior. The divine Names contain in summary all the stations of created things, the planets, the elements, the days of the week, and so on. The process of creation is represented as the infusion of the "breath of the merciful" (*nafs-i raḥmānī*) through all things.

Each of the two arcs functions like an immense set of concentric circles: universal reason encompasses within it the circle of the universal soul, down through the heavens and the planets and all the way to the center of the earth. What bridges these two aspects of being is the intermediate chord between them, which represents the reality of man (*ḥaqīqat-i insānī*). Here the author draws heavily on Ibn 'Arabī's cosmology, in which man becomes the *barzakh* combining within himself the divine Names and the realm of all created things.

The Circles

For the Shattaris, the human reality is the *barzakh-i ṣuġhrá* or the smaller *barzakh*, and they elaborated a system of interior discipline based on this notion of the human body. The *Jām-i Jahān Numā* and the three Shattari commentaries on it sketch out both the larger macrocosmic universe and its parallel microcosm in the human body. In combination with Shaikh Muḥammad Ġhauṣ Gvāliyārī's writings, to which we now turn, these texts form the framework for Shattari Sufi practice, which they termed the *mashrib-i Shaṭṭār* or the Shattari way.

In the *Kalīd-i Makhāzin,* Shaikh Muḥammad Ġhauṡ elaborates parts of the wider cosmological structure of Maġhribī's *Jām-i Jahān Numā* into a system of three *dā'irahs* or circles. The first circle, an image of the stages of self-disclosure of the divine mystery, establishes the key terms for Shattari Sufi practice. The second circle thematizes the Shattari spiritual cosmos through the Qur'ānic account of the six days of creation, incorporating created entities, stars, angels, and jinns into six concentric circles representing the days of creation. The third large circle is the one of the nine heavens (*nuh aflāk*), which takes up a segment of Maġhribī's arc of manifest knowledge and coordinates the planets and constellations into a set of nine concentric circles ruled by the Names of Allah. The concentric structure of this *dā'irah* is important both in visualizing the Shattari body as a symbolic field and in establishing Shattari links with the Mughal court.

In the first circle, Shaikh Muḥammad Ġhauṡ connects the stages of divine manifestation with the key terms of the Shattari worldview. The moving energy for the manifestations is love or desire, following the famous tradition (*ḥadīṡ qudsī*): "I was a hidden treasure, and longed to be known. I created the world in order that I may be known." The hidden treasure of divinity was manifested only because of the force of desire, which forms the link between the successive manifestations in the form of light, love, the soul, and reason. All the terms in this circle have both an open and a mysterious side, which are manifested together in each stage.

In the second *dā'irah,* the text of the *Kalīd-i Makhāzin* elaborates the Qur'ānic narrative of the six days of creation into a cosmological diagram. The text incorporates into each day of creation a stage of manifestation, from the unmanifested Essence, down through the station of the light of the Muḥammadan reality, to the world of sensible forms, the world of bodies, and finally to the world of existence (*vujūd*). The description of the second *dā'irah* also contains an account of the creation of the twenty-eight letters of the Arabic alphabet, which are the building blocks of the Shattari discipline of the self: "The twenty-eight letters are the material for the composition of the Names which are the aggregate of all created things. Every letter has a spiritual guardian/agent (*muvakkil-i rūḥānī*), and in each agent the form of a station and of all the stations within the Essence of the divine throne (*ẕāt al-kursī*) have been created."[36]

Each letter of the alphabet has a distinct spiritual agency, an efficacy derived from its creation by the divine Essence, visualized as an angel or spiritual guardian, and these angels control all the stations of the Shattari cosmology. The letters, each connected with a Name of Allah, encode an entire elaborate system of interior discipline and visualization. The seeker manipulates the equation between the microcosm and macrocosm in order to gain specific spiritual and material goals, as well as to predict the future.

The third and final *dā'irah* or circle in Shaikh Muḥammad Ġhauṡ Gvāliyarī's key to hidden spiritual treasuries develops a segment of Maġhribī's arc of manifest knowledge, the nine heavens (*nuh aflāk*), into a set of concentric circles. The circles of the nine heavens are matched not only with the Names of Allah, which unlock each planetary station, but also with the human faculties in their internal or real sense (*ḥaqīqat*) as well as their outer form (*ṣūrat*). The *dā'irah* provides an important conceptualization of the Shattari body as a symbolic field, containing within itself the planets that control the heavens. The two outermost circles, the crystalline sphere and the sphere of the constellations, contain the twelve signs of the zodiac and a set of twenty-eight angels, each of whom corresponds to a letter of the alphabet. The nine concentric circles establish the set of correspondences among Names, planets, and internal faculties, as seen in Table 7.1.

The set of correspondences outlined above adds to Maġhribī's set of the planetary spheres a dual set of names for unlocking and controlling the planets for specific spiritual and material goals, and they coordinate these spheres with the human reality (*ḥaqīqat-i insānī*). Each bodily faculty is linked with a

Table 7.1. Shaikh Muḥammad Ġhauṡ Gvāliyārī's Third *Dā'irah*

Planetary Spheres	Real Names (Ḥaqīqī)	Faculties	External Names
Signs of the Zodiac			
28 angels/letters			
Saturn	The Opener (al-Fattāḥ)	Life (*ḥayāt*)	The Wise (al-Ḥakīm)
Jupiter	The Protector (al-Ḥafīẓ)	Knowledge (*'ilm*)	The Sustainer (al-Qayyūm)
Mars	The Wrathful (al-Qahhār)	Power (*qudrat*)	The Holy (al-Quddūs)
Sun	The Master (al-Malik)	Sight (*baṣar*)	The Controller (al-Qābiẓ)
Venus	The Subtle (al-Laṭīf)	Hearing (*samā'*)	The Cause (al-Bā'iṡ)
Mercury	The Encompasser (al-Vasi')	Speech (*kalām*)	The Dispenser (al-Bāsiṭ)
Moon	The Elevated (al-Rafī')	Will (*irādah*)	The Sublime (al-Subḥān)

Source: Rampur Raza Library, Persian ms. 912.

planet that is supposed to rule it, and the practitioner can gain control over these senses and planets through invoking the divine Names. The Shattaris' practice of interiorizing the Names of Allah within their bodies and adapting yogic practices into their *ẕikr* is based entirely on the circles and letters of this cosmology, which forms the backdrop for the poetics and theology of the *Madhumālatī*.

The Five Jewels

In addition to his *Kalīd-i Makhāzin* ("The Key to Hidden Treasuries"), Shaikh Muḥammad Ġhauṣ also composed the most famous work of Shattari asceticism, a widely circulated *summa* of spiritual practice, the *Javāhir-i Khamsah* ("Five Jewels"). A brief discussion of the practices described in the "Five Jewels" will flesh out the references to asceticism in the *Madhumālatī* and set the stage for the erotic encounter between the heroic yogi and the beautiful princess.

Shaikh Muḥammad Ġhauṣ opens his text with the Arabic verse, "Verily Allah created Adam in the form of the Compassionate One" (*inna Allāh khalaqa Ādam ilá ṣūrati raḥmāni*),[37] which sanctions the approximation of macrocosmic geometry to microcosmic body that follows. The text is arranged in "five jewels" that ascend from ordinary prayers to the inheritance and realization of divine truth. The first *jauhar* or jewel is on worship, and gives various complex procedures for reading prayers (*namāz*) at various times of the day and night. These include regular prayers as well as prayers for special occasions such as traveling, putting on new clothes, bringing home a new bride, or curing a sick person. The Shaikh begins to gesture toward the larger purpose of the work when he describes the *namāz-i qalb*, the "prayer of the heart," in which the seeker asks God for whatever he wants, prays for forgiveness (*istiġhfār*), and then visualizes the spiritual guide in his mind.[38] The chapter ends with special prayers for every day of the week and every month of the year, an enhanced regimen of piety that the disciple had to go through in order to make himself perfect in all the exterior requirements of faith.

Once a person becomes strong in external prayers to Allah, then he has to perform internal exercises (*akhyār*) to purify his heart and dispel the dangers of the spiritual path. The second *jauhar*, on asceticism (*zuhd*), gives detailed instructions for performing the exercises necessary to accomplish goals such as gaining closeness to God, dispatching fear or perturbation of mind, ending laziness on the spiritual path, obtaining the right means of livelihood, satisfying various needs, gaining victory over one's carnal soul, and having visions of the higher stations of the path on which one has embarked. For example, if one wishes to have a vision of the Prophet Muḥammad and his companions, one should go outside the city to a clean place at the edge of a river, lake, or tank and read the specified prayers and Names. Then one must look up to the sky, walk three steps forward, three back, three right, and three left, and keep one's face continuously in the direction of the Ka'ba. After the vision of the Prophet that ensues from the correct execution of this procedure, one can open one's eyes and ask him to overlook one's faults and forgive all one's sins.[39] Shaikh Muḥammad ends the chapter by citing a Prophetic tradition derived from Abū Hurairah: "There are Ninety-nine Names of God, that is, one less than a hundred, and whoever remembers them and acts on them will enter into Paradise without any accounting of sins or punishment."[40] There follows a list of all the Names, which the disciple (and the hero Manohar) has to internalize in order to enter the next stage of practice.

The third *jauhar*, the longest in the book, is about invocation of the Divine Names. This mode of practice includes elaborate prescriptions for purity and directions for gaining various sorts of powers. Shaikh Muḥammad's account of the coming into being of all created things is encoded within the twenty-eight letters of the Arabic alphabet.[41] In Shattari letter mysticism, combinations of letters signified selected Names of Allah in sequence as well as places in the Shattari cosmology, and each was the abbreviated code for a different Shattari practice. In addition to interior visualization, the Shattari cosmology had another application: to predict or influence the future by calling up the angels or spiritual agents of each station in order to make them perform whatever task was desired, or to make an efficacious talisman or amulet (*ta'vīẕ*).[42] Each of the twenty-eight letters was matched with a numerical or *abjad* value, a Name of Allah, a quality, either terrible or benevolent, a perfume or incense, an element, a zodiacal sign, a planet, a jinn, and a guardian angel. These were called up in rituals of invocation that varied with the particular goals of the seeker.

Certain conditions had to be met for the invocation or *da'vat* to be successful: the invoker had to maintain ritual purity, eat only *ḥalāl* foods, wear unsewn garments, act only under the supervision of a perfected spiritual guide (*murshīd-i kāmil*), keep an open heart, control the carnal soul, and so on. Depending on whether the invoker was using *jamālī, jalālī*, or composite (*mushtarik*) Names of Allah, he had to meet other dietary conditions. For *jalālī* Names, he had to abstain from meat, fish, eggs, honey, musk, and sexual intercourse, while *jamālī* invocations required avoiding butter, milk, yoghurt, vinegar, dates, and salt. The *jauhar* as a whole is divided into fifteen chapters (*faṣls*), on the invocations that are to be used for purposes such as satisfying worldly or religious needs, gaining glory or happiness or money or a desired object, getting rid of a bad temperament, finding lost objects, getting rid of sin and iniquity (*fisq va fujūr*), killing one's enemies, escaping from a tyrant's clutches, subduing jinns, controlling the king of the world, and bringing animals back to life. One of the final chapters deals with procedures for wiping out invocations or magic spells cast on the invoker; reading specific verses from the Qur'ān after the *maġhrib* prayers cancels particular invocations that have caused the petitioner difficulty.

The seeker now must enter the fourth *jauhar*, on the way of the Shattaris (*mashrib-i Shaṯṯār*), after he has mastered the earlier stations of piety and ascetic exercises and passed through "the mysteries of invocation."[43] This is the most detailed evocation we have of Shattari asceticism. It begins with a genealogy of the order and a paradigmatic initiation. Shaikh Muḥammad Ġhauṣ first quotes Najm al-dīn Kubrá, the famous Central Asian Sufi master who formulated an elaborate system for visualizing and internalizing divine lights. According to the founder of the Kubrawi order, those who travel the usual road of mystical stages (*sā'irīn*) chose the path to God, while those who flew along it were birds or flyers (*ṯā'irīn*).[44] According to Shaikh Muḥammad Ġhauṣ, the Shattaris were the people of love (*ahl-i 'ishq*), superior to all these others in both intoxication (*mastī*) and perspicacity (*hushyārī*) because they achieved mystic absorption (*jaẕbah*) at the beginning of their quest rather than the end (as was the case for other Sufi orders). The source of their practice was a tradition of the Prophet Muḥammad, who said: "I am the city of knowledge and 'Alī is its door."[45] Shaikh Muḥammad Ġhauṣ gives a long genealogy for the order from 'Alī through the first five Imams down to Ja'far al-Ṣādiq (d. 765), Bāyazīd Bisṭāmī (d. 879), Muḥammad Shīrīn Maġhribī (fl. 1385), Yazīd 'Ishqī, Abū'l Muẕaffar Maulānā Turk-i Tūsī, Abu'l Ḥasan al-Kharaqānī (d. 1033), Khudā Qulī Māvrā al-Naḥrī, his son Muḥammad al-'Āshiq, Muḥammad ibn al-'Ārif, 'Abdullāh Shaṯṯār (d. 1485), Qāẕin Shaṯṯār, Abū' l-Fatḥ Hidāyatullāh Sarmast, Shaikh Zuhūr Ḥājī Ḥuẓūr, and finally down to Shaikh Muḥammad Ġhauṣ himself.

There are some chronological problems with this genealogy, which follows in its earliest links the "golden chain" (*silsilat al-ṣahab*) of the usual Sufi claim to physical and spiritual descent from the Prophet to 'Ālī through the line of Imams to Ja'far al-Ṣādiq. As Hamid Algar has noted in an essay on the Naqshbandi order, initiation of Bāyazīd Bisṭāmī by Ja'afar al-Sādiq has to be understood as "dispensed by the spiritual being (*rūḥāniya*) of the departed preceptor."[46] This is *a fortiori* the case in view of the temporal gap between Bāyazīd Bisṭāmī and the fourteenth-century poet Maġhribī, which is a good example of such a retrospective "spiritual initiation." Further, Shaikh Muḥammad Ġhauṣ creates the sanction for the initiatic pattern of Shattari *ẕikr* by citing a paradigmatic initiation of 'Alī by the Prophet:

> 'Alī said to the Prophet: "O Prophet! Teach me the easiest and best path for reaching God." The Prophet said to 'Alī: "You have to persist in the mentioning (*ẕikr*) of God in privacy (*ḵhalvat*)." 'Alī said: How, O Prophet of Allah?" The Prophet said: "Close your eyes and listen to

me three times!" The Prophet said, "*Lā ilāha 'illā!*" three times and 'Alī listened and then 'Alī said it three times and the Prophet listened.

This is presumably the ritual with which a disciple was initiated into the *mashrib-i Shaṭṭār*, and it introduces a long discussion of the various kinds of *ẕikr* that he had to learn under the direction of a Shattari master. They involve breath control and physical exercises along with repetition of the Divine Names, and range from "one-stroke" *ẕikr* (*yak-ẓarbī*) up through practices involving more "strokes" or "blows" and physical manipulations.

Once he masters these *aẕkār*, the seeker begins letter-mystical practices that use the cosmological and spiritual codes of the Arabic alphabet to internalize different attributes of Allah and to recreate himself in the image of the macrocosm. A passage from a hitherto unknown Persian manuscript, the *Shajarat al-Tauḥīd* ("The Tree of Unity"), a treatise on letter mysticism and on the invocation of the Names of Allah, attributed to Haẓrat 'Abdullāh Shaṭṭāri, the founder of the Shattari *silsilah*, illustrates this process well:

> The first authoritative Shattari practice is obtained in the form *Alif Bā Ṣād*. *Alif* is for Allah, i. e. the Being of the ultimate reality (*ḥaqq-i ta'ala*), which is qualified by the attributes of majesty and beauty, and has to be visualized inside the seeker. The seeker should bind his senses to this image and become completely absorbed in it, so that no other thought remains. After this, when he descends from this stage, just the suspicion of a thought appears, and he comes to the station of the greater *barzakh*. *Bā* is the sign of that place. In it the seeker imagines his inner space to be the greater *barzakh*, which is unity itself (*vaḥdat-us-sarf*) and the reality of Muhammad. Know that this station of Being is qualified with the attributes of majesty and beauty, and it enters inside the seeker. In this state all the senses open up...and when he descends from this state, he can open his eyes and examine himself and the station of the smaller *barzakh*, which is called the unity of all things (*vāḥidiyat-i jame'ah*) and the reality of man. After this every attribute of Allah appears, and *Ṣād* consists of these seven divine attributes (*ṣifāt*),...he should inspect them so that all inner secrets become manifest and he can progress from the reality of man to the station of the reality of Muhammad, and he can carry on till he reaches the station of ultimate Being (*ẕāt-i mutlaq*) by busying himself in this technique, and move along on the stages of ascent and descent.[47]

This long quotation shows how the Sufi matched the cosmological circles with states in his consciousness, point for point. The basic division between Divine Essence and Attributes is signified by the *alif* and *ṣād*. The letter *bā* indicates the two *barzakhs* (intermediate states) that are the central lines on the circles of manifestation, the reality of Muḥammad and the reality of man. The Names of Allah represent attributes with which the Shattari attempts to imbue his own body. The Sufi seeks to replicate the account of the self-manifestation of Divine Being in his body, and the Shattari commentaries on the *Jām-i Jahān Numā* elaborate this bodily structure. The Sufi can, after inculcating the appropriate powers, travel up and down on the stages of ascent and descent.

Thus these letters were used to conceptualize an elaborate system of interior discipline and visualization, and to manipulate the equation between the microcosm and macrocosm to gain certain powers. Perhaps the most elaborate example of how the seeker's body becomes a microcosm for Shattari cosmology is to be found in Shaikh Muḥammad's use of "the niche for lights" or the *mishkāt al-anvār*, the famous Qur'ānic passage in which Allah's radiance is compared to a lamp set within a niche (Q 24: 35).[48] Introducing the diagram that the seeker has to superimpose on himself, Shaikh Muḥammad Ġhauṡ remarks that the heavens are the macrocosm (*'ālam-i kabīr*) and man is the microcosm (*'ālam-i ṣaġhīr*).[49] The interior self matches the exterior cosmological structures elaborated by the Shattaris. The seeker has to imagine the form of a niche for lights, in which he himself is the lamp and the world is a niche. From the perspective of the Essence, man is the niche and the Divine Essence is the lamp. Further, he is to view the heart (*qalb*) as a clean glass (*ābgīnah*) through which light shines like a star. Or he can imagine it as water, which itself is colorless but can take on a hundred thousand colors. The seeker must purify the glass of all impurities, internal and external (Figure 7.1).

In the figure, Shaikh Muḥammad Ġhauṡ takes his cue from two Qur'ānic verses describing hellfire and the nineteen guardian angels who tend it: "darkening and changing the color of man. Over it are nineteen" (Q 74:29–30). His gloss serves as a verbal frame for the diagram: "and concerning the nineteen, they are: the world of man, in whose station there are nine heavens…and ten who were promised good news, and these are the ten perfect ones on the human tablet." Moving in toward the core of the diagram, we see that the nine are matched to nine interior organs or faculties on the esoteric side and ten exterior senses on the exoteric side of the human body. At the center is the rope of the jugular vein, which stretches from the brain to the heart. The brain contains within it the throne of God (*'arsh*) and is the place of the human soul. The heart or *qalb* is the lamp (*al-miṣbāḥ*), and around it stretches the lampshade or *zujājah* of the carnal soul. Only if the seeker cleans the glass shade can the light of the heart shine through. The prescription for effecting this transformation is encapsulated in the Qur'ānic verse that is inscribed along the jugular vein: "To Him mount up (all) words of purity: it is He who exalts each deed of righteousness" (Q 35:10). Thus all the words and deeds that the Shattaris prescribe are part of the Sufi's progress toward God.

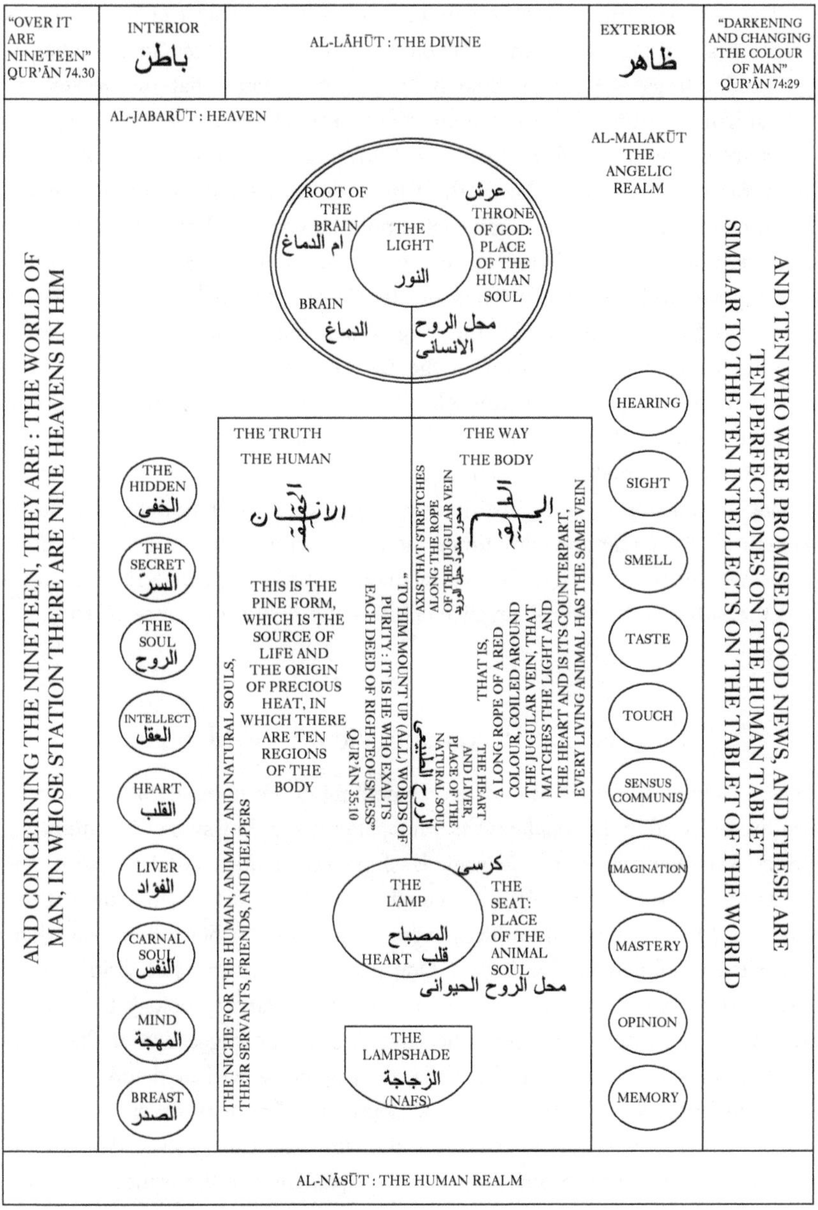

FIGURE 7.1 Man as a Niche for Lights.
Source: Javāhir-i Khamsah, India Office Library, Ethé ms. 1875.

The fifth and final *jauhar*, on inheritance of truth (*varṣat al-Ḥaqq*), begins by citing a Qur'ānic verse on the good news of divine grace: "give the believers good tidings" (Q 10:87). Shaikh Muḥammad states that the seeker can now affirm the truth of the statement that "these will be the heirs" (Q 23:10).[50] Heirs are of two kinds: formal/external (*ṣūrī*) and spiritual (*ma'navī*). A formal inheritor is recognized at the death of his father. In spiritual inheritance, the inheritor receives an internal gift that cannot be conceived except by someone intelligent who grasps divine grace. Shaikh Muḥammad goes on to discuss God's grace, and then the mastery of His Names, which leads to the unveiling of the invisible world of witnessing. When man looks at his own beauty he finds himself endowed with all the Divine Names and able to have mastery of them, recognizing in himself all the Names and becoming a place of manifestation for them. There follow several practices focused on visualizing each Name and making oneself into an image of it. In the philosophy of *vaḥdat al-vujūd* or identity in difference, the seeker will find himself to be sometimes the circle and sometimes the point, sometimes the seer and sometimes the mirror. In short, he will actualize within himself both the object and the subject of mystical practice. This is the true inheritance of truth (*irṣ al-ḥaqq*).

The Ascetic Praxis and Victory of Manohar

These disciplines of the "Jewels," and something of the necessity of ascetic practice, are reflected in the *Madhumālatī* when, after his night vision of Madhumālatī, Prince Manohar sets out as a yogi, is shipwrecked on a desolate shore, and meets in a dark forest the Princess Pemā, "Love," who acts as his guide at this juncture. She is a heavenly princess who used to live in her father's kingdom, "the shadow of paradise on earth." One day she goes with her girlfriends or *sakhīs*, who suggest virginal souls in paradise in Shattari cosmology, to a picture pavilion in a mango grove near the city, allegorically suggestive of the world of images. While she and her friends are playing, a wicked demon captures Love and brings her down to this dark, depressing forest. In order to fulfill his quest, Manohar must rescue Love from the clutches of the wicked demon. The description of this trial begins with Pemā's explanation to the prince:

"Listen, here is how you can kill the enemy.
In the garden you see towards the south,
is a tree heavy with immortal ambrosial fruit.
It is dense, shady, and laden with fruit,
and in it lives the demon's soul.
Until that tree is destroyed,

there is no way to slay the demon.
To uproot the tree is to kill the demon,
otherwise he will never be slain.
Let us go now, you and I, to the garden to destroy the tree with its fruit of immortality.
When you wound the demon, his heart will break, and he will die easily enough" [269].

When he heard about the fruit
that granted immortality, the prince
rose up and looked towards the south.
Now he knew in his mind with certainty
how the demon lived on after being killed.
"Pemā," he said, "Come with me,
and show me this immortal, ambrosial fruit."
The two of them set off together,
just as the demon came by
with fire blazing from all his heads.
But Pemā led the prince onwards
on to the tree with the fruit of immortality.
When he saw the tree, his heart rejoiced and his soul was overcome with joy.
He became certain that now God would grace him with the pennant of victory [270].

The prince examined the tree carefully.
He saw that it was dense of leaf,
a karṇikāra *tree laden with fruit.*
When he saw it his heart filled with pity,
for a fruit-bearing tree should not be cut down.
Then that excellent maiden asked the prince:
"Why do you delay over an enemy's life?
If one can overcome one's enemy,
tell me, O prince, why should one delay?
Take careful heed of what I say.
No fire is too small—do not underestimate
even a glimmering, a flicker of fire!
Hurry up and delay no more, if you are thirsty for your enemy's blood.
If you find him in your power, do not even let him draw breath!" [271]

When Pemā had explained this to the prince,
his consciousness became aware again.
He stood up and approached the tree.

Flexing his arms, he made firm his resolve.
He grasped the tree with both hands.
Calling on the name of Hari, he pulled up
the tree of immortality by its roots.
Then he took all its leaves, branches, and fruits,
and burnt them up in a fire he made.
The prince then took the painful trunk
of the tree, and cast it into the bonfire.
Having uprooted the tree of immortality and burnt it down to ashes,
happily the prince and princess returned to their four-cornered pavilion [272].

Night passed and the sun spread its rays,
and the demon came roaring to the door.
Black was his form and fearsome to behold,
and he had a discus in either hand.
When the prince heard him coming,
he took his bow in his hand,
and strapped on his sword, thirsty for blood.
He gathered up a spear and an axe,
and smeared ashes on his face and body.
He took staff, discus, and trident,
and prayed to the Lord for protection.
Recollecting Hari in his heart, he came out looking like Death incarnate.
The demon saw him and grew angry, and let loose a discus to kill him [273].

The demon hurled his discus in wrath,
but the prince shielded himself successfully.
The demon then threw his second discus,
but Manohar warded it off with his shield.
When the discus hit the shield,
the sparks of fire reached the heavens.
Then Manohar took his chance and pounced.
He wounded the demon in his head.
The demon's fifth head, endowed with special power,
fell to the ground, gashed by the sword.
When he was wounded thus fatally, the demon picked up his head.
He flew towards where the garden was, in the direction of the south [274].

The prince then ran towards the garden,
to find out about what would happen

with the demon and the tree of immortality.
He saw the demon staggering about,
fatally wounded in a vital place.
The demon came and threw down his head
in the place where the tree had been.
When he did not find the tree,
he despaired and knew his end was near.
Fire was ravaging the house of his life,
his spirit was about to leave his body.
Just as a tree whose roots have been hacked up suddenly falls
to the ground,
so the demon dropped to the earth when the spirit departed
from his frame [275].

The *karṇikāra* (*Pterospermum acerfolium, kanaka-champa,* Hindi) is a large tree with fragrant, small white flowers in March to June; its fruit ripens in the cold season. Mañjhan's suggestive use of the common folkloric motif of the tree in which the demon's soul dwells suggests that the root of egotism is pleasure, here signified by a dense and shady forest laden with ambrosial fruit.

The image of the dangerous tree was already known to the author of the first of the Hindavī romances, and, behind that text, from the symbolism of classic Sanskrit poetry. Early on in the narrative of the *Cāndāyan,* a wandering bard (*bājir*) falls senseless to the ground after a vision of the beautiful heroine of the love story. When he wakes up, he presents his experience as a riddle to the assembled crowd:

People say, "He is a fool, a madman."
I say I am telling you what's in my heart.
You'll understand it, if you're wise.
I saw a great tree, its fruits in the sky,
no hopes of plucking them with one's hands.
Tell me, who is powerful enough
to stretch out his arms around it?
Who can encompass the branches of that tree?
Night and day, guards keep watch,
and whoever sets eyes on it, is killed.
When I saw a serpent on the tree,
encircling its fruits and branches,
my heart shrivelled up like a lotus closing.
I, a tender shoot, withered away like a yellow leaf without life.
When the wind of separation blew, I fell from the branch rustling" [C 57].

The serpent in this tree becomes a demon in Manohar's tree.

Manohar's struggle with the demon is thus an allegory of the seeker's struggle with the egotism and lust that pervade his carnal soul. His victory over the demon and over the tree of immortality is his mastery of the ordeals of the ascetic praxis, which qualifies him to win the ultimate union with his princess, to realize his identity with his God.

The Magic Carpet

A final Shattari cosmological text that is essential to our understanding of this period is embedded in the *Qānūn-i Humāyūnī* ("The Institutes of Humāyūn"), written by one of Humāyūn's court chroniclers, the historian Khvānd Amīr. Khvānd Amīr describes weaving a carpet for the imperial audience hall, to establish a hierarchy of rule for Humāyūn's newly won kingdom. The carpet was patterned in concentric circles, with each circle matching a planetary sphere or one of the four elements:

> Among the fascinating innovations which emanated from the world-adorning mind of this victorious emperor was also the *bisāṭ-i nishāṭ* (carpet of pleasure).... It was a round carpet divided into circles corresponding to the orbits of the planets, and the number of elemental spheres, and was made of valuable stuffs. The first circle, which represented the crystalline sphere, was white like the book of deeds of the virtuous; the second blue; the third black in accordance with the colour of the planet Saturn; the fourth, which was ascribed to the most fortunate planet Jupiter, was of a sandal-wood colour; the fifth, which related to Mars, was red; the sixth, representing the Sun, was made of gold-embroidered cloth; the seventh, representing Venus, was bright green; the eighth, ascribed to Mercury, was of violet colour...the ninth circle representing the Moon was, like the face of the Moon of fourteenth night, white. After the circle of the moon were placed, in sequence, the circles of fire and air; and then those of earth and water were outlined; and the division of the inhabited quarters of the globe was confined to seven climes. For the sake of amusement of his exalted mind, the Emperor sometimes had this carpet spread on a circular wooden platform which was equal to it in area. And himself occupying the circle of the gold-embroidered cloth, he, like the Sun, reflected to it beauty, light and purity. Each section of the people was ordered to sit, in accordance with one of the seven planets appropriate to it, in the circle to which it corresponded. For instance, officers of Indian extraction and Shaikhs would sit in the circle of Saturn, which is black; the Saiyids and the learned in the circle of Jupiter, which is of a

> light brown colour; and so on in the other circles. And sometimes while people were seated in the above-noted circles, they used to throw dice on various sides of which figures of persons in different postures were painted by the creative pen; and whichever figure turned up on the throw from the hand of a person, he assumed the same position in his circle. For instance, if the picture of a standing person turned up he stood up, and if a seated one was presented he sat down, while if the reclining position was cast he lay down and even went to sleep...[among other uses of the carpet, a good one is that] each of the seven circles is divided into 200 grades, so that there are 1400 seats in the 7 circles...thus there can be no rivalry when people come to the carpet.[51]

The order of these circles stretches from the two spheres above Saturn on the left-hand side of the second *dā'irah* of Maġhribī's *Jām-i Jahān Numā*, down through the planets and the four elements. As we have seen, Shaikh Muḥammad Ġhauṯ elaborated on this section of Maġhribī's text in his circle of the nine heavens (*nuh aflāk*). Humāyūn uses it to order a subject population into an ideal cosmological scheme that is then animated through court ritual. A throw of the dice determined the position adopted by any of the players who were on the carpet. Humāyūn himself sat in the fifth circle, the sphere of the sun who governs the fate of rulers and kings.

What makes this remarkable reordering of a subject population more than an elaborate and humorous board game is that the emperor divided up the seven days of the week according to the planets and colors, and transacted all business according to the appropriate planetary influence of each day of the week. The people who sat in the carpet were divided into three large classes: the *ahl-i daulat* ("people of power"—noblemen, state officials); the *ahl-i sa'ādat* ("pious people"—Sufis, learned judges, poets, philosophers); and the *ahl-i murād* ("people of pleasure"—companions, friends, and lovers of pleasure). Thereafter,

> Saturdays and Thursdays were fixed for the pious people, and on these days audiences were granted to the literary and religious persons...[A]nd the reason why these two days were allotted to this class was, that Saturday is ascribed to Saturn, who is the patron of the respected Shaikhs and persons of old respectable families; and Thursday is appropriated to Jupiter, which is the star of the Saiyids, the learned and the strict followers of the Muhammadan Law. Sundays and Tuesdays (were fixed) for the State officials; and all royal affairs and the duties connected with the management of the government were discharged on these days....The advantage in appointing these two days for the holding of the court...was that Sunday appertains to Sun, who in accordance

> with the pleasure of the Almighty regulates the destiny of the rulers and the Sultans; while Tuesday is the day of Mars; and Mars is the patron of warriors. Hence it is clear and evident...that to adorn the throne of sovereignty in the public court-hall by his royal sessions on these two days...was more appropriate than on other days. Mondays and Wednesdays, on the other hand, were designated the days of pleasure (parties), and on these two days some of the old companions and chosen friends and parties of people of pleasure and distinction were invited to the heavenly assemblies, and all their wishes fulfilled.[52]

Thus Humāyūn adapted the Shattari cosmology into the machinery of rulership, with the planets determining the appropriate daily actions from the emperor's "throne of sovereignty." The emperor also arranged all government departments according to the four elements, earth (buildings, land grants, agriculture), water (cellars, canals, irrigation), fire (military), and air (wardrobe, kitchen, stable), and the officials of each department had to dress in the appropriate astrological color.

The Symbolics of Power

Although space prohibits full treatment of all the innovations of Humāyūn's court, what is clear from this account is that Humāyūn extended the Shattaris' conception of planetary spheres to articulate his political authority. (The seven planets and their corresponding colors and numbers were also famously used in Persian literature in Niẓāmī's *Haft Paikar*, where the seven princesses whom Bahrām Gūr visits each night are fitted into a planetary scheme where the day, planet, number, and clime of origin of the princess all match.[53]) Humāyūn's "carpet of delight" made the court a mirror of cosmic order implemented through administrative ordinance, with Humāyūn as the Sun who imparts "beauty and light" to the entire cosmological scheme. This symbolism is not taken from Humāyūn's Central Asian or Timurid origins, but is an extension of the emperor's interest in occult, mystical, and astrological matters. In an atmosphere where Sufi shaikhs and orders competed for political and economic patronage from the Mughal and Afghan courts, the Shattaris were guaranteed success at Humāyūn's court. That success, as we have seen, also led to bitter rivalries. Like the Chishtis of the previous chapter, the Shattaris are part of a dominant order seeking to establish itself in a position of cultural and political hegemony.

After Shaikh Phūl's murder in 1538 (see below), Sher Shāh Sūrī displaced Humāyūn from the throne in 1540, precipitating a political crisis for many Sufis close to the Mughal court. Since Shaikh Muḥammad Ġhauṡ had been instrumental in the Mughal capture of Gwalior from the Afghans, as well as in the taking of another fortress, Chunar, in the service of the Mughals,[54] he fled from Gwalior in fear of the Afghan conqueror. The *Kulliyāt-i Gvāliyārī*, by his disciple Fażl 'Alī Shaṭṭārī, recounts the shaikh's flight from the advancing armies of Sher Shāh into the forests of Bundelkhand:

> When Humāyūn left for Iran and the rule passed into the hands of Sher Khan, Shaikh Muḥammad Ġhauṡ left for Bundelkhand before Sher Khan could reach Gwalior. In Bundelkhand, the local landowners served him hospitably. When Sher Shah learnt this, he sent his sister's son Bakhtiyār Jang to Bundelkhand with an army of 12,000 men to pursue the shaikh and to behead him, while he himself entered Gwalior. When the army reached the place where Muḥammad Ġhauṡ was staying, they attacked the house. When they had reached the women's quarters, the shaikh's mother asked him, "When is your *vilāyat* (spiritual authority) and *ġhauṡiyyat* (claim to be the spiritual lode-star of an age) going to manifest itself? These people are very ill-mannered." Then all at once the shaikh took thought and declared aloud, "Mars, where are you? Do your work!" And the moment these words left his mouth a glittering sword came out of the east and went shining into the west. Then he addressed the attacking army and said, "Go back! Follow the Sharī'a and leave me alone. Emperors should only take prayers from *faqīrs*—do not tangle with an ascetic!" But Bakhtiyār Jang said, "Sher Khan has ordered us to cut your head off without any delay." When he heard this, the shaikh became angry and said, "Mars, kill them all!" As soon as he said this, 12,000 heads were separated from their bodies. After this Shaikh Muḥammad Ġhauṡ went to Gujarat.[55]

Despite elements of supernatural hagiography mixed into this account, it seems that Shaikh Muḥammad's power was evident to all those surrounding him, and that the spiritual exercises he had perfected were regarded as efficacious. As a recognized Sufi, his goal was to gain power over events and men, by whatever natural and supernatural forces he could command, and we have seen how Humāyūn adapted his spiritual cosmology even into court ritual and the articulation of political authority.

Whether this hagiographic account conceals a victory over the Afghans or an ignominious flight, Shaikh Muḥammad Ġhauṡ did reach Gujarat safely. Sher Shāh left Gwalior to besiege the massive fort of Kalinjar and sent a letter to Sultan Maḥmūd Shāh threatening to take violent measures if the shaikh was not delivered to him. When the letter reached the sultan, he sent some men to the shaikh to tell him about the contents of the letter. Fażl 'Alī's account continues:

> Shaikh Muḥammad Ġhauṡ was very distressed and before the assembled men he bowed his head down to the ground in contemplation. Then he

> said, "They have martyred this *faqīr*'s brother at Bayana and hung his head on the door, and now they have come for the *faqīr*. Whatever God wills, will happen." Then he went back into contemplation (*murāqiba*) and bowed his head down to the ground. After a little while he raised his head and with great anger picked up the ewer which he used for ablutions (*vuzū'*) and banged it on the ground violently, saying, "Today I have killed that tyrant. Tomorrow, God will kill him!" Smoke began to rise from the ewer. When those present asked, "What is happening?" he said, "Sher Khan has been burnt up in Kalinjar from a pipe of gunpowder, and his son Jalal Khan has become king under the name of Islām Shāh."[56]

The account of Shaikh Muḥammad's curse and its malevolent effect so frightened Islām Shāh that, according to Faẓl 'Alī, he came to Muḥammad Ġhauṣ and begged pardon for his (now deceased) father's violent actions against the shaikh's life. Although the shaikh, his supremacy established, pardoned the new sultan, he did not go back to Gwalior or Agra, refusing to come into Afghan-held territory, but stayed in Gujarat, where he acquired a coterie of followers and disciples. In his stead, his disciple Mañjhan (author of the *Madhumālatī*) was among the retinue of poets and courtiers around Islām.

The emperor Humāyūn wrote to Shaikh Muḥammad Ġhauṣ from his political exile in Iran expressing sympathy over Sher Shāh's harsh measures against him, and the shaikh responded by invoking the mysteries of the Divine Names:

> Thank you for your royal letter. I conveyed to your well-wishers here the happy news of your life and safety. I came to know also about the welfare of your servants and attendants. Everything is exactly as you have written. There is no formality between us, for:
>
> "Words that come from the heart, reach another's heart direct."
>
> I pray to God that unfortunate circumstances may not trouble your heart!
>
> Whenever exalted God wishes any of his good creatures to reach the degree of perfection, He sends down heavenly sustenance, alternatively terrible (*jalālī*) and merciful (*jamālī*), upon him. A merciful and gentle age has passed. Now for a few days it is a terrible and wrathful age. God says, "Verily there is ease with hardship."[57]

Shaikh Muḥammad invokes God's divine attributes, which correspond to particular stations in Shattari cosmology, to order the periods of history through which the world passes (*daur*). Their use here subordinates time to the power of the person who knows how to control the divine attributes and names (i.e., Shaikh Muḥammad) and whose authority gives the practice its political power.[58] Sufi cosmological schemes create bases for gaining power, both spiritual and political.

Thus Sufis are involved in approving or denying the legitimacy of kings at the same time as they are dependent on them for patronage. Kings seek the shaikh's supernatural authority to legitimate their rule and, in Humāyūn's use of Shattari cosmology, to articulate their political sovereignty. As Richard Eaton has incisively remarked in the course of a similar argument about the political claims of the Bengali Sufis:

> Being in theory closer to God than warring princes could ever hope to be, Muslim saints staked a moral claim as God's representatives on earth. In this view, princely rulers possessed no natural right to earthly power, but had only been entrusted with a temporary lease on such power through the grace of some Muslim saint. This perspective perhaps explains why in Indo-Muslim history we so often find Sufis predicting who would attain political office, and for how long they would hold it. For behind the explicit act of "prediction" lay the implicit act of appointment—that is, of a Sufi's entrusting his *wilāyat*, or earthly domain, to a prince.[59]

The Sufis thus interpret the course of history as the arena for supernatural intervention, and mysterious events such as the smoke rising from Shaikh Muḥammad's ewer can have hidden meanings, as with Sher Shāh's death, caused by his violence against the Shattaris. But Sufis were in practice dependent on the flow of alms and patronage (*futūḥāt*) from political rulers, so that their claims to superiority were tempered by the economic necessity of finding a patron to establish and maintain a *k͟hānaqāh*. Within this conception of superiority-yet-dependence, the authority of kings and that of Sufis are interdependent, each seeking legitimacy or patronage from the other, renouncing the world (*duniyā*) and ruling it through faith (*dīn*).

How was this Shaikh Muḥammad Ġhaus̱ Gvāliyārī related to the Sūrī court during the period of the Afghan interregnum (1540–1556)? Since he and the Shattari *silsilah* played a role in the defeat of the regional Afghan sultanates by the Mughal state centered in Delhi and Agra, they were enemies of the Sūr Afghan sultans. The poet's simultaneous addresses to Shaikh Muḥammad and Islām Shāh conceal a history of political intrigue in which Chishtis, Naqshbandis, and Shattaris took sides with Mughals or Afghans in the struggles for sovereignty over northern India in the sixteenth century.

The Shattaris' involvement with this complicated world of competitive religious politics began when 'Abdullāh Shaṭṭār founded the *silsilah*. Not much is known about him except that he came from Transoxiana in the latter half of the fifteenth century. Trying to establish his authority over an area (the Sufi idea of *vilāyah*) proved to be no easy task for the shaikh, who toured Delhi, Jaunpur, Bihar, Bengal, and Malwa in search of patronage and disciples. He conducted his tour in a militant style, as K. A. Nizami describes it, citing the later Shattari chronicler Muḥammad Ġhauṣī Shaṯṯārī's *Gulzār-i Abrār*:

> Fond of itinerancy, he travelled from place to place with great pomp and eclat. He used to put on royal dress, while the huge retinue of his disciples who accompanied him wore military uniform. This army of followers marched with banners and drums. Most of the preceding saints considered itineracy a part of the spiritual education of the traveller himself. Shah 'Abd-u'llah travelled, not for the sake of his own spiritual perfection, but to show others the "path of God." While all other organizers of *silsilahs* had always settled at one place and attracted people to themselves by their piety and kindness, Shah 'Abd-u'llah invited people to come to him. He proclaimed in every village and town which he visited by beat of drums: "Is there anyone who wishes to be shown the way to God?"[60]

Shaikh 'Abdullāh's method was distinctly a militant arrogation of territory to himself, a declaration of superiority based on his claim to be privy to the secrets of *tauḥīd* or the unity of God. He wrote the treatise *Laṭā'if-i Ġhaibīyyāh* ("Subtleties of the Invisible World") as well as the *Shajarat al-Tauḥīd* ("The Tree of Unity"), which we noted earlier in this chapter.

The shaikh's claims of spiritual supremacy brought him into competition with several Sufis who were prominent in the regional sultanates. For instance, the Chishti Shaikh Ḥusām al-Dīn Mānikpurī is reported to have come outside the town of Manikpur in response to the shaikh's challenge and to have told Shaikh 'Abdullāh that "he had nothing to offer him, neither could he himself learn anything in return for he was still preoccupied in absorbing what his *pir* had imparted to him." The Sultan of Jaunpur, Ibrāhīm Shāh Sharqī, is reported to have been alarmed by the shaikh's military pomp and show, and Shaikh Muḥammad Qāẓin 'Alā', a Bengali Sufi, "ignored the challenge, derisively replying that Sufis from Khurasan and Fars had often arrived with a battery of outlandish claims."[61] Shaikh 'Abdullāh eventually settled down in Mandu under the patronage of Sultan Ġhiyāṯ al-dīn Tuġhlaq.

What is remarkable about the shaikh's life and achievements is the style of spiritual practice that he forged, as well as his military, overtly political method of work. Even the hostile Bengali Shaikh Muḥammad Qāẓin 'Alā' became his disciple following a miraculous dream:

> The Shaikh...retired for a forty-day retreat (*chilla*). During this period his deceased father appeared in a vision and told him that his ascetic exercises were useless as his spiritual future was then in the hands of a sufi whom he had called 'the prattling fellow of Khurasan.' So Shaikh 'Alā' left for Mandu and for three days stood outside the Shah's house. Finally, moved by Shaikh 'Alā's humility, Shah 'Abdullah took him as disciple after obtaining a pledge that he would leave his ancestral sufic path and learn Shattariyya practices.[62]

Shaikh 'Alā (d. 1495) became Shaikh 'Abdullāh's principal *ḳhalīfah* or successor, and took the Shattari method of spiritual practice to Bengal and eastern India. He was followed by the two able Shattaris Shaikh Ẕuhūr Hājī Ḥamīd (d. 1523) and Shaikh Abū 'l-Fatḥ Hadīyatullāh 'Sarmast' (d. 1539), who established a Shattari presence in Bihar and had many links with local orders such as the Firdausis as well as with the rulers of Bihar.[63]

Shaikh Muḥammad Ġhauṯ carried on the *silsilah*'s tradition of conquering new territory. According to a disciple's account, the *Kulliyāt-i Gvāliyārī*, he went to his *pīr* to ask him to tell him where to go, and Shaikh Ḥamīd gave him leave to go anywhere he pleased:

> On hearing Shaikh Ḥamiduddīn's words he left his native place and came to Gwalior...[T]he political reason for Shaikh Muḥammad Ġhauṯ's coming to Gwalior could be that the fort was taken from Vikramāditya Tomar between 1518 and 1520 and brought under Muslim rule. The Muslim population of Gwalior was increasing. Therefore, in order to give spiritual guidance to these people, [Shaikh Muḥammad] finished his austerities around Chunar in 1523 and came to Gwalior. By 1526 he was famous within the fort and an acknowledged influence on the local population.[64]

From this position within a fort held by the Afghan Tātār Khān Lodī, Shaikh Muḥammad Ġhauṣ was able to take sides in the growing struggle between Afghans and Mughals for control over north India after Bābur's victory at the battle of Panipat in 1526.

Gwalior was a key strategic fort in this war, and Bābur, the first Mughal emperor, mentions Shaikh Muḥammad:

> After the pagan took Kandar and was close to Biana, Dharmankat, one of the Gwalior rajas, and another pagan styled Khan-i Jahan, went

> into the Gwalior neighbourhood and, coveting the fort, began to stir up trouble and tumult. Tatar Khan (an Afghan noble, the ruler of the fort), thus placed in difficulty, was for surrendering Gwalior to us.... We joined to Rahim-dad Khan's force a few Bhira men and Lahoris, [and] Mulla Apaq and Shaikh Ghuran went also with them. By the time they were near Gwalior, however, Tatar Khan's views had changed and he did not invite them into the fort. Meanwhile Shaikh Muhammad Ghaus, a darwish-like man, not only very learned but with a large following of students and disciples, sent from inside the fort to say to Rahim-dad, "Get yourself into the fort somehow, for the views of Tatar Khan have changed, and he has evil in his mind." Rahim-dad sent to say to Tatar Khan, "There is danger from the Pagan to those outside. Let me bring a few men into the fort and let the rest stay outside." Tatar Khan agreed, and Rahim-dad posted his troop near the Hathi-Pol (Elephant Gate). Through that gate he brought in the rest of his force at night. Next day, Tatar Khan, reduced to helplessness, willy-nilly made over the fort and set out to come and wait on me in Agra. A subsistence allowance of 20 *laks* was assigned to him in Bianwan *pargana*.[65]

Such service does not go unrewarded, and Bābur gave Shaikh Muḥammad a land grant of over a thousand *bīghahs* near Gwalior to set up his hospice. His establishment was a favored site for aristocratic patronage through the reigns of Bābur and Humāyūn, and his yogic and ascetic practices enjoyed full state support.

This was in marked contrast to the Chishti lineages, who had long-standing historical connections with the local Afghan sultans and nobility and did not back the Mughals in their fight for supremacy; therefore they were not patronized to the same extent by the Mughal rulers after the defeat of Ibrāhīm Lodī at Panipat in 1526. For example, the Chishti Shaikh 'Abdul Quddūs Gangohī wrote angry letters to the Mughal emperor Bābur asking that the lands that religious personages, Sufis, and learned men held as rent-free tenures (*madad-i ma'āsh*) from the emperor should not be subjected to *'ushr*, a tithe of a tenth of the produce from the land.[66] The shaikh also demanded that all non-Muslims should be excluded from state service and revenue-free grants.[67] After the accession of Humāyūn, he again wrote to the emperor restating "the need for the emperor to support the religious classes for the good of the empire, and recommends that any revenue-producing lands given to these groups should be in tax-free tenure."[68] The shaikh thus linked the moral argument for the betterment of the empire to support for the (Chishti) Sufi *silsilahs*, which were conceived to have an ideological claim to the revenue of the land.

Humāyūn, who was extremely interested in occult and mystical practices, was however much more favorably disposed to the Shattaris. One imperial chronicle relates that Shaikh Muḥammad Ġhauṡ and his brother, Shaikh Phūl, taught the emperor occult sciences and were very much in favor at court. Eventually, in a Thomas à Becket-like scenario, Shaikh Phūl was brutally murdered by a group of jealous courtiers, a crime over which Humāyūn felt great remorse, according to al-Badāyūnī:

> And in the year 945 H. [1538 A.D.] Mīrzā Hindāl, at the instigation of certain turbulent innovators, put to death Shaikh Buhlūl, brother of Shaikh Muḥammad Ġhauṡ of Gwāliār, who was one of the chief exponents of the art of invocation and incantation, and who enjoyed the full confidence of Humāyūn.[69]

What the mystical practices that the brothers taught Humāyūn might have been, and how the emperor used them, has not hitherto been very clear.

The Seeker as Microcosm

The Shattaris sought to act in a world beset by these struggles between Mughals and Afghans, and these larger cosmological and political contexts shed light on the ascetic and erotic passages of the *Madhumālatī*. The Names of Allah are vital for reading the allegorical centerpiece of the female body of the heroine. In the prologue to the *Madhumālatī*, Mañjhan briefly discusses ascetic practice and refers to the yogic and letter-mystical practices[70] that the Shattari Sufis used to refashion their bodies into microcosms of the elaborately patterned Shattari cosmos. The ideal seeker transformed his consciousness using Shattari cosmological and practical notions. These constructions of asceticism had a direct bearing on the text of the *Madhumālatī*, since Mañjhan refers to them in his erotic encounters between lover and beloved, and the hero's quest presents a shadowy allegory of the Shattari ascetic regimen. Accordingly, this section discusses the male body of the seeker that the Shattaris sought to discipline through their ascetic regimen.

Mañjhan's prologue refers to the Nāth yogic system of "airs" circulating in the channels of the subtle body, which had to be harnessed through breath control and used to purify the body from all worldly things:

Sit in meditation, focus on the Absolute.
Seize the upward breath from your body,

blow at the fire in your heart.
When the flame rocks, it showers sparks,
and burns the blackness off your body! [MM 32]

Many mystical practitioners and Sufis in north India after the thirteenth century adapted Nāth yogic practices.[71] The reference here to their techniques employs the vernacular terminology for asceticism that the Hindavī romances adapted into an equivalent for Sufi practice in the fantasy world.

The Shattaris took Nāth yogic practices and translated them into their own ascetic regimen. In addition to being the author of the *Kalīd-i Makhāzin* and the *Javāhir-i Khamsah*, Shaikh Muḥammad Ġhauṡ also translated into Persian the *Ḥauẓ al-Ḥayāt*, the Arabic version of the Sanskrit text on yoga known as the *Amṛtakuṇḍa* ("The Pool of Nectar").[72] Yusuf Husain has proposed that the Persian text is "syncretic," combining "Islamic and Hindu systems of practice."[73] Richard Eaton has disputed this, suggesting that "the work consists of two independent and self-contained worldviews placed alongside one another—a technical manual of yoga preceded by a Sufi allegory—with later editors or translators going to some lengths to stress their points of coincidence... [H]ere, at least, yoga and Sufi ideas resisted true fusion."[74]

I would like to propose an alternative solution to this crux: that the Persian "Pool of Nectar" appropriated yogic practices and adapted them into a larger Shattari system of practice, explained and legitimized with the help of Qur'ānic verses and traditions of the Prophet Muḥammad. Rather than undergoing systemic articulation within the Nāth yogic texts on practice, yogic practices now work within the Shattari *pīrs'* system of invoking the Names of Allah (*da'vat al-asmā'*), which is in turn based on the cosmology outlined above. This text, in conjunction with practical manuals left by the order, prescribes a complex set of doctrines, yogic asceticism, and letter mysticism for the Shattari acolyte.

Within the competitive religious scene of northern India, it was not unexpected for the shaikh and his *silsilah* to assert their separate and superior status while using practices that were comprehensible within Indian ascetic systems. As Carl Ernst has pointed out, the *Gulzār-i Abrār* describes Shaikh Muḥammad Ġhauṡ's translation of yogic practice as a militant assertion of dominance:

> The *Baḥr al-Ḥayāt* is the translation of the ascetical work and manual of the society of Jogis and Sannyāsis, in which occur interior practices, visualization exercises, description of holding the breath, and other types of meditation.... These two groups are the chief ascetics, recluses, and guides of the people of idolatry and infidelity. By the blessings

> of these very practices and repetitions of names (*azkār*), [they have] arrived to the ladder of false spirituality (*istidrāj*) and the excellent rank of visions.... He (Muḥammad Ġhauṣ) separated all these subjects from the Sanskrit language that is the tongue of the infidels' flimsy books, dressed them in Persian, loosed the belt of infidelity from the shoulder of those concepts, and adorned them with...unity and *islām*, thus freeing them from the dominance of blind adherence with the overwhelming strength of true faith. The master of realization bestowed aid and assistance with Sufi repetitions of names (*azkār*) and practices. He fashioned the Truth (*al-ḥaqq*), which is a single casket (*ḥuqqa*) of precious jewels, and a case for kingly rubies, from the spoils of "they are like cattle, nay, more erring" (*Qur'ān* 7.171)...into an ennobling crown for the Lord of "religion, for God, is *islām*" (*Qur'ān* 3.19).[75]

Far from being populist syncretizers, the Shattaris cite the Qur'ānic passages likening infidels to erring "cattle" who need to be driven into the fold of the "true Islam." The single casket of "truth" that the shaikh forged may have had elements in it from many different esoteric systems, but it was controlled by the authority of the shaikh. Thus, in the Persian translation of the *Ḥauẓ-al-Ḥayāt*, Shaikh Muḥammad Ġhauṣ begins his treatment of the body, its seven *cakras* (nerve centers) and their planetary correlates, by declaring that his yogic interlocutor said, "Know that the microcosm contains that which is in the macrocosm."[76] This microcosmic body contains seven ganglia or *cakras* that constitute the nerve centers of the spinal column. Each of these is coordinated with a different planet in the Shattari cosmological system, and endowed with a Name of Allah that is to be recited inwardly by the novice. The planets are part of the larger cosmological system of concentric circles or spheres called *dā'irahs*. The planets and their invocations are arranged as shown in Table 7.2.

Each station is associated with a tutelary deity, as well as a Name of Allah, repetition of which unlocks the powers and mysteries of that station.[77] The order of these planets is the same as it is in a section of the second *dā'irah* in Maġhribī's *Jām-i Jahān Numā*, with the exception of the interchanged positions of Jupiter and Mars. The Shattari planetary scheme of the seven heavens is here used to give new meanings to the Nāth yogic *cakras*, which are six (not seven) in number and are matched with mantras and deities different from the ones in this text.[78] Although the Shattaris took from the Nāths general concepts and forms of yogic practice such as the *cakras*, inverted meditation (*ulṭī sādhanā*, taken over by the Sufis as *namāz-i ma'kūs*), and the cleansing of the body through *prāṇāyāma* or breath control (Persian, *ḥabs-i dam*), they often emptied out the specific instructions within these frameworks and replaced

Table 7.2. The *Cakras* According to Shaikh Muḥammad Ġhauṡ Gvāliyārī

Planet	Mantra	Ẕikr	Deity
Saturn (Zuḥal)	HUM	*yā rabb*	Kālī
Mars (Mirrīkh)	AUM	*yā qadīm*	Bātarmī
Jupiter (Mushtarī)	RHIN	*yā khāliq*	Mangal
Sun (Shams)	BRINSRĪN	*yā karīm*	Badamtā
Venus (Zahra)	BRAY	*yā musakhkhir*	Sarasvatī
Mercury ('Utārid)	YUM	*yā 'alīm*	Nārī
Moon (Qamar)	HANŚĀYAŚYĀ	*yā muḥyī*	Tūtlā

Note: This table has been simplified slightly in order to give only the elements essential to my argument here.

Source: Carl Ernst, *The Arabic Version of "The Pool of the Water of Life"* (*Amṛtakuṇḍa*) (forthcoming).

them with Sufi concepts and terminology. The larger Shattari cosmology of planetary circles helps to place this competitive appropriation and reworking (rather than direct translation) of yogic practice within a Shattari worldview.

Further, it is clear from Maġhribī's second *dā'irah* that the realms of the seven planets occupy a set of spheres in the middle of the cosmology, not the highest reaches of the manifestation of divine Being. This is consistent with Shaikh Muḥammad Ġhauṡ's views of bringing infidel practices from false spirituality (*istidrāj*) to the true faith. The distinctive Shattari invocation of the Names of Allah (*da'vat al-asmā'*), their letter codes, their astrological manipulations, and their modes of divination provide a larger context for the yogic postures and exercises that the Shattaris used. The Shattari materials also allow us a rare glimpse into the exact historical referents of the ascetic quest of the hero in the Hindavī Sufi romances, who has to disguise himself as a yogi in order to attain the divine heroine.

The Shattaris formulated elaborate methods for superimposing cosmological diagrams on their bodies, and the practical manuals of the order contain directions for their use. Shaikh Muḥammad Ġhauṡ's followers developed the Shattari system of divination and invocation with great elaboration, and many manuscripts, such as Ismā'īl Farḥī's *Makhzan-i Da'vat* ("The Treasury of Invocation") or Shaikh 'Īsá Jundullāh's *'Ain al-Ma'ānī* ("The Essence of Meaning"), apply these principles and methods in differing contexts of visualization and prediction.[79] These applications of Shattari cosmology—yogic, magical, and visionary – thus show a common system that runs through all these cultural domains, encoded in the letters of the Divine Names, which are the loci for visualization and interior discipline. These practices, which were carried out in Shattari *khānaqāhs*, were the esoteric side of the *silsilah*'s social positioning of itself vis-à-vis kings and political leaders. The next chapter examines the face-to-face erotic encounters between Manohar and Madhumālatī in Mañjhan's Sufi romance, within the context of the theology and cosmology of the Shattaris.

8

The Seasons of Madhumālatī's Separation: The Madhumālatī, *Part 2*

The Love Play of Manohar and Madhumālatī

As he glimpses the beautiful Madhumālatī sleeping, the prince's soul is overcome with *viraha* or love in separation. The prince responds to her as if to a spiritual vision:

Seeing her sleeping so peacefully on her bed,
the pain of restless passion was aroused in the prince's body.
Spontaneously his consciousness was freed of all attachments,
and love in separation came and overwhelmed his soul.
Seeing Love's bow in splendor on her brow, his senses left him instantly.
"Blessed is that man's life for whom love is born in this maiden's heart"
[MM 98.4–6].

Mañjhan's text is unusual because, alone among the Hindavī romances, he goes on from *viraha* to depict a scene of union at the beginning of the love story. This replicates the Shattari spiritual practice in which the novice tastes absorption or union right at the beginning of his spiritual quest.

This initial encounter is followed by a conversation between Manohar and Madhumālatī that has many theological and cosmological references and defines love for the genre in terms of the Shattari aesthetics of form or beauty (*rūpa*). The princess seems divine beauty incarnate as she wakes up:

The maiden raised her arms above her head.
Lazily she yawned and stretched her limbs.
Her eyes awakened and became alert

like a hunter's arrows raised in ambush.
When a natural frown appeared upon her brow,
it seemed the God of Love had drawn his bow.
Her eyebrows were arched like the drawn bow of Kāmadeva,
and the triple world trembled in anticipation of her arrows
[MM 99.3–6].

She is astonished when she looks about her, for there is another bed spread out beside her, with a mighty prince lying upon it. She gathers up her courage and asks him how he has come to her inaccessible heavenly realm:

"Are you a demon or some ghostly apparition?
Can this body of yours be human?
Did you get miraculous power through a guru's words?
Or did you apply magic kohl to your eyes?
Is it a spell which has given you this power?
Did your guru make you drink some special herb?
Have you come so silently to my chamber
borne on a vehicle by the winds of the mind?
On all four sides the doorways are impassable
and many guards are awake all around.
Seven twisting paths lead to this chamber and countless warriors
are awake to guard them.
How have you come to this place to which even the wind has
no access?" [MM 102]

Madhumālatī's kingdom is a heavenly realm to which the magic power of the *apsaras*es has transported Manohar. The seven twisting paths or labyrinths here refer obliquely to seven stages that may tentatively be identified as the seven planetary circles of Shattari cosmology. These seven circles with their tutelary angels and mantras are also found in Humāyūn's court rituals and within the Shattari symbolic body, as we saw in Chapter 7.

The initial state of spiritual absorption of the Shattari neophyte is represented as a spontaneous loss of selfhood in the prince. When he hears the princess's words, his body is transformed:

When he heard these words as sweet as nectar,
the prince's body became immortal.
When he saw her he was perplexed and astonished,
and lost all consciousness of himself.
His heart was struck by pointed arrows,

as though her glances had been sharpened on a stone.
As sugar instantly dissolves in water,
so did the prince's soul surrender its own selfhood [MM 104.1–4].

The prince's self dissolves (*fanā*) like sugar in water; he is transformed by the moment of vision. He introduces himself to Madhumālatī as a royal prince who is dazzled by her transcendent beauty, and explains his plight:

"... The city of Kanaigiri is a most wonderful place.
The whole world knows my father, King Sūrajbhānu.
My own name is Prince Manohar.
I am of the Rāghava line, and belong to Kanaigiri.
I had scarcely closed my eyes in sleep,
and now I see I've woken up here.
I do not know who brought me here
so that our glances might meet" [MM 105.2–5].

In this meeting of glances, the classic moment of the awakening of desire, a moment of revelation and vision, the lover and beloved recognize one another after being parted for many lives.

Madhumālatī, who comes from the kingdom of Mahāras, the great *rasa*, responds to his query:

The princess began her story, full of rasa,
like a waterlily blossoming for love of the moon.
"Mahāras," she said, "is a city without equal.
Vikram Rāi, my father, is its mighty king.
My name, Madhumālatī, is radiant
both in this world and the hereafter.
I, a maiden, am my father's only child.
In this palace I am the darling of the king" [MM 110.1–4].

Rasa is the juice in her words that enables Shattari absorption as well as pleasure in hearing stories. The impact of her words on the prince is profound:

Although he tried to understand, her words robbed him of intelligence.
Like salt dissolving easily in water, he spontaneously lost his selfhood [MM 110.6].

Here the *rasa* in her words is the agent that causes the mystical dissolution of self, captured in the figure of salt (or, as above, sugar) dissolving in water.

It is thus the bond between lovers as they come together, but the word also links the text with its audience, forming a bond of literary pleasure between the poem and its readers.

Since the prince has fainted, the princess has first to revive him. She fans him and sprinkles ambrosial water on his face. Wiping the prince's face with the border of her sari, she raises his head from the ground. When he recovers, she asks him to tell her the truth (*ḥaqīqat/sat*) about his condition. Manohar invokes a spiritualized primal love between them; he proclaims to Madhumālatī that they are the same matter, and that they have been together since the beginning of creation:

> *"Listen, dearest one!" the prince then said,*
> *"In a former life God created love between you and me.*
> *Now that he has brought us into the world,*
> *I have given you my soul in exchange for sorrow.*
> *It is not just today that I grieve for you:*
> *I have known this sorrow from the first creation.*
> *The grief I feel separated from you was revealed*
> *the day the Creator fashioned this body of mine.*
> *O best of maidens, God mixed into my body's clay*
> *the pure cool water of your love" [MM 113.1–5].*

The poetic image of water mingling in clay refers to the Qur'ānic narrative of God's creation of Adam out of clay. If the dust from which God created humans is the stuff of creation, Manohar suggests, the water that leavens it into clay is love. In Manohar's speech to Madhumālatī, separation is what brings the soul into existence, since the universe emerges only by leaving God.

In the Shattari scheme of emergence and return, the pain of separation is a constant reminder of the demand of love, of the world's separation from God.

> *"To die is to taste immortality:*
> *Now I carry the burden of this grief,*
> *sacrificing all the pleasures of the two worlds.*
> *I have given myself to you and accepted this pain.*
> *Through dying I have tasted immortality.*
> *O Madhumālatī, the pain of love for you brings happiness to the world.*
> *Blessed is the life of the man in whose heart is born the pain of love for you" [MM 115.4–6].*

Because the pain of separation prompts the human return to God, it is the source of happiness; sorrow is the precondition for joy. Manohar welcomes it into his heart:

> *"I have heard that on the day the world was born,*
> *the bird of love was released to fly.*
> *It searched all the three worlds*
> *but could not find a resting place.*
> *So it returned and entered the human heart,*
> *liked it and never flew elsewhere.*
> *The three worlds asked it then:*
> *'Why are you attached to the human heart?'*
> *'Suffering' it answered, 'is the only hope for humans.*
> *Where there is sorrow, there I dwell'" [MM 116.1–5].*

Love chooses the human heart because it is affected by sorrow.

Manohar defines love and separation in his final address to Madhumālatī. Here the characteristic ambiguity of reference makes it difficult to fathom whether courtly poetry is being used to express an erotic theology or erotic theology is being used to give courtly poetry an added charge:

> *"You and I have always been together.*
> *Always we have been a single body.*
> *You and I, we two, are one body,*
> *two lumps of clay mixed with the same water.*
> *The same water flows in two streams,*
> *one lamp alone lights two homes.*
> *One soul enters two bodies,*
> *one fire burns in two hearths.*
> *We were one but were born as two:*
> *one temple with two doors.*
> *We were one radiant light, one beautiful form, one soul and one body:*
> *how can there be any doubt in giving oneself to oneself?"*

> *"You are the ocean, I am your wave.*
> *You are the sun and I am the ray that lights the world.*
> *Do not think that you and I are separate:*
> *I am the body, you are my life.*
> *Who can part us, a single light in two forms?*
> *I see everything through the eye of enlightenment,*
> *but who knows how long we have known each other?" [MM 117–8.4]*

The imagery makes embodiment the common experience between them. Here the body is the niche in which the flame of divine light burns, refracted through the glass and shining out from the niche throughout the world (as in Qur'ān 24:35).[1]

Madhumālatī's beauty is God's beauty, yet in seeing her Manohar recognizes his own identity with divinity:

> *"Till now I have lived my life without my soul,*
> *but today, on seeing you, that soul have I now found.*
> *I recognized you the moment that I saw you,*
> *for this is the beauty that had held me in thrall.*
> *This is the beauty that before was concealed.*
> *This is the beauty that pervades creation.*
> *This is the beauty that is Śiva and Śakti.*
> *This is the beauty that is the soul of the three worlds.*
> *This is the beauty that is manifest in many guises.*
> *This is the beauty found alike in king and beggar.*
> *This same beauty lives in all three worlds: earth, heaven and the nether world.*
> *This very same beauty I now see manifested, radiant upon your face" [MM 119].*

The word used here for beauty is *rūpa*, which also means form. All concrete forms in the Shattari cosmos share in God's beauty and can be read for signs of God's presence. The Shattari formulation of the moment of recognition makes contemplation of this *rūpa* true spiritual meditation.

Madhumālatī recognizes the prince as her lover and falls in love with him. She loses her heart to the tale he tells:

> *As she listened to his words,*
> *full of love's savor and feeling,*
> *the maiden's heart was at once intoxicated.*
> *Her soul delighted in the tale of love she heard,*
> *and the love of a previous life*
> *was kindled again in her memory.*
> *Just as fragrance mingles with the breeze,*
> *so did these two merge and become a single body.*
> *...Spontaneously their souls united and could not be told apart.*
> *When that love which had been born in a former life entered their hearts, they both sighed deeply, reflecting on their previous acquaintance.*
>
> *Then, touched by love, the maiden smiled and said:*
> *"You have overwhelmed me with these words of love.*

I was so overcome I could not speak.
Hearing your words I tasted the joys of love.
...My soul has found its place within your body,
and, through me, your name is manifest.
Mine is the beauty and your body is its mirror.
I am the sun and you are its light in the world [MM 121–2].

Though Manohar and Madhumālatī are tied together in this mirrored longing, they cannot consummate their desire immediately.

Mañjhan introduces the social implications of the spiritual or *ḥaqīqī* love that Manohar has defined so well for the princess. Before pledging herself to Manohar, the princess is worried about a second possible consequence of love: public disgrace for her for taking a lover before marriage. But as the prince sees Madhumālatī before him, his desire gets the better of him and he stretches out his hands toward her in lust:

The prince turned pale and rampant was his desire.
His pulse raced and from his body came a sigh.
Pierced by the arrows of the God of Love,
he could contain himself no longer.
He stretched his hands towards the maiden's breasts.
Leaving his finely adorned bed,
the prince sat upon the lovely maiden's couch.
That excellent maiden stopped his hands
and rose and moved to the prince's bed.
"O prince," she said, "why should we do wrong?
Why should we bring disgrace upon our parents?
Who would throw away everything for one fleeting moment of pleasure?
In this world the slightest indiscretion brings disgrace upon a woman" [MM 125].

To keep the prince at bay, the princess invokes a misogynistic gender hierarchy. Woman, she says, is a house to sin itself, and needs to be contained by the family in order to prevent her from disgracing herself and her clan:

"If a woman seeks to commit a sin,
in vain she destroys herself completely.
Womankind is the abode of sin.
But if a woman has a family,
then they will keep her from sinning.
Otherwise, who can contain her?

The clan is the only obstacle to sin.
Why become a sinner for a moment of pleasure?
Why sin and lose everything forever?" [MM 126.1–4]

The lovers must not consummate their desire, nor reveal their love to the world. The seeker must not disclose the secret identity of lover and beloved.

Madhumālatī is only willing to go as far as good girls go. She proposes a consummation of desire only within the framework of righteous conduct, which could mean both marriage and Islamic *sharī'ah* law:

"How can one whose heart is righteous
fall into the raging fire of sin?
Family and righteousness are the two protections,
so let no one abuse their mother or their father.
He who destroys himself for a momentary pleasure
has already reserved his place in hell.
But he who stood by the truth,
even if while on the path of sin,
will taste the heavenly fruit of immortality" [MM 127.2–5].

Correct action lies in promising to be true to one another while not overstepping the bounds of the mystic path. Public disgrace is the consequence of not following the strictures of righteous conduct. The path of truth (*ḥaqīqat*) referred to here is Shattari self-purification, polishing the mirror of the heart until one is fit to receive the divine revelation, or in this situation not giving way to lust when temptation beckons. Once the oath is taken, Manohar has promised to be true to her eternally, and to be silent about the details of their lovemaking for fear of public disgrace.

Therefore, they cannot make love fully, but only engage in lovers' play. The poet draws a curtain over the scene by referring only obliquely to what transpires, again suggesting *jalālī* and *jamālī* aspects of Madhumālatī's love play:

She made him fall and faint with love,
then sprinkled nectar to revive him.
Sometimes they enjoyed the ecstasies of love,
sometimes they feared the pain of separation.
Their eyes were gardens of beauty,
and their hearts given to the passions of youth.
Now they tasted the supreme bliss of love,
now they dedicated their hearts to one another [MM 134.1–4].

They exchange their jeweled signet rings as tokens of their undying love, and then fall asleep on one another's beds. The promise of truth (*sati bacana*), the lovers' pledge, which the rings signify, is brought up every time the couple meet.

Avoiding direct physical description, the poet moves directly to the point where the *apsaras*es return to find the beds all creased, the flowers withered, and the signs of lovemaking on both bodies:

They had exchanged their rings
and wore each other's on their hands.
Some of the maiden's bangles lay broken on the bed,
and her bodice was ripped open at the bosom.
Clothes had been torn from her limbs,
and the scratchmarks of nails were visible on her breasts.
The necklace and garlands at her breast were broken,
her parting was gone, and her plaits were undone.
Her bed was in total disarray,
and the beauty spot on her forehead had been wiped off.
Marks of collyrium could be seen on the prince's lips,
while red betel juice adorned the maiden's kohl-lined eyes
[MM 136].

The nymphs are shocked, and consider what to do next. They pick up the sleeping prince and take him back from heaven to earth, from Mahāras to his own kingdom of Kanaigiri. The first major turning point of the narrative, the meeting between the lovers, is concluded. Manohar and Madhumālatī are separated again. The rest of the plot revolves around their efforts to consummate their love, to change separation into union.

The Twelve Months of Separation: The Bārah-masā (Reprise)

The *bārah-māsā*, a generic set piece of the *premākhyān*, which we have seen in the tale of Mainā in the *Cāndāyan*,[2] occurs in the poetic sections that follow, which tell the story of Manohar's second meeting with Madhumālatī.

When Prince Manohar and Pemā arrive in King Citrasena's kingdom after vanquishing the demon, there is much rejoicing and jubilation. The entire town comes out to meet the pair, and everyone celebrates their homecoming. The king welcomes the prince, and Pemā takes care of him. But he is still distraught over Madhumālatī and cannot forget the object of his quest. Under the spiritual guidance of Pemā, he is ready to forget all but the divine.

In effect, he extinguishes his rational mind in the town of Citbisarāuṉ. Pemā reminds him that the second day of the month has come, and Madhumālatī will come to meet him. She arranges a meeting for them in the *citrasārī* or picture pavilion in the mango grove around the city, and the two lovers meet to renew their promise of true love. Rūpamañjarī, Madhumālatī's mother, discovers them and is outraged at the prospect of public disgrace for her daughter. She casts a spell that puts Manohar into an enchanted sleep and carries him back to Kanaigiri, and she bears Madhumālatī home to Mahāras. To punish her daughter for her misconduct, she bewitches her and transforms her into a beautiful bird, with green feathers and eyes like glittering jewels. Madhumālatī roams the forests, desolately searching for her love.

Tārācand, a prince who is out hunting, traps her with pearls. As a bird caught in the fowler's net, Madhumālatī represents the divine trapped in human and concrete form at the lowest level of the Shattari cosmology. She is forced to assume this embodied form in order to search for Manohar. At first, Tārācand is entranced with her beauty and in love with the beautiful bird, but when he finds out who she is, he talks of the value of leaving home in the service of the world and vows to help Madhumālatī with her quest. She tells Tārācand her whole story, and he promises to help her and sets out to return her to her own heavenly kingdom of Mahāras. He represents the Sufi quality of *k͟hidmah-i k͟halq* or selfless service, and acts as the guide or intermediary to Madhumālatī, just as Pemā has been the guide for Manohar. He takes her back home to her mother, the grief-stricken Rūpamañjarī, who removes her spell from the fabulous bird. But Madhumālatī is still distraught in separation from Manohar.

Here begins the generic set piece of the *bārah-māsā*, which in Mañjhan's text takes the form of a letter from Madhumālatī to Pemā describing her misery through the twelve months of the year and begging her desperately for help in finding Manohar. The *bārah-māsā*, as Charlotte Vaudeville has noted, is commonly composed around the theme of *viraha* or separation, the other side of *prema* or love, "the pain of separation (*viraha*) endured by a young wife pining for the return of her beloved all through the twelve months of the year. In such songs, the description of nature is intimately and attractively joined to the expression of the heroine's sorrow."[3] In the Hindavī Sufi romances, the *bārah-māsā* is spoken by the deserted wife of the hero, pining for her husband's return from his ascetic quest:

> While the main heroine of the Sūfī *mathnavīs* symbolises divine Beauty for which the hero is pining in the torments of *viraha*, it is a secondary heroine, usually the hero's first wife, who appears as the traditional *virahiṇī* and sings the *viraha-bārahmāsā*; thus the Muslim authors of

> *mathnavīs* in Avadhi respect the Hindu tradition of the *viraha bārahmāsā* in attributing the song to a neglected wife.[4]

The *bārah-māsā* is a message to the seeker entreating him not to forget his responsibility to the world and to take into account her agony. The seeker comes back, bringing his divine beloved with him, and the two wives fight. Only after the hero persuades the two women to make peace can he consummate his love with both of them, reconciling the claims of the world and of spirituality.

In the *Madhumālatī*, however, Mañjhan uses this Hindavī literary convention in a new way, to deliver a generic set piece without explicit allegorical coding. There is no second wife, as there is in the *Cāndāyan;* in her place, Pemā is Manohar's spiritual guide to his beloved Madhumālatī. After Manohar and Madhumālatī are separated, she roams the forests for twelve months, seeking her lost love, as God comes into the world in search of man. The *premākhyān* poets generally used this set piece to turn human desire artfully toward the divine, but the *bārah-māsā* of Madhumālatī represents a movement in the other direction, expressing the longing of the celestial Madhumālatī for her human lover, drawing the divine into a situation of reciprocal longing (*ḥubb-i ilāhī*).

> *She begins by summoning a messenger:*
> *Then Madhumālatī, unbeknownst to her mother,*
> *entreated the messengers with folded hands,*
> *to explain everything to Pemā thus:*
> *"You kindled this fire in my heart.*
> *Friend, I have wandered the earth for my love,*
> *but the fire in my heart was never quenched.*
> *Maybe, O princess, you can find him.*
> *If you do, re-unite me with my match" [MM 401.1–4].*

In the letter, Madhumālatī recounts all the past sufferings she has endured, parted from the prince and still enchanted in the form of a bird. The imagery employed interlaces Madhumālatī's incarnation as a bird with the cycle of nature, using the description of the passing of the seasons to connect her body with nature.

She begins her letter to Pemā with the month of the rains, Sāvan, when the dark masses of clouds thundered and her eyes rained tears and the scarlet ladybirds came out:

> *"When my tears of blood fell to the earth,*
> *they became the scarlet ladybirds of Sāvan.*

She who enjoys in this difficult season
the delights of the couch and the excitement of love,
enjoys the blessings that life has to offer.
I wandered as a cuckoo through every garden,
eyes bloodshot, body burning in separation.
Only a stubborn soul can stay in its body without a lover in the month of Sāvan,
with its massing clouds and torrents of rain, its endless nights and flashing lightnings" [MM 402.3–6].

The rainy season continued in the month of Bhādon̲, with its dark cloudy nights:

"In the fearsome nights of the dark month of Bhādon̲,
only separation's fierce fire shared my bed.
In the rains, the constellations of Maghā and the Lion
tossed my body to and fro in pain.
The water of love dripped from my two eyes.
All the eight physical signs of love
were aroused in my body, and the seven skies
bowed down low to touch the earth.
Thunder crashed frighteningly all around me.
I was sure my soul would leave me at last" [MM 403.1–4].

During the rains, the season in which lovers are united in poetry, she sought desperately for her lover, but found him nowhere:

"I wandered alone through wood and forest, with the pain of separation in my heart.
My shameless soul was such a sinner, it still did not leave my body" [MM 403.6].

She continued to wander without hope. The season changed with the month of Kun̲vār or Aśvin, but Madhumālatī's agony did not abate:

"The nine nights of the festival of Navarātra
heralded the cruel month of Kun̲vār.
The wind whistled of the winter to come.
In the crisp autumn nights, the moon
shone cool and bright in the sky.
Everyone was celebrating the festive season,
but I was alone, exiled to the forest" [MM 404.1–2].

In her bitter exile, she saw all the signs of nature returning to normalcy after the torrential rains:

"Night after night, cranes screeched in the lakes.
The colorful wagtails returned to the world.
As the birds re-appeared, the rains subsided,
and the wet earth became firm again.
The season of Kuṉvār was happy and festive,
and young women blossomed with joy" [MM 404.3–5].

Despite the festivities around her, she could not find her Manohar anywhere. She assures Pemā that she can barely speak, let alone write, of the agonies she went through in early autumn. In Kārtik, the cool month when the moon shines forth in silvery radiance, she was tortured by the moonlight:

"The full moon of Kārtik tormented this girl.
Its rays of nectar streamed down like poison.
Maidens were blossoming like lotuses,
night lotuses in the radiance of the moon.
They delighted in the cool nights of autumn,
spent in their lovers' passionate embraces.
My body was consumed with the fire of separation.
In the cool autumn moonlight,
I made my bed on burning embers" [MM 405.1–4].

Madhumālatī could not enjoy those autumn nights of moonlit radiance because no sweet-talking lover (*ravanh miṭhbolā*) shared her bed. She watched everyone celebrate Dīpāvalī while she wandered alone in the forest.

Winter came with the month of Aghan, and it was bitterly cold. Madhumālatī's body wasted away in the winter months, but she could not die because she was searching for her lover in the phenomenal, embodied world. Time itself became implicated in Madhumālatī's sorrow; the poet links the shortening of the days in the dark and cold winter to the forcible shortening of Madhumālatī's joys:

"Through the month of Aghan,
the cold weather was at its prime,
Bodies trembled in the bitter cold,
warm fire felt good. The days
and my joys drew shorter together.
Every moment, nights and sorrows grew longer.

Each dark night passed like an age,
as I wandered from branch to branch in the forest.
Only she knows this harrowing agony,
who has suffered separation while in love.
My gravest fault, dear friend, was this:
I did not die when I parted from my love" [MM 406.1–5].

Each winter night passed like an age, and the following month of Pūs was even more difficult because of the coincidence of this time with the time of Madhumālatī's coming of age:

"The nights of Pūs were intolerably difficult.
I, a weak woman, could barely endure them and survive.
How can a woman's nature bear a night
in which each watch passes like an age?
Everyone's heart held desire for their love,
and I wandered alone through the forest,
making my nest on the branches of trees....
Fortune turned away from me, O friend, when my lover turned his face away.
How could my lover abandon me blossoming in the prime of youth?" [MM 407.1–3, 6]

Even though her love was far away, she was constantly reminded of him. Her soul could not leave her body, and her body had no peace. Here the poet invokes her form as a bewitched bird:

"Listen, dear friend, how hard the month of Māgh:
my love was in a foreign land,
and I had no friend but separation.
How could I bear the harsh cold winter,
without a lover in my bed, and I a young girl?
Suffering the agony of parting,
I perched on wintry branches all night.
Hail and snow beat down on me.
How did Madhumālatī endure difficult Māgh,
her days of separation growing longer each moment?
Happiness went along with my love, and sorrow stayed to keep me company.
Separation's shears hacked at me, cutting away at bone and flesh" [MM 408].

The next three verses describe the seasons turning into spring. First, the month of Phāgun comes with the festival of Holī and its riotous colors. The pyre that burns the effigy of Holikā, the evil stepmother of Viṣṇu's devotee Prahlād, is lit, and Madhumālatī feels herself burnt on it in her agony. The image is conventional to the imagery of the *bārah-māsās* in the *premākhyāns*, but the poet links it with the red flowers of the flame-of-the-forest, the *ḍhāk* tree, spreading through the woods like a forest fire. Madhumālatī alone of all the birds remains, and the dry thorn bushes convey the desolation that spring has wrought upon her:

> *"In the month of Phāgun, my friend,*
> *a disaster befell my suffering body:*
> *I was burnt on the pyre like Holikā.*
> *Not a single leaf remained on the trees,*
> *the forest-fire of separation destroyed them.*
> *Forests suffered a fall of leaf,*
> *and all the gardens turned to dry thorns.*
> *All the birds renounced the woods,*
> *when they saw red blossoms*
> *light up the flame-of-the-forest.*
> *Not a tree remained in the world,*
> *to which I did not cling weeping in despair.*
> *Dear friend, I had not yet found my love—I was sobbing myself*
> *to death.*
> *My body, bursting with new youth, wasted away into dry thorn*
> *bushes" [MM 409].*

With the month of Caita, nature decked itself out like a young woman blossoming with fresh new life, greenery, and color; but Madhumālatī just longed for Manohar, calling him *sāīṉ* or lord, which could mean either her husband or God:

> *"Tender new leaves came out in Caita,*
> *and nature put on a fresh green sari.*
> *Black honey-bees hummed everywhere,*
> *and leaves and flowers adorned the branches.*
> *Blossoms raised their heads from the bough,*
> *and trees grew fresh flowering limbs.*
> *The trees which shed all their leaves in Phāgun*
> *grew green and fresh with leaf once more.*
> *Without my Lord, my own fall of leaf*
> *has not, dear friend, grown green again" [MM 410.1–5].*

In the month of Baisākh, Madhumālatī watched spring continue with a riot of fresh colors. The last line contains a pun, as it uses part of Madhumālatī's own name, which means "night jasmine," to convey her withering away in the forest, like jasmine blossoms drying up:

"Sorely I suffered, dear friend, in Baisākh,
when the forest was green but my body was burning. . . .
Forests and gardens clothed themselves with flowers.
For me, spring was barren without my love.
How was Madhumālatī to survive Baisākh,
when the fire of separation consumed her every moment?
Petals and leaves of every color,
clothed the trees yellow, green, and red.
Without my dear lord, O companion of my childhood, my youth bore no fruit,
its blossoms withered and fell to the ground, jasmine in the wood" [MM 411.1, 3–6].

Soon, continues Madhumālatī, in the hot summer month of Jeṭh, the sun ignited a fire in the world:

"My heart cried out, 'My love! My love!'
in the cruel hot month of Jeṭh.
The sun shone a thousand times more fiercely.
The flames of separation raged inside my heart,
and the sun rained fire for all to see.
Secretly, separation burnt me up,
and openly, the sun's fire consumed me:
how could a woman survive between two fires?" [MM 412.1–3]

Scorched between these two blazing fires, she could barely survive. She sums up her separation in a *dohā* that explains the reasons for her anguish. The last reason invokes the term *rūpa*, "form" or "beauty," implying Madhumālatī's original divine form, which she has had to leave behind because of her mother's enchantments. She has now lost her beauty, *jamāl*, so important in the initial encounter at midnight:

"First, I was separated, second, in exile, third, without friend or companion, fourth, I was without form or beauty: when I sought to die, death would not come" [MM 412.6].

The last verse in the *bārah-māsā* brings the progress of the seasons full circle, as after the summer the rains come again with the month of Asāḍh. For Madhumālatī, the tumult in the skies signaled regeneration of all nature:

> *"Dear friend, lightning flashed in the heavens*
> *to herald the unbearable month of Asāḍh.*
> *Dark clouds like elephants turned to look back,*
> *at the lightning which goaded them on.*
> *Crickets and grasshoppers clamored in tumult.*
> *The scorched grass grew back,*
> *mango trees blossomed once more.*
> *The earth sprouted with life again,*
> *but love never sprouted in my love's heart. . . .*
> *Asāḍh passed in torment for me, dear friend, like all twelve months.*
> *Now please, for the sake of the Creator, help me so I may*
> *be redeemed" [MM 413.1–4, 6].*

The rains came again, but Madhumālatī was not reborn. She ends the letter by begging Pemā to help her be united with Manohar. The entire *bārah-māsā* thematizes the longing for passionate fulfillment that, in Shattari terms, is the existential condition of both humans and the divine.

Consummation and Happy Ending

Once the message is sent to Pemā, she does all she can to unite Manohar with the anguished Madhumālatī. Manohar has recovered from his forced return to Kanaigiri under a magical spell and become a yogi again. In his search for Madhumālatī, he reaches Pemā's city of Citbisarāuṉ, and she relays Madhumālatī's pain-filled *bārah-māsā* to him. They send the messengers back with a reply from Pemā telling Madhumālatī of the yogi, and Manohar writes a secret letter to his love telling her of his sorrows and entreating her to be kind to him. When the message reaches Mahāras, there is great rejoicing. Madhumālatī's parents, acting on the advice of her spiritual guide Tārācand, set off with a huge entourage to negotiate Madhumālatī's wedding. When they reach a convenient campsite near Citbisarāuṉ, they send equerries to King Citrasena to announce their arrival.

The two royal families meet and arrange the wedding of Manohar and Madhumālatī, which is held with great pomp and show at the auspicious astrological moment. The idealized caste hierarchies of both kingdoms are on display, and the poet constructs the wedding rituals as an elaborate exercise in the display of courtly power. There are dancing girls and grand processions, and musicians sing songs of celebration in the streets. Manohar is still in yogic guise, as befits an ascetic, but once the wedding night comes he throws off his yogic clothes and becomes a prince again, reunited with his beloved. Madhurā, Pemā's mother, has the women's quarters (*ranīvāsā*) prepared, and the wedding ritual takes place. The prince and princess exchange garlands in the rite of the *jaimālā*, and finally the fire of separation that has raged in both their hearts is satisfied.

After they celebrate the ritual of tying the knot and circling the sacred fire, the lovers retire to a private bedchamber. The night of love (*suhāga rāta*) that follows is described with brio and panache:

Manohar took her arm and said,
"My sorrowing heart, which longed for you,
is now at peace. Give up your former cruelty,
abandon modesty and embrace me!"
All shyness gone, they spoke of love
and gazed directly into each other's eyes.
Those eyes which had thirsted in hope
now drank in love and beauty to the full.
Their grieving hearts were cooler now,
the fire subsiding as their hearts united.
Their eyes were joined in longing and their hearts enmeshed in love.
As both their hearts became one, their souls began to share in each other.

Their eyes drank in beauty till sated.
Somehow this sun and moon became one.
Still they could not turn face to face,
their hearts trembling before their first union.
The prince sought to kiss her lips
but Madhumālatī averted her mouth
and turned her face away from him.
Mistaking them for lamps, she blew on jewels,
only to make their light even brighter.
She covered her face with both her hands.
When the prince bit her lips she trembled in fear.
First, their hearts were madly in love; moreover, this was their very first time.
Third, modesty overcame them, so the desire to make love was not aroused.

Then a handmaiden hidden there said,
'Why did you study the arts of love?'
Hearing what the maiden said,

Madhumālatī was truly astonished.
But she remained caught between shame
and her knowledge of what to do.
Should she display her arts, she would lose
her modesty; should she remain shy,
her skills in love-making would go to waste.
She recalled with amusement the story of the woman,
with a snake-charmer for a father-in-law,
who was bitten by a snake in her most private parts
but could not speak out for modesty.
The prince scratched with the goad of his nails
her breasts, round like the swellings
on the forehead of an elephant.
Like a parrot he bit into her coral lips.
Looking at the depth of the waters of her youth, he could contain himself no longer.
Embracing her golden pitcher-breasts, he swam across the river of heir shyness.

In the grip of love and passion they embraced,
and then her untouched jewel was pierced.
The bodice on her bosom was torn to pieces,
and the parting in her hair was all washed away.
The vermillion from her parting ran
into the spot on her forehead,
and the mascara on her eyes turned red
from the betel juice on his lips.
So heavily did he press upon her
that the garland round her neck broke,
and the sandal paste on her breasts rubbed off.
Her source of nectar broke forth then,
and the raging fire in their hearts
was quenched, the quest fulfilled.
Under the power of desire they spent the night, unable to turn from one another.
But their burning hearts were only cooled when the heavens opened and a stream flowed forth [MM 448–51].

Narrative and erotic consummation coincide as Mañjhan works the arts of love into the scene of the wedding night. The prince, appropriately aroused, presses forward to gain the object of his desire.

The scene after the lovemaking is described in images of Madhumālatī's ripped bodice and the mingled *tilaka*s of the lovers. On the next day, Madhumālatī's girlfriends ask her how the night of love passed, and press her for every detail of the night's lovemaking:

She awoke as if she had swum in a sea of bliss.
Her companions then adorned her
and put on her both clothes and ornaments.
They took sweet delight in asking her about the rasa *of love.*
"Tell us," they said,
"How was your juicy night of love? Promise us you'll tell every passionate detail!" [MM 45.4/2–6]

She replies by invoking the necessity of secrecy and silence, the pledge to which the lovers are bound:

"Do not tell your secret to anyone;
what madwoman exchanges loss for gain?
One should keep love hidden within the heart.
Whoever reveals the mystery to the world
gives his life on the scaffold.
If I tell you my secret,
what good would it be to me?
Water cannot stay in a broken pot,
but leaks away drop by drop" [MM 454.2–5].

Here the reference is to Manṣūr al-Ḥallāj, who lost his life by declaring the greatest secret of Sufi thought, that of the human soul's identity with God.

This great secret is also indicated by the reversal of the *bārah-māsā* in this text, which goes further than any of the other *premākhyān*s in declaring God's need for man. Though her handmaidens continue to press Madhumālatī, she will not reveal her secret. In a reference to the opening of Rūmī's great *Masnavī*, Mañjhan says:

"Look at the pen carved of wood—what did it do when it was a reed in the forest?
As long as its head was not cut open, it never revealed its mystery to anyone" [MM 454.6].

In the Shattari stages of manifestation, concrete forms (*ṣūrat*) exemplify and are shadows of invisible but real spiritual processes on higher planes.

Metaphysically, God is the sole existent, as existence is intrinsic to Him and identical with His essence, while the "existence" of all else is extrinsic and superimposed on its essence, which is pure nonbeing. Although human beings are thus radically different from the divine Absolute, they share in the process of refracting divine essence through layers of grosser and grosser materiality. Manohar and Madhumālatī come together after each of them has been both the seeker and the object sought, interchangeable as subject and object of desire.

In Mañjhan's romance, the hero does not have to reconcile his two wives, who signify this world and the next, in order to reach narrative consummation. Instead Manohar and Madhumālatī are united in a marriage of love requited. But there still remain two major characters whose fate is to be resolved before the conclusion of the text: Pemā and Tārācand, who have functioned as guides for Manohar and Madhumālatī. Events transpire formulaically, as the two princes go hunting after the wedding. On their way back they stop in the mango grove with the painted pavilion, and Tārācand sees Pemā happily swinging among the lush mango trees. He is overwhelmed by the revelatory vision of her beauty, which is described in another *sarāpā*. Pemā is equally struck by the handsome prince, and a marriage is arranged between these two lovers. This royal wedding, too, is celebrated with great splendor, the lovers are blissfully united, and no major characters are pining away in separation any more.

But the story goes on. Following this second wedding ceremony, the plot takes another twist: the two brides depart from their parents' houses to go to their husbands as sexually mature women, in the ritual of the *gavana* or "going" away.[5] Here the valence of Mahāras and Citbisarāuṉ, both of which have been heavenly cities, shifts. They now signify the world, and the two brides leave them for paradise, their beloved husbands' house, where their love is consummated and they can live happily ever after. The event resonates both with the death anniversaries of Sufi shaikhs (*'urs*) in India, which are celebrated as the wedding of the shaikh with God, and with the common poetic symbolism of bridal songs, which depict with great pathos the departure of the bride from her father's house. Mañjhan consummates the desire of both pairs of lovers in the Sufi value of *baqā'* or eternal subsistence in God rather than in the evanescence and annihilation of all things to God. Unlike the other *premākhyāns*, the *Madhumālatī* ends not with the death of every major character but with a fairy-tale happy ending, two pairs of happy lovers.

The doubled ending and the ambiguous reference of the second ending, either to a bridal song depicting the departure from home of the bride or to the Sufi value of *baqā'*, would have worked well with the multiple courtly and Sufi audiences of the text. Throughout, the text shows a multiplicity of reference that informs the logic of the narrative transformation of desire into love. The *Madhumālatī* has a circular plot within which doubles and the intersections between characters form the turning points of the narrative. The plain text, *'ibārah*, conceals and reveals a play of referentiality, *ishārah*, as well as allegory and exemplification, *tams̱īl*. The sanction for this poetics of suggestion may perhaps be found in Shaikh Muḥammad Ġhaus̱'s statement in his cosmological treatise about the kind of crooked vision that is needed to see an object, for as he puts it, "Humans are the origin of a true reality that cannot be found, for an object cannot see itself by itself."[6] In Mañjhan's contribution to the genre of the Hindavī Sufi romance there is no annihilation, no folding back of the world into a mysterious Godhead. The only annihilation is of the seeker's own carnal nature, which gives him the concrete power simultaneously to stay in the world and to transcend it, echoing the Shattari *silsilah*'s own cosmology and the practices that turned the novice into a shadowy mirror for God.

9

Hierarchies of Response

Responding to the Hindavī Romances

In the previous chapters, we have sketched out the facets of a generic logic, privileging a spiritual reading of the text. There are limits to the allegoresis, however, and certain sections and details fall outside a strictly allegorical reading, raising the question of whether this privileged reading is justified. To resolve this crux, we turn from the texts of the romances to their listeners and readers, to see how different audiences received these works at the time when they were composed. The fragmentary cultural remains and the few and scattered references to contexts of reception make reconstructing the mixed Persianate and Hindavī aristocratic literary culture of the Delhi sultanate a nearly impossible task. But shadowy as our picture of this culture necessarily must remain, the framing verses in the prologues that describe the poet's aesthetic sense of his work (which we considered in Chapter 2), when read in conjunction with the Persian political and military chronicles of the period and the rare historical accounts of performances before groups of listeners, flesh out our picture of the larger cultural world and the generic expectations of the audiences of the Hindavī romances. The Hindavī poets use the formal features of the Persian generic model to depict their generous patrons as the exemplary readers who would best understand and appreciate their poems. Although these panegyrics to ruling sultans and provincial nobles were admittedly idealized and conventional poetic forms, they nevertheless delineate the qualities of the ideal reading subjects whom the poets would imagine for their poems. And the few available participatory descriptions of audience response point to two enduring features of poetry in Hindavī: its powerful and explicit imagery, and its continuing popularity among groups of cultivated listeners in courts, Sufi hospices (*k͟hānaqāhs*), and other spaces where poetry was sung or recited.

As with any broader contextual enquiry, we must marshal several sorts of materials to clarify the process of reception. The available contextual evidence of reception among the genre's audiences, both courtly and Sufi, suggests how the Sufi shaikhs and their disciples who composed the Hindavī romances also constructed a hierarchy of response in which the Sufi novice was the most ideal reader for their sensuous poems. The courtly and Sufi accounts of audience response show how these poems were performed and received within the aristocratic and mystical cultures of the day. Moreover, the Chishti composers of the genre recognized that the suggestive character of Hindavī verse and its explicit imagery had a powerful effect on the listener by arousing his desire. Careful control had to be exercised over the experience of listening to poetry, so that the desire could be directed toward Allah. Sufi recognition of the power of poetry was accompanied by elaborate glosses for correct interpretation and procedures for training the self of the listener toward Allah. Descriptions of the performance of Hindavī poetry in the courts of Afghan and Turkish nobles and sultans, supplemented by evidence for the Chishti Sufi practice of *samā'* (musical audition), indicate how these romances were understood during the period in which they were composed and allow us to sketch out the theory of reading that ideal readers or listeners were expected to bring to bear on the poems.

Not all readers are created equal. In fact, not all readers are readers; some are listeners. In Indian theories of response, the ideal receiver was the *sahṛdaya*, the "person with heart" who could open himself up to the meanings and nuances of poetry, music, and dance. Aesthetic experience was seen as a transsubjective communication of the *rasa* or juice of a performed or recited piece. Evening gatherings (*majlis*, pl. *majālis*) for Persian and Hindavī poetry, music, and dance were a common entertainment in the cultivated life of the Delhi sultanate. Poetry was performed at such gatherings at aristocratic courts, as well as in the context of the Sufi ritual audition of music (*samā'*).

In both these contexts of reception, words had power. For instance, when the prince in Quṯban's *Mirigāvatī* sets out as a yogi, he comes to a country whose king questions him about his ailment. He responds by feigning to refuse, then launching into this description:

> *The prince responded, "This is not a matter for words.*
> *Do not ask me, O king!*
> *I can't tell this sorrow to anyone—both speaker and hearer*
> *will burn up alive!"*
>
> *Then he began the tale of his separation,*
> *and of his sorrow in love. Whoever heard him*
> *could not stay conscious any longer.*
> *As he told love's story full of* rasa*,*
> *the king forgot his own consciousness.*
> *When he spoke of separation, his audience wept,*

washing their hands with the streams from their eyes!
Strife, agitation, restlessness, and conflict—
whoever heard that song remained entranced.
That yogi knew no other story at all
except for the romance of Mirigāvatī! [M 110.6–111.1–5]

The yogi's song makes the king and his populace faint and weep. Theories of response from the period emphasize this affective power of poetry, whether couched in terms of theories of audition or courtly protocols of presentation. They also recognized the links between reading or listening to poetry and the ascetic regimen.

Courtly Accounts of Audience Response

Ideological forms, however élitist and closed they may seem, generally circulate within larger contexts of reception. Let us begin with the literary culture of the aristocratic patrons of Hindavī and Persian verse in the Delhi sultanate. The Hindavī poets expected their readers to be familiar with the classical backgrounds, but especially to appreciate the skill with which they put together well-wrought verse in the newly fashionable *desī* literary language Hindavī.

From the few scattered references in the chronicles of the period, it seems that musical parties for singing Persian and Hindavī verse were a widespread practice. They were part of a larger culture of evening entertainments, called *Jashn*, which the historian K. M. Ashraf has described:

> When they spoke of organizing a *Jashn*, it usually brought to [mind] entertainments [such] as vocal and instrumental music, dainty wines, dried fruits and indoor games such as chess, *chaupar*, etc. It was usual to decorate the rooms where the guests assembled with rich carpets. Aloe-wood and incense were constantly burning there. Rose-water was frequently sprinkled over the party for its refreshing and cooling effect. Fruits were neatly served in silver and golden fruit trays. But the most entertaining item was the wine which was served by very handsome cup-bearers together with some spiced and seasoned dishes (like *kababs*) for relish....The serious business commenced after sunset when the musicians and dancers began their performance, and the wine cups went around. When the performers had stirred the emotions of the audience to fever heat, gold and silver were frequently showered on them at intervals. In the small hours of the morning the whole scene began to fade away before the weary eyes, and people dropped into sleep through sheer exhaustion.[1]

These nightly musical parties were also part of official state celebrations and public holidays, produced for the people who flocked to the court at Delhi and its festive occasions.

The historian Baranī speaks, with nostalgia and regret, of the vanished parties of his youth. The setting for his evocative picture of a courtly culture of poetry, song, and dance is the reign of ʻAlāuddīn Khaljī's uncle Jalāl al-dīn Khaljī (d. 1296):

> The *ġhazal* singers of the Sultan's *majlis* (evening gathering) were the noble Amīr and Ḥamīd Rājah. Every day Amīr Khusrau would bring a new *ġhazal* to the gathering. The Sultan was in love (*sheftah*) with the *ġhazals* of Amīr Khusrau and gave him much largesse. And the cupbearers (*sāqīs*) of the Sultan's *majlis* were the boys Haibat Khān and Niẕām Kharīṭah-dār. Yildiz was the head *sāqī*. They had beauty, and loveliness, and miraculous grace (*karishma*), such that every ascetic and devout worshipper who even glanced at them put his sacred thread down in the middle of the town (*bastī*) and made his prayer-rug the reed mat of the wine-shop! In the grip of obsessive love for those matchless ones, destroyers of the repentance of the devout (*taubah*), they became disgraced and notorious (*rusvā*). Of the musicians of the Sultan, Muḥammad the Harpist played the harp (*cang*), Futūḥā...and Nuṣrat Khātūn recited poetry (*surūd*) and from the beauty of just their plain voices the birds came down from the air. The listeners would be left without consciousness, their hearts would be aflame, and their lives in tumults...wherever these [singers] looked, and every grace that they displayed, and every flirtatious glance that they let loose, they spilled open a mine of salt! And there were dancers in the *majlis* of the Sultan, and everyone who saw the dancing, its marvellous grace and proud airs, wanted to take his life and offer it up...[in short], the *majlis* of the Sultan was one that cannot be seen outside of dreams.[2]

This is a vivid description of the aristocratic way to have fun in the Delhi sultanate: good company, wine, beautiful people, poetry, song, and dance. Saltiness, in the above passage, signifies sexiness, and the passage goes on to describe the flirtations and amusements that surrounded the performance of poetry. It is not unreasonable to assume that this was a model for aristocrats and others to emulate in their own evening gatherings for entertainment (*majālis*).

Ḥusain Shāh Sharqī of Jaunpur, at whose court-in-exile Quṭban composed and recited the *Mirigāvatī*, was a poet and a noted patron of the distinctive Sharqī style of architecture. He was also an accomplished musician.[3] This is the context for the end of prologue to the *Mirigāvatī*, in which Quṭban describes with immediacy the performance of his romance in front of Ḥusain Shāh:

> *Then I recited this story of mine,*
> *that I had adorned and polished well.*
> *I followed what that Indra among men had said!*
> *Lend me your ears, and I'll recite it well. [M 12.1–2]*

Here Quṭban refers, presumably, to a royal command to recite the poem in court. His exhortation to the reader to listen to his ornate romance accords well with a regular courtly culture of musical performances and recitations. Ḥusain Shāh, the illustrious "Indra among men" (*nariṃda*) invoked here, was a key figure in the recreation and transmission of Indian music and sung texts. Given the shared literary and musical culture of the day, it should come as no surprise that Ḥusain Shāh was also an important resource for another ruler of the time, Raja Mān Singh Tomar (1468–1517) of Gwalior. Raja Mān Singh collected all the new melodies and techniques invented at the courts of Delhi and the regional sultanates in his *Māna Kutūhala* ("The Curiosity of Mān Singh"). Later musicians and theorists drew extensively on the *Māna Kutūhala*, and the tradition of singing Hindavī lyrics in the *k͟hayāl* style (rather than the more somber *dhrupad* style, derived from Indian temple chants) can be traced back to Ḥusain Shāh's complex and creative part in the history of Indian music.[4] Ḥusain Shāh was thus a knowledgeable and appreciative sponsor of *k͟hayāl*, as well as of poetic genres such as the Hindavī romances. This courtly culture for the reception of these romances extends well into the sixteenth century. The regional courts in which the Hindavī romances were recited were provincial cousins of the imperial court at Delhi, outposts of civilized life in the *mofussil* (the provincial and rural parts of India). In the prologue to the *Cāndāyan*, Dā'ūd mentions his own oral presentation of his *sa-rasa* poem (*kabi sarasa ubhāsī*) at the court of Malik Mubārak, the local *iqṭā'-dār* of Dalmau in Avadh (C 17.1ff).

Already in the late thirteenth century, Ġhiyās̱ al-dīn Balban's successor in Delhi, his grandson Sultan Mu'izz al-dīn Kaiqubād (r. 1287–1290), was famous for his love of courtesans, musicians, wine, and pleasure parties. Young girls "whose breasts had not yet developed" were trained in archery, riding, dancing, and singing Hindavī and Persian songs for presentation to the court. The Sultan handsomely rewarded the girls and their teachers.[5] After two years of his reign had passed, his father, Sultan Nāṣir al-dīn of Bengal, summoned him to a sternly admonitory meeting. The young and newly repentant Kaiqubād returned from the meeting sobered by the strict counsels of good government he had received, and the royal camp proceeded without any merrymaking or revelry.

On his way home through Avadh, however, he met an artful and beautiful courtesan. She was "a piece of the moon, coquettish and wily, devastatingly lovely, clad in a gold-embroidered robe, a gold-worked quiver of arrows at her waist,... [and] a royal cap covering half her ears across her head."[6] Baranī describes the meeting:

> *She laid herself on the ground in front of the sultan and recited this verse in a dainty voice and with a heart-ravishing melody:*
> *"If on my eye you'd place your foot,*
> *I'd spread my eyes out on your path, that you may advance!"*[7]
> *And then she said to the sultan: "King of the world, the opening couplet of this ġhazal is more appropriate in your service, but I am afraid and I cannot recite it!"*
> *The sultan was amazed at this vision, and intoxicated by her words. He brought his horse to a halt and said, "Recite it, and don't be afraid!" And that breaker of the resolve of many abstinent ones said,*
> *"O silver cypress! You are going into the countryside—*
> *A virtuous promise-breaker you are, that you're leaving without me!"*[8]

The sultan immediately halted his advance and responded by exchanging some aptly flirtatious verses with her. As he was drawn into her seductive converse, he called for wine and companions and held a party of music and poetry right there. When he returned to Delhi, the populace rejoiced because the sultan had returned to his old ways. Vats of wine were broken open and the contents distributed publicly; Delhi celebrated Kaiqubād's return as the return of the good times.

A later historian, 'Abd al-Qādir Badāyūnī, also mentions the royal patronage of Hindavī and Persian verse in Delhi and its musical and recitative performance in his account of the reign of Fīrūz Shāh Tuġhlaq (r. 1351–1388). He notes that Fīrūz Shāh was interested in astrology and books of omens, some of which he had translated from Sanskrit into Persian with the help of Brahmins. Moreover, says Badāyunī, "I saw a few other books that had been translated in the name of Sultan Fīrūz. Some of them were about the science of *piṅgala*, that is, the art of music, and about the types of assemblies (*akhāra*) called *pātur-bāzī*, and some were on other subjects."[9] *Pātur-bāzī* signifies frequenting courtesans and their music and dance parties, while *piṅgala* is the art of prosody. There are also some scattered verses and a *ġhazal* by Amīr K͟husrau about the cruelty of separation, spoken, in macaronic Persian and Hindavī lines, from the perspective of an Indian woman who knows both languages.[10] I reproduce a quatrain by him that mixes Persian and Hindavī in a way that could have been appreciated only by a bilingual audience:

Look at the Hindu boy, how wondrously beautiful he is!
When he opens his mouth to speak, he rains flowers.
I said to him, "I'll take a kiss from your ruby lip."
He said, "Aré Rām! What is the 'Turuk' doing now?"[11]

The verse, with its cleverly mixed lines, even reproduces the rustically charming Gujarati accent in the boy's pronunciation, demanded for reasons of scansion, of Turk as "Turuk." In its lines one can read both an erotic and a linguistic encounter, the mutual desire and fascination that is part of any contact zone between people. Taken together, the *ġhazal* and the other macaronic verses by Khusrau are the work of someone with a mixed background, equally at home in the conjoint and interactive linguistic worlds of Persian and Hindavī. Although he wrote panegyric after inflated panegyric about the Islamic conquest of Hindustan in his professional career as court poet to several successive sultans of Delhi, he was a half-breed who represented himself both as an aristocratic Muslim poet with a Turkish father and as an Indian with an Indian mother and proud of India's unique beauty.

"The Pleasure of Desire"

In addition to these scattered references, we are lucky to have, surviving only in a single manuscript still extant from the period, a nearly complete manual, from a provincial Tuġhluqid court, on performing and understanding Indian music and dance. This rare work on aesthetic frameworks and ideal performance conditions translates many of the categories of Sanskrit aesthetics into Persian for the ruling élite. Composed around 1374 or 1375 by an unknown author, the *Ġhunyat al-Munyah* ("The Pleasure of Desire") is an explanatory guide for the Persian-speaking audience, written for the indigenized Turkish élite that had adopted Indian culture, language, and musical taste in addition to the Persian poetry and music they already enjoyed. The *Ġhunyat al-Munyah* is the only surviving source from the 1370s that documents in detail the Tuġhlaq aristocracy's interest in Indian poetry, music, and dance.

The author was part of the retinue of one of the nobles of Fīrūz Shāh Tuġhlaq, Malik Shams al-dīn Ibrāhīm Ḥasan Abū Rajā', whose family had served the Delhi sultans in prominent administrative posts for two or three generations. In 776/1374–75, Malik Shams al-dīn Abū Rajā' was appointed governor (*niyābah*) of Gujarat and undertook administration of that territory.

He had been connected with the imperial court for years, and he based his administration on the traditions of the Sharī'ah, on statesmanship, and on the law of equity and justice; his rule was said to have brought prosperity and happiness to the common people.[12] As the *Ġhunyat al-Munyah* notes, in a musical verse, "No one sighed except over the melody of the *cang* (harp) / and no one cried except over the singing of the tambour."[13] The verse suggests the activities that filled the leisure hours of the utopia ensured by the rule of this member of the Tuġhlaq provincial ruling élite.

When he was feeling the strain of hard work, this noble and discriminating patron refreshed his temperament (*ṭabī'at*) by finding "a refined or civilized hour" (*sā'at-i laṭīf*) to listen to the Persian *samā'* and the Hindavī *sarūd*, which the text defines as a compound of voice, words, and melody.[14] The function of music and poetry was to allure, to give pleasure to a temperament sensitive to nuances of meaning and expression in voice and melody. Musical evening gatherings for Persian and Hindavī poetry and dance were a common practice in the cultivated life of the Delhi sultanate. Given this cultivation of the pleasures of poetry, dance, and song, it is not surprising that the *Ġhunyat al-Munyah* should have been written as a guide for provincial nobles at the court of the official appointed to Gujarat from Delhi. The author goes on to state the reasons for the composition of his work:

> The companions of his assembly stated that the difficulties of the poetry had defeated them, and from the surging up of the waves of that encircling ocean of eloquence some pearls of meaning came to the surface of the water. Sometimes they asked about the difficulties of the sound, and from the quivering of the temperament of that emperor on the throne of rhetoric the veil of the bride of music was separated thread by thread. But due to the excessive fineness of each thread it could not be separated from the weave.[15]

Therefore, the patron assigned the author the task of lifting "the veil from the face of the heart-enchanting bride" and showing off her revelatory splendor (*jalvah*). And so he translated into Persian, to instruct the companions of the assembly, the relevant sections of Sanskrit works on poetics, music, and dance, including Bharata's *Nāṭya-Śāstra*, Mataṅga's *Bṛhaddeśī*, Śārṅgadeva's *Saṅgīta-Ratnākara*, and Somabhūpāla's *Saṅgīta-Ratnāvalī*. The Sanskrit sources listed by the author include several works now lost to us in Sanskrit and known only through their Persian summaries in the *Ġhunyat al-Munyat*.

Rasa theory, which we considered in detail in Chapter 2, was received into Persian as part of an Indian aesthetic culture, a weave or *pūd*, in the terms of the author of the *Ġhunyat al-Munyah*, of performed poetry, music, and dance.

In form, the text is a thoroughgoing application of Sanskrit *rasa* aesthetics and the principles and techniques of music and dance. The author describes *rasa* itself as a *kaifiyah-i laṭīfah*, which can be variously translated as a "subtle emotional state" or a "subtle poetic ecstasy." The text spells out the meanings of each of the *rasas*, here named in their Hindavī forms:

> *Rasa* is the meaning (*ma'ānī*) of musical performance (*sarūd*) and there are nine *rasas*: (1) *singār*: the description of passion and love, and the detailing of the beauty, the dress, and the adornment of the beloved; (2) *hās*: having to do with laughter; (3) *karuṇā*: that which excites compassion; (4) *raudra*: those meanings that have to do with anger and wrath (*ġhuṣṣah o ġhaẓab*); (5) *bīr*: the description of bravery and generosity and what is necessary to them; (6) *bhayānak*: the description of those things that increase our fear and dread; (7) *bībhica*: the mention of ugly things, from listening to which the temperament recoils in hate; (8) *adbhut*: the mention of marvelous things; (9) *śānt*: mention of religious practice and renunciation and distance from the world.[16]

Thus the subtle poetic feelings evoked by each *rasa* and their appeal to the temperament (*ṭab*) were carefully brought over into Persian, and the lyrics that accompanied the music were understood in terms of *rasa* theory. Similarly, in the section on dance, the instructions for understanding the motions of the dancer's eyes and her gestures translate entirely the system of the *rasas*, the *bhāvas* or permanent emotions, and the transitory emotions.[17] The dancer becomes an aesthetic vehicle for the *rasa* of the piece she is performing.

Moreover, aesthetic appreciation entailed a proper setting for a performance, which is described as a large and open-roofed space with trees all around it, perfumed with musk, ambergris, camphor, and rose. The audience should all sit facing the head of the assembly according to their social rank (*martabah*). The connoisseurs who understand and appreciate music and dance should sit on the left, and the performers must all be in front of them. The sponsor and head for such an assembly (*ṣāḥib-i majlis*) should be generous, noble, and knowledgeable, and he should dress better than everyone else. The companions who accompany him should be without excessive anger and wrath, and be prepared to listen and judge each piece justly and calmly. They should defer to the head of the assembly, as well as to better-informed connoisseurs.[18] The musicians, singing girls, and dancers who were the performers in these assemblies often had special neighborhoods in large cities like Delhi.

The Arab traveler Ibn Baṭṭūta, who visited Delhi in the early fourteenth century, describes the area around the Ḥauẓ-i Khāṣ in Delhi as follows:

> Along its sides there are forty pavilions, and round about it live the musicians. Their place is called Ṭarab Ābād ("City of Music") and they have there a most extensive bazaar, a Jāmi' mosque, and many other mosques besides. I was told that the singing girls living there, of whom there are a great many, take part in a body in the *tarāwiḥ* prayers in these mosques during the month of Ramaḍān.... The male musicians do the same.[19]

The performance of Persian and Hindavī poetry was thus part of the grand occasions of courtly life, and public recitation part of the cultivated lifestyle sponsored by the aristocracy. The patronage for these performers and their assemblies frequently came from the court of the sultan and set the style for cultivating poetry and music among lesser aristocrats and people of taste.

Persian Accounts of Audience Response

When the author of the *Ġhunyat al-Munyah* claimed that the meaning or *ma'ānī* of the performed Hindavī poetry was its *rasa*, he was equating the Sanskrit term with the Persian and Arabic traditions of rhetoric and interpretation. The Hindavī poets' version of *rasa* poetics has important analogues in Persian poetry. Islamic artistic traditions characterized the poet's capacity to create imaginative universes as, in Johann Christoph Bürgel's phrase, the "licit magic" (*siḥr al-ḥalāl*) of the arts. Commenting on the brilliant critic al-Jurjānī's (d. 1078)[20] theory of poetry and the innovative magic of the poet, Bürgel elaborates:

> Speaking of the astonishment or surprise effected by the poet's fantasy, he says "it is the very trustee... of poetry, the producer of its magic and the keeper of its secret." The idea that poetry is magic returns time and again in his book. Thus, we come across it in a passage where the author seeks to indicate the high value he attributes to a certain kind of comparisons: "Now you must know that by virtue of this method, comparisons are filled with some sort of magic (*ḍarb min as-siḥr*), which is hardly describable in its property.... For this magic reaches, at times, such a degree, that it is capable of converting the misogynist to a flirt, of distracting people from the sorrow caused by their children's death, of conjuring away the awe of loneliness, of retrieving your lost joy. It bears witness to the intrinsic glory of poetry and brings to light the rank and power it possesses!"[21]

Persian literary critics have been suspicious of such a view of poetry and its aura as "licit magic," with the power to transform people, to make the poet a rival to God, the Creator, and they have distinguished it carefully from the black magic (*siḥr al-ḥarām*) that can be used to control jinns, influence events, and so on. Much of al-Jurjānī's analysis of literature was focused on figures of speech and their precise workings, but "he also looked at them in terms of literary history and with a view to their ethical implications, i. e., he raised the question of their veracity." If poetry was based on lies, exaggeration, and word play, what accounted for its power? The suspicion lingered, in Arabic and Persian literary criticism, that the effectiveness of poetry was linked to its degree of departure from the truth ("The best poetry is the most untruthful").[22]

Bürgel points out that what was at stake in this question was the very status of fiction, which the later Arabic scholar of poetics, the thirteenth-century Ḥāzim al-Qarṭājanni, called *ikẖtilāq* or creation:

> Creative poetry, he said, may...remain within the limits of the possible, in which case it is hardly different from poetry based on experience. Transgression of these limits is, according to Qartajanni, achieved mainly in two ways: one is exaggeration, i. e., by means of hyperbole; the other is by talking of things that do not exist except in fantasy, such as a man with a lion's claw, etc.[23]

Bürgel goes on to demonstrate how Persian poets made the long narrative poem, the *mas̱navī*, the stage on which to represent neo-Platonic Sufi ideas about the perfect man (*insān al-kāmil*) and to transmute ordinary reality into a poetic medium with multiple planes of meaning. Both theoretically and in terms of literary history, this perspective is important because of the prestige of Persian in India and the frequent citation of Persian poets such as 'Aṭṭār, Sanā'ī, Niẓāmī, and Rūmī in the discourses of Indian Sufi Shaikhs.[24] These were the models for the Indian Islamic traditions that émigré and newly converted Muslims forged in the sultanate courts and provincial centers of Hindustan.

Bürgel uses Niẓāmī, the most famous poet of Persian romance, to provide persuasive examples of these points. His discussion of the poetic manipulation of words and elaborate rhetorical plays is particularly subtle when he shows how a master poet such as Niẓāmī can create a suggestive poetic texture:

> *The rose-buds tore their gowns like joyful lovers*
> *out of happiness in the exultant springtime.*
> *The rose hoisted the flag of joy in the garden,*
> *and the host of doves drove away the ravens.*

Jasmine was the cup-bearer, the narcissus had a cup in hand,
the violet was intoxicated and the red rose drunk.
...The violets had thrown their curls on their shoulders
and the wind had opened the ear-lobes of the jonquils.
The basil plants were brides, with hands upon their faces,
their blossoming flowers the combs in their hair.
The navel of the earth appeared pregnant
and brought forth all kinds of growth.
The breeze had twisted pearls amid the greenery,
tying mother-of-pearl to emerald.
Gazelle fawns played around the green ground
under the tender guard of their mothers.[25]

The passage is taken from the early part of the story of *Khusrau va Shīrīn*, where the sultan and his ravishing bride are enjoying a spring frolic in a green flowering meadow. As Bürgel notes, "Features of fancy and of reality are intertwined here almost imperceptibly. Nevertheless, the imagery is not random: images of love, marriage, pregnancy and child rearing, reaching from metaphor to reality, have been chosen quite deliberately for the loving couple going to enjoy the scenery."[26] The suggestiveness of the images, their textured presentation, and Niẕāmī's ability to imply psychological and aesthetic realities beyond the literal level of expressed meaning have made the *Khamsah* one of the most widely imitated and read oeuvres in the Persian-speaking world.

The magical power of poetry and mystical symbolism to reach people and the suggestiveness of Niẕāmī's romantic imagery are not far removed from the Sanskrit critics' painstaking analysis of literary and generic appropriateness (*aucitya*), the power of *rasa* and suggestion (*dhvani*), and the infinite possible variety of poetic universes. In the Indian formulation of "how newness enters the world," freshness of poetic invention is never a problem. New poetic universes, in the words of Abhinavagupta's *Locana* (L), can be produced and extended infinitely because of the power of poetic imagination:

Poetic imagination (*pratibhāna*) is a special insight (*pratijñā*) into the matter to be described. Because of the limited number of things worthy of description and because these have been touched on by the first poet [Vālmīki], a poetic imagination that takes these things for its object would be the same as his; and the poetry resulting therefrom would be the same. Accordingly, the profession of poet would by now have become obsolete. But through the multiplicity [of *dhvani*]...these same things become limitless; hence there arises an infinity of poetic imagination taking them as its object. The *Kārikā* explains the result which is

> attained by this infinity of poetic imagination by saying, speech acquires a fresh color....That can come about only if the poetic imagination is endless; and that only if the objects to describe are endless; and that only because of the variety of *dhvani* [L 4.2].

Thus we owe the inexhaustibility of speech to its powers of infinite suggestiveness, and this principle allows both Persian and Sanskritic poetic traditions to extend indefinitely a limited set of topoi and narrative and generic conventions. A poet can create new themes and topoi, or manipulate old ones for the delight of his audience, so that skill and inventiveness are measured by the innovative use of a given set of conventions. These theories of poetry locate poetry's power in its ability to communicate aesthetic meanings effectively, to enable sympathetic readers to experience the *rasa* of the Hindavī poems.

The use or applicability of these theories of meaning in the new Indo-Aryan literatures of the fourteenth century is as yet imperfectly understood. For eastern Hindavī, two surviving documents allow us a rare glimpse into the shaping of new linguistic and literary media out of Sanskrit and Apabhraṃśa. The *Ukti-Vyakti Prakaraṇa* of Paṇḍita Dāmodara is a Sanskrit grammar of Kosali that treats verbs, case endings, and usages common to the new Indo-Aryan speech of the eastern part of the Ganga-Jamuna doab.[27] Although the grammar and language of the manual probably predates the *Cāndāyan* by about two centuries, in it Paṇḍita Dāmodara does try to delineate the new usages and phraseology common to an eastern dialect of the spoken language. The transfer of literary forms from Sanskrit into eastern Hindavī before the *Cāndāyan* is also evident from the Maithili *Varṇa-Ratnākara* ("Ocean of Descriptions"), which the editor described as "a lexicon of vernacular and Sanskrit terms, a repository of literary similes and conventions dealing with the various things in the world and ideas which are usually treated in poetry."[28] The well-known Sanskrit author Kaviśekharācarya Jyotirīśvara Ṭhakkura wrote the *Varṇa-Ratnākara* at the court of Tirhut in northern Bihar, probably in the first quarter of the fourteenth century. In this poet's manual, Jyotirīśvara translates into Maithili the Sanskrit conventions for writing poetry. This text serves as a theoretical analogue for literary and linguistic transfer of conventions that Maulānā Dā'ūd also achieved, as well as a valuable source of information about the conventions that were popular at the time.

Reading Practices in the Prologues of the Hindavī Romances

These strong critical traditions in both Persian and Indic poetics explored the literary effects of poetry, delineating the proper conventions and topoi for versification and celebrating the poet's capacity to create surprising and new fictional universes, literary artifacts constructed for aesthetic pleasure. Although the deliberations of Arab and Persian literary critics, the romances of Niẕāmī, and the theoretical treatises and poetic manuals of critics provide important models for understanding the sources and allure of the Hindavī poems, they cannot be applied directly to Hindavī poetry. We must therefore turn again to the prologues of the genre to understand how the Hindavī poets defined poetics with these earlier models in view, as well as how they placed their literary efforts socially and ideologically. In their addresses to courtly patrons and to readers of their poems, the poets of these romances created a theory of reading, that is, a theory about what made the Hindavī poems both intelligible and a source of pleasure to audiences.

The prologue of the *Cāndāyan* describes the patrons of the Hindavī poets as ideal reading subjects, whose capacity to read the texts properly is fundamentally tied to their ability to perceive multiple meanings in poetry. The Khān-i Jahān Jūnā Shāh, Dā'ūd's ideal reader and patron, used this talent to confound pandits, scholars of Sanskrit:

God has given him much profound wisdom.
He has studied the fourteen sciences
and knows them well in his heart.
He interprets books and scriptures in so many ways
that pandits are left completely speechless [C 10].

The fourteen sciences are a reference to the *caturdaśa vidyā*, the traditional branches of Sanskrit learning that include the Vedas, Purāṇas, and Upapurāṇas. Whatever the state of Jūnā Shāh's knowledge of the Sanskrit classics, what is important here is the ideal reader's ability to find multiple meanings in poetry, an attribute also important to connoisseurs of Arabic and Persian poetry.

Similarly, Quṭban in his *Mirigāvatī* addresses his patron Ḥusain Shāh Sharqī as the ideal reader, who shared the poet's understanding of language. The move is clear in the following verse from the prologue, which the manuscripts entitle "*ṣifat paḍhne kī*" ("description of reading"):

He reads the scriptures, difficult of access,
and speaks the meanings aloud and explains them.
A single word can have ten meanings:
pandits are struck dumb with amazement [M 10.1–2].

The "scripture" or *purāṇa* that Quṭban refers to, in the Hindavī reinscription of Islamic religious terms, is the Qur'ān. Why was it necessary for the ideal reader in Hindavī to be able to interpret the Qur'ān? Fundamental to Persian and Arabic traditions of rhetoric and interpretation was the idea of the unique and unrepeatable miracle of eloquence of the Qur'ān (*i'jāz al-Qur'ān*), explored through the disciplines of grammar, rhetoric, and theology.[29] Nevertheless, since the book is not only a linguistic artifact but the revealed Word, there is a need for an explanation of words (Ar. *lafz̤*/Hind. *bola*) and meanings (Ar. *ma'ānī*/Hind. *aratha*), as well as their construction (*naz̤m*).[30] Qut̤ban is therefore ascribing to Sultan Ḥusain Shāh mastery over the science of meanings, the *'ilm al-ma'anī* that explores in exhaustive detail the workings of metaphor, simile, imagery, and figures of speech, analyzing them with sophistication and rigor.[31] The interpretation of figures of speech, considerations of form and meaning, and the powers of poetic imagination to create hyperbole and fantasy were significant features of literary criticism in Arabic and Persian.

The range of lexical and suggested meanings and the figurations of rhyme and thought that make up patterned verse are the key attributes of poetry for the Hindavī poet. The sultan as ideal reader stuns wise men with his capacity to read difficult texts and interpret them aloud. Qut̤ban implies also that language is not a straightforward representation of reality, but rather a surface that needs to be read for hidden signs. Among the Sufis, such a view has Qur'ānic sanction, as for instance Qur'ān 2:115, "And wheresoever you turn there is Allah's face," or Qur'ān 41:53, "Soon we shall show them our signs upon the horizons and within themselves, until it be manifest to them that this is the truth."[32] In Islamic theology, the signs that are spread out on the face of the earth (and within the seeker) can only point to the truth; they are not themselves identical with the divine essence. A long Arabic and Persian interpretive tradition extended the procedures of Qur'ānic exegesis into the realm of poetic topoi such as walled gardens, erotic exchanges between lovers, and dealings between the cupbearer (*sāqī*) and those desirous of wine.[33]

Qut̤ban's address to his royal patron signals the two main protocols of interpretation, scriptural exegesis and elucidation of hidden meanings in poetry. He goes on to describe his linguistic place and the metrical forms that he used in composing his poem. In an address to the reader, he names the most popular meters of Sanskrit, Apabhraṃśa, and Hindavī narrative poetry and then invokes an opposition between classical (*sāsatarī* < *śāstrīya*) and local or regional (*desī* < *deśī*) languages:

I have used the meters gāthā, dohā, arill, *and* ārajā,
and the soraṭhā *and* caupā'ī *to adorn my poem.*
I know my classical letters well,
but have selected and used the local forms.
Read out this pleasurable poem nicely,

and listen to it attentively. When you hear this,
you will not like any of the others.
Two months and ten days it took me to put it together and to finish it.
Each word is a pearl I have strung. I speak with all my heart and mind
[M 11.3–6].

He has chosen the sweet and pleasurable *desī* or local language, thus distancing himself from Sanskrit (*ārajā* < *āryā*) and Apabhraṃśa, even while drawing on older literary and metrical conventions.

Quṭban's stance toward Persian and Sanskritic models of poetic understanding is also distinctive, as is evident from his *envoi* to the love story:

First, this was a Hindavī story,
then some poets told it in Turkī.
Then I opened up its multiple meanings:
asceticism, love, and valor are its rasas.
When it was the year 1566 [1503],
I composed this tale in caupāīs.
If you read its six languages without a wise man,
evening will fall and you'll still be reading....
There are many meanings in this tale; use your wit and you'll understand.
I have told you whatever I could, all that was in my heart
[M 426.1–4, 6].

The poet assumes a readership that understands the various *rasas* that constitute the soul of poetry. He also assumes a knowledge of six languages, whose identity is not certain but must surely include Sanskrit, Persian, Arabic, Turkish, and some regional languages. With respect to Sanskrit, Quṭban has taken some liberties with the classical model of the nine *rasas*. He uses the emotions of *singār* (< *śṛṅgāra*, love) and *bīr* (< *vīra*, valor) in conformity with Sanskrit aesthetics, but in his *desī* articulation he adds a new *rasa*, the mood of asceticism (*joga* < *yoga*). Quṭban's story, indeed the entire genre, explores the connection between Sufi asceticism and eroticism. His use of *joga* here reimagines Sufi ideology within an Indian landscape and reshapes *rasa* poetics in Sufi terms.

Here the distinctive double distancing that is characteristic of the genre comes into play. In framing his aesthetics of asceticism and eroticism, Quṭban is not limited to adapting and rejecting classical Indian models. His story is different also from the versions that he may have drawn on in Persian or Turkish. His reference to the circulation of ideas and stories between Hindavī and Persian draws attention to the existence of a separate Hindavī literary and linguistic identity, which a multilingual reader can understand and put in its proper place. Such a reader would not only be familiar with Persian theories of *ma'ānī* and the Indian poetics of *rasa*, but would appreciate Quṭban's fashionably ethnic *desī* poetics and colorful local imagery.

The later poets of the genre develop this classicizing Hindavī literary tradition, and the many implications of the term *rasa*, into a genre of great sophistication. In his prologue to the *Padmāvat*, Malik Muḥammad Jāyasī uses graphic imagery in speaking of the centrality of the hidden meanings of his poem and the *rasa* of love:

My heart is a treasury full of gems.
I have unlocked it with my tongue, the key.
My tongue sings the matter of the jewel and essence,
full of rasa *and the priceless honey of love.*
Whoever speaks of the wounds of separation,
what is hunger to him, or shade from the sun?
He changes his guise, becomes an ascetic.
He is a ruby hidden in the dust [P 23.4–7].

As Thomas de Bruijn astutely indicates, this verse resonates with a tradition of the Prophet Muḥammad that reads, "By God, under the heavenly throne is a treasure, the keys to which are the tongues of the poets."[34] Moreover, the "matter" or *bola* of the jewel (*ratan*) and essence (*padāratha*) is a coded reference to Ratansen and Padmāvatī, the hero and heroine of Jāyasī's love story. The word *padāratha*, aside from meaning the substance or essence of a thing, can also be broken down into its component parts as "the meaning of a word," or even the "meaning of poetry," since *pada* can signify both a word and a verse of the north Indian devotional poets. Jāyasī thus foreshadows one of his major poetic strategies: using words that have multiple valences and can thus suggest multiple meanings. The verse also outlines the central elements of Jāyasī's aesthetics: *prema* (love), *viraha* (separation),[35] and ascetic practice. The last lines make explicit that love has important metaphysical implications and can be gained only through the Chishti Sufi path. The final evocative image, the ruby covered in dust, makes it the reader's task to recover the shining yet hidden meanings that are not apparent to the eye that sees only the dirty surface.

Critics have ignored the subtlety of this poetics of secrecy and the "scent of the invisible world" that a fully informed reader would take from the poems of the genre, preferring to explain them through rigid allegorical schemes. In the courtly poetic culture of the time, discerning and appreciative patrons were surrounded by brilliant and accomplished men who recited their poems in luxurious surroundings. The last poet from the period under consideration, Mīr Sayyid Mañjhan Shaṯṯari Rājgīrī, the author of the *Madhumālatī*, is mentioned in the

Afsānah-i Shāhān ("Tale of the Kings"), a chronicle of life in the Afghan interregnum that has come to us in the form of the recollections of a retired Afghan soldier:

> Wherever he [Islām Shāh] happened to be, he kept himself surrounded by accomplished scholars and poets. Kiosks [*khūshak*] were set up, scented with '*ghāliā*' (a compound of musk, ambergris, camphor and oil of bennuts), and provided with betel leaves. Men like Mīr Sayyid Mañjhan, the author of *Madhumālatī*, Shāh Muḥammad Farmūlī and his younger brother, Mūsan, Sūrdās and many other learned scholars and poets assembled there and poems in Arabic, Persian and Hindavī were recited.[36]

Within this mixed and multilingual courtly milieu, which included Vaiṣṇava poets such as Sūrdās, poetic performance was seen as a cultivated pleasure to be savored with betel (*pān*) and enjoyed in opulent assemblies. Mañjhan recited his poem in front of his noble patron and his courtiers against the tapestried and *khus*-scented walls of the Sūrī court. And Mañjhan's prologue contains the most developed set of frameworks for understanding his poem. He sketches out three key elements of his aesthetic: the ideology of love (*prema*), the importance of ascetic practice, and the privileged status of language in disseminating the truth embodied in poetry.

Mañjhan's view of love can be traced back to Persian *maṡnavī* prologues, which frequently include short philosophical reflections on love or poetry. For instance, Amīr K͟husrau's *Shīrīn va K͟husrau* contains the following lines in praise of love or *'ishq*:

> *The world without love does not have any foundation.*
> *The heavens do not revolve without love.*
> *Nor is there a man who is free of love,*
> *because man is love, the rest is clay and water.*
> *Reason and religion are the lamp of the entire world.*
> *Become a lover, for that is better than all these things [KS 261].*

These sentiments are echoed in several verses about love in Mañjhan's prologue. He asserts its importance in the creation of the world in Sufi cosmology:

> *Love made an entrance at the beginning,*
> *then the world came into existence.*
> *From love all creation sprang:*
> *love filled each created form.*
> *Only he enjoys life's reward on earth*

in whose heart is born love's anguish.
The man whose soul does not know love,
does not know the simple mystery.
Fate gives some the pain of separation,
gives them the crown of the triple world.
Do not think separation is pain; from it, joy comes into the world.
Blessed is the man whose sorrow is the sorrow of separation.
[MM 27.1–6].

The verse refers to the line popular among Sufis: "I was a hidden treasure, and longed to be known." From Allah's love for seeing His own beauty, the universe came into being as a mirror for Allah's face. Love and beauty (*rūpa*) are central to the aesthetics of the *Madhumālatī*.

Mañjhan's prologue explicitly links this aesthetic of the *rasa* of love with the path of asceticism. Among his group of Shattari Sufis, initiates practiced an intensive regimen of fasting and vegetarianism, supererogatory prayers, and a program of yogic exercises and letter mysticism. Mañjhan describes the method and goal of their spiritual practice:

Abandon consciousness, wisdom and knowledge,
focus on meditation, not on your body.
When you reach the state of union,
there you will find your own true self.
In the place of the Absolute, the Pure,
the Void, will be your self without any selfhood.
Beyond all knowledge, unknowing rules,
where your self will lose all knowledge of itself.
There, in the mystical, self-born union of Sahaja,
your own true self will be revealed.
Stay in absorption in the deep cave, motionless as if in sleep,
in the union where there is no "you," no other, and no action
[MM 33.1–6].

The terms *nirguṇa* (the attributeless Absolute), *nirañjana* (the Pure or Untainted One), and *sūnā* (the Void) describe the place where the seeker can remain absorbed in Allah. The deep cave, or fathomless void, is the ground for revealing the mystery of the self to itself. The allusion is to Ibn 'Arabī's theory of the unity of all existence (*vaḥdat al-vujūd*), in which created forms are refractions of divine essence but need spiritual practice in order to realize their identity-in-difference with divinity.

In the verse cited above, the poet also uses the terms *sahaja bheda*, the "simple or spontaneous mystery," and *sahaja-samādhi*, the "mystic union of Sahaja." In Kabīr and the other devotional poets of the fifteenth and sixteenth centuries, the term *sahaja* refers to the soul's "self-born" unity with the attributeless or *nirguṇa* Rāma, the transcendence in immanence to which the seeker has to awaken.[37] Among the Sufi poets, *sahaja* represents the internalization of the Sufi paradox of the identity, yet radical difference, of the being of divinity and human beings. This carries through into Mañjhan's view of language, which encapsulates the paradox:

Word, O word, where is your home?
From where did your light shine forth?
Where were you born? My mind cannot fathom it.
My mind has puzzled over this,
and no one can say what it means:
if words arise from mortal mouths,
then how can the word be imperishable?
If man, the master of words, can die,
then how does the word remain immortal?
Reflect on my words, and you will see:
the word is alive in every heart, like Him [MM 24.1–6].

Language becomes the currency of immortality for the poet, since it encompasses the divine and the human. Words last, though humans are perishable; the word, like divinity, is perpetually alive because it is refracted in every heart.

This topos is directly traceable to Persian prologues, as for instance the address to discourse (*sukhan*) in Niẓāmī's *Haft Paikar*. Here Niẓāmī focuses on the creative power of the word "*Kun*" or "Be," with which Allah created the heavens and the earth:

That which at once is new and old
is discourse; let its tale be told.
The mother "Be!" *hath never borne,*
than discourse, any better son.
Say not the eloquent are dead;
'neath waves of speech they've disappeared.
But should you mention one by name,
fish-like, he'll raise his head again.
Discourse—like to a flawless soul—
the keys to unseen treasure holds.

It knows the story yet unheard,
and reads the yet unwritten word.
Look round: of all that God has made,
what else, save discourse, does not fade? [HP 7.1–5][38]

Mañjhan takes these sentiments a step further in his Hindavī prologue. In the very next verse, he makes the word the foundation of all poetic discourse, but then he continues:

If the Maker had not made the word,
how could anyone hear stories of pleasure?
Before the beginning, before first creation,
the word was incarnate in Hari's mouth.
First, word, one word, the sound of Oṃ,
good and bad, it pervaded the cosmos.
The Creator gave the word a high place in creation,
it distinguishes man from beast.
Everyone knows about the word,
God is incarnate within it [MM 25.1–5].

Here Mañjhan resolves the paradox of identity-in-difference through his claim that divinity is manifest (*pargaṭa*) in the word, an incarnationist view that it would be heretical to express in Persian. Language, in Hindavī poetics, becomes the ground for understanding and representing the revelation of divinity to humans.

Language thus embodies poetic pleasure, but it also becomes the medium for another sort of embodiment: the refraction of the divine essence in visible form. It is through language that the heroine can signify the divine revelation, the allegorical centerpiece of the heroic quest for mystical union. For the Hindavī Sufi poets, the body of the heroine provokes a blinding flash of revelation in the eyes of the seeker, which pushes the seeker on to his quest for love, to realize the union that he has only glimpsed in his vision. At the end of his prologue, Mañjhan asks his audience to cultivate the taste for this supreme *rasa* of kings:

A story sweet as nectar I will sing to you:
O experts in love, pay attention and listen!
Such juicy matters only connoisseurs know,
tasteless stuff is tossed out by them.
Termites run away from wood without juice;
will camels eat cane without any sugar?

Whatever has rasa, *is enjoyed as such,*
and the man who does not have the taste
will find even the tasteful tasteless.
Many tastes are found in the world, O connoisseurs!
But listen: I shall describe love, the royal savor of savors [MM 43.1–6].

Rasa is the pleasure that listeners or readers take in stories as well as the lovers' consummation of desire in love (*prema*). The Sufi cosmology within which this aesthetic of *prema-rasa* is set allows the Hindavī Sufi poets to refer suggestively to the relation of mirrored desire between God and creatures. It is in this sense that the Hindavī romances are susceptible to interpretation in multiple ways. The next section of this chapter explores their performance and reception within the context of Sufi shrines.

Music and the Listening Self: The Chishti Sufi Practice of Samā'

The promise and pledge that I made to God (on the Day of Creation) was in Purbi rhyme.

—Niẓām al-dīn Auliyā'[39]

These words, apparently spoken by the great Chishti shaikh in a moment of spiritual exhilaration, point to the assimilation of Hindavī verse into a controversial practice that was the distinctive mark of Chishti Sufi ideology during the Delhi sultanate: *samā'* or listening to poetry accompanied by music. At its core, producing and performing this poetry within the context of the Sufi hospice was aimed at transforming the subjectivity of the listeners and redirecting it toward Allah. The basic ideology of love that is presented both in the text and in the protocols for its reception among Sufis was the theory of ordinate love, in which each object of desire is loved for the sake of one higher than itself, leading all the way up to God. The Chishtis believed in arousing desire for a worldly object of devotion and then training the disciple toward annihilating himself first in the person of his guide and then by a series of steps toward absorption in Allah. The narrative poetics of the Hindavī romances, as we have seen, are built around precisely this arousal of desire and its gradual transformation into a mutually fulfilling love. But the reception of this poetry among the Chishti Sufis was based on the principle of strict ritual control over the experience of audition. Since the practice was a controversial one, it brought the Sufis into conflict with the *'ulamā'* or legal scholars, and the Chishtis had often to defend their practice in court. Yet the practice of *samā'* maintained the Hindavī romances within a context of reception with its own complex and logocentric theory of reading, as well as within an ascetic regimen based on fasting, prayer, and rigorous spiritual exercises.

The conventions of address to the Sufi masters in the poems reflect the basic principles of the mystical agenda within which they were articulated. Each of the four Hindavī Sufi romances is dedicated to a Sufi *pīr* or spiritual guide, and sometimes to one or more spiritual lineages that were especially important to the poet. This was a Persian convention reimagined in Hindavī verse.

The Dedication of the *Cāndāyan*

Maulānā Dā'ūd's prologue to the *Cāndāyan* begins with praise of Allah and the Prophet, but before his praise of worldly rulers he adds a praise poem dedicated to his Sufi teacher. In doing this, he diverges from the model of Niẓāmī's *Khamsah* in one significant respect: Niẓāmī did not dedicate his romances to any particular teacher or Sufi shaikh. Instead, Maulānā Dā'ūd here follows the pattern of the prologues of Amīr Khusrau's Indo-Persian *maṣnavīs*, which generally include a section in praise of Shaikh Niẓām al-dīn Auliyā' (Khusrau's spiritual preceptor and beloved friend) in addition to all the other panegyrics. The explicit claim is that all worldly rulers depend on Niẓām al-dīn, that the shaikh is an emperor without the paraphernalia of royalty. Thus, in the *Majnūn va Laylī*, Khusrau introduces the shaikh as the embodiment of ascetic piety and the source of all worldly power:

In his hermit's cell, he is an emperor.
*In the world of the heart, he is the refuge of the world (*jahān-panāh*).*
...He is an emperor without throne or crown,
and kings are desperate for the dust of his feet.
*...He stands in the world of divine unity (*waḥdat*),*
with a foot in this world, and one in the hereafter [ML 150].

The shaikh holds the spiritual jurisdiction (*vilāyah*) and mastery over both this world and the invisible world of the hereafter. It is through him that devotees have access to God, since it is his closeness to Allah in the divine court that allows him to be a conduit for grace or *barakah*. Khusrau similarly extols these qualities in his *Shīrīn va Khusrau*, where the grace of the shaikh's court (*taufīq-i dargāh*) is the source of all territorial authority (*vilāyah-dārī*; SK 250). The poet uses the terms of political authority, but supersedes them by showing that the shaikh is a pure human mirror for the perfection embodied in the Prophet. The shaikh's piety, beauty, and attributes make him superior to any worldly ruler.

Maulānā Dā'ūd adapts this convention of the praise of the spiritual preceptor to express his own devotion to his guide in Hindavī. His teacher was Shaikh Zain al-dīn Chishti, the nephew of Shaikh Naṣīr al-dīn Maḥmūd 'Chirāġh-i Dihlī,' the successor to Shaikh Niẕām al-dīn Auliyā'. Dā'ūd praises him in the following terms:

> *Shaikh Zainuddīn showed me the way,*
> *the right path on which my sins were destroyed.*
> *I let my sins flow away in the Gaṅgā,*
> *and climbed into the boat of faith.*
> *He opened my eyes, filled my heart with light.*
> *I was able to write new letters in black,*
> *and gained correction in writing.*
> *I wrote in Turkish and sang in Hindukī.*
> *My shaikh extended his mercy and my sins were gone,*
> *just as smugglers and thieves are killed [C 9].*

Shaiḳh Zain al-dīn, who enabled Dā'ūd to climb into "the boat of faith," was Shaiḳh Naṣīr al-dīn's sister's son, and he is mentioned in a number of episodes in the *K̲hair al-Majālis* of Ḥamīd Qalandar and other Chishti works.[40] He was the caretaker of the shrine in Delhi, but his competition with Sayyid Muḥammad Gesūdarāz, his uncle's prize pupil, led to a dispute that ended when the spiritually charged material relics (*tabarrukāt*) that indicated succession and authority were interred with the body of the great shaikh. The conflict was part of the frequent pattern of rivalry in which the lineal descendants of Sufi shaikhs argued with their spiritual disciples over succession. The possession of the *tabarrukāt* was often the key to making any claims to authority.[41] Although Shaikh Zain al-dīn took care of the shrine in Delhi after the death of Shaikh Naṣīr al-dīn Maḥmūd, the interment of his uncle's relics effectively ended the chain of succession.

Devotion to Gurus in the Hindavī Romances

Dā'ūd uses the Hindavī trope of the teacher as the steersman who guides the disciple across the ocean of this world, washing away his sins and navigating the boat of faith (*dharma*). Learning how to write and compose poetry in Hindavī or Hindukī is dependent on his shaikh's grace. The later poets of the genre create a local language of devotion to Sufi masters. Thus Quṭban describes himself, in the prologue to the *Mirigāvatī*, as a disciple of Shaikh Buḍḍhan Suhravardī, his spiritual preceptor:

Shaikh Buḍḍhan is the true pīr *in the world.*
Take his name and your body is purified.
Quṭban took his name and fell at his feet.
He is a Suhravardī, pure in both the worlds.
He washed off all my previous sins,
all the old sins, as well as the new ones....
If anyone walks along the path that he has shown to the world,
he reaches his goal in an instant, if he holds fast to the
truth [M 6.1–3, 6].

Quṭban's terms of praise express the idea of the *pīr* or spiritual guide as the pure teacher for both the worlds, purifier of all the devotee's sins. The true path that he teaches is the way to enlightenment, if one's intentions are pure.

The identity of this Shaikh Buḍḍhan, whose name means simply "the eldest one," is a matter of some controversy. S. A. A. Rizvi notes that Shaikh Buḍḍhan was "the disciple of Shaikh Muhammad Isa Taj of Jaunpur. Although Shaikh Isa Taj was a distinguished Chishti, Shaikh Buḍḍhan seems to have been initiated into both the Chishtiyya and Suhrawardiyya orders."[42] S. M. Pandey has suggested that Quṭban was affiliated to a Chishti Shaikh Buḍḍhan, a "great musician, [who] lived during the time of Husain Shāh Sharqī in Barnawa in Meerut district near Delhi."[43] Barnawa's proximity to Delhi puts the town quite far from Ḥusain Shāh's court in exile in Bihar after the Lodis took Jaunpur in 1483, and directly in the path of the invading armies of the Lodis and the Sharqis. Moreover, Shaikh Buḍḍhan's solely Chishti affiliation makes Quṭban's discipleship with him an unlikely possibility.[44] In any case, Quṭban drew on mystical ideas common to both the Chishtis and the Suhrawardis in his romance, as well as on the model of the *Cāndāyan* of Maulānā Dā'ūd.

Both Dā'ūd and Quṭban compress their panegyrics to their spiritual guides into a single verse unit of a *caupāī-dohā*, five short rhymed pairs of lines with a longer couplet at the end. The next two poets of the genre, Malik Muḥammad Jāyasī and Mīr Sayyid Mañjhan Rajgīrī, use the model to express their admiration in much more elaborate terms. Malik Muḥammad Jāyasī addresses his *Padmāvat* to two separate spiritual lineages from which the poet derived instruction, the Mahdavis and the Chishtis. He begins with the great fifteenth-century Chishti Shaikh Ashraf Jahāngīr Simnānī (d. 1436/1437),[45] a famous peripatetic Sufi who traveled throughout Bengal and Jaunpur in search of a *vilāyah*:

Sayyid Ashraf is my beloved pīr,
He has illuminated the path for me.

He has lighted love's lamp in my heart.
The flame rose high and made my heart pure....
Jahāngīr is a Chishti, pure and spotless like the moon.
He is the master of the world, I am the slave of his house [P 18.1–2, 8].

Since the lifespan of this Chishti shaikh is separated from his own by several decades, a heated controversy rages about Jāyasī's precise link with Ashraf Jahāngīr.[46] The latter's guide was Shaikh Alā' al-Ḥaqq, among whose disciples was Shaikh Nūr Quṭb-i 'Ālam of Pandua.[47] The prologue to the *Padmāvat* mentions three disciples of Ashraf Jahāngīr, a certain Ḥājī Shaikh, called a "flawless jewel," and Shaikh Mubārak and Shaikh Kamāl, referred to as "shining lamps" (P 19). Shaikh Kamāl had been converted to Islam by Ashraf Jahāngīr but formerly wandered the world as Kamāl Jogī. This points to the constant interaction of Sufis and yogis on the cultural landscape of northern India, on the territories of the doab and central and eastern India, the land of Hindustan. These two sets of complex spiritual lineages were constantly responding to each other and competing for devoted followers and ascetically minded disciples. In addition to the spiritual descendants of Shaikh Ashraf Jahāngīr, going all the way to Kamāl Jogī or Shaikh Kamāl, the prologue gives a second Sufi genealogy in the person of a Mahdavi Shaikh named Burhān, mentioned as the actual *pīr* of Malik Muḥammad Jāyasī.[48]

The last poet under consideration, Mīr Sayyid Mañjhan Rājgīrī, addresses his praises to Shaikh Muḥammad Ġhauṣ Gvāliyārī (d. 1562), the poet's teacher and the fourth in a line of Shattari Sufi masters.[49] Shaikh Muḥammad was intimately involved in politics at the Mughal courts of Gwalior and Agra. The verses addressed to him emphasize his years of long asceticism and his importance in defining Sufi practice for seekers at his hospice:

There is a holy man great in the world,
a shaikh beloved of God,
profound in knowledge, matchless in beauty.
Whoever comes to touch him, calling on his name,
is cleansed from sin and gains enlightenment.
Whomever the shaikh loves from his heart,
he calls him gently and crowns him king.
The man whom his gaze touches is protected,
the stain of his body is washed away.
The disciple who understands his guru's glance
himself triumphs over his death!
A sight of the guru washes away sorrow, bless those who cherish that vision!

The disciple whom the guru nurtures is the king of all four aeons.
[MM 14.1–6].

The poet notes two crucial aspects of the shaikh's power: the transformative power of his gaze (*disṭi*) and the figurative kingship of even a disciple of his. The first of these refers to the power of the gaze of the spiritual guide, which can reach within a disciple's being and change his way of being in the world. The disciple can then triumph over "death," a reference to the Sufi experience of *fanā*, self-annihilation on the path, and the stage of subsistence after annihilation, *baqā'*. Here the poet uses the Hindavī *disṭi* to approximate the Persian *tavajjuh*, the absorbed attention of the shaikh that transforms the consciousness of the disciple. Such a disciple becomes not merely an earthly king like the one the poet has been praising, but king over all the ages of the world.

Losing oneself, however, involves giving oneself up to the authority of the shaikh. Among the Shattaris, as among other orders of Sufis, annihilating one's being in the teacher (*fanā fi'l-shaikh*) was an important step along the Sufi path:

If you want the guru's grace,
give up all argument, know him in your soul.
Everyone knows his manifest form,
but few recognize his secret nature.
The Lord has made mighty kings and saints who steady the world,
but Muḥammad Ġhauṣ transcends the attainments of both [MM 17].

Here, as elsewhere, the Sufi distinction between the interior (*bāṭin*) meaning and exterior (*ẓāhir*) form is invoked to comment on the double reality of the spiritual guide. The shaikh has a visible worldly form and an invisible significance in the spiritual cosmos of the Shattaris. From this station he transcends the attainments and powers of both kings and saints, and is thus the focal point of Shattari asceticism. As spiritual guides and teachers for the Hindavī poets, these shaikhs from the Chishti, Suhrawardi, and Shattari *silsilahs* formulated different ascetic regimens for their disciples and interacted in complex ways with political rulers and each other, asserting their superior claims to spiritual authority in their own spheres of influence.

What did Hindavī poetry mean to them, and how did they interpret it? One of the earliest descriptions comes from the fourteenth-century discourses of Sharf al-dīn Manerī, the Firdausī Shaikh of Maner Sharif in Bihar.[50] The Firdausīs were a local branch of the Suhravardis who had also adopted the practice of *samā'* formulated by the Chishtis, despite the wider rivalry between the two *silsilahs*. The shaikh emphasizes the ability to listen receptively and to respond to poetry as part of the Sufi training of the self. After the noonday prayers, the assembly in the shrine listened to the singing of first Persian verses, then Hindavī ones. The shaikh commented on the quality of response the Hindavī verses elicited:

> Hindavi verses are very forthright and frank in expression. In purely Persian verses, there is a judicious blend of allusions and what can be fittingly expressed, whereas Hindavi employs very frank expressions. There is no limit to what it explicitly reveals. It is very disturbing. It is extremely difficult for young men to bear such things. Without any delay, they would be upset....[51]

This recognition of the power of Hindavī verse to stir the passions because of its graphic and lush descriptions is coupled with anxiety over its uncontrolled use, which would lead to unbridled sensuality.

Although the practice of *samā'* was common to many Sufi *silsilahs*, the Chishtis in the thirteenth and fourteenth century were the distinctive formulators of the practice and the first Hindavī Sufi poets. The controversial practice of *samā'* allowed the Chishti Sufis to link sympathetic response to poetry to the taste (*z̤auq*) for things spiritual. The Chishtis of the Delhi sultanate were the inheritors of a system of musical theory in which music and ecstasy (*vajd/ḥāl*) were means to spiritual advancement. As Bruce Lawrence has put it in a pioneering article,

> [I]n the Indian environment from the period of the Delhi Sultanate through the Mughal era samā' assumed a unique significance as the integrating modus operandi of the Chishtī silsilah. Chishtī apologists adopted a distinctive attitude to samā': far from being an embarrassment to them, as the literature sometimes suggests, samā' was aggressively defended as an essential component of the spiritual discipline or ascesis incumbent on all Sufis. The Chishtī espousal of samā' also served a valuable practical function: it separated the Chishtī saints from the Suhrawardīya, their major mystical rivals in the pre-Mughal era of Indian Islam, and also opposed them to the 'ulamā, those too comfortable spokesmen for official, i. e., government sanctioned, Islam. Samā' became, if not the monopoly of the Chishtīya, the preeminent symbol crystallizing their position vis-à-vis other Indo-Muslim leadership groups.[52]

Though the Chishtis were not free from their own dependence on court patronage, their enthusiastic and longstanding espousal of Hindavī and Persian *samā'* against all rivals and opponents allowed them to make major advances in terms of musical and poetic theory.

The Eros of *Samā'*

The discourses of the Chishti Shaikhs frequently use exceedingly erotic language and imagery. For them, eroticism was embedded within the framework of ordinate love, in which each object of desire is loved for the sake of one higher than itself, all the way up to Allah. The Chishti practice of *samā'*, embedded within this larger eroto-mystical agenda, entailed a theory of reading specific to the Sufi context and an explicit theorization of the effects of sung poetry on the subjectivity of the listener.

The historian Badāyūnī chronicles public recitation of Maulānā Dā'ūd's *Cāndāyan* at the Friday prayer meeting at the great mosque in Delhi. In the passage that follows, a renowned Sufi reads the love story from the *minbar* or pulpit of a Jāmi' mosque built in Delhi as a visible sign of political and religious sovereignty:

> In the year 772 H. (1370 A.D.), K͟hān-i-jahān the *Vazīr*, died, and his son Jūnā Shāh obtained that title; and the book *Chandāyan* which is a *Maṣnavī* in the Hindī language relating the loves of Lūrak and Chāndā, a lover and his mistress, a very graphic work, was put into verse in his honour by Maulānā Dā'ūd. There is no need for me to praise it because of its great fame in that country, and Mak͟hdūm Shaik͟h Taqīu-d-Dīn Wāiz̤ Rabbānī used to read some occasional poems of his from the pulpit, and the people used to be strangely influenced by hearing them, and when certain learned men of that time asked the Shaik͟h saying, what is the reason for this Hindī Maṣnavī being selected? he answered, the whole of it is divine truth and pleasing in subject, worthy of the ecstatic contemplation of devout lovers, and conformable to the interpretation of some of the Āyats of the Qur'ān, and the sweet singers of Hindūstān. Moreover by its public recitation human hearts are taken captive.[53]

In explaining the appeal of Hindavī poetry, the phrase used in the Persian to describe the *Cāndāyan* is *ḥālat-bak͟hsh* ("worthy of ecstatic contemplation," or more literally, "ecstasy-inducing"). The shaikh's words explaining his selection of this text are crucial: all of it is divine truth (*ḥaqā'iq*), worthy of ecstatic contemplation by devout lovers (*muvāfiq-i vajdān-i ahl-i shauq-va 'ishq*) despite its graphic nature. Unlike the Persian *maṣnavīs*, Hindavī is seen as a sensuous, erotically charged language with a powerful poetic tradition that the Sufis have discovered and adapted. Further, it is recognized that the Hindavī verses describing feminine beauty excite desire in the listeners, and can be justified only by adducing Qur'ānic referents. Thus the shaikh explains the Sufistic interpretation of the text in terms of *tafsīr* (Qur'ānic interpretation): devout lovers, or more accurately, the people of desire (*shauq*) and love (*'ishq*), can appreciate the poem because it is conformable (*muṯābiq*) to certain Qur'ānic verses.

This passage implies a theory of reading in which erotic attributes and passages were transferred to the divine beloved, the distant Allah whose nearness the Chishtis sought so assiduously to cultivate. Audition attracted, because of its controversial nature, many theoretical statements in defense of a practice that the orthodox jurists condemned as forbidden to true believers. Already in classic manuals of Sufi practice such as Suhravardī's *'Avārif al-Ma'ārif* and 'Alī 'Us̱mān al-Hujvīrī's *Kashf al-Maḥjūb* ("The Unveiling of the Hidden"), the controversial practice of listening to music and poetry had been defended as a means to a spiritual state of ecstasy.[54] As Shihāb al-dīn Abū Ḥafṣ 'Umar Suhravardī (d. 1234) put it in his textbook of practice, listening to music entails a physical and emotional response:

> *Samā'* is audition, about which believers are not divided. It has been decided about the (ideal) listener that he is a man of intellect and rightly guided. *Samā'* is that which, influencing his heat with the coolness of faith, becomes the cause of a rain of tears from his eyes. Sometimes these are tears of sorrow and regret, because there is heat in sorrow and regret. Sometimes these are tears of enjoyment (*ẕauq*) and passion (*shauq*), and passion is also hot by nature. When *samā'* endowed with these qualities affects a man of heart who is full of the coolness of faith, the opposition (of heat and cold) makes tears flow.[55]

This bodily theory of heat and cold and the condensation that results from their commingling indicates the physicality of the response to poetry and music. It is part of a set of attitudes toward hearing that place listening to the Qur'ān at the top, and then extend the praiseworthiness of this practice to the permissibility of listening to poetry and music. Thus, 'Alī bin 'Us̱mān al-Hujvīrī (d. ca. 1071) begins his chapter on audition with these words: "The most beneficial audition to the mind and the most delightful to the ear is that of the Word of God, which all believers and unbelievers, human beings and peris alike, are commanded to hear. It is a miraculous quality of the Koran that one never grows weary of reading and hearing it."[56]

From the miraculous quality of listening to the Qur'ān, the Sufi commentators extended the powers of hearing to many sorts of objects. They drew on a body of musical theory that acknowledged the power of song and music to move human beings and made distinctions that were based on listeners' responses to music.

There were independent treatises about the practice of *samā'*, and the anecdotal compendia and discourses of Sufi shaikhs mentioned it. As Lawrence points out, assessing the available literature,

> There are two extant treatises on *samā'*, one in Arabic by a disciple of the foremost Chishtī saint of Delhi, Nizām ad-dīn (Awliyā), the other in Persian by Ṣūfī Hamīd ad-dīn Nāgaurī, a successor to the first Indian Chishtī Shaykh, Mu'in ad-dīn Sanjarī Ajmerī. Both *Uṣūl as-Samā'* and *Risālah-i Samā'* contrast with one another but even more with the sole extant treatise from an early non-Indian devotee of *samā'*. *Bawāriq al-ilma'* of Aḥmad Ghazzālī is a brilliant, independent work by one of the most influential Baghdadian Sufis who is just now beginning to receive the attention he deserves from scholars, after having been eclipsed for centuries by the fame of his older brother, Imām Ghazzālī.[57]

Aḥmad Ġhazzālī linked music to apprehension of hidden spiritual meanings and viewed it as a necessity for practitioners and disciples. In his treatise, the *Bawāriq al-Ilma'*, he states:

> Audition...is a reference to the observation of strange secrets in the delicate poems which the *qawwāl* (singer) recites while joined to the ecstasy which arises in the heart of the gnostic (*'ārif*) who works and the novice (*murīd*) who is perfect. It induces them to put off resistance, to be drawn to the presence of the One, the Powerful, and to ponder delicate things and secrets. And for the removal of these veils they have chosen audition with beautiful voices at most times, after fulfilling the things which are commanded, simply because man's nature is inclined to the voice.[58]

The subtle or delicate things (*laṭā'if*) hidden in poetry, and the spiritual mysteries attached to them, are brought up in the heart as part of the training of a novice. The power of the voice is such that it attracts the heart toward what is sung, and it is this power that the Sufis sought to use in their spiritual practice.

In his discussion of the two Chishti treatises, Lawrence emphasizes this link of music with emotion. The *Uṣūl al-Samā'* ("Principles of *Samā'*") of Faḳhr al-dīn Zarrādī is a detailed consideration of aspects of *samā'*, and its argument proceeds along well-defined lines:

> (1) the reality of *samā'* precludes a female vocal accompaniment (*al-ghinā*) but (2) depends on a beautiful male voice (*al-ṣawt al-ḥasan*) comparable to the Prophet David's. Of musical instruments the reedpipe alone is forbidden by the Prophet Muḥammad's directive, while (3) the use of other instruments, such as the drum and the tambourine is permitted by analogy to the Prophet's example. (4) Since inspired verse comes from the Creator, its use is not only permitted but encouraged for Sufis of all stages. (5), (7) and (8) Numerous citations from the Qur'ān and sound traditions support both the beautiful voice and recitation of verse but (6) it is necessary to establish the appropriate setting in which *samā'* is to be conducted. (9) Examples and quotations from early saints, including Shaykh Niẓām ad-dīn, in support of *samā'* are not lacking, and they indicate (10) that one of the chief effects desired in *samā'* is *tawājud*, which Zarrādī defines as "graceful movement that voluntarily emanates from the listener when he is overcome by *samā'*."[59]

Other Chishti sources define music and its effect on its audience in ways that echo this idea of the ecstatic movement of the listener overcome by the music. Muḥammad bin Mubārak 'Alavī Kirmānī begins a detailed chapter on audition in his *Siyar al-Auliyā'*, a compendium of anecdotes and maxims relating to practice, by citing the great Chishti Shaikh Farīd al-dīn Ganj-i Shakar (d. 1265) on the subject: "*Samā'* is a pleasant voice that makes the hearts of the listeners tremble and ignites the fire of passion in their chests. If it is out of control it is seen as right, and if within limits, it is diseased (*ma'lūl*) *samā'*."[60] The power of music to cross bounds and the potential it has for exciting passions that can then be trained toward God is underscored by the other major work on *samā'*, Ḥamīd al-dīn's *Risālah-i Samā'* ("Treatise on *Samā'*"), a brief meditation on the benefits of audition. As Lawrence points out, Ḥamīd al-dīn links *samā'* with *vajd* or ecstasy; they are both "wings of the spirit by which it takes flight till it reaches the Divine Presence."[61] There are numerous instances of Sufis expiring in an ecstasy of *samā'*, the most famous of these being Quṭb al-dīn Baḳhtiyār Kākī, who died in a *samā'* assembly in Delhi in 1232.

The perceived capacity of *samā'* to break all limits, its potential for spiritual advancement, and the dangers posed by the sensual effects of poetry occasioned fierce controversy and a focus on the variety of audience response. Chishti theorists answered the legal opposition to *samā'* by formulating a classificatory scheme distinguishing lawful from unlawful effects of music. Thus al-Hujvīrī resolved the controversial question by appealing to the effect of audition on the mind: "Its lawfulness depends on circumstances and cannot be asserted absolutely: if audition produces a lawful effect on the mind, then it is lawful; it is unlawful if the effect is unlawful, and permissible if the effect is permissible."[62] The passage indicates the seriousness with which the Chishtis used the idea of sympathetic response, which to them had to be directed to Allah to be properly devotional. Whether in Persian or Hindavī, the meanings of poetry had to refer back to the invisible anchor of the world to allow musical audition to be a defensible part of Sufi devotion.

The fourteenth-century Chishti sources on *samā'* share these classifications and also explain the states of mind in which listeners hear music. Muḥammad Kirmānī's *Siyar al-Auliyā'* cites Niẕām al-dīn Auliyā' on the four types of audition. *Samā'* is legal (*ḥalāl*) where the listener is totally inclined toward God (*ḥaqq*), but illegal (*ḥarām*) where he is totally inclined toward the world (*majāz*). Recognizing the mixed character of human intentionality, Kirmānī introduces a further division: *samā'* is reprehensible (*makrūh*) when the listener is mostly inclined toward the world, but permissible (*mabāḥ*) when he is mostly inclined toward God. Playing on Arabic grammatical terminology, the text separates various aspects of hearing: what is needed is a speaker (*musamma'*), a listener (*mustama'*) and a text that is heard (*masmū'*). He also lays out the requirements for permissible *samā'*: the speaker must be a man, not a woman or child. The listener must not be neglectful of remembering God. What is heard should not be obscene or ridiculous. There should not be musical instruments such as the *cang* (a sort of harp) or the rebeck or *rabāb*.[63]

Given the Chishti focus on sympathetic response and effect, what does lawful practice of *samā'* do to the listening self? The answer involves the *ādāb-i samā'* or prescriptive rules for performance and right behavior among the Chishtis. The *Siyar al-Auliyā'* provides valuable information about the practice and what was perceived as necessary to it. The place and time of performance were important, so that it was necessary to choose a "good time which was conducive to the opening of the heart and not the scattering of the temperament, a pleasant place which attracts everyone's soul at sight, the good company of the *ahl-i samā''* ('the people of *samā'*") who are harmonious like brothers and restrained, and a perfumed place and clean clothes."[64] The author cites Zarrādī on proper behavior for the novice who is allowed to listen to *samā'*:

> (1) he should listen to *sama'* with a conscious ear (*gosh-i hosh*) and he should pay little attention to and restrain his eyes from looking at the other listeners, he should not yawn and stretch and throw his head up in thought, and he should restrain his heart from clapping and dancing and movement and other inclinations; (2) he should not snap his fingers or cry, but instead restrain his spirit and not cry for sorrow or dance just for the sake of movement; (3) he should aim for a sameness

> of community. If at a particular place those of a single group stand up in ecstasy then it is a true ecstasy (*vajd-i ṣādiq*).[65]

Although audition is meant to make the seeker mindful of the distant but all-powerful Allah, it is in a communal setting that his ecstasy becomes true ecstasy (*vajd-i ṣādiq*). The seeker's quest for nearness to God was thus tied to a social setting where his affective responses were on display and could be channeled through prayer and ascesis into what his Sufi teacher thought appropriate for him. Moreover, the affective response, by being socially visible, was implicitly tied to a whole set of Chishti attitudes to the interpretation of performed poetry and music.

The goal of poetry that was sung in a beautiful voice was to open the seeker's subjectivity to a succession of spiritual states and stations. As Niẓām al-dīn Auliyā' put it in a famous passage in the *Favā'id al-Fu'ād*, these are the benefits of listening to recitation of the Qur'ān and to music:

> The devotee experiences a sense of spiritual bliss which may be manifest as celestial lights (*anvār*), mystical states (*aḥvāl*), and physical effects (*āṣār*). Each of these derives from three worlds: the present world, the angelic sphere, and the potential realm, this last being the intermediate between the first two. And these three manifestations of spiritual bliss may occur in one of three places: the spirits (*arvāḥ*), the hearts (*qulūb*), or the bodily limbs. At first celestial lights descend from the angelic sphere (*muluk*) on the spirits, then mystical states descend from the potential realm (*malakūt*) on the hearts, and finally physical effects from the present world (*jabarūt*) alight on the bodily limbs. In other words, during the state induced by listening to music, celestial lights descend from the angelic sphere upon the spirits. What subsequently appear in the heart are called mystical states, because it is from the potential realm that they descend on the hearts. Next, crying, movement, and agitation appear, and they are called physical effects because they alight from the present world on the bodily limbs.[66]

Each part of the body is here matched to an appropriate state in the invisible world. The scheme of the spiritual effects of audition is part of a Chishti cosmology in which God is of a different essence from the world and hence inaccessible, yet part of a cosmic unity of being (*vaḥdat al-vujūd*). However, the successive states of reflection or refraction of this essence (*ẕāt*) in increasingly concrete realms are available to the seeker as part of his mystical journey through the stages of love and asceticism.

The ability to open up to these eroto-mystical processes had to be carefully cultivated, and involved *ẕauq* or the taste for spiritual things. Such a taste could even be fostered by the perceived intervention of a supernatural agency:

> One day Haẕrat Niẕām al-dīn Auliyā', the sultan of shaikhs, was sitting on the threshold of his house and Sāmit the singer sang in front of him. It had an effect on the sultan of shaikhs, and tears and ecstasy overcame him. None of his friends was there, and therefore when he began dancing those present were worried. Meanwhile a man came in from outside, put his head on the ground, then began to dance. The sultan of shaikhs did the same thing in conformity, and for a while they enjoyed the taste of *samā'*. When the gathering was over the man went outside again. The shaikh said, "Look for that man from the invisible world." Men went out all together in search of that dear one left and right, but they could not find him.[67]

The story underscores the importance of an appropriate setting for communal enjoyment of the grace of musical ecstasy.

Reading the Hidden Meanings

The sense of an invisible world was already known to musical theory in the early formulation of Aḥmad Ġhazzālī, who states in his treatise on the benefits of *samā'*:

> Then when there arises in him increase of arrangements of notes and spiritual analogies which are called music, [man's nature] prefers them to everything else. So when a person hears the analogies which pertain to notes, which include the realities (*ma'ānī*) which pertain to taste (*ẕauq*) and the truths which pertain to the Unity, the being inclines to all those, and every bodily member receives its portion separately. The hearing [receives] the things of the unrestrained analogies; the sight, the analogies of the movements; the heart, the delicate things of the realities; and the intellect, the inner consciousness.[68]

Music thus reveals the truths of hidden meanings (*ma'ānī*) to each bodily sense. Whether they are the subtleties of the realities (*ḥaqā'iq*) of Allah, or their physical analogues in the sensible world, the response to music unites all the levels of reality known to Sufi theory. The theory of reading implied by this spiritual principle unites for Sufi readers all the disparate images and details of sung poetry, eliciting a deep response within the listening self.

This logocentric understanding of *samāʿ* and its benefits is carried over into Sufi schemes for interpreting poetry. The danger of sensual misdirection and misunderstanding of the poetry necessitated a system of interpretation among the Sufis that guided audience response away from the worldly love described in the poetry and redirected it toward God. Since poetry was recognized to have the singular effect of transforming the listener, the Sufi interpretive communities that wrote and read Hindavī and Persian poetry exercised strict control over the range of interpretations that were held to be valid. Both the principle of multiple meanings developed in Arabic and Persian literary theories and the poetics of infinite suggestiveness that is part of the Sanskrit theory of *rasa* were subordinate to the overarching sense of a cosmos overshadowed by the hidden presence of divinity. As Niẕām al-dīn Auliyā' put it, "Every letter one hears in *samāʿ* is an attribute one hears of the attributes of God the Glorious and Supreme and All High so that the meaning of that letter is praised with those qualities."[69]

The Chishtis termed the specific theory of reading that formulated this restriction on multiple meaning *taḥmīl-i alfāẕī*, or verbal transfer. This entailed, according to the *Siyar al-Auliyā'*, carrying the figurative meanings of poetry over to the qualities of Allah. For example, Niẕām al-dīn Auliyā' would explain a line of verse in which a lover wishes to be close to a lock of hair (*zulf*) from his beloved to mean that he wishes to be close to Allah. He would interpret a reference to the lovely eyes of the beloved as a desire for the divine glance of compassion.[70] Indeed, as Zarrādī put it in the *Uṣūl al-Samāʿ*:

> The transfer of the words expressing the qualities of God is such that it always happens from the apparent words towards something that is appropriate (*munāsib*) to the words. From the command of God the Majestic and Supreme then the words of the couplets are as if allegorical (*imṡālī*); the aim of the allegory is the thing which is thought appropriate and the place of use of that allegory is not the place of the external meaning—this is the meaning.[71]

Thus the true meaning of poetry is precisely its ability to present to listeners and readers the likeness (*miṡl*) of Allah. This *miṡl* (or *tamṡīl*), an allegory or exemplum of invisible spiritual meanings, was more important than the literal or "external" meaning. To understand poetry, on the Chishti path, was to open oneself up to the hidden spiritual processes of the cosmos and witness within oneself the unfolding of divine essence into the world. Signs of the invisible divine presence, according to the Chishtis, were sent to seekers in the revealed books as well as in the words of the Prophet, and finally in the actions and words of their Sufi shaikhs, their own preceptors.

Such a strong principle of reading poetry, directed only toward the single goal, Allah, requires that the creation of endless meanings by poets and readers be severely curtailed and subject to a single interpretive rule. This applies to poetry in all the languages used by the Chishtis: poetry's power is here redefined as its ability to represent the theoretically unrepresentable absolute through language. The power of *samāʿ* is due to its overwhelming capacity to remind men of their link with Allah:

> Then Badr al-dīn Ġhaznavī asked Shaikh Niẕām al-dīn, "Where does the unconsciousness (*bīhūshī*) of the people who listen to *samāʿ* come from?" He answered, "They heard the sound of 'Am I not your Lord?' and become unconscious. From that day forward a certain unconsciousness is centered in them, and whenever they hear *samāʿ*, that unconsciousness that is within them has an effect and produces amazement and movement."[72]

Man's affirmative response to God's question of the day of Creation, "Am I not your Lord?" (*alastu bi-rabbikum*, Qur'ān 7:171), sealed a covenant or pledge (*mīs̱āq*) that endures through time. Its renewal in the Indian Sufi ideology of *samāʿ* is indicated by the words attributed to Niẕām al-dīn Auliyā' quoted at the head of this section: "The promise and pledge that I made to God (on the Day of Creation) was in Purbi rhyme." Purbi or eastern Hindavī, the Avadhi love poetry that was sung in the Chishti assemblies along with Persian and Arabic verses, was thus an intrinsic part of Sufi musical practice in the Delhi sultanate and thereafter.

Moreover, the Indic notion of the sensitive reader or *sahṛdaya* who understands the flow of the *rasa* of Hindavī verse is paralleled by and merged with the Chishti idea of the soul that is open to *ẕauq*, the spiritual taste of erotic poetry. The Chishti Sufi notion of the ideal reader allows us to specify another Hindavī reader and context of performance: the novice being trained by his shaikh and guided on the spiritual path. Chishti sources celebrate the sensitivity of these ideal readers or receptive novices and even arrange them in a hierarchy of response:

> Certain people are overcome by *ḥāl* (ecstasy) in *samāʿ* such that they have no decorum (*tamīz*), and some, while they feel a mystical state, are not overcome and their perfection is precisely in this that they are not overcome. Some people become so heedless in *samāʿ* that even if an iron nail were to go into their foot they would not know it, while others are so present to Allah in *samāʿ* that even if a flower-petal were underfoot they would know it. This is the perfected stage they are in.[73]

The Chishti notion of the perfected listener, who would feel even a flower petal underfoot, shifted the taste for poetry from a relation between text and audience to a relation between the seeker and Allah. Thus the Chishti commentators exploited to the full the inherent capacity of *rasa* to excite a response in the sensitive listener.

This responsiveness entailed a recognition of the power of Hindavī verse in its own right, yet yoked its effects to an ascetic regimen based on the Qur'ān and Islamic traditions and teachings. The following passage from the *Favā'id al-Fu'ād* about the spiritual discipleship of Shaikh Aḥmad Nahrvānī attests to the Chishti move to turn Hindavī to the service of mystic practice and belief:

> Faqih Mādho...was the prayer leader at the congregational mosque of Ajmer. One day Shaykh Ahmad was singing a Hindavī song, for in his youth he had a fine voice and used to sing beautiful Hindavī tunes. When Faqih Mādho heard of this, he berated Shaykh Ahmad: 'With a voice such as yours, what a shame to waste it on Hindavī music (*sarūd-i Hindavī*)! Memorize the Qur'ān instead!' Shaykh Aḥmad then committed the Qur'ān to memory; he also became a Muslim.[74]

This episode of conversion proves the ideological superiority of Islam, but also the enduring appeal of the Hindavī verses and melodies that in other contexts of performance were even equated with Qur'ānic verses. Hindavī poetry and music (*sarūd-i Hindavī*), therefore, was a distinctive part of Chishti Sufi practice. The ascetic imagery and erotic allure of Hindavī were used to express the Sufi ideology of fasting, prayer, and ascesis, all aimed at gaining access to the invisible spiritual cosmos (*'ālam-i ġhaib*). An invisible divinity hedged ordinary physical events and shaped causes and effects in mysterious ways. The aesthetic goal of the Sufi poets and their audiences was to catch the scent of this invisible world, undergirded by adepts and the mysterious divine will. In performances in shrines, the Sufis sought to contain the proliferation of multiple meanings implicit in poetry by interpreting the erotic resonances of Hindavī poetry as referring to Allah.

But the authority of interpretive communities is not absolute, and the Chishti projections of the ideal reader as receptive Sufi novice should be supplemented by recalling the celebration of polysemy that is part of the genre. Hindavī poetry circulated beyond the court and *k͟hānaqāh*, to be read without courtly ceremonial or Sufi glosses. One later account of readership comes from a very unusual document, the autobiography of a Srimal Jain merchant, Banārsīdās. Writing in 1641 at the age of forty-five, Banārsīdās describes his life's vicissitudes in a book that he called *Ardhakathānaka* ("Half a Tale"), since he believed at this point that he had spent half his allotted lifespan. Banārsīdās periodically lost all his money in risky ventures and spent parts of his life in destitute poverty. At one such juncture, he entertained a number of persons in his house by reciting and singing large portions of the eastern Hindavī or Avadhi love stories:

> I had only a few coins left. I would remain sitting at home, and stopped visiting the market-place. But I spent my evenings singing and reciting poems. A small group of about ten or twenty people used to visit me regularly and to them I sang *Madhumalati* and *Mirgavati*, two grand books. My visitors continually praised my singing and conversation. My evenings were thus spent pleasantly, though I was so miserably poor that I had nothing to eat the next morning. One of my regular listeners was a halwai who sold kachauris—a kind of stuffed, deep-fried pancake. I bought large quantities of kachauris from this man's shop on credit.... I ate kachauris for all my meals, breakfast, lunch or dinner; often eating them cold or even stale. My halwai friend was unaware of my true circumstances. But one day, when I was alone with him, I told him all, confessing that I had no money left with me and that I even owed a lot. I warned him not to give me any more kachauris for he might never get his money back. The halwai was a kindly soul. He gave me leave to eat kachauris worth twenty rupees from his shop, assuring me that he would not bother me for money... my evening sessions of story-telling continued in this manner for six months.[75]

Therefore dissemination and reception of the Hindavī Sufi romances was not limited to the institutional contexts of court and shrine. Nor were the protocols of interpretation laid out for these contexts the sole determinants of the meanings of these poems. Often a group of cultivated men, *rasika*s or connoisseurs, gathered to listen to love poetry privately. Familiar with the language and the generic features of these poems, they came together for the pleasure of a good story told in elegant verse. The notion of *rasa* as a relationship between text and reader, a relationship of mutual understanding and aesthetic pleasure, enabled the circulation of these texts among different social groups. Through the manuals of performance and anecdotes of audience response, it has been possible to delineate a theory of reading which allowed the Sufi romances to circulate and to be understood differently in different contexts. The courts of nobles and rulers, Sufi shrines, bazaars and mosques, and the houses of the affluent were the contexts of reception for enjoying the pleasure of the text.

Epilogue: The Story of Stories

An Indian Ocean of Stories

What of the sources of the stories, and the source of story itself? More particularly, Where do the stories in the Hindavī Sufi romances come from? To answer this question ontologically, we would have to account for the universal human urge to tell stories. This being ultimately unanswerable, we can at least investigate two or three smaller questions, with particular reference to our texts: Who uses common narrative motifs to tell stories? At which particular historical moments do people tell particular stories, and what do they mean at that time and in that place? Can one string together a genealogy of such narrative moments, revealing a story about the stories people tell?

To begin to answer these questions, we can interpret stories within their particular historical moments, as being explanatory of social roles, historical and material changes, and, in this particular instance, Sufi spiritual direction. And even though poetic fictions of imaginary worlds can be set apart from the author's historical and social world, the narrative motifs woven into their formulaic patterns have a history of their own and reinscribe larger historical processes within the landscape of fantasy. The fictional universes of the Hindavī Sufi romances, set in exotic locales such as Serendib or the City of Gold (Kancanpura), are constructed out of well-known sequences of narrative motifs in the various storytelling traditions in the languages surrounding the Indian Ocean. The narrative motifs that the poets use reveal a history of complex interactions among Persian, Arabic, Sanskritic, and local story traditions.

Stories are part of larger historical worlds with their own struggles and interactions. The primary purpose of the poet who creates an imaginary universe may not be to represent historical events, but poetic uses of individual motifs and larger narrative sequences are linked with larger historical processes and have a history of their own. The travels of narrative motifs mark deep and long cultural interactions between peoples in premodern global economies. People who trade merchandise also swap stories and translate beast fables and borrow larger narrative frameworks. In these narrative exchanges, culture and society are shaped as mixed, polyglot, and ever-changing. Stories themselves change and shift, signifying different things to different audiences and being used differently by poets and storytellers.[1] They travel along with the spices, jewels, and textiles that have always been staple commodities in trade. Movements of people, in K. N. Chaudhuri's phrase, necessarily involve the "exchange of ideas, economic systems, social usage, political institutions, and artistic traditions."[2] Narrative motifs are common to many traditions and consequently have widespread appeal, but they are also historically marked, have a history of their own, and occur in unexpected places. The consolidation of the Delhi sultanate produced new regional polities, allowed local artistic and literary traditions to be adapted to new ends, and enabled wandering holy men to set up networks across the provinces of Hindustan.

The movements of scholars, Sufis, traders, and travelers through the familiar and less familiar parts of the known world engendered not just travel narratives but also geographies, nautical guides, and accounts of the marvels found in the lands and oceans stretching from India to China. The fantasy world of the Hindavī Sufi romances is part of a regional or Hindustani literary tradition with its own poetics and politics, but Hindustan itself was part of a larger Islamicate world in which stories, people, and merchandise traveled freely. The trade in stories that went along with the mercantile (and sometimes martial) encounters among cultures in this world changed forever with the arrival of the Portuguese on the Malabar coast in the last decade of the fifteenth century. The Hindavī Sufi romances share in this historical moment.

In tracing the sources of these narrative motifs and sequences, we are not looking for the origin of a story, but for how that story has traveled, has been linguistically manipulated in translation from one language to another, has been adapted into numerous ideological frameworks in new situations. Narrative sources are not to be mined merely as an exercise in *Quellenkritik*, but as representative of historical agents, people in situations of hostility and alliance, encounter and exchange. Earlier ages too knew phenomena like the wildly enthusiastic reception given to the *Arabian Nights* in eighteenth- and nineteenth-century Europe, England in particular,[3] the hundreds of versions, translations, abridgements, magazine excerpts of the "Oriental tale," lushly Orientalized dramatizations, alluring fancy dress costumes, exotic fabliaux, and folkloric recountings.

One example of such a successful reception of a genre is the premodern transmission of the beast fables of the *Pañcatantra*, the now-lost original "mirror for princes"[4] famously composed by Viṣṇu Śarmā in Sanskrit.[5] The tales are said to have occasioned a special mission to India from the sixth-century court of Khusrau Anūshīrvān the Just, who sent Burzoe, an ancient Iranian sage, on a search for a magic life-restoring herb, a search that culminated in his theft of the book.[6] Translated into Arabic from Pahlavi by Ibn al-Muqaffa' ca. 750 A.D., as the tales of the wise sage Bidpai or, in Sanskrit, Vidyāpati, the fables were disseminated as the narrative exchanges of Kalīlah and Dimnah, a pair of jackals who told these easy to-understand-stories illustrating just about every trick in the book to young princes in training for rulership.[7] Kalīlah and Dimnah are modeled on the Sanskrit Karaṭaka and Damanaka, two Indian jackals who similarly instruct princes on statecraft and strategy.

These beast fables traveled as folklore, courtly literature, song, fable, and wonder tale through the courts and languages of the Middle East and Europe.[8] They circulated with the merchandise and money whose routes Janet Abu-Lughod has delineated so deftly in her account of the premodern global system of the Islamicate world:

> Ships sailing to China from Mesopotamia exited the Persian Gulf and then skirted the western coast of Sind (today's Pakistan) and Hind (today's India), making frequent port calls and seldom out of sight of land. The monsoon winds allowed them to cross the open sea from Muscat-Oman to India, but boats were small and navigational methods were still primitive. In the tenth century, the Arabs had only the sidereal rose, a method of plotting locations via the polar star that the Persians had used before them. By the thirteenth century if not before, however, Arab navigators were supplementing star navigation with the floating compass the Chinese had employed a century or so earlier.[9]

In this milieu, it is no surprise that there are many extant examples, full of linguistic manipulations of various sorts, of later retranslations of Arabic tales back into Indian Persian or other regional languages, as well as folkloric versions and fresh translations from the Sanskrit. In 1919, in an exhaustive tracing out of *Pañcatantra* story motifs in later folkloric renditions, W. Norman Brown stressed the continuous back-and-forth borrowing of motifs and frames by the tellers of oral tales and the composers of literary fictions, and the high degree of coincidence between oral and written tales.[10] There are also continuous instances of interlinguistic transfers back and forth. The Mughal emperor Akbar, apparently dissatisfied at the degree to which the *Anvār-i Suhailī* ("Lights of Canopus") and Abū 'l-Faẓl's *'Iyār-i Dānish* ("Touchstone of Wisdom") departed from the Sanskrit original of the *Pañcatantra,* sponsored a fresh Persian translation of a Jain Sanskrit version of the tales called the *Pañcākhyāna.* The translator, Muṣṭafá Khāliqdād 'Abbāsī, who apparently used a copy of the Jain recension in the imperial library, was also responsible for a complete Persian translation of the famous Sanskrit collection of tales entitled the *Kathā-sarit-sāgara* ("The Ocean of the Streams of Story," commonly called "The Ocean of Story").[11] We have the itinerary of another such traveling literary phenomenon, the Sanskrit *Śuka-saptati*, the "Seventy Tales of a Parrot."[12] Translated into Persian as the *Tūṭī-Nāmah* by the fourteenth-century north Indian Chishti disciple Ẓiyā' al-dīn Nakhshabī, these tales illustrate a misogynistic stereotype of the age, the cupidity and lustful nature of women.[13] They were translated back into Deccani Urdu, a local or regional language, by Ġhavvāṣī, the celebrated poet laureate (*malik al-shu'rā'*) at the Golkonda court of Sultan 'Abdullāh Quṭb Shāh in the seventeenth century.[14]

These examples demonstrate the polyglot worlds in which tales traveled, both in the cosmopolitan Persian-speaking Islamicate world and in the multilingual local worlds of Hindustan and the Deccan. Moreover, as Richard Eaton notes about the rise of tales about the phenomenon of travel itself,

> Nowhere is this Islamic "world system" more vividly captured than in the genre of travel literature that emerged after the thirteenth century. The Qur'an itself enjoins its community to "Journey in the land, then behold how He originated creation" (29:20). From the earliest days of Islam, pious Muslims followed this injunction quite literally; indeed the tradition of peripatetic scholars and saints is traceable in part to this verse. In the fourteenth and fifteenth centuries yet another purpose for "journeying in the land" appeared when increased European demand for spices...triggered trade diasporas throughout the Indian Ocean and Sahara Desert. For both pious and commercial reasons, Muslims during these two centuries began moving through the known world in unprecedented numbers. They also recorded their experiences.[15]

The Arabic- and Persian-speaking world encountered cultural difference through its accounts of marvels, and framed its fantasy literature within a metaphysics derived from the Qur'ān and the essentials of the faith that merchants carried with them throughout the Indian Ocean, which links the port cities of Asia to the clearinghouses of the Arab world and the markets of Europe

In this trajectory, the Hindavī Sufi romances produce and reproduce a generic logic that is quite particular. The characters in the usual love triangle of the genre all have Indian names and practice local religious customs such as going to temple on important and holy days, enjoying the pleasures of *pān* chewing and chess, the appeal of the new Hindavī story and song, playing and swinging in forest groves or mango orchards, even when they exemplify states of being or spiritual processes. Indeed, the genre is a re-presentation of Islamic models of piety and poetry in Indian dress, the Persian sugar candy in the form of jaggery or raw golden sugar. Although the Hindavī Sufi romances are modeled in part on Persian allegorical poems such as 'Aṭṭār's *Manṭiq al-Ṭair* or *The Conference of the Birds*, along with richly symbolic and suggestive poems such as the *Khamsah* of Niẓāmī, they fully reimagine these Persian concepts and models through local aesthetics and narrative conventions.

This realm of crisscrossing polities, erotologies, ascetic lineages, literatures, and languages was also part of the larger Islamicate world and pre-Islamic world of the Indian Ocean. Parallel to the process of consolidating and expanding Turkish and Afghan rule over Hindustan, there was an expansion of trade and travel networks[16] through the extensive Indian Ocean trade that was revitalized by the Arabs after the eighth century.[17] The Arab traders took over the classical Greek and Roman trade with India and worked alongside the existing trading systems of the Indians, Indonesians, and Chinese.

Following the pioneering work of K. N. Chaudhuri, scholars have treated the littorals of the Indian Ocean as a group of societies linked by trade, the annual compulsion of the monsoon winds, commonalities of culture and social practice, and networks of circulation and exchange.[18] In tandem with this process of cultural and mercantile exchange based on transoceanic trade, there were significant overland developments. The *pax Mongolica* enabled overland trade between Europe and China and linked Asia, the Middle East, and Europe in what Abu-Lughod has termed a premodern world system.[19] This world system was "Islamicate" in the sense that it was not always linked "directly to the religion, Islam, itself, but to the social and cultural complex historically associated with Islam and the Muslims, both among Muslims themselves and even when found among non-Muslims."[20] As Phillip Wagoner indicates in his study of the court dress code of the south Indian kingdom of Vijayanagara, this systemic shift also entailed a civilizational change. In the world of the Indian Ocean, people adopted cultural and discursive practices from the Turkish sultanate of Delhi and the regional Afghan kingdoms while maintaining indigenous forms as part of their useful symbolic repertoire.[21]

Fantasy and the Fantastic

Nowhere is the process of cultural exchange more vivid than in the accounts of the marvels and wonders that travelers found in new places. The sense of the marvelous, that which causes astonishment (*'ajab*), can be construed both as an imaginative escape from humdrum existence and as a mark of cultural encounter and exchange. It can thus be examined within a larger historical and cultural trajectory. In one way, these fantasies liberated readers and listeners from the bounds of ordinary experience and allowed them to travel to faraway lands and unlikely places populated by marvelous beasts and beings. Yet this invitation away from the brute realities of history into a world of exotic wonders and romantic quests had its own historical status within the struggles of the age that produced it.

In another context of cultural encounter, the European apprehension of the "new" world of the Americas, Stephen Greenblatt has spoken of wonder as "the decisive emotional and intellectual experience in the presence of radical difference."[22] In the Islamicate world of the sultanate period, accounts of marvels or wonders (*'ajā'ib*) that travelers saw were marked by a similar sense of astonishment (*'ajab* or *ta'ajjub*). Their astonishment had a double referent, as it was provoked by the extraordinary monuments of classical antiquity as well as by the marvels encountered in distant lands. Early accounts, such as the tenth-century Captain Buzurg bin Shahryār's *Kitāb 'Ajā'ib al-Hind* ("The Book of Wonders of India"), were, as C. E. Dubler insists, "no wanton inventions of fancy, but [were] often based on a minute and exact observation of nature."[23] However, as the geographical accounts and cosmographies of Arab writers grew more elaborate, they ventured more into the realms of fantasy and imaginative literature:

> The taste for the fantastic was so pronounced in the medieval Arab world that it spawned a distinctive genre of literature, that of *aja'ib* (marvels), and books were written on the marvels of Egypt, of India and of the cosmos as a whole. Such books were hugger mugger compilations of improbable information about the stupendous monuments of antiquity, strange coincidences, the miraculous powers of certain plants, stones, and animals, and feats of magic. Many of the marvels first found in "non-fiction" works on cosmography eventually made their way into the *Nights*. The Sinbad cycle, which is a fictional reworking of mariners' yarns about the wonders to be found in the Indian and China seas (among them the wak-wak tree with its human-headed fruit, the Old Man of the Sea and the fish as large as an island), is the most obvious example of this process.[24]

The sense of astonishment over the radically different, as well as over the stupendous and magical, comes to a person "at the time of that person's ignorance of the *sabab* (cause) of something."[25] Amazement is frequently accompanied by a formulaic affirmation of Allah as the supreme creator of all things found in the universe. Marvels are thus fitted into the totalizing frame of the divine will that is expressed through creation, signs of wonder that make humans aware of Allah's omnipotence.

The subsequent creation of imaginative literature seems to demonstrate this insight from Henry James:

> The only general attribute of projected romance that I can see...is the fact of the kind of experience with which it deals—experience liberated, so to speak: experience disengaged, disembroiled, disencumbered, exempt from the conditions that we normally know to attach to it and...drag upon it, and operating in a medium which relieves it, in a particular interest, of the inconvenience of a related, a measurable state, a state subject to all our vulgar communities.[26]

In one sense, these fantasies liberated readers and listeners from the bounds of ordinary experience and allowed them to travel to faraway lands and unlikely places populated by wondrous beasts and beings. Although such audiences were bounded by an overarching sense of a cosmic and natural order overshadowed by God, the marvels and wonders of creation stretched the limits of the imagination and of what James calls "all our vulgar communities."

In another sense, as Tzvetan Todorov notes in his study of the fantastic, fantasy is dependent on notions of the real because they provide a basis for comparing the imaginary world with the ordinary one:

> The reader and the hero...must decide if a certain event or phenomenon belongs to reality or to imagination, that is, must determine whether or not it is real. It is therefore the category of the real which has furnished a basis for our definition of the fantastic. No sooner have we become aware of this fact, than we must come to a halt—amazed.[27]

Todorov's well-staged amazement or hesitation between the real and the imaginary is the focus for a thoroughgoing analysis of a variety of fantastic texts and discourses. As Graham Seymour indicates, "The real constitutes a linchpin for the analysis of the reading of literary fantasy in so far as it indicates the point from which the subject is suspended in the hesitation of his/her desire—a hesitation and a division which...is both aimed at and provoked by the fantastic."[28] Todorov himself comments on the origins of this "linchpin" as follows: "The nineteenth century transpired, it is true, in a metaphysics of the real and the imaginary, and the literature of the fantastic is nothing but the bad conscience of this positivist era. But today, we can no longer believe in an immutable, external reality, nor in a literature which is merely the transcription of such a reality. Words have gained an autonomy which things have lost."[29]

The universe of words of the Avadhi or eastern Hindavī *premākhyāns* is a fantasy world of marvels and exotic locales, of supernatural helpers and agencies who aid the hero along his way. The linchpin of the genre, however, is not some positivist notion of the real, but an aesthetic of *rasa* that is adapted from Sanskrit poetics to suggest new and varied Sufi and secular meanings. The literary mechanism by which the poetry could be interpreted in multiple ways was the Sanskrit theory of *dhvani* or suggestion, which allowed poets and readers to go beyond the literal and figurative levels of meaning in poetic texts.[30]

This theoretical move holds a mimetic form of literary and artistic representation to be secondary to the enterprise of writing literature. In reading any genre that follows this poetic system, one cannot assume a straightforward link between a particular time and space and its representation in poetry. As Abhinavagupta puts it, in his *Locana*, "A poet has no need to carry out a mere chronicle of events. That is a task accomplished by the historian" (L 3.10–14e). Instead, the poet invents a new universe through the innumerable varieties of suggestion that can be created from the old subjects of poetry. In this determinedly anti-mimetic universe, experience is liberated and disembroiled from the travails of everyday life. This constitutes the appeal of the poetic effort. As Todorov notes, "The fantastic requires . . . a reaction to events as they occur in the world evoked. . . . In short, the fantastic implies fiction."[31]

Todorov construed the fantastic as the staging of amazement over marvelous events and phenomena, as a hesitation over whether they are real or imaginary. The authors of romances may construct fantasy worlds to liberate the imagination, but we must delineate their generic and narrative outlines against the shadowy background of the material fragments and literary remains of the sultanate period. As Stephen Greenblatt put it, "It is . . . a theoretical mistake and a practical blunder to collapse the distinction between representation and reality, but at the same time we cannot keep them isolated from one another. They are locked together in an uneasy marriage in a world without ecstatic union or divorce."[32]

When the fictions we examine are about the victors and vanquished in a particular historical situation, how can we separate our readings from these political and theological resonances? How can we sidestep the theoretical dualism of real and imaginary, of having to decide between truth and falsity in some perpetually unsatisfactory positivist operation? Rosemary Jackson, writing about fantasy, indicates the beginnings of a productive line of inquiry by urging an emphasis on ideology, which she characterizes as "roughly speaking, the imaginary ways in which men experience the real world, those ways in which men's relation to the world is lived through various systems of meaning such as religion, family, law, moral codes, education, etc."[33] Understanding the many meanings of fantastic literature lies precisely in unpacking the ideological frames and uses of narrative.

Formulaic Structures

In formulaic literature, "Originality is to be welcomed only in the degree that it intensifies the expected experience without fundamentally altering it."[34] As John G. Cawelti notes, "Since the pleasure and effectiveness of an individual formulaic work depends on its intensification of a familiar experience, the formula creates its own world with which we become familiar by repetition. We learn in this way how to experience this imaginary world without continually comparing it with our own experience."[35] The pleasure of entering this fantastic world can be maximized by the author's use of the most widespread and conventional social and narrative forms. This factor allows many different audiences to enjoy the formulaic plots of the Hindavī romances, much as they enjoy the Indian cinematic extravaganzas of the present day.

Like these films, the generic formula of the Hindavī Sufi romances contains a set of easily predictable conventions and motifs. Originality consists of using the formula in new ways, but the basics remain the same: the hero's quest for self-transformation impelled by an initial dream, vision, or encounter; the use of abstract characters or narrative options in the progress of true love; the entwined articulation of erotics and asceticism in the service of an ideal of mystical love; and the use of an aesthetics of *rasa* that is reworked from its classical sources to express a distinctive Hindavī agenda of Sufi love. As Cawelti noted:

> Conventional story patterns work because they bring into an effective convention a large variety of existing cultural and artistic interests and concerns. This approach is different from traditional forms of social or psychological determinism in that it rejects the concept of a single fundamental social or psychological dynamic in favor of viewing the appeal of a conventional literary pattern as the result of a variety of cultural, artistic, and psychological interests. Successful story patterns like the western persist, according to this view, not because they embody some particular ideology or psychological dynamic, but because they maximize a great many such dynamics. Thus, in analysing the cultural significance of such a pattern, we cannot expect to arrive at a single key interpretation. Instead, we must show how a large number of interests and concerns are brought into an effective order or unity.[36]

Nowhere is this dictum better illustrated than in the Avadhi *premākhyāns*.

Vladimir Propp spoke of the capacity for transformation inherent in such formulaic tales.[37] Studying stories, for Propp, was analogous to "the study of organic formations in nature,"[38] and from this insight he developed a system to find the quasi-biological "morphology" of a given set of stories by analyzing their structure and motifs. Propp's analysis of themes and their place in actions that advance the narrative, called functions, reduces narrative structure to the combinations and recombinations of the component parts of a tale. Emblematic functions, rather than people, trundle through the plot, strangely reminiscent of wheeled robots in contemporary formulaic science fiction. People, idealized or otherwise, do not matter; what is important is the overall structure of the plot and the options that move it along. These emblematic characters help or hinder the hero's progress toward the satisfaction of his perpetually deferred desire, his arrival and dispatch, the ordeals that structure his ascetic quest, the action of the plot. Propp's analysis clearly is limited by the relatively simple and formulaic nature of the Russian folk narratives he discusses. Yet something like the concept of "function" may be necessary whenever we think about individual emblematic or allegorical characters, for it allows us to discuss the movement and action of the plot. On a larger scale, the notion of function gives us a way to link what happens in the whole course and design of the narrative with the social logics surrounding it, the action itself as emblem of the larger cultural and psychological tensions of the polyglot cultural scene of northern India or Hindustan.

Although the use of formulaic motifs may be repetitive, it is not static but dynamic, exciting and enhancing the enjoyment of the poem through every detail. The abstraction is useful in that it allows us to analyze the representation of historical events as well as fictional ones, but begs the question of how the historical and social world is implicated in the narrative world of fantasy. The problem is especially acute in highly formulaic genres of literature such as the Hindavī Sufi romances, which use common Indian, Islamic, and folkloric narrative motifs of wider provenance but arrange them according to a very specific overall design. Although Propp and the French structuralists have attempted to construct morphologies or generative grammars[39] of narrative, the move separates the fantasy world from the social world and creates an abstract structure that is ultimately indefensible.

As a partial solution to the problem, Peter Brooks developed a theory of narrative desire, based on what Roland Barthes called *la passion du sens*, the "passion of/for meaning" that animates us as readers of narrative.[40] Brooks links "the reading of plot as a form of desire that carries us forward, onward, and through the text" with the psychology of the reading subject to construct what he calls a "textual erotics."[41] Something analogous is required of us as readers of the Hindavī romance.

Translations and Wider Influences of the Hindavī Romances

In the *Cāndāyan*, Dā'ūd created an Indian narrative genre for cultivated people who already enjoyed the exquisite Persian romances of the great Niẓāmī Ganjavī, with their subtly suggestive texture and imagery, as well as Indian music, poetry, and dance in evening parties and gatherings. In return, there were two partial translations of the *Cāndāyan* into Persian[42] and one Persian translation of the Hindavī *Mirigāvatī*. In the years immediately preceding the death of Akbar, the rebellious Prince Salīm was ensconced in a provincial court in Allahabad that his father Akbar had newly endowed with a secure fort upriver of the confluence of rivers. There Salīm sponsored a subimperial atelier of painters, calligraphers, and book binders that produced the Indo-Persian prose version of the *Mirigāvatī*, the *Rāj-Kuṉvar*, "Prince." This important Mughal imperial manuscript was a lavishly illustrated codex made for the rebel prince as he waited for his father's demise.[43]

There are in addition no fewer than eleven translations of the *Padmāvat* into Persian, and even an opera that the librettist Laloy composed on the theme and that was performed in Paris in 1923.[44] The eleven Persian translations are evidence of the close interlinguistic links and resonances of a culture that was equally at home in Persian and Hindavī. They include the version of 'Āqil Khān Rāzī, a prominent courtier at the camp of Aurangzeb in Burhanpur, entitled the *Sham' va Parvānah* ("The Lamp and the Moth").[45] Dr. S. A. H. Abidi, the doyen of Indo-Persian and Persian studies and discoverer of many rare works, provides a discussion of all the translations of the *Padmāvat*.[46] The eighth of the twelve translations of Jāyasī's *Padmavat* that Dr. Abidi lists, the *Ḥusn-va-'Ishq* of Ḥusām al-dīn, is actually a translation of Mañjhan's *Madhumālatī* by Mirza Ḥusām al-dīn Ḥusāmī, the father of the eighteenth-century Persian lexicographer and litterateur Sirāj al-dīn 'Alī Khān Ārzū.[47] The translator was related to the Shattari *silsilah* by marriage if not spiritual lineage, for his wife was one of the granddaughters of Shaikh Muḥammad Ġhauṣ Gvāliyārī. Two other Persian translations of the *Madhumālatī* were made by various persons connected with the Shattari *silsilah*, including the indefatigable 'Āqil Khān Rāzī, who was also a disciple of the later Shattari shaikhs of Burhanpur. Much further work needs to be done on all these versions.

The literary tradition of Sufi romances in Hindavī did continue under the Mughals, although Akbar and his successors were more interested in patronizing mannerist or *rīti* poetry and the poetry devoted to Kṛṣṇa in Braj Bhāṣā, another premodern literary language hailing from the region around Mathura,[48] and the later romances of the genre waned in popularity after this shift in patronage. Later poets who composed romances following the model of the great sultanate Hindavī love stories did not create such elaborate narratives as the *Padmāvat* and the *Madhumālatī*.[49] But in the seventeenth century, 'U<u>s</u>mān of Ghazipur (ca. 1613) composed his *Citrāvalī*,[50] which represents the Creator as a painter (*citerā*) who looks at the world and paints it full of imaginal forms as a kind of picture pavilion or *citra-sārī*. A prince, Sujāna, magically transported to the picture pavilion of Princess Citrāvalī of Rūpa-nagara, sees a ravishing picture of the princess, is transfixed, and draws a picture of himself next to it. When the princess sees his picture, she falls in love, and the rest of the plot covers the adventures of the prince and princess as they try to consummate their mutual desire. These adventures include being blinded and eaten by a python, finding a magic ointment for regaining sight, and surviving a subplot involving a second heroine, Kaulāvatī. Nūr Muḥammad of Azamgarh, a prominent eighteenth-century *premākhyān* poet, wrote works including the *Indrāvat* (1744)[51] and the *Anurāg-Bānsurī* or "Flute of Love," completed in 1764.[52] Romances such as these continued to be composed till the beginning of the twentieth century, though under the Mughals the genre became a local literary tradition without significant imperial political sponsorship.

It is natural to wonder about the "impact" of a genre of literature, if that can ever be measured. Subsequent to the era of the great sultanate romances, narrative genres such as *qiṣṣah* and *dāstān* in the new literary languages of the eighteenth and nineteenth centuries, Hindi and Urdu, were recreated out of earlier genres.[53] Still later, the makers of Bombay films drew upon performance traditions such as *nauṭankī* and Parsi theater. In short, even after the sultanate had been obliterated, both individual motifs, such as becoming a yogi in love, and the larger cultural space of storytelling and formulaic fantasy that the Hindavī Sufi romance poets carved out continued to be reconstituted. Just as Quṭban used the voyages of Sindbād and the marvels of India as motifs in the *Mirigāvatī*, his text and the other Sufi romances were a source for later *qiṣṣah* and *dāstan* writers, as well as novelists, filmmakers, and opera composers. The literary, artistic, and musical echoes continue to resonate.

Shantanu Phukan has unearthed rare and interesting accounts of the later reception of the Hindavī Sufi romances. Of these, perhaps one can be singled out as exemplary of the process by which the genre became a "classical" received tradition for later listeners and readers. In 1739, a nobleman by the name of Anand Rām, with the Persian pen name of Mu<u>kh</u>liṣ ("Sincere"), went to the death-anniversary celebrations at a Sufi shrine. On his first night there he could not sleep, so he requested his servant to tell him a tale to while away the night:

> [M]y servant told the colorful tale that Jāyasī, author of the Hindi *Padmāvat*, had written entirely in the Eastern dialect (*pūrabī*)—as

> though it were an Eastern melody brimming over with pain. Jāyasī had based its wording on uncommon ideas and rare metaphors; however, since the work contains the bewitchments and marvels of love, it compels the heart to feel pain.[54]

In his analysis of this quote, Phukan demonstrates that Mukhliṣ felt the "unmistakable pull of its language upon his sensibility—it moved him, as does a soulful melody 'brimming over with pain' (*sar tā sar chūn pardah-yi pūrabī labrīz-i dard*). The Eastern dialect of Hindi evidently evoked associations of musicality, rhythm, and cadence."[55] This was precisely the reason the Hindavī Sufi romances were prized and enthusiastically translated and retold numerous times.

Moreover, as Phukan shows, Ānand Rām Mukhliṣ went on to use a sartorial metaphor to explain the intention behind his translation of the tale into Persian. As he puts it:

> And I said to myself, "If this Hindi Beloved were to be displayed in the robes of a Persian writer (*qalamkār-e Fārsī*) then it is possible that this work of art might appear elegant and permissible in the estimation of the people of taste (*dar naẓar-e ahl-e ẕauq īn fan mustaḥsan numāyad*). Therefore, my pen laid the foundations of this literary project and, having completed it within the span of a week, called it *Hangāma-e 'Ishq* (the clamor of love)."[56]

Here *qalamkār-i Fārsī* refers not to a "Persian writer" but more properly to the "work of the pen," or writing. A charming ambiguity is conveyed by the fact that the word *qalamkār* also refers to a certain type of patterned cloth produced to this day in Iran, especially around Isfahan. The phrase should read "in Persian robes patterned by the pen."

Phukan overstates the case when he claims that this passage has to be understood in an oppositional way: "Here Hindi is defined by opposition: if Persian robes refine the Hindi-beloved, making her fit for the eyes of the literati, then Hindi by implication lacked polish, elegance, and taste."[57] Hindavī was hardly the poor provincial cousin that Phukan makes her, but rather a sophisticated regional literary tradition that had its own polished sweetness and charm, which is why appealing examples from it were rendered into Persian so many times. The Hindavī romances were fully part of the mental furniture of the sultanate male aristocrats, just as much part of their cultural and literary canon as were the older works of Sa'dī or Firdausī. The patrons and audiences of these texts were Indian Muslims, frequently intermarried, sometimes converted, tracing their genealogy back to Arabia or Persia or Central Asia but very much part of the *desī* landscape and celebrating their love of their native land in Hindavī poetry. The metaphor of dress is interesting, too, when one considers how the Hindavī romances constitute a Persian genre that is completely reinvented in Indian form. The characters of the Hindavī romances are Muslims in local dress, questing princes in the garb of yogis, as much a part of a cross-dressing colonial élite as a Simla fancy-dress party during the summer seasons of the Raj or a Richard Burton in the robes of a Persian doctor on the hajj.

Amīr Khusrau once described himself as a parrot using his beak to break Indian sugar rather than refined Persian sugar candy. Echoing this choice, the Hindavī poets celebrated the *desī* mixture of ghee and jaggery, the raw golden *guṛ* made from sugarcane juice. It is not hard to imagine a cosmopolitan *desī* literary and devotional culture newly created in the provinces of the Delhi sultanate and the Afghan kingdoms, centered around evening gatherings at court or private musical sessions at Sufi shrines. These contexts of reception shaped a range of responses to these beautiful and conventionally patterned narratives in the spoken language of Hindustan. The pleasure of a long formulaic genre, such as the Persian *dāstān*, the Hindavī Sufi *masnavī*, or the modern Indian film, consists of abandoning oneself to the events and descriptions in the story, the set pieces that every instance of the genre must include, and tasting the juice of love that is the express aesthetic agenda of the poets and storytellers of these media. Along with the poem, courtly audiences would have enjoyed the usual intoxicants—the pleasurably narcotic red juice of *pān*, wine, and other stimulants—as well as the luxurious atmosphere of *khus*-scented kiosks hung with tapestries and perfumed with incense. If the stories resolved the perceived cultural tension between eroticism and asceticism, so much the better. They fit perfectly into a cultural scene that knows gods such as the erotic ascetic Śiva,[58] in which there were and are many competing ascetic lineages with distinct poetic and devotional practices, and in which kings as famous as Raja Bhartṛhari renounced their kingdoms and went wandering as yogis on a quest for the divine beloved and the savor of *prema-rasa*.

Notes

CHAPTER 1

1. Sheldon Pollock, "India in the Vernacular Millennium: Literary Culture and Polity, 1000–1500," *Daedalus*, volume 127, no. 3, 1998, p. 42.
2. See, for instance, Kanwar Muhammad Ashraf, *Life and Conditions of the People of Hindustan* (Delhi: Munshiram Manoharlal, 1969 [1928]); or R. C. Majumdar, *The Delhi Sultanate*, Series: The History and Culture of the Indian People, vol. 6 (Bombay: Bharatiya Vidya Bhavan, 1990).
3. On the vagueness of the limits of this geographical unit, generally understood to comprise the Indo-Gangetic doab with a capital at Dilli or Dehli, modern Delhi, see Ashraf, *Life and Conditions of the People of Hindustan*, pp. 1–4.
4. Colin P. Masica, *The Indo-Aryan Languages* (Cambridge: Cambridge University Press, 1991), p. 25.
5. On the history of the Delhi sultanate, see Peter Jackson, *The Delhi Sultanate: A Political and Military History* (Cambridge: Cambridge University Press, 1999); Tapan Raychaudhuri and Irfan Habib, eds., *The Cambridge Economic History of India* (Cambridge: Cambridge University Press, 1982), A. B. M. Habibullah, *The Foundation of Muslim Rule in India: A History of the Establishment and Progress of the Turkish Sultanate of Delhi, 1206–1290* A. D. (Allahabad: Central Book Depot, 1961). For an account of the social changes that took place at this time, see I. H. Siddiqui, "Social Mobility in the Delhi Sultanate," in *Medieval India I: Researches in the History of India, 1200–1750*, ed. Irfan Habib (Delhi: Oxford University Press, 1992).
6. See André Wink, *Al-Hind: The Making of the Indo-Islamic World, Volume II: The Slave Kings and the Islamic Conquest, 11th–13th Centuries* (Leiden: E. J. Brill, 1997), esp. pp. 162–293, for a detailed account of the interaction of Central Asian nomadic cultures and South Asian sedentary agricultural kingdoms, and for the consolidation of garrisons and regional sultanates. For a sophisticated and multifaceted study of establishment of rule in a particular region, see Richard M. Eaton, *The Rise of Islam on the Bengal Frontier* (Berkeley: University of California Press, 1993).

7. See Irfan Habib, "Formation of the Sultanate Ruling Class of the Thirteenth Century," in idem, ed., *Medieval India. 1: Researches in the History of India 1200–1750* (Delhi: Oxford University Press, 1992), pp. 1–21.
8. On the perceived opposition between asceticism and sensual pleasure during the period, see Simon Digby, "The *Tuḥfa i naṣā'iḥ* of Yūsuf Gadā: An Ethical Treatise in Verse from the Late-Fourteenth-Century Dehlī Sultanate," in Barbara D. Metcalf, ed., *Moral Conduct and Authority: The Place of* Adab *in South Asian Islam* (Berkeley: University of California Press, 1984), p. 105. On the coincidence between asceticism and eroticism, see Wendy Doniger (O'Flaherty), *Asceticism and Eroticism in the Mythology of Siva* (Oxford University Press, 1973; retitled *Siva: The Erotic Ascetic*, 1981).
9. K. A. Nizami, "Early Indo-Muslim Mystics and Their Attitude Towards the State," *Islamic Culture*, vol. 22, 1948, p. 397. See also his *Some Aspects of Religion and Politics in India During the Thirteenth Century* (Delhi: Idarah-i Adabiyat-i Delli, 1974).
10. I. A. Zilli, "Successors of Shaikh Nasiruddin Mahmud and the Disintegration of the Chishti Central Organization," *Proceedings of the Indian History Congress*, vol. 44, 1984, p. 324.
11. Iqtidar Alam Khan, "Shaikh 'Abdul Quddūs Gangohī's Relations with Political Authorities: A Reappraisal," *Medieval India: A Miscellany*, vol. 4, 1977, p. 80ff.
12. Simon Digby, "The Sufi Shaikh as Source of Authority in Mediaeval India," in *Islam et Société en Asie du Sud: Collection Puruṣārtha 9*, ed. Marc Gaborieau (Paris: École des Hautes Études en Sciences Sociales, 1986), pp. 57–77.
13. Aziz Ahmad, "The Sufi and the Sultan in Pre-Mughal Muslim India," *Der Islam*, vol. 38, 1963, pp. 142–53.
14. See Digby, "The Sufi Shaikh," pp. 57–77.
15. Idem, p. 63.
16. Amīr Ḥasan Sijzī, *Favā'id al-Fu'ād*, ed. with an Urdu translation by Khwaja Hasan Sani Nizami (Delhi: Urdu Academy, 1990), p. 320. See also the notable English translation by Bruce B. Lawrence, *Morals for the Heart: Conversations of Shaykh Nizam ad-din Awliya recorded by Amir Hasan Sijzi*, p. 294. I have cited the English translation, with occasional emendations.
17. Sijzī, *Favā'id al-Fu'ād*, 232–34, and Lawrence, *Morals for the Heart*, p. 97.
18. See Farīd al-dīn 'Aṭṭār, *The Conference of the Birds*, tr. D. Davis and A. Darbandi (London: Penguin Classics, 1984). For a concise treatment of Islamic allegory, see Peter Heath, *Allegory and Philosophy in Avicenna (Ibn Sīnā), with a Translation of the Book of the Prophet Muḥammad's Ascent to Heaven* (Philadelphia: University of Pennsylvania Press, 1992), pp. 4–10.
19. Sijzī, *Favā'id al-Fu'ād*, 498, and Lawrence, *Morals for the Heart*, p. 186.
20. See K. A. Nizami, *Some Aspects of Religion in India During the Thirteenth Century* (Delhi: Idarah-i Adabiyat-i Delli, 1974), pp. 231–35, for a description of some of the formalizations of the mystical path drawn on by the Chishti

Sufis, based on theoretical compendia such as Suhravardī's *'Avārif al-Ma'ārif* and 'Alī al-Hujvīrī's *Kashf al-Maḥjūb*.

21. Sijzī, *Favā'id al-Fu'ād*, pp. 390–92, and Lawrence, *Morals for the Heart*, pp. 151–52. See also K. A. Nizami, "Introduction," in *Morals for the Heart*, pp. 11–12.
22. Sir George Abraham Grierson, *The Modern Vernacular Literature of Hindustan* (Calcutta: Royal Asiatic Society of Bengal, 1889), pp. xviii, p. 18.
23. See Richard A. Williams, "The *Ḍholā-Mārū Rā Dūhā* and the Rise of the Hindi Literary Tradition" (unpublished Ph. D. dissertation, University of Chicago, 1976), pp. 4–11, for a detailed discussion of literary periodization in the formation of the Hindi literary canon.
24. See now Vasudha Dalmia, *The Nationalization of Hindu Traditions: Bhāratendu Hariścandra and Nineteenth-century Banaras* (Delhi: Oxford University Press, 1997), pp. 146–221; and Christopher Rolland King, *One Language, Two Scripts: The Hindi Language Movement in Nineteenth Century North India* (New York: Oxford University Press, 1995), for detailed and thorough accounts of the movement for the propagation of modern standard Hindi.
25. For a succinct account of the five major literary languages that constitute premodern Hindi poetry, see Karine Schomer, *Mahadevi Varma and the Chhayavad Age of Hindi Poetry* (Berkeley: University of California Press, 1983), pp. 1–5.
26. Ramchandra Shukla, *Hindī Sāhitya kā Itihās* (Varanasi: Nāgarīpracāriṇī Sabhā, 1957), p. 1.
27. Ganapatichandra Gupta, "*Premākhyān-kāvya*," in *Hindī Sāhitya kā Itihās*, ed. Nagendra and Sureshchandra Gupta (NOIDA: Mayūr, 1991), p. 144.
28. On this point, see Iqtidar Husain Siddiqui, "Introduction," *Perso-Arabic Sources of Information on the Life and Conditions in the Sultanate of Delhi* (New Delhi: Munshiram Manoharlal, 1992), pp. xi–xvi.
29. Sir Henry Myers Elliot, "Original Preface," in H. M. Elliot and John Dowson, *The History of India as Told by Its Own Historians* (Delhi: Low Price, 1990 [1867–77]), vol. 1, pp. xviii–xxiii.
30. See Ronald Inden, "Orientalist Constructions of India," *Modern Asian Studies*, vol. 20, no. 3, 401–446; and Thomas R. Metcalf, *Ideologies of the Raj* (Cambridge: Cambridge University Press, 1995), esp. pp. 1–27.
31. On this point, see also Carl W. Ernst, *Eternal Garden: Mysticism, History, and Politics at a South Asian Sufi Center* (Albany: State University of New York Press, 1992), 18–37, esp. pp. 18–20.
32. Elliot, "Original Preface," pp. xxi–xxii.
33. On the historiography of Hindus and Muslims as separate nations, see the essays collected in Romila Thapar, Harbans Mukhia, and Bipan Chandra, *Communalism and the Writing of Indian History* (Delhi: People's, 1969).
34. Gyanendra Pandey, *The Construction of Colonialism in Colonial North India* (Delhi: Oxford University Press, 1990), p. 10.

35. See also Ronald B. Inden, *Imagining India* (Oxford: Basil Blackwell, 1990); and Thomas Metcalf, *Ideologies of the Raj*.
36. I. H. Qureshi, *The Struggle for Pakistan* (Karachi: University of Karachi, 1987), p. 13.
37. Tara Chand, *Influence of Islam on Indian Culture* (Allahabad: Indian Press, 1946), p. 137.
38. Aziz Ahmad, "Epic and Counter-Epic in Medieval India," *Journal of the American Oriental Society*, vol. 83, no. 4, 1963, p. 470.
39. Annemarie Schimmel, *Classical Urdu Literature from the Beginning to Iqbāl*, Series: A History of Indian Literature, vol. 8, part 1, fasc. 3 (Wiesbaden: Otto Harrassowitz, 1975), p. 128.
40. Asim Roy, *The Islamic Syncretistic Tradition in Bengal* (Princeton: Princeton University Press, 1984), p. 58.
41. On this point, see Muzaffar Alam, "Competition and Co-existence: Indo-Islamic Interaction in Medieval North India," *Itinerario*, vol. 13, no. 1, 1989, pp. 37–59.
42. Shantanu Phukan, "The Lady of the Lotus of Gnosis: Muhammad Jayasi's *Padmavati*," unpublished paper, pp. 2–3. I am grateful to Shantanu Phukan for sharing his unpublished work with me.
43. Richard M. Eaton, *Sufis of Bijapur, 1300–1700: Social Roles of Sufis in Medieval India* (Princeton: Princeton University Press, 1978); and *The Rise of Islam on the Bengal Frontier, 1204–1760 (*University of California Press, *1996)*.
44. Ernst, *Eternal Garden*.
45. P. M. Currie, *The Shrine and Cult of Mu'īn al-Dīn Chishtī of Ajmer* (Delhi: Oxford University Press, 1989); and Paul Jackson, S. J., *The Way of a Sufi: Sharfuddin Maneri* (Delhi: Idarah-i Adabiyat-i Delli, 1987).
46. Mohammad Habib, "Chishti Mystics [sic] Records of the Sultanate Period," in his *Politics and Society During the Early Medieval Period: Collected Works of Professor Mohammad Habib*, ed. K. A. Nizami (New Delhi: People's, 1974), vol. I, pp. 385–433; and Bruce B. Lawrence, *Notes from a Distant Flute: The Extant Literature of pre-Mughal Sufism* (Tehran: Imperial Iranian Academy of Philosophy, 1978).
47. See Lawrence, *Notes from a Distant Flute*, pp. 27–59, for a review of the meager literary output of the early Chishtis and the "voluminous corpus" of later Chishti authors.
48. See Abdul Ḥaqq, *Urdū kī ibtidā'ī nashv va numā meṉ Ṣūfiyī-i kirām kā kām* (Delhi: Anjuman-e Taraqqī-e Urdū Hind, 1939). See also S. H. Askari, "Avvalīn musalmān aur desī bhāshā'eṉ," *Patna University Journal*, 1954, pp. 59–80.
49. Ernst, *Eternal Garden*, p. 168.
50. Cynthia Talbot, "Inscribing the Other, Inscribing the Self: Hindu-Muslim Identities in Pre-Colonial India," *Comparative Studies in Society and History*, vol. 37, no. 4, 1995, p. 694.

51. Shantanu Phukan, "'None Mad as a Hindu Woman': Contesting Communal Readings of *Padmavat*," *Comparative Studies of South Asia, Africa, and the Middle East*, vol. 16, no. 1, 1996, p. 42, quoting Aziz Ahmad, "Epic and Counter-epic in Medieval India," p. 475.
52. Scholars who have rendered problematic the idea of a single Indian Muslim community in the post-Independence years include M. Mujeeb, *The Indian Muslims* (London: Allen and Unwin, 1967); Frances Robinson, *Separatism Among Indian Muslims: The Politics of the United Provinces' Muslims, 1860–1923* (Cambridge: Cambridge University Press, 1974); and Rafiuddin Ahmed, *The Bengal Muslims 1871–1906: A Quest for Identity* (Delhi: Oxford University Press, 1988).
53. Richard M. Eaton, "Introduction," *Indian Islamic Traditions, 711–1800*, ed. idem, Series: Themes in Indian History (Delhi: Oxford University Press, forthcoming), pp. 3–4.
54. See Sumathi Ramaswamy, *Passions of the Tongue: Language Devotion in Tamil India, 1891–1970* (Berkeley: University of California Press, 1997), pp. 22–78.
55. Edward C. Dimock, Jr., et al., *The Literatures of India: An Introduction* (Chicago: University of Chicago Press, 1974), pp. 20–21.
56. Pollock, "India in the Vernacular Millennium," p. 42.
57. Baburam Saksena, *Evolution of Awadhi (A Branch of Hindi)* (Allahabad: Indian Press, 1937), pp. 6–8.
58. Dalmia, *The Nationalization of Hindu Traditions*, pp. 152–54.
59. Grierson, *The Modern Vernacular Literature of Hindustan*, xviii, p. 18.
60. Shukla, *Hindī Sāhitya kā Itihās*.
61. Ganapatichandra Gupta, "*Premākhyān-kāvya*," p. 144; and Parashuram Chaturvedi, *Bhāratīya Premākhyān* (Allahabad: Bhāratī Bhaṇḍār, 1985).
62. S. M. Pandey, *Madhyayugīn Premākhyān* (Allahabad: Lokabhāratī Prakāśan, 1982); and R. S. McGregor, *Hindi Literature from Its Beginnings to the Nineteenth Century*, Series: A History of Indian Literature, vol. 8 (Wiesbaden: Otto Harrassowitz, 1984), p. 10.
63. Peter Gaeffke, "Alexander in Avadhī and Dakkinī *Mathnawīs*," *Journal of the American Oriental Society*, vol. 109, 1989.
64. S. M. Pandey, "Kutuban's *Mirigāvatī*: Its Content and Interpretation," in *Devotional Literature in South Asia: Current Research, 1985–1988*, ed. R. S. McGregor (Cambridge: Cambridge University Press, 1992), pp. 186–87.
65. S. C. R. Weightman, "Symmetry and Symbolism in Shaikh Manjhan's *Madhumālatī*," in *The Indian Narrative: Perspectives and Patterns*, eds. Christopher Shackle and Rupert Snell (Wiesbaden: Otto Harrassowitz, 1992), pp. 208–9.
66. V. S. Agraval, "Introduction," *Padmāvat: Malik Muhammad Jāyasī kṛta Mahākāvya (mūla aur sanjīvinī vyākhyā)* (Chirganv, Jhansi: Sāhitya Sadan, 1956), p. 57.
67. John Millis, *Malik Muhammad Jāyasī: Allegory and Religious Symbolism in his* Padmāvat (unpublished Ph. D. dissertation, University of Chicago, 1984), p. 108.

68. Phukan, "The Lady of the Lotus of Gnosis," pp. 2–3.
69. Thomas de Bruijn, *The Ruby Hidden in the Dust: A Study of the Poetics of Malik Muḥammad Jāyasī's* Padmāvat (Leiden: Rijksuniversitaet Proefschrift, 1996), pp. 104–6.
70. Alam, "Competition and Co-existence," p. 44.
71. Gaeffke, "Alexander in Avadhī and Dakkinī *Mathnawīs*," p. 528.
72. S. A. A. Rizvi, *A History of Sufism in India* (Delhi: Munshiram Manoharlal, 1983), vol. II, p. 155, n. 2.
73. For excellent summary accounts of these texts, see McGregor, *Hindi Literature from Its Beginnings to the Nineteenth Century*, pp. 26–28, 65–73.
74. McGregor, *Hindi Literature from Its Beginnings to the Nineteenth Century*, pp. 150–54.
75. See, for instance, Northrop Frye, *Anatomy of Criticism: Four Essays* (Princeton: Princeton University Press, 1957), pp. 187–88; and Fredric Jameson, "Magical Narratives," in his *The Political Unconscious: Narrative as a Socially Symbolic Act* (Ithaca, NY: Cornell University Press, 1981), pp. 103–50.
76. Gavin R. G. Hambly, "Becoming Visible: Medieval Islamic Women in History and Historiography," in his *Women in the Medieval Islamic World: Power, Patronage, and Piety* (New York: St. Martin's Press, 1998), p. 19.
77. Hambly. "Becoming Visible," p. 21.
78. Ashraf, *Life and Conditions of the People of Hindustan*, pp. 166–76.
79. For a discussion of *'ishq*, see Chapter 3.
80. Shaikh Mīr Sayyid Mañjhan, *Madhumālatī*, ed. Mataprasad Gupta (Allahabad: Mitra Prakāśan, 1961), verse 44, line 2, tr. Aditya Behl and Simon Weightman, with S. M. Pandey, *Madhumālatī: An Indian Sufi Romance*, Series: Oxford World's Classics (Oxford: Oxford University Press, 2000).
81. Malik Muḥammad Jāyasī, *Padmāvat*, ed. Mataprasad Gupta (Allahabad: Bhāratī Bhaṇḍār, 1973), 27.1–2, translation mine. In addition, I have referred to the edition of V. S. Agraval (Chirganv, Jhansi: Sāhitya Sadan, 1956), as well as the 1675 manuscript of the *Padmāvat* now held in the Rampur Raza Library (Hindi ms. 6). I have also consulted A. G. Shirreff's pioneering translation, *Padmavati of Malik Muhammad Jaisi*, Series: Bibliotheca Indica, Work No. 267 (Calcutta: Royal Asiatic Society of Bengal, 1944).
82. Maulānā Dā'ūd, *Cāndāyan*, ed. Mataprasad Gupta (Varanasi: Viśvavidyālaya Prakāśan, 1967), 82.1–2.
83. Shaikh Quṭban Suhravardī, *Mirigāvatī*, ed. D. F. Plukker (Amsterdam: Universiteit van Amsterdam Academisch Proefschrift, 1981), 74.6. I have also consulted the editions of Mataprasad Gupta (Agra: Pramāṇik Prakāśan, 1968), as well as Parameshvarilal Gupta (Varanasi: Viśvavidyālaya Prakāśan, 1967).
84. McGregor, *Hindi Literature from Its Beginnings to the Nineteenth Century*, p. 64.

CHAPTER 2

1. Translated in J. L. Masson and M. V. Patwardhan, *Aesthetic Rapture: The Rasādhyāya of the Nāṭya-Sāstra* (Poona: Deccan College Postgraduate and Research Institute, 1970), vol. I, p. 46. For a clear account of Bharata's theory, see David L. Haberman, *Acting as a Way of Salvation: A Study of Rāgānugā Bhakti Sādhana* (Oxford: Oxford University Press, 1988), pp. 13–16.
2. *Rasādhyāya* p. 1.47.
3. See the image of the tree, in Chapter 7.
4. For Indian theories of linguistic meaning in Sanskrit, see K. Kunjunni Raja, *Indian Theories of Meaning* (Madras: Adyar Library and Research Centre, 1963), especially pp. 17–77, 149–87, and 229–73. The same volume also contains a brief treatment of suggestion, variously termed *vyañjanā* and *dhvani*, pp. 275–315, which discusses the objections that a number of philosophical schools had to the theory of *dhvani* before it became generally accepted.
5. E. Gerow, *Indian Poetics: A History of Indian Literature* (Wiesbaden: Harrassowitz, 1977), p. 256.
6. Ānandavardhana's *Dhvanyāloka*, K 3.34A.
7. On *rasa* in Tantric practice, see David Gordon White, *The Alchemical Body: Siddha Traditions in Medieval India* (Chicago: University of Chicago Press, 1996). On specifically Muslim uses of rasa in the context of spiritual practice, see David Cashin, *The Ocean of Love: Middle Bengali Sufi Literature and the Fakirs of Bengal* (Stockholm: Association of Oriental Studies, 1995), esp. pp. 185–98.
8. For a brief account, see Jan Rypka, *History of Iranian Literature* (Dordrecht: D. Reidel, 1968), pp. 210–13.
9. Examples of the genre include Hubert Darke, trans., *The Book of Government or Rules for Kings: The Siyāsat-nāma or Siyar al-Mulūk of Niẓām al-Mulk* (London: Routledge and Kegan Paul, 1960), and Julie Scott Meisami, tr., *The Sea of Precious Virtues (Baḥr al-Favā'id): A Medieval Islamic Mirror for Princes* (Salt Lake City: University of Utah Press, 1991).
10. Niẓāmī Ganjavī, *Laylī-va Majnūn*, ed. B. Sarvatiyān (Teheran: Maktaba Tus, 1986), pp. 25–6. Future quotations will be integrated in the text by verse and section number following the abbreviation LM.
11. Amīr Khusrau, *Shīrīn va Khusrau*, in his *Khamsah-i Amr Khusrau Dihlavī* (Teheran: Intishārāt Shaqā'iq, 1362), p. 244. The translation is my own. Future quotations will be integrated in the text by page number following the abbreviation SK. On Amīr Khusrau, see Muhammad Wahid Mirza, *The Life and Works of Amir Khusrau* (Delhi: Idārah-i Adabiyāt-i Delli, 1935).
12. Amīr Khusrau, *Duwal Rānī Khazir Khān*, ed. Maulana Rashid Ahmad Salim Ansari, with Introduction and Notes by K. A. Nizami (Delhi: Idarah-i

Adabiyat-i Delli, 1988), p. 1. Further quotations from this text will be indicated by page number after the cited portion; the title is henceforward abbreviated as DRKK.

13. Maulānā Dā'ūd, *Cāndāyan*, ed. M. P. Gupta (Varanasi: Vishvavidyālaya Prakāśan, 1967), p. 1. Future quotations will be incorporated into the text by verse number following the abbreviation C.
14. For a detailed treatment, see G. H. Schokker, "The Language of Bhakti," in *Studies in Mysticism in honor of the 1150th anniversary of Kobo-daishi's nirvāṇam*, Acta Indologica, VI, 1984.
15. Quṭban, *Mirigāvatī*, verse 1. Further citations will be indicated by verse number in the body of the text following the abbreviation M.
16. The literature on Ibn 'Arabī (1165–1240) is voluminous. For a summary account, see Henri Corbin, *History of Islamic Philosophy*, tr. L. and P. Sherrard (London and New York: Kegan Paul International and Islamic Publications for the Institute of Ismaili Studies, 1993), pp. 291–96. For a brief treatment of the philosophy, see William Chittick, *The Sufi Path of Knowledge* (Albany: State University of New York Press). For an excellent intellectual biography, see Claude Addas, *Quest for the Red Sulphur: The Life of Ibn 'Arabi* (Cambridge, UK: Islamic Texts Society, 1993). After the fourteenth century, Ibn 'Arabī's theory had become the accepted version of creation for most Indian Sufi orders, and therefore it is not surprising to see the poets after Dā'ūd using different aspects of his ideas.
17. Jāyasī, *Padmāvat*, verse 1. I have used the editions of M. P. Gupta (Allahabad: Bharati Bhandar, 1973) and Vasudev Sharan Agraval (Cirganv, Jhansi: Sahitya Sadan, 1956). Further citations will be indicated by verse number in the body of the text following the abbreviation P. All translations are my own.
18. A. Yusuf Ali, tr., *The Holy Qur'ān* (1934; reprint, Beirut: Dār al-Qur'ān al-Karīm, 1982), pp. 907–8.
19. Mañjhan, *Madhumālatī*, ed. M. P. Gupta (Allahabad: Mitra Prakashan, 1968), verse 1. Aditya Behl, Simon Weightman, and S. M. Pandey, trs., *Madhumālatī: An Indian Sufi Romance* (Oxford: Oxford University Press, Series: Oxford World's Classics, 2001). All future references are indicated by verse number in the body of the text following the abbreviation MM.
20. On the role of such orthodox voices in shaping public opinion, see Kanwar Muhammad Ashraf, *Life and Conditions of the People of Hindustan* (Delhi: Munshiram Manoharlal, 1969 [1928]), pp. 20–21, and Simon Digby, "The *Tuḥfa i naṣā'iḥ* of Yūsuf Gadā: An Ethical Treatise in Verse from the Late-Fourteenth-Century Dehlī Sultanate," p. 105.
21. Ashraf, *Life and Conditions of the People of Hindustan*, p. 47.
22. A. K. S. Lambton, "Islamic Mirrors for Princes," *Quaderno dell'Accademia Nazionale dei Lincei*, no. 160, 1971, pp. 419–42.

23. Keykāvūs ebn Eskandar, *Qābūs Nāmeh*, ed. G. H. Yusofi (Tehran: Bazmgāh-i Tarjumah va Nashr-i Kitāb, 1967). Translated by Reuben Levy as *A Mirror for Princes: "The Qābūs Nāma" by Kai Kā'ūs ibn Iskandar, Prince of Gurgān* (New York: Dutton, 1951).
24. Niẓām al-Mulk Tūsī, *Siyāsat-Nāmah*, translated by Hubert Darke as *The Book of Government, or Rules for Kings: The Siyar al-Muluk or Siyasat-nama of Nizam al-Mulk* (London: Routledge and Kegan Paul, 1978).
25. Julie Scott Meisami, tr. and ed., *The Sea of Precious Virtues (Baḥr al-Favā'id): A Medieval Islamic Mirror for Princes* (Salt Lake City: University of Utah Press, 1991).
26. Julie Scott Meisami, *Medieval Persian Court Poetry* (Princeton: Princeton University Press, 1987), p. 180.
27. Peter Jackson, *The Delhi Sultanate: A Political and Military History* (Cambridge: Cambridge University Press, 1999), pp. 1–2.
28. Ibid., p. 2.
29. Fakhr al-dīn Rāzī, *Jāmi' al-'Ulūm*, ed. M. K. Malik al Kuttab, cited by Richard Eaton, *The Rise of Islam and the Bengal Frontier, 1204–1760* (Berkeley: University of California Press, 1993), pp. 29–30.
30. Eaton, *The Rise of Islam and the Bengal Frontier, 1204–1760*, p. 30. See Eaton, pp. 23–32, for a concise summary of the use of Persianate ideas of kingship in the sultanates formed in the Indian subcontinent.
31. For detailed dynastic lists, see C. E. Bosworth, *The New Islamic Dynasties: A Chronological and Genealogical Manual* (New York: Columbia University Press, 1996), pp. 185–89, 199–200.
32. Niẓāmī Ganjavī, *Khusrau va Shīrīn*, ed. B. Sarvatiyān (Teheran: Maktaba Tus, 1988), pp. 88–89. Future quotations will be integrated in the text by verse number following the abbreviation KS.
33. Niẓāmī, *Haft Paykar: A Medieval Persian Romance*, tr. Julie Scott Meisami (Oxford: Oxford University Press, 1995), p. 15.
34. See Simon Digby, "The *Tuḥfa i naṣā'iḥ* of Yūsuf Gadā: An Ethical Treatise in Verse from the Late-Fourteenth-Century Dehlī Sultanate," pp. 105, 121.
35. On this figure, see Jackson, *The Delhi Sultanate*, p. 185.
36. See Ẕiā al-dīn Baranī, *Tārīkh-i Fīrūzshāhī*, pp. 531–38 (translated in Elliot Dowson, *The History of India as Told by Its Own Historians, III*, Delhi: Low Price, 1990 [1867–1877]); Yaḥya bin Aḥmad bin Sirhindi, *Tārīkh-i Mubārakshāhī*, ed. Maulvi Hidayat Hosain (Calcutta: Asiatic Society of Bengal, 1931), pp. 120–23; and M. Habib and K. A. Nizami, *A Comprehensive History of India, Vol. V: The Delhi Sultanat (A. D. 1206–1526)* (Delhi: People's Publishing House, 1970), pp. 570–73.
37. For further details concerning Jūnā Shāh's succession to the political office of *vazīr* under Fīrūz Shāh Tuġhlaq, see Shams-i Sirāj 'Afīf, *Tārīkh-i Fīrūz Shāhī*, pp. 426–27.

38. For a more detailed history of the period, see Habib and Nizami, *A Comprehensive History of India,* pp. 630–732. For a detailed history of the Sharqī kingdom, see M. M. Saeed, *The Sharqi Sultanate of Jaunpur: A Political and Cultural History* (Karachi: University of Karachi, 1972).
39. Saeed, *The Sharqi Sultanate of Jaunpur,* p. 111. See also S. H. Askari, "Qutban's Mrigavat: A Unique Ms. in Persian Script," *Journal of the Bihar Research Society,* vol. 41, no. 4, December 1955, pp. 457–58; idem, "Bihar Under Later Tughlaqs and Sharqis," in his *Medieval Bihar: Sultanate and Mughal Period* (Patna: Khuda Bakhsh Oriental Public Library, 1990), pp. 22–31; and D. F. Plukker, *The Miragāvatī of Kutubana,* p. xviii, n. 4.
40. For details see Saeed, *The Sharqi Sultanate of Jaunpur,* pp. 111–12 and pp. 206–7, and A. Halim, "History of the Growth and Development of North-Indian Music During Sayyid-Lodi Period," *Journal of the Asiatic Society of Pakistan,* vol. 1, no. 1, 1956, pp. 46–64.
41. See Dirk H. A. Kolff, Naukar, *Rajput, and Sepoy: The ethnohistory of the military labour market in Hindustan, 1450–1850* (Cambridge: Cambridge University Press, 1990), for an excellent account of Sher Shāh's rise to power as an Afghan warlord.

CHAPTER 3

1. The classic art-historical statement on sultanate painting is Karl Khandalavala and Moti Chandra, *New Documents of Indian Painting—A Reappraisal* (Bombay, 1969). For a summary of the published scholarship on the painted manuscript traditions of the romance of Lorik and Cāndā, see Basil Gray, "The Lahore Laur-Chandā Pages Thirty Years After," in *Chhavi 2: Rai Krishnadasa Felicitation Volume* (Banaras: Bharat Kala Bhavan, Benares Hindu University, 1981), pp. 5–9. For a larger discussion of the manuscript culture of the Delhi sultanate, see Jeremiah P. Losty, *The Art of the Book in India* (London: British Library, 1982), pp. 37–73; and B. N. Goswamy, "In the Sultan's Shadow: Pre-Mughal Painting in and Around Delhi," in R. E. Frykenberg, ed., *Delhi Through the Ages,* pp. 129–42.
2. See, for instance, Kunwar Muhammad Ashraf, *Life and Conditions of the People of Hindustan (1200–1550)* (Delhi: Munshiram Manoharlal, 1969 [1928]).
3. A critical edition by Richard Cohen and Mehr Afshan Faruqi is awaited, which will, it is hoped, resolve the question of Dā'ūd's original text.
4. For a detailed statement of some of the problems of the field, see Simon Digby, "The Literary Evidence for Painting in the Delhi Sultanate," *Bulletin of the American Academy of Benares,* vol. 1, 1967. Despite these problems, however, there are good studies of particular painting traditions of the period. See *inter alia* B. N. Goswamy, *A Jainesque Sultanate Shahnama and the Context of pre-Mughal Painting in India* (Zurich: Museum Rietberg, 1988).

5. B. N. Goswamy, *A Jainesque Sultanate Shahnama and the Context of pre-Mughal Painting in India*, p. 6. For details about the incident of the picture showman, see Shams-i Sirāj 'Afīf, *Tārīkh-i Fīrūz Shāhī* (Calcutta: Baptist Mission Press, 1890), pp. 379–81, and also the discussion in B. N. Goswamy, "In the Sultan's Shadow: Pre-Mughal Painting in and around Delhi," in R. E. Frykenberg, ed., *Delhi Through the Ages* (Delhi: Oxford University Press, 1986), pp. 134–36.
6. Simon Digby, "The Literary Evidence for Painting in the Delhi Sultanate," *Bulletin of the American Academy of Benares*, vol. 1, 1967, p. 58.
7. For a discussion of a Jain narrative theme in conjunction with a larger cultural logic of conquest and romance, see Chapter 6.
8. For more on the Rajputs and their response to the Delhi sultanate, as well as their participation in the larger cultural logics of the day, see Chapter 6.
9. Rukn al-dīn Quddūsī, *Laṭā'if-i Quddūsī* (Delhi: Mujtabā'ī Press, 1894), pp. 99–100. See also Simon Digby, "'Abd al-Quddūs Gangohī (1456–1537 A. D.): The Personality and Attitudes of a Medieval Indian Sufi," *Medieval India: A Miscellany*, vol. 3, 1975, pp. 54–56; and S. M. Pandey, "Maulānā Dāūd and His Contributions to the Hindi Sūfī Literature," *Annali dell'Istituto Orientale di Napoli*, vol. 38, 1978, pp. 87–88.
10. See Chapter 7.
11. See S. A. H. Abidi, ed., *'Ismat Nāmah yā Dāstān-i Lorik va Mainā* (New Delhi: Markaz-i Taḥqīqāt-i Zabān-o Adabiyāt-i Fārsī dar Hind, 1985).
12. M. M. Bakhtin, "The Problem of Speech Genres," in his *Speech Genres and Other Late Essays*, tr. Vern W. McGee (Austin, Texas: University of Texas Press, 1986), p. 91.
13. For examples of Persian *sarāpās*, see Niẓāmī Ganjavī, *Khusrau va Shīrīn*, ed. Behruz Sarvatiyan (Teheran: Tus, 1987), pp. 140–49, Waris Kirmani, ed., *Dreams Forgotten: An Anthology of Indo-Persian Poetry* (Aligarh: Kitab-khana-yi Shiraz, 1986), p. 39, and elsewhere. For *sarāpā*s in Urdu, see Mīr, "Mu'āmalāt-i 'Ishq," in *Kulliyāt-i Mīr* (Lahore: Sang-i Mīl, 1987), especially pp. 921ff; and Jur'at, "Bāl suljhānā terā kanghī se dil uljhā'e hai," in *An Anthology of Classical Urdu Love Lyrics*, edited by D. J. Matthews and Christopher Shackle (London: Oxford University Press, 1972) pp. 75–79. In Hindi, the tradition of Rīti poetry took up the Sanskrit *nakha-śikha varṇana*, which describes the heroine in the opposite direction, "from the tips of her toes to the crest of her head," and so is distinct from the Persian model for the Hindavī *premākhyān*s.
14. See Chapter 2.
15. Edited and translated by Frances Wilson as *The Love of Krishna: The Kṛṣṇakarṇāmṛta of Līlāśuka Bilvamaṅgala* (Philadelphia: University of Pennsylvania Press, 1975).
16. Edited and translated by Barbara Stoler Miller as *Love Song of the Dark Lord: Jayadeva's* Gītagovinda (New York: Columbia University Press, 1977).

17. Lee Siegel, *Sacred and Profane Dimensions of Love in Indian Traditions as Exemplified in the* Gītagovinda *of Jayadeva* (Delhi: Oxford University Press, 1978), p. 21.
18. Līlāśuka, *Kṛṣṇakarṇāmṛta*, I. 4, in Wilson, *The Love of Krishna*, p. 96.
19. For an account of the sources and composition of the *Bhāgavata Purāṇa*, see Friedhelm Hardy, *Viraha-bhakti: The early history of Kṛṣṇa devotion in South India* (Delhi: Oxford University Press, 1983), pp. 483–552. For good general accounts of adaptation of South Indian *bhakti* ideology into the formation of north Indian devotional sects, themselves composed out of numerous regional traditions, see *inter alia* Hardy, *Viraha-bhakti*; and Vasudha Narayanan, *The Way and the Goal: Expressions of Devotion in the Early Śrī Vaiṣṇava Tradition* (Washington, DC, and Cambridge, MA: Institute for Vaishnava Studies and Center for the Study of World Religions, Harvard University, 1987). See also Edward C. Dimock, Jr., *The Place of the Hidden Moon: Erotic Mysticism in the Vaiṣṇava-sahajiyā Cult of Bengal*; Sudhindra Chandra Chakravarti, *Philosophical Foundation of Bengal Vaiṣṇavism*; Richard Barz, *The Bhakti Sect of Vallabhācārya*; Krishna Sharma, *Bhakti and the Bhakti Movement: A Study in the History of Ideas*; and David L. Haberman, *Acting as a Way of Salvation: A Study of Rāgānugā Bhakti Sādhana*.
20. Jayadeva, *Gītagovinda*, I. 46, in Miller, *Love Song of the Dark Lord*, p. 77.
21. Siegel, *Sacred and Profane Dimensions of Love*, p. 69.
22. See, for instance, Edward C. Dimock, Jr., and Denise Levertov, tr., *In Praise of Krishna: Songs from the Bengali* (New York: Anchor Books, 1967).
23. Subhadra Jha, ed. and tr., *Vidyāpati-gīta-saṃgraha or The Songs of Vidyāpati* (Benares: Motilal Banarsidass, 1954), p. 14 (translation emended considerably).
24. Siegel, *Sacred and Profane Dimensions of Love*, p. 45.
25. Edward C. Dimock, Jr., *The Place of the Hidden Moon: Erotic Mysticism in the Vaiṣṇava Sahajiyā Cult of Bengal* (Chicago: University of Chicago Press, 1966), p. 177.
26. Richard Barz, *The Bhakti Sect of Vallabhācārya* (Delhi: Munshiram Manoharlal, 1976), pp. 83–84.
27. See James D. Redington, *Vallabhācārya on the Love Games of Kṛṣṇa* (Delhi: Motilal Banarsidass, 1983).
28. See Charlotte Vaudeville, *A Weaver Named Kabīr* (Delhi: Oxford University Press, 1993), pp. 109–30. I have drawn extensively on Vaudeville in the summary account of Kabīr that follows.
29. Kabīr, Sākhī 10, tr. Vaudeville, *A Weaver Named Kabīr*, pp. 179–80.
30. Kabīr, Ślok 2, tr. Vaudeville, *A Weaver Named Kabīr*, p. 297.
31. See S. W. Fallon, *A New Hindustani-English Dictionary, with Illustrations from Hindustani Literature and Folklore* (Banāras: Medical Hall Press, 1879), pp. 1015–16; and William Crooke, *A Rural and Agricultural Glossary for the North West Provinces and Oudh* (Calcutta: Thacker, Spink, 1888), pp. 104–5.

32. Kabīr, Pad 8, tr. Vaudeville, *A Weaver Named Kabīr*, pp. 274–75.
33. Cited in Lois Anita Giffen, *Theory of Profane Love Among the Arabs: The Development of the Genre* (New York: New York University Press, 1971), p. 85.
34. Ibid., p. 64.
35. Ibid., pp. 19–20.
36. For a more extensive list of topoi, as well as complete references to the Platonic and Aristotelian sources of these ideas, see Joseph Norment Bell, *Love Theory in Later Ḥanbalite Islam* (Albany: State University of New York Press, 1979), pp. 4–5.
37. Annemarie Schimmel, *Mystical Dimensions of Islam*, pp. 137–38.
38. Bell, *Love Theory*, p. 9.
39. See, for instance, Ibn Hazm, *The Ring of the Dove*, tr. A. Arberry (London: Luzac, 1953).
40. See P. K. Agravala, *The Unknown Kamasutras* (Varanasi: Books Asia, 1983).
41. Vātsyāyana, *Kāma-Sutra*, 1.2. 11. *The Kamasutra of Vatsyayana.* A new translation, introduction, and commentary. By Wendy Doniger and Sudhir Kakar. London and New York: Oxford World Classics, 2002.
42. D. H. H. Ingalls, tr., ""Love in Enjoyment," *An Anthology of Sanskrit Court Poetry: Vidyākara's "Subhāṣitaratnakoṣa"* (Cambridge, MA: Harvard University Press, 1965), p. 198.
43. D. H. H. Ingalls, "Love in Enjoyment," p. 199.
44. Bruce B. Lawrence, *Notes from a Distant Flute*, p. 42. On Nakhshabī's translation of the Sanskrit *Śūka-saptati*, the "Seventy Tales of a Parrot."
45. Al-Hujvīrī, *Kashf al-Maḥjūb*, p. 306.
46. See ibid., p. 310.
47. Muḥammad Kirmānī, *Siyar al-Auliyā'* (Delhi: Maṭba' Muḥibb al-Hind, 1885), p. 476.
48. Ibid., p. 463.
49. See Al-Hujvīrī, *Kashf al-Maḥjūb*, pp. 210–11.
50. See Bruce B. Lawrence, *Notes from a Distant Flute: Sufi Literature in Pre-Mughal India* (Tehran: Imperial Iranian Academy of Philosophy, 1978), p. 31.
51. For a full discussion of *samā,'* audition, see Chapter 9.
52. Ḥamīd Qalandar, *Khair al-Majālis*, ed. K. A. Nizami (Aligarh: Department of History, Aligarh Muslim University, 1959), pp. 42–43.
53. Giffen, *Theory of Profane Love*, p. 108.
54. Stansley Insler, "Les dix étapes de l'amour (*daśa kāmāvasthāh*) dans la littérature indienne," *Bulletin d'Études Indiennes*, vol. 6, 1988, p. 311. See also *Nāṭya-Śāstra*, ed. Manmohan Ghosh (Calcutta: Manisha Granthalaya, 1967), XXIV.169–91, and *Kāma-sūtra*, 5.1.4–5.
55. I am indebted to Mujeeb Rizvi for the idea of the fluctuation of the heroine's attributes as mirroring the gentle and terrible divine attributes and Names.

56. Bilgrāmī, Abdul Vāḥid, *Ḥaqā'iq-i Hindī*, Aligarh: Maulana Azad Library; trans. into Hindi by S.A.A. Rizvi (Varanasi: Nagaripracarini Sabha, 1957), p. 39. See also Aligarh ms., Ahsanullah Collection 297.7/11, f. 192. For a detailed account of the transcendent references of the *sarāpā* in the *Cāndāyan*, see especially S. M. Pandey, "*Candāyan* meṉ nakhśikh aur uskā ādhyātmik svarūp," in his *Sūfī Kāvya Vimarśa*, pp. 1–26. In another essay on the *sarāpā*, Pandey convincingly compares Niẓāmī's *sarāpās* to Malik Muḥammad Jāyasī's, to conclude that Jāyasī's text represents an Indianization of the form with much greater emphasis on the transcendent or supernatural referentiality of the heroine's body. See, in the same volume, "Jāyasī aur fārsī kavi Nizāmī kā nakhśikh: ek tulnātmak adhyayan," pp. 88–96, esp. pp. 95–96.
57. More detailed consideration of the *sarāpā* is the focus of Chapter 7 (on the *Madhumālatī* of Mañjhan Shaṭṭari), in which I contrast the poetic description of the female body with the male ascetic body and place it within the context of Sufi cosmology and practices.
58. Bruce B. Lawrence, "The Lawa'ih of Qazi Hamid ud-din Nagauri," *Indo-Iranica*, vol. 20, 1975, p. 38. In view of the reluctance of the early Chishti shaikhs to write books, the survival of this fragment assumes great importance as evidence of the mystical ideology of the *silsilah*.
59. *Bī-'āshiq va 'ishq kār-i ma'shūq habā ast,*
Tā 'āshiq nīst nāz-i ma'shūq kujā ast?
60. Lawrence, "The Lawa'ih of Qazi Hamid ud-din Nagauri," p. 39.
61. Ibid., p. 41.
62. S. M. Pandey, "Love Symbolism in *Candāyan*," in Monika Thiel-Horstmann, ed., *Bhakti in Current Research, 1979–82* (Berlin: Dietrich Reimer, 1983), p. 281.
63. For the Nāth-yogic symbolism of the raising of the sun, see R. S. McGregor, *Hindi Literature from its Beginnings to the Nineteenth Century* (Wiesbaden: Otto Harrassowitz, 1984), p. 28, and Chapter 5.
64. Bilgrāmī, *Ḥaqā'iq-i Hindī*, p. 60. See also Aligarh Ms., Ahsanullah Collection 297.7/11, f. 197.
65. See Premchandra Jain, *Apabhraṃśa Kathākāvya evaṃ Hindī Premākhyānak* (Amritsar: Sohanlal Jaindharm Pracharak Samiti, 1973), pp. 267–343, for an exhaustive list of descriptive topoi and motifs.
66. Premchandra Jain, *Apabhraṃśa Kathākāvya evaṃ Hindī Premākhyānak*, pp. 333ff.
67. Suniti Kumar Chatterji, ed., *Varṇa-Ratnâkara of Jyotirīśvara-Kaviśekharâcārya* (Calcutta: Royal Asiatic Society of Bengal, 1940). See also S. M. Pandey, *Hindi aur Fārsī Sufī Kāvya*, pp. 39–40.
68. Jyotirīśvara-Kaviśekharācārya, *Varṇa-Ratnākara*, p. 2.
69. Verrier Elwin, *Folk-Songs of Chhattisgarh* (Oxford: Oxford University Press, 1946), pp. 338–70.
70. Satyendranath Ghoshal, "Sati Mainā aur Lor-Candrālī," *Vishva Bharati*, 1956, cited in Vishvanath Prasad, "Prastāvanā," *Candāyan* (Agra: Agra University, 1962), p. 23.

71. S. M. Pandey, *The Hindi Oral Epic Loriki: The Tale of Lorik and Canda* (Allahabad: Sahitya Bhawan, 1979), pp. 9–10.
72. S. M. Pandey, "Cāndāyan aur Lorikāyan," in his *Hindī aur Fārsī Sūfī Kāvya,* pp. 31–45.
73. McGregor, *Hindi Literature,* pp. 14–15.
74. Joyce B. Flueckiger, "Caste and Regional Variants in an Oral Epic Tradition," in Stuart H. Blackburn, Peter J. Claus, Joyce B. Flueckiger, and Susan S. Wadley, eds., *Oral Epics in India* (Berkeley: University of California Press, 1989), p. 35.
75. The following brief synopsis is based on S. M. Pandey, *The Hindi Oral Epic Loriki,* pp. 11–15. For other versions of the story, see idem, *The Hindi Oral Epic Tradition: Bhojpurī Lorikī* (Allahabad: Sāhitya Bhavan, 1995) and *The Hindi Oral Epic Canaini* (Allahabad: Sāhitya Bhavan, 1982).
76. Flueckiger, "Caste and Regional Variants in an Oral Epic Tradition," p. 42.
77. Ibid., pp. 47–52.
78. Joyce B. Flueckiger, *Gender and Genre in the Folklore of Middle India* (Ithaca: Cornell University Press, 1996), p. 134.
79. S. A. H. Abidi, ed., *'Iṣmat Nāmah yā Dāstān-i Lorik va Mainā* (New Delhi: Markaz-i Taḥqīqāt-i Zabān-o Adabiyāt-i Fārsī dar Hind, 1985).
80. Ibn Hazm, *The Ring of the Dove,* tr. A. Arberry, p. 197.
81. Bharata, *Nāṭya-Śāstra,* XXIV.169–171. Of course later authors freely adapt these lists to different narrative and poetic purposes; a varied set of representative lists is given in Insler, "Les dix étapes de l'amour," p. 311.
82. For representative lists, see Bell, *Love Theory,* pp. 157–59; and also Mir Valiuddin, *Love in Its Essence: The Sūfi Approach* (Delhi: Indian Institute of Islamic Studies, 1967).
83. For the yogic practice of the Gorakhnathis, see *inter alia* Agehananda Bharati, *The Tantric Tradition;* Hazariprasad Dwivedi, *Nāth Sampradāya* (Allahabad: Lokbhāratī Prakāśan, 1981); George Weston Briggs, *Gorakhnāth and the Kānphaṭa Yogīs* (Delhi: Motilal Banarsidass, 1989); Mircea Eliade, *Yoga: Immortality, and Freedom,* tr. W. R. Trask (Princeton: Princeton University Press, 1969); and David G. White, *The Alchemical Body: Siddha Traditions in Medieval India* (Chicago: University of Chicago Press, 1996).
84. For further details about the competitive interaction between Sufis and yogis, the specific imagery of the Gorakhnāth panth, and its adaptation by the Hindavī Sufi poets, see Chapter 5.
85. Peter Gaeffke, "Alexander in Avadhī and Dakkinī *Mathnawīs,*" *Journal of the American Oriental Society,* vol. 109, 1989, p. 529.
86. Giffen, *Theory of Profane Love,* pp. 102–3.
87. Annemarie Schimmel, *Mystical Dimensions of Islam* (Raleigh: University of North Carolina Press, 1978), p. 143.
88. Muḥammad Kirmānī, *Siyar al-Auliyā',* p. 463.

89. Jyotirīśvara-Kaviśekharācārya, *Varṇa-Ratnākara*, p. 14.
90. But see Lokesh Chandra Nand, *Women in Delhi Sultanate* (Allahabad: Vohra, 1989), for a review of sources in which women are mentioned.
91. Simon Digby, "The *Tuḥfa i naṣā'iḥ* of Yūsuf Gadā: An Ethical Treatise in Verse from the Late-Fourteenth-Century Dehlī Sultanate," p. 110.
92. Ḥamīd Qalandar, *Khair al-Majālis*, p. 61 *et passim.*
93. Ibid., p. 90.
94. Simon Digby, "The Sufi Shaikh as a Source of Authority in Mediaeval India," *Puruṣārtha* 9, 1986, p. 67.
95. See Aziz Ahmad, "The Sufi and the Sultan in Pre-Mughal Muslim India," *Der Islam*, vol. 38, 1963, pp. 142–53.
96. Niẓām al-dīn Aḥmad, *Ṭabaqāt-i Akbarī*, ed. Brajendranath De (Calcutta: Asiatic Society of Bengal, 1913), vol. I, p. 62, and trans. Brajendranath De (Delhi: Low Price, 1992 [1911]), vol. I, p. 70.
97. Niẓām al-dīn Aḥmad, *Ṭabaqāt-i Akbarī*, p. 62, and trans. Brajendranath De, p. 71. For further stories of Sufis as kingmakers, as well as a detailed analysis, see Simon Digby, "The Sufi Shaikh and the Sultan: A Conflict of Claims to Authority."
98. Bilgrāmī, *Ḥaqā'iq-i Hindī*, p. 60. See also Aligarh Ms., Ahsanullah Collection 297.7/11, f. 197.
99. It is significant that Cāndā is stung by a snake only once in the versions of the tale collected by S. M. Pandey. Further research into the recensions of Dā'ūd's text is required to see if the second episode is superfluous here.
100. Jyotirīśvara-Kaviśekharācārya, *Varṇa-Ratnākara*, pp. 18–20.
101. For the significance of the various houses and planets, as well as interpreting and predicting the future from them, see Gopesh Kumar Ojha, *Hindu Predictive Astrology* (Bombay: D. B. Taraporevala Sons, 1972).
102. For the evil aspect or *dṛṣṭi* of Mars as well as other planets and their effects in the houses of the horoscope, see P. V. Kane, *History of Dharmaśāstra* (Poona: Bhandarkar Oriental Research Institute, 1930–1962), vol. V, pt. 1, p. 589ff.
103. M. P. Gupta, "Introduction," *Cāndāyan*, p. 32.

CHAPTER 4

1. For a full discussion of the context of the *Mirigāvatī*, as well as a complete translation, see *The Magic Doe: Shaikh Quṯban Suhravardī's* Mirigāvatī. *A New Translation by Aditya Behl*, ed. Wendy Doniger. New York: Oxford University Press, 2011.
2. Northrop Frye has noted that these structuring principles are widespread in romance genres all over the world. See his *The Secular Scripture: A Study of the Structure of Romance* (Cambridge, MA: Harvard University Press, 1976).

3. R. S. McGregor, *Hindi Literature from its Beginnings to the Nineteenth Century* (Series: A History of Indian Literature, vol. 8 (Wiesbaden: Otto Harrassowitz, 1984), p. 66.
4. For more on this theme, see Umapati Rai Chandel, *Hindī Sūfī Kāvya meṉ Paurāṇik Ākhyān* (Delhi: Abhinav Prakāśan, 1976), an exhaustive listing and tracing out of all the epic and puranic references in the Hindavī Sufi romances.
5. See Stith Thompson, *Motif-Index of Folk-Literature: A Classification of Narrative Elements in Folktales, Ballads, Myths, Fables, Mediaeval Romances, Exempla, Fabliaux, Jest-Books, and Local Legends* (Copenhagen: Rosenkilde and Bagger, 1956), vol. II, p. 34, motif D361.1.
6. See Stith Thompson and Jonas Balys, *The Oral Tales of India* (Bloomington: Indiana University Press, 1958), p. 325, motif K 1335. For an example of the use of the motif of the magic sari to ensnare a heavenly nymph, see the Kannada folk-tale "Adventures of a Disobedient Son," in A. K. Ramanujan, *Folktales from India* (New Delhi: Viking Penguin, 1991), pp. 274–85.
7. Vladimir Propp, *Morphology of the Folktale*, tr. Laurence Scott et al. (Austin: University of Texas Press, 1968), pp. 114–15.
8. For Bluebeard, see Charles Perrault, "La Barbe Bleue," in Andrew Lang, ed., *Perrault's Popular Tales* (Oxford: Clarendon Press, 1888), pp. 23–29. For extensive parallels in European folklore, see Lang's introduction to the collection, pp. lx–lxiv. For the literary origin of the European Bluebeard in Charles Perrault's tale, see "Bluebeard," in D. A. Leeming and M. Sader, eds., *Storytelling Encyclopedia: Historical, Cultural, and Multiethnic Approaches to Oral Traditions Around the World* (Phoenix, Arizona: Oryx Press, 1997), pp. 81–82.
9. McGregor, *Hindi Literature*, p. 66.
10. See Farīd ud-dīn 'Attār, *The Conference of the Birds*, trans. Afkham Darbandi and Dick Davis (Harmondsworth: Penguin Books, 1984); and James Winston Morris, "Reading *The Conference of the Birds*," in *Approaches to the Asian Classics*, ed. Wm. Theodore de Bary and Irene Bloom (New York: Columbia University Press, 1990), pp. 77–85.
11. See Homer, *The Odyssey*, ed. W. B. Stanford (London: St. Martin's Press, 1959), IX.105–566, vol. I, pp. 134–48.
12. See Roy P. Mottahedeh, "*'Ajā'ib* in *The Thousand and One Nights*," in Richard G. Hovannisian and Georges Sabagh, eds., The Thousand and One Nights *in Arabic Literature and Society* (Cambridge: Cambridge University Press, 1997), pp. 30–32, for a discussion of the role of astonishment in creating narrative suspense in the frame-story of the *Arabian Nights*.
13. I am grateful to Simon Digby for first pointing out Indian genealogy of some of the motifs of the Sindbād cycle, and for his subsequent willingness to discuss the finer points of narrative transmission with me.

14. Husain Haddawy, tr., *The Arabian Nights II: Sindbad and Other Popular Stories* (New York: Norton, 1995), pp. 18–19.
15. Mia I. Gerhardt, *The Art of Story-Telling: A Literary Study of the Thousand and One Nights* (Leiden: Brill, 1963), pp. 236–63.
16. Ferial J. Ghazoul, *Nocturnal Poetics:* The Arabian Nights *in Comparative Context* (Cairo: American University in Cairo Press, 1996), pp. 68–81, esp. pp. 77ff.
17. Peter D. Molan, "Sinbad the Sailor: A Commentary on the Ethics of Violence," *Journal of the American Oriental Society*, vol. 98, no. 3, pp. 237–47.
18. Haddawy, tr., *The Arabian Nights II*, p. 19.
19. Elliot Colla, "The Popular Imagination of Sindbad: Towards a Historical Understanding of the Variant Texts of *Alf Laylah wa Laylah*," unpublished ms., pp. 20–21. Colla notes that the words *ta'ajjub* and *tavakkul* recur frequently in the text and perceptively contextualizes his analysis of the variant endings of the Sindbād cycle within Abbasid and Mamluk mercantile cultures. I am grateful to him for sharing his unpublished work with me.
20. Haddawy, tr., *The Arabian Nights II*, pp. 19–20.
21. Muhsin Mahdi, "Exemplary Tales in the *1001 Nights*," in *The 1001 Nights: Critical Essays and Annotated Bibliography, Mundus Arabicus*, vol. 3, 1983, pp. 1–24. Mahdi is a little too severe in his judgment that "most of the secondary literature makes use of one unknown source to prove the existence of another unknown source; speaks of Indian sources and prototypes of which we find only meager and scattered fragments today, and suggests that they were transmitted through many centuries and countries ... all this belongs to the history of mythology and is itself quasi-mythological in character" (p. 4). As I hope to show through the rest of this chapter, the sources are not necessarily fragmentary or meager, and each context of narration encodes within it significant historical and ideological processes.
22. Husain Haddawy, "Introduction," *The Arabian Nights* (New York: Norton, 1990), pp. xii–xiii.
23. Buzurg bin Shahryar, *The Book of the Wonders of India: Mainland, Sea and Islands*, ed. and trans. G. S. P. Freeman-Grenville (London and the Hague: East-West, 1981), pp. 106–7. A *ratl* is approximately equal to half a pound.
24. Ibid., p. 108.
25. Ibid., pp. 109–10.
26. Muhsin Jassim Ali, *Scheherazade in England: A Study of Nineteenth-Century English Criticism of the* Arabian Nights (Washington, DC: Three Continents Press, 1981), pp. 19–20.
27. G. E. von Grunebaum, *Medieval Islam: A Study in Cultural Orientation* (Chicago: University of Chicago Press, 1946), p. 298.
28. Robert Irwin, *The Arabian Nights: A Companion* (London: Penguin Books, 1994), p. 71.

29. For the enormously complicated history of the manuscripts, editions, and translations of the *Arabian Nights*, see Duncan Black Macdonald, "The Earlier History of the Arabian Nights," *Journal of the Royal Asiatic Society*, 1924, pp. 353–97; E. Littman, "Alf Layla wa-Layla," *Encyclopaedia of Islam (New Edition)*, vol. I, pp. 358–64; as well as Robert Irwin, *The Arabian Nights: A Companion*, pp. 14–62. The following account is mostly drawn from these works, to which the reader may refer for more detailed coverage, and my differences from them are noted in the text.
30. Al-Mas'ūdī, *Les Prairies d'or*, ed. and trans. C. Barbier de Meynard (Paris, 1861–1877), vol. IV, pp. 89–90, cited and translated in Robert Irwin, *The Arabian Nights: A Companion*, p. 49.
31. Bayard Dodge, ed. and tr., *The Fihrist of al-Nadīm: A Tenth-century Survey of Muslim Culture* (New York: Columbia University Press, 1970), vol. II, pp. 713–14.
32. W. A. Clouston, *Popular Tales and Fictions: Their Migrations and Transformations* (Edinburgh: William Blackwood and Sons, 1887), vol. I, p. 9, n. 1.
33. See B. E. Perry, "The Origin of the Book of Sindbad," *Fabula*, Band 3, Heft 1/2, 1959, pp. 1–94; and Stephen Belcher, "The Diffusion of the Book of Sindbād," *Fabula*, Band 28, Heft 1/2, 1987, pp. 34–58.
34. See Josef Horovitz, "The Origins of 'The Arabian Nights,'" *Islamic Culture*, vol. 1, 1927, pp. 36–57.
35. See B. E. Perry, "The Origin of the Book of Sindbad," p. 5, n. 7. For a treatment of translation into Arabic, see Ulrich Marzolph, *Arabia Ridens: Die humoristische Kurzprosa der frühen adab-Literatur im internationalen Traditionsgeflecht* (Frankfurt am Main: Vittorio Klostermann, 1992), 3 vols.
36. Dodge, *The Fihrist of al-Nadīm*, vol. II, p. 715. For the Arabic passage, see Muḥammad Ibn Isḥāq al-Nadīm, *Fihrist*, ed. Yusuf Ali Tawil (Beirut: Dār al-Kutb al-'Ilmiya, 1996), p. 476.
37. On the textual history of the *Bṛhat-kathā* and its transmission, see M. Winternitz, *History of Indian Literature*, tr. with additions by Subhadra Jha (Delhi: Motilal Banarsidass, 1963), vol. III, part 1, pp. 346–70.
38. The discoverer and first critical editor of the Nepali manuscript, Félix Lacote, places the date of composition sometime between the eighth and ninth centuries, while later commentators have placed it variously in the "fifth or sixth century A. D." (Moti Chandra) and "the Gupta age" (U. N. Roy). See F. Lacote, *Essai sur Guṇāḍhya et la Bṛhatkathā* (Paris: Ernest Leroux, 1908), pp. 146–49; Moti Chandra, *Trade and Trade Routes in Ancient India* (New Delhi: Abhinav, 1977), p. 129; and U. N. Roy, "The Bṛhatkathā-Śloka-Samgraha on Maritime activities in the Gupta Age," in M. Rao, S. Pande, and B. N. Misra, *India's Cultural Relations with South-East Asia* (Delhi: Sharada Publishing House, 1996), p. 59.
39. See Moti Chandra, *Trade and Trade Routes in Ancient India*; E. H. Warmington, *The Commerce Between the Roman Empire and India* (Cambridge: Cambridge

University Press, 1928); J. C. van Leur, *Indonesian Trade and Society: Essays in Asian Social and Economic History*, tr. J. S. Holme and A. van Marle (The Hague and Bandung: W. van Hoeve Ltd., 1955); and Janet Abu-Lughod, *Before European Hegemony*, pp. 261–90. For materials and modes of travel and transport, see Radha Kumud Mookerji, *A History of Indian Shipping* (Allahabad: Kitab Mahal, 1962); and now Jean Deloche, *Transport and Communications in India Prior to Steam Locomotion*, tr. James Walker (Delhi: Oxford University Press, 1994), particularly vol. II, "Water Transport."

40. The classic study of this phenomenon is G. Coedes, *The Indianized States of Southeast Asia*, ed. W. F. Vella and tr. S. B. Cowing (Honolulu: East-West Center Press, 1968). For bibliographic references as well as a somewhat skeptical review of the extensive literature on the Indianization of Southeast Asia, see Janet Abu-Lughod, *Before European Hegemony*, pp. 299–302. For a narrative account, see D. G. E. Hall, *A History of South-east Asia* (London: Macmillan, 1968), pp. 3–227.
41. Pāṇini, *Gaṇapāṭha* V.3.100, cited in Moti Chandra, *Trade and Trade Routes in Ancient India*, p. 53.
42. Budhasvāmin, *Bṛhat-kathā Çlokasamgraha*, ed. F. Lacote (Paris: Ernest Leroux, 1908), book 18, verses 486–95, trans. J. A. B. van Buitenen, *Tales of Ancient India* (Chicago: University of Chicago Press, 1959), p. 246.
43. Budhasvāmin, *Bṛhat-kathā Çlokasamgraha*, book 18, verses 499–510, trans. J. A. B. van Buitenen, *Tales of Ancient India*, p. 247.
44. For the voyages of Cārudatta, see Moti Chandra, *Trade and Trade Routes in Ancient India*, pp. 130–31. For a discussion of the ideological significance of the *Vāsudeva-hiṇḍī*, see Jagdish Chandra Jain, *Prākrit Sāhitya kā Itihāsa*, pp. 381–93.
45. Sylvain Lévi, "Maṇimekhalā, a Divinity of the Sea," *Indian Historical Quarterly*, vol. 6, no. 4, 1930, p. 608.
46. See Paula Richman, *Women, Branch Stories, and Religious Rhetoric in a Tamil Buddhist Text* (Syracuse, NY: Maxwell School of Citizenship and Public Affairs, Syracuse University, 1988), for a careful and critical study of the text.
47. Shattan, *Manimekhala (The Dancer with the Magic Bowl)*, tr. Alain Daniélou with T. V. Gopala Iyer (New York: New Directions Books, 1989), pp. 64–65. See also the more restrained and literal translation in Paula Richman, *Women, Branch Stories, and Religious Rhetoric in a Tamil Buddhist Text*, pp. 39–42.
48. Shattan, *Manimekhala*, p. 65.
49. I have preferred to cite Paula Richman's translation of the final speech of the chief, since it brings out more clearly his recognition of the appropriateness of the goods he offers to Sāduvan's world of trade and exchange. See her *Women, Branch Stories, and Religious Rhetoric in a Tamil Buddhist Text*, p. 42.
50. For a more detailed commentary on the story of Sāduvan, see Richman, *Women, Branch Stories, and Religious Rhetoric in a Tamil Buddhist Text*,

pp. 42–52. Richman's work also remains the most detailed and insightful consideration of the rhetorical pattern and message of the entire *Maṇimekhalai.*

51. E. B. Cowell, ed., *The Jātaka or Stories of the Buddha's Former Births,* tr. W. H. D. Rouse (Cambridge: Cambridge University Press, 1895), vol. 2, p. 90. For the Pali text, see V. Fausboll, ed., *The Jātaka Together with Its Commentary Being Tales of the Anterior Births of Gotama Buddha,* vol. 2 (London: Trubner, 1879), pp. 127–30. I have amended the translation only to change the rendition of *yakkhinī* from "goblin" into "she-devil."

52. See R. H. Major, "Introduction," *India in the Fifteenth Century. Being a Collection of Narratives of Voyages to India, in the Century Preceding the Portuguese Discovery of the Cape of Good Hope; from Latin, Persian, Russian, and Italian Sources, Now First Translated into English* (London: Hakluyt Society, 1857), pp. xxxi–xlv.

CHAPTER 5

1. Henri Lefebvre, *The Production of Space,* tr. D. Nicholson-Smith (Oxford: Blackwell Publishers, 1991), p. 15.
2. Ibid., pp. 33–46 *et passim.*
3. Ibid., p. 17.
4. Jonathan Z. Smith, "Map Is Not Territory," in idem, *Map Is Not Territory: Studies in the History of Religions* (Chicago: University of Chicago Press, 1993), pp. 292–93.
5. James S. Duncan, *The City as Text: The Politics of Landscape Interpretation in the Kandyan Kingdom* (Cambridge: Cambridge University Press, 1990), p. 22.
6. Ali al-Hujviri, *Kashf al-Mahjūb,* trans. Reynold A. Nicholson (1911; reprint, Lahore: Islamic Book Foundation, 1976), pp. 210–13.
7. Simon Digby, "The Sufi Shaikh as Source of Authority in Mediaeval India," in *Islam et Société en Asie du Sud: Collection Puruṣārtha 9,* ed. Marc Gaborieau (Paris: École des Hautes Études en Sciences Sociales, 1986), p. 63.
8. Abdul Ḥaqq, *Akhbār ul-Akhyār* (Delhi: Mujtabā'ī Press, 1891), p. 153, my translation.
9. Thomas de Bruijn, *The Ruby Hidden in the Dust: A Study of the Poetics of Malik Muḥammad Jāyasī's* Padmāvat (Leiden: Rijksuniversitaet Proefschrift, 1996), p. 131.
10. For a detailed discussion of this system, see Ānandavardhana's *Dhvanyāloka,* K 3.10, and the references cited in Chapter 2.
11. A. G. Shirreff, "Introduction," *Padmavati of Malik Muhammad Jaisi,* Series: Bibliotheca Indica, Work No. 267 (Calcutta: Royal Asiatic Society of Bengal, 1944), p. ix.
12. For the notion of love poetry expressing an "interior landscape," I am indebted to the work of A. K. Ramanujan on South Indian poetry. See his *The Interior*

Landscape: Love Poems from a Classical Tamil Anthology (Bloomington and London: Indiana University Press, 1967), pp. 97–115.

13. See John Millis, *Malik Muhammad Jāyasī: Allegory and Religious Symbolism in his* Padmāvat (unpublished Ph. D. dissertation, University of Chicago, 1984), pp. 32–39, for a review of the controversy. On Sayyid Ashraf Jahāngīr Simnānī, see M. M. Saeed, *The Sharqi Sultanate of Jaunpur: A Political and Cultural History* (Karachi: University of Karachi, 1972), pp. 241–45.
14. The full Chishti genealogy descending from Shaikh Niẓām al-dīn Auliyā' is given in Shirreff, *Padmavati*, pp. 16–17, note 54. The last Shaikh mentioned by Shirreff, Shaikh Muḥyī al-dīn, on the basis of Grierson and Shukla's readings of verse 20, was not actually Malik Muḥammad's preceptor, as Millis has made clear in his rereading of the text. See the discussion below, as well as Millis, *Malik Muhammad Jāyasī*, p. 36.
15. Shirreff, "Introduction," *Padmavati*, p. vi.
16. Simon Digby, "Sufis and Jogis" (unpublished manuscript, n. d.), pp. 92–93. I am indebted to Digby for sharing his unpublished work with me.
17. Ibid., p. 96.
18. *Guru mahadī khevaka main sevā/ calai utāila jinha kar khevā// aguvā bhayeu sekha burhānu/ panth lāi jehiṃ dīnha giyānu//*. For the correct text, see V. S. Agraval, *Padmāvat: Malik Muhammad Jāyasī kṛta Mahākāvya (mūla aur sanjīvinī vyākhyā)* (Chirganv, Jhansi: Sāhitya Sadan, 1956), verse 20, line 1. On the Mahdavis, see Saeed, *The Sharqi Sultanate of Jaunpur*, pp. 284–92.
19. Millis, *Malik Muhammad Jāyasī*, pp. 38–39. See also 'Abd al-Qādir Badāyūnī, *Muntakhab ut-'Tawārīkh*, ed. Maulavi Ahmad Ali (Calcutta: College Press, 1869), vol. III, pp. 6–7; and Abu-l Faẓl 'Allāmī, *Ā'īn-i Akbarī*, trans. H. Blochmann and H. S. Jarrett (1927–1949; reprint, Delhi: Low Price, 1989), vol. I, p. 539. On Shaikh Burhān's verses, see S. H. Askari, "A Newly Discovered Volume of Awadhi Works Including Padmāwat and Akhrāwat of Malik Muhammad Jāisī," *Journal of the Bihar Research Society*, vol. 39, 1953, pp. 35–36.
20. 'Abd al-Qādir Badāyūnī, *Muntakhab ut-Tawārīkh*, vol. III, p. 7.
21. Peter Brown, *Authority and the Sacred: Aspects of the Christianisation of the Roman World* (Cambridge: Cambridge University Press, 1997, Canto Edition), pp. 3–4.
22. See Simon Digby, "Hawk and Dove in Sufi Combat," in Charles Melville, ed., *Pembroke Papers 1: Papers in Honour of Peter W. Avery*, 1990, pp. 7–25.
23. I. A. Zilli, "Successors of Shaikh Nasiruddin Mahmud and the Disintegration of the Chishti Central Organization," *Indian History Congress* 44, 1984, pp. 324–25.
24. For a concise history, see S. A. A. Rizvi, *A History of Sufism in India* (Delhi: Munshiram Manoharlal, 1983), vols. I–II.
25. Digby, "Sufis and Jogis," p. 94.

26. *śūfī nihād dām va sar-i ḥuqqah bāz kard/ buniyād-i makr bā falak-i ḥuqqah-bāz kard// ai kabk-i khush-khirām kih khush mīravī ba-nāz/ ghurrah mashau kih gurbah-yi zāhid namāz kard.* See Ḥāfiẓ, *Dīvān*, ed. Qazvini Ghani.
27. Digby, "Sufis and Jogis," pp. 94–95.
28. See Richard M. Eaton, "Approaches to the Study of Conversion to Islam in India," in Richard C. Martin, *Approaches to Islam in Religious Studies* (Tucson: University of Arizona Press, 1985), pp. 106–23.
29. Digby, "Sufis and Jogis," p. 95.
30. On the Islamic notion of paradise as a garden, see the essays in Richard Ettinghausen, ed., *The Islamic Garden* (Washington, DC: Trustees for Harvard University, Dumbarton Oaks, 1976); as well as Elizabeth B. Moynihan, *Paradise as a Garden in Persia and Mughal India* (New York: George Braziller, 1979). On artistic and architectural representations of the celestial garden, see Sheila S. Blair and Jonathan M. Bloom, eds., *Images of Paradise in Islamic Art* (Hanover, NH: Hood Museum of Art, Dartmouth College, 1991). On allegorical gardens in Persian poetry, see Julie Scott Meisami, "Allegorical Gardens in the Persian Poetic Tradition: Nezami, Rumi, Hafez," *International Journal of Middle Eastern Studies*, vol. 17, 1985, 229–60.
31. *jabahi dīpa niyarāvā jāī/ janu kabilāsa niyara bhā āī.*
32. Abū 'l-Majd ajdūd Sanā'ī, Dīvān, ed. M. Razavi (Teheran, 1962), pp. 30–35. On Sanā'ī in general, see J. T. P. de Bruijn, *Of Poetry and Piety: The Interaction of Religion and Literature in the Works of Ḥakīm Sanā'ī of Ghazna* (Leiden: Brill, 1983).
33. Annemarie Schimmel, "The Celestial Garden," in *The Islamic Garden*, ed. Richard Ettinghausen (Washington, DC: Trustees for Harvard University, Dumbarton Oaks, 1976), p. 23.
34. This refers to the *māsa-vāsīs*, ascetics who wander everywhere and stop for just a month in each place. For further details on the various sects of ascetics, see Shirreff's footnote to this verse, *Padmavati*, p. 25, note 33.
35. See M. Shahidullah, *Les Chants Mystiques de Kānhipā*; and Nilratan Sen, *Cāryagītīkośa* (Simla: Indian Institute of Advanced Study, 1977).
36. David Gordon White, *The Alchemical Body: Siddha Traditions in Medieval India* (Chicago: University of Chicago Press, 1996), p. 57.
37. Sen, ed., *Cāryagītikośa*, p. 132, translation slightly emended.
38. P. D. Barthwal, ed., *Gorakhbānī* (Prayāg: Hindī Sāhitya Sammelan, 1979), pp. 120–21, translation mine.
39. A kāpālī ascetic is one who carries a human skull. For more detailed readings of yogic symbolism in the *Padmāvat*, see Millis, *Malik Muhammad Jāyasī*, pp. 168–82. Millis takes the view that this yogic symbolism shows the "influence" of the Nāth panth on Jāyasī; rather, I argue that Jāyasī takes certain elements from the Nāth panth, as well as from other sources, and

that this "syncretism" is to be explained not simply by its resolution into constituent parts but by its workings and narrative logic.

40. Barthwal, ed., *Gorakhbānī*, p. 120.
41. Millis, *Malik Muhammad Jāyasī*, p. 181.
42. Not entirely coincidentally, the *Amṛta-kuṇḍa* is also the title of a Sanskrit work on Tantric yoga, which the Shattari Shaikh Muḥammad Ġhauṣ Gvāliyarī translated into Persian as the *Baḥr al-Ḥayāt*. The work is being translated into English by Carl Ernst as *The Pool of Nectar: Muslim Interpreters of Yoga*. The text was widely known among the *silsilahs*, as the numerous manuscript copies that are found in shrine libraries attest.
43. Charlotte Vaudeville, *A Weaver Named Kabīr* (Delhi: Oxford University Press, 1993), p. 116.
44. White, *The Alchemical Body*, p. 41.
45. Barthwal, ed., *Gorakhbānī*, pp. 120–21.
46. Malik Muḥammad Jāyasī, *Padmāvat* (Rampur Raza Library Hindi ms. 1), f. 12. A threefold classification of lords of horses (*aśvapati*), men (*narapati*), and elephants (*gajapati*) appears in numerous Sanskrit and new Indo-Aryan texts from the sultanate period. Cynthia Talbot has interpreted the image as a tripartite geographical scheme referring to the kings of Orissa (known as the lords of elephants), the northwestern Muslim dynasties who controlled the best horses in the subcontinent (lords of cavalry), and the southern kingdoms such as Vijayanagara (lords of infantry). Jāyasī adds *gaṟhapati*, lords of forts, to the scheme. The title could refer to the massive forts built by many of the Turkish and Afghan Sultans to garrison the provinces controlled from Delhi and the regional centers. See Cynthia Talbot, "Inscribing the Self, Inscribing the Other: Hindu-Muslim Identities in Pre-colonial India," *Comparative Studies in Society and History*, vol. 37, no. 4, 1995, pp. 708–10.
47. Schimmel, "The Celestial Garden," p. 18.
48. Ibid., p. 16.
49. See Chapter 2.
50. See Chapter 3.
51. The Sanskrit text runs: *bhavati kamalanetrā nāsikākṣudrarandhrā aviralakucayugmā cārukeśī kṛśāṅgī/ mṛduvacanasuśīlā gītavādyānuraktā sakalatanusuveśā padminī padmagandhā*. Cited in V. S. Apte, *The Practical Sanskrit-English Dictionary* (Kyoto: Rinsen Book Company, 1986), 962.
52. Thomas de Bruijn, *The Ruby Hidden in the Dust*, p. 191.
53. See D. C. Sircar, *Cosmography and Geography in Early Indian Literature, Sir William Meyer Endowment Lectures in History 1965–66, University of Madras* (Calcutta: Indian Studies Past and Present, 1967), pp. 47–51.
54. More recent researches suggest that *jambu* may not mean rose-apple after all, but perhaps plum-tree or jackfruit.

55. David Cashin, *The Ocean of Love: Middle Bengali Sufi Literature and the Fakirs of Bengal* (Stockholm: Association of Oriental Studies, 1995), p. 194.
56. Ibid., p. 195.
57. Ibid., p. 195.
58. See White, *The Alchemical Body*, p. 486, n. 200, for references to the "curved duct" in yogic texts. White notes that the term also has an alchemical application: it is "a curved tube which, tapered at one end, is used as a blowpipe for ventilating a flame."
59. See Chapters 3 and 8.
60. This verse is omitted in the editions of Mataprasad Gupta and V. S. Agraval, but it does appear in the 1675 Rampur manuscript (f. 107) as well as in Ramchandra Shukla, ed., *Jāyasī Granthāvalī*, p. 167. I include it against the judgment of the two later editors because it indicates how a Sufi reading community would have interpreted the events of the narrative.

CHAPTER 6

1. See Muhammad Habib, tr., "The Campaigns of 'Alauddin Khalji," in his *Politics and Society During the Early Medieval Period*, ed. K. A. Nizami (Delhi: People's Publishing House, 1981), vol. II, pp. 188–90.
2. M. Habib and K. A. Nizami, *A Comprehensive History of India, Vol. V: The Delhi Sultanat (A.D. 1206–1526)*, p. 370.
3. James Tod, *Annals and Antiquities of Rajasthan* (New Delhi: Oriental Books Reprint, 1983 [1829–1832]), vol. I, pp. 212–16.
4. For a detailed treatment of the later reception of the Padmāvatī story in Rajasthani and Bengali, see Ramya Sreenivasan's doctoral dissertation at Jawaharlal Nehru University, "Gender, Literature, History: The Transformation of the Padmini Story." I am grateful to Ramya Sreenivasan for sharing her unpublished work with me. [Editor's note: for Ramya Sreenivasan's later published work, see her book, *The Many Lives of a Rajput Queen: Heroic Pasts in Indian History c. 1500–1900*, Permanent Black (New Delhi) and University of Washington Press, 2007; and her relevant articles, "Alauddin Khalji Remembered: Conquest and Gender in Medieval Rajput Narratives," *Studies in History*, 2002, special issue on Gender in History, ed. Kumkum Roy and Tanika Sarkar; and "Genre, Politics, History: Urdu Traditions of Padmini," in Kathryn Hansen and David Lelyveld, eds., *A Wilderness of Possibilities: Urdu Studies in Transnational Perspective*, Oxford University Press, 2005.]
5. Ramya Sreenivasan, "Gender, Literature, History: The Transformation of the Padmini Story," p. 6.
6. Aziz Ahmad, "Epic and Counter-Epic in Medieval India," *Journal of the American Oriental Society*, vol. 83, no. 4, 1963, p. 470.

7. R. S. McGregor, *Hindi Literature from Its Beginnings to the Nineteenth Century* (Wiesbaden: Otto Harrassowitz, 1984), pp. 68–69. On the versions of the poem, see Narottamdas Swami, *Rāso-sāhitya aur Pṛthvīrāja-Rāso* (Bikaner: Bhāratīya Vidyāmandir Śodh Pratiṣṭhān, 1963), pp. 53–81. For an analysis of the basic story of the *Rāsau*, see Frances W. Pritchett, "Prithviraj Raso: A Look at the Poem Itself," *Indian Literature*, vol. 23, no. 5, 1980, pp. 56–75. For the text of the *Padmāvatī Samaya*, see M. V. Pandya and Shyamsundar Das, eds., *Pṛthvīrājarāso* (Benares: Nāgarīpracāriṇī Sabhā, 1993), vol. 1, pp. 575–83.
8. See Muhtā Naiṇsī, *Muhtā Naiṇsī rī Khyāt*, ed. B. Sakariya (Jodhpur: Rajasthan Oriental Research Institute, 1960), 4 vols.
9. The term *Rajput* is a retrospective invention, as most of the martial literature of resistance to Turkish conquest dates only from the mid-fifteenth century onward. As Dirk Kolff has noted in his *Naukar, Rajput and Sepoy: The Ethnohistory of the Military Labour Market in Hindustan, 1450–1850* (Cambridge: Cambridge University Press, 1990), the invention of "Rajput" identity can be dated to the sixteenth-century narratives of nostalgia for lost honor and territory. On the retrospective invention of the Rajput identity in the early period, see also B. D. Chattopadhyaya, "Origin of the Rajputs," in his *The Making of Early Medieval India* (Delhi: Oxford University Press, 1994).
10. See Chapter 5.
11. W. Norman Brown, *The Story of Kālaka: Texts, History, Legends, and Miniature Paintings of the Śvetāmbara Jain Hagiographical Work the* Kālakācāryakathā (Washington, DC: Freer Gallery of Art, Oriental Studies No. 1, 1933), p. 3.
12. P. H. L. Eggermont, "The Purāṇa Source of Merutuṅga's List of Kings and the Arrival of Śakas in India," in A. L. Basham, ed., *Papers of the Date of Kaniṣka* (Leiden: E. J. Brill, 1961), pp. 67–86.
13. Brown, *The Story of Kālaka*, p. 1.
14. See H. Jacobi, ed. and tr., *The Kalpasūtra of Bhadrabāhu* (Leipzig: F. A. Brockhaus, Abhandlungen für die Kunde des Morgenlandes, 1879).
15. Brown, *The Story of Kālaka*, p. 3.
16. The following brief summary is based on Brown, *The Life and Works of Amīr Khusrau* q. v.
17. Ibid., p. 58.
18. Ibid., p. 59.
19. Ẕiyā-ud-dīn Baranī, *Tārīḵh-i Firūz Shāhī*, pp. 259–83. Translated in Elliot Dowson, *The History of India as Told by Its Own Historians, III* (Delhi: Low Price, 1990 [1867–1877]), pp. 162–79. A brief summary of these invasions is also given in Muhammad Wahid Mirza, *The Life and Works of Amir Khusrau*, pp. 89–94. For a treatment of Baranī's vision of history, so different from the panegyrics of Amīr Khusrau, see Peter Hardy, *Historians of Medieval India: Studies in Indo-Muslim Historical Writing* (London: Luzac, 1960), pp. 20–39.
20. On warfare in the period, see Simon Digby, *Warhorse and Elephant in the Dehlī Sultanate* (London: Orient Monographs, 1971).

21. Amīr Khusrau, *Khazā'in al-Futūḥ*, translated by Muḥammad Habīb as *The Campaigns of 'Alā'u'd-dīn Khiljī, being the Khazā'inul Futūḥ (Treasures of Victory) of Hazrat Amīr Khusrau of Delhi* (Madras: D. B. Taraporevala, Sons, 1931).
22. These include his *Miftāḥ al-futūḥ* ("The Key to Conquests"), his *Khazā'in al-futūḥ* ("The Treasures of Victories"), and his *Deval Rānī Khiẓr Khan* ("Deval Rānī and Khiẓr Khān"). For a brief account, see Muhammad Wahid Mirza, *The Life and Works of Amīr Khusrau*, pp. 176–81.
23. Nayacandra Suri, *Hammīra-mahākāvya*, ed. Fateh Singh (Jodhpur: Rājasthān Oriental Research Institute, 1968). For another version of the story, in Hindi rather than Sanskrit, see Jodhrāj Kavi, *Hammīr-rāso*, ed. Shyamsundar Das (Varanasi: Nāgarīprachāriṇī Sabhā, 1950).
24. For a summary of the story, see also Muhammad Wahid Mirza, *The Life and Works of Amir Khusrau*, pp. 177–81. For a detailed summary and extensive comparisons to the historian Firishta's account of these events, see Mohammad Habib, *Hazrat Amir Khusrau of Delhi* (Lahore: Islamic Book Service, 1979 [1927]), pp. 56–66.
25. For examples of such imagery in Persian poetry, see Annemarie Schimmel, *A Two-Colored Brocade* (Chapel Hill: University of North Carolina Press, 1992), pp. 138–43.
26. Mohammad Habib, *Hazrat Amir Khusrau of Delhi*, pp. 64–65.
27. Kanwar Muhammad Ashraf, *Life and Conditions of the People of Hindustan* (Delhi: Munshiram Manoharlal, 1969 [1928]), pp. 54–55.
28. For a scholarly study of the *Kānhaḍade Prabandha* as a chivalric romance, see I. M. P. Raeside, "A Gujarati Bardic Poem: The Kānhaḍade-Prabandha," in C. Shackle and R. Snell, *The Indian Narrative: Perspectives and Patterns* (Wiesbaden: Otto Harrassowitz, 1992), pp. 137–53.
29. Padmanābha, *Kānhaḍade Prabandha*, edited by K. B. Vyas (Jaipur: Rajasthan Oriental Research Institute, 1953), and translated by V. S. Bhatnagar as *Kānhaḍade Prabandha (India's Greatest Patriotic Saga of Medieval Times)* (New Delhi: Aditya Prakashan, 1991). All references to the text, hereafter abbreviated as KP, are correlated with page numbers in Bhatnagar's translation, although I have sometimes emended his translation to follow the original more closely.
30. For an insightful account of Rajput state structure and the historical changes that were occurring at this time, see B. D. Chattopadhyaya, "Political Processes and Structure of Polity in Early Medieval India," in his *The Making of Early Medieval India* (Delhi: Oxford University Press, 1994), pp. 183–222. On construction of the myth of Rajput ancestry, see, in the same volume, "Origin of the Rajputs: The Political, Economic, and Social Processes in Early Medieval Rajasthan," pp. 57–88.
31. The *locus classicus* for classical Indian notions of polity is Kauṭilya's *Artha-śāstra*, ed. and tr. R. P. Kangle. These notions are taken up by rulers and poets in later centuries in differing ways to provide both an ideal language for kingship and a practical manual of statecraft. For Rajput uses, see Chattopadhyaya, "Political Processes and Structure of Polity in Early Medieval

India"; and Norman Ziegler in J. F. Richards, *Kingship and Authority in South Asia.* For Islamic kingship, see Nizam ul-Mulk Tusi, *The Book of Rules for Government,* tr. Hubert Darke (London: Routledge and Kegan Paul, 1960), and A. K. S. Lambton, *Theory and Practice in Medieval Persian Government* (London: Variorum Reprints, 1980).

32. For more examples of this common occurrence, as well as a fine discussion of the cultural politics of image worship and seizure of images in India in the sultanate and later periods, see Richard H. Davis, *Lives of Indian Images* (Princeton: Princeton University Press, 1997).
33. Bruce B. Lawrence, "Honoring Women Through Sexual Abstinence: Lessons from the Spiritual Practice of a Pre-Modern South Asian Sufi Master, Shaykh Nizam ad-din Awliya," *Journal of Turkish Studies,* vol. 18, 1994, p. 149–61.
34. For an account of this literature, see Hiralal Maheshwari, *History of Rājasthānī Literature* (New Delhi: Sahitya Akademi, 1980), pp. 51–92.
35. Aziz Ahmad, "Epic and Counter-epic in Medieval India," *Journal of the American Oriental Society,* vol. 83, 1963, p. 475.
36. On this point, see also the summary discussion in Shantanu Phukan, "'None Mad as a Hindu Woman': Contesting Communal Readings of *Padmavat,*" *Comparative Studies of South Asia, Africa and the Middle East,* vol. 16, no. 1, 1996, esp. pp. 45–46.
37. Aziz Ahmad, "Epic and Counter-epic in Medieval India," pp. 475–76.
38. Kolff, *Naukar, Rajput and Sepoy,* p. 96. For a detailed account of the events, see Kolff, pp. 96–110, and Niẓām al-dīn Aḥmad, *Ṭabaqāt-i Akbarī,* vol. III, pp. 355–66.
39. See Nārāyaṇa Dāsa's *Chhitāī-vārtā,* ed. Mataprasad Gupta (Varanasi: Nāgarīpracāriṇī Sabhā, 1959).
40. See Nayacandrasūrī, *Hammīra Mahākāvya,* ed. Fateh Singh (Jodhpur: Rajasthan Oriental Research Institute, 1968), pp. 100–101.
41. Mohamed Kasim Ferishta, *History of the Rise of the Mahomedan Power in India Till the Year* A.D. *1612,* tr. John Briggs (Delhi: Atlantic, 1929 [1829]), vol. I, pp. 206–7.
42. Most of the historical sources for the period ('Abdullāh's *Tārīḳh-i Dā'ūdī,* Ni'matullāh's *Tārīḳh-i Khān-i Jahānī va Maḳhzan-i Afġhānī,* Aḥmad Yādgār's *Tārīḳh-i Salāṭīn-i Afāġhinā,* Niẓām al-dīn Aḥmad's *Ṭabaqāt-i Akbarī,* and Abū 'l-Faẓl's *Akbar Nāmah*) agree on Sher Shāh's use of this trick. One historian who disagrees is 'Abbās Khān Sarvānī, who was connected to Sher Shāh's family by marriage and cites an eyewitness who was at Sher Shāh's capture of Rohtas to discredit the story as false. See 'Abbās Khān Sarvānī, *Tārīḳh-i Sher Shāhī,* tr. B. P. Ambasthya (Patna: K. P. Jayaswal Research Institute, 1974), pp. 264–65. See ibid., chapter IV, n. 58, pp. 323–27, for a review of all the other historical sources on the capture of Rohtas.
43. Shantanu Phukan, "The Lady of the Lotus of Gnosis," pp. 20–21.
44. Ibid., p. 21.

CHAPTER 7

1. Bruce B. Lawrence, "Honoring Women Through Sexual Abstinence: Lessons from the Spiritual Practice of a Pre-Modern South Asian Sufi Master, Shaykh Nizam ad-din Awliya," *Journal of Turkish Studies* 18 (1994: 149–61), p. 151.
2. Ibid., p. 158.
3. See Lokesh Chandra Nand, *Women in Delhi Sultanate* (Allahabad: Vohra, 1989), pp. 128–63.
4. On Rābi'ah, see the classic Margaret Smith, *Rabi'a the Mystic and Her Fellow-Saints in Islam* (Cambridge: Cambridge University Press, 1928).
5. Shaikh Rizqullah Mushtāqī, *Wāqi'āt-i Mushtāqī*, British Museum Add. Ms. 11633, ff. 19b–20. Translated by Iqtidar Hussain Siddiqui as Shaikh Rizqullāh Mushtāqī, *Wāqi'āt-i Mushtāqī: A Source of Information on the Life and Conditions in Pre-Mughal India* (New Delhi: Indian Council of Historical Research and Northern Book Centre, 1993), pp. 48–49. I have modified the translation only very slightly. For a similar story, see Simon Digby, *Wonder-tales of South Asia* (Oxford: Oxford University Press, 2006), pp. 239–40.
6. For *'ishq*, see Chapter 3.
7. See I. H. Siddiqui, "Shaikh Muhammad Kabir and his History of the Afghan Kings," *Indo-Iranica*, vol. 19, no. 4, 1966, p. 75.
8. S. C. R. Weightman, "Symmetry and Symbolism in Shaikh Manjhan's *Madhumālatī*," in *The Indian Narrative: Perspectives and Patterns*, eds. Christopher Shackle and Rupert Snell (Wiesbaden: Otto Harrassowitz, 1992), p. 196, n. 6.
9. S. A. A. Rizvi, *A History of Sufism in India* (Delhi: Munshiram Manoharlal, 1983), vol. 2, pp. 151–52.
10. Weightman, "Symmetry and Symbolism," pp. 208–9.
11. For a more complete reading of the narrative than it is possible to provide in this chapter, see the introduction to the annotated translation by Aditya Behl and Simon Weightman, *Madhumālatī: An Indian Sufi Romance* (Oxford: Oxford University Press, Series: Oxford World's Classics, 2000).
12. See Pierre Bourdieu, *Outline of a Theory of Practice*, trans. Richard Nice (Cambridge: Cambridge University Press, 1977), esp. pp. 78–87.
13. The *Yogasūtra* of Patañjalī is the classical Sanskrit source for yoga and Sāṃkhya philosophy, the *Amarakoṣa* is a compendium of the conventions used in constructing a poetic universe, and the *Kokaśāstra* is a classical Sanskrit work on erotics.
14. Bilgrāmī, *Ḥaqā'iq-i Hindī*, tr. S. A. A. Rizvi p. 64.
15. *jo koī kahai ki biddhi pasārā tehi kara sunahu subhāū bidhi guputa jaga mānhi kāhun na dekhā kāū*
16. See Chapter 3.
17. Bilgrāmī, *Ḥaqā'iq-i Hindī*, p. 40.

18. Ibid., p. 41.
19. Ibid., p. 42.
20. The male gaze in the context of Western cinema has been famously analyzed by Laura Mulvey, who argues that the cinematic gaze is gendered and objectifies women in an obsessive scopophilia and fascination with the female form. Though there is some similarity between Mulvey's analysis and, in Roland Barthes's term, the "corporeal striptease" being described here, the Sufi text is distinct in recognizing that the female gaze overwhelms the male looking at her. For Mulvey's argument, see her "Visual Pleasure and Narrative Cinema," in Laura Mulvey, *Visual and Other Pleasures* (Bloomington: Indiana University Press, 1989), pp. 14–26. For a perspective that questions Mulvey's views and comments on the difficulties of women's recovery of an empowered gaze, see E. Ann Kaplan, "Is the Gaze Male?" in *Powers of Desire: The Politics of Sexuality*, ed. Ann Snitow, Christine Stansell, and Sharon Thompson (New York: Monthly Review Press, 1983), pp. 309–27.
21. On the notion of the *barzakh* in Shattari cosmology, see the discussion of macrocosmic geometries below.
22. Mīrzā Asadullāh Khān Ġhālib, *Dīvān-i Ġhālib* (Lahore: Majlis-i Yādgār-i Ġhālib, 1969), p. 20. *balā-yi jāṉ hai Ġhālib us kī har bāt//'ibārat kyā ishārat kyā adā kyā.*
23. For detailed information about the shaikh, see in particular the excellent Urdu biography by Masūd Aḥmad, *Shāh Muḥammad Ġhaus̱ Gvāliyārī* (Mirpur Khas: Aftab Press, 1964). My account here largely concerns the Shaikh's political connections, as well as Mañjhan's depiction of him in the prologue of the *Madhumālatī*. For a treatment of the Shattari *silsilah* that lists most of the available manuscript sources, see Qazi Moinuddin Ahmad, *History of the Shattari Silsilah* (Ph. D. dissertation, Aligarh Muslim University, 1963).
24. Shaikh Muḥammad Ġhaus̱, *Kalīd-i Makhāzin* (Rampur Raza Library Persian ms. 912), f. 75. *insān hamchū kitābast, va har ḥarf ṣūrat-i mis̱ālast. har chih ṭalab kunī yābī, nā-yāb naravī.*
25. Ibid., ff. 3–4.
26. Ibid., ff. 6–7.
27. See William Chittick, *The Sufi Path of Knowledge* (Albany: State University of New York Press, 1989), for a detailed review of the theory. For an incisive spiritual and intellectual biography of Ibn 'Arabī, see Claude Addas, *Quest for the Red Sulphur: The Life of Ibn 'Arabi* (Cambridge, UK: Islamic Texts Society, 1993).
28. This account of the stages of divine manifestation is based on the *Fuṣūṣ al-Ḥikam*, tr. R. W. J. Austin, in *The Bezels of Wisdom* (New York: Paulist Press, 1908). For another account of the emanations, see Toshihiko Izutsu, *Sufism and Taoism: A Comparative Study of the Key Philosophical Concepts* (Berkeley: University of California Press, 1984), pp. 11ff.

29. *Kalīd-i Makhāzin*, ff. 17–18.
30. Chittick, *The Sufi Path of Knowledge*, p. 14.
31. For a more detailed account, see M. Takeshita, *Ibn 'Arabī's Theory of the Perfect Man and Its Place in the History of Islamic Thought* (Tokyo: Institute for the Study of the Languages and Cultures of Asia and Africa, 1987).
32. For my account of the *Jām-i Jahān Numā*, I have used the manuscript preserved in the Pirmohammedshah Library in Ahmedabad (Persian ms. 1326), as well as the Asiatic Society of Bengal ms. 1302.
33. The only copy of the *Davā'ir-i Rashīdī* I have been able to locate is held in the Salar Jung Museum and Library, Hyderabad (cat. no. 3269).
34. Manuscripts of Shaikh Vajīh al-dīn 'Alavī's *Sharḥ-i Jām-i Jahān Numā* exist in various *khānaqāh* libraries in India. I have used the Khanqah Mujeebia, Phulwari Sharif copy, as well as the Asiatic Society of Bengal (Persian ms. 1302). Shaikh Ibrāhīm Shaṭṭārī's *Ā'īnah-i Ḥaqā'iq Numā* has, unfortunately, been available to me only in two incomplete manuscript copies, one from the Pirmohammedshah Library in Ahmedabad (Persian ms. 1329), the other from the Rampur Raza Library (Persian ms. 873). The third commentary, that of Shaiḳh Bahlūl, seems to survive only in a manuscript held in the Khuda Bakhsh Oriental Public Library in Patna.
35. For this later Shattari rendition of Maġhribī's cosmological structure, see Khaja Khan, *The Secret of Ana'l Ḥaq* (1926; reprint, Lahore: Shaikh Muhammad Ashraf, 1965). This is a translation of a seventeenth-century treatise on Maġhribī's two *dā'irahs* by Shaikh Muḥammad Ibrāhīm Shāṭṭarī'Gāzūr Ilāhī of Shakarkot, Nagpur.
36. *Kalīd-i Makhāzin*, ff. 49–50.
37. Muḥammad Ġhaus Gvāliyārī, *Javāhir-i Khamsah* (India Office Library Ethé ms. 1875), f. 1a. The verse is frequently quoted in the text, although often without the reference to the Compassionate One, i.e., God created Adam in his own image.
38. *Javāhir-i Khamsah*, ff. 29b–30a.
39. Ibid., ff. 66b–67a.
40. Ibid., ff. 67b–68a.
41. For a different "philosophical alphabet" for divination (*jafr*), see Louis Massignon, *Essay on the Origins of the Technical Language of Islamic Mysticism*, translated by Benjamin C. Clark (Notre Dame, IN: University of Notre Dame Press, 1997), pp. 68–72.
42. A detailed account of this practice, as well as an extensive table containing all the stations and all their corresponding elements, is given in Thomas Hughes, "Da'wah," in *Dictionary of Islam* (1885; reprint, Calcutta: Rupa, 1988), pp. 72–78. For more details about Shattari magical practices, see Ja'far Sharīf, G. A. Herklots, and William Crooke, *Islam in India or the Qānūn-i Islām: The Customs of the Musalmāns of India* (1921; reprint, New Delhi: Oriental Books,

1972), pp. 218–77. For a review of the scholarship on Indo-Muslim esoteric practices, see Marc Gaborieau, "L'Ésotérisme Musulman dans le Sous-continent Indo-pakistanais: un point de vue ethnologique," *Bulletin d'Études Orientales*, vol. 44, 1992, pp. 191–209.

43. *Javāhir-i Khamsah*, f. 205b.
44. Ibid., f. 206a. See also S. A. A. Rizvi, *A History of Sufism in India*, vol. II, p. 160.
45. *Javāhir-i Khamsah*, f. 206b.
46. Hamid Algar, "The Naqshbandī Order: A Preliminary Survey of Its History and Significance," *Studia Islamica*, vol. XLIV, 1976, p. 130.
47. 'Abdullāh Shaṭṭar, *Shajarat al-Tauḥīd* (Khanqah Mujeebia Persian ms.), f. 1.
48. See Chapter 2.
49. *Javāhir-i Khamsah*, f. 240b.
50. Ibid., f. 263b.
51. Khwāndamīr, *Qānūn-i Humāyūnī*, tr. Baini Prashad (Calcutta: Royal Asiatic Society of Bengal, 1940), pp. 80–81.
52. Ibid., pp. 26–28.
53. See Georg Krotkoff, "Colour and Number in the *Haft Paykar*," in *Logos Islamikos: Studia Islamica in honorem Georgii Michaelis Wickens*, eds. Roger M. Savory and Dionisius A. Agius (Toronto: Pontifical Institute of Medieval Studies, 1984), pp. 97–118.
54. See al-Badāyūnī, *Muntakhabu-'t-Tawārīkh*, ed. Maulavi Ahmad Ali (Calcutta: Asiatic Society of Bengal, 1868), vol. 2 [trans. Lowe], p. 62.
55. Fazl 'Ali Shattari, *Kulliyāt-i Gvāliyārī*, f. 12, cited in Gulāb Khān Ġhorī, *Gvāliyar kā Rājnaitik aur Sānskritik Itihās* (Delhi: B. R., 1986), p. 234.
56. Ibid., ff. 12–13.
57. These letters were collected by Ġhausī Shaṭṭarī, the compiler of the *Gulzār-i Abrār*. The Persian text and English translation are quoted in K. A. Nizami, "The Shattari Saints and Their Attitude Towards the State," *Medieval India Quarterly*, vol. 1, no. 2, 1950, pp. 63–64. I have emended the translation to match the original more closely.
58. For the later history of Shaikh Muḥammad Ġhauṣ, which includes his controversial claim to have undergone a *mi'rāj* or ascension to heaven, his competition with the Naqshbandi Shaikh Gadā'ī, and his political decline under Bairam Khān's regency and Akbar's rule, see K. A. Nizami, "The Shattari Saints," and S. A. A. Rizvi, *A History of Sufism in India*, vol. 2, pp. 151–73.
59. Richard M. Eaton, *The Rise of Islam and the Bengal Frontier, 1204–1760* (Berkeley: University of California Press, 1993), p. 83.
60. K. A. Nizami, "The Shattari Saints," p. 57.
61. S. A. A. Rizvi, *A History of Sufism in India*, vol. 2, p. 153.
62. Ibid., p. 154.

63. For details of the spread of the *silsilah* in Bihar, see the writings of S. H. Askari, especially his "Gleanings from the Malfuz of the 17th Century Shuttari Saint of Jandaha," *Current Studies*, 1963, pp. 1–26, and his "A Fifteenth Century Shuttari Sufi Saint in North Bihar," *Journal of the Bihar Research Society*, vol. 37, 1951, pp. 66–82.
64. Ġhorī, *Gvāliyar kā Rājnaitik aur Sāṉskritik Itihas*, p. 229. The manuscript of the *Kulliyāt-i Gvāliyārī*, which is held in private hands in Gwalior, has been unavailable to me, necessitating dependence on secondary sources for an account of the Shaikh's stay in Gwalior.
65. Zahiru'd-din Muhammad Bābur Padshah Ghazi, *Bābur-Nama*, tr. Annette S. Beveridge (1921; reprint, Delhi: Low Price, 1989), pp. 539–40. See also Al-Badāyūnī, *Muntakẖabu-t-Tawārīkẖ*, vol. 1, ed. Maulavi Ahmad Ali (Calcutta: Asiatic Society of Bengal, 1868); and tr. George S. Ranking (1898; reprint, Delhi: Atlantic, 1990), vol. 1, p. 445.
66. Iqtidar Alam Khan, "Shaikh Abdul Quddus Gangohi's Relations with Political Authorities: A Reappraisal," in *Medieval India: A Miscellany*, vol. IV, p. 83.
67. Simon Digby, "'Abdul Quddūs Gangohī (1456–1537 A. D.): The Personality and Attitudes of a Medieval Indian Sufi," *Medieval India: A Miscellany*, vol. 3, 1975, pp. 33–34.
68. David Damrel, "The 'Naqshbandî Reaction' Reconsidered" (paper presented at the Shaping of Indo-Muslim Identity Workshop, Duke University, April 1995), p. 13.
69. al-Badāyūnī, *Muntakẖabu-t-Tawārīkẖ*, vol. 1, tr. Ranking, p. 459.
70. I use "letter mysticism" rather than *cabbalism* to characterize Shattari practices of invocation because of the specifically Judaic associations of the Kabbalah. The classic study of technical language in Sufi practice remains Massignon, *Essay on the Origins of the Technical Language of Islamic Mysticism*.
71. See S. A. A. Rizvi, "Sufis and Nâtha Yogis in Mediaeval Northern India (XII to XVI Centuries)," *Journal of the Oriental Society of Australia*, vol. 7, nos. 1–2, 1970, pp. 119–33.
72. For a detailed study of this text, see Carl Ernst's translation and introduction to the text, in *The Pool of Nectar: Muslim Interpreters of Yoga* (forthcoming); as well as Yusuf Husain, "Haud al-Hayat: La Version arabe de l'Amratkund," *Journal Asiatique*, vol. 113, 1928, pp. 291–344. For a listing of the numerous manuscript versions of the Persian and Arabic versions of the text, see Eaton, *The Rise of Islam and the Bengal Frontier, 1204–1760*, p. 78, n. 23.
73. Yusuf Husain, "Haud al-Hayat: La Version arabe de l'Amratkund," p. 292.
74. Eaton, *The Rise of Islam and the Bengal Frontier, 1204–1760*, p. 81.
75. Muḥammad Ġhauṡī Shaṭṭārī, *Gulzār-i Abrār* (Asiatic Society of Bengal Persian ms. 259), ff. 327b–328a, cited and translated in Carl W. Ernst, "Sufism and Yoga According to Muḥammad Ghawth" (paper presented at the American Academy of Religion Conference, Anaheim, CA, 1989), p. 6. As Ernst notes,

the modern Urdu translation by Fazl Ahmad Jivari, *Aẕkār-i Abrār: Urdū Tarjumah-i Gulzār-i Abrār*, mutes the disparaging language of this passage and replaces "idolators" and "infidels" simply with *Hindus*.

76. Carl Ernst, *The Pool of Nectar: Muslim Interpreters of Yoga*, p. 33. I am indebted to Ernst for sharing his unpublished translation with me.

77. The tutelary deities are not the standard Nāth figures, and seem to be taken from a wide range of sources. Here they are being used to approximate the spiritual agents (*muvakkil-i rūḥānī*) that are the guardians of each letter in Shattari cosmology.

78. See George W. Briggs, *Gorakhnāth and the Kānphaṭā Yogis* (1938; reprint, Delhi: Motilal Banarsidass, 1989), p. 310, for a list of the six Nāth *cakras* and their positions in the body; and David White, *The Alchemical Body: Siddha Traditions in Medieval India* (Chicago: University of Chicago Press, 1996), for detailed accounts of the various physiological concepts employed among the Tantric practitioners. For a reading of these notions as they are deployed in Hindavī Sufi romances, see Chapter 5.

79. See, for instance, Shaikh Ibrahim Shāṭṭarī, *Ā'īnah-i Ḥaqā'iq Numā* (Rampur Raza Library Persian ms. 873), and Ismā'īl Farḥī, *Makhzan-i Da'vat* (Asiatic Society of Bengal Curzon ms. 437). On Shaikh 'Īsā Jundullah, a Shattari Sufi who lived in Burhanpur in the Deccan, see the Urdu monograph by Shaikh Farīd, *Ḥaẓrat Shāh 'Isā Jundullāh* (Hyderabad: National Fine Printing Press, 1975), which contains an account of Shaikh 'Īsā's system for invoking all the ninety-nine Names of Allah. For a good account of visualization in other Sufi orders, notably the Chishtis and the Naqshbandis, see Mir Valiuddin, *Contemplative Disciplines in Sufism*, ed. Gulshan Khakee (London and the Hague: East-West, 1980).

CHAPTER 8

1. See Chapter 2.
2. See Chapter 3.
3. Charlotte Vaudeville, "Preface," in *Bārahmāsā in Indian Literatures* (Delhi: Motilal Banarsidass, 1986), p. x.
4. Idem, "Bārahmāsā Literature in Indo-Aryan Vernaculars," in *Bārahmāsā in Indian Literatures*, pp. 38–39.
5. For more details on the imagery of the *gavana*, see the discussion of Kabīr in Chapter 3.
6. Shaikh Muḥammad Ġhauṣ, *Kalīd-i Makhāzin* (Rampur Raza Library Persian ms. 912), f. 80.

CHAPTER 9

1. Kanwar Muhammad Ashraf, *Life and Conditions of the People of Hindustan* (Delhi: Munshiram Manoharlal, 1969 [1928]), pp. 229–30.

2. Ẕiā al-dīn Baranī, *Tārīḳh-i Fīrūzshāhī*, pp. 531–38, (translated in Elliot Dowson, *The History of India as Told by Its Own Historians, III* (Delhi: Low Price, 1990 [1867–77]), p. 199.
3. For details see M. M. Saeed, *The Sharqi Sultanate of Jaunpur: A Political and Cultural History* (Karachi: University of Karachi, 1972, pp. 111–12, 206–7); and A. Halim, "History of the Growth and Development of North-Indian Music During Sayyid-Lodi Period," *Journal of the Asiatic Society of Pakistan*, vol. 1, no. 1, 1956, pp. 46–64.
4. See A. Halim, "Music and Musicians of the Court of Shāh Jahān," *Islamic Culture*, vol. 18, no. 4, 1944, pp. 354–60, esp. 355–56.
5. M. Habib and K. A. Nizami, *A Comprehensive History of India, Vol. V: The Delhi Sultanat (A.D. 1206–1526)* (Delhi: People's Publishing House, 1970), p. 304.
6. Baranī, *Tārīḳh-i Fīrūz-shāhī*, p. 158.
7. *gar qadam bar chashm-i mā ḳhvāhī nihād/dīdah bar rāh mī-naham tā mīravī.*
8. *sarv-i sīmīnā ba-ṣaḥrā mīravī/nīk bad-'ahdī kih bī-mā mīravī.* Baranī, *Tārīḳh-i Fīrūz-shāhī*, pp. 158–59. The *ġhazal* recited by the courtesan is by Sa'dī Shīrāzī. The closing couplet is also on the theme of the departing beloved: *dīdah-i Sa'dī va dil hamrāh-i tū'st/tā na pindārī kih tanhā mīravī* ("The eyes and the heart of Sa'dī go with you / So you will not feel that you go alone"). For the text, see Sa'dī, *Kulliyāt-i Sa'dī*, ed. M. A. Furoghi, p. 691. For a commentary on the opening verse, as well as responses to the theme in the works of later Persian and Urdu poets, see Frances W. Pritchett, *Nets of Awareness: Urdu Poetry and Its Critics* (Berkeley: University of California Press, 1994), pp. 96–103.
9. 'Abd al-Qādir Badāyūnī, *Muntaḳhab ut-Tawārīḳh*, ed. Maulavi Ahmad Ali (Calcutta: Asiatic Society of Bengal, 1868), vol. I, p. 249, and tr. George S. Ranking (1898; reprint, Delhi: Atlantic, 1990), vol. I, p. 332. With his characteristic disdain for popular practices, Badāyūnī judges the worth of these works: "I found most of them to be profitless, and their paucity of interest is for the most part due to the triviality of their subject matter, and the difficulty of explaining it, as is evident."
10. The opening couplet of this *ġhazal*, often sung still by qawwals, is:

    ze ḥāl-i miskīn makun taġhāful daurah-yi nainān̠ banā'e batiyān̠/
    ze tāb-i hijrān̠ na-dāram ai jān̠ na leho kāhe lagāve chhatiyān̠.

11. *hindū baccah bingar ke 'ajab ḥusn dhare chhe*
    bar vaqt-i suḳhan guftan mukh phūl jhaṛe chhe
    guftam ze lab-i la'l-i tū yak bosah bigīram
    guftā ke are rām! turuk kā'īn̠ kare chhe!

These verses and the preceding couplet, cited in note 10, are cited in A. Halim, "Growth of Urdu Language and Literature During Sayyid-Lodi Period," *Journal of the Asiatic Society of Pakistan*, vol. III, 1958, p. 53. The translation is my own.

12. Shahab Sarmadee, ed., "Introduction," in *Ġhunyat-ul-Munya: The Earliest known Persian Work on Indian Music* (Bombay: Asia, 1978), p. 6.
13. Ibid., p. 3.
14. Ibid., p. 33.
15. Ibid., pp. 3–4.
16. Ibid., p. 32.
17. Ibid., pp. 72–4.
18. Ibid., pp. 108–9.
19. Ibn Battutah, *The Travels of Ibn Baṭṭūṭa* A.D. *1325–1354*, tr. H. A. R. Gibb (Cambridge: Cambridge University Press, for the Hakluyt Society, 1971), vol. III, p. 625.
20. On al-Jurjānī, see Margaret Larkin, *The Theology of Meaning: 'Abd al-Qāhir Jurjānī's Theory of Discourse* (New Haven, CT: American Oriental Society, 1995); and K. Abu Deeb, *Al-Jurjānī's Theory of Poetic Imagery* (Warminster: Aris and Phillips, 1979).
21. J. C. Bürgel, *The Feather of Simurgh: The "Licit Magic" of the Arts in Medieval Islam* (New York: New York University Press, 1988), p. 57.
22. Ibid., p. 67.
23. Ibid., p. 68.
24. See K. A. Nizami, *State and Culture in Medieval India* (Columbia, MO: South Asia Books, 1985), pp. 209–38.
25. Cited in Bürgel, *The Feather of Simurgh*, pp. 73–74. I have modified the translation somewhat, using the Persian text in Niẕāmī Ganjavī, *Khusrau va Shīrīn*, ed. Behruz Sarvatiyan (Teheran: Maktaba Tus, 1987), pp. 253–54.
26. Bürgel, *The Feather of Simurgh*, p. 74.
27. Pandita Damodara, *Ukti Vyakti Prakaraṇa*, ed. Acharya Jina Vijaya Muni (Bombay: Bharatiya Vidya Bhavan, 1953).
28. Suniti Kumar Chatterji, "Introduction," *Varṇa-Ratnâkara of Jyotirīśvara-Kaviśekharâcārya* (Calcutta: Royal Asiatic Society of Bengal, 1940), p. xxi.
29. Margaret Larkin, *The Theology of Meaning: 'Abd al-Qāhir Jurjānī's Theory of Discourse*, p. 9.
30. K. Abu Deeb, *Al-Jurjānī's Theory of Poetic Imagery*, pp. 24–25.
31. Ibid., p. 25.
32. A. Yusuf Ali, tr., *The Holy Qur'ān* (1934; reprint, Beirut: Dār al-Qur'ān al-Karīm, 1982), pp. 49, 1302. On application of this Qur'ānic verse even to the physical sciences, see S. H. Nasr, *An Introduction to Islamic Cosmological Doctrines* (Albany: State University of New York Press, 1993), pp. 6, 10 *et passim*.

33. Julie Scott Meisami, "Allegorical Gardens in the Persian Poetic Tradition: Nezami, Rumi, Hafez," *International Journal of Middle Eastern Studies*, vol. 17, no. 2, May 1985, pp. 229–30. On the exegesis of the *Qur'ān* see also Paul Nwyia, *Exégese Coranique et langue mystique: nouvel essai sur le lexique technique des mystiques musulmans* (Beirut: Dar al-Machreq, 1970), pp. 314–16.
34. Thomas de Bruijn, *The Ruby Hidden in the Dust: A Study of the Poetics of Malik Muḥammad Jāyasī's* Padmāvat (Leiden: Rijksuniversitaet Proefschrift, 1996, p. 157.
35. On the inseparability of *viraha* and *prema* in Jāyasī's text, see Charlotte Vaudeville, "La Conception de l'Amour Divin chez Muhammad Jāyasī: *virah* et *'ishq*," *Journal Asiatique*, 1962 (250:4), esp. pp. 356–57.
36. Muḥammad Kabīr, *Afsānah-i Shāhān* (British Library Ms. Add. 24409), f. 105b. The Persian text and Hindi translation are also given in P. L. Gupta, ed., introduction to *Miragāvatī* (Varanasi: Viśvavidyālaya Prakāśan, 1967), p. 39; and cited in S. C. R. Weightman, "Symmetry and Symbolism in Shaikh Manjhan's *Madhumālatī*," in *The Indian Narrative: Perspectives and Patterns*, eds. Christopher Shackle and Rupert Snell (Wiesbaden: Otto Harrassowitz, 1992), pp. 195–96. I have slightly amended the translation to follow the manuscript more closely.
37. See Charlotte Vaudeville, *A Weaver Named Kabir* (Delhi: Oxford University Press, 1993), p. 115.
38. Niẕāmī, *Haft Paykar: A Medieval Persian Romance*, tr. Julie Scott Meisami (Oxford: Oxford University Press, 1995), pp. 22–23.
39. Dārā Shikūh, *Ḥasanat al-'Ārifīn*, Nadwat-ul-Ulama Ms., Lucknow No. 202, p. 21, cited in K. A. Nizami, "Introduction," in Bruce B. Lawrence, *Morals for the Heart: Conversations of Shaykh Nizam ad-din Awliya Recorded by Amir Hasan Sijzi* (New York: Paulist Press, 1992), p. 17.
40. For a compilation of sources on Shaikh Zain al-dīn, see S. M. Pandey, "Maulānā Dāūd's Teacher Shaiḳh Zainuddīn," in A. W. Entwhistle and Françoise Mallison, eds., *Studies in South Asian Devotional Literature: Research Papers, 1988–1991* (Paris: École Française d'Extrême Orient, 1994), pp. 285–97.
41. For an analysis and detailed account of the rivalry, see Simon Digby, "*Tabarrukāt* and Succession Among the Great Chishti Shaikhs," in R. E. Frykenberg, ed., *Delhi Through the Ages: Essays in Urban History, Culture and Society* (Delhi: Oxford University Press, 1986), pp. 77–89.
42. S. A. A. Rizvi, *A History of Sufism in India* (Delhi: Munshiram Manoharlal, 1978), vol. I, p. 367.
43. S. M. Pandey, "Kutuban's *Miragāvatī*: Its Content and Interpretation," in R. S. McGregor, ed., *Devotional Literature in South Asia: Current Research, 1985–1988* (Cambridge: Cambridge University Press, 1992), p. 180.
44. M. M. Saeed has suggested another possibility for Quṯban's teacher: the Mahdavi Shaikh Burhān al-dīn Anṣārī of Kalpi (d. 1562–63). Shaikh Burhān

al-dīn was also a Hindavī poet and instructed Malik Muḥammad Jāyasī, the author of the *Padmāvat.* However, in view of Quṭban's reference to Shaikh Buḍḍhan Suhravardī in the text, the ascription cannot stand. See Saeed, *The Sharqi Sultanate of Jaunpur,* p. 200, and below for Shaikh Burhān as Jāyasī's teacher.

45. On Shaikh Ashraf Jahāngīr Simnānī, see M. M. Saeed, *The Sharqi Sultanate of Jaunpur: A Political and Cultural History* (Karachi: University of Karachi, 1972), pp. 241–45.
46. See John Millis, *Malik Muhammad Jāyasī: Allegory and Religious Symbolism in his* Padmāvat (unpublished Ph. D. dissertation, University of Chicago, 1984), pp. 32–39, for a review of the controversy.
47. For the full Chishti genealogy, see sources listed in note 14 on p. 360, above.
48. For a detailed discussion, see Chapter 5.
49. For detailed information about the shaikh and his *silsilah,* see in particular the excellent Urdu biography by Mas'ūd Aḥmad, *Shāh Muḥammad Ġhauṡ Gvāliyārī* (Mirpur Khas: Aftab Press, 1964), and Chapter 7.
50. For a discussion of the shaikh's life and work in Bihar, see Fr. Paul Jackson, S.J., *The Way of a Sufi: Sharf al-dīn Maner* (Delhi: Idarah-i Adabiyat-i Delli, 1987).
51. *Mukh al-Ma'ānī,* Majlis 35, cited in Annemarie Schimmel, *As Through a Veil: Mystical Poetry in Islam* (New York: Columbia University Press, 1982), p. 135. On the audiences for Sufi literature at *khānaqāhs,* see also Richard M. Eaton, *Sufis of Bijapur, 1300–1700: Social Roles of Sufis in Medieval India* (Princeton: Princeton University Press, 1978), pp. 142ff.
52. Bruce B. Lawrence, "The Early Chishtī Approach to Samā'," in Milton K. Wagle, ed., *Islamic Society and Culture: Essays in Honour of Aziz Ahmad* (New Delhi: Manohar Books, 1984), pp. 73–74.
53. 'Abd al-Qādir Badāyūnī, *Muntakhab ut-Tawārīkh,* ed. Maulavi Ahmad Ali (Calcutta: Asiatic Society of Bengal, 1868), vol. I, p. 250, and tr. George S. Ranking (1898; reprint, Delhi: Atlantic, 1990), vol. I, p. 333.
54. For a history of the controversies surrounding *samā',* see *inter alia* Annemarie Schimmel, *Mystical Dimensions of Islam* (Chapel Hill: University of North Carolina Press, 1975), pp. 178–86; Lawrence, "The Early Chishtī Approach to Samā'"; Sirajul Haq, "Samā' and Raqṣ of the Darwishes," *Islamic Culture,* vol. 18, no. 2, pp. 111–30; and Jean During, *Musique et Extase: L'audition mystique dans la tradition soufie* (Paris: Albin Michel, 1988). For an account of the opposition to *samā'* in fourteenth-century Delhi and Niẓām al-dīn's successful defense of *samā'* at the court of Ġhiyāṡ al-dīn Tuġhlaq, with references to the controversy in Baghdad and other Islamic centers, see Muḥammad bin Mubārak 'Alavī Kirmānī, *Siyar al-Auliyā'* (Delhi: Maṭba' Muḥibb al-Hind, 1885), pp. 535–42.

55. Shihāb al-dīn Abū Ḥafṣ 'Umar Suhravardī, *'Avārif al-Ma'ārif*, translated into Urdu by Shams Barelvī (Delhi: Arshad Brothers, 1986), p. 320.
56. Alī bin Uthmān al-Hujwīrī, *The Kashf al-Mahjub: The Oldest Persian Treatise on Sufiism*, tr. Reynold A. Nicholson (Lahore: Islamic Book Foundation, 1976), p. 394.
57. Lawrence, "The Early Chishtī Approach to Samā'," pp. 74–75.
58. James Robson, ed. and tr., *Tracts on Listening to Music* (London: Royal Asiatic Society, 1938), p. 71.
59. Lawrence, "The Early Chishtī Approach to Samā'," pp. 75–76.
60. Muḥammad Kirmānī, *Siyar al-Auliyā'* (Delhi: Maṯba' Muḥibb al-Hind, 1885), p. 502.
61. Lawrence, "The Early Chishtī Attitude to Samā'," p. 77.
62. Al-Hujwiri, *Kashf al-Mahjūb*, p. 402.
63. Muḥammad Kirmānī, *Siyar al-Auliyā'*, pp. 501–2. See also *Favā'id al-Fu'ād*, pp. 1020–23; and Lawrence, *Morals for the Heart*, pp. 355–56.
64. Kirmānī, *Siyar al-Auliyā'*, p. 503.
65. Ibid., pp. 503–4.
66. Sijzī, *Favā'id al-Fu'ād*, p. 304; and Lawrence, *Morals for the Heart*, p. 121.
67. Muḥammad Kirmānī, *Siyar al-Auliyā'*, p. 520.
68. James Robson, ed. and tr., *Tracts on Listening to Music*, p. 71.
69. Muḥammad Kirmānī, *Siyar al-Auliyā'*, p. 505.
70. Ibid., p. 504.
71. Cited in Kirmānī, op. cit., p. 505.
72. Ibid., pp. 509–10.
73. Ibid., p. 509.
74. Sijzī, *Favā'id al-Fu'ād*, p. 764; and Lawrence, *Morals for the Heart*, p. 276.
75. Banārsīdās, *Ardhakathānaka*, ed. and tr. Mukund Lath (Jaipur: Rajasthan Prakrit Bharati Sansthan, 1981), pp. 49–50 (translation slightly emended).

EPILOGUE

1. Wendy Doniger, *The Implied Spider: Politics and Theology in Myth* (New York: Columbia University Press, 1998).
2. K. N. Chaudhuri, *Trade and Civilization in the Indian Ocean: An Economic History from the Rise of Islam to 1750* (Cambridge: Cambridge University Press, 1985), p. 34.
3. See Muhsin Jassim Ali, *Scheherazade in England: A Study of Nineteenth-Century English Criticism of the* Arabian Nights (Washington, DC: Three Continents Press, 1981).
4. See Chapter 2 for early Persian versions of the "mirror for princes."

5. For the *Pañcatantra*, see Patrick Olivelle, *The Pañcatantra: The Book of India's Folk Wisdom* (Oxford: Oxford University Press, Series: Oxford World's Classics, 1997).
6. See Alexander Mackie Honeyman, *The Mission of Burzoe in the Arabic Kalilah and Dimnah* (privately printed Ph. D. dissertation, distributed from Chicago: University of Chicago Libraries, 1936).
7. Thomas Ballantine Irving, "Introduction," *Kalilah and Dimnah: An English Version of Bidpai's Fables Based upon Ancient Arabic and Spanish Manuscripts* (Newark, DE: Juan de la Cuesta, 1980), p. x. See also I. G. N. Keith-Falconer, *Kalīlah and Dimnah, or, The Fables of Bidpai, Being an Account of Their Literary History, With an English Translation of the Later Syriac Version of the Same, and Notes* (Cambridge: Cambridge University Press, 1885).
8. See the excellent essays collected in Ernst J. Grube, *A Mirror for Princes from India: Illustrated Versions of the* Kalilah wa Dimnah, Anvar-i Suhayli, Iyar-i Danish, *and* Humayun-Nameh (Bombay: Marg, 1991); as well as Esin Atil, *Kalilah wa Dimnah: Fables from a Fourteenth-Century Arabic Manuscript* (Washington, DC: Smithsonian Institution Press, 1981).
9. Janet Abu-Lughod, *Before European Hegemony: The World System A.D. 1250–1350* (New York: Oxford University Press, 1989), p. 200.
10. See W. Norman Brown, "The *Pañcatantra* in Modern Indian Folklore," *Journal of the American Oriental Society*, vol. 39, 1919, pp. 1–54.
11. See Muṣṭafá Khāliqdād 'Abbāsī, *Panjākyānah*, ed. Tara Chand and Sayyid Amir Hasan Abidi (Aligarh: Aligarh Muslim University, 1973).
12. See Richard Schmidt, *Die Çukasaptati: Textus Simplicior* (Leipzig: F. A. Brockhaus, Abhandlungen für die Kunde des Morgenlandes, 1893).
13. See Ziya'u'd-din Nakhshabi, *Tales of a Parrot*, tr. and ed. Muhammed A. Simsar (Cleveland, OH and Graz, Austria: Cleveland Museum of Art and Akademische Druck u. Verlagsanstalt, 1978).
14. Ġhavvāṣī, *Ṭūṭī-Nāmah*, ed. Mīr Sa'dat 'Alī Rizvī (Hyderabad: Silsilah-yi Yūsufiyya, 1357 A.H.).
15. Richard M. Eaton, "Introduction," in Hans J. Kissling et al., *The Last Great Muslim Empires: History of the Muslim World*, tr. F. R. C. Bagley (Princeton: Markus Wiener, 1996), pp. xiii–xiv.
16. Genevieve Bouchon and Denys Lombard, "The Indian Ocean in the Fifteenth Century," in Ashin Das Gupta and M. N. Person, eds., *India and the Indian Ocean, 1500–1800* (Calcutta: Oxford University Press, 1987), pp. 46–70. For a survey of seagoing trade in the period, see Simon Digby, "The Maritime Trade of India," in Tapan Raychoudhuri and Irfan Habib, eds., *The Cambridge Economic History of India*, vol. I: c. 1200–c. 1750 (Cambridge: Cambridge University Press, 1982), pp. 125–159.

17. Chaudhuri, *Trade and Civilization in the Indian Ocean*, p. 44. See also George F. Hourani, *Arab Seafaring in the Indian Ocean in Ancient and Early Medieval Times* (Princeton: Princeton University Press, 1995), pp. 51–84.
18. Chaudhuri, *Trade and Civilization in the Indian Ocean*, pp. 34–36.
19. Janet L. Abu-Lughod, *Before European Hegemony*, pp. 153–84.
20. Marshall G. S. Hodgson, *The Venture of Islam: Conscience and History in a World Civilization* (Chicago: University of Chicago Press, 1974), vol. I, p. 59.
21. Phillip B. Wagoner, "'Sultan Among Hindu Kings': Dress, Titles, and the Islamicization of Hindu culture at Vijayanagara," *Journal of Asian Studies*, vol. 55, no. 4, November 1996, pp. 851–80.
22. Stephen Greenblatt, *Marvelous Possessions: The Wonder of the New World* (Chicago: University of Chicago Press, 1991), p. 14. On that encounter see also Tzvetan Todorov, *The Conquest of America: The Question of the Other*, tr. Richard Howard (New York: Harper and Row, 1984).
23. C. E. Dubler, 'Adjā'ib, *Encyclopaedia of Islam (New Edition)*, vol. I, p. 203.
24. Robert Irwin, *The Arabian Nights: A Companion* (London: Penguin Books, 1994), p. 182.
25. Rāġhib al-Iṣfahānī, *al-Mufradāt fī Ġharīb al-Qur'ān*, ed. M. Kailani, p. 322, cited in Roy P. Mottahedeh, "*'Ajā'ib* in *The Thousand and One Nights*," in Richard G. Hovannisian and Georges Sabagh, eds., The Thousand and One Nights *in Arabic Literature and Society* (Cambridge: Cambridge University Press, 1997), p. 30.
26. Henry James, *The American* (New York: Scribner, 1907), p. xvii.
27. Tzvetan Todorov, *The Fantastic: A Structural Approach to a Literary Genre*, tr. R. Howard (Ithaca: Cornell University Press, 1975), p. 167.
28. Graham Seymour, "On Reading Literary Fantasy: Towards an Aesthetics of the Fantastic," *Paragraph: The Journal of the Modern Critical Theory Group*, vol. 5, no. 4, March 1985, p. 65.
29. Todorov, *The Fantastic*, p. 168.
30. For more about *dhvani*, see Chapter 9.
31. Todorov, *The Fantastic*, p. 60.
32. Greenblatt, *Marvelous Possessions*, p. 7.
33. Rosemary Jackson, *Fantasy: The Literature of Subversion* (London: Methuen, 1981), p. 61.
34. Robert Warshow, *The Immediate Experience* (Garden City, NY: Doubleday Anchor Books, 1964), p. 85, cited in John G. Cawelti, *Adventure, Mystery, and Romance: Formula Stories as Art and Popular Culture* (Chicago: University of Chicago Press, 1976), p. 9.
35. Cawelti, *Adventure, Mystery, and Romance*, p. 10.
36. Ibid., p. 30.

37. Vladimir Propp, *Morphology of the Folktale*, tr. Laurence Scott et al. (Austin: University of Texas Press, 1968), pp. 114–15. See the discussion in Chapter 4.
38. Vladimir Propp, "Transformations of the Wondertale," in his *Theory and History of Folklore*, tr. A. Y. Martin and R. P. Martin (Minneapolis: University of Minnesota Press, 1984), p. 82.
39. See, for instance, Tzvetan Todorov, *Grammaire de Décameron* (Hague: Mouton, 1969), and also Roland Barthes, "Introduction to the Structural Analysis of Narratives," in Susan Sontag, ed., *A Barthes Reader* (London: Jonathan Cape, 1982), pp. 251–95.
40. Barthes, "Introduction to the Structural Analysis of Narratives," p. 295.
41. Peter Brooks, *Reading for the Plot: Design and Intention in Narrative* (Cambridge, MA: Harvard University Press, 1992), p. 37.
42. See Chapter 3.
43. Published in Linda Y. Leach, *Mughal and Other Indian Paintings from the Chester Beatty Library* (London: Scorpion Cavendish, World of Islam Festival Trust, 1995), pp. 189–232.
44. For a complete listing of later versions of the *Padmāvat*, see now Thomas de Bruijn, *The Ruby Hidden in the Dust: A Study of the Poetics of Malik Muḥammad Jāyasī's* Padmāvat (Leiden: Rijksuniversitaet Proefschrift, 1996), pp. 24–34.
45. For a discussion of interlinguistic resonances in this version, see Shantanu Phukan, "'None Mad as a Hindu Woman': Contesting Communal Readings of Padmavat," *Comparative Studies of South Asia, Africa, and the Middle East*, vol. 16, no. 1, 1996, esp. pp. 47–53.
46. For a brief account of Persian versions of the *Padmāvat*, see S. A. H. Abidi, "The Story of Padmavat in Indo-Persian Literature," *Indo-Iranica*, vol. 15, no. 2, pp. 1–11.
47. An illustrated manuscript copy of the translation exists in the private collection of Simon Digby, to whom I am indebted for showing it to me.
48. For an introduction, see Rupert Snell, *The Hindi Classical Tradition: A Braj Bhāṣā Reader* (London: School of Oriental and African Studies, University of London, 1991).
49. For details, see R. S. McGregor, *Hindi Literature from Its Beginnings to the Nineteenth Century* (Series: A History of Indian Literature, vol. 8, Wiesbaden: Otto Harrassowitz, 1984), pp. 150–54.
50. 'Usmān, *Citrāvalī*, ed. Jaganmohan Varmā (Benares: Nagaripracharini Sabha, 1912–13).
51. Excerpt published in G. P. Dwivedi, *Hindī Premgāthā-kāvya* (Allahabad: Hindustani Academy, 1953), pp. 239–309.
52. Nūr Muḥammad, *Anurāg-Bānsurī*, eds. R. C. Shukla and Chandrabali Pande (Allahabad: Hindi Sahitya Sammelan, 1997).
53. See Frances W. Pritchett, *Marvelous Encounters: Folk Romance in Urdu and Hindi* (Delhi: Manohar Books, 1985) for an excellent account of the genre.

54. Ānand Rām Mukhliṣ, *Hangāmah-yi 'Ishq* (Patna: Khuda Bakhsh Library, Persian ms. 8918), f. 5, cited in Phukan, "The Rustic Beloved: Ecology of Hindi in a Persianate World," *Annual of Urdu Studies*, no. 15, 2000, p. 4.
55. Phukan, "The Rustic Beloved," p. 5.
56. Mukhliṣ, *Hangāmah-yi 'Ishq*, f. 5, cited in Phukan, "The Rustic Beloved," p. 4.
57. Phukan, "The Rustic Beloved," p. 5.
58. Wendy Doniger (O'Flaherty), *Asceticism and Eroticism in the Mythology of Siva* (Oxford University Press, 1973; retitled *Siva: The Erotic Ascetic*, 1981).

Index

as courtier, 55, 109, 111, 290, 300. *See also* Ḥusain Shāh Sharqī, Sultan
other authors or texts and, 41–44, 55, 109, 118, 200, 216, 310, 336
on *rasa*, poetry, or language, 115–16, 287, 300–2
as Sufi, 309–10

race, 13, 19
Rādhā, 68
Rāghav Chetan (*Padmāvat* character), 201–3, 208–9
Raisen, 200
Rāj Kuṉvar (Indo-Persian text), 335
Rāj Kuṉvar, Prince (*Mirigāvatī* hero), 109, 111–22, 125, 139–40
Rajasthan, 178
Rajputs, 17, 24, 27–28, 61, 88, 173, 176, 178–81, 185, 189–95, 197–200, 204, 207, 215–17, 364n9
Rāma (or Rām), 11, 63, 69–70, 82, 158, 203, 305
Rāmāyaṇa, 111
Ranthambhor, 185–86, 203–4, 206–7
rasa (essence; poetic sentiment), 16, 26, 30–32, 34, 53, 57, 63–68, 78–79, 99, 114, 147, 166, 170, 266–67, 287, 293, 295, 298, 306–7, 321–23, 332–33, 338
definition or types of, 31, 64, 294, 301
elements of, 31–33, 294
physical, 31, 68, 169
prema- (pure love), 63, 65, 67, 81–82, 88, 91, 104, 107, 168–69, 203, 205, 215, 217, 220, 303, 307, 338
śṛṅgāra (erotic), 67, 73–74, 116, 159, 205, 294, 301
rasāyaṇa. *See* alchemy
Rashīd, Shaikh, 236
rasika (connoisseur of *rasa*), 31, 100, 324
Ratansen (*Padmāvat* hero), 23, 27, 147, 166–67, 169–70, 172–77, 179–80, 198, 201–4, 206–8, 210–13, 215–16, 302
readers, ideal or cultivated (*sahṛdaya*), 31, 34, 287, 299–300, 322–23
reading
desire and, 334
Sufi theories of, 287, 299, 308, 313–15, 321–22
revelation, divine. *See* manifestation, divine
revivalism, Hindu, 11
rhetoric
dualistic. *See* dualisms, rhetorical
of warriors, warfare, or conquest, 2, 22, 24–25, 54, 143, 184, 198, 200
Risālah fi'l-'Ishq va 'ln-Nisā' ("Essay on Love and Women"), 71
Risālah-i Samā' ("Treatise on *Samā'* ") of Ḥamīd al-dīn, 316–17
Rizvi, S. A. A., 221, 310
romances, 24, 218, 331, 336
conquest and, 27, 185, 189. *See also under* Hindavī Sufi romances (*premākhyāns*)
European chivalric, 134
Hindavī Sufi. *See* Hindavī Sufi romances (*premākhyāns*)
Persian, 27, 31, 34, 46, 48–49, 59, 296, 335. *See also* Niẓāmī Ganjavī
Roy, Asim, 15
Rukn al-dīn Quddūsī, 62
Rūmī, Jalāl al-dīn, 8, 283, 296
rūpa (form; beauty), 32, 46, 89, 112, 155, 165, 264, 269–70, 279
Rūpcand, King (*Cāndāyan* character), 64, 76–77, 80, 83, 91–92
Rūpminī (*Mirigāvatī* character), 117–20

Sāduvan (*Maṇimekhalai* character), 135–36
sahaja (mystical absorption), 22, 304
sahaja bheda (simple mystery), 1, 305
sahṛdaya ("person with heart"; cultivated reader). *See* readers, ideal or cultivated
Śaivas, 41, 158